Understanding Business Law

second edition

Understanding Business Law

second edition

Brendan Pentony LLB(ANU)
Barrister of the Supreme Court of NSW
Senior Lecturer in Law
University of Canberra

Stephen Graw BCom, LLB(Qld)
Solicitory of the Supreme Court of Qld
Associate Professor of Business Law
James Cook University of North Qld

Jann Lennard BA, LLB(Hons)(ANU)
Barrister of the Supreme Court of NSW
Barrister and Solicitor of the Supreme Court of the ACT
Barrister of the High Court
Lecturer in Commercial Law
University of Canberra

David Parker BCom(Hons), BEd, LLM(Melb)
Barrister and Solicitor of the Supreme Court of Vic
Senior Lecturer in Law
Victoria University of Technology

Butterworths
Sydney — Adelaide — Brisbane — Canberra — Melbourne — Perth
1999

AUSTRALIA	BUTTERWORTHS Tower 2, 475–495 Victoria Avenue, Chatswood NSW 2067 On the internet at: www. butterworths.com.au
CANADA	BUTTERWORTHS CANADA LTD, Markham, Ontario
HONG KONG	BUTTERWORTHS ASIA (HONG KONG) Hong Kong
INDIA	BUTTERWORTHS INDIA New Delhi
IRELAND	BUTTERWORTH (IRELAND) LTD Dublin
MALAYSIA	MALAYAN LAW JOURNAL SDN BHD Kuala Lumpur
NEW ZEALAND	BUTTERWORTHS OF NEW ZEALAND LTD Wellington
SINGAPORE	BUTTERWORTHS ASIA Singapore
SOUTH AFRICA	BUTTERWORTH PUBLISHERS (PTY) LTD Durban
SWITZERLAND	STAEMPFLI VERLAG AG Berne
UNITED KINGDOM	BUTTERWORTHS London
USA	LEXIS LAW PUBLISHING Charlottesville, Virginia

National Library of Australia Cataloguing-in-Publication entry

---

Understanding business law.

2nd ed.
Includes index.
ISBN 0 409 313696.

1.Business Law — Australia. I. Pentony, Brendan.

346.9407

©1999 Reed International Books Australia Pty Limited trading as Butterworths
Reprinted 2000 (twice).
First edition 1995.

Edited and desktop published by Indigo Ink Pty Ltd

Inquiries should be addressed to the publishers.

Printed in Australia by Robert Burton Printers Pty Ltd.

Contents

Preface

This second edition of *Understanding Business Law* has been prepared taking into account the comments — favourable and critical — of the readers of the first edition. We hope we have improved the book.

As repeat collaborators we knew what we were letting ourselves in for in writing the second edition and we thank the many people who extended forbearance as we worked on it. We wish particularly to thank Rowena Oldfield who maintained her cool and professional skill in the face of missed deadlines, sick authors and all sorts of problems. Tiffany Hutton at Indigo Ink was a tower of strength in the hectic days as the book was being readied for the printer. We thank her too.

The writing task was shared — Brendan Pentony wrote part of Chapter 1 and Chapters 7, 8, 9, 10, 17, 18 and 19. Stephen Graw wrote Chapter 6 and Chapters 11–16. Jann Lennard contributed to Chapters 1 and 18 and was responsible for Chapters 2, 3, 4 and 5. David Parker also contributed to Chapter 1 and wrote Chapters 20, 21 and 22.

The law is as stated at 1 October 1998.

Queanbeyan
November 1998

Brendan Pentony
Stephen Graw
Jann Lennard
David Parker

Table of Cases

references are to paragraphs

references are to paragraphs

Table of Cases

references are to paragraphs

references are to paragraphs

references are to paragraphs

references are to paragraphs

Table of Cases

references are to paragraphs

references are to paragraphs

references are to paragraphs

references are to paragraphs

Table of Cases

Table of Statutes

references are to paragraphs

references are to paragraphs

Table of Statutes

references are to paragraphs

references are to paragraphs

Table of Statutes

references are to paragraphs

references are to paragraphs

references are to paragraphs

references are to paragraphs

references are to paragraphs

references are to paragraphs

references are to paragraphs

SOUTH AUSTRALIA

references are to paragraphs

references are to paragraphs

references are to paragraphs

references are to paragraphs

UNITED KINGDOM

references are to paragraphs

1

The Australian Legal System

What this chapter does ...

The legal system is an essential feature of Australian society. It affects business as well as individuals. A business enterprise must comply with the laws governing its operations and in some cases it relies on the law for its very existence.

To understand how the legal system works it is necessary to be aware of the way in which Australia's law developed from its link with the United Kingdom. In this respect it is important to be aware of the Constitution, which was the document which brought the Commonwealth of Australia into existence and which determines our system of government. This chapter discusses the process by which Australia emerged as an independent nation and the impact that process had on the development of law.

The legal system involves the courts, which are an important institution for resolving disputes and also for developing the law. This chapter examines the court systems — how a matter goes to court and the procedure in court. It also discusses the way in which the courts develop the common law. In this context the important doctrine of precedent is discussed.

The unsatisfactory aspects of the formal legal system have led to a demand for other ways of resolving disputes. Alternative dispute resolution is discussed, as are particular industry-based schemes.

The sources of law	**[1.1]**
The historical background	**[1.2]**

The sources of law

[1.1] To understand the way in which the legal system works in Australia it is necessary to examine its history and origins. Laws made by parliament and judge-made law are the product of centuries of thought and learning, human and commercial activity and changes in society. For instance, 200 hundred years ago there would have been no motor car law, whereas today there is very little traffic law dealing with horses and carriages.

To find the law on a particular matter the first source to be examined will be legislation and reports of what the courts have said in the cases. These are the primary sources of law. The secondary sources are textbooks and legal journals. They supply commentaries, explanations and speculation about the primary law and often generate debate about the state of the law or the need for reform. An article in a law journal about the need to change the law about company directors' duties may prompt parliament to change the legislation, or influence a judge when making a judgment.

The historical background

[1.2] Australian law can be traced back to England before 1066. The Anglo-Saxon law was maintained, though gradually changed, by William the Conqueror after the Norman conquest. He began the process of centralising the justice system and developing a system for the administration of justice.

At the time of King William all law-making power was with the Crown. By 1100, however, his son Henry I began to meet and seek advice from the 'Counsel of Barons'. These were people of importance such as knights, bishops and barons. A significant event took place in 1215 when King John was forced to sign the Magna Carta which represented the gradual lessening of the King's absolute power, as well as granting the first 'charter' of rights.

By the fourteenth century, knights, town leaders and important citizens began to meet separately from the barons and the bishops. Citizens began to represent different regions of the country and this part of the council began to evolve into what is now the House of Commons. The barons and bishops in their more eminent role formed the House of Lords. Over time the two Houses of Parliament began to assume greater power and the King would only issue proclamations on law approved by the two houses. These proclamations were the origins of modern legislation. The King maintained the prerogative powers, which enabled him to dissolve parliament since he was the head of all government. Over time parliament asserted its authority and became the supreme law-making body. The monarch, however, remains as the head of state in the United Kingdom and Australia.

The introduction of English law to Australia

[1.3] Although it involves events and principles of the eighteenth century and earlier, the question of the reception of English law into Australia was an important consideration in *Mabo v Queensland* (1992) 175 CLR 1; 107 ALR 1. The decision in that case, despite its historical basis, was and continues to be, of profound practical importance for modern Australia.

The *Mabo* case arose from a challenge by Eddie Mabo, David Passi and James Rice against the Queensland Coast Islands Declaratory Act 1985 which purported to extinguish their traditional land rights. The plaintiffs argued that their people, the Meriam, had enjoyed rights over the Murray Islands since time immemorial. It followed, they argued, that they owned certain land in the islands. They said that their rights in the land arose because they held it under traditional native title or they enjoyed the right to possession or they owned it by way of customary title.

In the course of the leading judgment, Brennan J discussed the reception of English law into Australia:

Reception of the common law

…

According to Blackstone, English law would become the law of a country outside England either upon first settlement by English colonists of a 'desert uninhabited' country or by the exercise of the Sovereign's legislative power over a conquered or ceded country. Blackstone did not contemplate other ways by which sovereignty might be acquired. In the case of a conquered country, the general rule was that the laws of the country continued after the conquest until those laws were altered by the conqueror. The Crown had a prerogative power to make new laws for a conquered country although that power was subject to laws enacted by the Imperial Parliament. The same rule applied to ceded colonies, though the prerogative may have been limited by the treaty of cession. When 'desert uninhabited countries' were colonised by English settlers, however, they brought with them 'so much of the English law as [was] applicable to their own situation and the condition of an infant colony'. English colonists were, in the eye of the common law, entitled to live under the common law of England which Blackstone described as their 'birthright' …

When British colonists went out to other inhabited parts of the world, including New South Wales, and settled there under the protection of the forces of the Crown, so that the Crown acquired sovereignty recognised by the European family of nations under the enlarged notion of terra nullius, it was necessary for the common law to prescribe a doctrine relating to the law to be applied in such colonies, for sovereignty imports supreme internal legal authority. The view was taken that, when sovereignty of a territory could be acquired under the enlarged notion of terra nullius, for the purposes of the municipal law that territory (though inhabited) could be treated as a 'desert uninhabited' country. The hypothesis being that there was no local law already in existence in the territory, the law of England became the law of the territory (and not merely the personal law of the colonists). Colonies of this kind were called 'settled colonies'. Ex hypothesi, the indigenous inhabitants of a settled colony had no recognised sovereign, else the territory could have been acquired only by conquest or cession. The indigenous people of a settled colony were thus taken to be without laws, without a sovereign and primitive in their social organisation. In *Advocate-General of Bengal v Ranee Surnomoye Dossee* (1863) 2 Moo NS 22 at 59; 15 ER 811 at 824; 9 Moo Ind App 391 at 428; 19 ER 786 at 800 Lord Kingsdown used the term 'barbarous' to describe the native state of a settled colony:

> Where Englishmen establish themselves in an uninhabited or barbarous country, they carry with them not only the laws, but the sovereignty of their own State; and those who live amongst them and become members of their community become also partakers of, and subject to the same laws.

...

The common law thus became the common law of all subjects within the Colony who were equally entitled to the law's protection as subjects of the Crown. Its introduction to New South Wales was confirmed by s 24 of the Australian Courts Act 1828 (Imp). As the laws of New South Wales became the laws of Queensland on separation of the two Colonies in 1859 and, by the terms of the Queensland Coast Islands Act 1879 and the Governor's Proclamation, the Murray Islands on annexation became subject to the laws in force in Queensland, the common law became the basic law of the Murray Islands. Thus the Meriam people in 1879, like Australian Aboriginals in earlier times, became British subjects owing allegiance to the Imperial Sovereign entitled to such rights and privileges and subject to such liabilities as the common law and applicable statutes provided. And this is so irrespective of the fact that, in 1879, the Meriam people were settled on their land, the gardens were being tilled, the Mamoose and the London Missionary Society were keeping the peace and a form of justice was being administered.

...

The facts as we know them today do not fit the 'absence of law' or 'barbarian' theory underpinning the colonial reception of the common law of England. That being so, there is no warrant for applying in these times rules of the English common law which were the product of that theory. It would be a curious doctrine to propound today that, when the benefit of the common law was first extended to Her Majesty's indigenous subjects in the Antipodes, its first fruits were to strip them of their right to occupy their ancestral lands ...

The law

Common law and civil law systems

[1.4]   Australian law is based on what is called a common law system. Similar systems are found in England, the United States, New Zealand and Canada. The term 'common law' has two meanings. One is a reference to a system of law where legal principles are developed by judges through case law; another meaning is a reference to the workings of this particular legal system, where the mode for solving disputes within the court system is adversarial. The procedures used by common law courts are based on English courts where each side has responsibility for presenting its case.

A common law system is distinguished from civil law systems found in Europe and some Asian countries. The civil law system has its origins in Roman law and later the Napoleonic Codes. Civil law systems do not rely on case law or for the development of that law by judges. They have the law set out in codified legislation, such as the criminal law in Queensland, Western Australia and Tasmania which is designed to cover every aspect of the relevant law. The procedural style in civil law jurisdictions is generally non-adversarial or inquisitorial with the judge taking the leading role rather than the lawyers involved.

Development of the common law

[1.5]   As mentioned earlier, the judicial development of law through the common law system began during the twelfth and thirteenth centuries when a centralised court system began to form. In that period there was no equivalent of the modern form of legislation and the law was based on customary practices according to the place a person lived. This was referred to as customary law and was determined by communal or feudal courts.

In the thirteenth century the King began to send professional judges to the different regions of England. They applied the customary law of the region, unless it was considered to be bad, and on returning to London judges would discuss cases. At around this time decisions began to be recorded and began to form an identifiable and readable body of legal principles which could be used in future cases. Judges began to apply customary law uniformly throughout the land, hence the term common law. As new situations called for decisions the law began to develop and still does.

Common law emerged from the development and refinement of legal rules by the courts as they heard successive cases. Eventually a body of law evolved for each branch of the law. It is sometimes referred to as judge-made law.

Case Example

The House of Lords had to decide an appeal by Miss Donoghue. She was out with a friend who bought her a bottle of ginger beer. After drinking part of the contents of the bottle she discovered the decomposed remains of a snail. She became physically ill and sued the manufacturer of the ginger beer for damages in negligence.

A major obstacle stood in her way. The courts had hitherto decided that a person can sue in negligence only where there is a duty of care arising from a contract. Miss Donoghue had a contract with nobody. The only contract in existence was that between her friend and the shopkeeper who sold him the bottle of ginger beer. There was no contract between her or her friend and the manufacturer of the drink but if anyone should be liable for the snail being in the bottle it should be the manufacturer.

The court found in her favour. It did so by identifying a principle of law which supported the view that each person has a duty of care to all others, who they could reasonably foresee as being affected by their actions: *Donoghue v Stevenson* [1932] AC 562.

This case is an example of judge-made law which set a legal standard on which the courts will assess liability for negligent acts. The principle which was expounded became part of the law in Australia and has been the basis for further development of the law of negligence. It applies not only to the duty owed by manufacturers of ginger beer but to the duty of care owed by a wide range of persons.

Legislation and common law

[1.6]   The modern growth of government has brought with it the development of legislation (or statute law). Legislation operates in a close and complementary fashion with common law and is often a product of common law. The parliament may have decided to gather up the different principles set out in case law, and consolidate and codify them into legislation thus making the law more accessible. Legislation is also the means by which a common law principle can be overturned. An example of such a use of legislation is the way in which the law on insurance was modernised in the Insurance Contracts Act 1984: see Chapter 17.

While judges effectively make law through their decisions in court, they are kept in check by parliament. This occurs in several ways. Whenever there is a conflict between legislation and a judge-made rule, the legislation will always prevail. Another check is that if a court's decision reflects an outdated or unfair legal principle or is politically unacceptable, then, rather than waiting for a superior court to overrule it, parliament will be asked to pass legislation to do so. This could be brought about by pressure exerted by the media, the community or politicians. The reaction to the *Mabo* case was an example. Following *Mabo* the Commonwealth Parliament passed the Native Title Act 1993. This Act was unsuccessfully challenged by the state of Western Australia. Then, in 1995, the High Court decision in *The Wik Peoples v Queensland* (1996) 187 CLR 1; 141 ALR 129 upheld the position of the Wik people. Legislation was enacted to accommodate the strong political reaction to the High Court's decision.

Sometimes the government overhauls the whole of a particular area of law by requesting a responsible government department to analyse and revamp an area of law into a more useable form. Alternatively, a law reform body may be given a reference to examine and develop an area of law into a more modern format. Legislation is then passed to incorporate the recommendations which are acceptable to the government. The significant changes in insurance law followed the government's acceptance of recommendations of the report of the Australian Law Reform Commission — ALRC 20.

Another avenue of reform is the system of parliamentary committees such as in the Federal Parliament. The House of Representatives Standing Committee on Legal and Constitutional Affairs undertook an inquiry into insider trading, published a report and, eventually, the government introduced legislation into parliament to modernise the law on the subject.

Where a principle has been developed by the common law it is always open to parliament to reverse it. What Australians regard as traditional freedoms guaranteed by the common law could be abolished overnight by an Act of Parliament, especially in the case of state parliaments because the Federal Parliament has limited power in such areas. A common law principle confirmed by the High Court in 1993 that no police officer has the power to arrest a person merely for the purpose of detaining him or her was reversed by a New South Wales statute in 1994. This illustrates the subordinate nature of common law.

Precedent

[1.7]   The Australian common law system is underpinned by the doctrine of precedent. This means that once a legal principle is established through a decision in a case, then future cases will be decided according to the same legal principle. This provides fairness by treating like cases in the same way and thus contributes certainty about the law. It removes the undemocratic practice of arbitrary application of the law. The doctrine of precedent is also referred to as *stare decisis*, or settled principle.

Precedent depends for its application on the hierarchy of the court system where a court is bound to follow precedents set by superior courts in the same hierarchy. The use of precedent allows for some flexibility and principles of law may be developed as the need arises but this is a slow method as the courts must wait until an appropriate dispute arises. Precedent relies on the reasoning of judgments being recorded in law reports. It is not so much the results of cases as the way in which the courts reached them that is important. Without a record of the reasoning there is no way of knowing what is the precedent. Access to those reasons is through the published reports and, to a growing degree, to the unreported judgments. Law reports are reliable since they are regulated by appropriate legal bodies who check whether they can be accepted as an official statement of a court.

The significance of the judgment

[1.8]   When a decision is made by a court the judge or judges will publish a single decision if it is unanimous, or sometimes several judgments if they use different reasoning or come to a different conclusion. What is important about the decision is the reasoning that led the court to make it. It is important that the reasoning is published because the way in which the judges reached their decision is thus exposed to scrutiny and that acts as a brake on arbitrary decision-making and the supplanting of parliament's role in making the law.

The reason for the decision of the judge is called the *ratio decidendi* and is essentially the legal principle which will be referred to by other courts. The ratio decidendi might be stated by the judge in one or two sentences. Alternatively, the whole judgment may have to be read to summarise the legal principle stated by the judge. The judge may make a variety of comments in coming to a conclusion on a principle of law. These comments are known as *obiter dicta* — comments made by the way.

The doctrine of precedent

[1.9]   A precedent set by a court is said to be binding on all courts lower in the hierarchy. This means that in cases where the facts are identical the lower courts are bound to follow a superior court's legal reasoning. Courts are not bound to follow their own precedents but normally a judge would be persuaded to do so for the sake of consistency. While each court is bound to follow the decisions of a superior court, there is no court superior to the High Court and it is not bound by any other court nor by its own past decisions. In the case of *Cole v Whitfield* (1988) 165 CLR 360; 78 ALR 42 the court took the opportunity to review its decisions on s 92 of the Constitution and in that process overturned several of its earlier decisions.

Persuasive precedent

[1.10]   A court within each state is bound by the reasoning of higher courts within its hierarchy and the High Court. Courts will, however, take note of decisions outside their hierarchy, for instance in other states or in other common law countries. A Victorian court may be persuaded to follow a New South Wales precedent where it represents a more modern development of the law or, perhaps, where a legal issue is being heard in Victoria for the first time and the reasoning in another court was compelling.

Courts will be persuaded to follow a precedent outside their jurisdiction where it was established by an eminent court with respected judges. Thus the reasoning of a Supreme Court of another state, the English House of Lords or the New Zealand Supreme Court may persuade a state court. Once a court is persuaded by an outside precedent then the judgment becomes part of its own precedent.

Reversing, overruling, disapproving and distinguishing

[1.11]   Precedent is both protected and developed by various techniques used by the judges. If a court is incorrect in its application of law a superior court may reverse the decision on appeal and state the correct law. This does not change the law, but applies and preserves the original law.

An appeal court may decide that a decision made in a lower court is outdated or not an appropriate application of the precedent and overrule that decision. By overruling the original decision, the court may be changing the law and setting a new precedent to be followed by courts further down in the hierarchy.

A court bound by a precedent may feel that it is bound to follow that legal principle, even though it believes it is not the appropriate decision to make. The judge may state that the precedent is being applied reluctantly. This signal from the lower court may prompt the losing party to appeal to a higher court in the hope of having the precedent overruled.

Sometimes a lawyer will ask the court to avoid an otherwise binding precedent by demonstrating that the facts in the case are sufficiently different so that the precedent does not apply. This technique is not a sharp lawyer's trick. It recognises that in the doctrine of precedent the facts are important and that precedents are binding only when the facts in the later case are similar. This is known as distinguishing a precedent.

Advantages of precedent

[1.12]   Underpinning the role of the courts are certain legal conventions which a judge must keep in mind when deciding the law. These conventions, or practices of the law, require a court to interpret and implement the law to community standards, to ensure the rights and freedom of all citizens, and to be seen to be making a fair decision according to the purpose of the law before them.

Many supporters of the doctrine of precedent believe that it is a good system which enables judges to develop and change the law in line with developments in community standards. The use of precedent provides consistency and coherence which makes the law predictable with consequently fewer disputes.

Some of the reasons given for retaining the use of precedent are that:

- judge-made law is much more flexible and adaptable to modern times and unforeseen circumstances than statute;
- judges are less open than politicians to pressure from community groups for a quick change in the law;
- a court can uphold the rights of weaker members of society who are unable to receive political help by changing statutory law; and
- the court deals with real life situations before them, and they are compelled to apply the standards of society at that time, whereas the parliamentary draftsman can only guess at the effectiveness of the legislation.

Disadvantages of precedent

[1.13]   The critics of the use of precedent claim that it is an inefficient way of using law. Some criticisms are that:

- A judge's decisions are often difficult to understand and can contain contradictory statements. It can be very difficult to separate the ratio decidendi from other comments made by the judge.

- There can often be several different precedents on the one area of law which makes it difficult to work out what is the correct legal principle.
- Judges can be very conservative and not want to change the law.
- If judges do distinguish precedent from a case before them then it makes the law uncertain.
- Development of the law is slow and uncertain because courts must wait for cases to arise before principles can be changed.

Development of law in Australia

[1.14]   In 1823 the United Kingdom government passed the New South Wales Act which gave New South Wales full status as a colony. The Governor of the colony was then able to pass laws provided they did not conflict with English law. The Australian Courts Act was enacted in 1828 and it stipulated that all relevant English case law and legislation in force on 25 July 1828 would apply to the colonies of New South Wales and Van Diemen's Land. English statutes passed after that date did not automatically become law in the Australian colonies. Any later English law would apply only to the colonies if it was expressly intended to do so. Such laws were said to apply by paramount force.

As new colonies formed, English law applied up to the point of their creation. In the case of Western Australia this was until 1829 and for South Australia, 1836. The Australian colonies then began gradually to receive the power to pass their own legislation. In 1865 the Colonial Laws Validity Act of the Imperial Parliament gave them the right to pass their own legislation provided it was not contrary to any British law specifically intended for the colony.

Loosening the ties

[1.15]   Australia became a self-governing nation in 1901 with the passing by the United Kingdom Parliament of the Commonwealth of Australia Constitution Act. That parliament maintained power to pass laws affecting Australia, though in practice it would not. In 1931 it passed the Statute of Westminster which became law in Australia as the Statute of Westminster Adoption Act in 1942. The effect of the Statute of Westminster was that no law could be passed by the United Kingdom Parliament for Australia, unless requested by Australia. The Statute of Westminster was a significant stage in the emergence of Australia as an independent nation.

The Australia Act — finally independent

[1.16]   It was not until 1986 that the Commonwealth and state parliaments relying on the Statute of Westminster requested the United Kingdom Parliament to pass the Australia Act 1986. That gave full independence in law-making to Australia. The Commonwealth, with the agreement of the states, passed the Australia Act 1986. The long title of that Act provides a summary of its purpose and effect:

An Act to bring constitutional arrangements affecting the Commonwealth and the States into conformity with the status of the Commonwealth of Australia as a sovereign, independent and federal nation.

Since the Australia Act, the United Kingdom Parliament no longer has power to legislate for the Commonwealth, a state or a territory. State parliaments are no longer fettered by the Colonial Laws Validity Act. Appeals to the Privy Council from decisions of Australian courts are no longer possible.

The Constitution

Introduction

[1.17] In 1900 the United Kingdom Parliament passed the Commonwealth of Australia Constitution Act 1900. The significance of the Act was that it created a federal Commonwealth comprising the Commonwealth of Australia and the states. It also incorporated the Constitution which came into effect on 1 January 1901.

The Constitution itself is a broad charter of principles which sets out how government institutions will work, and their relationships with each other. It stipulates the operation and make-up of parliament, the federal courts, the functions of the Commonwealth government and relations between the Commonwealth and the states. It is essentially a political document — setting up the political institutions for the newly created Commonwealth. The former colonies, now called states, retained their pre-federation political structures. The Constitution does not pay much attention to civil rights or personal freedoms. They are assumed to exist as part of the common law tradition.

Conventions in the Constitution

[1.18] The Constitution is silent on some matters and relies on conventions which are the 'unwritten laws' which regulate the way in which things are done. For example, it is the convention that the leader of the political party which commands a majority in the House of Representatives will be appointed Prime Minister. The Constitution refers to ministers but at no time does it mention the Prime Minister. The Governor-General is also able to dismiss the Prime Minister as occurred in 1975. The authority to do so is said to be found in a convention or in the reserve powers of the Governor-General. Another of the constitutional conventions is that the Governor-General has the power to dissolve parliament. The usual practice is for the Prime Minister to recommend that an election be held and, if the Governor-General agrees, parliament will be dissolved.

Responsible government

[1.19] When the Constitution was being drafted in the 1800s, the Westminster model of responsible government was incorporated. This means that the members of the executive must be responsible to the parliament.

Responsible government was described in the parliamentary debate leading to the Commonwealth of Australia Constitution Act as follows:

> the greatest institution which exists in the Empire and which pertains to every Constitution established within the Empire. I mean the institution of responsible government, a government under which the executive is directly responsible to — nay, is almost the

creature of — the Legislature. (Lord Haldane (as he later was) quoted in the *Engineers* case — *Amalgamated Society of Engineers v Adelaide Steamship Co Ltd* (1920) 28 CLR 129.)

The nature of the relationship between executive and legislature makes the system of government in Australia fundamentally different to that of the United States of America. In the US system of government there is no equivalent of the Australian system of elected ministers. The persons who hold similar offices are appointed by the executive, subject to scrutiny by Congress.

The origins of the Constitution

[1.20] As *Cole v Whitfield* (1988) 165 CLR 360; 78 ALR 42 (see **[1.22]**) shows, in order to understand the Australian Constitution, and perhaps its defects, it is sometimes necessary to examine the social, political and economic history of Australia. It is also relevant to note that federation came about through a political process rather than by revolution. In the last half of the nineteenth century Australia was a collection of six colonies which operated like separate countries. Each colony had its own laws, customs barriers, monetary regulations and immigration policies. There were many differences between the colonies, with New South Wales having a comparatively large population and developed industry, while Tasmania was economically very small.

The federation

[1.21] The Constitution was the legal document that formed a federation of the Australian colonies. It did so by establishing them as states and by joining them through the creation of a central government with specific powers. This federation could be described as a political and economic union. The economic impetus was a major driving force in the creation of the federation. The idea of a national market was very persuasive.

Section 92 — free trade

[1.22] The federation and free movement of people and goods was seen as vital by the framers of the Constitution. Section 92 of the Constitution states that interstate trade, commerce and intercourse among the states shall be absolutely free, and this freedom cannot be impeded by either state or federal governments.

The landmark case of *Cole v Whitfield* (1988) 165 CLR 360; 78 ALR 42 arose from the purchase by Mr Whitfield of crayfish in South Australia. He worked for a company that conducted a crayfish farm in Tasmania. The crayfish were of legal size in South Australia but were under size in Tasmania. He was prosecuted in a Magistrates Court for breaking the Sea Fisheries Regulations 1962. The magistrate dismissed the charge but an appeal was made to the Supreme Court of Tasmania. The matter was then removed to the High Court with the Commonwealth and five states joining the case in support of Tasmania.

Mr Whitfield's defence was that the transaction was in the course of interstate trade and therefore he was entitled to be protected by s 92 of the Constitution. His argument was that the Tasmanian law impeded the freedom of interstate trade.

The High Court reflected on the difficult history of s 92 cases. It referred to Mason J who said that '... there is now no interpretation of s 92 that commands the acceptance of a majority of the Court'. The High Court considered other comments and said (at 49):

They identify what we see as a quite unacceptable state of affairs.

... it is not surprising that the Court is now pressed to reconsider the approximately 140 decisions of this Court and the Privy Council which have attempted to illuminate the meaning and operation of the section.

The court engaged in an examination of the background of the section and concluded (at 54) that:

> The purpose of the section is clear enough: to create a free trade area throughout the Commonwealth and to deny to Commonwealth and States alike a power to prevent or obstruct the free movement of people, goods and communications across State boundaries ... The enemies of free trade were border taxes, discrimination, especially in railway freight rates and preferences ...

The term 'absolutely free' as it appears in s 92 could not be interpreted always to mean totally free of regulation. To do so would be to permit a state of anarchy to exist. While the section does not say what trade, commerce and intercourse among the states are 'absolutely free' from, the High Court has established that it is to be free from regulation that discriminates against interstate trade and protects the local trade.

The High Court in *Cole v Whitfield* accepted that the Tasmanian law was constitutional. It did not breach s 92 because, even though it imposed a burden on trade, it did not discriminate against interstate trade and commerce. Crayfish caught in Tasmanian waters were subject to the same law. Although the law protects the Tasmanian crayfish industry, it did not give Tasmanian crayfish a competitive advantage over crayfish from outside the state.

The extension of s 92 to guarantee freedom of intercourse between the states was demonstrated in the case of *R v Smithers; Ex parte Benson* (1913) 16 CLR 99. The state of New South Wales attempted to prohibit a person who had been imprisoned in Victoria from entering New South Wales. The High Court found this to be unconstitutional and against the principle of free movement.

Another case which illustrated the capacity of s 92 to protect personal freedoms was *Gratwick v Johnson* (1945) 70 CLR 1. In that case, wartime restrictions on interstate travel were struck down by the High Court as unconstitutional because they impeded intercourse between the states. This was despite the fact that the country was on a war footing and that the power of the Commonwealth in wartime to make laws with respect to defence was very wide.

The freedom of individuals to move between the states can be subject to much less regulation than trade and commerce. The appropriate level of permissible regulation of interstate movement is illustrated by the traffic rules.

The structure of the Constitution

[1.23]   The Constitution is divided into eight chapters made up of 128 sections. The first three chapters deal with the parliament, the executive government and the judicature. These three chapters appear to reflect and reinforce the doctrine that legislative, executive and judicial functions should be separate. This arrangement of governmental powers is described as the doctrine of separation of powers. It means, ideally, that those who pass the laws should not enforce them or administer them as an executive body. Similarly, those who adjudicate on disputes, especially in criminal matters, should be independent of the other arms of government. The separation of powers cannot apply in Australia because of the institution of responsible government. The close relationship of the executive and the legislature makes it impossible. What does seem to respect the doctrine is the way in which the independence of the judicial function is maintained.

Parliament

[1.24]   Section 1 of the Constitution states that the legislative power of the Commonwealth shall be vested in a Federal Parliament consisting of the Queen, a Senate, and
a House of Representatives. This means that the law-making power for the Commonwealth is exercised by parliament.

As a matter of convention the government of the day is formed from the House of Representatives. The Constitution does not stipulate how the leader of the government will
be appointed. Indeed, it makes no reference to the office of Prime Minister and the existence of that office is a matter of convention.

The Constitution provides that the House of Representatives is composed of members
who represent a particular electorate within a state. The Senate is elected on a state-wide
basis, and every state elects 12 senators irrespective of its size. The fact that a less populated state can elect the same number of senators as a larger one reflects the concerns of
the original colonies. The smaller states feared they would be dominated by the more
populated states, who would have the majority of members in the House of Representatives. The Senate was intended to be the states' house and to look after their interests. The
Constitution allows, in s 122, for representation in parliament of the territories. Accordingly, the people of both the Australian Capital Territory and the Northern Territory are
represented in the Federal Parliament.

The Constitution prescribes who is eligible to stand for parliament and who is able to
vote. In this respect it makes it clear that the government of Australia is to be conducted
according to democratic principles.

In s 51 (discussed in [1.28]) the powers of the Federal Parliament are enumerated. The
section sets out the areas in which the parliament is able to make laws. The Constitution
anticipated the possibility of hostility between the Houses of Parliament and in s 57 has
provided the means of overcoming an impasse between the House of Representatives and
the Senate through a double dissolution and, if necessary, a joint sitting of both houses.

The executive government

[1.25]   The second of the traditional pillars of government is the executive. The Constitution, in s 61, expresses the executive power as follows:

> The executive power of the Commonwealth is vested in the Queen and is exercisable by
> the Governor-General as the Queen's representative, and extends to the execution and
> maintenance of this Constitution, and the laws of the Commonwealth.

The body that advises the Governor-General in the government of the Commonwealth
is the federal Executive Council: s 62. There is provision in s 64 of the Constitution for
ministers and they are members of the federal Executive Council.

In practice, the government of the country is in the hands of the Cabinet which is made
up of ministers who, in turn, are drawn from the parliament. The Governor-General is
appointed by the Queen (of Australia) on the advice of the Prime Minister. By this process the notion of democracy is upheld as the elected head of government determines who
should be the head of the executive.

In the words of Mason J in *Victoria v Commonwealth and Hayden* (1988) 134 CLR
338; 7 ALR 277 at 327, explaining the nature of the executive power:

> ... there is to be deduced from the existence and character of the Commonwealth as a
> national government and from the presence of ss 51(xxxix) and 61 a capacity to engage in
> enterprises and activities peculiarly adapted to the government of a nation and which can-
> not otherwise be carried on for the benefit of the nation.

It is through the executive power that the Commonwealth Government is able to exercise the common law prerogative powers of the Crown which include the power to declare war, to enter into treaties and to conduct diplomatic relations. It is also able to undertake Royal Commissions, to conduct inquires or appoint advisory bodies. In these matters the Commonwealth does not need legislation to authorise its activities.

The judicature

[1.26] The third arm of government is the judicature and, under s 71 of the Constitution, the Commonwealth's judicial power is vested in the High Court and such other federal courts as the parliament creates.

The nature and importance of this power in the government of the country can be seen in the judgment of Griffith CJ in *Huddart Parker v Moorehead* (1909) 8 CLR 330 where he said (at 357):

> … the words 'judicial power' as used in s 71 of the Constitution mean the power which every sovereign authority must of necessity have to decide controversies between its subjects, or between itself and its subjects, whether the rights relate to life, liberty or property. The exercise of this power does not begin until some tribunal which has power to give a binding and authoritative decision (whether subject to appeal or not) is called upon to take action.

In a democratic society the courts are expected to be independent. In this regard s 72, which deals with the appointment, tenure and remuneration of the Justices of the High Court, attempts to enshrine their independence by:

- making it difficult to remove them;
- making it impossible to reduce their remuneration; and
- fixing their term so that they retire at the age of 70 years (before a referendum in 1977 members of the High Court were appointed for life).

The importance of the High Court as an institution can be seen from the fact that it is the court with jurisdiction to determine disputes involving the Commonwealth, and disputes between states. It is also, most importantly, the court with the final jurisdiction to interpret the Constitution. In this respect the High Court plays a role as adjudicator of disputes between the Commonwealth and states about their respective constitutional powers. It is viewed as the custodian of the Constitution. With the abolition of appeals to the Privy Council the High Court is also the final court of appeal from federal and state courts.

Alteration of the Constitution

[1.27] It is very difficult to change the Commonwealth Constitution. It can be done only in accordance with s 128, which requires an Act of the Federal Parliament, followed by a referendum. The referendum must be accepted by a majority of voters in a majority of states and by a majority of voters throughout the country.

The states, by contrast to the Commonwealth, can more easily change their Constitutions by Act of Parliament, though each state has its own procedures. Some states require special procedures to change the Constitution.

There have been many attempts to change the Australian Constitution by referendum. Between 1901 and 1988 there have been 18 referendums to vote on 42 possible changes to the Constitution. The voters of Australia have agreed to only eight alterations. The difficulty in amending the Constitution has been a factor in the High Court's approach to interpretation.

The resistance to constitutional change by Australian voters has puzzled governments and commentators, particularly as some referenda have been preceded by extensive advertising campaigns to inform the public. Along with a lack of understanding of the Constitution, there appears to be a distrust of change, or perhaps a perception that politicians are trying to hoodwink the public. Another reason for the lack of change might be that political parties oppose changes to the Constitution on political grounds. It has also been suggested that voters in smaller states fear the influence of the population in the larger states.

The legislative powers of the Federal Parliament

[1.28]   Upon federation, the new political entity, the Commonwealth, needed law-making powers and some of the powers previously exercised by the colonies were transferred to it through the Constitution. The main areas in which the Federal Parliament has power to make laws are set out in s 51 of the Constitution which provides:

PART V. — POWERS OF THE PARLIAMENT

51. The Parliament shall, subject to this Constitution, have power to make laws for the peace, order, and good government of the Commonwealth with respect to:–

(i)   Trade and commerce with other countries, and among the States;

(ii)   Taxation; but so as not to discriminate between States or parts of States;

(iii)   Bounties on the production or export of goods, but so that such bounties shall be uniform throughout the Commonwealth;

(iv)   Borrowing money on the public credit of the Commonwealth;

(v)   Postal. telegraphic. telephonic, and other like services;

(vi)   The naval and military defence of the Commonwealth and of the several States, and the control of the forces to execute and maintain the laws of the Commonwealth;

(vii)   Lighthouses, lightships, beacons and buoys;

(viii) Astronomical and meteorological observations;

(ix)   Quarantine;

(x)   Fisheries in Australian waters beyond territorial limits;

(xi)   Census and statistics;

(xii)   Currency, coinage, and legal tender;

(xiii) Banking, other than State banking; also State banking extending beyond the limits of the State concerned, the incorporation of banks, and the issue of paper money;

(xiv)   Insurance, other than State insurance; also State insurance extending beyond the limits of the State concerned;

(xv)   Weights and measures;

(xvi)   Bills of exchange and promissory notes;

(xvii) Bankruptcy and insolvency;

(xviii) Copyrights, patents of inventions and designs, and trade marks;

(xix)   Naturalisation and aliens;

(xx)   Foreign corporations, and trading or financial corporations formed within the limits of the Commonwealth;

(xxi)   Marriage;

(xxii)   Divorce and matrimonial causes; and in relation thereto, parental rights, and the custody and guardianship of infants;

(xxiii)   Invalid and old-age pensions;

(xxiiiA) The provision of maternity allowances, widows' pensions, child endowment, unemployment, pharmaceutical, sickness and hospital benefits, medical and dental services (but not so as to authorise any form of civil conscription), benefits to students and family allowances;

(xxiv)   The service and execution throughout the Commonwealth of the civil and criminal process and the judgments of the courts of the States;

(xxv)   The recognition throughout the Commonwealth of the laws, the public Acts and records, and the judicial proceedings of the States;

(xxvi)   The people of any race, other than the aboriginal race in any State, for whom it is deemed necessary to make special laws;

(xxvii)   Immigration and emigration;

(xxviii) The influx of criminals;

(xxix)   External affairs;

(xxx)   The relations of the Commonwealth with the islands of the Pacific;

(xxxi)   The acquisition of property on just terms from any State or person for any purpose in respect of which the Parliament has power to make laws;

(xxxii)   The control of railways with respect to transport for the naval and military purposes of the Commonwealth;

(xxxiii) The acquisition, with the consent of a State. of any railways of the State on terms arranged between the Commonwealth and the State;

(xxxiv) Railway construction and extension in any State with the consent of that State;

(xxxv)   Conciliation and arbitration for the prevention and settlement of industrial disputes extending beyond the limits of any one State;

(xxxvi) Matters in respect of which this Constitution makes provision until the Parliament otherwise provides;

(xxxvii) Matters referred to the Parliament of the Commonwealth by the Parliament or Parliaments of any State or States, but so that the law shall extend only to States by whose Parliaments the matter is referred, or which afterwards adopt the law;

(xxxviii)The exercise within the Commonwealth, at the request or with the concurrence of the Parliaments of all the States directly concerned, of any power which can at the, establishment of this Constitution be exercised only by the Parliament of the United Kingdom or by the Federal Council of Australasia;

(xxxix) Matters incidental to the execution of any power vested by this Constitution in the Parliament or in either House thereof, or in the Government of the Commonwealth, or in the Federal Judicature, or in any department or officer of the Commonwealth.

The division of powers between the Commonwealth and states

[1.29]   Law-making powers which are not stated in the Constitution as belonging to the Commonwealth remain with the states. There are some areas where both the Commonwealth and the states have power to make laws — these are concurrent powers, for example, the taxing power. The states can, however, be excluded from these areas if their laws are inconsistent with those of the Commonwealth: s 109. Some powers are stated to be exclusive to the Commonwealth. These include the defence power (s 114), the power to impose excise and customs duties (s 90), the currency, coinage and legal tender power (s 51(xii)) and the making of laws for the government of a territory: s 122. The Commonwealth Parliament also has exclusive power under s 52 to make laws for the peace, order and good government of the Commonwealth in respect to the government of the Commonwealth, public service matters and other Commonwealth areas.

While the Commonwealth is restricted on the areas for which it can make laws, the states can pass laws on many of the Commonwealth areas, as long as they are within the jurisdiction of the state. Where the Commonwealth has not been specifically given a power to legislate, then those remaining powers are exclusive to the states, for instance motor law, criminal law and contract law. Most business law is made as state law.

As can be expected, the states guard their powers from encroachment by the federal government. For example, when the federal government attempted to take over all regulation of corporations through legislation, the states challenged that right under the Constitution in *New South Wales v Commonwealth* (1990) 169 CLR 482; 90 ALR 355. The High Court interpreted s 51(xx) of the Constitution as giving the Commonwealth power to make laws concerning the activities of corporations, but not concerning the process of incorporation. That is a state power. The Commonwealth's legislation was invalid in that regard and in order to establish uniform legislation it was necessary to obtain the cooperation of the states. Under s 51(xxxvii) the state parliament can refer or exchange powers to or between the Commonwealth. These powers were used in 1980 to examine issues concerning off-shore powers, and in formulating the Australia Act of 1986.

Expanding the role of the Commonwealth

[1.30]   The originators of the Constitution envisaged that the states would remain essentially independent of the Commonwealth government which was expected to deal only with the national issues. Responsibility for the provision of services such as transport, health, education and business regulation was to be a matter for the states.

Over the years the Commonwealth has become the dominant political and economic entity even in areas where it has no particular power. One way in which the Commonwealth increased its power was by exercising its income taxing powers during the Second World War. The states did not recover their taxing position, and became dependent on the Commonwealth for grants under s 96 of the Constitution. They have been reluctant to rely on their own income taxation power for political reasons.

The Commonwealth generates considerable revenue through the collection of income tax and under s 96 is able to make grants to the states with attached conditions. This has increased the power of the Commonwealth considerably since these grants can be tied to purposes requested by the Commonwealth and for which it does not have power through s 51. In matters such as health, housing and education, where it has no direct constitutional power, it can influence those areas of Australian life with its power over state grants.

In some areas where it appears that the Commonwealth powers have increased it has been not a widening of the powers as much as an interpretation of the powers which has favoured the Commonwealth's submission. There have been examples of using a combination of powers, thus allowing the Commonwealth to regulate activities where it has not previously entered. The Trade Practices Act 1974 is one such example where the use of the corporations power, the trade and commerce power, the postal power, the territories power and s 52 enabled the Commonwealth to pass laws with respect to consumer protection — an area previously within the province of the states. Similarly, the external affairs power has been used to support regulation of environmental activity. An example of that was in the *Tasmanian Dam* case, *Commonwealth v Tasmania* (1983) 158 CLR 1; 46 ALR 625, where the Commonwealth relied on the external affairs power, and some others, to prevent the construction of a dam which it regarded as environmentally unacceptable.

Personal rights and guarantees under the Constitution

[1.31]   Unlike the Bill of Rights which is set out in an amendment to the United States of America Constitution, the Commonwealth Constitution does not define the rights of citizens. They are left to be protected by the courts through the common law. Some would argue that it is better to leave this situation as it is, since to enshrine the common law rights in legislation could create problems such as those of interpretation or limitation of the freedoms. Others would argue that the rights should be stated.

The Commonwealth Constitution does, however, provide personal rights such as:

* the right to vote (s 41);
* the right to compensation on just terms where the Commonwealth compulsorily acquires property (s 51(xxxi));
* the right to trial by jury for an indictable Commonwealth offence (s 80);
* freedom of movement within Australia (s 92);
* freedom of religion (s 116); and
* equal treatment of residents in other states: s 117.

The High Court has recognised that the form of representative government as established in the Constitution brought with it an implied right to freedom of political communication. For developments in this area see *Nationwide News Pty Ltd v Wills* (1992) 177 CLR 1; 108 ALR 681; *Australian Capital Television v Commonwealth* (1992) 177 CLR 106; 108 ALR 577; *Theophanous v The Herald And Weekly Times Limited* (1994) 182 CLR 104; 124 ALR 1; *Lange v Australian Broadcasting Corporation* (1997) 189 CLR 520; 145 ALR 96.

The courts

Hierarchy of courts

[1.32]   The courts are vital to the operation of law since they dispense justice, resolve disputes and punish wrongdoers. The courts also play an important role in the development of common law, central to which is the hierarchy of courts.

The hierarchy refers to the ranking of courts according to their importance. Each level of the court system has a particular jurisdiction, or lawful authority to hear certain legal matters. The higher the court in the hierarchy, the more serious are the matters it can consider, the more likely is it able to hear appeals from lower courts and the greater the effect of its decisions in terms of precedent. The more serious the crime, or the greater the monetary amount claimed in a civil matter, the further up in the court hierarchy will the matter be heard.

When a court has jurisdiction or authority to hear a legal matter for the first time, without that matter being referred to any other court, then the court has what is known as original jurisdiction over that legal area. For instance, the County Court of Victoria and the District Court of New South Wales would have original jurisdiction over a civil claim for $80,000, but would not have original jurisdiction to hear a charge of murder, which comes within the original jurisdiction of the Supreme Court. Similarly, courts which are lowest in the hierarchy have original jurisdiction over minor offences and for small claims of money.

Power to hear appeals

[1.33] The hierarchy of the courts will also determine the appellate jurisdiction of a court. The appellate function of a court refers to its jurisdiction or authority to hear appeals from courts lower in the hierarchy. The lowest court in the hierarchy has no appellate jurisdiction. Thus, the High Court can hear appeals from any court in the Australian system, whereas a magistrates court has no jurisdiction to hear appeals.

The highest court for Australia was originally the Judicial Committee of the Privy Council. This was a court located in England and composed of judges from Commonwealth countries including judges from the House of Lords. Appeals to this court were gradually eroded by Australian legislation, and were finally abolished in 1986 with the Australia Act. The final appellate court in Australia is now the High Court of Australia.

Each of the states of Australia has its own court hierarchy, as does the federal court system. The High Court of Australia is a federal court and is at the peak of both the federal and state court hierarchy. The state courts generally have jurisdiction to hear matters falling within state law. These would be matters such as civil disputes involving contract law, property law and claims for injuries, as well as criminal law.

The state courts

Courts of summary jurisdiction

[1.34] At the lowest rung of the state hierarchy are the courts of summary jurisdiction; they hear more than 90 per cent of all matters in the system. They are known as a summary courts because they deal with minor or summary offences, as well as small claims for compensation and other lesser civil matters.

Summary courts are presided over by a magistrate. A magistrate is not a judge, but rather a judicial officer of lower rank. In some states a Justice of the Peace is permitted to preside over this court. The magistrate is usually addressed in court as 'your worship'.

The decisions of summary courts are not recorded in law reports. Summary courts are less formal than other courts in the hierarchy. For instance, less emphasis is given to procedure and dress, and solicitors will often appear rather than a barrister. Matters before the court are generally heard very quickly, with the magistrate more likely to give a lesser penalty than a higher court, possibly a bond or community service for a minor conviction. It is said by some that the summary courts dispense a rough brand of justice.

The summary courts are known as the Magistrates Court in Victoria, Queensland, South Australian and the Australian Capital Territory. In New South Wales they are know as Local Courts. In Western Australia the summary courts are the Court of Petty Sessions and Local Court, and in Tasmania they are the Courts of Petty Sessions and Courts of Request.

[1.35] Jurisdiction Summary courts generally hear non-indictable offences which require only a summons for the person to appear in court rather than an arrest and charge. Summary offences include matters such as petty crimes, traffic infringements or non-payment of fines. Usually it is the police who prosecute in this court, but officers from government departments might also conduct a prosecution.

[1.36] **Indictable offences**   Where a person has been charged with an indictable offence, it is considered to be more serious and the person may be remanded in custody or released on bail. Summary courts have the jurisdiction to hear some indictable offences, for instance shoplifting, but only where the accused is given the option of having the case heard before a judge and jury in a higher court. There can be appeals from the summary courts on questions of law, or where there has been a mistake as to the facts.

In each of the states the Act which determines the jurisdiction of the court will also set out the offences which fall within the authority of the court. Similarly, the Act will determine the civil jurisdictional limits, which varies between states.

[1.37] **Committal hearings**   Another function of a summary court is the conduct of committal hearings. A committal hearing takes place when a person has been apprehended and charged with a serious crime. Before the person can be held in custody and subsequently brought to trial, the police or appropriate authority must present sufficient evidence to convince a magistrate that the person has a case to answer. If the magistrate is satisfied that there is enough prima facie evidence to make a finding of guilt likely, the person will be committed for trial. This procedure is known also as a preliminary hearing, and is designed to protect the liberty of individuals, since a judicial officer rather than the police must be satisfied of a case to answer before detaining a person.

[1.38] **Other courts of summary jurisdiction**   At the same level in the court hierarchy are some other courts which have a specialist jurisdiction. The Children's Court, for instance, can hear most matters concerning children, including many serious criminal offences. This court would also hear applications for the welfare or protection of children up to the age of 18. Another summary court, the Coroner's Court, investigates situations where there has been a violent, unnatural or suspicious death. This is like an inquiry where witnesses are called and some conclusion reached as to the cause of death. The Coroner may find grounds for committing a person to trial.

Intermediate courts

[1.39]   Intermediate courts are the middle rung in the hierarchy. They are known as District Courts except in Victoria where they are the County Courts. There are no intermediate courts in Tasmania, the Northern Territory or the Australian Capital Territory.

[1.40] **Jurisdiction**   The intermediate courts have an original jurisdiction to hear important civil matters, involving disputes and claims for substantial amounts of money. The civil jurisdiction of this level court varies between states and is set out in the legislation of each state. A jury may be used in some civil matters, such as defamation.

Intermediate courts have a criminal jurisdiction over serious criminal offences, with a jury appointed when a criminal matter is heard for the first time. There is a limit to the criminal jurisdiction of the court with serious crimes such as murder removed from this court's authority.

The intermediate courts have an appellate jurisdiction. A judge sitting alone may hear an appeal from a decision of a magistrate's court. These courts are more formal than the inferior courts, with greater attention given to procedure and the rules of evidence. This is because the cases will be more serious than those heard in the summary courts. It is therefore likely that a barrister rather than a solicitor will represent a client at this level.

Superior courts

[1.41] The Supreme Court is at the top of each state court hierarchy. This court hears very serious matters, such as crimes of murder. The Supreme Court also hears civil matters where the monetary amount exceeds the jurisdiction of the intermediate level court in its system. A jury is used for criminal matters heard for the first time, and for some civil claims. There is no limit to the jurisdiction of this court, except for matters which fall within the jurisdiction of the federal courts or the High Court.

[1.42] **Appeals** A Supreme Court has an appellate jurisdiction and hears appeals from the two lower courts before a single judge. The Supreme Courts also have an appeals division from their own court. A party may be given leave to appeal on the grounds of mistaken facts or law to a number of judges. The appeal will take place before either three judges or the full bench of five judges.

The Supreme Court is very formal with strict procedures being followed in the preparation and presentation of material to the court. The decisions are often reported in law reports and of course determine the law which must be followed by lower courts. Supreme Court justices are appointed from the legal profession — often they are leading barristers, or judges of the intermediate courts.

The High Court

[1.43] The High Court is the pre-eminent Australian court. It was established under the Constitution and has a wide original jurisdiction. It is especially important because it has the jurisdiction to determine disputes between states, or between the states and the Commonwealth. Under the Constitution there is an appellate jurisdiction which results in the High Court being the final appeals court from all courts — state, territory and federal. Not all cases are able to go on appeal to the High Court and it is necessary to seek leave to appeal.

The High Court is the ultimate court in constitutional matters and its role makes it an important participant in the system of government in Australia.

The High Court comprises seven members known as justices. Decisions by the High Court are studied carefully because all Australian courts are bound by a decision or legal principle determined by the High Court.

Other federal courts

[1.44] The Federal Court and the Family Court are courts exercising federal jurisdiction. Both were established in 1976.

The Federal Court has two divisions, the Industrial Division which hears industrial issues and disputes, and the General Division which hears matters concerning bankruptcy, trade practices and administrative law. It has an appellate division which hears appeals on decisions made by a single Federal Court judge. The court can also hear appeals from territory Supreme Courts on both civil and criminal matters or state courts on certain federal matters such as bankruptcy, patents and trademarks. Appeals from the Federal Court are heard by the High Court.

The Family Court of Australia came into existence in 1976 with the passing of the Family Law Act 1975 (Cth). This court hears matters dealing with family law such as divorce, custody of children and property disputes. It also has jurisdiction in some taxation matters.

Cross-vesting of jurisdiction

[1.45] When a legal matter arises, whether it is a civil claim or criminal offence, the issues involved might overlap state and Commonwealth jurisdictions. For instance, a family dispute might involve both Commonwealth family law and state contract law. The cross-vesting of jurisdiction legislation makes it possible for one court to hear the whole case. This means that there is an arrangement between the states and the Commonwealth whereby they give, or vest, each other with jurisdictional power so that the whole case can be heard by one court.

Cross-vesting of jurisdiction between the Supreme Courts of the states and the Commonwealth is possible under the Jurisdiction of Courts (Cross-vesting) Act 1987 (Cth). The state and territory Supreme Courts have the power to hear legal issues normally outside their jurisdiction, such as trade practices issues and family law but not criminal matters. Similarly, the Federal Court and the Family Court can now deal with original jurisdiction in state matters. Cross-vesting of jurisdiction can apply only where there are overlapping jurisdictional issues. Not every matter can be heard by a state court. Industrial relations is one area which would be transferred from a state court to the Federal Court.

The adversary system

[1.46] A characteristic of the common law system of law is the use of an adversarial approach to resolve disputes between litigants, and to prosecute offenders. The adversarial approach is combative. It involves a judicial officer such as a judge or magistrate, or a judge and jury, hearing argument from the parties involved in a case and making a decision on what has been presented. This approach is competitive and encourages lawyers to use a range of techniques to achieve a favourable result. Witnesses are subjected to robust cross-examination as each party attempts to weaken the other's case and strengthen its own. Where a jury is involved it is not uncommon for lawyers to make emotional appeals. The judge's role appears to be limited to ensuring that court procedure is followed, and that each party is given sufficient time to present their case. Ultimately, however, the judge must dispense justice to the parties.

Taking a matter to court

[1.47] The adversary system translates differences between the state and a citizen and disputes between one citizen and another into battles. The method of naming cases reflects this: *R v Chamberlain, Commercial Bank of Australia v Amadio*.

The aim of court proceedings, whether they be civil or criminal in nature, is not to investigate the matter but to arrive as nearly as possible at the truth, based on the evidence presented by the parties. In this battle the initiative is said to be with the parties. This means that the conduct of the litigation is primarily in the hands of the parties. Each party must make out each aspect of the case being argued, whether by way of positive assertion or defence.

Parties do this by presenting evidence and submitting legal arguments as to what law is relevant and how it should be applied. Evidence is elicited by tendering of documents and examination of witnesses; the judge does not call witnesses or examine them on the facts. Both facts and law must be argued by the parties — it is not enough to say 'here are the facts judge, now tell us who wins'.

Common law and equity

A brief history

[1.48]   The case law which makes up what is referred to as the common law is divided into two categories — common law and equity. This classification is not easily understood and the two bodies of law take their names from the courts in which they were developed. Common law means that part of the law which was created by the older English common law courts, as opposed to the law developed in the courts of equity. This was a system of courts which developed later and is sometimes referred to as the Chancery Courts.

In the late medieval period the common law courts were concerned only with certain types of cases: crimes, property, contracts and civil actions in tort. In civil, non-criminal matters the courts offered only a limited range of remedies which were an order to restore property to a person or an order to pay damages as compensation for a wrongful act. These civil actions were normally commenced by a writ.

There were faults with this system, the worst of which was that it came to be more concerned with the processes of the court rather than with doing justice. The procedural rules for achieving a remedy became dominant and the aim of dispute settling was sometimes lost sight of. There were many kinds of writ and the plaintiff had to select the correct one. If the wrong writ was used the claim would fail. The form of the writ could also determine the form the proceedings would take and the type of remedy that was available,.

These situations where the common law was seen to be defective gave rise to the development of another body of legal principles known as equity. Persons who were not able to bring their case before the common law courts or whose only remedy in those courts was inadequate, would petition the King or Queen in Council. These petitions were referred to the Chancellor — the conscience of the King or Queen, and eventually became addressed specifically to him.

The petitions for justice could not be dealt with according to the law, because it was the inadequacy of the law which caused the petitions in the first place. They were decided on the basis of equity and good conscience; that is, on the merits and justice of the case. From these beginnings there developed the court of chancery, exercising the equitable jurisdiction of the Chancellor.

In every Australian jurisdiction the courts may exercise both common law and equitable jurisdictions. Should the principles conflict the rules of equity prevail.

Some equitable remedies

Injunction

[1.49]   The common law would provide the remedies of orders for the return of property or the payment of compensation for a wrongful act. The courts in the exercise of their equitable jurisdiction have the power to restrain a person from doing a certain act such as committing a nuisance or breaching a contract. They also have power to require a person to do a specified act, such as requiring a public servant to make a decision. The remedy is referred to as an injunction and refusal to comply with an injunction is a contempt of court.

Specific performance

[1.50]   An order for specific performance compels a person to complete a contract. Such orders are most commonly given in respect of contracts for the sale of land or for other unique items such as works of art. This remedy is a good illustration of the way in which equity fills the gaps of the common law or allows the courts to do justice where the common law remedy is clearly not adequate.

Equity in action

[1.51]   The decision in *Commercial Bank of Australia v Amadio* (1983) 151 CLR 447; 46 ALR 402 is an illustration of equity in action.

Case Example

The Amadios were an elderly couple who could read little English and were first misled by their son and then used by the bank to whom he owed hundreds of thousands of dollars. In 1977 Giovanni and Cesira Amadio believed their son Vincenzo to be a successful businessman with a prosperous lifestyle to match. When Vincenzo asked them to help him over a temporary financial problem by mortgaging their land for up to six months for a maximum of $50,000, they agreed. But he had not told them the whole truth.

The mortgage was unlimited as to both time and amount. His business was insolvent and his bank knew it. Vincenzo and his bank manager met daily to decide which cheques should be honoured and which should be allowed to bounce. His parents were not aware of their son's true financial state and they were never told, not even when they signed the mortgage documents in front of the bank manager.

A few months later Vincenzo's company collapsed and the bank wanted to enforce its mortgage. It was only then that the Amadios realised the true nature of what they had signed. This was a landmark decision in the High Court. Mason J said in the course of his judgment:

If A having actual knowledge that B occupies a position of special disadvantage in relation to an intended transaction, so that B cannot make a judgment as to what is in his own best interests, takes unfair advantage of his (A's) superior power or bargaining position by entering into that transaction, his conduct in so doing is unconscionable.

And if instead of having actual knowledge of the situation, A is aware of the possibility of that situation existing or is aware of facts that would raise that possibility in the mind of a reasonable person, the result will be the same.

In this case:

(1) It was obvious to the bank that they had not understood and the bank closed its eyes to that fact. Vincenzo had not seen the document at the time he 'explained' it to them, and the bank manager did not correct Mr Amadio when he said that the thought the mortgage was limited to six months. The bank could not shelter behind its failure to make proper inquiry.

(2) The Amadios were operating under a special disadvantage that is their lack of English and lack of knowledge of commerce.

> The court said that relief against unconscionable dealing is a purely equitable remedy; the concept underlying the jurisdiction to grant the relief is that equity intervenes to prevent the stronger party to an unconscionable dealing acting against equity and good conscience by attempting to enforce or retain the benefit of that otherwise valid dealing. Mr and Mrs Amadio were entitled to have the whole transaction set aside unconditionally.

The doctrine as developed in *Amadio* has been applied widely by the courts in personal and commercial settings.

Civil law and criminal law

[1.52]   Proceedings in a court are either civil or criminal. A civil matter is a dispute concerning the rights and obligations between one citizen and another. In a civil case the plaintiff, the person making the claim and therefore the person who commences the action, must prove each fact of the case argued. The standard of proof required in civil cases is on the balance of probabilities. This means the plaintiff must convince the court that the facts necessary for the case to succeed are more likely than not true.

In a criminal case, the enforcement of the criminal law by the state against a citizen, the prosecution must prove the facts in issue more convincingly. The criminal standard of proof is beyond a reasonable doubt.

Terminology

[1.53]   There are different terms used to describe the parties to a proceeding, depending on whether the matter is civil or criminal. The rules of the court in which the matter is being heard and the application of some legislation can also lead to differing descriptions being applied to the parties.

In civil claims the person bringing the action is variously called the plaintiff, petitioner, applicant or complainant. The person answering the claim is called the defendant or the respondent. If the matter goes to appeal the parties become the appellant or respondent. The terms plaintiff and defendant will be used for the purposes of this chapter.

The state conducts the case in criminal matters and is referred to as the prosecution or the Crown. Where the police conduct the case they may be referred to as the informant or complainant. The person charged with an offence is referred to as the defendant or the accused. The terms prosecution and accused will be used for the purposes of this chapter.

A civil action

[1.54]   Most parties to civil litigation are represented by lawyers. Each party through his or her lawyer prepares the case in advance of the trial by investigation of the facts and the law and the gathering and preparation of the evidence. The pre-trial procedures have two aims: to bring the best and most useful evidence to the court and to narrow the area of dispute as to both fact and law between the parties. This means that the court has only to deal with the issues between the parties and the hearing is shorter and less expensive than if the court had to hear every aspect of the matter.

Identifying the issues

[1.55]   The process of preparing a case for court involves several steps. Because the trial is a method of assisting the court to establish the truth of allegations it is not appropriate to engage in any trickery or to present last minute surprise evidence. The formal steps in preparation for trial are:

1. *Pleadings*   The plaintiff formally begins the battle by lodging with the court a document which sets out the essential facts of the case which, if true, would establish the plaintiff's claim at law. The defendant answers with a pleading which may admit some of the facts alleged by the plaintiff but deny others.

   The defendant may raise other facts to counter the arguments of the plaintiff. This identifies the facts which are in issue between the parties. In some cases the defendant will admit all the facts alleged by the plaintiff but submit arguments that the law to be applied is either different from that argued by the plaintiff or will produce a result different from that which the plaintiff seeks.

2. *Interrogatories*   Each party may discover facts by the process of interrogatories. Interrogatories are questions on facts in issue. The questions and answers are in writing and the answers must be given on oath. The interrogating party may use interrogatories to:
   • confirm facts already known. This saves the bringing of evidence to prove them;
   • discover facts known only to the other party. The party answering is bound by the answers which may be used as evidence of those facts.

3. *Discovery*   Discovery of documents is a procedure by which one party may require the other to produce documents relevant to the facts in issue. It prevents one party surprising the other at the trial with evidence which may have settled or disposed of the matter and thus avoids unnecessary litigation. The parties usually voluntarily show each other documents which prove the facts alleged.

Witnesses

[1.56]   The parties and their lawyers cannot rely on witnesses voluntarily appearing to give evidence, and so witnesses are served with subpoenas prior to the trial to ensure their attendance. Subpoenas are court orders commanding attendance. There are two types: to attend and give evidence, and to attend to give evidence *and* produce specified documents.

Most witnesses who give evidence in court give evidence of facts — what is done or not done, what was said or not said. Some witnesses are called as experts to give evidence based on their particular expert knowledge — accountants, medical practitioners, engineers and forensic scientists, for instance. These witnesses may, once the court has accepted their competence, give expert opinions based on their observations — the likely effect of physical injury or the presence of blood.

Conduct of the hearing

[1.57]   The plaintiff's lawyer will open the hearing with a statement which broadly sets out the case against the defendant. The witnesses for the plaintiff are then called and examined. Once the witnesses for the plaintiff (who may include the plaintiff) have testified, the plaintiff's case is closed and the defendant's case will be presented.

[1.58]   Examination of witnesses   The witness is first examined by the lawyer for the calling party. This is called examination-in-chief. In examination-in-chief the lawyer asks questions, the answers to which will bring out the evidence he or she wishes to put before the court. Documents supporting this evidence may be tendered.

In cross-examination the lawyer for the other party may ask wide questions both to challenge the evidence-in-chief and elicit new facts favourable to his or her client's case.

After cross-examination the first lawyer may re-examine the witness to explain or clarify evidence given in cross-examination.

When the witnesses for both sides have given evidence the lawyers make closing addresses. Closing addresses review the evidence, raise the differences as to both facts and law between the parties and make submissions as to the law which should be applied to the facts. The lawyers attempt by legal argument to persuade the court to adopt the interpretation of the law that favours their client's case.

The court's role

[1.59]   A civil trial is a legal battle between the two parties. It is the parties' role to conduct their cases so as to bring the relevant facts and legal arguments before the court. The court plays no part in the presentation of the cases.

The judge or magistrate has a twofold role:

- to ensure that the contest is conducted according to the rules of procedure and evidence; and
- to identify the relevant law and apply it to the facts presented, in order to reach a decision which finishes the matter between the parties.

A criminal action

[1.60]   A crime is an act or conduct which is prejudicial to the community and it renders the guilty person liable to punishment by fine or imprisonment. A crime may be committed even though no person has been harmed. The criminal legal system is concerned with the enforcement of the law by the state and for this reason legislation is the major source of criminal law. A feature of criminal proceedings is that the accused is afforded special protection in order to redress the advantages the state has in respect of resources and size. One form of protection is the presumption of innocence. The Crown must prove an accused's guilt beyond reasonable doubt. Another is that in most Australian jurisdictions the accused may give an unsworn statement from the dock instead of giving evidence on oath; this avoids the accused being subject to cross-examination.

Launching criminal proceedings

[1.61]   A range of public officials have the power to investigate conduct and initiate criminal proceedings but in the majority of cases the police conduct investigations. In some instances the police will initiate the action and conduct the prosecution while in others the Director of Public Prosecutions (DPP) will do so. The steps in the process of bringing an accused person to court to stand trial are as follows.

[1.62]   Investigation   The police have considerable powers to investigate crimes; these include the power to detain and interrogate people; to arrest suspects; to enter and search premises; and to seize property. These powers, although wide, are restricted and normally require authorisation in the form of warrants. Legislation has, however, expanded the powers to include the power to take fingerprints, photographs and body samples. The rules relating to the questioning of persons and the gathering of evidence by police must be strictly followed. Evidence unlawfully obtained, especially of alleged confessions, cannot be used against the accused person.

If the police are interviewing a suspect and decide to arrest, the suspect must be cautioned. The police are required to inform the suspect of the right to remain silent and that there is no obligation to answer their questions but if the person does answer the questions those answers may be taken down and used as evidence in court.

[1.63] Arrest Arrest and charging are formal procedures which commonly take place in the police station. The process of charging informs the accused person of the precise nature of the charge and the crime alleged. It also informs the accused and the court of the details of the case alleged. If bail is granted the accused will be required to appear in court on a specified date. If bail is not granted the accused will be remanded in custody until the date of the trial.

Summary and indictable offences

[1.64] Crimes that are not regarded as serious enough to be tried by a judge and jury may go straight to trial before a magistrate. These are called summary offences — dealt with in summary courts as discussed in **[1.34]**. Indictable offences are the more serious matters and are tried by a judge and jury. The first step for the trial of an indictable offence is the committal proceeding conducted by a magistrate to decide whether the prosecution has established that there is a prima facie case to answer. On some occasions indictable offences may be summarily heard, either because the accused opts for that or because the magistrate at the committal proceedings decides to try the matter.

Trial

[1.65] When the time of the trial arrives the accused is brought before the court and the charge is read, the accused is asked to plead guilty or not guilty. If the plea is not guilty, the jury is selected and empanelled. Jury selection is usually by ballot and each side has the right to challenge.

The roles of the jury and the judge in a trial are different. The jury must decide the facts by determining which evidence is true. Its role is then to decide the guilt or innocence of the accused. It is the judge's role to ensure that the proceedings are conducted properly and to determine the law which applies. Lawyers when addressing the jury should be assisting the jury in the discovery of the truth rather than arguing which law should be applied to determine guilt or innocence.

Arguments on points of law may be made at any time during the trial but the judge, not the jury, will determine them. After each side has made final addresses to the jury, the judge will sum up the case for the jury. The judge decides questions of law and will direct the jury as to the application of the law.

Remedies outside the court system

[1.66] The test of the value of legal rights is in whether they can be enforced. It is notorious that the cost of using the formal court system is beyond the means of most individuals. For many it becomes a comparison between cost and benefit. On that basis many legal rights are lost by default. There are some persons who will fight for the principle of the matter but that can be an expensive attitude. To some degree there have been improvements since the 1970s when small claims jurisdictions were established.

Recently, the banking, general insurance and life insurance industries have established dispute resolution schemes.

Self-help

[1.67]   It is often possible to resolve a problem without resorting to the courts. Merely by returning a defective item the consumer is able to enforce the statutory rights. For example, the rights under the Trade Practices Act are that if an item is defective the consumer has a primary right to be refunded the price. The supplier cannot insist on some other remedy such as repair or replacement. Signs that say 'We exchange but do not give refunds' are legally wrong and in fact are illegal under s 53(g) of the Trade Practices Act.

Government agencies

[1.68]   Another form of self-help for an aggrieved consumer is to enlist the support of the consumer affairs authorities. They usually and quite properly require that the consumer first attempts to resolve the issue with the supplier. In some cases the agency is the only one that can react; for example, where the conduct complained of amounts to a breach of s 53 of the Trade Practices Act. That is a matter requiring prosecution and the consumer is not able to do that. The consumer could become a witness in a prosecution and of course could launch action for damages sustained as a result of the breach: s 82.

Small claims jurisdiction

[1.69]   Small claims tribunals exist in New South Wales, Victoria, Queensland and Western Australia. In the other parts of Australia the existing court structure has been adjusted to accommodate small claims. While the difference between a court and a tribunal is not immediately apparent, it does have legal significance. A court has the capacity to enforce its own decisions whereas if a tribunal decision were ignored, further action in a court would be necessary to have it enforced.

   The object of the small claims jurisdiction was to provide a means of resolving disputes between traders and consumers that was cheap, informal and speedy. The legislation that set up the system makes it impossible to contract out the right to use a small claims body. In that way the consumer's rights are preserved. In Queensland and the Australian Capital Territory, for example, a trader is able to use the system in a dispute with another trader.

Operation of a small claims/consumer claims tribunal

[1.70]   The style of a small claims body is different to that of a court. Usually there is a referee who plays a more active role in finding a solution to the problem between the parties. The formal rules of evidence are dispensed with and legal representation is not permitted. This is probably appropriate in view of the factual nature of most disputes. For this reason also there is no right of appeal. A court may become involved in proceedings but only when it exercises its supervisory role over inferior bodies. It would do so where, for example, the tribunal was entering into a matter over which it had no jurisdiction or where natural justice was being abused.

   While the small claims system provides a robust form of justice which no doubt satisfies the parties, the style of its operations makes it necessary to impose financial limits on its jurisdiction. It is simply the fact that, despite the formality, the procedures of courts are much better at resolving complex disputes. For that reason the jurisdiction of the tribunals remains 'small':

- New South Wales: $10,000 ($25,000 for building disputes);
- Victoria: $5000;
- Queensland: $5000;
- South Australia: $2000;
- Western Australia: $6000;
- Tasmania: $2000;
- Australian Capital Territory: $5000; and
- Northern Territory: $5000.

Relevant legislation

[1.71] The relevant legislation for the states and territories is shown in the following table.

Relevant Legislation

Jurisdiction	Legislation
New South Wales	Consumer Claims Tribunals Act 1987
Victoria	Small Claims Tribunals Act 1973
Queensland	Small Claims Tribunals Act 1973
South Australia	Magistrates Court Act 1991
Western Australia	Small Claims Tribunals Act 1974
Tasmania	Magistrates Court (Small Claims Division) Act 1989
Australian Capital Territory	Small Claims Act 1974
Northern Territory	Small Claims Act 1974

Alternative dispute resolution

[1.72] Once a dispute has arisen in a commercial transaction it is necessary to consider means of resolving it. As stated earlier, the court system, through litigation, provides a mechanism for resolving disputes and declaring the rights of the parties. The court system is, however, expensive, very formal and time-consuming. The average individual cannot afford to use the courts and in most cases the parties solve the problem themselves — a form of self-help. There is often a commercial settlement where one party decides that the amount at stake is not worth fighting over. This approach recognises that, for a business, time is money and uncertainty is unwelcome.

[1.73] The non-court methods of bringing a dispute to an end are numerous. The mere threat of going to court is often enough to provide an effective solution. The more orthodox methods include compromise, negotiation, agreeing to disagree, accepting defeat, or imposing one's own penalties on the other party such as a boycott at some future date. In the commercial setting a traditional means of resolution has been arbitration. It has become part of a modern movement towards what is described as alternative dispute resolution (ADR) which also includes negotiation, conciliation, the use of experts, mini-trials and mediation. In some jurisdictions in Australia the courts have embraced ADR through court-annexed arbitration, conciliation and mediation. Variations of the court process of adjudication have been introduced in the form of 'inferior tribunals' such as the Small Claims Tribunals, the Administrative Appeals Tribunal and Commercial Tribunals. There are also industry-based systems for resolving disputes such as the Banking Ombudsman and the General Insurance Claims Review Panel.

Voluntary arbitration

[1.74]   It is not uncommon for parties to provide in their legal documents that any disputes which arise in the course of a transaction should be referred to an arbitrator. Quite often, the arbitrator is also specified; for example, a person nominated by the President of the Civil Engineers Society. The parties are, however, not prevented from deciding independently of any previous agreement to submit a matter to arbitration; the decision can be made at the time a dispute breaks out. Resolution of a dispute in this way involves a third party imposing a settlement.

Although arbitration is classified as a form of ADR, it can be undertaken with the rigour of a court action and with almost the same degree of formality and legalism. It offers the advantage of being cheaper, private and less time-consuming. In measuring the cost of settling a matter it is not only the direct financial cost that is relevant. The distraction that a drawn out court case can create for executives and the emotional strain are significant considerations. The privacy aspect is also important as court proceedings can result in the airing of dirty linen or the release of sensitive commercial information. Another advantage of arbitration is that the person chosen as arbitrator is more likely to have technical expertise in the area under dispute than a judge.

Arbitration is a process chosen by the parties with the procedures also being chosen by them if they wish. Despite the fact that arbitration is often described as part of the ADR style it is, like the formal court system, adversarial and it often incorporates procedures similar to those used by courts. These procedures, such as sworn evidence and subpoenas, make it easier to establish the facts of a dispute and, in that way, contribute to a better quality determination.

Commercial Arbitration Act

[1.75]   The decision to have a matter arbitrated is made by the parties but the general principles of arbitration are subject to legislation. In all of the states and territories there is modern and largely uniform legislation which deals with matters the parties may have overlooked or which they are unable to make provision for. The legislation (in this chapter the Commercial Arbitration Act 1984 (NSW)) recognises the importance of the arbitration agreement between the parties but it provides procedures where the agreement did not and, more importantly, it lays down general rules about the way in which the arbitration is to be carried out. The Act covers situations that the parties did not or could not provide for.

The relevant legislation in each state is shown in the following table.

Relevant Legislation

Jurisdiction	Legislation
New South Wales	Commercial Arbitration Act 1984
Victoria	Commercial Arbitration Act 1984
Queensland	Commercial Arbitration Act 1990
South Australia	Commercial Arbitration Act 1986
Western Australia	Commercial Arbitration Act 1985
Tasmania	Commercial Arbitration Act 1986
Australian Capital Territory	Commercial Arbitration Act 1986
Northern Territory	Commercial Arbitration Act 1985

The arbitrator

[1.76]　The Act provides that, unless the agreement provides otherwise or the parties subsequently agree, there will be a single arbitrator: s 6. The arbitrator's authority is irrevocable, subject to the agreement: s 50. Subject to any other arrangement, the Act provides that if there are more than two arbitrators one will be appointed as president and matters will be decided by majority vote: s 15. It is possible for the arbitrators to appoint an umpire whose role is to break any deadlock between arbitrators: s 12. The umpire becomes part of the process but only when the two appointed arbitrators are unable to make an award. The ability to appoint an umpire ultimately contributes to a decision being made.

Should the appointment of an arbitrator as required by an agreement not proceed, or a vacancy occur, the court can make the appointment: ss 10, 11.

Arbitration procedure

[1.77]　In an arbitration, the arbitrator has the power, subject to the agreement, to decide how to conduct proceedings: s 14. This power is, however, ultimately supervised by the court. If the arbitrator has misconducted proceedings — in other words, has ignored the rules of natural justice — the court has the power to set aside the award: s 42. Likewise, if the arbitrator is misconducting proceedings the court has a power of removal: s 44. The parties to an arbitration agreement are able to provide that the arbitrator can require evidence to be given on oath, by affirmation or by affidavit: s 19. This is a significant power as it formalises the hearing and improves the capacity to make a finding of fact. If a person refuses to give sworn evidence the arbitrator, or one of the parties, is able to seek an order from the court requiring the person to appear before the court: s 18. It is also possible for the arbitrator, or one of the parties, to apply to the court for a subpoena to be served on the other party: s 17. The subpoena, once issued, orders the person to appear before the arbitrator and/or bring documents to the hearing. The remedy under s 18 to seek an order to have the person appear before the court is available should the person disobey the subpoena.

The formal nature of arbitration is illustrated by s 22 which says that in the course of the arbitration any questions that arise must be determined according to law. The Act also allows considerations of general justice and fairness to be taken into account.

The formality of proceedings, the importance of questions of law and the fact that issues of natural justice could be at stake raise the question of legal representation before the arbitrator. The parties are free to agree that legal representation is to be allowed. The Act also specifies other circumstances where representation is possible. These are where the other party is represented, where the amount which is subject to the arbitration exceeds $20,000 or if the arbitrator gives leave for representation: s 20(1). The arbitrator must give leave where it is shown that to have legal representation will shorten proceedings or that, without it, a party is disadvantaged: s 20(3).

Alternatives to arbitration

[1.78]   The parties are always free to seek other ways of settling a dispute. Section 27 provides that even if there is an arbitration agreement the parties may seek to settle their dispute by 'mediation, conciliation or similar means'. They may abandon the arbitration process and authorise the arbitrator to perform as a mediator or conciliator or in some other capacity. If a party to an arbitration agreement launches court proceedings the other party is able to seek to have those proceedings stayed which means that they could be stopped by the court: s 53. The application will be granted if the court is satisfied that the party who is applying is ready and willing to proceed with the arbitration and the matter is one that can go to arbitration.

Arbitration and litigation

[1.79]   Prior to the Act the parties were able to include what was called a *Scott v Avery* clause. The effect of such a clause was to prevent the parties to an agreement going to court until there had first been arbitration. Section 55 of the Act has made these clauses inoperative but the ability of a party to seek a stay of proceedings under s 53 means that parties are not able to ignore the arbitration agreement and litigate rather than arbitrate.

The award

[1.80]   Once a matter has gone to arbitration the Act provides that, unless otherwise provided in the agreement, the award shall be final and binding: s 28. In this way the arbitration process is different from mediation and other methods in that it is an imposed settlement of the dispute whereas the others are agreed resolutions. When an award is made, the Act requires it to be in writing, signed and supported by reasons but the parties are able to vary this: s 29. The Act provides that the arbitrator is able to make awards as to costs but the agreement may make other arrangements: s 34.

The final and binding quality of the award is emphasised by s 38(1) of the Act which states a general rule that the court has no power to set aside an award. An exception is that an appeal can be heard on a question of law: s 38(2). In the course of the hearing, an arbitrator can ask the court to determine a question of law. The court will agree to the request if it is satisfied that to do so could result in 'substantial savings in costs to the parties' and it is a question on which the court would give leave to appeal: s 39. Another circumstance where the court will intervene is where there has been misconduct on the part of the arbitrator or the proceedings have been misconducted or the award has been improperly procured: s 42. Misconduct in this context means fraud, partiality, bias or an absence of natural justice. Similar grounds can justify the court in removing the arbitrator — where there has been misconduct, undue influence or if the arbitrator is incompetent or unsuitable: s 44. The arbitrator is not liable in negligence but is liable in fraud: s 51.

Enforceability of awards

[1.81] The enforceability of awards is dealt with by the Act. If the matter is one where the court could order specific performance — the party who has lost the case is required to perform what was promised under a contract — the arbitrator is able to make the same order unless the arbitration agreement provides otherwise: s 24. An award is enforceable by leave of the court in the same way as a judgment or order of a court: s 33.

International arbitration

[1.82] Arbitration lends itself to the settlement of disputes in international commerce. It overcomes the problems of different legal systems and different laws. The critical issue of enforcement has been solved through work undertaken by the United Nations. The United Nations Commission on International Trade Law (UNCITRAL) developed a set of rules which have become part of Australian law. The 1985 UNCITRAL Model Law was made law in Australia through an amendment to the Arbitration (Foreign Awards and Agreements) Act 1974 (Cth). That Act and the Commercial Arbitration Acts provide for the recognition and enforcement of foreign arbitration awards.

Other alternative methods

[1.83] Apart from arbitration there are other methods of settling a dispute outside the formal court system. The parties may negotiate a settlement between themselves so that no third party is involved. They may resolve the matter by agreement through a variety of assisted forms.

Mediation

[1.84] This is a process whereby a neutral third party works towards encouraging the parties to discover a settlement formula. Unlike arbitration or the court, there is no imposed settlement. The role of the mediator is to provide the encouragement to bring about what otherwise would be a negotiated settlement. What resolves the dispute is determined by the parties. The mediation process is not governed by legislation and does not have a particular form.

Conciliation

[1.85] Conciliation is like mediation to the extent that a third person is involved. The role of the third person is more active in conciliation because it can involve discussions with and counselling of the parties, giving of advice and offering suggestions for resolution. The conciliator intervenes to a greater degree than the mediator and the views and conduct of the conciliator could be significant factors in the outcome. The conciliator is not as decisive as an arbitrator and if a matter cannot be conciliated arbitration is the next step.

Expert opinion

[1.86] In this situation the parties agree to be bound by the opinion of an independent expert. The parties could agree, for example, that an engineer's opinion about the cause of damage to a building will provide the basis for a settlement. The person acting as an expert does no more than what is necessary to give a technical, unbiased opinion. The expert opinion may be sought on such a technical matter or it might be a finding of fact or a legal opinion or it might be an opinion by a merchant banker about the fairness of a share price.

The courts and the alternative schemes

[1.87]   The courts do not operate exclusively by way of the traditional style of trials. There have been developments at both state and federal level to provide mediation, conciliation and arbitration. Court-annexed arbitration allows some courts to impose a compulsory form of arbitration in civil cases. Courts are also able to refer a matter to arbitration with the agreement of the parties.

In a number of jurisdictions, cases can be referred to mediation or conciliation, sometimes by judges and other times by the court registrar. The Federal Court, for example, in its court rules provides a facility for 'mediated resolution of proceedings'.

Industry-based resolution schemes

[1.88]   Since the late 1980s several industry-based forms of dispute resolution have emerged. This has been the result of community and government pressure reflecting the fact that access to the formal court system is limited. In some cases overseas examples have inspired Australian industries to establish schemes. The areas where the developments took place are typically where there is an imbalance between the parties — where individuals are in dispute with large institutions.

The Trade Practices Commission (now the Australian Competition and Consumer Commission) was interested to ensure that the industry-based codes of conduct were not anti-competitive and that they complied with the consumer protection law. It was not unknown in Australia for a industry association to establish a code of practice or code of ethics which was no more than a public relations exercise. The code very often protected members of the association from competition. For example, a code could provide that price cutting was unethical and, by so doing, it would enshrine price fixing within that industry. Another reason for the interest in the codes of conduct was that they incorporated mechanisms for the processing of complaints.

Banking and insurance industry schemes

[1.89]   On a wider scale, schemes have been developed in the banking and insurance sectors. These are the longest established schemes and have been influenced by similar schemes in the United Kingdom.

The Banking Ombudsman

[1.90]   This scheme was introduced in May 1989, three years after its United Kingdom model. It comprises the private banks who finance the scheme according to the number of disputes they each generate. This form of financing offers an incentive for institutions to settle a dispute before it reaches the Ombudsman.

The independence issue

[1.91]   For a scheme such as this to succeed it must have public acceptance which makes it is necessary to create the perception of independence. Although the scheme is financed by the banks it is accepted as independent because the Ombudsman is separated from the banks by the Australian Banking Industry Ombudsman Council which is the governing body of the scheme. It comprises equal representation by consumer and banking industry members with an independent chair (the first of whom was Sir Ninian Stephen, a former

Governor-General of Australia and High Court justice). The first report of the Banking Ombudsman contained the following statement:

> Independence lies at the very heart of the ability to deliver justice — whether that be through the courts, by mediation, arbitration or other forms of alternative dispute resolution.

Jurisdiction

[1.92] The Banking Ombudsman is guided by Terms of Reference which specify the jurisdiction and procedures. According to the Ombudsman's first annual report:

> The Ombudsman has chosen to adopt the more innovative practices of alternative dispute resolution rather than the more formal evidentiary process of the court system or the formal interview processes of parliamentary ombudsmen in resolving disputes. The processes of mediation, conciliation, negotiation and arbitration have been identified as working particularly well in situations where the disputing parties need to re-establish relationships. They also work well where parties can neither afford the time nor cost of a court's formal adversarial processes but need a forum to simply clarify information. Most importantly, they provide the opportunities for parties to reach their own solutions and settle matters amicably.

General Insurance Claims Review Panel

[1.93] The General Insurance Claims Review Panel ('the Panel'), which comprises an independent chair, a person nominated by the insurance industry and one nominated by the federal government, was established in September 1991. It is part of the Insurance Industry Complaint Resolution Scheme. The participating insurance companies are bound by contract with Insurance Enquiries and Complaints Ltd to observe the determinations of the Panel.

The Panel is last in the line of procedures where there is a complaint. Under the General Insurance Code of Practice the initial inquiry is conducted by an Internal Dispute Resolution panel within the insurer's organisation.

The Code of Practice was largely formulated by the industry but the Insurance Act 1973 s 113 requires that general insurers subscribe to the Code as a condition of conducting general insurance business.

Jurisdiction of the Panel

[1.94] The Panel has jurisdiction to deal with disputes governed by the Insurance Contracts Act. This means that effectively all forms of consumer insurance is subject to the Panel. It is also able to deal with some small business policies. Without the backing of an Act of Parliament the Panel, like all other non-statutory tribunals, is unable to require sworn evidence, nor can it compel witnesses to attend or to produce material. As a result, the procedure adopted when the Panel conducts a hearing is inquisitorial. Cases which involve allegations of fraud are dealt with by a referee who has wide powers to investigate the allegations but who is as procedurally limited as the Panel.

The monetary limit for the Panel is set out in its Terms of Reference which provides for adjustment in line with CPI movements. The definition of a small business for the purposes of the Panel is one operated by an individual, partnership or company; with no more than five employees (including working proprietors) and an annual turnover also adjusted according to the CPI.

Basis of decisions

[1.95] In arriving at its determination the Panel 'shall have regard to what is fair and reasonable in all the circumstances; it must also have regard to good insurance practice, the terms of the policy, and established legal principle'. A matter may be withheld from the Panel if the factual issues are beyond the capacity of its procedures or if it raises an important issue of law of general application. These provisions quite properly recognise the limitations of an informal dispute resolution system and keep from the Panel matters that are better resolved within the formal court system where the interests of the parties can be protected through the procedures of a court.

Independence

[1.96] The Panel is funded by participating insurers. Between the Panel and the insurers stands a company, Insurance Enquiries and Complaints Ltd, which acts as a buffer between the participating companies and the Panel. It provides administrative support for the Panel and is the conduit for the funding. Participating insurers pay a membership fee and are charged for each matter involving them that reaches the Panel. If the matter is decided against them a further fee is charged. In this way there is pressure on insurers to resolve disputes before they reach the Panel.

Summary and key terms

[1.97]   This chapter has set out to explain:

- Where Australia's law came from — the sources of law and the importance of the historical *connections*.
- The significance of the Constitution in our legal system. In particular the way in which it established the institutions of government — parliament, the executive and the judicature — the way it divided power between the Commonwealth and the states and the provisions it makes for guaranteeing personal freedoms.
- How the courts are organised — the state and federal systems, the difference between summary and indictable matters, the significance of the hierarchy of courts.
- Why *common law* is part of the Australian legal tradition and how our system of common law differs from the civil law systems.
- The way in which *legislation* is the supreme form of law-making and the relationship between common law and legislation.
- What it means to refer to *'judge-made' law*.
- The *doctrine of precedent* and how it affects the development and application of law.
- The relative importance of binding and persuasive precedent.
- How a precedent can be overcome by the way courts are able to overrule a precedent.
- The way in which equity developed and its place in the system.
- Civil and criminal law and their differences.
- Remedies that exist outside the formal court system. These include the *Small Claims* jurisdictions, *Alternative Dispute Resolution* and industry systems such as the *General Insurance Claims Review Panel*.

2
Contract: Formation

What this chapter does ...

The first stage of a contract is its formation and there is a considerable amount of law about that. This chapter examines:

- the rights and obligations which exist between the parties to contracts;

- the formation of a contract — offer, acceptance, agreement, consideration and the intention to be legally bound;

- who may enter a contract — capacity;

- who may be liable on or enforce a contract — privity; and

- what happens where the parties do not have a valid contract but it would be unfair or unjust to deny one party the benefit of the transaction — part performance and estoppel.

The law of contract is about the processes involved in making and performing contracts. This law is at the heart of every commercial transaction. The legal relationships created by contracts have been regulated by the law for at least one thousand years. The law is constantly changing and contract law provides many examples of the courts using equity to develop the law and reduce the harsh result of a strict application of the common law rules.

Australian contract law is comprised of legislation as well as judge-made law. The federal and state parliaments have legislated to control particular types of contract (Sale of Goods Acts); the enhance the rights of consumers as parties to a contract (Fair Trading Acts); to provide relief from contracts in certain cases (Contracts Review Act 1980 (NSW)); and to determine the rights and obligations of parties at the end of a contract: Frustrated Contracts Act 1988 (SA).

Introduction

Contracts

[2.1]   Entering into a contract, whether private or commercial, is the most common legal transaction undertaken. If persons voluntarily give promises to each other and assume an obligation to make good those promises a contract may come into existence. Every day of the year people enter into contracts — leases, purchases, loans, mortgages, guarantees, purchases of goods and services, to name but a few. Whether the contract is for the purchase of a loaf of bread or for a loan to finance a $10 million undertaking it will be governed by the law.

The law of contract revolves around the question of enforceability of promises. Many of the other topics discussed in this book are related to the law of contract — agency, consumer transactions, intellectual property, insurance and banking law among others.

The law governing contracts and the rights and obligations of the parties to them consists of case law — both common law and equity — and legislation. Australian contract law has its foundation in the common law rules developed over centuries, but takes much of its structure from later legislative rules. There is a tension between the common law's view of contract as private law reflecting the self-imposed, or freely assumed obligations of a contract and recent developments in equity and legislation which reflect public values and impose standards of commercial conduct.

Is there a contract?

[2.2]   The law relating to formation of contracts deals with both the 'legal' requirements — offer, acceptance, agreement, consideration, the intention to be legally bound and capacity — and the question of what happens where the parties' actions have not resulted in a valid contract but it would be unfair or unjust to deny one party the benefit of the transaction. The formation of a contract may be affected by the conduct of one party: what appears to be a valid contract may be vitiated or rendered ineffective by unfair pressure, mistake, deceit, misrepresentation or unconscionable conduct. Both the common law and legislation provide remedies in these situations.

What does the contract say and what does it mean?

[2.3]   Even where the parties believe they are in agreement, it will not always be clear just what terms make up the contract and, even where the content of the contract is agreed, the meaning of the words may be in dispute. The determination of a remedy will require the identification of the terms of the contract and an assessment of the importance of the terms breached or of the effect of the breach on the contract.

What happens when the contract ends?

[2.4]   Contracts may be discharged in a variety of ways; for example, by performance, breach or frustration. The method of discharge will influence the remedies available to any party who suffers damage.

Commercial transactions are the foundation of the business world; in everyday life people enter into contracts continually. Each party to a contract needs to know the content and meaning of that contract, and, if things go wrong, each party needs to know what rights, obligations, liabilities and remedies exist. Common sense tells us that a large percentage of business people make contracts and solve disputes without any, or with only minimal reference to, the applicable legal principles: litigation is often not a commercial or realistic path. Litigation is expensive, time-consuming and often will not give the parties what they want. Arbitration and alternative dispute resolution are discussed in **[1.72]**–**[1.88]**.

What is a contract?

[2.5]   A contract may be described as an agreement or set of promises that the law will enforce. Not every promise to do something will be enforced: the law has to determine which promises give rise to legal obligation and which give rise to merely moral obligation. Where a promise does give rise to a legal obligation, that obligation may arise irrespective of the existence of a contract; for example, in the tort of negligence or under the doctrine of estoppel.

The term 'contract' refers to a binding agreement: an agreement which will be enforced by the courts. This notion of enforceability is central to contract law: an aggrieved person is seeking a remedy and forcing the other party to honour its obligations is, to many, the first and most obvious remedy. Classical contract theory saw the role of the courts as being to give effect to the intention of the parties. This was based on the notion that the wishes or intention of the parties created rights and obligations, which once identified would be enforced. The common law of contract is therefore centrally concerned with the rules relating to the formation, the meaning, the breach, the termination and the enforcement of legally binding agreements. The courts have developed the equitable principles relating to contract by applying standards of reasonableness, fairness, good faith and good conscience to the conduct of the parties. Both state and Commonwealth legislation has reflected these developments; for example, the Contracts Review Act 1980 (NSW) allows a court to undo and rewrite a contract if circumstances render the contract harsh or unjust. As a result of these developments the body of law which governs contracts now does much more than apply common law rules.

Which promises will be performed?

[2.6]   How does one determine whether any particular promise will be enforced as contractual? There are three essential elements which must be present before any set of promises will be a legally enforceable contract. These are:

- actual agreement — the parties must have concluded their negotiations and have 'struck a deal';
- the intention to be legally bound — the parties must expect that legal rights and obligations will arise from their agreement; and
- consideration — there must be a bargain or exchange underlying the agreement; something is to be given in return for the promise (unless the agreement is contained in a deed: see **[2.7]**).

Although all three elements are necessary for the existence of a contract, their presence does not mean that every such agreement is an enforceable contract. There may be other factors which will prevent legal obligation to perform arising; for example, one of the parties may lack capacity, the agreement may not be real if consent was obtained by force or fraud, or the contract may be for the performance of an illegal act.

[2.7] A promise which is gratuitous, that is 'free' or not supported by consideration, will only be enforceable if it is contained in a deed. The promises contained in deeds are called covenants. Covenants can be enforced at common law, but, because equity will not assist a volunteer, the parties to a deed do not have access to equitable remedies such as specific performance. Equity may, however, intervene to stop the maker of a deed from denying the deed. Deeds are often used to ensure that gifts, contracts not supported by consideration and trusts are enforceable.

A deed is an instrument that is:

- written on paper, parchment or vellum;
- signed by the party or parties to the deed. The party to be bound by the deed must sign or put their mark on the instrument;
- sealed: very few people still use personal seals and so most Australian jurisdictions have legislation which deems instruments to be sealed if they are expressed to be so;
- delivered: while a deed is only operative on delivery this is not confined to a physical handing over of the instrument. Delivery relates to an act done which shows that the maker of the deed intends to be legally bound;
- intended to operate as a deed; that is, the maker of the deed by signing shows that there is true intent to do the action required by the deed; and,
- affects the legal interests or position of the parties.

Freedom of contract

[2.8] It is an underlying theme of the common law that contracts freely entered into will be enforced by the courts. The doctrine of freedom of contract has two key aspects: that every person is free to enter into a contract with any person they choose and to contract on any terms they want. Presumably it could also be said that every person has the freedom to refuse to contract if either the terms or the other party are not suitable. This doctrine, along with the principle of caveat emptor (let the buyer beware), arose from the law merchant because the courts saw their role as one of upholding contracts.

> If there is one thing which more than another public policy requires it is that men of full age and competent understanding shall have the utmost liberty of contracting, and that their contracts, when entered into freely and voluntarily shall be held sacred and shall be enforced by the courts of justice. (Jessel MR in *Printing & Numerical Registering Co v Sampson* (1875) LR 19 Eq 462 at 465)

The doctrine of freedom of contract is still recognised today, although it is often in conflict with commercial and legal reality. The widespread use of standard form contracts and the 'take it or leave it' approach of business mean that often one party to the contract is not exercising freedom of choice, indeed there is little evidence of bargaining in most consumer contracts. Legislation has also whittled away the freedom of contract so that the terms of some contracts are implied by statutes such as the Trade Practices Act 1974 (Cth) and the terms on which parties do contract may be set aside by judicial review under legislation like the Contracts Review Act 1980 (NSW). In addition, the state has imposed the obligation to contract on citizens in some circumstances, such as compulsory third party injury insurance and workers compensation issuance.

How do you know that you have a contract?

[2.9]   The formation of a contract usually follows negotiation by the parties and in the case of commercial contracts these negotiations can be long and complex. Before a court can adjudicate on any transaction, it must be able to determine its legal nature. Two basic themes are present in the process of identifying any particular transaction as a contract: agreement and bargain.

There will always be two or more parties to a contract, but at times there will be no readily identifiable negotiations; for example, the purchase of a shirt in a department store may involve no more than selecting the shirt and paying for it. Where there are at least two promisors, and each has promised to do something in return for a promise from the other, the contract which results is a bilateral contract; for example, a repairman promises to come to a house and fix the television and the householder promises to pay for that service. A unilateral contract will arise where only one party is obliged to perform its promise: reward cases are an example where the finder is not under obligation to search.

The traditional approach to determining whether there is a contract centres on agreement. It seeks to identify the time at which the parties have concluded their negotiations and can be said to have formed a contract. This is done by labelling the stages of negotiation (offer, acceptance and agreement), and confirming both the consideration supporting the contract and the parties' intention to be legally bound. While this approach was well suited to a commercial environment where negotiations were conducted by post and where the pace of commerce was steady, it is not always appropriate given today's complex commercial environment and rapid communication technology.

Agreement

[2.10]   A contract cannot be formed in the absence of agreement. The parties must have reached *consensus ad idem* (a meeting of the minds): this will usually be when they are finally agreed and negotiations are complete. Simply put this means that each party has clearly and without qualification accepted the offers made by the other. Usually the agreement will be express; for example, contained in a formal contract or in a spoken agreement sealed by a handshake. Where it is not express the courts are willing to find agreement in the conduct of the parties; for example, if a store receives an order for a television set by facsimile and then signs and returns the facsimile with minor amendments and then delivers the television. It is likely that a contract for the purchase of the television will be found to exist even though the second facsimile is not acceptance but a counter-offer: see **[2.29]**.

Whether or not a binding agreement has been reached depends upon whether the parties commonly intended to do so. This common intention will be objectively determined by the courts by interpreting the overt actions of the parties as a reasonable, objective bystander would. In *Smith v Hughes* (1871) LR 6 QB 597 at 607, Blackburn J said:

> … I apprehend that if one of the parties intends to make a contract on one set of terms, and the other intends to make a contract on another set of terms, or as it is sometimes expressed, the parties are not ad idem, there is no contract, unless the circumstances are such as to preclude one of the parties from denying that he agreed to the terms of the other … If, whatever a man's real intention may be, he so conducts himself that *a reasonable man would believe that he was assenting to the terms proposed by the other party*, and that other party upon that belief enters into the contract with him, the man thus conducting himself would be equally bound as if he intended to agree to the other party's terms. [emphasis added]

Offer

[2.11]   Offer may be described as the opening statement of the negotiations between the parties or the statement which signifies the willingness to contract. Offer may be defined as a statement capable of giving rise to a contract on acceptance. To classify a statement as an offer the statement must be more than a mere expression of interest in doing business, and it must be shown that the offeror intended to be bound upon acceptance. That is, an offer is promissory in nature. The person making the offer is called the offeror and the person to whom the offer is made is called the offeree.

It is not always easy to determine whether a statement amounts to an offer. A statement may be an invitation to treat, mere puff or a request for information; which it is will depend on whether the person to whom the statement was directed can reasonably infer that the maker of the statement intended it as an offer. Suppose John owns a farm and Bob wants to buy it, so Bob sends a facsimile to John and asks 'Will you sell me your farm? Fax lowest price.' John, who has not considered selling his farm, nevertheless sends the following reply: '$200,000 lowest price.' Will there be a binding contract created by Bob's next fax: 'I agree to buy your farm for $200,000'? Was there ever an offer to sell the farm made? In *Harvey v Facey* [1893] AC 552 correspondence similar to this was characterised as a request for information and the supply of that information. It could not be reasonably inferred that John was offering to sell his farm.

Mere puff

[2.12]   Mere puff is a representation in exaggerated and often non-specific language, which clearly over-exaggerates the characteristics of a product or service. If a statement is mere puff it will not be an offer because the maker of the statement did not intend it to be so. The Carbolic Smoke Ball Co published in London newspapers an advertisement promoting the use of the Carbolic Smoke Ball for the prevention of influenza. The advertisement was as follows.

> One hundred pound reward will be paid to any person who contracts the increasing Epidemic Influenza, colds or any disease caused by taking cold, after having used the CARBOLIC SMOKE BALL according to the printed directions supplied with each Ball. £1000 is deposited with the Alliance Bank showing our sincerity in the matter.

Mrs Carlill, on the faith of the advertisement, purchased one of the balls, used it according to the directions, but nevertheless contracted influenza.

When Mrs Carlill applied for the £100 reward, the Carbolic Smoke Ball Company refused to pay, arguing, inter alia, that the advertisement was not a binding promise to pay, or an offer to contract, but mere puff. In *Carlill v Carbolic Smoke Ball Co* [1883] 1 QB 256 at 261–2, Lindley LJ said:

> We must first consider whether this was intended to be a promise at all, or whether it was a mere puff which meant nothing. Was it a mere puff? My answer to that question is No and I base my answer on this passage: '£1000 is deposited with the Alliance Bank, showing our sincerity in this matter'. Now for what was that money deposited or that statement made except to negative the suggestion that this was a mere puff and meant nothing at all? ... advertisements offering rewards. They are offers to anybody who performs the conditions named in the advertisements and anybody who does perform the conditions

accepts the offer. In point of law this advertisement is an offer to pay £100 to anybody who will performs these conditions and performance of the conditions is the acceptance of the offer.

[2.13]   The claim of mere puff as used in *Carlill* was often a 'defence' in relation to advertising claims and there are today many advertisements in which the claims made for a product can be said to be mere puff. The fact that a statement would be considered mere puff at common law does not mean that it cannot be misleading and deceptive conduct for the purposes of s 52 of the Trade Practices Act 1974.

In Western Australia a builder said in an advertisement '*If you don't get Collier to build your home you won't be getting the best deal*'. A competitor claimed that the statement was misleading and thus in breach of s 52. The Federal Court said that it would not be correct to say that even if a statement was classified as mere puff that statement could not be characterised as conduct that was misleading and deceptive, and that in some circumstances a representation that something was 'bigger and better' could be both mere puff *and* misleading and deceptive. Any reasonable person would understand the statement as conveying no more precise meaning than that the builder regarded itself as offering the best deal. The statement did not breach s 52: *Collier Constructions Pty Ltd v Foskett Pty Ltd* (1990) 97 ALR 460;19 IPR 44; ATPR (Digest) 46–063.

Invitation to treat

[2.14]   An invitation to treat is merely an expression of interest in doing business and carries no legal obligation. An invitation to treat is not a positive undertaking, it is an expression of willingness to enter negotiations. Most displays of goods on shop shelves, catalogues and advertisements are not offers but invitations to treat. This means that if a person responds to an advertisement for goods but is not able to purchase them because, for instance, the seller has run out of stock, no remedy is available in contract. The Trade Practices Act 1974 or related consumer legislation may provide remedies.

In *Pharmaceutical Society of Great Britain v Boots Cash Chemists (Southern) Ltd* [1953] 1 QB 401 the display of priced goods on a shelf was held not to infringe a statute prohibiting the sale of drugs except under the supervision of a registered pharmacist. The display was merely an invitation to treat and not an offer to sell; the customer made an offer to buy by taking the goods to the checkout. The cashier could either reject or accept the offer. The court said that in the case of an ordinary shop, although goods are displayed and it is intended that customers should go and choose what they want, the contract is not completed until customers have indicated the articles needed, and the shopkeeper accepts that offer. In a modern supermarket the display of goods on shelves is an invitation to treat; selecting goods and placing them in the trolley is not an offer — it carries no obligation to buy or even to offer to buy — the goods can be replaced on the shelf. There are two times when the offer could be said to arise: either the customer makes an offer to buy by placing the goods on the checkout counter, and the checkout operator accepts that offer by putting the goods through the register; or the checkout operator makes an offer to sell by putting the goods through the register, and the customer accepts that offer by payment.

Tenders

[2.15]   Suppose a corporation wishes to construct an office block and calls for tenders from interested building companies. Those interested building companies will, after considering the detailed requirements of the project, submit tenders. Is the corporation bound to accept the best tender? In general a call for tenders is not regarded as an offer but as an invitation to treat. The caller is doing no more than gathering information from which a willingness to negotiate may emerge.

Where the tenders called for are for the supply of goods or services for a stated period then the acceptance of a bid may or may not result in a binding contract. This depends on the ostensible intention of the parties. Acceptance may bind one party to supply and the other to accept the goods or services for the contract period, or it may be merely a selection by the buyer of the party from whom the goods and services will be acquired. In the latter case no binding contract is created until a specific order is placed.

Use of the word 'offer'

[2.16]   A description of a statement by one party to negotiations as an offer or as an invitation to treat will not of itself determine the matter. *Harvela Investments Ltd v Royal Trust Co of Canada (CI) Ltd* [1985] 1 All ER 261 illustrates the point that it is the underlying intention of the speaker and not the words used which is crucial. The Royal Trust Co had a parcel of shares for sale and invited two possible purchasers 'to make a single offer' for the parcel of shares. The offer was to be made by sealed tender and Royal Trust undertook to accept the higher of the two. The court had to determine whether a binding contract came into existence on the receipt of the higher tender. There are two interpretations to be put on the actions of the parties: the invitation was an offer to buy from the highest bidder and acceptance of that offer was achieved by bidding the highest, or the invitation was merely an invitation to make an offer, the bid was the offer and acceptance required another step by the Royal Trust. The first interpretation was accepted by the court and despite the use of the phrase 'make an offer' the invitation was found to be an offer. Waller LJ said (at 265):

> If it were not for the words 'We bind ourselves to accept', this would have been a mere invitation to treat; but those words … make it an offer which the bidder being highest accepted.

To whom may an offer be made?

[2.17]   An offer need not be directed to an identified person but may be made to a particular person, a class of persons or to the whole world. Rewards and advertisements are examples of offers made to a wide class; the contract is formed only with the person who accepts by acting in response to the offer. In *Carlill v Carbolic Smoke Ball Co* [1883] 1 QB 256 it was argued that the offer was not valid because it is not permissible to contract with the whole world, but the court said (Bowen LJ at 268):

> it is not a contract made with the whole world … it is an offer made to all the world; and why should not an offer be made to all the world which is to ripen into a contract with anybody who comes forward and performs the condition.

The offer must be communicated to the person[s] for whom it was intended

[2.18]   Without communication of the offer there can be no acceptance. Unless the second party is acting in response to the offer there can be no *consensus ad idem*. It follows from this that any acceptance must be in reliance on the offer. This means that doing an act without knowledge of an offer cannot ever be acceptance.

Termination of offers

[2.19]   A binding contract will result only from the acceptance of an offer while the offer remains operative or in existence. An offer will cease to be operative if it is revoked by the offeror or lapses with the passing of time, for example.

Options

[2.20]   A promise to hold an offer open for a specified time or a statement that an offer will remain open for a stated time, indicates the date at which the offer will lapse. The offeror can revoke the offer prior to the time indicated, unless the offeree has purchased an option; that is, given consideration, or paid for, the promise. Such options are most commonly purchased in relation to the acquisition of land or shares. Griffith CJ said in *Goldsbrough Mort & Co Ltd v Quinn* (1910)10 CLR 674 at 678:

> ... an offer may be withdrawn at any time before acceptance. A mere promise to leave it open for a specified time makes no difference, because there is, as yet, no agreement, and the promise if made without some distinct consideration is nudum pactum and not binding. But if there is ... a consideration for the promise it is binding. This is often expressed by saying that an option given for value is not revocable.

Conditional offers

[2.21]   An offer may be made on condition and cannot be accepted unless the condition is fulfilled. Such conditions usually require that either a specified state of affairs continues to exist or that acceptance is not possible until some other act is complete or state of affairs achieved. Commonly offers to purchase land are conditional on the purchaser being able to obtain finance.

Revocation of an offer

[2.22]   Revocation may occur at any time before acceptance and it brings the offer to an end. Revocation must be communicated to the other party but direct communication is not necessary — it is enough that the offeree is reliably informed. This principle is seen in *Dickinson v Dodds* (1876) 2 Ch D 463, where Dodds offered in writing to sell his property to Dickinson and the document stated, 'This offer to be left open until Friday, 9 o'clock am, 12 June 1874'. On the afternoon of Thursday 11 June Dickinson was told that Dodds had agreed to sell the property to another. Dickinson then 'accepted' the offer by delivering a note to Dodds' house on the Thursday evening and again by handing Dodds a written acceptance on the Friday morning. Dodds said this was too late as the property had already been sold. Could Dickinson accept an offer which he knew had been revoked, or was Dodds bound to keep the offer open as promised? The court said (at 472–3):

> ... this promise ... was not binding, and that at any moment before a complete acceptance by Dickinson of the offer, Dodds was as free as Dickinson himself ... It may well be that one man is bound ... to let the other man know that his mind with regard to the offer has been changed ... it is ... quite clear that before there was any attempt at acceptance [Dickinson] was well aware that Dodds had changed his mind ... It is impossible therefore to say that there was ever that existence of the same mind between the two parties which is essential in point of law to the making of the agreement.

There are problems with the actual revocation of some offers, such as that made to the whole world in *Carlill*. Revocation by the same method as the original offer would be effective: if an offer is made in a newspaper advertisement, its revocation should be made in a similar newspaper advertisement.

Further special difficulties arise from some unilateral contracts; for example, if a person promises to give you $2000 if you stop smoking for two years. The principle of *Carlill* that the performance of the action amounts to acceptance of the offer means that you cannot have accepted the offer until you have stopped smoking for two years. Would this mean that the person can revoke the offer at any time before acceptance, say, when you have not been smoking for 22 months? The courts take the view that once the offeree has begun to perform there is an implied obligation that the offer will not be retracted. If there is such a retraction of the offer this would probably be regarded as a breach of contract.

A person making an offer may specify a time for acceptance, after which the offer lapses and cannot be accepted. A person offering to sell a house to another, may say 'I promise to keep the offer open until 9.00 am on 12 June'. That offer may be accepted at any time up to 9.00 am 12 June but cannot be accepted after that. Where no time is specified an offer must be accepted within a reasonable time.

Lapse

[2.23]   It is a general rule that an offer not expressly limited in time must be accepted within a reasonable time, or, put another way, offers do not remain on foot forever but lapse after the passage of a reasonable period of time. The High Court in *Ballas v Theophilos* (No 2) (1957) 98 CLR 193 said that the question of what is a reasonable time is a question of fact, but that offerees must act with promptness after consideration of the information contained in the offer. This is especially so in commercial contracts where time and the vicissitudes of business may result in changing conditions.

This rule was applied by the Supreme Court of the Australian Capital Territory in *Dencio v Zivanovic* (1991) 105 FLR 117. A person who had suffered personal injury offered on 28 September 1990 to settle for $20,000 plus costs but, having received no reply after eight weeks, continued to prepare for the litigation. On 6 August 1991 the other party purported to accept the offer. The court held that this acceptance was not valid because it was not within a reasonable time and noted that the offeror had incurred more costs as a result of the delay.

Rejection

[2.24]   Rejection of an offer destroys that offer. Once an offer is rejected it cannot be revived — there must be a new offer. An offer is terminated by any express rejection from the offeree. Offers are often answered by the making of a counter-offer. A counter-offer is a rejection of the original offer. It may be either a counter-proposal (say where a house is for sale at $150,000 and someone offers $140,000) or an 'acceptance' which varies the terms. There are some difficulties in determining which of a series of statements made in the course of negotiations between the parties can be labelled as the offer and which will be the acceptance which results in a binding contract being formed.

Death

[2.25]   If the offeror dies before the offer is accepted then the offer will lapse, but it is not clear from the authorities whether it lapses automatically or only once the offeree has notice of the death. In *Fong v Cilli* (1968) 11 FLR 495 the court accepted the proposition that an offer cannot be accepted after the death of the offeror by an offeree having notice of the death. The implication of this is that, unless the offer is personal to the offeror, it may be accepted by the offeree if there is no actual knowledge of the offeror's death.

This was considered by the High Court in *Laybutt v Amoco Australia Pty Ltd* (1974) 132 CLR 57; 4 ALR 482, a case which considered the question of whether an option to purchase land could be exercised after the death of the vendor. The court confirmed the decision in *Fong v Cilli* and said:

- as a general rule, upon the death of a party to a contract all liabilities under the contract pass to the deceased's personal representative.
- this general rule will not apply if the performance of the contract depended upon the personal skill or judgment of the deceased party or if the contract was intended to be enforceable only against that party.

[2.26] It would seem then that the same rule applies to offers and that the estate of an offeror may be bound by an offer which was accepted after the death of the offeror provided that it was not personal to the deceased and that the offeree had no notice of the death of the offeror. The general rule in relation to an offeree is that an offer which is personal to the offeree is not capable of being accepted after the death of the person to whom it was made. In *Carter v Hyde* (1923) 33 CLR 115 the High Court had to consider the question of whether the estate of an offeree could accept an offer made to him before he died. It was held that the personal representatives of the offeree could create a valid contract by accepting the offer. If the offer is personal to the offeree — for instance, it calls for the exercise of personal skills or discretion — it can be accepted only during the offeree's lifetime and lapses on death. But if the offer is not personal to the offeree then on death the benefit of the offer passes to the personal representatives.

Acceptance

[2.27] An offeree may either accept or reject an offer. The traditional or formal rule is that an unqualified acceptance in the precise terms of the offer will form a contract from the moment of acceptance. This is because anything else is not agreement. Any later communications cannot alter the rights and obligations of the parties unless they amount to waiver, variation or discharge. Until the parties have reached a *consensus ad idem*, a meeting of the minds, neither party will be legally bound. This is the approach of traditional contract law; however, the Trade Practices Act 1974 and the doctrine of estoppel could mean that parties may incur legal liability even though the negotiations are not complete.

Conditional acceptance

[2.28] An acceptance on condition will not be binding unless the offeror agrees to the condition: the condition will need to be fulfilled before a legally binding contract arises There are two common examples of conditional acceptance: 'subject to contract' and 'subject to finance'. Each case turns on its own facts and the words used by the parties must be given meaning in order to determine what the parties intended. Where the parties have reached an agreement expressed to be 'subject to contract' the courts must determine whether the parties intended to be immediately bound or were postponing their legal obligations until after the execution of a formal contract. In each case the issue is the intention of the parties which must be objectively ascertained from the terms of the agreement in the light of the surrounding circumstances. In *Masters v Cameron* (1954)

91 CLR 353 at 360–2 the High Court said that where parties have been in negotiation and reach agreement about the terms of their contract and also agree that the agreement shall be dealt with by a written contract, then one of three situations applies:

- the parties have reached finality in the terms of the bargain and intend to be immediately bound to the performance of those terms but propose to have the terms restated in a form which will be fuller or more precise but not different in effect;
- the parties have agreed upon all the terms of their bargain but nevertheless have made performance of one or more terms conditional on the execution of a formal document; or
- the parties intend not to make a concluded bargain at all unless and until they execute a formal contract.

Case Example

Mr Leitch and his associated companies alleged that they had an action for damages against the Natwest Australia Bank. Leitch had many meetings with the bank and alleged an oral agreement to reorganise the finances of the group of companies. This oral agreement dealt with a debt of $10 million dollars owed to the bank, mortgages and charges over the properties of the companies and their directors and the provision of finance for the construction of private hospitals on land owned by the companies. The bank denied that a concluded agreement had been reached. The question was whether there was a contract or merely a preliminary agreement.

The court held that the situation fell within the third category of *Masters v Cameron* and found that neither Leitch nor the bank intended to be immediately contractually bound. The oral agreement dealt only with the basic terms of the agreement and a formal contract was intended which would also deal with subsidiary issues and consequential details.

In reaching this decision the court made the following observations:

- that in determining objectively what the common intention of the parties was, the subjective intentions and personal beliefs of the parties were not relevant;
- in making an objective determination of intention it is appropriate to have regard to the circumstances and the subject matter of the negotiations and the agreement. This was a very complex matter, involving a large amount of money, and the parties and their legal advisers continued correspondence relating to the contract for a further two weeks after the date of the alleged oral contract.

The court concluded that in these circumstances either party was free to retire from the contract if on looking at the document they found that it represented what was said but not what they meant it to say: *David Henry Leitch v Natwest Australia Bank Limited* (1995) ATPR (Digest) 46-153.

Who can accept?

[2.29] Only the persons to whom the offer was addressed can accept it, although as was said in *Carlill* an offer can be made to the whole world. Can a person accept an offer made to another? In *Lang v James Morrison & Co Ltd* (1911–12) 13 CLR 1;17 ALR 530 it was held by the High Court that a purported acceptance of an offer directed to another person is the making of a new offer. An offer from A to B accepted by B and C or accepted by B as agent for B and C, is not an acceptance of the original offer, but is a new offer — an offer by B and C to make a contract on the terms of the original offer, and neither party is bound by the new offer until it is accepted.

Where the personality of the offeree is important to the offeror, or the contract is personal by virtue of its subject matter, then the offer can only be accepted, and the contract can only be performed, by the person to whom it was directed. This principle was applied by the High Court in *Bruce v Tyley* (1916) 21 CLR 277; 22 ALR 215 to prevent the assignment of a contract with the Commonwealth to remove refuse from an army camp by the original offeree. So if, for example, Bobbie asks Jo to play at a party, Kim cannot agree to play instead.

The form of acceptance

[2.30] There is no general rule as to what form of words is necessary for a valid acceptance. A person's behaviour can be acceptance if it reasonably indicates that this is the case. Acceptance must be communicated to the person making the offer but there is no general requirement for the acceptance to be in writing or for any particular form of words to be used. Where the offeror does not specify any particular form of acceptance the presumption is that the acceptance should be in the same form as the offer.

Some offers can be accepted by performance consistent with the existence of the contract. The communication of the acceptance will be either express or implied from the conduct of the offeree. A railway company sent a draft written contract to Brogden, who had been supplying the railway with coal for many years without the benefit of any formal agreement. Brogden, on receipt of the draft contract, inserted the name of an arbitrator in the space left for that purpose and wrote 'approved'. He sent the document back to the railway company and nothing further was ever done to execute or implement the agreement. The parties continued to deal with each other by ordering, delivering and paying for coal until a dispute arose, and then Brogden denied that there was a binding contract. The application of the traditional formula would have left the parties with an unaccepted counter-offer (after Brogden altered the document). In *Brogden v Metropolitan Railway* (1877) 2 App Cas 666 it was held that a contract came into existence when the first order was placed by the railway company after the return of the draft contract or at the latest when Brogden filled that order. This fairly vague reasoning has come to be accepted to stand for the proposition that it is possible to accept an offer by conduct consistent with the existence of the alleged contract.

[2.31] Some circumstances have been held to give rise to a contractual relationship between a large number of parties engaged in common conduct. Suppose a person enters a marathon race and agrees with the organisers to abide by their published rules: could it be said that the competitor was in a contract with every other person participating in the marathon? Would the published rules be the terms of the contract? In *Clarke v The Earl of Dunraven, The Santanita* [1897] AC 59 it was held that competitors in a yacht race who had agreed to be bound by the rules of the yacht club conducting the race were in a contractual relationship with each other.

In such ongoing relationships it is difficult to fit the lawyer's analysis of offer and acceptance to the actions of the parties and the question will sometimes be whether the circumstances give rise to a tacit understanding of agreement: *Integrated Computer Services Pty Ltd v Digital Equipment Corp (Aust) Pty Ltd* (1988) 5 BPR 11,110. However, it is not every case of acting in response to a representation that results in the formation of a contract, only where there is a connection between the representation and the action in response to it is this likely to occur.

Case Example

The question of whether there was such a connection is considered in another case concerning yachtsman. Forbes and Bandock were two sailors who competed at the highest international level in Tornado class yacht racing. The Australian Yachting Federation sent to them documents which set out the criteria for selecting the Australian Olympic Yachting Team. Forbes and Bandock competed in the races specified in the selection documents and were the best performing crew. When they were not selected for the Olympic team they brought an action alleging that a binding contract had arisen because the Australian Yachting Federation's selection criteria was an offer and an undertaking that the Australian Yachting Federation would consider persons for selection only on the basis of the published criteria; and Forbes and Bandock accepted the offer by performance. A unilateral contract was said to be inferred from performance of the act required by the offer, and that this performance was also the consideration for the contract.

The court held, inter alia, that the documents setting out the selection criteria did not constitute an offer because they did not make a request that any crew participate in the specified races, merely stated that such participation was a precondition to being considered for selection. Therefore no action on the part of the two sailors could bind the Australian Yachting Federation to a contract: *Forbes v Australian Yachting Federation Inc* (1996) ATPR (Digest) 46-158.

Acceptance must be communicated to the offeror

[2.32] A contract is formed when the offer is accepted, and a contract cannot be formed without the knowledge of one of the parties. The general rule is that the acceptance is complete when it is communicated to the offeror. Reward cases or unilateral contracts are exceptions to this rule. In *Carlill* it was held that a person may accept an offer by performance and in these cases it is not necessary directly to communicate acceptance to the offeror.

The offeror may waive the requirement of communication of acceptance but the offeror cannot impose a condition that silence on the part of the offeree will amount to acceptance. In *Felthouse v Bindley* (1862) 11 CB (NS) 869; 142 ER 1037 a man wrote to his nephew, offering to buy a horse and said 'if I hear no more I consider the horse is mine'. The court held that even though the nephew intended to sell the horse to his uncle, there could be no binding agreement unless the offer to buy had been accepted.

The time of formation

[2.33]   The time of acceptance determines the time of the formation of the contract, which can be important for a number of reasons such as taxation, insurance, liability for loss. A binding contract is formed when the acceptance of the offer is communicated to the offeror. Where communication of the acceptance of the offer is face to face the agreement is concluded at the time the offeror actually receives the acceptance. In such cases little time passes between the uttering of the acceptance and its receipt.

In many cases the actual time of making the contract will not have to be pinpointed; but if the court is trying to determine whether or not it has jurisdiction to hear a matter, when and where acceptance occurs will be crucial because the law of the place in which the contract was formed will, in the absence of express intention to the contrary, be the law which governs the outcome of any dispute.

Many acceptances are communicated by methods other than face to face and so the rule that formation occurs at the time of acceptance is modified to meet these circumstances. Whenever the parties contemplate that an offer may be accepted by post, the offer will be accepted at the time a properly addressed letter is put into the hands of the post office and a binding contract is formed at the time when, and the place where, the letter of acceptance is posted. Any letter of acceptance would have to be correctly addressed and stamped before being put in the hands of the post office. The party asserting the contract was formed by posting an acceptance would have to prove the letter was posted at the time and place alleged. This is best done by sending the letter of acceptance by registered mail. Once this is shown the postal rule will apply and even if an offeror denies receipt of the letter of acceptance a binding contract will be formed. The postal rule also applies to acceptance by telegram.

In *Tallerman & Co Pty Ltd v Nathan's Merchandise (Vic) Pty Ltd* (1957) 98 CLR 93 at 111–12, the High Court said:

> The general rule is that a contract is not completed until acceptance of an offer is actually communicated to the offeror, and a finding that a contract is completed by the posting of a letter cannot be justified unless it is to be inferred that *the offeror contemplated and intended that his offer might be accepted by the doing of that act.* [emphasis added]

If the offeror specifies another method of acceptance or that a contract will not be formed until actual receipt of the acceptance, the postal rule cannot be invoked. While the postal rule operates to protect offerees against denials of receipt of acceptance by offerors, it has been criticised because it can result in the offeror being bound to a contract before he or she has actual knowledge of its formation. The basis of the rule is that the offeror will have contemplated acceptance by post; it is always open to the offeror to specify some other method of acceptance.

Instantaneous communications

[2.34]   The postal rule does not apply to instantaneous methods of communication such as telephone, telex, email and facsimile. The general rule that a contract is formed at the time and at the place where acceptance is communicated to the offeror is applied. There may be problems in determining that an instantaneous message has been received and understood. The approach to indistinct or faulty transmissions was clarified by Lord Denning in *Entores Ltd v Miles Far Eastern Corp* [1955] 2 QB 327; 2 All ER 493 at 495:

> Suppose that I make an offer to a man by telephone and in the middle of his reply the line goes dead so that I do not hear his words of acceptance. There is no contract at that

moment. The other man may not know the precise moment when the line failed. But he will know that the telephone conversation was abruptly broken off, because people usually say something to signify the end of the conversation ... suppose that the line does not go dead but is so indistinct that I do not catch what he says and I ask him to repeat it. He then repeats it and I hear his acceptance. The contract is made not on the first time when I do not hear, but only on the second time when I do hear. The contract is complete only when I have his answer accepting the offer.

[2.35]   Facsimile (fax) transactions are used by business people every day in negotiations and contracting. If an acceptance of an offer is sent by fax the contract will be formed at the time that the person to whom it was addressed received it. There may be questions as to what is meant by received — is that when the fax comes out of the machine or is it when the fax is handed to the person named on the front page? The courts will look to all the circumstances of the transaction to decide what the reasonable person would have thought the parties intended to be the time of acceptance. The House of Lords has cautioned that 'no universal rule can cover all such cases: they must be resolved by reference to the intentions of the parties, by sound business practice and in some cases by judgment of where the risks should lie': *Brinkibon Ltd v Stahag Stahl und Stahlwarendhandel GmbH* [1983] 2 AC 34 at 42; [1982] 1 All ER 293.

Case Example

In a recent Australian case which considered the question of whether sending a letter by facsimile was a proper giving of notice, the court said that there was:

> ... no reason for finding that a notice sent by facsimile transmission is any less a notice in writing than one which is sent and received in any other fashion. The piece of paper which results from the transmission is not the original document nor does it contain an original signature. It may therefore be inadequate in cases where a signature is required.

This could mean that in circumstances where a duly executed acceptance is required a facsimile transmission is not acceptance. However, it would also mean that where the parties required acceptance in writing, or had not specified a method of acceptance, a valid acceptance of an offer can be made by fax.

The court considered the time of receipt of the facsimile. If modern forms of communication are used and equipment is kept available for the receipt of messages then service by that medium is sufficient even though the document may arrive outside of normal business hours. The time of receipt of a facsimile is usually the same as the time it was sent plus the few minutes it takes for transmission, and is usually recorded on the fax or transmission slip. It is always open to the parties to bring evidence to show that although the machine was on there was no person in authority to actually receive the document. Acceptance by facsimile would, unless the contrary is proved occur at the time that the facsimile is received by the offeror's machine: *NM Superannuation Pty Ltd v Baker* (1992) 7 ACSR 105.

Acceptance must correspond to the offer and be in response to it

[2.36] A person cannot accept an offer while unaware of it. Where an offer is made for a reward to be paid in return for the performing of some act, the mere chance that a person happens to do that act while ignorant of the offer will not result in any contract being formed, and the other party will have no legal obligation to pay the reward. This is because there was no agreement between the parties. In order for a contract to be formed the person performing must be acting on or in pursuance of or in reliance upon or in return for the consideration contained in the offer: see *R v Clarke* (1927) 40 CLR 227; 34 ALR 97.

If two persons send corresponding offers to each other at the same time (the letters cross in the mail) no contract would result, because two offers do not amount to an agreement. If the offer calls for acceptance by the performance of some act and a person begins performing in ignorance of the offer, but subsequently becomes aware of the offer and then completes performance, such continuing performance could be seen as acceptance.

Agreement

[2.37] Agreement is said to follow from an offer and acceptance in corresponding terms. This approach is often out of step with the commercial realities. The traditional approach of using the offer and acceptance to identify the time the contract was formed is firmly entrenched in the common law and will serve most purposes. There are times, however, when the nature of the relationship between the parties will make it difficult to identify the elements of offer and acceptance.

> It is often difficult to fit a commercial arrangement into a common lawyer's analysis of a contractual arrangement. Commercial discussions are often too unrefined to fit easily into the slots of 'offer', 'acceptance', 'consideration' and 'intention to create a legal relationship'. In classical theory, the typical contract is a bilateral one and consists of an exchange of promises by means of an offer and its acceptance together with an intention to create a binding legal relationship ... the question [is often] whether the conduct of the parties viewed in the light of the surrounding circumstances show a tacit understanding or agreement. (McHugh JA in *Integrated Computer Services Pty Ltd v Digital Equipment Corp (Aust) Pty Ltd* (1988) 5 BPR 11,110)

> Where the parties are in a continuing commercial relationship or involved in protracted negotiations, which involve the exchange of documents and other correspondence, it may be possible to state that the parties are in a contractual relationship, but difficult genuinely to label one action as an offer and another as its acceptance. Wherever businesses use their own standard forms it may be difficult to label the steps in any negotiation as offer and acceptance, especially if each party is sending its own forms to the other. In such cases the court will either determine, as a matter of fact, which form contains the offer or acceptance, or decide that a contract exists in accordance with the circumstances. In dynamic commercial relationships it may be difficult to pinpoint the precise moment when the requirements for a contract have been met — indeed, the conduct of the parties may mean that new terms are being added and old terms superseded. It will in such cases be necessary to examine the whole relationship.

> It may be more sensible to ask not whether one party has accepted the other's offer, but whether in the circumstances it can be shown that each party has assented to the contract.

This is what Kirby P asked in *Empirnall Holdings Pty Ltd v Machon Paull Partners Pty Ltd* (1988) 14 NSWLR 523. The court had to decide whether the terms of a written agreement, not signed by one party, were binding. A series of meetings had taken place between Empirnall, a property developer, and Machon Paull, a firm of architects. Work on drawings, plans, council approval and demolition was done by the architects, who then submitted a claim for payment and sent a signed contract to the developer. They were told that the developer never signed contracts, and with their next claim for payment the architects sent a letter which said 'we are proceeding on the understanding that the conditions of the contract are accepted by you and works are being conducted in accordance with those terms and conditions'. Work continued although the developer did not ever sign the contract. When a dispute as to liability for payment arose the court was asked to decide whether the terms of the unsigned contract applied. This would only be so if it could be said that the developer had accepted the offer of the architect to do the work on the terms and conditions set out in the contract.

The court agreed that Machon Paull could not bind Empirnall to the contract by the letter above: 'an offeror may not impose a contractual obligation upon an offeree by stating that if the latter does not expressly reject the offer as made, it will be taken to have accepted it'. McHugh JA saw this as not so much a case of acceptance by conduct but one where Empirnall had taken the benefit of the work done so that an objective bystander would say that it had accepted the offer made by Machon Paull. Kirby P examined the whole of the surrounding circumstances and concluded that at the time of the first payment for work done there was a binding agreement of some sort in existence, and an objective bystander would conclude that Empirnall had accepted that the work was to be done according to the printed contract, and thus, Empirnall had assented to the contract.

Standard form contracts

[2.38]   The concept of an offer and acceptance giving rise to an agreed contract between parties contemplates that the parties have, after negotiations, freely entered into an agreement and are informed of the rights and obligations which each has. However, many business enterprises use pre-printed standard forms — these may be purchase orders, delivery dockets, confirmation of order forms or invoices. If firms engage in an exchange of these pre-printed forms it can be difficult to identify which form constitutes an offer and whether other, later, forms are acceptances or counter-offers. In most cases when there is a battle of the forms a contract is formed when the last of the forms is sent and received without objection from the other party to its contents.

> ### Case Example
>
> Butler Machine Tool Company gave a quotation of £75,535 for supply of a machine, with delivery in March 1970. They used their own quotation form, which had printed on its back certain terms and conditions, one of which was that if there was an increase in costs the price of the machine could be varied. The purchasers of the machine, Ex-Cell-O Corp, placed an order for the machine at the quoted price, but used their own order form which said 'Please supply on conditions and terms below and overleaf'.

The terms and conditions printed on its back did not include a price variation clause. At the foot of the buyer's order was a tear-off slip which said 'We accept your order on the terms and conditions stated thereon …'. This was signed and returned by Butler Machine Tool Company, with a letter acknowledging receipt of the order and saying that delivery would be in accordance with the quotation. The machine was not delivered until November 1970 and Butler Machine Tool Company claimed an extra £2892 under the price variation clause.

The court had to determine which form won the battle to be the offer accepted by the other party. The quotation for £75,535 was an offer by Butler Machine Tool Company. The order by Ex-Cell-O Corp, since it was not in the same terms as the offer, was a counter-offer and therefore a rejection of the original offer. The return of the tear-off slip was then acceptance of the counter offer. This meant that the contract did not contain the price variation clause. See *Butler Machine Tool Co Ltd v Ex-Cell-O Corp (England) Ltd* [1979] 1 WLR 401.

Re-negotiation

[2.39]   An accepted offer amounts to agreement and therefore the rights and obligations between the parties cannot be altered by any later negotiations unless these negotiations are a waiver, variation or discharge.

- *Waiver*   One party voluntarily waives or abandons rights which accrue under the original agreement and accepts something less than strict performance by the other party. Once a right has been waived it cannot be relied upon to found a breach of contract action. A waiver requires no consideration.

- *Variation*   Variation may be viewed in two ways: it is either a repudiation of the first contract and the formation of a new contract on different terms, or a contract to vary the terms of the original contract (two contracts). A variation must be supported by consideration to be enforceable and must observe the same formalities as the original contract. Common law will not enforce an informal variation but equity may.

- *Discharge*   Discharge occurs where the parties agree that no further performance is required of the obligations contained in the contract.

Intention

[2.40]   Agreement alone will not create a contract binding in law. A critical factor in the formation of a contract is the necessity for intention by the parties to create legally binding obligations. Unless the intention of the parties is to constitute an agreement enforceable at law, there will be no contract. The parties must prove the existence of an intention to be legally bound to perform the contract in order to call upon the court to provide a remedy for non-performance. In general, where agreement can be shown it will be rare that a court will hold that there has been no intention to create a legally binding obligation.

The law requires evidence of the express or implied intention of the parties. However, most contracts do not contain an express statement of the parties' intention to be legally bound. There are two presumptions at law which may assist in determining the intention of the parties. These are both able to be rebutted by evidence as to the true intention of the parties, and both are concerned with the nature of the relationship between the parties:

- where the parties are in a commercial relationship, the presumption is that they intended to create a legally binding contract by their agreement; and
- where the parties are in a purely domestic or social agreement, the presumption is that it was not intended to create a legally binding contract.

[2.41]   Where the parties have expressly declared their resolve that the agreement is not to affect their legal position, the actual language used may take a number of forms. The following is a simple example in which the court held that no legally binding obligation was created. A football pools coupon contained the following provision:

> It is a basic condition of the sending in and acceptance of this coupon that it is intended and agreed that the conduct of the pools and everything done in connection therewith and all arrangements related thereto (whether mentioned in these rules or to be implied) and this coupon and any agreement or transaction entered into or payment made by or under it shall not be attended by or give rise to any legal relationship, rights, duties or consequences whatsoever or be legally enforceable or the subject of litigation, but all such arrangements, agreements and transactions are binding in honour only: *Jones v Vernon's Pools Ltd* [1938] 2 All ER 626.

It must not be assumed that the courts will always accept the ordinary meaning of the words used by the parties. What the courts are looking for is not the meaning of the words so much as the intention of the parties to the agreement, as evidenced by the words they use.

The question of what was the actual intention of the parties most often falls to be decided in domestic agreements. The courts take all the surrounding circumstances into account to determine what a reasonable person would say was the intention of the parties at the time of formation of the agreement (this is the objective intention of the parties).

The intention must be shown to be that of all parties. No party will be permitted to prove an intention which is not in conformity with what has passed between them. There are four factors which may be of particular relevance in determining whether a social or family agreement was objectively intended to create legal relations:

- Clarity of terms: where the alleged rights and obligations are clearly spelt out the courts are more likely to find a contract. At the same time, the courts recognise that formal contracts will probably not be used in family agreements.
- If the agreement invites one party to incur expense, inconvenience or substantial detriment, there is more likely to be a contract. In *Todd v Nicol* [1957] SASR 72 an intention to enter into a contract that was legally binding was found in the circumstances where one party gave up her employment and sold her household effects in Scotland to journey to Australia to live with a relative.
- The flavour of the agreement can influence the court. A car pool or weekly lottery ticket has a social flavour, but where there has been an account opened for lottery winnings this tends towards the more formal or commercial flavour.
- Was it contemplated that either party would engage in litigation to recover damages or obtain specific performance if the other party failed to perform?

Case Example

Mrs Woodward agreed to help her husband salvage and repair a dredge and barge in order to establish a gravel supply business and in return her husband promised her 10 per cent of the business. For a period of 18 months she did substantial physical work on most weekends; chipped and scraped away rust, cleaned and hosed down the barge, assisted in painting, tarring and gravelling the deck, as well as collecting spare parts and helping with the paperwork involved. Nevertheless her husband retained all the profits of her labours and refused to formalise her interest in the business. Cooper J said:

> The question is what was the intention of the parties at the time the arrangement was entered into ... One takes into account the language used and the circumstances which existed at the time the arrangement was made, including any serious consequences of the arrangement not being legally enforceable, to determine whether the necessary intention can be inferred.

The arrangement was found to be one where she was free to do the work if she chose to but it could not be said that if she had failed to do the work she would have exposed herself to an action for damages at the suit of her husband: the arrangement was a purely family arrangement and therefore not a contract: *Woodward v Johnston* [1992] 2 Qd R 214 at 225–6; (1991) 14 Fam LR 828.

Some transactions will occur in situations which are neither wholly domestic nor commercial. In *Teen Ranch Pty Ltd v Brown* http://online.butterworths.com.au/unrep/95/9504248.htm, the court had to consider the case of a young person who was injured while working at a Christian camp for teenagers and determine whether there was a contract between the volunteer worker and Teen Ranch, a non-profit organisation. Brown worked at the camp from time to time under an informal arrangement — usually Teen Ranch wrote asking whether Brown was available to work. Brown was never paid wages, but was provided with accommodation and meals. While at the camp Brown was subject to the camp rules and discipline and could not leave without permission. The court found that there was no contract between Teen Ranch and Brown because there was nothing in their arrangement that pointed to an intention that there should be a binding contract. Brown did not do the work for the board and lodging but to further the purposes of the Christian group which ran the camp. Persons who combine to further a common end or interest such as a religious one must clearly and truly indicate an intention to enter legal relation in order to create an enforceable contract.

[2.42]   It cannot be said that every commercial transaction results in a binding contract. The courts will look for actual promissory intention on the part of each party. Statements of intention to act in a particular way, which will not give rise to a contract, have been distinguished from promissory statements which carry an intention to be bound and so do give rise to a contract. Recent cases on letters of comfort illustrate the approach of the courts — to examine the words used by the parties and to enforce promissory statements unless there is a clear indication that both parties did not intend them to be binding. Letters of comfort are similar to good references for companies wishing to borrow money and are usually given by a parent company to a lender to that parent's subsidiary. Traditionally letters of comfort were not regarded as legally binding. Both the New South

Wales and Victorian Supreme Courts have said that whether the letters would be binding was a matter of construction. Parties to commercial dealings are free to enter into transactions which will not give rise to legal obligation but there must be a clear expression of that intention. See *Commonwealth Bank of Australia v TLI Management Pty Ltd*. [1990] VR 510 and *Banque Brussels Lambert SA v Australian National Industries Ltd* (1989) 21 NSWLR 502 at 532 where Rogers J said:

> There should be no room in the proper flow of commerce for some purgatory where statements made by businessmen, after hard bargaining and made to induce another business person to enter into a business transaction would, without any express statement to that effect, reside in a twilight zone of merely honourable engagement. The whole thrust of the law today is to attempt to give proper effect to commercial transactions. It is for this reason that uncertainty...has fallen into disfavour as a tool for striking down bargains. *If the statements are appropriately promissory in character, courts should enforce them when they are uttered in the course of business and there is no clear indication that they are not intended to be legally enforceable.* [emphasis added]

Consideration

What is consideration?

[2.43] Persons who call on the courts to enforce promises given to them must show that the promises were paid for, or supported by consideration. Consideration is the price paid for a promise. Consideration is an essential requirement for an enforceable simple contract. Without consideration a promise, unless contained in a deed, is not enforceable at law. There are two different views of the basis of consideration: bargain and reliance. The first is the idea that whatever one party gives in a contract is bought or bargained for by the other: a promise in response to a promise, a promise for an act. The second is that if one party gives a promise and the other acts in reliance on that promise, so as to confer a benefit or incur a detriment, consideration will be present. Consideration may be viewed as a technicality which only has real importance when the courts use it to draw the line between those promises which will be enforced and those which will not, or between legal and moral obligations.

[2.44] The rules of consideration can be summarised as follows:
- consideration is (something of value) exchanged for the promise (see [2.45]);
- consideration must move from the promisee (see [2.46]);
- past consideration is no consideration (see [2.47]);
- consideration must have value to the promisor (see [2.48]);
- consideration need not be adequate — but it must be sufficient: see [2.49]–[2.52].

Consideration is something of value exchanged for the promise

[2.45] There is no one simple definition or description of consideration. It helps to view consideration in terms of the role it plays. It may be said that offer, acceptance and intention are clearly matters relating to the formation of the contract, whereas consideration and privity (see [2.64]) serve to mark off those promises or agreements which are actionable under the law of contract. A simple contract (that is, one not under seal or contained in a deed) will be enforced if the plaintiff can prove that it is supported by consideration.

The classic definition of consideration is found in *Currie v Misa* (1875) LR 10 Exch 153 at 162:

> A valuable consideration in the eyes of the law may consist either in some right, interest, profit, or benefit accruing to one party, or some forbearance, detriment, loss, or responsibility given, suffered or undertaken by the other.

The widely used definition of consideration found in *Dunlop Pneumatic Tyre Co Ltd v Selfridge & Co Ltd* [1915] AC 847 at 855 reflects the bargain theory:

> An act or forbearance of one party, or the promise thereof, is the price for which the promise of the other is bought, and the promise thus given for value is enforceable.

The High Court adopted the bargain theory in *Australian Woollen Mills Pty Ltd v Commonwealth* (1954) 92 CLR 424; 61 ALR 453 and said at CLR 456–7:

> In cases of this class it is necessary, in order that a contract may be established, that it should be made to appear that the statement or announcement which is relied on as a promise was really offered as consideration for the doing of the act, and that the act was really done in consideration of a potential promise inherent in the statement or announcement. Between the statement or announcement, which is put forward as an offer capable of acceptance by the doing of an act, and the act which is put forward as the executed consideration for the alleged promise, there must subsist, so to speak, the relation of a *quid pro quo*.

In *Beaton v McDivitt* (1987) 13 NSWLR 162 consideration was seen as an element of the bargain struck between the parties by an exchange: consideration must be satisfied in the form of a price in return for the promisor's promise or a quid pro quo. The price can be in the form of an act, forbearance or promise. In *Bluebird Investments Pty Ltd v Graf* (1994) 13 ACSR 271 at 293–5, the Supreme Court of New South Wales said that the removal of a detriment (such as the discharge of an existing liability) is sufficient benefit to the promisor to constitute consideration for the contract.

Consideration must move from the promisee

[2.46]   The person who alleges that the contract was breached must show that the promise breached was bought or bargained for: consideration is said to flow from the promisee. Dunlop sold tyres to wholesalers under an agreement as to the retail price to be charged. The wholesalers sold to Selfridge on the same terms; that is, that they would not sell the tyres below a certain specified price. Selfridge sold below that price and Dunlop sued for breach of contract. The House of Lords said that Dunlop could not enforce Selfridge's promise not to sell below that price because Dunlop had given nothing in return for the promise: *Dunlop Pneumatic Tyre Co Ltd v Selfridge & Co Ltd* [1915] AC 847.

Although consideration must flow from the promisee it need not flow to the promisor. As part of a round of transactions Mrs Arcadiou mortgaged her property in favour of her son and daughter-in-law who in turn mortgaged their property to a bank which lent money to Mr Arcadiou (her husband) for business purposes. When Mrs Arcadiou was declared bankrupt the trustee tried to remove the mortgage from her land to make the land available for her creditors. It was argued that there was no consideration flowing from the son and daughter-in-law to support the mortgage. The question for the court was whether the granting of the mortgage to the bank could be consideration. The court adopted a common sense approach and found that in the ordinary commercial sense they gave consideration for the mortgage of Mrs Arcadiou's property. That consideration was real and substantial. It is not to the point that the mother received no financial advantage from the agreement. What is important is that consideration moved from the son and daughter-in-law: *Official Trustee in Bankruptcy v Arcadiou* (1985) 8 FCR 4.

Where there are two or more persons receiving a benefit under the contract (joint promisees) it is sufficient that consideration move from one of them. See *Coulls v Bagot's Executor and Trustee Co Ltd* (1967) 119 CLR 460; [1967] ALR 385.

Past consideration is no consideration

[2.47] A contract is only enforceable if the consideration is either executory (yet to be performed) or executed (already performed), but not if the consideration for the giving of the promise is already past. The promise received must have been bargained for. Suppose Allan promises to mow Barbara's lawn and Barbara promises to wash Allan's car. Allan's promise is the consideration for Barbara's promise and vice versa. These mutual promises taken together are a valid contract supported by executory consideration.

What if Allan promises to mow Barbara's lawn and Barbara in return for the promise pays him $20? The actual payment of the $20 is executed consideration. In both of these examples the promises are enforceable. Consideration is said to be past when the promise is made after the performance of an act and independently of it. If Allan mows Barbara's lawn and then she says that she will pay him $20, Allan cannot enforce the promise because his consideration is past.

These examples reflect the rules that a promise cannot be enforced unless it was bargained for and the relation of quid pro quo must exist between the promise and its price. There will be cases where a promise to pay for an already completed act will be good consideration if the already completed act was done at the request of the promisor and the promise to pay and the action can be described as part of the one transaction.

> **Case Example**
>
> Braithwait had killed a man and asked Lampleigh to do all he could to obtain a pardon. Lampleigh made considerable effort, including undertaking several trips to London at his own expense, and Braithwait then said he would pay him £100. When Lampleigh sued for the £100 Braithwait argued that the promise to pay was not enforceable because the consideration for it was past. The court held that the services of Lampleigh were procured by a request from Braithwait, which was coupled with the promise to pay £100 and that the promise to pay *and* the efforts to secure a pardon could be seen as part of the one transaction. It could also be said that the request to Lampleigh to use his best endeavours to secure a pardon carried with it an implied promise to give compensation for the service and that the promise of £100 was merely setting the value: *Lampleigh v Braithwait* (1615) 80 ER 255.

Consideration must have value to the promisor

[2.48] The promisee's act or promise must be looked at in the context of the whole trans-action to determine whether it has any value to the promisor. In *Australian Woollen Mills Pty Ltd v Commonwealth* (1954) 92 CLR 424 at 457; 61 ALR 453, the High Court used the following example:

> A in Sydney, says to B in Melbourne: 'I will pay you £1000 on your arrival in Sydney.' The next day B goes to Sydney. If these facts alone are proved, it is perfectly clear that no contract binding A to pay £1000 to B is established. For all that appears there may be no relation whatever between A's statement and B's act. It is quite consistent with the facts proved that B intended to go to Sydney anyhow, and that A is merely announcing that, if and when B arrives in Sydney, he will make a gift to him. The necessary relation is not shown to exist between the announcement and the act. Proof of further facts, however, might suffice to establish a contract. For example, it might be proved that A, on the day before £1000 was mentioned, had told B that it was a matter of vital importance to him (A) that B should come to Sydney forthwith, and that B objected that to go to Sydney … might involve him in financial loss. These further facts throw a different light on the statement on which B relies as an offer accepted by his going to Sydney … A's going to Sydney to be consideration must be of value to B.

Even where the promisor discards as rubbish the thing which constitutes considera-tion, this will not of itself render the consideration valueless to the promisor. In such cases the court will examine all the factors relating to the consideration in the context of the whole transaction. In *Chappell & Co Ltd v Nestlé Co Ltd* [1960] AC 87 Nestlé, as part of an advertising campaign, offered to send records to any person who sent to it a postal order for 1/6d (15 cents) plus three Nestlé chocolate wrappers. The court had to decide whether the chocolate wrappers were part of the consideration. It was said that the wrappers were of no value to Nestlé and that they were thrown away when received. Lord Somervell of Harrow said (at 114–15):

> A contracting party can stipulate for what consideration he chooses. A peppercorn does not cease to be good consideration if it is established that the promisee does not like pepper and will throw away the corn. As the whole object of selling the record … was to increase the sale of chocolates, it seems to me wrong not to treat the stipulated evidence of such sales as part of the consideration.

Consideration need not be adequate, but it must be sufficient in the eyes of the law

[2.49] To say that a contract is supported by sufficient consideration is to say that it has satisfied the law's usual demands for the existence of valid or good consideration: it has moved from the promisee, it is not past, it has value, and it was given in exchange for the promise or act of the other party. Where these are all present the courts will not refuse to enforce a contract on the grounds that the consideration was not equal in value to the act or promise of the other party.

In cases where the parties have agreed on consideration the courts will not inquire as to its sufficiency. In *Woolworths Ltd v Kelly* (1991) 22 NSWLR 189; 4 ACSR 431; 9 ACLC 539, Kirby P listed six reasons for not inquiring into the sufficiency of consider-ation. They may be summarised as follows:

1. each party in the marketplace will place different values on the bargain — this value can arise from idiosyncratic, sentimental, ethical and economic reasons;

2. the expertise of the courts does not extend to substituting its opinion as to the value of the bargain for that of the parties;

3. once the courts began to inquire as to the adequacy of consideration the litigation would flood the courts;

4. the prospect of such litigation would introduce a great deal of uncertainty into commercial transactions;

5. the law already provides means to challenge the adequacy of a bargain where some wrong or moral fault can be shown; and

6. the approach of respecting the right of parties to enter their own bargains, untroubled by the paternalistic supervision of the courts as to the adequacy of their bargains, is one protective of economic freedom.

What constitutes sufficient consideration?

[2.50] The law values consideration from the point of view of the promisor — if the price given for the promise is sufficient to the promisor then even if it be trivial it is accepted. To be sufficient consideration must be real, not vague, illusory or deceptive. This rule may be linked to the element of intention. In the example of the peppercorn rent it could be said that the intention to be bound is signified by the giving of a symbolic consideration; whereas illusory, vague or deceptive consideration may be evidence that one party had no intention of incurring legal obligation.

Promises to perform an existing obligation to the promisor

[2.51] The promise to perform an existing obligation is traditionally regarded as no real consideration because although it appears to be real, on examination it lacks content; the person making such a promise is really asking for something in return for nothing. If the obligation is one arising from an existing contract, any new promise to fulfil an old obligation will be illusory and therefore will not be sufficient.

The High Court said in *Wigan v Edwards* (1973) 1 ALR 497 at 512:

> … the general rule is that a promise to perform an existing duty is no consideration, at least when the promise is made by a party to a pre-existing contract, when it is made to the promisee under that contract, and it is to do no more than the promisor is bound to do under that contract. The rule expresses the concept that the new promise, indistinguishable from the old, is an illusory consideration. And it gives no comfort to a party who by merely threatening a breach of contract seeks to secure an additional contractual benefit from the other party on the footing that the first party's new promise of performance will provide sufficient consideration for that benefit.

The statement of the principle that the performance by A of a contractual duty which A already owes to B is no consideration for a promise made by B to A comes from *Stilk v Myrick* (1809) 170 ER 1168. In that case some sailors deserted a ship, which left it short-handed. The captain promised those sailors who remained that if they worked the ship home the wages that the deserters would have received would be divided between them. The owners of the ship refused to make this payment. There was no consideration given by the sailors — they were only doing what they were already bound to do.

However, in a 1991 English decision it was held that A's promise to B to perform an existing duty owed to B may be consideration notwithstanding the general rule that a promise to perform an existing duty is not good consideration. The rule is avoided only where the promisor obtains an additional benefit or avoids a detriment from the performance of an existing promise: see *Williams v Roffey Bros & Nicholls (Contractors) Ltd* [1991] 1 QB 1; [1990] 1 All ER 512. This has been applied and expanded upon by the

New South Wales Supreme Court in *Musumeci v Winadell Pty Ltd* 34 NSWLR 723; (1995) Aust Contract Reports 90-050. A landlord of a shopping centre granted a rent reduction to a tenant who alleged that it had suffered damages as a result of the landlord allowing a competing business into the shopping centre. When a dispute arose the tenant sought a declaration that the rent reduction was an enforceable variation of the lease. Santow J held that the rent reduction was an enforceable variation to the lease because it was supported by consideration. The consideration was the practical benefit to the landlord of having the tenant stay in occupation, and therefore maintain a full shopping centre Therefore a promise by A to perform an existing contractual obligation owed to B may be good consideration where B obtains a real or practical benefit from the performance of the obligation. In addition, consideration will be found if A, as a result of performing the existing obligation, suffers a detriment. In this case the detriment to the tenant was staying in occupation and taking the risk of its business being damaged by the competition, rather than leaving the premises to set up elsewhere and maybe having to pay damages to the landlord. Without the rent reduction, leaving was their preferred option.

Therefore it can be said that an important qualification to the general principle is that a promise to do precisely what the promisor is already bound to do is a sufficient consideration when it is given by way of a bona fide compromise of a disputed claim, the promisor having asserted that he or she is not bound to perform the obligation under the pre-existing contract or that he or she has a cause of action under that contract. This avoids some of the harsher results of a strict application of the *Stilk v Myrick* rule, which required absolute adherence to the promises contained in an original contract. The reality of commercial transactions is that contracts may often be altered during their performance, and those alterations may be concession made by one party to the other in order to retain the contract, or reach a compromise in a dispute.

Promises to perform an existing obligation to a third party

[2.52] If A owes a contractual duty to C the performance of that duty can be good consideration for the promise of B to do some thing for A. In *Hill Equipment and Refrigeration Co Pty Ltd v Nuco Pty Ltd* (1992) 110 FLR 25, for example, Nuco ran a construction business which on 7 March 1989 entered into a contract with Hill Equipment for the supply of goods. Hill refused to deliver the goods until a guarantee was signed by the directors of Nuco. A guarantee was signed on 9 March 1989 and then Hill performed the contract by delivering the goods. Nuco did not pay for the goods and when Hill sought to enforce the guarantee the directors argued that it was unenforceable because the consideration for it was either:

- the entering into of the contract to supply goods and therefore past; or
- the promise to perform the contract, that is to do an act which they were already bound to do, and therefore empty or illusory.

The Northern Territory Supreme Court accepted the argument that the consideration for the guarantee was not the act of concluding the contract (which was past consideration) but the performance of the contract. Kearney J applied the High Court's reasoning in *Port Jackson Stevedoring Pty Ltd v Salmond and Spraggon (Aust) Pty Ltd* (1978) 139 CLR 231; 18 ALR 333 to hold that the performance of a pre-existing obligation to a third party can be a valid consideration. This was performance that was owed by Hill to Nuco, not to the guarantors, and therefore good consideration.

Equitable estoppel

[2.53] The obligation to keep a promise deliberately given for value is central to contract law. The failure of the common law to provide a remedy for broken non-contractual promises has resulted in increased reliance on equity. Equity acts to soften the harsh results of strict application of the common law rules and so allows the courts to achieve the best justice between the parties.

At common law a promisor is not obliged to keep either a promise not given for value or a promise given for value but where the required legal formalities were not observed. Estoppel is the equitable doctrine which allows a remedy where one party is prevented from relying on common law rights to walk away from a promise. That party is said to be estopped because in the circumstances it would be against good conscience for that party to be able to ignore or refuse to act on the assumptions or expectations of the other. This is known as equitable estoppel.

[2.54] The saga of estoppel begins with the decision of the House of Lords in *Hughes v Metropolitan Railway Co* (1877) 2 App Cas 439; [1874–80] All ER 187. In October 1874 the lessor gave the lessee six months notice to repair the premises or forfeit the lease. On 28 November the parties entered into negotiations for the sale of the lessee's interest in the property and the repairs were deferred. An offer to surrender the lease for £3000 was rejected. Six months after the date of the notice to repair the premises the lessor purported to forfeit the lease and sued to eject the lessee. The House of Lords held that the operation of the notice was suspended during the period of negotiations and that time began to run afresh from the rejection of the offer to surrender the lease. Lord Cairns said (at 448):

> It is the first principle upon which all Courts of Equity proceed, that is parties who have entered into definite and distinct terms involving certain legal results … afterwards by their own act or with their own consent enter upon a course of negotiations which has the effect of leading one of the parties to suppose that the strict rights arising under the contract will not be enforced, or will be kept in suspense or held in abeyance, the person who otherwise might have enforced those rights will not be allowed to enforce them where it would be inequitable having regard to the dealings which have taken place between the parties.

In some cases it will not be sufficient for equity to look only to the contract which exists between the parties: estoppel may operate when the parties are in a contractual relationship but the doctrine may also have effect where the parties are not in a contract. Estoppel may affect the pre-contractual negotiations, the question of formation of a contract, the issue of consideration, the existence of facts and the negotiation of a settlement where there has been a breach of contract.

The doctrine of estoppel will operate where one party to a transaction has, through the giving of a promise, the making of a representation or by conduct, caused a second party to assume that a particular legal relationship exists between them or that facts exist or that a particular course of conduct will be followed, and the second party has in reliance on that promise, representation or conduct, acted on that assumption in a way that would make it unconscionable for the first party to act in a manner which is inconsistent with the assumption.

Case Example

The modern form of equitable estoppel emerged from the judgment given by Lord Denning in *Central London Property Trust v High Trees House Ltd* [1947] KB 130. During the Second World War many people moved out of London to avoid the bombing. This meant that many houses and flats were empty. The landlord of one block of flats agreed to accept one half of the rent due on the block. After the war people returned to live in London and it was no longer necessary to charge the low rent. The landlord then not only put the rent back to full price but sued the tenants to recover the full amount of rent for the war years. Since there had been no alteration to the lease for the flats, and there had been no consideration given to the landlord for the lowering of the rent, at common law the rent was due to the landlord. Lord Denning said that the landlord was not able to recover his rent as the landlord had promised to accept half the rent, and the law, while not enforcing that promise, would not allow a departure from it: *Central London Property Trust v High Trees House Ltd* [1947] KB 130.

The doctrine has been accepted as part of Australian law. The doctrine, as originally adopted by the High Court in *Legione v Hateley* (1983) 152 CLR 406; 46 ALR 1, was confined to parties in a pre-existing contractual relationship, and could be used only in a defensive manner. There were three requirements for the application of the doctrine:
- the parties must be in a pre-existing contractual relationship;
- there must be a clear representation or promise; and
- the person alleging the estoppel must have relied upon the promise so that if the other was allowed to depart from it the promisee would be materially disadvantaged.

Waltons Stores (Interstate) Ltd v Maher (1988) 164 CLR 387; 76 ALR 513 extended the doctrine and recognised that promissory estoppel could be used as the basis for an individual cause of action in the absence of a pre-existing contractual relationship.

Case Example

In October 1983, Mr and Mrs Maher negotiated with Waltons Stores for Waltons to lease their land at Nowra; the existing building was to be demolished and rebuilt according to Waltons' specifications. Waltons required that the building be completed by 5 February 1984. On 7 November 1983 Waltons' solicitors sent to the Mahers' solicitors a contract of lease and specification documents which had been orally approved by Waltons and said 'we will let you know by tomorrow if these are not approved'. The Mahers' solicitors heard nothing more and so had the Mahers sign the contract. These executed documents were sent to Waltons' solicitors for signing and exchange. Waltons, however, was having second thoughts and, knowing that it was not legally bound until it had executed and exchanged contracts, told its solicitors to go slow. The Mahers began demolition of the building and this was known to Waltons by 10 December 1983. The Mahers had completed the demolition and 40 per cent of the reconstruction when, on 19 January 1984, Waltons advised that it did not intend to proceed with the lease.

Exchange of contracts had not occurred and so there was no binding contract or contractual relationship between the parties.

The Mahers, despite this, commenced an action in the Supreme Court of New South Wales for specific performance, or alternatively damages for breach of contract. Both at first instance and on appeal the Supreme Court found in favour of the Mahers, on the basis that they had assumed that a valid contract had existed, and the demolition and reconstruction of the building were undertaken in reliance on that assumption. This reliance had resulted in a detriment to the Mahers.

Waltons appealed to the High Court, and argued that the representation upon which the Mahers relied was not one of existing but future fact (that a contract would be signed), but since they were not in a contractual relationship, the Mahers could not rely on promissory estoppel to prevent a departure from the assumptions created by that representation. The High Court upheld the decisions of the New South Wales courts on the grounds of estoppel: the judges differed in their reasons. It was held that Waltons was estopped from denying that it was bound:

- by Mason CJ, Wilson, Brennan and Deane JJ on the ground that it was estopped from retreating from its implied promise to complete the contract because Waltons knew that the Mahers were acting to their detriment on the basis of a false assumption, and it was unconscionable to adopt a course of inaction, which encouraged them in that action;
- by Deane J on the ground that Waltons' deliberate silence and inaction had caused the Mahers to believe that a binding contract existed and to act to their detriment on that assumption; and
- by Gaudron J on the ground that Waltons' failure to inform the Mahers that exchange might not take place caused the Mahers to assume that it had and it would be unjust not to compel adherence to the rights to which the Mahers believed that assumed exchange had given rise.

In the course of their judgment Mason CJ and Wilson J recognised (at 400) that using promissory estoppel to aid the Mahers would 'drive promissory estoppel one step further by enforcing directly in the absence of a pre-existing relationship of any kind a non-contractual promise on which the representee has relied to his detriment'. Equity does not enforce promises unsupported by consideration in such circumstances, but rather comes to the relief of plaintiffs on the footing that it would be unconscionable conduct on the part of the other party to ignore the assumptions created by the promise (at 404):

> [T]he doctrine extends to the enforcement of voluntary promises on the footing that a departure from the basic assumptions underlying the transaction between the parties must be unconscionable. As failure to fulfil a promise does not of itself amount to unconscionable conduct, mere reliance on an executory promise to do something, resulting in the promisee changing his position or suffering detriment does not bring promissory estoppel into play. Something more would be required.

This is that a departure from the assumptions created by the representation would amount to unconscionable conduct.

Brennan J set down six elements which a plaintiff has to prove to established equitable estoppel:

[1] the plaintiff assumed that a particular relationship then existed between the plaintiff and the defendant or expected that a particular relationship would exist between them and, in the latter case, that the defendant would not be free to withdraw from the expected legal relationship;

[2] the defendant has induced the plaintiff to adopt that assumption or expectation;

[3] the plaintiff acts or abstains from acting in reliance on the assumption or expectation;

[4] the defendant knew or intended him or her to do so;

[5] the plaintiff's action or inaction will occasion detriment if the assumption or expectation is not fulfilled; and

[6] the defendant had failed to act to avoid that detriment whether by fulfilling the assumption or expectation or otherwise.

Waltons Stores (Interstate) Ltd v Maher (1988) 164 CLR 387; 76 ALR 513.

[2.55] In *Waltons v Maher* (1988) 164 CLR 387 at 406, the court said that failure to fulfil a promise does not itself amount to unconscionable conduct — mere reliance on an executory promise to do something, resulting in the promisee changing his or her position or suffering detriment does not bring estoppel into play. Something more would be required. That something is the unconscionable conduct of the promisor in moving away from the assumptions created by his or her words or conduct. The focus of estoppel is the unconscionable nature of the departure by one party from an assumption created by that party and upon which the other party has relied to its detriment. This means that the belief or assumption created by the words or conduct of the first party has been relied upon by the second party, who has thereby altered his or her position in such a manner that this second party would suffer loss, damage or detriment if the first party were allowed to resile.

Case Example

HMAS *Voyager* was involved in a collision at sea and some Australian sailors were injured. Mr Verwayen was one of these and he sued the Commonwealth government for damages. The Commonwealth had indicated a number of times that it would not rely on two defences available to it at law:

- that the claim was out of time; and
- the public policy that members of the armed forces cannot claim against the government for injury suffered in the course of their duty.

Verwayen commenced his action well out of time and then the Commonwealth sought and was granted leave to amend its defence to include these two defences.

The High Court decided that the Commonwealth was not able to rely on the defences. In this case Mason CJ expressed the view (at 55) that the purpose of estoppel is:

> protection against the detriment which would flow from a party's change of position if the assumption or expectation that led to it was deserted ... the consistent trends in the modern decisions point inexorably towards the emergence of one overarching doctrine of estoppel rather that a series of independent rules.
>
> *Commonwealth v Verwayen* (1990) 64 ALJR 54; 170 CLR 394.

Relief based on estoppel

[2.56] The relief appropriate to a case of estoppel will vary from case to case. The court's aim is to relieve the detriment caused by an unconscionable departure from an assumption created by the party estopped, not the enforcement of the promise. The relief should be no more than is necessary to relieve the detriment. There are several possible remedies available: stopping one party from departing from the promise, damages for any loss suffered as a result of such a departure or restoring the innocent party to the position which existed before the assumption was relied on. There may be circumstances where the relief which is needed to remove the detriment is the enforcement of a non-contractual promise. For example, if one party promised the other that a run-down bush shack was to be given to them as a gift, and the second party expended money in making the shack habitable, is the minimum relief necessary to relieve the detriment the cost of the improvements or the transferring of ownership of the shack? Relief in equity is discretionary and the court will probably determine relief after examining the cost to the estopped party of making good the assumption.

The question of the 'minimum equity' required to do justice between the parties was examined by the Victorian Supreme Court in *The Commonwealth v Clark* (1994) 2 VR 333. This case also concerned a sailor injured in the *Voyager* collision. In 1985 Mr Clark was advised through his solicitor that the Commonwealth would not rely on the defences available to it and so he commenced proceedings for damages arising from the Commonwealth's negligence. Mr Clark borrowed a substantial sum of money to pay for the litigation, and underwent various medical examinations in preparation for the trial. In 1986 the Commonwealth indicated that it would rely on the defences. Mr Clark became ill once he learned of the Commonwealth's change of attitude. The trial judge found that the Commonwealth was estopped from relying on the defences and awarded Mr Clark $650,000 damages.

The Supreme Court on appeal agreed that the Commonwealth was estopped from relying on the defences and in determining that the appropriate remedy was to hold the Commonwealth to its promise not to exercise its right to rely on the defences, considered the High Court's judgments in both *Verwayen* and *Waltons v Maher*. To obtain the minimum equity the relief should avoid unconscionable conduct and do justice between the parties. In determining the remedy there were two interrelated questions to be addressed: whether Mr Clark acted to his detriment in reliance on the assumptions, and whether, if he so acted, it would be unconscionable to allow the Commonwealth to depart from those assumptions. The court concluded that justice cannot always be measured in terms of money and that the representation that the defences would not be relied upon had raised false hopes in Mr Clark. He had, in reliance on those false hopes, borrowed money and endured the considerable strain of preparing for litigation. When the Commonwealth resiled from its promise he suffered mental ill health and was likely to suffer further detriment if the Commonwealth was allowed to rely on the defences. It would, therefore, be unconscionable to do other than hold the Commonwealth to the promise not to rely on the defences.

Capacity

[2.57]   Certain classes of persons are regarded by law as incapable, either wholly or partly, of entering into contractual obligations binding on them. This is either because they are unable to assess the meaning of the contract, and therefore the rights and obligations arising from it, or the legal status of such persons imposes limits on their ability to contract. A contract may not be valid and enforceable if one or both of the parties lacks the necessary legal capacity.

Minors

[2.58]   The capacity of minors (persons under the age of 18) to contract is governed by the common law or the common law as altered by state legislation.

Minors' contracts at common law

[2.59]   At common law there are two types of contract which will be binding on a minor — contracts for necessaries and contracts for the provision of beneficial services. The common law aims to:

- protect minors from harsh or oppressive contracts; but
- allow minors to contract where it is essential or to their benefit; and
- give persons who have contracted with minors some protection.

Contracts for necessaries are not confined to the bare necessities of life. It is not possible to give an exhaustive list of what goods would be necessaries, but luxuries are excluded. 'Necessaries' includes at least food, clothing, medical treatment, education and accommodation. The circumstances of each minor and his or her actual requirements at the time of entering into the contact must be considered in deciding whether the contract is for necessaries. Contracts for the provision of beneficial services are similar in nature and cover contracts of employment, training or apprenticeship. Where the contract is one of these then the minor is liable to pay for the goods or services.

Case Example

Les Darcy was 20 years old in 1916 and therefore a minor lacking in contractual capacity. He was also a professional boxer, who could not get enough bouts in Australia to make a living and therefore wanted to go to America where he would find not only fighting engagements but also be able to undertake specialised instruction and training. Darcy needed a passport to travel to America, and because he believed that he could not present his case adequately he hired a solicitor, McLaughlin, to represent him. McLaughlin went to Melbourne and interviewed the relevant authorities. Although he did not succeed in obtaining a passport for Darcy, he did extract a promise to consider Darcy's request favourably.

> The court held that the contract was one for necessaries and that the services rendered and the work done were essential to the welfare of Darcy, and therefore that McLaughlin was able to sue for his fee: *McLaughlin v Darcy* (1918) 18 SR (NSW) 585; 35 WN (NSW) 174.

Continuing contracts such as those involving the sale of property, leases, mortgages, share contracts and loans, which are of some benefit to the minor, are likely to be voidable by the minor. This means the contracts are binding on the minor unless and until the minor takes steps to avoid them. Any person who deals with the minor will be bound by the contract, but the minor may repudiate the contract at any time before reaching the age of majority. All other contracts will not be binding on minors, either before or after the minor reaches the age of majority, unless ratified.

Minors' contracts and legislation

[2.60]   The Minors (Property and Contracts) Act 1970 (NSW) makes civil acts which are for the minor's benefit presumptively binding on the minor: s 19. A civil act is defined by s 6 to mean a contract, disposition of property or any act relating to contractual or proprietary rights or obligations or to any chose in action. Where a minor enters into a contract for his or her benefit, it will be binding unless it is proven that the minor, by reason of youth, lacked the understanding necessary for participation in the civil act: s 18. The question of whether or not a civil act is for the minor's benefit is not answered by reference to necessaries, but encompasses a wider range of contracts and is a question of fact in each case. If a minor has entered into a contract which is not presumptively binding it cannot be enforced by the other party unless affirmed. These contracts may be affirmed by the court while the minor is still under 18 or by the minor on obtaining majority: s 30. The minor may repudiate such a contract at any time before turning 19 (s 31), and the court has the power to adjust the interest of the parties, and to order restitution where appropriate: s 37. See also Minors Contract (Miscellaneous Provisions) Act 1979 (SA).

Corporations

[2.61]   A corporation is an artificial legal person, but has the legal capacity of a natural person: Corporations Law s 161. Since a corporation is an artificial entity it is only able to operate through human agents. Section 182 of the Corporations Law provides that:

(1) So far as concerns the formalities of making, varying or discharging a contract, a person acting under the express or implied authority of a company may make, vary or discharge a contract in the name of or on behalf of, the company in the same manner as if that contract were made, varied or discharged by a natural person.

(2) The making, variation or discharging of a contract in accordance with subsection (1) is effectual in law and binds the company and other parties to the contract.

The need for a corporation to act through human agents may give rise to problems for persons who deal with corporations. The human agents of the corporation may act in a way which is beyond their actual authority and then the person dealing with them has no certainty as to the binding nature of the transaction. Section 164 of the Corporations Law allows persons dealing with corporations to assume the authority of the agent: these assumptions clarify the situation.

Persons of unsound mind and intoxicated persons

[2.62]   A contract made by a person who has been declared by a court to be of unsound mind is absolutely void, even though it has been made during a lucid interval. Contracts made with persons of unsound mind not so declared and contracts made by intoxicated persons are prima facie valid.

These persons can repudiate contracts entered into by them only if they can show that:

- they were so incapable at the time of entering into the contract as not to know what they were doing; and
- the other party knew of their condition.

These contracts must be repudiated within a reasonable time of the party becoming sane or sober. However, should the mentally incapacitated or intoxicated persons confirm the contract upon becoming sane or sober they cannot subsequently refuse to be bound by it on the grounds of unsoundness of mind or intoxication.

Bankrupts

[2.63]   A bankrupt is not by reason of the bankruptcy deprived of capacity to contract but the Bankruptcy Act imposes some limits on the dealings of bankrupts. A person who is a declared bankrupt cannot carry on business as a partner in a legal firm, nor enter into certain contracts to purchase goods worth more than $3000 without disclosing that he or she is an undischarged bankrupt: s 269 of the Bankruptcy Act 1966 (Cth).

Privity of contract

[2.64]   This doctrine owes a lot to the bargain theory of contract. If each party bargains for or gives some thing in return for the promise or performance of the other party it makes sense that *only* the parties to the contract have incurred obligations under the contract and only the parties to the contract have gained enforceable rights from it. A contract only binds those persons who are parties, or privy, to the contract — persons who are not parties to a contract cannot have rights imposed or enforceable benefits conferred on them.

Up until the judgment of the High Court in *Trident General Insurance Co Ltd v McNiece Bros Pty Ltd* (1988)165 CLR 107; 80 ALR 574 there was no doubt that the doctrine of privity was a strong force in Australian law, and that it was linked to consideration. The doctrine of privity has been the subject of criticism. The strict application of the doctrine of privity has both substantial and procedural problems.

> **Case Example**
>
> What happens when one person contracts for a group, but cannot properly be described as an agent for each individual? In *Jackson v Horizon Holidays* [1975] 3 All ER 90, Jackson entered into a contract with a travel agent for a holiday for himself, his wife and his children. The holiday was a disappointment. The resort they had booked into was not available and the hotel they stayed in did not answer the description — it did not have the promised facilities, it was dirty and had mildew and fungus growing on the walls. Only Mr Jackson could sue because only he was a party to the contract. Jackson made the contract himself for the benefit of the whole party. Lord Denning said: 'the only one who can sue is the one who made the contract. None of the rest of the party van sue, even though the contract was made for their benefit'. Mr Jackson recovered damages which took into account the discomfort, vexation and distress of the whole party.

While the result in this case may be satisfactory, there remains a procedural barrier to recovery by persons for whose benefit the contract was made. What happens if the contracting party will not or cannot sue, or has suffered no personal loss, and, how can the courts ensure that the damages awarded to the contracting party are passed on to those who suffered the actual loss?

Contracts for the benefit of a third person

[2.65]   Where two parties contract for the benefit of a third person, that third person cannot sue to enforce the contract. In most cases neither will either of the true parties. The true parties can sue each other for breach of contract where there is a refusal to perform; but specific performance cannot be obtained if damages are available and adequate. The measure of damages will be the loss sustained by the plaintiff, not the benefit which has not been conferred on the third person.

There is a lot of sense in saying that if Allan and Barbara are parties to a contract they cannot impose any obligations or burden on Charlie; but where Allan and Barbara enter a contract which confers a benefit on Charlie it is not as easy to defend the rule that Charlie cannot enforce that contract so as to obtain the benefit.

The problem for the law is that while the doctrine of privity is useful and necessary to draw the line around the persons who may sue or be sued on a contract, there will be cases where the operation of the doctrine results in injustice. Some legislative changes have been made, so that in some contracts a third party is able to enforce a benefit expressly conferred by contract. The promise must be one that intended to confer a legal benefit and there must be an intention to create legal relations between the promisor and the beneficiary.

The Insurance Contracts Act 1984 (Cth), for example, extends the coverage of insurance contracts to persons who are not parties to contracts of insurance but are often the claimants. Section 48(1) provides that where a person who is not a party to a contract of general insurance is specified or referred to in the contract, whether by name or otherwise, as a person to whom the insurance cover provided by the contract extends, that person has a right to recover the amount of his or her loss from the insurer in accordance with the contract notwithstanding that he or she is not a party to the contract.

Part performance

[2.66]   Under this doctrine, equity may intervene to give relief to a claimant who has partly performed a valid contract which is unenforceable because the formalities required by the legislation based on the Statute of Frauds have not been observed. For example, the Conveyancing Act 1919 (NSW) provides that only those contracts for the transfer of an interest in land which are evidenced in writing are enforceable: an oral contract for a lease may be valid but cannot be enforced in court. The basis of the doctrine is that it would be against good conscience to allow a defendant to set up the statute to deny relief to a claimant who has performed the whole or part of his or her obligations in reliance on the contract (by claiming that the contract is unenforceable because it does not meet the requirement of the relevant statute). Part performance is only available where the contract is one which is capable of specific performance. The claimant must prove:

- an oral agreement; and
- acts done in reliance on that oral agreement; and
- that these acts are referable to the contract in the sense that the doing of the acts is inexplicable except on the assumption that the contract alleged had been made (that is, they are done with no other view or intention but to perform).

Case Example

The decision in *Re Wardle: Widin v Australia & New Zealand Banking Group Ltd* (1990) ALR 613 illustrates this doctrine. The ANZ bank provided finance to Wardle, in return for which he agreed to give a mortgage on his house. Wardle went to the bank and signed a blank mortgage document and an authority for the bank to fill in the blanks. The bank then proceeded to do all things a bank usually does under the finance agreement, including assuming liability as an endorser of bills in the market. At some stage the bank filled in the blanks on the mortgage. Wardle went bankrupt. While the mortgage was not complete it was not a sufficient memorandum in writing to satisfy the statute, but once filled in it was. Widin, the trustee in bankruptcy, argued that since the bank had not completed the form at least six months prior to Wardle's bankruptcy it was void as a preference. The bank argued that it had done sufficient acts of part performance from the time the blank form was signed and that therefore the bank had a valid and enforceable mortgage prior to the preference period.

The court at first instance held that the acts were unequivocally and by their nature referable to the existence of an agreement of the general nature of that which existed between Wardle and the bank. The bank, in rendering itself liable on the bills, altered its position on the faith of the oral agreement. On appeal the Federal Court held that there was no relevant act of part performance relating to the agreement affecting an interest in land. The act relied upon must be seen as referable only to the contract alleged; the payment of money and the endorsing of the bills were ordinary commercial transactions and did not point to the existence of the mortgage. The mortgage was therefore void against the trustee.

Summary and key terms

[2.67]   This chapter has set out to explain:
- What a contract is — a set of promises which the law will enforce.
- The tension which exists between the doctrine of freedom of contract and commercial reality, as well as the effect of legislation such as the Trade Practices Act.
- The five elements which must be established before a contract can be formed — offer, acceptance, agreement, consideration and intention.
- The ways in which promises may still have some legal force even though not contained in a contract — estoppel and part performance.

3

Contracts: Interpretation

What this chapter does ...

Before a person can complain about a breach of contract it will be necessary to establish what was agreed to by the parties. Then it is necessary to assess the importance of the terms breached or to establish the effect of the breach on the contract. This chapter examines:

- *what the contract says — express and implied terms, collateral contracts;*

- *how important the terms are — conditions and warranties; and*

- *what the terms mean — limitation and exclusion clauses.*

What did the parties agree to?

[3.1] Once it has been established that the parties have made an agreement which the courts will enforce, the next likely area of dispute is what they have agreed to do. What are the respective rights and obligations of the parties under the contract? There are two factors to consider:

- what does the contract say; and
- what does it mean?

This involves an exploration and identification of the terms of the contract followed by interpretation of those terms to determine what the parties have agreed to do.

Many contracts are not contained in formal written documents, although most commercial contracts are reduced to writing and formally executed by the parties. These entirely written contracts will be formed after and based upon agreement reached during negotiations between the parties. Some contracts are formed by a handshake at the end of spoken negotiations: these informal contracts are called oral contracts. Other contracts may be made up of both oral statements and written documents.

Identifying the contents of a contract

[3.2] When giving effect to the agreement between the parties, courts do not rewrite the contract nor do they rectify oversights. If a contract has not worked the way a party expected it to work that is bad luck. The court identifies what the parties intended to agree to and will not change what is in the contract, even where it may operate unfairly. An example of this approach can be seen in the decision of Menzies J in *The South Australian Railway Commissioner v Egan* (1973) 130 CLR 506, where he gave effect to an agreement between a contractor and the railway even though, in his opinion, it was 'perhaps the most wordy, obscure and oppressive contract that I have come across'. His attitude illustrated the role of the courts in a contractual dispute.

The terms of a contract are called different things — clauses, conditions, provisions, elements, stipulations, warranties and covenants. Each term is a separate item of agreement between the parties, and each is a contractual promise capable of being breached.

[3.3] Except in a few cases (for example, dealings in land), there is no particular way in which a contract must be expressed or recorded. The parties may record their contract entirely in writing, or the whole contract may be oral, or it may be a combination of both. Of course, even though a contract does not have to be in writing, there are practical reasons for reducing it to writing. A written contract goes a long way to establishing what the parties actually agreed to, but there are sometimes arguments about what was said between the parties in negotiations prior to formation. It could be argued that the written contract supersedes any statements made during the course of negotiations: the final contract contains all that has been agreed to. On the other hand, pre-contractual statements are the foundation of the agreement and particular statements may have been important enough to have persuaded a person to enter into the contract. An analysis of the offer and acceptance resulting in the formation of the contract may therefore be an important first step to determining the contents of a contract.

Terms must be known to the parties prior to formation of the contract

[3.4]   Only those matters to which the parties have agreed can be terms of the contract. The actual terms of a contract are those which the parties intended. Therefore each party must know of and consent to each term. In cases where the document said to contain the terms of the contract is produced and given by one party to another the general rule is that only those matters which were brought to the attention of the parties prior to agreement will be terms.

Ticket cases

[3.5]   Tickets for transport, admission to entertainment, parking stations and for the collection of dry cleaning or items left for repair are common examples of standard form contracts. Suppose Bob goes to a railway station and asks for a ticket, pays the fare and is given a ticket: that ticket may have terms printed on its face or back and may also refer Bob to terms displayed on a notice. When will those terms have contractual force?

The general rule is that the issue of the ticket is the offer; the passenger is said to have an opportunity to consider the terms of the offer and the making of the journey is the acceptance by the passenger. This rule cannot apply where the contract is in fact formed before the issue of the ticket. In this circumstance the terms will be a part of the contract, if and only if, they were sufficiently brought to the attention of the passenger prior to the formation of the contract.

Case Example

In *Dillon v Baltic Shipping Co 'The Mikhail Lermontov'* (1991) 22 NSWLR 1, the court was asked to decide whether the terms printed on a ticket were part of the contract between the parties. Mrs Dillon saw an advertisement for a 14-day cruise to New Zealand, to commence on 7 February 1986. On 30 October 1985 Mrs Dillon paid a deposit and received an acknowledgment of her booking. On 9 November 1985 she received a booking form and was invited to pay the balance of the cost of the cruise. This booking form set out the name of the vessel, cruise number, sailing date, Mrs Dillon's personal details, type of cabin, fare and balance owing plus penalties which would be incurred by Mrs Dillon should she cancel her booking. On 6 January Mrs Dillon paid the balance of the fare, and she received her ticket on 24 January. The ticket contained terms and conditions limiting the shipping company's liability for personal injury and loss of personal effects.

The *Mikhail Lermontov* sank off the New Zealand coast as a result of negligent navigation by the ship's pilot. Mrs Dillon suffered physical injury and nervous shock. The Baltic Shipping Company sought to rely on the limitation clauses contained in the ticket. In deciding whether or not these clauses were part of the contract the court examined two issues: when was the contract formed, and were these clauses sufficiently drawn to Mrs Dillon's attention prior to that formation? The shipping company argued that these terms were part of the contract. It said that the contract was made after the issue of the ticket, by which time Mrs Dillon had had an opportunity to examine its contents and opted to take the cruise.

The booking form stated that the contract would arise only at the time of the issuing of the tickets, and further that there were terms and conditions on the tickets.

The court found that the contract of carriage was actually made when Mrs Dillon received the ticket. She would only be bound by the terms printed on the ticket if they had been sufficiently drawn to her attention before she received the ticket. The reference on the booking form to the existence of the terms was not sufficient compliance with the company's duty to bring unusual or harsh terms to the notice of passengers. Therefore the terms were not part of the contract between the parties. This meant that Mrs Dillon was not bound by the limitation clause and could recover damages.

Terms of the contract

[3.6]   Before parties to a contract agree on its terms, they will have negotiated a range of issues — some important to the contract and some not. Therefore, if a written contract does not contain a statement made during the negotiations, or if the parties later disagree as to what was in an oral contract, the court will have to decide what it was that the parties can be said, objectively, to have agreed to. It can be difficult to say precisely what the contents of a contract are because the express terms may be found in what was said by the parties prior to agreement or in any document prepared by the parties to give effect to their agreement. The contract may also contain terms not expressly agreed to by the parties: both the common law and legislation will imply certain terms into the contract. Documents external to the contract may contain terms which are by the conduct of the parties added to the contract.

Parol evidence rule

[3.7]   Where a contract is written the general rule is that the writing contains all of the contract. In the process of establishing the express terms, wholly written contracts are subject to a rule of evidence — the parol evidence rule. The rule is based on the proposition that the writing is the entire contract between the parties, and the 'broad purpose of the parol evidence rule is to exclude external evidence, including direct statements of intention and antecedent negotiations, to subtract from, add to, vary or contradict the language of a written instrument': Mason J in *Codelfa Construction Pty Ltd v State Rail Authority of New South Wales* (1982) 149 CLR 337 at 347.

The rule operates to limit the introduction of extra terms based on oral statements into the contract. Thus, once a court determines that a contract is wholly in writing it will not admit any evidence to alter its terms. A strict application of the parol evidence rule can be seen in *British Movietone News Ltd v London & District Cinemas* [1952] AC 166. There was a written contract for the supply of film, which contained a clause allowing termination by either party on the giving of four weeks notice. Legislation passed during the Second World War required the parties to ratify the contract. The parties ratified their agreement and in the second contract agreed that the contract between them would continue to have effect until the relevant legislation was withdrawn. In 1948 one party served notice on the other that it intended to terminate the contract in four weeks. The other party refused to accept this because the legislation was still in force. The court refused to admit evidence that the second contract was meant to have effect for only so long as there was war. It was held that it was wrong to consider extraneous circumstances when attempting to interpret the validity of the second agreement. It should be considered according to its contents alone. The words of the contract were perfectly clear and unambiguous and meant that while the legislation was still in force the contract could not be terminated.

[3.8]   Such strict applications of the rule lead to hardship. Therefore some exceptions have been developed. Parol evidence:

- is admissible to show that a custom or trade usage is applicable to the contract even though not specifically referred to;
- may be given that the operation of the written contract was subject to a condition, which has not yet been fulfilled — for example, approval by a third party;
- may be admitted to show that the contract was not wholly in writing but was in fact partly in writing and partly oral;
- may be given to identify either the subject matter of the contract or a party to it; and
- is always admissible to show that either the contract does not operate — for example, because it was obtained by unconscionable conduct — or that it does not accurately reflect the agreement of the parties.

Categories of terms

[3.9]   There are several categories of contractual terms. They can be:

- express;
- implied; or
- incorporated.

Express terms

[3.10]   These are the terms which the parties have specifically made and which they intended to be part of the contract. In oral contracts this will be what was actually agreed between the parties. Any term in writing is an express term.

If it was as simple as that there would be no disputes, but it is sometimes necessary to take account of statements made in pre-contractual negotiations between the parties. They may be express terms of the contract. At common law the problem is to distinguish statements which are mere representations — statements which are not intended to have contractual force — and those which are intended to be terms of the contract.

The significance of the problem is that if a mere representation turns out to be untrue, but not fraudulent, the only remedy at common law will be rescission of the contract. This will often not be an adequate remedy, and will not allow the plaintiff to ask for damages to make good the representation. If, however, the statement is a term of the contract and it turns out to be untrue, that is a breach and damages as well as possible rescission are available to the injured party. As discussed in **[4.1]–[4.10]** the common law on misrepresentation has been affected by the introduction of the Trade Practices Act 1974. It may be that the untrue statement, even if it is not a term of the contract, is misleading and deceptive conduct under s 52 of that Act and, if that is so, there will be wider remedies available.

[3.11]   The intention of the parties is examined to determine whether or not an express pre-contractual statement is a term of the contract. The courts require the plaintiff to show three things:

- a statement of fact;
- reliance on the statement; and
- that the representor intended to guarantee or warrant the truth of the statement.

The objective approach to the intention of the parties can be seen in the case of *Oscar Chess v Williams* [1957] 1 WLR 370, where Lord Denning posed the crucial enquiry as 'was the statement a binding promise or only an innocent misrepresentation? ... Was it intended as a promise or not?'

Australian courts look not only to the question of intention and reliance but to the intention to be liable for the truth of the statement. They therefore look to the circumstances existing at the time of the representation and the formation of the contract, particularly:

- what form the statement took — opinion or fact;
- the time of the making of the representation in relation to the formation of the contract;
- the existence of any evidence as to the importance of the representation to the contract; and
- the knowledge and expertise of the representor.

Case Example

Ross wanted to purchase a harvester; he hoped to make enough money as a contract harvester to pay for the hire–purchase of the machine, and told the salesperson that he had budgeted for doing 120–130 acres per day. The salesperson, who had done similar work himself, said 'In my experience the best this one could do is 90 acres per day'. Ross bought the machine but found that it would not do even 90 acres per day. He sued, alleging a breach of the warranty that the harvester would do 90 acres per day. The High Court, after examining the question of whether the statement was meant to be promissory in nature, concluded that it did not amount to a warranty because it was merely a statement of opinion based on experience. The salesperson had not intended the statement to be binding in the sense of being liable if it turned out to be untrue: *Ross v Allis-Chalmers Australia Pty Ltd* (1980) 32 ALR 561; (1981)55 ALJR 8.

[3.12]   Where the contract is oral the express terms will be discovered by the identification of the words actually used by the parties at the time of formation. This will be a question of fact for the court to decide on the evidence of the parties.

Case Example

The decision in *Ross v Allis-Chalmers Australia Pty Ltd* (1980) 32 ALR 561; (1981)55 ALJR 8 was applied by the Supreme Court of New South Wales in a recent case. Hill carried on business as a haulage contractor. In 1992 Allied Express Transport was looking for someone to deliver Arnotts' biscuits to eight towns in the Riverina area.

Shea, a representative for Allied Express Transport, negotiated with Hill. A written contract was prepared by Allied Express Transport. This contract set out the towns to which biscuits were to be delivered, the eight-week schedule for delivery, that the deliveries were expected to take three to four days each week and that Hill would be paid $1000 per week. Shea said to Hill during negotiations that the payment of $1000 would be for an average of 800 km per week. When Hill asked what happened on all kilometres over 800, Shea replied 'There won't be any'. Hill then signed the contract.

When Hill began performing the contract he found that he was travelling much more than 800 km per week. The court had to determine whether the statements made by Shea during negotiations were promissory in nature, thereby giving rise to a warranty within the contract, or merely representational, and therefore not a part of the contract. The court said that it had to look at what was said in the particular context: was a definite statement made at the time that the parties were considering the terms of the contract? The basis for payment is a most important item in a contract, and furthermore Shea, who made the statement, could be assumed to know the distances involved. Hill could not have calculated the distance in advance because the delivery involved more than just driving between towns — delivery to various shops within some towns meant driving a further 60 km.

It was held that the words constituted a promise that for $1000 per week Hill would be required to travel no more that 800 km in an average over each week of the eight-week delivery period. Allied Express Transport was in breach of contract and required to pay damages. *Allied Express Transport P/L v Hill* 12524/96 28 FEBRUARY 1997 http://www.austlii.edu.au/do2/disp.pl/au/cases/nsw/supreme_ct/96012524

Collateral contracts

[3.13]   Another complicating factor in the process of establishing what the parties agreed to is that the matters to which the parties have agreed are not necessarily found in one place. There may be two contracts which taken together contain the entire agreement between the parties. This raises the issue of collateral contracts.

A collateral contract may be described as a subsidiary contract, the main purpose of which is to vary or add to the terms of the principal contract. The courts are reluctant to find a collateral contract where the purpose is to add a term to the contract which the parties could have, but did not, include themselves. Often the collateral contract is found in pre-contractual representations which have not found their way into the principal contract.

Case Example

Before the formal exchange of contracts for the sale of a house, the purchaser inquired as to whether there were any white ants in the house, and the vendor replied, 'No, no, no, if there had been any I would have taken steps to eradicate them'. After the sale was complete, the purchaser discovered white ants in the house and sued for breach of the term that the house was ant-free.

This pre-contractual statement had not been included in the written contract and the purchaser had to find a way to avoid the application of the parol evidence rule. One way was to show that the statement was a collateral contact. Wolff CJ said, 'the primary rule is that you cannot have parol statements to vary the terms and conditions of a written contract … if it can be proved that there was a collateral contract or something which the parties intended to form a consideration for their ultimate bargain, then that may be established by evidence': *Van den Esschert v Chappell* (1960) WAR 114 at 115–16.

This sort of statement was of such importance to anyone buying a house in the particular area that it would be promissory. It was not inconsistent with the main contract and because the written contract was a standard form, not a term usually included. Therefore the statement that the house was free of white ants was a contract collateral to the main contract for the sale of the house.

Collateral contracts will only be found where the following conditions are satisfied:

- the terms of the collateral contract cannot be inconsistent with the terms of the main contract;
- the terms of the collateral contract cannot be terms which would ordinarily be found in the main contract; and
- the terms of the collateral contract must be promissory in nature.

It is not enough to show that the statement induced the contract. To establish a collateral contract two things must be shown: a promise contained somewhere outside the main contract, and entry into the main contract being the consideration which makes the promise effective: *JJ Savage & Sons Pty Ltd v Blakney* (1970) 119 CLR 435; 44 ALJR 123.

Implied terms

[3.14]	The most detailed written contract cannot provide for every possibility, and in less formal or oral contracts there will be terms not discussed by the parties. Although it is common to say that the courts imply terms into contracts, it is more accurate to say that the courts give expression to terms which were always part of the contract, but had not been expressed by the parties. In the case of implied terms, this deficiency is caused by the failure of the parties to direct their minds to a particular eventuality and to make provision for it: *Codelfa Construction Pty Ltd v State Rail Authority of NSW* (1981) 149 CLR 337. The implication of terms into contracts by the courts is based on a presumed common intention of the parties to have a workable and effective contract.

The common law draws a distinction between terms which are implied in fact and terms which are implied by law. A term implied in fact purports to give effect to the presumed intention of the parties to the contract in respect of a matter that they have not mentioned but which they presumably would agree should be part of the contract. A term implied by law, on the other hand, arises from the nature, type or class of contract in question: see *Breen v Williams* (1996) 158 ALR 259; 70 ALJR 772 at 787–8.

The courts will imply terms into a contract in the following circumstances:

- to give business efficacy to a contract; or
- from custom or trade usage.

Business efficacy

[3.15] The courts are willing to imply terms in fact to give a contract commercial meaning. Where a contract is complete on its face but cannot be given effect to, the court will consider the implication of terms. It is not enough, however, for it to be reasonable to imply a term, it must be necessary to do so to give business efficacy to the contract. The High Court has said in *Breen v Williams* (1996) 158 ALR 259; 70 ALJR 772 that the implication of a term in a contract is based upon the presumed or imputed intention of the parties. In the case of a formal contract which is complete on its face, it may be said in general that no implication arises unless it is necessary to give business efficacy to the contract or unless it is so obvious that it goes without saying (at 780–1).

The pre-conditions to the implication of terms to give business efficacy to a contract were set out in *BP Refinery (Westernport) v Hastings* (1977) 16 ALR 363; 52 ALJR 20. The term must:

- be reasonable and equitable;
- be necessary to give business efficacy to the contract, so that no term will be implied if the contract is effective without it;
- be so obvious that 'it goes without saying';
- be capable of clear expression; and
- not contradict any express terms of the contract.

Case Example

Codelfa Constructions contracted with the State Rail Authority of New South Wales to carry out construction work on the Eastern Suburbs railway line in Sydney. The work involved considerable excavation and blasting as well as the construction of tunnels. This work was in residential areas and created considerable noise and dust. The contract price and the time allowed for completion of the work were determined on the understanding that Codelfa would be able to carry out the work continuously because it would enjoy the Authority's statutory immunity from injunction to restrain nuisance. Construction work was commenced on a three shifts a day, six days a week timetable. Local residents sought an injunction and it was held that the Authority's statutory immunity from injunction did not extend to Codelfa. An injunction to restrain nuisance was granted and Codelfa was restrained from working between 10 pm and 6 am each day. This meant that the completion of the contract was delayed. Codelfa asked the court to imply a term to give business efficacy to the contract in relation to cost for the extra time taken. The High Court held that it was not possible to imply any such term because it was not satisfied that it went without saying that the parties would have agreed to the term if they had put their minds to the possibility of an injunction being granted and it was not necessary to give business efficacy to the contract.

Mason J made the following comments concerning the courts' role in implying contractual terms:

- the implication of terms is an exercise in construction — it is not a question of the content of the contract but one of its meaning;

- the problem is caused by a deficiency in the expression of the contract — the court is asked to give meaning not to a term the parties have actually agreed upon but to one which it is presumed they would have agreed upon if they had turned their minds to the circumstances in which they now find themselves — the objective framework of facts at the time of formation of the contract and the parties' presumed intention at that time must be examined;
- it is not enough that it would be reasonable to imply the term, it must be clearly necessary and the test to be applied is that set out in *BP Refinery (Westernport) v Hastings* (1977) 16 ALR 363; 52 ALJR 20.

Codelfa Construction Pty Ltd v State Rail Authority of New South Wales (1982) 149 CLR 337; 41 ALR 367.

Custom or trade usage

[3.16]   These terms arise from the nature of the contract and are implied in law on the basis that contracts entered into for particular trades or commercial purposes all contain the same unspecified terms. Some of these are general and implied by the common law to complete the legal effect of the contract. For example, when a tenant farmer leases a property there may be no mention of what will happen to crops sown but not harvested at the end of the tenancy. Where local custom decrees that the tenant farmer should have an allowance from the landlord for both the cost of the seed and labour, this will be a term of the contract even though not expressly mentioned: *Hutton v Warren* (1836) 1 M & W 466; 150 ER 517.

Other terms are implied from the custom or usual practice of the trade or industry. The High Court has, in the case of *Constan Industries of Australia Pty Ltd v Norwich Winterthur Insurance (Australia) Ltd* [1986] 160 CLR 226; 64 ALR 481, set out the rules under which custom or trade usage may form the basis for the implication of terms:

- it is a question of fact as to whether there is a custom or usage which will justify the implication of a term;
- the custom relied on must be so well known and acquiesced in that everyone making a contract in that situation can reasonably be presumed to have imported that term into the contract;
- a term will not be implied on the basis of a custom or trade usage where it is contrary to the express term of the contract; and
- a person may be bound by a custom even if unaware of it.

Case Example

Michael Jackson, who owned Dockside Fitness, agreed with the owner of the yacht *Parmelia* that he would pay $5000 for naming and advertising rights and for crew positions for himself and his son Jonathon when the *Parmelia* took part in the Sydney to Hobart yacht race. Jonathon Jackson was ill during the voyage to Sydney for the start of the race and the captain of the *Parmelia* refused to have him as a crew member. Michael Jackson brought an action for breach of contract and for return of the sponsorship money already paid. The *Parmelia's* owner asserted that an implied term of the contract arose from the customary powers of a captain to refuse to have any person as a crew member if that person's inclusion was not consistent with the fitness and safety of the vessel.

It was said that Jonathon Jackson's sea sickness made him unsuitable. The court said that it is an implied term of any 'sailing contract' that a person can only be a member of a ship's crew if that membership is not likely to jeopardise the safety of the vessel or other members of the crew. In this case the mere fact of Jonathon Jackson's sea sickness did not warrant his exclusion under that implied term, and therefore the yacht owners were in breach of their promise to provide him a place in the crew: *Dockside Fitness Pty Ltd, Michael Anthony Jackson and Jonathon William Jackson v Brian Woods* A81/1996 SC(Tas) http://www.austlii.edu.au/do2/disp.pl/au/cases/tas/supreme_ct/unrep799.

Implication of terms in informal contracts

[3.17]   The High Court has drawn a distinction between the implication of terms in informal contracts and the implication of terms in formal or commercial contracts. When examining informal contracts — that is, oral contracts where the parties have not spelt out the full terms of their contract — the court 'should imply a term by reference to the imputed intention of the parties if, but only if, it can be seen that the implication of the term is necessary for the reasonable or effective operation of a contract of that nature in the circumstances of the case': Deane J in *Hawkins v Clayton* (1988) 164 CLR 539 at 573.

Case Example

Ms Breen had silicone implants inserted into her breasts. Some time after this operation she consulted Dr Williams about some problems that had developed. Later another surgeon removed the implants. Ms Breen was interested in joining the litigation being pursued in the US against the manufacturers of the implants. She sought to gain access to the medical records which Dr Williams had in relation to her, but Dr Williams refused her access. Ms Breen argued that it was an implied term of the contract between herself and Dr Williams that she had a right of access to the medical records. In rejecting her argument the High Court said:

- the doctor–patient relationship is contractual, but given the informal nature of the relationship the contract rarely contains many express terms;
- because this is so the courts are obliged to formulate the rights and obligations of the parties to the contract;
- the court does so by establishing what the terms of the contract are by implying terms in fact or in law in accordance with established legal principles;
- into a contract between a doctor and patient the law would imply terms that the doctor agreed to advise and treat the patient with reasonable skill and care, that the patient would render payment to the doctor and that the patient would submit to the treatment proposed — these terms are implied in fact because they reflect what the parties intended.

Ms Breen argued for the implication of a term in law that the doctor was obliged to act in the best interests of the patient and that this would encompass providing access to medical records. This was rejected — the High Court refused to imply any such term because the contract was operative and effective without it — it was neither necessary to give business efficacy to the contract nor so obvious that it goes without saying: *Breen v Williams* (1996) 158 ALR 259; 70 ALJR 772.

Terms implied by statute

[3.18] These most commonly appear in consumer protection legislation such as the Fair Trading Acts and the Trade Practices Act 1974 (Cth). The terms implied by statute are terms of the contract and therefore where there is a breach of them the remedy available is for breach of contract. The statute itself does not give a right to a remedy although it may describe the remedy and prescribe the manner of obtaining it. This class of implied terms involves the intervention of the state into a commercial transaction — the parties agree to what they actually decide and to what the state has expressed in legislation. The terms implied by legislation will usually give certainty to the contract, redress the imbalance of negotiating power or overcome the operation of common law doctrines.

The Trade Practices Act 1974 (Cth) implies certain terms into consumer contracts; that is, those contracts where a person is purchasing goods for ordinary household use or worth less than $40,000. For example, s 71 implies conditions as to the quality or fitness of the goods.

[3.19] Before terms will be implied from the Trade Practices Act it must be shown that:
* the parties were in a contractual relationship (*E v Australian Red Cross Society* (1991) 31 FCR 299; 105 ALR 53; (1992) ATPR 41–156);
* the goods were supplied in the course of a business — this means that the conditions are not implied into non-commercial contracts;
* the purchaser was a 'consumer'; that is, that the goods were of a kind ordinarily acquired for personal, domestic or household use, or worth less than $40,000 and they were not acquired for resupply or use in manufacture: s 4B.

If there is a breach of these conditions then the consumer has all of the rights which would usually follow from a breach of contract. The Trade Practices Act also creates a statutory right to rescission of the contract following breach of an implied condition. This allows the consumer to return the goods, thus transferring property in the goods to the supplier and allowing the consumer to recover the purchase price as a debt owed: see s 75A of the Trade Practices Act 1974.

Incorporated terms

The rule in *L'Estrange v Graucob*

[3.20] Once a person has signed a document which he or she knows to contain contractual term, the signature is said to incorporate all the terms of the document. Unless the signature has been obtained by fraud the person is bound by its terms. It does not matter whether the person signing has read and/or understood the terms of the document. This is the rule in *L'Estrange v Graucob* [1934] 2 KB 394; All ER Rep 16.

Terms contained elsewhere than in the main contract

[3.21] Contracts, whether written or oral, may include terms contained in documents found elsewhere. These terms become part of the contract by the process of incorporation. The most common form of incorporation of terms is by notice. An everyday example is the ticket dispensed by a machine at the entrance to parking stations. This often contains a statement that the contract is subject to the terms and conditions displayed on a sign elsewhere within the parking station.

Many standard form contracts will refer the parties to more detailed terms contained in a separate document. This means that there is little real chance of the parties negotiating to determine the contents of a contract, particularly where there is an imbalance in bargaining power, such as in consumer contracts. The courts are often called upon to decide whether the alleged terms have been brought to the attention of the party in a manner sufficient to incorporate them into the contract. This is a common theme in the 'ticket cases': see **[3.5]**.

Terms contained in writing elsewhere than in the main contract may be incorporated by notice provided the terms are clearly brought to the attention of the other party before the formation of the contract. There are many situations in everyday life where there is no deliberate adoption of a document or acknowledgment between the parties as to the terms of their contract.

Case Example

A couple booked into a hotel for a week's stay and some furs and jewellery were stolen from their room. The hotel sought to rely on an exclusion clause displayed on a sign behind the door of the couple's room. This clause was held not to be a term of the contract because it had not been brought to their attention prior to formation of the contract: *Olley v Marlborough Court* [1949] 1 KB 532.

Case Example

On 17 February 1996 Carolyn Hutchins and others purchased tickets to attend the Australian Formula 1 Grand Prix to be held at Albert Park. On 7 March 1996 the plaintiffs entered the Grand Prix area in accordance with the licences granted to them as ticket holders and occupied seats in the rear row of the Fangio grandstand, in a prime position alongside the front straight and close to the finishing line. They had a large yellow banner which had in black print on it the words 'Save Albert Park'. Shortly after 10 am the plaintiffs proceeded to hold the banner aloft so that it was visible to other spectators. The plaintiffs' ultimate objective in doing so was to have the Grand Prix removed from Albert Park. The Australian Grand Prix Corporation expelled Ms Hutchins and the others from the area. Once they were outside the gate they were told by officials of the Grand Prix that they would not be permitted to re-enter the area, and that the Grand Prix had the authority to eject them because it was in the conditions of entry contained in the tickets. Ms Hutchins argued that the Corporation had no right to expel them from the designated area except for reasonable cause; and that they had given them no reasonable cause to do so in that they were doing no more than exercising their democratic rights to express their views concerning the Grand Prix and its location at Albert Park. They had caused no disruption to the Formula 1 Event.

The tickets issued to the plaintiffs have printed on their reverse sides amongst other things the words: 'This ticket is sold subject to the seller's Conditions of Sale, a copy of which is available for inspection at the time of purchase and/or collection of this ticket' and the words: 'The seller reserves the right to refuse admission with reasonable cause'.

> At every entrance gate to the prescribed area there is erected a large sign approximately 8 feet high and 30 inches wide displaying the conditions of entry to the designated area. Condition 5 reads: 'Patrons may not, without the consent of the Corporation, bring any of the following items into the Event: (i) any flags larger than 1 metre by 1 metre or with handles greater 1 metre.' Condition 8 reads: 'Any person who does not comply with these Conditions may be removed from the Event and have their Ticket and any object brought into the Event in contravention of these Conditions confiscated by an Authorised Person.'
>
> It was argued that the conditions of entry were not conditions of the plaintiffs' contract. The court found that these conditions were incorporated by reference into that contract. Therefore Ms Hutchins and the others were in breach of condition 5(i) and that that breach was sufficient to justify their expulsion: *Hutchins v Australian Grand Prix Corp,* Supreme Court of Victoria No 4722 of 1996.

Incorporation by a course of dealing

[3.22]   Where there has been a series of dealings in which a contract was signed or a sign displayed, the courts suppose that in later dealings the offeror is offering to deal on the usual terms. It is a question of fact for the court as to whether a particular term has been incorporated.

Terms sought to be incorporated by a course of dealings between the parties are usually found in unsigned documents such as invoices, order forms and delivery dockets. They might also appear on signs. If in a particular transaction these terms are not used or displayed or are shown to one party only after the making of the contract then for that transaction the terms may not be part of the contract, especially if they are terms which limit liability. The issue of whether or not terms from previous courses of dealing are part of the contract depends on the intention of the parties.

What do the terms mean?

Construction of terms

[3.23]   Disputes between parties to a contract can develop over what the terms of the contract mean. This is another area where the courts are used to resolve the dispute. Assuming a valid agreement has been proved and the terms of that agreement established, the court's role is to determine and declare what the terms mean. The primary guide in this process of interpretation is the objective intention of the parties which may be gathered from evidence as to the words they used and their conduct. The usual rules of legal interpretation apply and words are to be construed in the context of the document as a whole. Problem areas in this regard are where the words are ambiguous and exclusion clauses.

In *Schenker & Co (Australia) Pty Ltd v Maplas Equipment and Services Pty Ltd* [1990] VR 834 the Victorian Supreme Court recognised that contracts are not created in a vacuum and that their meaning is to be gathered not only from the words used but from the conduct of the parties and the background facts:

- in interpreting the words of a contractual term a court does more than give the words their plain and ordinary meaning;
- a contract is to be construed in the light of the circumstances existing and known to the parties at the time of formation — this includes the reason for the contract, the commercial purpose of the contract and the objective sense of what reasonable persons in the position of the parties would have in mind;
- courts should not give commercial contracts meanings which flout business common sense — they should strive to ascertain what reasonable business people in the position of the parties would have regarded the clause as meaning if they had put their minds to it at the time of formation;
- nevertheless, the words of the parties should not be given a strained meaning in order to give the contract operation which is fair or desirable. The law to be applied was stated by the High Court in *Darlington Futures Ltd v Delco Australia Pty Ltd* (1986) 161 CLR 500 at 510–11; 68 ALR 385 at 391–2:

> … the interpretation of a … clause is to be determined by construing the clause according to its natural and ordinary meaning, read in the light of the contract as a whole, thereby giving due weight to the context in which the clause appears including the nature and object of the contract …

Ambiguity

[3.24]   Two possible meanings for the words of a contract will not necessarily lead to the contract being void for uncertainty. The courts will take this view especially in commercial contracts or where one party has already acted in the belief that there was a binding contract. The courts will determine where possible which meaning is to be preferred. Where it is possible to extract two meanings from the words of the contract, one unreasonable and one not, the court will presume that the reasonable meaning was intended. If the clause being construed is an exclusion or limitation of liability clause the courts will choose the meaning least favourable to the party seeking to rely on it.

Exclusion clauses

[3.25]   It is common for contracts to contain terms, variously called exclusion, exemption or limitation clauses, which operate exclusively to the benefit of only one party. The effect of these clauses is to:

- exclude all liability for breach;
- limit liability for breach of contract or other wrongful conduct;
- exempt a party from the obligation to perform as promised; or
- limit the redress available to the other party where there is a failure to perform.

Almost invariably these clauses are not the subject of negotiation between the parties and many are contained in standard form documents which are exchanged in the course of performance.

It may be said that there are two basic types of exclusion clauses. The first denies facts which may in turn deny remedy for breach, for example:

> The seller does not make any representation as to the quality of the vehicle, and if any such representation was made then it was not intended to have any legal force.

Case Example

A hire–purchase agreement contained clauses which asserted that the customer had examined the car and, while not making known any purpose for which the car was required, acknowledged that the car was fit for that purpose. The court struck down the clauses holding that it is not competent for a contract to stipulate that the facts were other than they were. In no sense was this clause promissory so as to bind the customer: *Lowe v Lombank* [1960] 1 All ER 611.

The second form of exclusion clause is the 'all care but no responsibility' variety, whereby one party seeks to limit or exclude liability arising from a breach of contract, for example:

> Parking Station Company Pty Ltd does not accept any responsibility for the loss or damage to any vehicle or for loss or damage to any article or thing in or upon any vehicle or for any injury to any person howsoever such loss, damage or injury may arise or be caused. Any liability not otherwise excluded is limited to $200.

This is the most common type; it is usually imposed on one party by the other and is often found in standard form contracts or invoices, order forms and delivery documents.

[3.26]   Where there has been a breach of, or failure to perform, a contract which is alleged to contain an exclusion clause the courts are primarily called upon to determine two things:
- whether the exclusion clause is in fact a term of the contract; and, if so,
- what it means.

Once satisfied that the clause is a term of the contract — by, for example, incorporating it into the contract if it is not already in written form — the courts will allow it to work if it can be shown that the parties intended that it should have contractual force. The High Court has said that exclusion clauses should simply be construed in accordance with their language and that they should not be subjected to a strained construction in order to reduce their ambit of operation: *Darlington Futures Ltd v Delco Australia Pty Ltd* (1986) 161 CLR 500; 68 ALR 385. A court does not rewrite the contract of the parties but gives effect to the intention of the parties by construing the words used by them.

The construction of the clause by the courts will determine the plaintiff's remedies and the defendant's liability. In *Darlington Futures v Delco* the court said that it was not entitled to reject an exclusion clause however unreasonable if the words are clear and fairly susceptible of only one meaning.

Where wide exclusion clauses have been upheld the decision often reflects the view that commercial entities are capable of looking after their own interests. An exclusion clause is interpreted according to its natural and ordinary meaning giving due weight to the context in which the clause appears, including the nature and object of the contract. The courts will apply the contra proferentem rule in case of ambiguity. This means that where the clause is ambiguous the court will adopt the meaning which is least favourable to the party asserting the clause.

Case Example

May & Baker contracted with Thomas Nationwide Transport (TNT) for TNT to carry some packages from Melbourne to various interstate destinations. The packages were collected from May & Baker's premises by Pay, a subcontractor of TNT. His usual practice was to deliver all packages collected from various points in Melbourne to TNT's depot where they would be sorted and dispatched. Pay did not complete his collection round until 5.40 pm and as the TNT depot was shut he took the packages to his home, planning to deliver them to the depot the next day. During the night his truck caught fire and the packages belonging to May & Baker were damaged.

TNT sought to rely on clauses which purported to exempt TNT from any liability for any loss or damage to the goods while in transit or in storage. The High Court looked at the operation of the contract, and the expectations of the parties as to the manner of performance, and said:

> it must have been taken to have been implicit in the contract which TNT made with the respondent that its goods would be taken to TNT's depot and that the depot would be available for their reception at the conclusion of the pick-up round. It is, to our minds, unthinkable that it was within the contemplation of the parties than an extremely valuable consignment of goods was to be kept overnight … in the garden of a suburban cottage.

The storage of the goods in Pay's garage was seen as departing so far from the contract of carriage as to preclude TNT from relying on the exclusion clauses: *Thomas Nationwide Transport(Melbourne) Pty Ltd v May & Baker (Australia) Pty Ltd* [1966] 115 CLR 353.

The decision illustrates how the High Court construes exemption clauses in the light of the contract as a whole. Whether an exclusion clause covers any particular situation depends upon whether, properly construed, the clause is wide enough to cover the breach complained of.

Case Example

A container full of cartons of frozen prawns was stolen from a stack of container at the Glebe Island shipping terminal. The owner of the container sued the carrier for non-delivery. The contract contained a term which provided that the carrier was not liable for or in respect of 'any loss or damage to or in connection with the goods arising or resulting at any time from … any cause or event which the Carrier could not avoid or the consequence of which the Carrier could not prevent by the exercise of reasonable diligence'.

The question for the High Court was whether the clause protected the carrier in respect of the loss arising from non-delivery of the goods. The owner submitted that the main object of the contract of carriage was the delivery of the goods to the owner at Sydney and that to construe the exclusion clause as exempting the carrier from liability for loss or damage for non-delivery would defeat that object.

The judgment of the High Court in *Darlington Futures Ltd v Delco Australia Pty. Ltd.* (1986) 161 CLR 500 at 510 that: '... the interpretation of an exclusion clause is to be determined by construing the clause according to its natural and ordinary meaning, read in the light of the contract as a whole, thereby giving due weight to the context in which the clause appears including the nature and object of the contract, and, where appropriate, construing the clause contra proferentem in case of ambiguity', was relied upon.

The High Court had to decide what was the scope of the exclusion clause and what the phrases 'loss to goods' and 'loss in connection with goods' meant. The court said that:

> the meaning of that provision ultimately depends on its language, read in context, and not on any a priori notion that the non-delivery of goods was not intended to be protected. In determining whether an exemption clause should be construed so as to apply to an event which has defeated the main object of the contract, much must depend upon the nature of the events which the clause identifies as giving rise to the exemption from liability. If the happening of a stipulated event will always result in the defeat of the main object of the contract, there will be no scope for holding that that object requires the conclusion that the exempting clause is not applicable to that event. But even in cases where the occurrence of the events stipulated in the exemption clause will not always defeat the main object of the contract, the nature of those events may nevertheless give rise to the inference that the clause was intended to apply to those events even when they occur in circumstances which defeat the main object of the contract.

The conditions upon which the exclusion clause operated were causal events which would ordinarily occur without any fault on the part of the carrier. The loss and damage in respect of which the exclusion clause gives exemption, therefore, depend on events against the consequences of which a carrier might reasonably be expected to seek protection notwithstanding that those events might cause the non-delivery of goods accepted by the carrier for transportation. In the circumstances the main object of the contract provides no ground for concluding that non-delivery of the goods was outside the protection of the exclusion clause.

The words 'loss to goods' and 'loss in connection with goods' should be read as covering indirect, consequential or financial loss arising from the loss of the goods. The exclusion clause therefore exempted the carrier from loss or damage resulting from non-delivery of the goods: *Nissho Iwai Australia Limited v Malaysian International Shipping Corporation, Berhad* (1989) 167 CLR 219.

Exclusion clauses and consumer transactions

[3.27]   The attitude of the courts where an exclusion clause appears in a consumer transaction is somewhat different to that in commercial transactions but the principle is much the same. The court will interpret the clause in the context of the transaction and very often will recognise that a consumer does not have the same capacity to deal with an exclusion clause as a commercial entity. Typically, in a consumer transaction there is little or no opportunity to negotiate terms. Consumers are not able to alter the terms imposed by the supplier, cannot insure to cover any loss and do not have the resources to litigate to recover loss resulting from a breach of contract.

A more powerful factor in dealing with exclusion clauses is the modern consumer protection legislation. In contracts for the supply of goods and services to consumers, the legislation protects consumers by implying terms to the benefit of the consumer into the contract, and then by rendering void any term or clause which seeks to exclude those terms or limit liability for their breach.

Where the transaction has been induced by misleading and deceptive conduct an exclusion clause cannot be used to deprive the misled party of the remedy provided by s 52 of the Trade Practices Act, although it may avoid contractual liability. In *Byers v Dorotea Pty Ltd* (1986) 69 ALR 715; (1987) ATPR 40–760 purchasers were induced to enter contracts for the purchase of units on the Gold Coast by representations as to the existence of a swimming pool and the superior finish of the units. These representations were untrue and held to constitute misleading and deceptive conduct. Pincus J held that clauses stating that the purchasers had not relied on any representation by the vendor were not effective to prevent a claim under the Trade Practices Act.

The state consumer protection legislation may also be used by consumers to avoid the harsh results that would come from a literal and broad approach to exclusion or limitation clauses. In *John Dorahy's Fitness Centre Pty Ltd v Buchanan* http://www.austlii.edu.au/do/disp.pl/au/cases/nsw/supreme_ct/94040386, the Court of Appeal in New South Wales followed the High Court's approach in *Darlington Futures Ltd v Delco Australia Pty Ltd* (1986) 161 CLR 500; 68 ALR 385 by construing the clause narrowly and also considered the question of whether the contract which contained the clause was valid under the Contracts Review Act 1980 (NSW).

Case Example

In late 1995, in response to an advertisement, Carol Buchanan went to John Dorahy's Fitness Centre and inspected the premises. She signed on for a trial period of two weeks and then decided to become a permanent member. Carol Buchanan was on her way into a circuit training session when an employee of John Dorahy's Fitness Centre handed her a completed membership application form. Carol Buchanan signed the form, paid her annual membership fee and then went into the circuit training session. Carol Buchanan was severely injured while using unsafe equipment in the gymnasium. The equipment was unsafe as a result of a failure by the fitness centre to maintain it properly. When she sued for damages the fitness centre sought to rely on the following exclusion clause:

The member hereby absolutely releases John Dorahy's Fitness Centre its employees and agents from:

1) any claim howsoever arising either during the term of this agreement or at any time thereafter by reason of the Member suffering disease deterioration of health illness or aggravation of any condition of ill health as a result of participation in the programs acceptance of the advice or use of the facilities afforded to the Member by John Dorahy's Fitness Centre; and

2) any claim for personal injury sustained by the Member in on or about the Fitness Centre premises including (without limiting the generality of the foregoing) any claims for personal injuries arising from and arising out of the negligence of the Fitness Centre its employees or agents or the negligence of any other member of any other person using the Fitness Centre premises and the Member hereby acknowledges that he uses the premises and all facilities entirely at his own risk.

In relation to the meaning of the clause the court said that although exclusion clauses are to be construed according to their ordinary and natural meaning the purpose of the construction of them is to give effect to the intention of both the parties. It was not likely that the plaintiff would have agreed that she intended the meaning argued for by the fitness centre — if we fail to maintain the machines and so make them dangerous we will not be liable in contract or tort for any injury you suffer. It was found that the injury resulted from a breach of the implied term of the contract that the fitness centre would properly maintain its equipment and that the exclusion clause while it may operate to exclude liability in tort or for ill health occurring as a result of using the gymnasium, did not exclude liability for such a breach of contract.

Further, the court considered the contract to be harsh and oppressive under the Contracts Review Act 1980 (NSW), and that it should refuse to enforce the exclusion clause in so far as it operated to prevent the plaintiff from suing for damages in negligence or for breach of contract. The court said that Carol Buchanan had no opportunity to consider or negotiate the clause and the circumstances of formation showed that the contract was harsh and unjust in that there was an imbalance of bargaining power between the parties: *John Dorahy's Fitness Centre Pty Ltd v Buchanan* http://www.austlii.edu.au/do/disp.pl/au/cases/nsw/supreme_ct/94040386.

Summary and key terms

[3.28] This chapter has set out to explain:
- Courts are called upon to both identify and give meaning to the terms of the contract between the parties.
- That there is a variety of sources of terms of a contract.
- Terms of a contract may be express, implied or incorporated.
- Express terms will in general only be part of a contract if within the contemplation of both parties at the time of formation.
- Terms will be given their usual meaning, with the primary guide being the objective intention of the parties and the words being construed in the context of the document as a whole.
- Exclusion clauses are examined as an example of the identification and interpretation of terms.

4
Apparent Contracts: Lack of True Agreement

What this chapter does ...

Sometimes parties think that they have reached agreement and made a contract but some conduct on the part of either of them could create a problem. The formation of a contract may be affected by fraud or other misconduct.

This chapter examines such misconduct and the remedies available. Examples are:
- *duress;*
- *undue influence;*
- *unconscionable conduct;*
- *mistake;*
- *misrepresentation; and*
- *statutory remedies such as those available under the Contracts Review Act and the Trade Practices Act.*

It is easy enough to identify an apparent contract between two people. It will often be the case that the conduct of one party at the time that the contract was formed meant that the other had not truly agreed to that contract. This lack of true consent can arise from:
- *misrepresentation;*
- *mistake;*
- *duress;*
- *undue influence; and*
- *unconscionable conduct.*

Introduction

Vitiation of a contract

[4.1] There can be no contract without the true consent and agreement of the parties. If a party's consent to the contract is induced by a misrepresentation, obtained by duress, undue influence or unconscionable conduct or affected by an operative mistake, then there is no agreement and the innocent party may elect to treat the contract as invalid, that is, may rescind it. If the contract is rescinded the law treats it as a nullity and the parties are returned to their pre-contractual positions.

Misrepresentation

[4.2] A misrepresentation is a statement that is not true. Statements made by parties during the negotiations leading up to a contract may either be terms of the contract, collateral contracts or mere representations. As discussed at **[3.6]–[3.13]**, the statement has contractual force in the first two situations and if it proves to be untrue the person to whom it was made — the promisee or representee — has an action for breach of contract with remedies of damages and possibly rescission. In the third situation the statement has no true contractual force and if it proves to be untrue the representee may have remedies in tort or rescission of the contract for misrepresentation.

There are many rules relating to misrepresentation: the contract rules overlap with the rules of tort and fraud, and there is an ever-increasing amount of legislation. From a contract point of view the main concern is with the effect of non-promissory pre-contractual statements.

The many cases on misleading and deceptive conduct which contravenes s 52 of the Trade Practices Act have altered the law relating to misrepresentation, so that it may be said that s 52 (and other provisions of the Act dealing with false representations) has largely replaced misrepresentation in relation to commercial transactions. The common law can still be used in commercial situations, but need not be. In non-commercial transactions the common law provides the only remedy, because the Trade Practices Act and most Fair Trading Acts apply only to activities in trade or commerce. Thus if a car dealer sold Jo a car and said falsely that it had never been in an accident, Jo may use both the common law of misrepresentation or s 52. However, if Jo purchased the car privately from Kim, only the common law could be used.

Representation

[4.3]   A actionable misrepresentation is a pre-contractual statement of fact which induces entry into the contract. It may be made by words or conduct. Silence will amount to a representation in some circumstances; for example, where the contract requires full disclosure, such as a contract of insurance, or where the parties are in a 'relationship of confidence'.

Case Example

A real estate agent who had been engaged to sell a farm for a widow, swapped his house for her farm, at an advantage to himself. It was held that the relationship gave rise to a requirement of full disclosure so that suppression of information as to the true value of her property amounted to a positive misrepresentation: *McKenzie v McDonald* [1927] VLR 134.

Silence will be a representation in circumstances where the failure to speak gives a distorted view of a positive representation. Where there has been a positive representation made as to facts and there is a change in circumstances between the time of making the representation and the time of formation of the contract, silence may result in the 'continuing representation' giving a false impression.

Case Example

A medical practitioner made a true statement as to the number of patients his practice had, but during the time taken for negotiations for the sale of the practice this had considerably declined. It was held that failure to reveal the changed circumstances amounted to a misrepresentation: *With v O'Flanagan* [1936] Ch 575.

When is a representation significant?

[4.4]   To rely on the misrepresentation to avoid being bound by the contract, the plaintiff must prove three factors:

[4.5] **A representation of existing fact** Any representation must be one of fact not opinion or prediction and the fact must be existing or current. This is because a statement of opinion or intention as to future acts or events cannot be true or false at the time of being made. While the law will not bind a party by mere speculation, it recognises that parties can be influenced equally by statements of opinion, prediction or fact. Therefore the courts have interpreted the rule so that an opinion or a statement of intention to act in a certain way has been said to be a representation as to the current state of mind of the party and thus a statement of existing fact. A statement of intention or opinion is often held to embody a statement of fact; that is, that the representor currently holds that opinion or has that intention. In this the identity — the personality, qualifications or experience — of the representor may be important. Where the person making the representation is in a better position to know the facts than the representee, it may be presumed that the representor based his or her opinion on the facts. In *Smith v Land House Property Commission* (1884) 28 Ch D 7, the landlord said the tenant was creditworthy and he turned out not to be so. This was held to be not an expression of the landlord's opinion, but a statement of fact.

The traditional rule that representations to be actionable had to be representations of fact not law was described by the High Court in *David Securities Pty Ltd v Commonwealth Bank of Australia* [1992] 175 CLR 353 as difficult to apply and artificial. The distinction between law and fact was rejected, at least in relation to the recovery of moneys paid under a mistake.

[4.6] **The statement must be false** This is a question of fact for the court and is not necessarily related to the intention or knowledge of the representor. The question of whether a statement is true or false is to be determined at the time of the making of the representation.

[4.7] **The statement must have induced the contract** The plaintiff must show that the decision to enter the contract was affected by the representation and there are two elements to be considered:

* the person making the representation — the representor — must have intended that the other party would respond to or act on the representation; and
* the inducement must be actual, but it need not be the sole inducement to enter the contract.

Types of misrepresentation

[4.8] A misrepresentation may be either fraudulent, negligent or innocent, and each type gives rise to its own set of remedies.

A misrepresentation is fraudulent if it is made with knowledge of its falsity, or with reckless indifference as to whether or not it is true. The contract can be rescinded and an action for damages launched — in the tort of deceit — for fraudulent misrepresentation. A person who was induced to enter a contract by reason of a fraudulent representation may resist any attempt to enforce the contract.

Misrepresentations will be negligent if:

* the representor owed to the representee a duty of care — this often arises where the misrepresentation is made during the provision of information or the giving of professional advice;
* there was a breach of that duty of care; and,
* the breach resulted in loss or damage to the representee.

The representee's remedy for negligent misrepresentation is rescission of the contract and damages in the tort of negligence.

An innocent misrepresentation occurs when a person makes an untrue statement in good faith and without knowing that he or she has made a false statement or created a false impression. In such cases the representee may rescind the contract but not sue for damages.

Remedies for misrepresentation

[4.9] Where there has been a misrepresentation, the innocent party may obtain a remedy outside of the law of contract if he or she can show that:

- the statement was made negligently — then the remedy would be in tort; or
- the representation became a term of the contract — then the remedy is for breach of contract; or
- the representation gave rise to an operative common mistake and no contract was formed; or
- the representation amounts to misleading and deceptive conduct and therefore breaches s 52 of the Trade Practices Act or similar state legislation. The remedy could be either damages and/or orders for rescission.

At common law a representee will be bound to a contract induced by an innocent but false statement. There are no common law contractual damages available for innocent misrepresentation. Equity will allow the innocent party to rely on a misrepresentation either to rescind the contract or resist an action for specific performance. There may be a right to recover money or property transferred to the other party.

Only the person induced to enter the contract by the false representation may rely on that misrepresentation to bring the contract to an end. If that person wishes to do so the contract is rescinded by informing the other person, usually in writing. If this rescission is not accepted, the other party may sue to enforce the contract or regard the attempted rescission as a breach of contract. In such cases the court will be called on to determine whether there was a right to rescind for misrepresentation.

Bars to rescission

[4.10] When a person ends a contract because it was induced by a false representation, the rescission is from the time the contract was formed. This is referred to as rescission ab initio, which means that in law there never was a contract between the parties. Therefore, for an effective rescission the common law requires the return of the parties to the position they were in before the contract was made. Restitution must be available otherwise the innocent party will be bound to the contract and if any of the following events have occurred then the rescission will not be possible:

- the innocent party, after learning of the falsity of the representation, affirms the contract;
- there has been undue delay between learning of the falsity of the representation and the rescission;
- a third party has acquired rights under the contract, and rescission would prejudice those rights; or
- property has been transferred in execution of the contract— this rule, known as the rule in *Seddon's* case, applies only to contracts induced by an innocent misrepresentation. If the parties have executed the contract — that is, fulfilled their obligations — and property has been transferred then it is not possible to undo the contract. The rule in *Seddon's* case has been criticised because the innocent party will often only discover the misrepresentation after performance of the contract.

Equity recognised that where it was not possible to return the parties to their exact pre-contractual positions, but substantial restitution was possible the court could undo the contract and make orders to do appropriate justice between the parties. The approach of the High Court can be seen in *Alati v Kruger* (1955) 94 CLR 216.

Case Example

Kruger purchased a fruit business from Alati, by a contract dated 7 June 1954. There was a representation that the average takings in the shop were £100 per week. This representation induced Kruger to enter the contract. After Kruger began operating the business it was observed that the takings never reached £100, and it was discovered that for the nine weeks preceding his takeover of the business they had in fact averaged much less.

After three weeks Kruger rescinded the contract and began proceedings to recover the price paid for the business. The trial took place on 30 September 1954 and up until that time Kruger continued to run the business, despite low takings, but by the time judgment was given on 17 December 1954, the business had closed. The High Court in considering whether Kruger had a right to rescind for misrepresentation after he had completed the contract and begun running the fruit business, said (at 223–4):

> … it might have been argued that at the date when [Kruger] issued his writ he was not entitled to rescind the purchase, because he was not then in a position to return to the appellant in specie that which he had received under the contract … But it is necessary here to apply the doctrines of equity and equity has always regarded as valid the disaffirmance of a contract induced by fraud even though precise restitution in integrum is not possible, if … it can do what is practically just between the parties and restore them substantially to the status quo.

It was held that the further deterioration in the business was not the fault of the purchaser, and that the seller knew from November 1954 that the case had gone against him. When the seller made no effort to take back the business he ran the risk of its deteriorating. The court said (at 255) that the case 'was typical of the class of cases in which a defrauded purchaser is regarded by a court … as entitled to rescind the purchase and obtain a decree, on proper terms … giving effect to the rescission as an avoidance of the transaction from the beginning': *Alati v Kruger* (1955) 94 CLR 216.

Statutory reform

[4.11] The failure of the common law to give any adequate remedy for innocent misrepresentation and the limits on the operation of the remedies of rescission and damages has been the subject of much criticism. The law relating to misrepresentation has been significantly altered by statutory reform. Similar, if not identical, provisions have been enacted by both the state and Commonwealth parliaments in relation to false or misleading statements made prior to commercial transactions. This legislation overcomes many of the difficulties within the common law of misrepresentation and is able to be used to set aside contracts induced by false statements and to recover damages for any loss caused by relying on such false statements.

Some Australian jurisdictions have passed legislation which allow for rescission of contracts for misrepresentation in some circumstances and for damages where rescission is not available. They are the Misrepresentation Act 1971 (SA), the Goods Act 1958 (Vic), the Law Reform (Misrepresentation) Act 1977 (ACT) and the Sale of Goods Act 1923 (NSW).

The Law Reform (Misrepresentation) Act 1977 (ACT) which allows for damages for innocent misrepresentation and abolishes the rule in *Seddon's* case, provides:

(3) Where a person has entered into a contract after a misrepresentation has been made to him, the person shall ... be entitled ... to rescind the contract notwithstanding that —

(a) the misrepresentation has become a term of the contract;

(b) the contract has been performed; or

(c) a conveyance, transfer or other document has been registered ...

(4) Where a person enters into a contract after a misrepresentation has been made to him by —

(a) another party to the contract;

(b) a person acting for, or on behalf of, another party to the contract; or

(c) a person who receives any direct or indirect material advantage as a result of the formation of the contract,

and as a result of so entering into the contract he suffers loss, any person (whether or not he is the person by whom the misrepresentation is made) who would be liable for damages in tort in respect of the loss had the misrepresentation been made fraudulently, shall ... be so liable, notwithstanding that the misrepresentation was not made fraudulently.

Case Example

Wakefield had the exclusive rights to import and distribute the components of a domestic burglar alarm system (Alarmax). He advertised a franchise to conduct a business installing the alarms in Canberra. The advertisement read:

Distributor required to market exclusive lines of security products. Enormous market potential affords you the opportunity to net in excess of $2000 per week ...

Mr and Mrs Crawford answered this advertisement and were told by Wakefield and Parish, who was responsible for sales and training, that there was no competition in Australia. This was said to be so because the big firms were not interested in household burglar alarms and that similar products available in Australia were inadequate and unreliable. The Crawfords signed an agreement for the purchase of two franchise areas in Canberra.

Before starting to trade the Crawfords became aware that a competing system, Imperial Alarms, operated in Canberra, but continued with the Alarmax business. Imperial Alarm's prices were significantly cheaper and the Crawfords' Alarmax business suffered losses resulting from trading.

In their claim against Parish the Crawfords relied on s 4(1) of the Law Reform (Misrepresentation) Act and on s 52 of the Trade Practices Act.

Higgins J said (at 461):

... the Law Reform (Misrepresentation) Act alters the common law in relation to misrepresentations ... s 4(1) would give a cause of action to a contracting party against an agent of the other contracting party such as the defendant.

The plaintiff is not required by the legislation to show that the misrepresentation is fraudulent to recover damages; but must show

- that the misrepresentation induced the making of the contract;
- that he or she acted in reliance on the representation; and,
- that the inducement and the falsity of the statement is causally related to the loss or damage suffered.

Although the Crawfords continued to trade after they discovered that the representation was not true, this neither broke the chain of causation of loss nor reduced the amount of damages to be awarded: *Crawford v Parish* (1991) 105 FLR 361; (1992) ATPR (Digest) 46–087.

Misrepresentation and the Trade Practices Act

[4.12]   Section 52(1) of the Trade Practices Act provides that:

> A corporation shall not, in trade or commerce, engage in conduct that is misleading or deceptive or is likely to mislead or deceive.

It has been said that s 52 has transformed the law of misrepresentation. The case law relating to s 52 is extensive and the section has been the subject of a great deal of litigation; many of the cases show a novel approach to the section and its range of uses and applications has not been exhausted. The application of s 52 has been so broad that the shadow of the section must be felt to hang over every commercial transaction. See **[8.5]**ff for a detailed discussion of s 52.

The interaction of the law of contract and the Trade Practices Act in cases where false statements are made in pre-contractual negotiations is illustrated in the following case.

Case Example

Mr and Mrs Byers entered into a contract to purchase several units in a building on the Gold Coast 'off the plan'. Before execution of the contract representations were made by the seller that the building would contain an internal heated swimming pool and substantial lobby and that the units would be bigger and better than those in another building close by. There was in fact never any intention to include a heated swimming pool, and the units were not superior to those nearby. When the time for settlement and payment of the purchase price arrived Mr and Mrs Byers rescinded the contract for misrepresentation. The court found that the false representations had induced the Byers to enter into the contracts and pay the deposit on the units.

The written contract contained the following clause:

> The purchaser acknowledges that he has not relied on any representations by the vendor ... in or about entering into this contract other than as set out herein, and the conditions and stipulations hereof constitute the only agreement between the purchase and the vendor.

The written contract made no reference to the swimming pool, lobby or finish of the units and the court found that the exclusion clause defeated a claim based on innocent misrepresentation.

However, the court found that the vendor had, in making the false statements, engaged in misleading and deceptive conduct in contravention of s 52 of the Trade Practices Act 1974, and that the provisions of that Act could not be defeated by the exclusion clause. It was therefore possible to grant relief to the purchasers: *Byers v Dorotea Pty Ltd* (1987) ATPR 40-760.

Mistake

[4.13]   The fact that a party was acting under a mistake does not afford any general relief in contract law. The law takes a robust view about mistakes — parties should be careful enough to avoid them and if the contract appears to be regular the parties must live with the mistake. There are several types of mistake than can be made in the course of commercial transactions — a mistake at the time of entering the contract, payments made by mistake, property transferred by mistake. Parties may be mistaken about the identity of the other party or the subject matter of the contract or the quality of what is being sold. The legal significance of a mistake in contract is that the parties did not reach agreement. If one or both of the parties is mistaken then the parties cannot be said to be *ad idem*. Once it is seen that the parties are in agreement, the law will not set aside a contract just because one party later discovers facts, which if known earlier would have dissuaded that party from entering the contract.

The common law does not recognise any general right to relief in respect of mistake. The common law remedy where a contract has been affected by operative mistake is to render the contract void ab initio. This could have an adverse effect on the interests of third parties, especially bona fide purchasers of goods. Equitable principles give relief for mistake in more instances than does the common law, but rarely treats a contract as void from the start for mistake. A contract valid at common law may, however, be treated by equity as voidable for mistake. In these cases the contract must be avoided before the interests of third parties are affected. Such a voidable contract may be rescinded on terms which achieve justice between the parties.

Equity can rectify a mistake in any contract (that is, it can alter the words of a contract to reflect the true intention of the parties) and can take the factor of mistake into account when considering other equitable remedies such as specific performance. The modern approach is to narrow the application of the common law and to deal with problems of mistake according to equitable principles. The courts will rescind or rectify a contract affected by mistake if the interests of innocent parties will not be adversely affected and it would be unconscionable for one party to enforce rights or obtain benefits under the contract, given the mistake which has been made by both parties, or by one party to the knowledge of the other.

Common mistake

[4.14]   This is a shared mistake. Both parties make the same error. This mistake cannot affect formation of the contract since the parties are clearly in agreement, but it does affect performance. A common mistake has no effect at common law unless the mistake was a to a fact fundamental to the agreement, such as the existence of the subject matter of the contract. If the mistake otherwise affects the contract, the contract will be unenforceable but not voidable.

Common mistake has two dimensions:

- the existence of the subject matter of the contract; and
- the quality of the thing contracted for.

The existence of the subject matter of the contract

[4.15]   What the court decides in cases where the mistake is as to the existence of the subject matter of the contract seems to depend very much on the construction of the contract. It is not uncommon for parties to agree to convey title in property or goods which are not in existence at the time of the contract. This is an empty bargain for there can be no transfer of a thing which does not exist. Where the common mistake of the parties is as to the existence of the subject matter of the contract (*res extincta*), the approach of the courts is to characterise the mistaken assumption as either a condition precedent to liability — the non-fulfilment of which results in there being no obligation to perform — or, alternatively, the courts will say that there was a warranty the breach of which has a remedy in damages.

Case Example

There was a contract for the sale of a cargo of corn, which, unknown to either party, had deteriorated at sea and had been disposed of prior to the formation of the contract. The common mistake was therefore as to the existence of the corn. The vendor brought a claim for payment because, according to shipping law, once the vendor had delivered the shipping documents to the purchaser, property in the corn passed from the vendor to the purchaser. If the contract was valid the buyer would be obliged to pay for goods which he had never received. The court did not, however, hold the contract to be void for mistake as to the existence of the subject matter, but found that the existence of the corn was a condition precedent to liability to pay the price. That is, the purchaser was not obliged to pay for the corn unless it was in existence at the time of formation of the contract: *Couturier v Hastie* (1856) 10 ER 1065.

In the above case there was nothing for the parties to contract about — the contract was for the purchase of specific goods which had perished before the agreement was reached. The alternative approach is used in cases where the mistake resulted from one party making unfounded statements. This case below can also be said to stand for the proposition that if the mistake is the fault of one party, then that party is generally precluded from relying on it to escape from the contract.

Case Example

After the Second World War the Commonwealth Disposals Commission advertised for tenders to salvage an oil tanker, said to contain oil, wrecked on Jourmand Reef. The McRae brothers were the successful tenderers and equipped a vessel to salvage the tanker, but were not able to locate the tanker. As it happened there was no tanker — or reef — at the location specified by Commonwealth Disposals.

> If the contract was void for mistake as to the existence of the tanker, the McRae brothers would have no remedy, and could not recover the money spent in fitting out the salvage vessel and searching for the tanker. The court held that there was a contract and that there was a promise by the Disposal Commission that the tanker existed and was where they said it was. The buyers relied upon, and acted upon, the Disposal Commission's assertion that there was a tanker in existence. The Disposal Commission made an assumption that the tanker existed, but the plaintiffs knew nothing except what the Commission told them. There was a contract and the Commission promised that a tanker existed in the position specified. Since there was no such tanker, there was a breach of contract and the plaintiffs were entitled to damages for that breach: *McRae v Commonwealth Disposals Commission* (1951) 84 CLR 377.

[4.16]   The common mistake can be about title to the property which is the subject matter of the contract. If parties contract for the transfer of property which already belongs to the purchaser then the mistake renders the contract ineffective because the seller has nothing about which to contract. Suppose Bob's grandfather owns a warehouse. Bob reaches an agreement with his grandfather's agent to lease the warehouse but then discovers that at the time of the agreement his grandfather had died and left the warehouse to Bob in his will. The contract for lease would not be effective, since the lessee already owned the subject matter of the contract (*res sua*).

The quality of the thing contracted for

[4.17]   If the principles applied in cases where the subject matter of the contract either does not exist or is already owned by the purchaser were extended, then it could be said that there is a doctrine of common fundamental mistake; that is, if both parties are mistaken as to some fundamental fact, that mistake will always prevent the existence of the contract. There is, however, no judicial authority in strong support of this view. The courts have found that mistake as to a fundamental element of the contract — such as the existence of the subject matter, the identity of the other party or the very nature of the transaction — can prevent the formation of a contract. However, mistakes as to other less critical elements — the quality of the subject matter, the attributes of the other party, or the terms of the contract — are not capable of preventing formation of the contract.

The test applied is whether or not the parties are, in spite of the mistake, able to achieve the essential objectives of the contract even though it may be more difficult or more costly than contemplated. Where there is a contract but the subject of the contract has a quality different from that which was contracted for, then there will often be a question as to whether the quality is governed by a warranty or condition. At common law, where there is a contract that is clear in its terms and capable of being performed a party cannot avoid the contract for mistake as to quality but equity may treat the contract as voidable. There may be other grounds for setting aside the contract, such as misrepresentation.

Case Example

In 1944 Leaf purchased a painting thought by both parties to be by Constable. It was not. It was argued that there was an essential difference between what Leaf thought he was getting and what he in fact got, but the terms of the contract were clear. Lord Denning said (at All ER 694):'

> There was a mistake about the quality of the subject matter, because both parties believed the picture to be a Constable, and that mistake was in one sense essential or fundamental. Such a mistake, however, does not avoid the contract. There was not mistake about the subject matter of the sale. It was a specific picture of Salisbury Cathedral. The parties were agreed in the same terms on the same subject matter, and that is sufficient to make a contract: *Leaf v International Galleries* [1950] 2 KB 86; (1950) 1 All ER 693.

[4.18]   The courts rarely set aside a contract for mistake, and if they can give effect to the contract they will, even though the mistake results in loss to one party. The rigour of the courts is well illustrated where the mistake could have been avoided or where a party has not taken protective measures.

Case Example

Svanosio bought the Bull's Head Hotel in Bendigo from McNamara and discovered, after moving in, that the hotel was partly built on the Crown land next door. Svanosio asked the court to set aside the contract on the basis that it was void for a common mistake as to a fundamental fact, in that both parties had believed that the hotel stood wholly on the land sold. The High Court said that although there was a common mistake, this did not make the contract void. The decision in *McRae v Commonwealth Disposal Commission* was applied to prevent Svanosio relying on his own mistake to avoid the contract. The court said that as there was no question of fraud or failure of consideration the position depended on the terms of the contract. These were clear and the contract had been settled according to the usual conveyancing practices. There had been ample opportunity for the buyer to discover the defect in title but he had not availed himself of it. The High Court refused to set aside the contract for mistake but acknowledged that if Svanosio had known that the hotel was built on the Crown land, he would not have entered into the contract. In addition the court said that mistake could be a ground on which equity could refuse specific performance of a contract, and if the error had been discovered before completion of the contract, the court would have allowed Svanosio to resist completion: *Svanosio v McNamara* (1956) 96 CLR 186.

Mutual mistake

[4.19]   An example of this type of mistake is found in the case of *Raffles v Wichelhaus* (1864) 2 H&C 906, where Wichelhaus agreed to buy a shipment of goods to arrive aboard the ship *Peerless* sailing from Bombay in October. The seller, however, understood the goods to be aboard another ship called *Peerless* which was sailing later.

Mutual mistake occurs where the parties are in apparent agreement and the terms of the contract are clear but nevertheless the minds of the parties are at odds. The party seeking to escape the contract must show that, as a matter of fact, there is a misunderstanding. If the terms of the contract can be identified, defined and applied the contract will be valid and enforceable. If the terms cannot be identified or interpreted with certainty then the contract will be void — for uncertainty more often than for mistake. Where each party is mistaken about the other party's intention, but neither of them has realised it, the court's task is to identify the bargain by asking what a reasonable observer would have concluded was the real bargain.

Case Example

Houlahan entered into a contract with the ANZ Bank to guarantee the repayment of moneys advanced to Ultra Tune pursuant to an overdraft facility of up to $10,000. The ANZ Bank later advanced a greater amount to Ultra Tune. The parties did not agree as to the effect of the advance of this extra money — Houlahan argued that the amount guaranteed was limited to the original $10,000 but the bank argued that the guarantee extended to all money advanced.

The Supreme Court of the ACT said that where the parties are mistaken about each other's understanding of the agreement, the agreement has been entered into under a mutual mistake. The agreement can only be avoided if the mutual mistake destroys the apparent assent by the parties to the agreement which appears on an objective basis to have been reached. In this case the agreement related only to an account with an overdraft limit of $10,000. Therefore the bank could only enforce the agreement to that extent, but Houlahan was not entitled to rely on the bank's mistake to set aside the entire guarantee: *Houlahan v Australia and New Zealand Banking Group Ltd* (1992) 110 FLR 259.

Unilateral mistake

[4.20] When one party to the contract is mistaken this is a unilateral mistake. If one party is mistaken as to the terms or the effect of the contract and the other party does not know of the mistake then there is no legal consequence of the mistake. For example, John buys a carpet from a market stall and pays $4000 for it in the belief that it is silk. If the vendor does not know of John's mistake, and the carpet turns out to be synthetic, then John cannot be heard to say that there was a mistake.

[4.21] Unilateral mistake occurs where one party is mistaken as to the terms or the effect of the contract and the other party knows of that mistake. At common law the mistaken party cannot avoid the contract (unless the mistake is of a fundamental nature as discussed in **[4.17]**). In the typical case of a contract for the sale of goods, the doctrine of caveat emptor applies and the vendor is not obliged to tell the purchaser of any error. To find a remedy for unilateral mistake the mistaken party will have to turn to equity and, in addition to showing 'serious and unforeseen circumstances', will also need to show that some conduct on the part of the other party contributed to the party's mistake. The approach of the High Court is seen in the following example.

Case Example

Mrs Johnson had 10 acres of land for sale, and she granted an option to Taylor or his nominees to purchase the land for $15,000. She refused to complete the contract for the sale of land after the exercise of the option on the grounds that the contract was void for mistake — she had believed the price to be $15,000 per acre but the price in the option was $15,000 in total. The current value of the land was $50,000 and $195,000 after rezoning. Mrs Johnson was still willing to sell for a price that reflected the actual value of the land. Mrs Johnson was acting under a unilateral mistake as to a term of the contract — the price. Taylor brought an action for specific performance and Mrs Johnson sought rectification or rescission.

The case went to the High Court which decided that where a party to a formal written contract has entered into it under a mistake as to the existence or content of an actual term, at common law the contract is not a nullity from the beginning. This contract was not void ab initio. Any party seeking relief for unilateral mistake must turn to equity. While there is no hard and fast rule as to when equity will refuse specific performance or set aside a contract on the ground of mistake, it was acknowledged that the circumstances must be such as to show that it would be inequitable to hold a person to the contract, and that a contract would not be set aside unless there had been conduct approaching fraud. The contract was set aside. Parties who enter into contract under a serious mistake as to the contents of a fundamental term are entitled in equity to an order setting aside the contract if the other party was aware of the serious mistake and deliberately set out to ensure that the first party did not become aware of the mistake: *Taylor v Johnson* (1983) 151 CLR 422; 57 ALJR 197.

Mistake as to the identity of the other party

[4.22] Where the mistake is as to the identity of the other party, the law often does no more than determine which of two innocent parties will suffer least. There is a long line of cases relating to forged cheques and passing off as the owner of stolen property.

- A contracts to sell goods to B >
- A believes that B is C. If we stop there we have a unilateral mistake and a contract that is voidable, but in many instances B[C] will have sold the goods to D >
- will A's right to return of the goods under a void contract defeat D's claim to the goods?

Case Example

Lewis sold his car for £450 to a person who said he was Richard Greene, an actor then starring in the television series Robin Hood. 'Richard Greene' paid for the car with a cheque which turned out to be stolen. Avery later purchased the car from this person. Who owned the car? Lewis had not intended to pass property to any person other than 'Richard Greene' and so had not passed property to the thief. Therefore the thief could not pass property to Avery.

> Denning LJ said there was a contract between Lewis and the buyer but because of the mistake as to the identity of that buyer it was voidable by Lewis; the mistaken party can only avoid the contract if he or she does so before third parties have in good faith acquired rights under it. Avery kept the car as an innocent third party: *Lewis v Avery* [1971] 3 All ER 907.

This case can be contrasted with others where the identity of the other party is crucial to the making of the offer or acceptance.

Rectification of contracts

[4.23]   The common law does not recognise any unified doctrine of mistake and so it cannot be said that mistake always affects the formation of a contract. The approaches of the common law and equity are different. It is difficult to reconcile the cases, and the remedy available for mistake depends on a variety of factors, including the type of mistake. If the parties have reached an agreement and then drawn up a written document which by mistake does not record their agreement the court may rectify the document to reflect the actual agreement of the parties. The courts rectify the document, they do not rewrite the contract. Before a court will rectify a document the following conditions must be met:

* the parties must have reached the end of their negotiations and there must be a common continuing mutual intention to contract on certain terms;
* there must be a mistake in the manner in which the document records that agreement;
* the mistake is such that the document does not reflect the common intention of the parties — there must be a literal disparity between what the parties agreed and what is in the writing; and,
* the proposed rectification must be capable of clear expression and must reflect the actual intention of the parties.

Further, if there has been undue delay by either party or if third parties have acquired rights under the contract, the courts will not rectify the document.

Mistake as to the nature of the document — *non est factum*

[4.24]   The general rule is that any person who signs a contract will be bound by it because they are assumed to have read and understood and agreed to it: see *L'Estrange v Graucob Ltd* [1934] 2 KB 394. Where a person who signs a contract is mistaken as to the nature or character of the document the defence of non est factum could be pleaded and, where proved, would result in the contract being absolutely void. Whenever non est factum is pleaded there will be conflict between two propositions:

* the injustice of holding a party to a contract to which he or she has not truly consented; and
* the need to hold parties, who sign documents, to the contracts, especially where others have relied on the signature.

Non est factum results in the contract being void against the whole world, and so third parties who have relied on the signature (or the resulting contract) may be disadvantaged.

The defence of non est factum is narrow. The High Court said in *Petelin v Cullen* (1975) 132 CLR 355 at 359:

> The class of persons who can avail themselves of the defence is limited. It is available to those who are unable to read owing to illiteracy and blindness and who must rely on others

for advice as to what they are signing; it is also available to those who through no fault of their own are unable to have any understanding of the purport of a particular document. To make out the defence a defendant must show that he signed the document in the belief that it was radically different from what it was in fact and that, at least as against innocent persons, his failure to read and understand it was not due to carelessness on his part.

Therefore, to establish the plea of non est factum three factors must be proved:

- that there was a radical difference between what the mistaken party thought was being signed and what was actually signed;
- that the mistaken party, through no fault of his or her own, was not able to understand the nature of the document. This could come about, for example, through blindness or illiteracy so that the mistaken party was relying on others for advice as to what was being signed; and,
- that there was no carelessness or want of care on the part of the mistaken party. That is, that reasonable precautions were taken by the signing party to ascertain the nature of the document. If the other party knows of the mistaken understanding then lack of care will not be relevant.

The plea of non est factum is often used in cases where there is also a question of lack of mental capacity contributing to the failure to understand the nature of the document being signed.

Money paid under a mistake

[4.25]   The common law allows the recovery of money or property transferred whether under a mistake of law or a mistake of fact. A payer is prima facie entitled to recover moneys paid under a mistake if payment was made in the mistaken belief that there was a legal obligation to pay and that the payee was legally entitled to the payment. Carelessness by the payer is not relevant, nor is it necessary for the payer to show that it is not just for the payee to retain the moneys. In order to displace the obligation to repay, the recipient has to show that the repayment of the money would in all the circumstances result in injustice; for example, if the recipient had altered his or her position on the strength of the payment. See *David Securities Pty Ltd v Commonwealth Bank of Australia* (1992) 175 CLR 353; 109 ALR 57. It is necessary before repayment will be ordered for the payer to establish that the mistake caused the payment. If the payment arose from another factor then recovery may be denied.

Case Example

Miss Tancredi was involved in a motor vehicle accident and her car was damaged. She made a claim against the insurance company CIC and disclosed in the claim form that she had consumed alcohol before the accident. In such cases CIC's usual practice was to obtain a police report, but in this case this was not done. CIC wrote to Miss Tancredi saying that her car was a total loss and offering to pay her $12,000. This offer was subject to her signing a release which stated 'it is a condition of this discharge that the policy is cancelled'. She accepted the offer and signed the release. Later CIC was informed by the police that her blood alcohol level was over the legal limit. CIC sought to recover the $12,000 on the basis that it was mistaken as to its legal obligations and her legal entitlements at the time of payment.

> The Supreme Court of Victoria found that CIC had made the payment based upon a mistaken belief that it was obliged to do so and that Miss Tancredi was entitled to it, but that the payment was made not under the policy of insurance between them but under a new agreement. CIC was not giving effect to the existing rights and duties but had made a decision on how much to offer to relieve itself of any further obligation under the policy. Miss Tancredi did not have to repay the $12,000: *CIC Insurance Limited v Tancredi* (1996) Aust Contract Reports 90-064.

Elements affecting the consent of a weaker party

[4.26]   Consent to a contract must be voluntarily and freely given. Each party must enter the contract without any coercion or compulsion. Otherwise there is simply no agreement. Conduct which affects the consent of one party includes:

* duress (common law) (see **[4.27]**–**[4.28]**);
* undue influence (equity) (see **[4.29]**–**[4.31]**); and
* unconscionable behaviour (equity): see **[4.32]**–**[4.43]**.

These three doctrines are part of the general area of unconscionability which is affected by the common law, equitable doctrines and a growing body of legislation such as the Contracts Review Act 1980 (NSW) and Pt IVA of the Trade Practices Act 1974. There is no general relief available from a contract just because it is not fair or proves to have harsh consequences. Unconscionability examines the relief available where there has been procedural unfairness; that is, where there is some circumstance or factor which has affected the formation of the contract because the consent of one party has been obtained in a manner which is against good conscience.

Duress

[4.27]   It is a common law doctrine that any contract entered into under duress is voidable by the innocent party, which means that it can be rescinded by the party who has been subject to the duress. The doctrine was originally limited to physical duress but it will now be applied whenever there has been a coercion of the will of one party so that the consent was a result of the coercion, and thus the act of entering into the contract was not voluntary.

The application of the doctrine to a situation of threat of physical harm is well illustrated by the case of *Barton v Armstrong* [1976] AC 104, where a contract for the transfer of shares was set aside because the transferee had threatened to murder the family of the transferor unless he agreed to the deal. The court said that if there is pressure to enter the contract and that pressure is of a kind that the law does not regard as legitimate this will amount to duress. Once the threat of physical harm is established as a matter of fact, the party asserting the contract must show that the threat was no inducement to the bargain.

In *Crescendo Management Pty Ltd v Westpac Banking Corp* (1988) 19 NSWLR 40 at 45–6 McHugh J analysed the doctrine of duress and stated that the focus is on the illegitimate pressure applied by one party:

... [t]he rationale of the doctrine of economic duress is that the law will not give effect to an apparent consent which was induced by pressure exercised upon one party by another party when the law regards that pressure as illegitimate ... The proper approach in my opinion is to ask whether any applied pressure induced the victim to enter into the contract and then ask whether that pressure went beyond what the law is prepared to countenance as legitimate? Pressure will be illegitimate if it consists of unlawful threats or amounts to unconscionable conduct. But the categories are not closed. Even overwhelming pressure, not amounting to unconscionable or unlawful conduct, however, will not necessarily constitute economic duress.

[4.28]   Originally the doctrine of duress did not recognise that a threat to property or economic well-being could amount to duress. It is easy to appreciate that a threat to destroy a valuable Ming vase may be as effective an inducement to enter a contract as the threat of physical violence to a party or that party's family. The modern approach acknowledges that a contract entered into pursuant to a threat to injure one's economic interests is also voidable. There is line to be drawn between economic duress and legitimate commercial pressure. The law does not relieve parties from the consequences of hard bargains without some element which makes the pressure illegitimate. A person who has entered a contract as a consequence of economic duress may treat the contract as voidable or raise economic duress as a defence to enforcement by the other party.

Case Example

In a contract for the construction of a tanker, the price was fixed in US dollars. The US dollar devalued and the shipbuilder demanded a higher price to compensate, and threatened to breach the contract by failing to complete the ship unless it was paid. The tanker's owners had already negotiated a contract to charter the completed vessel to Shell and when they were unable to get the shipbuilders to go to arbitration, they paid the extra, and then sought to recover it on the grounds that it was paid under duress. The court held that the threat to break the contract was economic duress. Mocatta J said (at 718):

> The agreement to increase the price by 10 percent ... was caused by what may be called 'economic duress'. The [ship building] yard was adamant in insisting on the increased price without having any legal justification for so doing and the owners realised that the yard would not accept anything other than an unqualified agreement to the increase ... [t]he owners might have claimed damages in arbitration against the yard with all the inherent unavoidable uncertainties of litigation, but in view of the position of the yard vis-à-vis their relations with Shell it would be unreasonable to hold that this is the course they should have taken. The shipowners were not able to recover the payments, however, because it was held that they had affirmed the contract: *North Ocean Shipping Co Ltd v Hyundai Construction Co Ltd* [1979] QB 705.

In some instances where the pressure is more than ordinary commercial pressure but not sufficient to amount to physical or economic duress, the doctrine of duress merges with the equitable doctrines of undue influence and unconscionability. Commercial pressure beyond that which is legitimate may also fall under the unconscionable conduct provisions of the Trade Practices Act 1974.

Undue influence

[4.29]   It is quite common and legitimate for one person to persuade another to enter into a contract. But the fact of forceful persuasion alone is not sufficient to set aside the contract. Equity will intervene where one person has influence over another and abuses it to persuade that other to enter into a contract. What factors make the influence undue? If the influence brought to bear is such that the act of entering the contract was not the free and voluntary act of one party but arose from the pressure exerted then the influence will be undue. To some extent, then, the party asserting that the contract should be set aside is arguing that the influence was such that the transaction was the result of the actual undue influence over the party's mind and therefore not a free or voluntary act. Undue influence is in those cases not unlike duress. The nature of the relationship which existed between the parties prior to the entering into of the contract is the key to undue influence. Some relationships because of their nature give rise to a presumption of undue influence.

There are two types of undue influence:

- presumed undue influence, and
- actual undue influence.

Presumed undue influence

[4.30]   The court asks — what was the parties' relationship before there was any hint of a contract? If the relationship was one of trust and confidence then the court will presume that any contract or gift between the parties came about because undue influence was exerted. The undue influence will arise, if at all, from the nature of that relationship. Equity, once it sees influence, bends a long way towards protecting the influenced party.

Some classes of relationships automatically give rise to the presumption of undue influence: parent and child (and guardian and ward); solicitor and client; trustee and beneficiary; physician and patient; and religious leader and disciple. If one of these relationships exists, then the presumption arises and the person asserting the contract must prove that there was as a matter of fact no undue influence.

The presumption can also arise where the relationship was a relationship of confidence. Usually such relationships are characterised by one stronger party giving advice and guidance which is relied upon by the weaker party. The stronger party knows, or expects that, the advice will be relied upon. The courts will look to a number of factors in determining whether a relationship of confidence exists. It is not possible to give an exhaustive list of factors which point to the existence of a relationship of trust and confidence, but the list may include:

- the length of the relationship;
- the closeness of the relationship — taking into account matters such as whether the parties are related; whether they live in the same home;
- emotional dependence by one party on another;
- the need by one party for guidance and support especially in relation to finance or business matters;
- the weaker party's intelligence, education and business experience;
- whether the weaker party was independently advised; and,
- whether the transaction was one-sided — that is, particularly advantageous to the stronger party.

Once the court finds that there is a relationship of confidence the onus shifts to the person asserting the contract to show that although there was this relationship, there was no abuse of the position of influence and the contract is the result of the voluntary and spontaneous decision of the other. The evidence required will vary from case to case but includes:

- whether the party alleging undue influence had independent legal or financial advice;
- whether the party alleging undue influence was able to make a independent judgment as to whether the transaction was in their best interests;
- the adequacy of the consideration for the contract — was a fair price paid?; and,
- the effect of the transaction on the affairs of the weaker party.

Case Example

Mr Buttress was a man who relied on other people for guidance in his daily life, but quarrelled with whichever relatives sought to help him. He often altered his will to favour whoever was giving him guidance or support. Dixon J described Mr Buttress thus:

> … he was a man peculiarly dependent upon others. He was quite illiterate; he could not even write his own name. Whether because his hands were stiffened with labour, or through disuse of other faculties, he was quite unable to do anything but the roughest work. He was excitable and would give rein to his emotions, whether of anger, grief or dejection. He was easily moved to gesticulation and shouting. He had a tendency to loud and disconnected talk. Many people found him trying and he seems to have been regarded as an oddity.

Mr Buttress was not employed and was 66 years old when his wife died. He lived at different times with his son, his sister, and also had help from his stepson and another sister. Mr Buttress began to visit Mrs Johnson, who offered him advice in relation to tenants then living in his house and also cooked his meals. He expressed a desire to make a will in her favour and she took him to her solicitor's office where he made a will leaving all his property to her. Soon after this Mr Buttress began to live with the Johnson family. Mrs Johnson again took him to her solicitor and he transferred ownership of his house to her.

Later still Mr Buttress stopped living with the Johnsons and changed his will to leave the house to a niece. After Mr Buttress died his son asked the court to set aside the transfer on the ground of undue influence. The High Court found a relationship of confidence arose between Mrs Johnson and Mr Buttress, and since Mrs Johnson was not able to show that the transfer had been the result of the free exercise of will by Mr Buttress the transfer was declared void: *Johnson v Buttress* (1936) 56 CLR 113.

Actual undue influence

[4.31]   Actual undue influence arises where parties are not in a relationship of trust or confidence, but where the transaction in question was brought about by actual coercion or dominance. The party asserting that his or her decision to enter the contract was the result of actual undue influence must prove it. The evidence must show that the influence was exerted at the time of entering into the contract and that it was undue, which means that it was an unconscientious use of any special capacity or opportunity that may have existed or had arisen and which affected the weaker party's will or freedom of judgment. In the case of third party mortgages — that is, where A advances money to B on the security of a mortgage over a property owned by C — the transaction between A and C may be infected by the undue influence exerted by B over C to obtain agreement to the mortgage. The transaction is likely to be set aside unless A can show that he or she took reasonable steps to ensure that C entered into the transaction freely and with full knowledge of the relevant facts. In many cases the line between actual undue influence and presumed undue influence is blurred. In the case below one party was able to exert actual influence on another, but this ability arose from the history of their relationship.

Case Example

Lynette left school at 15 and was employed by WC Thomas & Sons as a clerical worker. There she met Charles Thomas — they married when she was 21 and he was 25. During their marriage she knew virtually nothing about their financial matters. Her husband gave her money for housekeeping but otherwise he paid all of the bills. Charles worked for the family company and Lynette's father-in-law, Frederick Thomas, was the dominating figure in their life.

When her father-in-law wished to borrow $2.7 million he offered the house owned and occupied by Lynette and Charles as part security for the loan. Lynette was never given any explanation of the financial and legal consequences of the loans and the mortgage, by either her husband, her father-in-law or the building society. The lender prepared the necessary documents and gave them to Frederick Thomas to be executed by his family members. Her husband and father-in-law came into her kitchen at about 5 pm when she was preparing to feed her three small children. He husband said, 'The old man has got some papers he needs us to sign'. She signed them and went back to feeding the children. She did not read the documents and did not understand that what she was signing was a legal document. She was only shown one page and told where to sign.

The court accepted that Lynette was very much under the influence of the husband and father-in-law. Frederick had opposed her marriage and she desired to show him that she was a good wife, mother and daughter-in-law — she was overawed and intimidated by him. Her father-in-law was described as a benevolent despot who since he had provided the house viewed it as an asset to be used for his own purposes without consultation with her. The court said that having regard to the circumstance of the transaction the influence of the father-in-law was undue.

The lender had not once during the transaction contacted or consulted with Lynette, but was content to allow Frederick to obtain the execution of the mortgage. It was held that the building society had both actual and constructive notice of facts that pointed to the likelihood of the exercise by Frederick of undue influence over his family in order to obtain the security of a mortgage over their property even though there was no benefit to them from the transaction. It was unconscionable for the lender to enforce the mortgage against Lynette: *Geelong Building Society (in liq) v Thomas* (1996) V Conv R 54-545; Aust Contract Reports 90-068.

Unconscionable conduct

[4.32] If one party to a contract takes advantage of the other's apparent weakness to achieve formation of a contract the weaker party may be entitled to rescind. The stronger party's conduct in taking advantage of the other's apparent weakness is unconscionable. The equitable jurisdiction to relieve against unconscionable transactions has long been recognised in Australia, and was clearly set out by Kitto J in *Blomley v Ryan* (1956) 99 CLR 362 at 415:

> ... This is a well known head of equity. It applies wherever one party to a transaction is at a special disadvantage in dealing with the other party because illness, ignorance, inexperience, impaired faculties, financial need or other circumstances affect his ability to conserve his own interests and the other party unconscionably takes advantage of the opportunity thus placed in his hands.

Unconscionable dealing involves the conduct of the stronger party in attempting to enforce, or retain the benefit of, a dealing with a person under a special disability in circumstances where it is not consistent with equity or good conscience to do so.

The test for unconscionable conduct

[4.33] Where one party to a transaction is found to have acted unconscionably in either procuring the transaction or the other party's consent to it, equity may intervene to declare the transaction void. In the typical case the innocent party will be able to resist enforcement of a contract such as a guarantee secured by mortgage or reverse a transfer of property.

To rescind the contract for unconscionable conduct the weaker party must prove:

- he or she was under a special disadvantage;
- that the disadvantage was, or ought to have been, evident to the stronger party; and
- that the disadvantage meant that the weaker party was not able to judge whether or not the transaction was in his or her own best interests.

These factors make it unconscionable for the stronger party to have procured or accepted the weaker party's consent to the contract. Once this is established the onus shifts to the stronger party to show that the transaction was fair, just and reasonable.

Case Example

Giovanni and Cesira Amadio were an elderly Italian couple who could read little English. They had a son, Vincenzo, who they believed was running a successful business. When Vincenzo asked his parents to help him over a temporary spot of financial trouble they agreed. Vincenzo asked them to mortgage their land for six months to a limit of $50,000. The bank manager brought the mortgage documents to their house for signature.

Unknown to the Amadios their son had lied as to the extent of his financial problems and about the documents they signed. The mortgage was unlimited as to both time and amount and Vincenzo's business was insolvent. The bank knew this. Every day Vincenzo and his bank manager met to decide which cheques should be honoured and which should bounce. His parents were not aware of his true financial state and they were never told, not even when they signed the mortgage in front of the bank manager.

> A few months later when Vincenzo's company went into liquidation and the bank wanted to enforce its mortgage the Amadios realised what they had done. The High Court set out the following test:
>
> > ... [i]f A having actual knowledge that B occupies a position of special disadvantage in relation to an intended transaction, so that B cannot make a judgment as to what is in his own best interests, takes unfair advantage of his (A's) superior power or bargaining position by entering into that transaction, his conduct in so doing is unconscionable. And if instead of having actual knowledge of the situation, A is aware of the possibility that that situation may exist or is aware of facts that would raise that possibility in the mind of a reasonable person, the result will be the same: *Commercial Bank of Australia Ltd v Amadio* (1983) 151 CLR 447; 57 ALJR 358 at 366.

The doctrine as developed in *Amadio* has been widely applied by the courts not only to contracts involving old persons, widows and orphans, but also between business people in a commercial context. The High Court of Australia has shown itself to be willing to read notions of unconscientious behaviour and unequal bargaining power widely in the context of both commercial and non-commercial transactions.

In the case of *Louth v Diprose* [1992] 175 CLR 621; 110 ALR 1; 67 ALJR 95 the High Court applied the doctrine to a gift of a house made by a solicitor to a woman with whom he was infatuated. The test was restated — the jurisdiction of equity to set aside transactions procured by unconscionable conduct arises from a chain of three circumstances:

- a relationship between the parties which, to the knowledge of the beneficiary, places the other party at a special disadvantage;
- the beneficiary's unconscientious exploitation of that disadvantage; and
- as a consequence the weaker party is not able to make a worthwhile judgment as to what is in his or her best interest.

What constitutes a special disadvantage?

[4.34] There is no exhaustive check list but some guidance can be had from what the courts have said. In *Blomley v Ryan* (1956) 99 CLR 362 at 405, the High Court said that:

> the circumstances adversely affecting a party which may induce a court to set aside a transaction on the grounds of equity are of great variety and can hardly be satisfactorily classified. Among them are poverty or need of any kind, sickness, age, sex, infirmity of body or mind, drunkenness, illiteracy or lack of education, lack of assistance or explanation where assistance or explanation is necessary. The common characteristic seems to be that they have the effect of placing one party at a serious disadvantage vis-à-vis the other.

Emotional dependence was found to be a factor giving rise to the requisite position of disadvantage in *Louth v Diprose* [1992] 175 CLR 621. Generally speaking the transaction which results from unconscionable conduct will be lopsided in some way. For example, in *Amadio* the bank received all of the benefit from the contract, but the Amadios received little. Inadequacy of consideration may also be a factor for the court to examine but it is not an essential factor.

Remedies for unconscionable conduct

[4.35] The traditional remedy for unconscionable conduct has been the rescission *ab initio* of the contract. Equity, however, has a wider range of remedies available to it. To achieve the best justice between the parties the court may make an order which partially rescinds the contract or allows only a part of the contract to be enforced. For example, a director of a company gives a guarantee for the debt owed to a supplier. The guarantee is expressed to cover all moneys which are now, or at any time may be, owing to the supplier. However, the director is told that only future indebtedness is being guaranteed. When the supplier sues on the guarantee the director asks for rescission of the contract. If the whole contract was set aside for the misrepresentation the supplier would have no way of recovering any money owed. To do practical justice between the parties the High Court said that the contract should be set aside as to the liability for past debts but that the director had guaranteed future debts and would be kept to that promise: *Vadasz v Pioneer Concrete Ltd* [1995] 184 CLR 102.

Legislative regulation of unconscionable conduct

[4.36]   Legislation has been enacted by the Commonwealth and the states to regulate unconscionable conduct. There are two primary aims of such legislation — to set standards of conduct in both commercial and consumer transactions; and to protect parties who are at a disadvantage in commercial transactions.

Trade Practices Act Pt IVA

[4.37]   The prohibition on unconscionable dealing is contained in Pt IVA of the Trade Practices Act 1974. Section 51AA provides:

> (1) A corporation must not, in trade or commerce, engage in conduct that is unconscionable within the meaning of the unwritten law, from time to time, of the States and Territories.

The term 'unconscionable' was deliberately chosen in preference to 'unjust', because it was a concept familiar to Australian law. In effect, the purpose of the section is to impose a duty to trade fairly. Unconscionable conduct in trade or commerce will constitute a contravention of the Act, this will affect a much wider range of conduct than the equitable doctrine of unconscionable conduct which focuses on formation of the contract. Unconscionable conduct in relation to all commercial activity is proscribed; the manner in which a contract is performed and enforced will also be covered by this provision.

[4.38]   The scope and impact of s 51AA is yet to be tested; much will depend on the interpretation of the phrase 'the unwritten law'. The unwritten law of unconscionable conduct is found within the doctrines of duress, undue influence and unconscionability. This means that as the courts develop and extend this area of law, the meaning to be given to s 51AA will alter. The legislature itself has not attempted to change the law and both the Explanatory Memorandum and Second Reading Speech stress that the law of unconscionable conduct cannot be applied to grant relief simply because a party has made a bad bargain. Section 51AA embodies the doctrine of unconscionability as enunciated by the High Court in cases such as *Amadio* and *Louth v Diprose* and does not extend the application of the doctrine beyond its current limits.

Case Example

The Australian Competition and Consumer Commission has instituted proceedings in the Federal Court, Perth, against the owners of Farrington Fayre Shopping Centre at Leeming, Perth in Western Australia. Certain directors and the asset manager representing the owners have also been joined in the proceedings.

The ACCC alleges that the owners dealt with certain tenants in an unconscionable manner in contravention of section 51AA of the Trade Practices Act. Section 51AA of the Act prohibits unconscionable conduct in commercial transactions. The ACCC believes that the term unconscionable conduct covers cases where:

- a party to a transaction suffered from a special disability, or was placed in some special situation of disadvantage, in dealing with the other party; and
- the other party was in a superior bargaining position; and
- the weaker party's disability was sufficiently evident that the stronger party knew, or ought to have known, about it; and
- the stronger party took unfair advantage of its superior position or bargaining power.

The ACCC alleges that in 1996 and early 1997 the owners implemented a strategy whereby they refused to grant renewals, variations or extensions of leases to three tenants unless those tenants withdrew from legal proceedings before the WA Commercial Tenancy Tribunal against the owners and/or agree not to pursue legal rights against the owners.

The ACCC believes that these tenants were at a special disadvantage when bargaining with the owners because of their financial dependence upon renewal, variation or extension of their leases. The ACCC alleges that it was unconscionable for the owners to take advantage of their superior bargaining position to have legal proceedings withdrawn and/or rights to future proceedings waived.

The ACCC is seeking orders against the owners and their representative which include:

- declarations that tenants were subject to unconscionable conduct in contravention of the Act;
- injunctions preventing the repetition of similar conduct;
- the publishing of public apologies; and
- the institution of corporate compliance programs to minimise the possibility of such conduct recurring.

Also, the owners, certain directors and the owner's representative may be liable for damages flowing from the alleged conduct, should the Commission take representative action on behalf of the tenants or should tenants take damages actions. *ACCC Press Release 6 April 1998.*

Section 51AB provides:

(1) A corporation shall not, in trade or commerce, in connection with the supply or possible supply of goods or services to a person, engage in conduct that is, in all the circumstances, unconscionable.

Section 51AB applies in respect of the supply or possible supply of goods or services of a kind ordinarily acquired for personal, domestic or household use or consumption: s 51AB(5). In this way the section is limited to what are, essentially, consumer transactions: see *Atkinson v Hastings Deering (Qld) Pty Ltd* (1985) 71 ALR 93 and *Jillawarra Grazing Co v John Shearer Ltd* (1984) ATPR 40-441 for discussion of the type of goods that would satisfy the requirements of s 51AB. The state and territory Fair Trading Acts contain similar provisions to protect consumers from unconscionable conduct.

Section 51AB applies not only to contracts but to other conduct as well. 'Unconscionable' is not defined in the Act and there have been few cases in which this section has been examined. In *Zoneff v Elcom Credit Union Ltd* (1990) ATPR 41–009 at 51,158 the Federal Court of Australia said:

> The cases have not sought to define unconscionability nor is it appropriate so to do because the criteria to be applied will depend upon all the circumstances. Nevertheless in general terms, it may be said that conduct will be unconscionable where the conduct can be seen in accordance with the ordinary concepts of mankind to be so against conscience that a court should intervene. At the least the conduct must be unfair. It invites comparison with doctrines of equity … where inequality of bargaining power or absence of the ability to bargain freely will be relevant to the finding that there has been an unfair advantage taken by one person of the other.

[4.39]   Although 'unconscionable' is not defined in the Act the courts are provided with guidance in the form of a shopping list of factors which may be considered. Section 51AB(2) sets out those matters:

* the relative bargaining strengths of the parties;
* whether the consumer was able to understand the documentation;
* whether undue influence or pressure was exerted or unfair tactics used;
* whether the consumer was required to comply with conditions which were not reasonably necessary for the protection of the legitimate interests of the supplier;
* the amount for which and the circumstances under which the consumer could have acquired equivalent goods or services from another party.

The list is not expressed to be exhaustive and the court could take into account any other factors which it sees as appropriate.

[4.40]   Remedies under the Act   Section 87(1) gives the court a wide discretion to make orders to compensate and protect persons who have suffered loss or damage as a result of a contravention of Pt IVA. These include but are not limited to:

* an order declaring the whole or part of a contract void;
* an order varying a contract;
* an order refusing to enforce the whole or part of a contract; and
* an order for payment of damages.

In *Akron Securities Ltd v Iliffe* (1997) ATPR 41-550 it was said that s 87 aimed to provide the appropriate remedy, and that it was possible to take into account the interests of both the defendant and the plaintiff. Rescission of contract is only one remedy available from the smorgasbord of remedies offered by the Act.

[4.41]   Changes to the Act   The House of Representatives Standing Committee on Industry, Science and Technology in its report *Finding a Balance: Towards Fair Trading in Australia,* recommended that Pt IVA be strengthened to provide small business with the same specific protection against unconscionable conduct as consumers. A new s 51AC has been enacted: Unconscionable conduct in business transactions. This provision extends the equitable doctrine of unconscionability as expressed in s 51AA to transactions involving small business. There is a limit of $1 million on transactions and publicly listed companies are not able to instigate action under this provision. The new section provides:

> (1)A corporation must not, in trade or commerce, in connection with:
> (a) the supply or possible supply of goods or services to a person (other than a listed public company); or

(b) the acquisition or possible acquisition of goods or services from a person (other than a listed public company);

engage in conduct that is, in all the circumstances, unconscionable.

There is a similar provision governing the conduct of corporations. In determining whether a person or a corporation has engaged in unconscionable conduct the court apply the equitable doctrine and the Act provides a check list of factors to which the court may have regard:

(a) the relative strengths of the bargaining positions of the supplier and the business consumer; and

(b) whether, as a result of conduct engaged in by the supplier, the business consumer was required to comply with conditions that were not reasonably necessary for the protection of the legitimate interests of the supplier; and

c) whether the business consumer was able to understand any documents relating to the supply or possible supply of the goods or services; and

d) whether any undue influence or pressure was exerted on, or any unfair tactics were used against, the business consumer or a person acting on behalf of the business consumer by the supplier or a person acting on behalf of the supplier in relation to the supply or possible supply of the goods or services; and

(e) the amount for which, and the circumstances under which, the business consumer could have acquired identical or equivalent goods or services from a person other than the supplier; and

(f) the extent to which the supplier's conduct towards the business consumer was consistent with the supplier's conduct in similar transactions between the supplier and other like business consumers; and

(g) the requirements of any applicable industry code; and

(h) the requirements of any other industry code, if the business consumer acted on the reasonable belief that the supplier would comply with that code; and

(i) the extent to which the supplier unreasonably failed to disclose to the business consumer:

(i) any intended conduct of the supplier that might affect the interests of the business consumer; and

(ii) any risks to the business consumer arising from the supplier's intended conduct (being risks that the supplier should have foreseen would not be apparent to the business consumer); and

(j) the extent to which the supplier was willing to negotiate the terms and conditions of any contract for supply of the goods or services with the business consumer; and

(k) the extent to which the supplier and the business consumer acted in good faith.

Contracts Review Act 1980 (NSW)

[4.42] This legislation focuses on the circumstances in existence at the time of the formation of the contract. The courts may declare contracts to be unjust. The courts have power to grant a wide range of remedies where those circumstances result in the contract being unjust. The application of this Act by the courts has resulted in law that is wider than any of the doctrines discussed above and different in approach to that which is anticipated under Pt IVA of the Trade Practices Act.

This Act is regarded by the courts as beneficial legislation and is liberally construed and applied. Section 7(1) of the Act gives a court power to make a variety of orders by way of relief where it finds a contract to be unjust in the circumstances relating to the contract at the time it was made. 'Unjust' is defined to include unconscionable, harsh or oppressive.

[4.43] Conduct affected by the Act The Contracts Review Act is confined in its application to formed contracts only, not to arrangements or negotiations. Not every contract entered into in New South Wales is governed by this Act. Section 6 provides:

> (1) The Crown, a public or local authority or a corporation may not be granted relief under this Act.
>
> (2) A person may not be granted relief under this Act in relation to a contract so far as the contract was entered into in the course of or for the purpose of a trade, business or profession carried on by him or proposed to be carried on by him, other than a farming undertaking (including but not limited to, an agricultural, pastoral, horticultural, orcharding or viticultural undertaking) carried on by him or proposed to be carried on by him wholly or principally in New South Wales.

From the beginning the courts have adopted a literal approach to s 6, so that the Act applies to a much wider range of contracts than might at first be thought. In fact in many cases the question of whether the Act applies is not asked, it seems to be assumed. The court's approach was illustrated in *Beaumont v Helvetic Corporation* (1982) ASC 55–194, which involved a medical practitioner who had guaranteed a loan to a company of which he was a shareholder (the company ran the medical centre) and said that since he was not in the business of giving guarantees, the contract was not entered into in the course of his trade, business or profession. From this it can be assumed that all non-commercial contracts will be covered; for example, the purchase of a house and any attendant contract which are not loans for a business but mortgages and guarantees connected to them.

When applying this Act the courts are able to look not only at the conduct of the parties to the contract, but the conduct of others who may have been concerned in the transaction but were not necessarily parties to the contract, and the effect of the contract and the remedies available to all parties. An examination of the circumstances relating to the formation of the contract may find that the contract is unjust, and an order for relief may be made, but it is not necessary for the court to find fault or apportion blame.

Many of the cases for which relief is granted concern contracts which were signed, but where one party later claims that he or she did not understand the contract, in particular the effect of the contract, and asks for relief on the ground that the lack of understanding plus other circumstances existing at the time of formation rendered the contract unjust. Even though the factors which gave rise to the unjust nature of the contracts were not the fault of, nor within the knowledge of, the other party, the court may still grant relief under the Contracts Review Act.

Case Example

Mr Bandeski owned and lived in a house and was approached by Mr van der Mark, who wished to purchase it for development. For the consideration of $1 he granted an option to purchase the house at a price of $150,000. Bandeski resisted an action for specific performance of the option, claiming that $150,000 was below the true value of the house which was found by the trial judge to be $200,000 or more and that he had not understood the effect of the option. The contract was held to be unjust because:

- the price was too low,

- the purchaser was a $2 company with no assets so that in practical terms Bandeski would have been unable to enforce the option against the purchaser, and,
- had Bandeski understood the consequences of granting the option he would not have entered into the contract.

The Court of Appeal noted, however, that Mr Bandeski had 'found his way into difficulty by not recognising his own limitations and his behaviour was not that of a reasonable man' and further that there had been no wrongdoing on the part of Mr van der Mark: 'the fact that within the terms of the legislation [the contract] is described as unjust does not imply any wrongful conduct on his part'. This is in contrast to the unconscionability doctrine which contemplates some degree of wrongful conduct in the positive action of taking advantage of the other's less favourable position: *Idameneo No 9 Pty Ltd v Bandeski* (1991) ASC 56-047.

This is a considerable broadening of the courts' ability to achieve not only 'balanced' justice, but to be seen to be achieving it. There is flexibility provided by the Contracts Review Act to allow the party seeking to resist enforcement of the contract to argue that there was a lack of understanding due primarily to a third person.

Case Example

The Smith family partnership owned and conducted a farming and grazing business. No member of the family was highly educated, their schooling having ended at about 14 or 15 and they had no training or experience in finance, accountancy or business matters. The partnership had been dealing with Elders for about 40 years. Elders sold their wool, organised the purchase of livestock, supplied goods and provided finance as needed.

In 1985 the partners borrowed money from Elders to purchase a property called Nuneham Park. This was not a successful venture and the investment did not return enough to repay the principal and interest as required. The court found that the contract was unjust and that while Elders was entitled to the repayment of the $750,000 advanced they could not enforce the compounded interest payments.

Elders had not acted unfairly but the following factor made the contract unjust:

- The contrast between the commercial position of Elders and its experience and understanding of the risks involved in the transaction and that of the Smiths was extreme. The Smiths were utterly out of their depth.
- The Smiths saw Elders' readiness to lend them the money as a recommendation as to the likely success of the investment, whereas Elders was lending the money not based on an assessment of the likely success of the venture, but on the basis that the security and collateral available from the Smiths made the investment not risky for Elders.
- The Smiths lacked the skill and business insight necessary to assess the risks involved for them in the transaction: *Smith v Elders Rural Finance Limited* (1995) Aust Contracts Reports 90-054.

Summary and key terms

[4.44] This chapter has set out to explain the factors which may influence the consent of one party to a contract and therefore affect formation of a contract.

Consent may be influenced by:

- the conduct of one party:
  - duress;
  - undue influence;
  - unconscionable conduct; or
  - misrepresentation; and
- the circumstances surrounding the parties at the time of the contract.

Remedies are available from the common law, equity and legislation, such as the Trade Practices Act.

5

Contracts: Termination and Breach

What this chapter does ...

This chapter looks at the way in which a contract may be brought to an end and the remedies available to a party who is wronged in the performance or discharge of the contract:

- *performance;*
- *termination* of contracts — *discharge, repudiation, rescission and frustration;*

If a contract is breached there is a variety of remedies available to the innocent party, and the chapter examines:

- *specific performance;*
- *injunction; and*
- *damages* — *causation, remoteness and mitigation.*

Bringing the contract to an end

[5.1]   A contract may be discharged or brought to an end at any time after formation and there are several ways in which this can happen. A contract may be avoided by one party — for example, for unconscionable conduct by the other; the contract may be terminated before performance is complete — for example, for breach by one party; or the contract may be performed to the satisfaction of the parties. Where the contract is discharged by performance rights arising under the contract can still exist. The contract of sale that takes place at a supermarket checkout is for all intents and purposes completed at the time the money is paid and the goods are given to the customer. The rights attached to the contract persist for longer; for example, it is an implied term of the contract that the goods are of merchantable quality and whether this is satisfied might not become known for some time after the checkout transaction.

The methods of ending a contract are described as termination or rescission:

* *Termination*   When a contract is terminated, the future rights and obligations of all parties cease, but the contract itself remains in existence in the sense that the rights and liabilities arising prior to termination may still be pursued. Where appropriate, damages are assessed on the basis of the contract and some terms may still be enforced. What has terminated is the obligation of either party to perform any outstanding promises in the contract. What the law is concerned with here is the circumstances in which a contract may be discharged by events that occur after formation. Some terminations are automatic; for example, where a clause of the contract operates to end the contract following the failure of a condition subsequent or where the contract is frustrated. Others are not; for instance, where one party is in breach of the contract and the other must give notice that the contract is terminated for that breach.

* *Rescission*   Rescission extinguishes the whole contract so that neither party is bound by the contract as to either past or future rights and obligations. Once a contract has been rescinded there can be no action for damages based on the contract. Rescission

is generally available to a party whose consent was not genuine as a result of duress, undue influence, unconscionable conduct, mistake or misrepresentation. The rescinding party is entitled to act as if there had never been a contract — this is sometimes called rescission *ab initio* (from the beginning). In the insurance context, for example, a contract is said in some circumstances to have been 'avoided' — it did not exist at any time.

Termination by performance

[5.2] Performance of the obligations imposed by the contract is the usual method by which a contract is discharged. When each party performs according to the terms of the contract, or at least to the satisfaction of the other party, the contract is said to have been terminated or discharged by performance. The standard of performance required to satisfy the contract terms and oblige performance or payment by the other party is a matter which has been developed through the cases.

Independent and dependent promises

[5.3] It may be that the contract imposes on each party a duty to perform promises whether of not the other has performed. For example, if a landlord has promised in a lease to keep premises in good repair, that duty is not dependant on the tenant keeping a promise to pay rent. These promises are said to be independent because each duty is owed independently of the other party's performance of their obligations.

In other contracts there will be a relationship of dependence between the duties. This relationship may mean that one party must perform before the obligation of the other is enforceable. For example, an employee must perform the work promised under the contract of employment before the employer is obliged to pay wages. It is also possible for contracts to require obligations to be performed at the same time. For example, in a contract for the sale of goods the vendor's obligation to transfer title to the goods is concurrent with the purchaser's obligation to accept delivery and pay the price.

Conditions precedent and conditions subsequent

[5.4] Conditions precedent and conditions subsequent are terms of the contract which may affect its formation, performance or discharge. A condition precedent refers to the happening of a specified event being the factor necessary for either the formation of the contract or the obligation of the other party to perform. A condition subsequent is a term of the contract which describes events, the happening of which will bring the obligation to perform or the contract to an end. It is often a matter of construction by the court to determine whether such conditions are precedent or subsequent.

Both conditions subsequent and conditions precedent may be events which the parties can bring about or they may be exclusively in the control of third parties. The parties may agree 'subject to contract' and this will impose a condition precedent to formation that a written contract be created and signed. (See the discussion of *Masters v Cameron* (1954) 91 CLR 353 in **[2.28]**.) An example of a condition precedent to performance can be seen in *Perri v Coolangatta Investments Pty Ltd* (1982) 149 CLR 537; 56 ALJR 445. The parties had entered into a contract for the sale of a block of land and the contract provided that 'This Contract is entered into subject to Purchasers completing a sale of their property No 9 Korokan Road, Lilli Pilli.' When the property at Lilli Pilli remained unsold for several months the vendor terminated the contract. This was possible because the condition precedent to performance — the sale of the Lilli Pilli land — had not been fulfilled. The law requires strict compliance with conditions precedent before an obligation to perform will exist: see *Tricontinental Corporation Ltd v HDFI Ltd* (1987) 21 NSWLR 689.

Strict or exact performance

[5.5] The common law requires each party to do exactly what is specified in the contract. Any departure from the actual terms will be viewed as a breach of contract. In some contracts imprecise terms — such as that goods will be reasonably fit for a known purpose or that a party will make reasonable endeavours — will have to be construed by the court to see whether there has been a failure to comply with them. The operation of this harsh and sometimes impractical rule is illustrated in *Re Moore & Co Ltd and Landauer & Co* [1921] 2 KB 519. The contract, which was for the sale of tins of fruit, specified that the fruit was to be packed 30 tins to the case. The seller delivered the correct number of tins of fruit, but some were packed 24 tins to the case. It was held that the buyer was entitled to reject the consignment because it was not packed and delivered in strict compliance with the terms of the contract. The seller was in breach of the contract for non-performance because he had not done precisely what the contract required.

Entire performance rule

[5.6] An extension of the requirement of strict performance is what is called the entire performance rule which provides that the entire contract must be performed before payment becomes due. Parties to a contract can always provide otherwise, and contracts do often require payment in stages. If the contract does not specify the method of payment, it will be interpreted so that performance of the whole contract is a condition precedent to the liability to pay. In *Sumpter v Hedges* [1898] 1 QB 673 there were contracts for the construction of two houses: the builder did some work and then asked for a progress payment before he would do more. It was held that where there is a contract to do work for a lump sum, the price cannot be recovered until the whole contract is completed.

The time for performance

[5.7] If the contract specifies a time for performance the strict performance rule requires that the parties complete performance by that time. Where performance by a specified time is crucial to the parties the contract should contain a 'time is of the essence' clause. In such a case failure to perform by the specified date will allow the innocent party to terminate the contract for breach. If the contract has not specified the time for performance the law will imply a term requiring the contract to be performed within a reasonable time. If time has not been specified or expressed to be essential then either party may, by giving a notice to complete, fix the time for performance and failure to perform within time will be a breach of contract.

Exceptions to the performance rules

[5.8] The strict application of the performance rules can lead to harsh results and therefore the law has developed a number of exceptions. They include:

- *de minimus non curat lex* — the law does not concern itself with trifles;
- substantial performance;
- the ready, willing and able rule; and
- divisible contracts.

De minimus non curat lex — the law does not concern itself with trifles

[5.9] This exception allows a court to disregard trifling departures from the requirements of the contract. Parties whose performance falls slightly short of perfection shall not be affected by the shortfall. In *Shipton, Anderson & Cos v Weil Bros & Co* [1912] 1 KB 574 the parties entered into a contract for the sale of 4950 tons of wheat. The vendor delivered 4950 tons and 55 pounds, and although the vendor only charged for 4950 tons, the purchasers refused to accept on the grounds that performance was not exact. It was held that the difference in weight was so insignificant that the de minimus rule applied to override the vendor's failure to render exact performance.

Substantial performance

[5.10] Where the difference between the contract and the performance is more than de minimus but not sufficient to warrant a denial of all of one party's rights then substantial performance may be enough. The acceptance of partial performance or of any variation must be the free and willing acceptance of the party. The innocent party may have a remedy in damages.

The ready, willing and able rule

[5.11] This rule applies where one party is unable to perform because of the actions of the other. If the attempted or refused performance is in accordance with the terms of the contract the 'performing' party is discharged from any further obligations, and may terminate the contract as well as sue for damages. The refusal or prevention of performance is regarded as a breach of the contract and can be compensated for: see **[5.39]**.

Case Example

Mahoney agreed to sell to Lindsay some land and the business conducted on it. Mahoney later made it clear that he did not intend to complete the transfer; Lindsay sued for specific performance and argued that he could not succeed because he had not done all that was required of him and so was not at the time of Mahoney's refusal ready, willing and able to perform. The court held that he was entitled to an order for specific performance because it was clear that any tender of performance would be rejected, and attempted performance would have been pointless. The court also said if any one party to a contract prevents the other from fulfilling a condition of the contract, that is equivalent to performance by the latter: *Mahoney v Lindsay* (1980) 33 ALR 601; (1981) 55 ALJR 118.

Divisible contracts

[5.12] Clearly not every contract contemplates the performance of the entire contract before payment or reciprocal performance becomes due. This will be a matter of construction for the court. Divisible or severable contracts are to be distinguished from entire contracts. They are contracts which clearly indicate that some performance less than the whole contracted for may suffice to confer rights on the performing party. Many construction contracts provide for payments in instalments or as and when certain steps are completed.

Termination by agreement

[5.13]   Just as parties are free to enter into any contract they are free to bring the contract to an end by agreement. Sometimes the contract itself will contain termination clauses which will give the parties a right to terminate it in certain circumstances. Termination clauses may also set out the method by which an agreement may be ended; for example, by notice in writing. At other times a new or further agreement will be required to terminate the contract. To be binding these agreements must be either a valid contract or enforceable as a deed. This can be an agreement to simply cancel the contract (discharge) or an agreement to vary or alter the terms so that performance is now different from that which was originally bargained for (variation). Such a termination by agreement may be a compromise reached to settle a dispute between the parties.

Discharge by the operation of the contract

[5.14]   There is nothing to prevent a contract containing a term that will allow the parties to bring the contract to an end or a term that provides for automatic discharge on the happening or failure of some specified event. A contract for the sale of land might provide that building approval from the local council must be obtained by the vendor by a certain date. Such a provision is a condition precedent to performance. The failure to obtain such approval will result in automatic termination of the contract and could be exploited for the benefit of the vendor. To overcome that possibility condition precedents are construed as not usually giving rise to an automatic termination but as giving the buyer the right to choose to terminate for non-fulfilment of the condition.

In long-term or continuing commercial contracts it is usual to find a clause which allows for termination of the contract by the giving of a notice in writing to terminate within a specified period. If the contract is silent on the matter of termination the courts may be willing to imply a term that the contract is terminable at will on the giving of reasonable notice: see *Crawford Fitting Co v Sydney Valve & Fittings Pty Ltd* (1988) 14 NSWLR 438.

Mutual discharge

[5.15]   Where there is some unperformed, executory consideration on both sides of the contract this presents no problem — one party's promise to abandon rights under the original agreement is consideration for a similar promise from the other. The same formalities that were observed in the original agreement should be used.

Release or waiver

[5.16]   Where one party's consideration is wholly executed — that is, complete — then that party may release the other from the obligation to perform or waive the right to terminate or sue for damages. To be enforceable this waiver must be a separate contract or contained in a deed. Waiver is usually characterised by one party being relieved of an obligation or liability and the other forgoing rights.

Novation or substitution

[5.17]   Here the parties discharge their original contract and enter into a new one. This can also be by way of variation of the first contract.

Abandonment

[5.18]   If the parties have abandoned a contract then that abandonment will terminate the contract. Mere lapse of a long period of time does not indicate that a contract has been abandoned. The court will infer that as a matter of fact the parties have been inactive and this inaction indicates that there has been an implied mutual discharge.

Discharge by operation of law

[5.19]   Certain events either automatically bring a contract to an end or give one of the parties the right to rescind or terminate. Equity allows parties to rescind contracts where consent has been obtained by fraud, duress, undue influence or unconscionable conduct. The common law brings to an end contracts which have been frustrated and may set aside illegal contracts. Legislation confers rights to terminate contracts for breach of terms implied by statute and empowers the court to rescind unjust contracts.

Frustration

[5.20]   The first and most obvious reason for discharge from the obligation to perform is that something has happened to make it impossible to perform the contract. In technical terms the contract is frustrated. The law's attitude to frustration is quite strict. Since the parties to a contract are free to provide for the happening of frustrating events, they will be bound to perform according to the terms of the contract, even where circumstances have changed so dramatically that it is not possible to do so. Failure to perform amounts to a breach of contract. The general principle is that where there is a contract to do a thing the promisor must perform it or pay damages for not doing it. This will be so even if the performance of the contract has become unexpectedly burdensome or even impossible.

The law asks whether the original promise made extends to performance in these particular circumstances. The matter must be examined from the viewpoint of each party to see whether the intervention of a frustrating event has ended the contract. This necessitates an inquiry into the scope of the contractual promises. Entering into contracts, especially commercial contracts, often entails running the risk that things will not go well or according to plan. The realisation of such risks will not be treated as frustration by the courts, especially when the parties could have provided for what should be done on the happening of certain events. An example is in the case of a construction contract — a builder could not claim frustration because bad weather prevented completion by a certain time. A court is likely to say that bad weather is an almost foreseeable risk and the builder should have made allowance for it.

If the purpose of the contract for one party is frustrated, this will not automatically be the same as the contract itself being frustrated. For example, a person had ordered a ball dress to be made but broke her leg and could not attend the ball — there was no need for the dress. From the dressmaker's point of view the not going to the ball was of no consequence. Events which make performance of the contract more expensive or arduous than expected will not amount to frustration.

[5.21] The modern doctrine is set out in *Davis Contractors Ltd v Fareham Urban District Council* [1956] AC 696 at 729:

> ... frustration occurs whenever the law recognises that without default of either party, a contractual obligation has become incapable of being performed because the circumstances in which performance is called for would render it a thing radically different from that which was undertaken by the contract ... It was not this that I promised to do.

Frustration will only arise where the following conditions are met:

- there must be a supervening event (that is, a post-contractual event — pre-contractual events which alter the contemplated performance are dealt with by the doctrine of mistake);
- that event must cause a fundamental change to the nature of the contractual rights and obligations;
- neither party should be the instigator of the supervening event (that is, it must not be the fault of any party to the contract);
- the supervening event must not have been in the contemplation of the parties at the time of formation; and
- it must be unjust to hold the parties to the contract as agreed upon.

[5.22] Most commercial contracts will be subject to the doctrine of frustration. The doctrine will operate to end those contracts where unforeseen events have frustrated the commercial purpose of the contract. This is provided for not only under the common law doctrine but in some instances legislatively. The Sale of Goods Act 1923 (NSW), for example, provides:

> 12   Where there is an agreement to sell specific goods, and subsequently the goods without any fault on the part of the seller or buyer perish before the risk passes to the buyer, the agreement is thereby avoided.

Contracts concerning the transfer of an interest in land may be frustrated by a supervening event which prevents the vendor transferring the interest. It is less clear as to whether a contract for the sale of land is frustrated by an event which merely alters the use to which the land can be put. There was for many years a restriction on the application of the doctrine to leases on the basis that a lease creates an interest in the land which cannot be destroyed by subsequent events although the use of the leased land may be radically altered. In 1981 the House of Lords held that the doctrine of frustration was capable of applying to a lease: *National Carriers Ltd v Panalpina (Northern) Ltd* [1981] AC 675. If this is followed by Australian courts, there seems no reason why, as a matter of legal principle, if a supervening event which renders it impossible for the lessee to use property in a manner contemplated by the contract frustrates the lease, the same could not apply to contracts for the sale of land.

Frustrating events

[5.23] The types of event which will frustrate a contract cannot be listed exhaustively, but the following are common:

- the destruction of the subject matter of the contract — goods perishing between contract and delivery;
- non-occurrence of an event which underlies the contract — contracts for the hire of balconies from which to watch the coronation parade of King Edward VII were frustrated by the cancellation of the coronation;
- the contemplated means of performance of the contract is rendered impossible — see *Codelfa Construction Pty Ltd v State Rail Authority of NSW* (1982) 149 CLR 337 below;
- delay of an extraordinary kind that the purpose of the venture is frustrated; and
- changes to the law subsequent to formation — legislation which renders it illegal to do the acts contemplated by the contract.

Case Example

Codelfa had a contract with the State Rail Authority for the construction of railway tunnels for the eastern suburbs railway in Sydney. The contract price had been calculated on the basis that work would be done for 24 hours a day and seven days a week. The excavation and construction work caused considerable noise and vibration. Local residents and the local council sought injunctions to restrain the work and Codelfa was ordered not to carry out work at night or on weekends. This meant that Codelfa could not complete the contract either on time or for the agreed price.

Codelfa argued that the contract was terminated by frustration on the grounds that:
- there was a supervening event in the form of the injunction;
- it had radically altered the contractual rights and obligations as it was not now possible to complete on time or within the price agreed;
- neither party to the contract had instigated the injunction;
- the parties had not allowed for such an event because their legal advice was that such an injunction would not be possible; and
- It was manifestly unjust to keep the parties to the contract because Codelfa would suffer a penalty.

The High Court held that the contract had been frustrated because the work envisaged by the contract had been so disrupted that the new situation was fundamentally different from the method of performance that had been contemplated by the contract: *Codelfa Construction Pty Ltd v State Rail Authority of NSW* (1982) 149 CLR 337

The consequences of frustration

[5.24] Frustration of a contract discharges both parties from the obligation to perform the contract. The discharge is automatic and applies from the time of the frustrating event. Rights which have already accrued under the contract are not necessarily lost. A breach of contract which occurred prior to frustration will allow an action in damages to compensate the innocent party. While all obligations to perform in the future cease on frustration, some terms will continue to have force. If a contract contains a term which requires confidentiality, the obligation of confidentiality may continue although the contract is ended.

The frustration brings the contract to an end, but how do the parties distribute the loss between themselves? If the obligations of one party have been performed such as by doing work or by payment of money, but the other party has not performed in return prior to the frustration, the loss will usually lie where it falls. The contract which has been frustrated is a perfectly good contract up to the time of frustration and so in some cases parties will be able to recover money paid for work promised but not performed. The common law is not able to treat every party to a frustrated contract evenly and so there are four possible problems identifiable in the common law's approach to the consequences of frustration:

• the unfairness in not being able to recover unless there is total failure of consideration;
• the injustice if benefits are conferred but not paid for prior to the supervening event;
• the loss resulting from frustration is often borne by one party alone yet the basis of the doctrine is that neither party is at fault; and
• unjust enrichment may result if one party enforces an action for damages resulting from a breach which arose prior to the frustration.

Statutory reform

[5.25]   New South Wales, South Australia and Victoria have legislation covering this area but it is not uniform. None of the Acts provides a means of determining when a contract is frustrated, but each deals only with the consequences of frustration. Each Act will apply only if under the common law the contract could be said to be frustrated.

The Frustrated Contracts Act 1978 (NSW) provides for a simple scheme whereby once a contract is frustrated there is an adjustment between the parties so that no one party is unfairly disadvantaged. Section 7 provides that a promise, due for performance before the frustrating event but not performed, is discharged except to the extent necessary to support an action in damages, and so preserves actions arising prior to frustration.

Where the obligations of one party have been wholly performed prior to frustration that party is entitled to compensation from the other party: s 10. Apportionment is provided for where one party has partly performed prior to frustration: s 11. If money has been paid under the contract and nothing has been done in return the whole sum is to be returned; if there is something received for the money then there is an apportionment of compensation: s 12. Likewise, where performance has been rendered by one side but not received by the other (for example, deposit paid) the loss is to be apportioned: s 13.

The South Australian Frustrated Contracts Act 1988 specifically preserves the common law as to the effect of frustration. It provides that frustration discharges all contractual obligations but that those obligations which the parties agreed were to continue after frustration and those actions for damages in respect of breaches before frustration would survive: s 6. The loss is to be adjusted after frustration so that no party is unfairly advantaged or disadvantaged by the frustration: s 7.

In Victoria all moneys paid before the frustration can be recovered, and any action arising before frustration can be compensated by a just sum: Frustrated Contracts Act 1959 (Vic) s 3.

Illegality

[5.26]   Given that a contract is a transaction that will be enforced by a court it is hardly surprising and certainly consistent that courts have been called upon to declare some contracts void, and others unenforceable either in whole or in part, for illegality. The word illegal has a wide meaning in contract law and extends beyond those acts which are prohibited by legislation. There are several ways in which a contract may be said to be 'illegal'. The rule against the courts enforcing contracts which are tainted with illegality arose from public policy, as explained in *Fitzgerald v FJ Leonhardt Pty Ltd* (1997) 143 ALR 569 at 593:

> The rule permitting a court to refuse its assistance to enforce a contract where to do so would be contrary to public policy is an ancient one ... The principle of public policy is this ... No court will lend its aid to a man who founds his cause of action upon an immoral or illegal act ... [T]he fundamental rational for withholding relief is one essentially of the court's self-regard. It will not (unless required to do so) lend its authority and assistance to a party seeking to invoke its process in connection with illegal or otherwise reprehensible conduct.

In the area of contract law some contracts are themselves illegal — either because they are to do an illegal act (murder, for example), or because it is illegal to form such a contract (to fix prices, for example). In some cases the illegality occurs in the giving of effect to the agreement. Contracts tainted by illegality may be either illegal as formed or rendered illegal due to some event between formation and performance. The former are void ab initio — that is, never truly formed — and the latter may be simply rendered unenforceable by the illegality. For example, Arnotts negotiated the takeover of Nabisco and, at that stage, there was a valid contract of purchase. However, the takeover was successfully challenged under the Trade Practices Act 1974 (Cth). Therefore the basic contract was not invalid but its performance was rendered illegal and it became unenforceable.

Statutory illegality

[5.27]   Statutory illegality does not necessarily mean that criminal activity is involved. It covers a much wider range of activity than entering into a contract to commit a crime. Broadly speaking, there are three types of statutory illegality:

* express statutory illegality;
* implied statutory illegality;
* a contract to breach a statute.

[5.28]   Express statutory illegality   This is where the formation of the contract is prohibited by statute. While these contracts are clearly tainted with illegality, the courts' policy is not to declare them void unless as a matter of construction the statute had that intention. The interpretation of legislation is influenced by its language, purpose and context. If legislation expressly prohibits the making of a particular contract then the contract is clearly illegal:

* if the legislation prohibits an activity then there is little room for doubt — for example, a contract for the sale of tobacco to a person under the age of 16 years would be void;
* s 45 of the Trade Practices Act 1974 (Cth) prohibits the entering into of a contract that has the effect of substantially lessening competition — these contracts will be unenforceable.

[5.29]   Implied statutory illegality   This will apply where there is no express prohibition on the making of the contract but, if the conduct surrounding the making of the contract breaches a statute, it might be implied that the contract is illegal. It does not always follow that a contract which results in the breach of a statute is illegal and thus unenforceable.

> **Case Example**
>
> An action was brought for specific performance of two contracts for the sale of shares. The defendant alleged that both contracts were illegal because the plaintiffs were persons connected with the company whose shares were to be sold and were in possession of information which was not generally available and would be likely materially to affect the price of the shares if it were. This was a breach of the insider trading provisions of the Securities Industry Code. Seaman J found that although the legislation was intended to protect the investing public this was done by way of penalty and compensation; it was not intended by the legislation that dealings which contravened the insider trading provisions should be rendered void: *Singh v Crafter* (1992) 10 ACLC 1,365.

[5.30]   A contract to breach a statute   Such a contract will be void on public policy grounds: the law will not allow persons to obtain benefits from an agreement to do an illegal act. Some statutes expressly declare void any provisions of a contract which seek to avoid the operation of the statute to oust the effect of the legislation. Section 68 of the Trade Practices Act declares void any term of a contract that purports to exclude, restrict or modify a right conferred by other provisions of the Act.

> **Case Example**
>
> The owner of land contracted with a licensed driller to drill some bores on his land. This was done and the bores produced water. Neither the owner nor the driller had obtained a permit to drill the bores as required by s 56 of the Water Act 1992 (NT). A dispute arose as to how much the owner should pay to the driller and the driller brought an action to recover his fee. The owner argued that no money was owed because the contract was illegal. The Water Act did not expressly prohibit the making of the contract, nor did performance of the contract call for the commission of any illegal act. The Water Act imposed a penalty on the owner for causing the drilling of bores without a permit.
>
> In determining that the contract was not void on public policy grounds the High Court applied the principles set out in *Nelson v Nelson* (1995) 184 CLR 538 that courts should not refuse to enforce legal or equitable rights simply because they arose out of or were associated with an unlawful purpose unless:
>
> (a) the statute discloses an intention that those rights should be unenforceable in all circumstances; or
>
> (b) (i) the sanction of refusing to enforce those rights is not disproportionate to the seriousness of the unlawful conduct;
>
>   (ii) the imposition of the sanction is necessary, having regard to the terms of the statue to protect its objects or policies; and
>
>   (iii) the statute does not disclose an intention that the sanctions and remedies contained in the statute are to be the only legal consequences of a breach of the statute or the frustration of its policies.
>
> Kirby J said (at 594):

> It would be absurd if a trivial breach of a statutory provision constituting ille-
> gality, connected in some way with a contract or contracting parties could
> be held to justify the total withdrawal of the facilities of the courts
>
> and that 'if the court were to withhold relief to the driller it would result in a wind-
> fall to the landowner which would itself be an affront to public conscience' (at
> 597): *Fitzgerald v FJ Leonhardt Pty Ltd* (1997) 143 ALR 569.

Common law illegality

[5.31]   The common law will not enforce an illegal contract because to do so would be against the public interest. Public policy requires contracts such as those to commit a crime, to interfere with the administration of justice, or to defraud the public revenue to be void.

In the commercial law context illegality becomes an issue in contracts which are in restraint of trade. Both the common law and Pt IV of the Trade Practices Act can apply to such contracts. Restraint of trade clauses are to be found in contracts of employment or for the sale of a business. The vendor of a business agrees not to set up or work for a business that would be in competition with the one being sold. Such clauses usually impose these restrictions over time and apply to any business within a certain distance of that being sold.

All restraints of trade of themselves are contrary to public policy and therefore void. This presumption may be rebutted if the restraint sought to be imposed affords no more than reasonable protection of something in the nature of a proprietary right. Reasonableness is a question of law to be determined by the court in the light of the circumstances of the case. The onus of proving special circumstances justifying the restriction as reasonable lies on the party alleging it to be so.

Case Example

Drake Personnel employed Beddison and the contract of employment provided that Beddison would not carry on the business of an employment agency
within a 25 km radius of Drake for 12 months after termination of his employment. Beddison left Drake and after one month set up in business less than
1 km away. Drake sought an injunction to restrain him.

The court held that such a clause may be used to protect business secrets but
Beddison's general skill and knowledge acquired while employed at Drake were
not trade secrets. Drake could be protected from Beddison soliciting its clients
but not from competition itself: *Drake Personnel Ltd v Beddison* [1979] VR 13.

Consequences of illegality

[5.32]   The general rule is that where a contract is void for illegality the courts will not assist either party to enforce it. However, it is possible to obtain a remedy notwithstanding the illegality. The first way is to allow the plaintiff to sue outside the contract; for example, by finding a collateral contract or by allowing an action in tort. If one or more terms of the contract are eliminated from the contract because they are tainted with illegality the remainder of the contract may still be enforced. Severance is only possible if the term can be eliminated without altering the essential nature or substance of the contract. The contract will not be rewritten by the court. As a general rule money or property transferred under an illegal contract cannot be recovered.

Discharge by breach

[5.33] Discharge by breach is a significant aspect of contract law because it brings into play the special quality of a contract as an agreement the law will enforce. If a party, without lawful excuse, fails to perform the things promised in the contract, that party is in breach of the contract. There are two types of breach which may terminate the contract — actual and anticipatory.

Actual breach occurs where one party fails to perform all or part of the contract at the time performance falls due. Such a breach usually involves not a complete and conscious repudiation of the whole contract but a breach of certain obligations under it. Actual breach will occur where there is non-performance, defective performance, late performance or where terms of the contract turn out to be untrue. If the promisee rejects defective or late performance that is treated as non-performance by the promisor.

Anticipatory breach occurs where one party to the contract indicates before performance is due an intention not to do whatever the contract requires. This is called repudiation. Anticipatory breach may, with the passing of time, become actual breach. In *Foran v Wight* (1989) 168 CLR 385 the High Court said anticipatory breach of a contract occurs when the threatened non-performance would deprive the innocent party of substantially the whole benefit which it was intended should be obtained from the contract. Repudiation by way of anticipatory breach does not end the contract unless the other party accepts the repudiation and terminates the contract. The innocent party does not have to accept the repudiation, but may continue to treat the contract as on foot and hold the repudiating party to the performance of the contractual obligations. If those obligations remain unperformed when the time for performance arrives, the anticipatory breach will be converted into actual breach.

[5.34] Repudiation is not in itself a discharge of the contract, but is evidence of an intention on the part of one party no longer to be bound by the terms of the contract. To found an anticipatory breach the renunciation must be an intimation of an intention to abandon altogether, or refuse performance of, the contract. The following is an illustration.

Case Example

In October 1985, Capalaba agreed to lease a shop in a Queensland shopping centre to Laurinda for a period of six years. Under the agreement, Capalaba was required to complete a number of blanks in the lease and to annex a sketch of the premises, so as to put the lease into registrable form, and then to register the lease or, at least, to deliver the lease in registrable form to Laurinda. This obligation was to be fulfilled by Capalaba upon the commencement of the lease 'or so soon thereafter as is practicable'. Laurinda went into possession in December 1985.

141

In March 1986, the lease not having been received, the accountants for Laurinda requested a copy. The lessor's solicitors said that the lease was in Melbourne, and that they expected it to be returned to them 'in the not too distant future', whereupon they would forward it to the lessee. At this time, Laurinda was seeking a buyer of the business that it was conducting on the premises and this was known to Capalaba.

On 21 August 1986 Laurinda's solicitors wrote to Capalaba's solicitors stating that the documentation should have been completed months ago and that it was crucial for their client's security of tenure that the lease be registered. The letter demanded that registration of the lease be completed within 14 days. The only response they received was a letter from the lessor's solicitors shortly before the expiration of the 14-day period, stating that they had referred the matter to the lessor for instructions which would be communicated as soon as they were received. On 5 September 1986 Laurinda terminated the contract on the ground that Capalaba's delay in registering the lease was a repudiation of the contract — the extraordinary delay was evidence of an intention not to perform the contract according to its terms.

The High Court concluded that Capalaba's conduct amounted to a repudiation of its obligations under the agreement and that this justified termination. The attitude of Capalaba was not only dilatory but also cavalier and recalcitrant and the lessor's intention was only to perform the contract in a manner substantially inconsistent with its obligations: *Laurinda Pty Ltd Capalaba Park Shopping Centre Pty Ltd* (1989) 166 CLR 623; 63 ALJR 372. See also *Gold Coast Oil Co Pty Ltd v Lee Properties Pty Ltd* (1985) 1 Qd R 416.

Consequences of breach

[5.35]   It is not always easy to decide whether the breach entitles the innocent party to terminate, or whether the contract is still on foot and the innocent party is merely entitled to sue for damages. The general principle is that actual breach by one party discharges the other party from performance if one of the situations stated by the High Court in *Shevill v Builders Licensing Board* (1982) 149 CLR 620 exists:

- One party renounces liabilities under the contract, by evincing an intention no longer to be bound by the contract, or shows an intention to perform the contract only in a manner substantially inconsistent with the contractual obligations and not in any other way (anticipatory breach).

- One party although wishing to perform proves to be unable to do so and the breach goes so much to the root of the contract that it makes further commercial performance of the contract impossible (frustration).

- There has been a breach of a condition — a fundamental or essential term of the contract (actual breach). Where there is a breach of a condition the contract may be terminated by the innocent party. Other remedies such as damages will still be available to that innocent party.

The right to terminate a contract for breach will only arise where the breach is of an essential term of the contract or where the effect of the breach is fundamentally to alter the performance offered by the party in breach.

Classification of terms

[5.36]   Where there has been a breach it is necessary to classify the term that has not been fulfilled. Terms which are promissory in nature are generally classified according to whether they are conditions or warranties. This classification will determine whether the innocent party can terminate the contract if one of the terms of the contract is breached.

Where there is a breach of a condition the innocent party may terminate the contract and sue for damages. Where there is a breach of a warranty the only remedy available is damages. The innocent party is not obliged to terminate the contract for breach of a condition. Unless the breach makes further performance impossible, the innocent party may elect to treat the breach as a breach of warranty and affirm the contract.

In some cases the parties 'classify' the terms for themselves but this is not always accepted by the court, though where the parties have specified the remedy to flow for breach of any particular term that remedy will usually be given effect to. Wherever the terms of a contract are implied by statute they are also classified by the statute; for example, s 71 of the Trade Practices Act 1974 (Cth) implies a *condition* as to fitness for purpose, whereas s 74 implies a *warranty* that services will be rendered with due skill and care.

The relevance of the classification of a term is its importance to the contract. A condition is defined as an essential term of the contract; a stipulation which goes to the root of the matter, so that a failure to perform it would render the performance of the rest of the contract a thing different from what the promisor has stipulated for: *Bettini v Gye* (1846) 1 QBD 183. A warranty is regarded as subsidiary to the main purpose of the contract and thus something of lesser significance than a condition. A breach of a condition deprives the innocent party of the whole benefit of the contract and therefore termination is allowed. A breach of a warranty does not go to the heart of the contract and therefore can be properly compensated for by damages.

In *Tramways Advertising Pty Ltd v Luna Park (NSW) Ltd* (1938) 38 SR(NSW) 632 at 642, the Supreme Court of New South Wales stated that when looking at the remedy for breach of contract the nature of the promise broken is one of the most important matters.

> If it is a condition that is broken that is, an essential promise, the innocent party, when he becomes aware of the breach, had ordinarily the right at his option whether to treat himself as discharged from the contract and to recover damages for loss of the contract, or else to keep the contract on foot and recover damages for the particular breach. If it is a warranty that is broken, that is, a non-essential promise, only the latter alternative is available to the innocent party: in that case he cannot of course obtain damages for loss of the contract ...

Some terms are not easily classified as always essential or always subsidiary. The effect of the breach of a particular term may need to be examined before it can be said that the innocent party is entitled to terminate because they have been deprived of substantially the whole benefit of the contract. In *Hongkong Fir Shipping Co Ltd v Kawasaki Kisen Kaisha Ltd* [1962] 2 QB 26 at 70 it was said:

> ... [t]here are some simple contractual undertakings ... of which it can be predicated that every breach of such an undertaking must give rise to an event which will deprive the party not in default of substantially the whole benefit which it was intended that he should obtain from the contract. And such a stipulation, unless the parties have agreed that breach of it shall not entitle the non defaulting party to treat the contract as repudiated, is a 'condition'. So too there may be other simple contractual undertakings of which it can be predicated that no breach can give rise to an event which will deprive the party not in default of substantially the whole benefit which it was intended that he should obtain from the contract; and such a stipulation, unless the parties have agreed that breach of it shall entitle the non

143

defaulting party to treat the contract as repudiated, is a 'warranty'. There are, however, many contractual undertakings ... which cannot be characterised as being 'conditions' or 'warranties'. Of such undertakings all that can be predicated is that some breaches will and others will not give rise to an event which will derive the party not in default of substantially the whole benefit which it was intended that he should obtain form the contract; and the legal consequences of a breach of such an undertaking, unless provided for expressly in the contract, depend upon the nature of the event to which the breach gives rise ...

The High Court has recognised that a term in a contract may stand somewhere between a condition and a warranty: see *Ankar Pty Ltd v National Westminster Finance (Australia) Ltd* [1987] 162 CLR 549. Such an intermediate or innominate term is capable of operating, according to the gravity of the breach, as either a condition or a warranty. The innominate term brings a greater flexibility to the law of contract — a serious breach of an innominate term entitles the innocent party to treat the contract as at an end but minor breaches only allow a suit for damages.

Electing to affirm or rescind the contract

[5.37]   Where there is anticipatory or actual breach of a condition or a substantial breach of an innominate term, the innocent party has the right to terminate the contract, but is not always obliged to do so, and may elect to treat the breach as a breach of warranty and so affirm the contract. Affirming means that the contract remains alive and the innocent party has remedies of damages and perhaps specific performance. Where one party is in a position to either affirm or terminate the contract there are three factors to be considered:

- *Knowledge*   There is some doubt as to the extent of knowledge required by the innocent party. Must there be knowledge of the facts of the breach which gives rise to a right to elect or must there also be knowledge of the consequences of the breach?

- *Unequivocal conduct*   Both rescission and affirmation of the contract must be evidenced by unequivocal conduct; sometimes the choice of the innocent party will be inferred from conduct. The test is whether their conduct is consistent with a choice having been made.

- *Finality*   Once the innocent party has chosen to either affirm or terminate, the right to choose the other is extinguished.

Case Example

A financial institution agreed to lend up to $750,000 to a building developer, but before the full amount had been advanced informed the developer that no further money would be advanced. The lender offered to advance $30,000 under a new loan arrangement and this offer was accepted. In finding that the financial institution's conduct amounted to a repudiation of the contract and that the acceptance of the offer of $30,000 amounted to a termination of the original loan contract Miles CJ stated:

- The breach must be of such magnitude to entitle the innocent party to treat the contract as at an end. The test is in *Shevill v Builders Licensing Board* (1982) 149 CLR 620 — a contract may be repudiated if one party evinces an intention no longer to be bound by the contract or shows that he or she intends to fulfil the contract only in a manner substantially inconsistent with his or her obligations and not in any other way.

- The right to terminate must be exercised by unequivocal words or conduct evincing an intention to terminate the performance of the contract and to sue for damages. The entering into of an independent and alternate contract would be such conduct.
- The cases are not clear on whether the relevant knowledge on the part of the innocent party is the awareness of the legal right to elect to terminate (rather that to elect to affirm) or the awareness of the facts which give rise to legal recognition of that right. A person confronted with a choice is not bound to elect at once, but may keep the question open so long as the delay foes not cause prejudice to the other side. An election takes place when the conduct of the party is such that it would be justifiable only if an election had been made one way or the other. A party to a contract may be held to have made an election, notwithstanding that that party was unaware of his or her actual rights — it is sufficient that the party is aware of the facts giving rise to the right to terminate.

Hill v Canberra Centre Holdings Ltd (1995) 122 FLR 434; see also *Sargent v ASL Developments Ltd* (1974) 131 CLR 634; *Khoury v Government Insurance Office (NSW)* (1984) 165 CLR 622.

Prevention or refusal of performance: the ready, willing and able rule

[5.38]   There is a general rule that whether the breach is actual or anticipatory the innocent party must either tender performance or be 'ready, willing and able' to perform. Otherwise the non-breaching party cannot be said to be innocent. This is essential before a cause of action can be said to exist.

Whenever one party prevents the other from performing the contract, or from tendered or attempted performance, that 'prevention' discharges the 'performing' party from any further obligations, and that party may exercise any right or remedy available. The refusal or prevention of performance is a breach of the contract.

Case Example

A contract for the sale of land to the value of $75,000 was executed on 24 December 1982, and $7500 deposit was paid. The contract provided that 22 June 1983 was the date for settlement and time was expressed to be of the essence. On 20 June 1983 the purchaser's solicitor telephoned the vendor's solicitor to ask what time on 22 June settlement would take place. The vendor's solicitor said that settlement could not take place because a right of way had not been registered as required by the contract. There was no further communication between the parties or their solicitors and on 24 June the purchasers rescinded the contract.

The vendor's statement that settlement could not take place because the right of way had not been registered was a repudiation of the contract, and may have allowed the purchaser to rescind for anticipatory breach.

nation[5.38]

> The rescission was, however, for actual breach since the vendors had failed to settle on 22 June as the contract required. The purchasers did not have finance on 20 June and so it was argued that they were not ready, willing and able to complete and that therefore their rescission was invalid. The High Court held that the purchasers were entitled to rescind and to have the deposit returned and said that in any action for breach of contract, the readiness and willingness of the plaintiff to perform those mutual obligations remaining to be performed by the plaintiff under the contract is a condition precedent to the right to recover. In cases of both anticipatory and actual breach readiness and willingness on the part of the plaintiff is part of the cause of action. In this case the vendor's anticipatory breach of the contract released the purchasers from having to offer tender of performance on the date settlement was due. What they had to show was 'that at the time of the repudiation, that is at the time they were absolved from future performance, there was not a "substantial incapacity" on their part or a "definitive resolve or decision" against the performance of their obligations' (at 455): *Foran v Wight* (1989) 168 CLR 385.

Remedies

[5.39] The law provides the means to enforce a right, or to prevent, redress or compensate for the infringement of a right. That is, it provides a remedy for the grievance of the injured party. Following a breach of contract the question is what remedy is available to the injured party but it is not the case that every contractual dispute is resolved in court. Settling disputes through litigation is only one of the roles of contract law. Litigation is costly, time-consuming and not always the best commercial or most practical solution for the parties. Most commercial contracts are performed in a way which is satisfactory to the parties, and where there is a problem the parties are often able to negotiate a solution.

An understanding of the range of remedies available will be the background for the settlement negotiations. The innocent party will want to know what can be done when something has occurred which prevents full and proper performance of the contract.

The law of contract is almost wholly concerned with the range of remedies provided by common law, equity and statute. The courts are able to determine and declare the exact obligations of the parties, to compel the parties to perform their obligations according to the terms of the contract, or to compensate for the loss caused by non-performance or defective performance.

Types of relief

[5.40] Where the cause of complaint is that the consent of one party to the contract was obtained by duress, undue influence or unconscionable conduct, or if the party was operating under a mistake or in reliance on a misrepresentation, the remedy sought will be the rescission of the contract. This is discussed in Chapter 4. This chapter discusses the remedies directly related to breach of contract: for a discussion of the related remedies of Mareva injunctions and Anton Pillar orders, see **[18.16]** and **[14.17]**.

[5.41] Where the cause of action is breach of contract the aggrieved party, the plaintiff, seeks either:

- enforcement of the contract; that is, specific relief — orders for specific performance, injunctions to prevent breach, or rectification of the contract. Specific relief is available from equity; or,

- the substitutionary remedy of damage: see **[5.46]–[5.57]**. Damages are substitutionary in the sense that damages are monetary compensation granted by the court as a substitute for the performance of the contract. Damages are usually awarded by the courts as a common law remedy, but it is possible for equity to grant damages to the innocent party. Common law damages aim to compensate the plaintiff for the loss suffered as a result of the breach; or,

- restitution. A restitutionary remedy is one which requires the party in breach of the contract to return to the plaintiff any benefit received at the plaintiff's expense. This could include the return of money paid under the contract or payment of the value of goods transferred under the contract.

Damages as compensation for the loss resulting from the breach is the principal common law remedy for breach of contract. Once the breach of contract is proved, damages are available to the plaintiff as of right. Equity steps in only where the common law is not able to provide an adequate remedy or where the operation of the common law rules would not achieve the best justice between the parties. Therefore specific relief is available only where common law damages is not an adequate remedy. Equitable remedies are available at the discretion of the court.

Specific performance

[5.42] If one were designing a set of remedies for breach of contract then a court order that each party perform as promised would be an obvious starting point; that is, an order for *specific performance*. If one party is refusing, without justification, to perform the contract, the other party may ask for a court order that the contract be performed according to its terms. 'Complete and perfect justice to a promisee may well require that a promisor perform his promise ...': *Coulls v Bagot's Executor & Trustee Co Ltd* (1967) 119 CLR 460 at 501; 40 ALJR 471. The specific enforcement of contractual promises makes sense since the key factor in contract is the voluntary assumption of mutual legally enforceable obligations. Orders of specific performance are given in equity to fill the gap in the common law which would not make orders to compel parties to do things, such as perform contractual promises. An order for specific performance is only available where damages is an inadequate remedy. Specific performance is available not as of right but at the discretion of the courts which apply the following general principles:

- Specific performance of a contract is available only where common law damages is not an adequate remedy. This rule was first developed in relation to contracts for the sale of land and it can be readily appreciated that money will often not be satisfactory if what was wanted was a particular piece of land. Contracts for the sale of goods will not usually give rise to specific performance because substitute goods or buyers are readily available. Where the goods are especially valuable to the buyer, or not readily obtainable elsewhere, specific performance will be possible. A contract for the sale of a taxi was specifically enforced because the car itself could be easily substituted for but the taxi licence made it valuable to the buyer: *Dougan v Ley* (1946) 71 CLR 147. For a case where it was arguable that damages were not adequate but specific performance was refused see *Co-operative Insurance Society Ltd v Argyll Stores (Holding) Ltd* [1996] 3 All ER 934.

- The courts will not order specific performance of a contract for personal service, even if damages is a less than adequate remedy. This comes from the undesirability of forcing parties to maintain ongoing personal relationships against their will. Therefore the courts will not order the performance of a positive covenant in a contract — that is, a promise to perform a personal service such as play football.

- The courts will not order specific performance if the circumstances indicate that continual supervision by the court will be necessary to ensure compliance with any order to perform. Damages will be awarded instead.

- Specific performance will not be ordered unless mutuality of performance is possible. That is, the court will not order one party to specifically perform contractual obligations if it cannot ensure that the outstanding obligations of the other party will also be specifically performed.

- Specific performance will not be ordered if it would cause great hardship to the defendant. The hardship may arise from the terms of the contract or from circumstances which have arisen since formation of the contract. Mere inconvenience or financial difficulties will not be sufficient.

Injunction

[5.43] The injunction is an equitable remedy available to a person who can show that the other party is about to breach the contract. An injunction is the natural remedy for a threatened breach of contract because it is prohibitory and restrains the breach. Suppose that Athol had contracted to deliver the first of the season's cherries to Bridget for $20 per kilo (a positive covenant): these cherries are always in high demand and any fruit vendor selling them makes a good profit and obtains a high level of publicity. If Bridget learns that Charlie has persuaded Athol to sell the cherries to him for $25 per kilo, she may ask the court to restrain Athol from breaching the contract by failing to deliver the cherries.

Before an injunction will be granted the plaintiff must show that:

- a legal right of a proprietary nature, such as a contractual right has been, or is likely to be, infringed;
- the infringement is likely to continue or be repeated;
- damages is an inadequate remedy; and
- the contract is the final expression of the parties' rights.

[5.44] Specific performance and injunction may achieve the same result for the plaintiff. If Athol is restrained from delivering the cherries to anyone else but Bridget, this could have the same practical result as an order to deliver the cherries to her.

If there is a contract for personal service, such as to perform in a play, sing in a concert or play a sport for a particular club, the courts will not order specific performance of any positive covenant in the contract. So if Gary promises to play football for Hawthorn Football Club for three years, the court will not order him to perform by keeping his promise. Many contracts for personal service require the exclusive services of the performer or player and so in addition to such a positive covenant the contract will contain a negative covenant. If Gary also promises not to play football for any other club for three years, Hawthorn may obtain an injunction to restrain him playing for any other club since that would be a breach of the negative covenant.

If playing football was the only way Gary could earn a living the practical result of such an injunction would be to force him to play for Hawthorn — a de facto specific performance. Where the courts are applying the rules of equity it is possible to arrive at a remedy which, while not offending good conscience, achieves practical justice between the parties. In *Buckenara v Hawthorn Football Club Ltd* (1988) VR 39 the Victorian Supreme Court was able to reconcile the matter by granting an injunction to prevent Buckenara from playing for any football club which was in competition with Hawthorn.

Rectification

[5.45]   Rectification is also an equitable remedy often asked for in conjunction with specific performance. The jurisdiction to rectify a contract is based on the common mistake of the parties and the court must be satisfied as to three things:

- that the parties had reached a complete agreement;
- that an error was made in reducing that agreement to writing; and
- that the intention of the parties remained unchanged up to the time of reducing the agreement to writing.

In *Maralinga Pty Ltd v Major Enterprises Pty Ltd* (1973) 128 CLR 336 the High Court said that the purpose of the remedy is to make the instrument conform to the true agreement of the parties, where the writing by common mistake fails to express that agreement accurately. The court must discover the common intention and agreement of the parties, as communicated the one to the other, and rectify the contract to give effect to that common intention: see also **[4.23]**.

Damages

[5.46]   At common law any breach of contract gives rise to a right to at least nominal damages. Where actual damage is proved substantial damages may be awarded. To determine whether an award of substantial damages will be made, the court will ask:

- was there a breach? if yes,
- did the breach cause the loss complained of? and, if so,
- is this the type of loss for which damages are awarded? if yes,
- is the loss claimed not too remote from the breach?

Purpose of damages

[5.47]   The aim of common law damages is to compensate the innocent party and they are measured by reference to the loss suffered by the innocent party. In contract law damages are never punitive. The principal reason for granting damages is to put the innocent party into the position he or she would have been in had the contract been properly performed; that is, had the breach not occurred: *Robinson v Harman* (1848) 1 Ex 850.

In general the innocent party will receive as damages an amount of money equal to the value that party expected to receive on performance of the contract. So if Andrew agreed to sell a car to Bruce for $10,000 but then refused to complete the contract, and Bruce had to pay $12,000 for a similar car, Bruce will have as damages the difference between the contract price and the market price — that is, $2000.

The return of money expended in reliance on the contract may be available as damages. The effect of this will be to put the innocent party in as good a position as before the promise was made. In *McRae v Commonwealth Disposals Commission* (1950) 84 CLR 377, where there was a contract for the salvage of a oil tanker, which was not found at the place indicated by the Disposals Commission, the plaintiffs were able to recover damages for the expense incurred in fitting out a salvage expedition and searching for the tanker. In incurring this expense the plaintiffs had relied upon and acted upon the assertion of the Commission that there was a tanker in existence: see **[4.15]**.

Measure of damages

[5.48] There is no hard and fast rule for quantifying the amount of damages to be recovered, for in every case the courts must discover what is reasonable in all the circumstances to put the innocent party in the position he or she would have been in had the contract been fully performed.

- *Market value* Where the action is for delay or non-delivery, the cost to the innocent party of obtaining an alternative or substitute supply is the primary measure of damages. This means that the market of substitute goods or services at the time of the breach is the measure of damages; this may be more or less than the contract price.

- *Diminution of value* Where the value the plaintiff receives from the contract is less than that bargained or paid for the damages will usually be the difference. Alternatively the plaintiff may ask to have the deficiency cured. In some cases the cost of curing the defect will be more than the loss in value and so there will be a conflict between the parties as to whether the damages should reflect the loss in value or the cost of making good the defect so as to give the innocent party what was bargained for. In *Bellgrove v Eldridge* (1954) 90 CLR 613 a house was constructed with inadequate foundations: the house owner argued for the cost of demolishing and rebuilding the house plus consequential loss while the builder argued for the difference in value. The High Court said the owner was entitled to recover the cost of curing the defect, because this would leave her with a house in conformity with the specifications and it was a reasonable course to adopt.

Causation

[5.49] The plaintiff must show that the breach of contract by the defendant was a cause of the loss. The courts in Australia apply the 'but for' test, and ask whether the breach of contract was *a* cause of the loss suffered by the plaintiff? Would the plaintiff have suffered the loss for which damages are sought *but for* the defendant's breach of contract? It is not necessary for the breach to be the only cause or the dominant cause. This is but the first step in the determination of damages: remoteness is also examined.

The 'but for' test is explained in *Alexander v Cambridge Credit Corp Ltd* (1987) 9 NSWLR 310 where the court had to decide whether a negligent audit had caused a company to keep trading and to suffer huge losses. Glass J said (at 350):

> The common law has followed the ordinary man's notion of causation instead of the theories espoused by philosophers and scientists … in the law of contract, it is sufficient that the breach 'causally contributed' to the loss … However, whether or not a particular act or omission attracts legal liability ultimately depends on policy and not logic. Thus the common law is concerned with whether on a particular occasion a particular act or omission contributed to the occurrence of a particular event [causation] and, if so, with whether responsibility should attach to the act or omission [remoteness]. In principle, therefore, there is no reason why the legal theory of causation should be considered with any question other than whether a particular act or condition was one of the conditions or relations necessary to complete the set of conditions which represent the total cause. This is the basis of the 'but for' test of causation which is championed by many legal writers and applied in practice by courts and juries. It accords with ordinary habits of thought and speech.

Therefore the plaintiff must establish that the defendant's default caused the damage suffered — where there is more than one cause of the damage suffered it is enough to establish that the default was one cause of that damage. The test is to be applied in a practical common sense way to determine whether the evidence shows that the loss would not have been suffered but for the action of the defendant.

Heads of damage

[5.50]   The law does not compensate for every loss that can be said to flow from a breach of contract: the next step in determining whether or not a loss is recoverable is to ask whether the loss is a recognised head of damage at contract law. Contracts are mainly concerned with commercial matters — money, property and profits — and so the most obvious head of damage at contract is financial loss. The profit which the plaintiff expected to make had the contract been fully and properly performed is the principal basis of damages commonly awarded for breach of contract in the commercial arena. Certainly in the early twentieth century the view was that damages in contract should be restricted to pecuniary loss and that damages for distress, upset or discomfort, injured feelings and damage to business reputation were not available. This approach has been modified by the courts and it is now possible to be compensated for other losses apart from pure economic losses, for example:.

* *Loss of the use of money*   Loss of the use of money as a result of a breach of contract is an example of loss that was, until recently, not recoverable as damages, but the High Court has said that loss suffered as a result of being denied the use of money may be recovered. When accountants, in breach of contract, wrongly estimated their client's tax liability and overpayments were made in respect of three tax years, the plaintiffs claimed as damages the cost of borrowing money in their business. They argued that had they had the money overpaid as tax they would not have paid as high an amount of interest on loans taken in the running of their business — this was the cost of the loss of the use of the money: *Hungerfords v Walker* (1990) 171 CLR 125; 84 ALR 119.

* *Damage to business reputation*   In *Flamingo Park Pty Ltd v Dolly Dolly Creations Pty Ltd* (1986) 65 ALR 500 a company was awarded damages for loss of reputation and the resulting loss of further profit arising from a breach of contract. Flamingo Park owned the designs of fashion designer Jenny Kee and had a contract with Dolly Dolly which allowed the use of those designs; an express term of the contract prohibited the use of the design otherwise than in accordance with the instructions of Flamingo Park. This term was breached and damages awarded.

Non-economic loss resulting from a breach of contract was once excluded as a matter of public policy but the courts have recognised that, so long as the loss suffered is not too remote from the breach, it should be compensated for. For example:

* *Physical injury*   Damages were awarded to compensate for the physical injury suffered as a result of contracting dermatitis from underwear which was, as a result of being impregnated with sulphur, not fit for the purpose. This was a breach of a term implied by statute: *Grant v Australian Knitting Mills Ltd* (1936) AC 85.

* *Distress and upset*   In general the rule is that damages are not available for distress and upset resulting from a breach of contract. However, there are some contracts which are not strictly commercial and which contemplate benefiting one party by delivering some form of enjoyment, relaxation or peace of mind and these are an exception to the rule that damages are not awarded for mental distress caused by a breach of contract. In *Dillon v Baltic Shipping Co (The Mikhail Lermontov)* (1991)

22 NSWLR 1 Mrs Dillon was awarded damages for the mental distress suffered and the loss of expected enjoyment which resulted from the sinking of the cruise ship on which she was holidaying. In another case, the mother of the groom ordered two silver Rolls Royces and two silver Mercedes to take the happy couple and their families to the wedding ceremony and then to the reception. The cars did not arrive and the wedding party had to take taxis to the church — they arrived late and dishevelled, the bride's mother ripped her dress getting into the taxi. The court awarded substantial damages for loss of enjoyment as well as the cost of the torn dress and the cost of the taxis — a wedding is a once in a lifetime event, spoiled by the breach of contract: *Cole v Rama* [1993] 5 Current Law (England) Monthly Digest 114.

Remoteness

[5.51] The party in breach of contract will not be held responsible for every consequence of the breach. Losses which result from the breach of contract are not compensable if they are too remote. Once it is found that the breach caused the loss, the next question to be asked is whether the loss was a natural consequence of the breach, or reasonably within the contemplation of the parties at the time of formation of the contract. In *Reg Glass Pty Ltd v Rivers Locking Systems Pty Ltd* (1968) 120 CLR 516 the High Court said that the measure of damages for breach of a contract involved two steps: first, to determine that the loss resulted from the breach and, second, to ask whether the loss suffered was, when the contract was made, reasonably foreseeable as likely to result from such a breach. This is not the same as reasonably foreseeable in tort but a narrower test which marks the limit of liability.

[5.52] **The rule in *Hadley v Baxendale*** In *Hadley v Baxendale* (1854) 156 ER 145 the owners of a mill had given the defendant, a carrier, a broken mill shaft to carry to the maker as a model for a new one. The carrier, in breach of contract, delayed the transport of the mill shaft. The carrier knew only that the plaintiffs were the owner of a mill and that the article to be carried was a broken mill shaft. The carrier did not know that the shaft was the only one available and required to operate the mill. It was held that the plaintiffs could not recover damages for the loss of profits arising from the mill being idle as the result of the delay of the defendants. That loss of profits was too remote as being neither arising in the 'usual course of things' nor within the contemplation of the carrier at the time of the making of the contract.

There are two limbs to the test to be applied to determine whether the particular loss caused by the breach is too remote to be compensated for by an award of damages. Where two parties have made a contract which one of them has broken, the damages which the other party ought to receive in respect of such breach of contract should be:

* such as may fairly and reasonably be considered as arising naturally — that is, according to the usual course of things from such breach of contract itself; or
* such as may reasonably be supposed to have been in the contemplation of both parties, at the time they made the contract, as the probable result of the breach of it.

[5.53] In *Victoria Laundry (Windsor) Ltd v Newman Industries Ltd* [1949] 2 KB 528 the defendant had sold a boiler to the plaintiff who was a launderer and dyer. A breach of contract meant that the delivery of the boiler was delayed, and the laundry was not able to take advantage of the offer of some especially profitable contracts. The defendant knew the nature of the plaintiff's business and that it intended to put the boiler to immediate use. It was held that damages could be recovered for the loss of ordinary business profits arising from delay in delivering the boiler (these fell within the first limb of the rule in *Hadley v Baxendale*), but not for the profits arising from the expectations of specially lucrative contracts which could only be fulfilled by punctual delivery (for these fell outside the second limb of the rule in *Hadley v Baxendale*). Six propositions relating to remoteness were set out and they summarise the modern approach to the assessment of damages:

- The governing purpose of damages is to put the party whose rights have been violated in the same position, so far as money can do so, as if his or her rights had been observed.
- The aggrieved party is only entitled to recover such part of the loss actually resulting as was at the time of the contract reasonably foreseeable as liable to result from the breach.
- What was at the time reasonably so foreseeable depends on the knowledge then possessed by the parties.
- For this purpose, knowledge possessed is of two kinds: imputed or actual. Everyone, as a reasonable person, is taken to know the 'ordinary course of things' and consequently what loss is liable to result from a breach in that ordinary course.
- It is not necessary that the contract breaker should actually have asked himself or herself what loss is liable to result from a breach.
- Nor, finally, to make a particular loss recoverable, need it be proved that upon a given state of knowledge the defendant could, as a reasonable person, foresee that a breach must necessarily result in that loss.

Mitigation

[5.54]   The final question relates not to liability so much as to the amount of damages due. The plaintiff is under a duty to mitigate his or her damages. That is, when there has been a breach the innocent party cannot sit back and allow damages to build up unchecked but must take reasonable steps to avoid extra losses. There are three rules which apply to the mitigation of damages:

- The plaintiff will not be able to recover any loss which could have been avoided by the exercise of reasonable care.
- If the plaintiff takes reasonable steps to avoid loss but suffers further loss then the defendant will be liable for that further loss.
- Where the plaintiff successfully avoids loss by taking mitigating action the defendant is only liable for the reduced loss.

Only the actual loss suffered can be compensated for by an award of damages. If the plaintiff acts in a way that is more than reasonable or mitigates to the extent that no loss is suffered the defendant will not be required to pay for the avoided loss. The question of whether or not the plaintiff has acted reasonably to avoid the loss is one of fact. Where the defendant argues that the plaintiff has failed to take reasonable steps to mitigate the loss, the onus of proof lies on the defendant. In general the innocent party is required to do only what would occur in the ordinary course of business and is not expected to go to extraordinary lengths to mitigate. If the breach is the failure to deliver goods the plaintiff may be required to purchase substitute goods in the market place, but is not required to search extensively for the cheapest price.

Even though the plaintiff's action in mitigation may be reasonable, the effect may be not to minimise the loss but to increase it. The law allows the innocent party to recover the increased loss. For example, if the breach of contract resulted in the destruction of the innocent party's property — a factory — and in order to save the business and thereby mitigate the loss the plaintiff has the factory rebuilt, the damages will be the cost of rebuilding. It does not follow that the defendant will be able to decrease the amount of damages for the advantage to the innocent party which flows from now having a new or modern factory: see *Harbutt's Plasticine Ltd v Wayne Tank and Pump Co Ltd* (1970) 1 QB 447.

The date of assessment of damages

[5.55] The general rule is that damages for breach of contract are assessed as at the date of the breach. Since the time at which the damages are assessed can greatly affect the amount actually awarded, this rule is applied in a flexible way so the courts can give an injured party that amount of damages which will most fairly compensate for the wrong suffered: *Johnson v Perez* (1988) 166 CLR 351.

Penalties and liquidated damages

[5.56] Parties are often in the best position to pre-estimate the loss that will flow from a particular breach or from the breach of a particular term. When the amount to be paid in the event of certain breaches is set out in the contract this is called a liquidated damages clause. If the amount set out in the contract is a genuine pre-estimate of the loss suffered as a result of the particular breach then it will be enforceable. However, if the amount inserted is more of a deterrent against breach than a genuine pre-estimate of damages it will be seen as a penalty clause and will not be enforced. Only the actual loss sustained can be recovered. If the contract does not say what amount is to be paid for the breach then the damages are unliquidated and determined by the court applying the rules discussed above.

Some problem areas

[5.57] There will be some cases where although there is a breach of contract there will either be no loss or the damages available do not reflect the expectation interest of the aggrieved party. The explanation of these cases is beyond the scope of this book; however, they are mentioned to show the different approaches possible:

• There is breach of contract but no loss is suffered. Suppose that Xavier agrees to sell Kim, a florist, 400 roses for $3 each to be delivered before Mothers' Day, and three days before delivery is due informs Kim that since a better price is available elsewhere the roses will not be delivered. Kim has a moment of panic but, after one hour of phone calls is able to obtain substitute supplies for $3 a rose. Since there is no actual loss there is no need for damages as compensation: see *Lazenby v Wright* [1976] 1 WLR 459.

• One party has paid more than they should. What is the case when the innocent party finds that the breach of contract results in no loss in the usual sense but performance has cost more than it need have? A local council employs a company to remove rubbish from the town parks and the contract provides that 20 persons and five trucks will be supplied for this task. In breach of contract the company only supplies three trucks and 15 persons, but the rubbish is always removed satisfactorily. The council has suffered no damage from the breach, but has paid more than it need have.

• Damages reflect loss in value but are not what was expected from the contract. A mining firm agreed with the owners of Ocean Island to revegetate the mined land so that it was as near as possible in the same condition as before the mining companies operation began. When the mining company failed to undertake the replanting the owners of the island brought an action for damages for breach of contract claiming an amount of $73,000 per acre as the cost of that replanting. It was held that the cost of replanting did not represent the loss to the island's owners and that the proper measure of damages was the difference between the value of Ocean Island in its undamaged state and its damaged state. This was $75 per acre: *Tito v Wadell (No 2)* [1977] 3 All ER 129.

Restitution

[5.58]   Restitution requires the defendant to give to the plaintiff the money equivalent of any benefit which the defendant received at the plaintiff's expense. The basis of restitution is the prevention of unjust enrichment of the defendant and does not need to be based on any implied promise or quasi-contract. Where the parties are in a contract any remedy will usually be based on a claim for damages for breach of contract. However, where there is no contractual right to recover money, or obtain compensation for non-monetary benefits transferred under a contract, the principles of restitution may provide a remedy. Restitution is a developing area of law.

Restitution may provide the following remedies:

* recovery of an amount equal to any received by the defendant from the plaintiff under the contract;
* payment of an amount equal to the value of any goods or services received by the defendant from the plaintiff — *quantum meruit*.

The Builders Licensing Act 1971 (NSW) requires all contract for building work to be in writing. If they are not they are not enforceable. A builder entered into an oral contract to build a house for Mrs Paul. Mrs Paul argued that the oral contract was not enforceable and that therefore she did not have to pay for the building work. The builder claimed payment on the basis of *quantum meruit* for the value of the work. This would avoid unjust enrichment of Mrs Paul. The builder was allowed to recover a reasonable sum for the work done even though the contract was not enforceable. The High Court held that this was based on restitution or the avoidance of unjust enrichment. Monetary restitution involves the payment of a fair and just compensation for the enrichment accepted by the other party: *Pavey & Matthews Pty Ltd v Paul* (1987) 162 CLR 221.

Summary and key terms

[5.59]   This chapter has set out to explain the following:

What happens if a contract cannot be performed:

* frustration; and
* illegality.

Where non-performance is the result of the conduct of one party the law provides remedies to the innocent party:

* specific performance;
* injunction;
* rectification;
* damages; and
* restitution.

In order to award the appropriate remedy the court will be required to:
- identify the terms of the contract:
- interpret the terms:
    - exclusion clauses;
- decide whether rescission of the contract is available:
    - conditions;
    - warranties; and
    - the effect of the breach on the contract;
- determine the amount of damages, if any:
    - causation;
    - remoteness; and
    - mitigation.

6

Sale of Goods

What this chapter does ...

Sale of goods contracts are among the most common contracts in our society. Each has its own specific aspects — subject matter, price, time and place of delivery, associated warranties — but they also have a number of common aspects: an intent to pass ownership, a money consideration payable either immediately or at some future time, and a range of common understandings about what will happen if the goods prove to be defective or if the buyer fails to pay the price. Therefore, it is perhaps not surprising that sale of goods contracts are regulated not only by the general law of contract but also by a number of both state and federal statutes which, in the main, provide both greater certainty in the law and a degree of consumer protection. This chapter will deal with the provisions of the various Australian state and territory Sale of Goods Acts. Those Acts are almost identical in content (because they are all based on the United Kingdom's Sale of Goods Act 1893) and they add to — rather than replace — the general law that was dealt with in Chapters 2–5. The impact of the Trade Practices Act 1974 (Cth) and the various state and territory Fair Trading Acts is dealt with in Chapters 7 and 9.

The sale of goods contract

[6.1]   For there to be a sale of goods contract there must be:
- a contract of sale;
- of 'goods'; and
- a money consideration called the price.[1]

A contract of sale

[6.2] The term 'contract of sale' is defined to include both a *sale* and an *agreement to sell*.[2] The Act explains the difference. A 'sale' occurs when property in the goods (the ownership) is transferred to the buyer at the point of sale. With an 'agreement to sell' the transfer takes place either in the future or subject to some condition.[3]

Therefore, under an agreement to sell the buyer does not *immediately* get a full proprietary interest in the goods. An agreement to sell will become a sale when the property is finally transferred (that is, when the time stipulated has elapsed or when the condition has been satisfied).[4]

[6.3] Contracts of sale should be distinguished from a number of other, similar dealings because, while they may be similar in effect, they are not subject to the Sale of Goods Act. The dealings in question include:

- barter contracts (that is, contracts involving a pure exchange of goods);
- hire–purchase contracts (under which there is no immediate or conditional transfer of property, merely an option to buy the goods at the end of the hiring period);
- chattel mortgages, bills of sale, pledges, pawns and other forms of security (which do not involve an absolute alienation of property in the goods);
- commercial leasing agreements (where there is no transfer of property, only a transfer of possession);
- contracts for work and labour (because what you buy is the skill or expertise of the other person, not just the end product of his or her labour. Therefore, when you choose a solicitor to write you a will, or a draftsman to draw you a set of plans or an artist to paint your portrait — see *Robinson v Graves* [1935] 1 KB 579 — the contract is not a sale of goods contract, it is a contract for the provision of services); and
- contracts for the provision of services where goods may be *incidentally* supplied. For example, in *E v Australian Red Cross Society* (1991) 105 ALR 53, the plaintiff contracted AIDS from a blood transfusion and sued the Red Cross, alleging the blood had been supplied under a sale of goods contract. He failed. The contract was for the provision of hospital, medical and nursing *services*. He had been provided with goods such as food, medications, dressings and blood but they had been supplied as an incident to that contract and not under a separate sale of goods contract.

'Goods'

[6.4] Goods includes all chattels personal other than things in action and money as well as emblements and things attached to or forming part of the land which are *agreed to be severed* before sale or under the contract of sale.[5]

Chattels personal, which include both choses (things) in possession and choses (things) in action, are discussed in more detail in Chapter 13. For present purposes a chattel personal includes any property other than land and 'things in action' are intangible forms of that property. Therefore, 'goods' only include tangible property other than land — essentially everything we would regard as 'goods' in normal everyday life.

---

1. ACT s 6(1), NSW s 6(1), NT s 6(1), Qld s 4(1), SA s 1(1), Tas s 6(1), Vic s 6(1), WA s 1(1).
2. ACT s 5, NSW s 5, NT s 5, Qld s 3, SA s 60, Tas s 3, Vic s 3, WA s 60.
3. ACT s 6(3), NSW s 6(3), NT s 6(3), Qld s 4(3), SA s 1(3), Tas s 6(3), Vic s 6(3), WA s 1(3).
4. ACT s 6(4), NSW s 6(4), NT s 6(4), Qld s 4(4), SA s 1(4), Tas s 6(4), Vic s 6(4), WA s 1(4).
5. ACT s 5, NSW s 5, NT s 5, Qld s 3, SA s 60, Tas s 3, Vic s 3, WA s 60.

Money is also excluded from the definition. But that only affects money actually used as currency, whether in Australia or elsewhere. Specifically, coins or notes sold as curios or as collectors' items are not affected. Therefore, a contract to buy US dollars in preparation for an overseas trip would not be a sale of goods contract, but a contract to buy a Roman coin or a 1930 penny would be: see *Moss v Hancock* [1899] 2 QB 111.

Emblements (that is, growing crops the annual result of agricultural labour (see **[13.10]**), and things attached to or forming part of the land can be goods *if* they are severed from the land before sale or if it is agreed that they will be severed under the contract of sale. This means that 'goods' includes crops which have been or will be harvested, fixtures (see **[13.5]**–**[13.9]**) and everything else growing on or forming part of the land (such as timber — see *Ashgrove Pty Ltd v DFC of T* (1994) 124 ALR 315; 94 ATC 4,549), which will be severed under the contract. It does not, however, include the land itself. If the 'thing' is part of the land — such as gravel, clay or shale — the contract will not be a sale of goods contract, it will be a profit à prendre (that is, a right to take the soil, etc from the land) and it will not be governed by the Act.

Case Example

Morgan agreed to sell Russell & Sons a quantity of cinders and puddle slag lying on land he leased or on land from which he had a licence to remove them. Russell & Sons removed some of the material but the lessor and the licensors (the owners of the respective properties) then intervened and stopped them — on the grounds that the cinders and slag were their property and not Morgan's. Russell & Sons sued Morgan alleging (inter alia) breach of his obligations under the Sale of Goods Act. The court held that the agreement was not a sale of goods contract. The cinders and slag had become part of the land, they were not merely *things* attached to it. Therefore, they could not be goods even if they were *agreed* to be severed (although, of course, if they had already been severed they would have been 'goods' for the purposes of the Act): *Morgan v Russell & Sons* [1909] 1 KB 357. See also *Mills v Stokman* (1967) 116 CLR 61.

Classifying goods

[6.5]   The Act allows goods to be classified as:
- Future goods — 'goods to be manufactured or acquired by the seller after the making of the contract of sale';
- Specific goods — 'goods identified and agreed upon at the time a contract of sale is made';
- Existing goods — goods which are currently in existence but which are not yet necessarily the seller's property;
- Unascertained goods — goods which are to be the subject matter of the contract but which have not yet been specifically appropriated to it (that is, the specific items have not yet been identified from the whole from which they are to be drawn or have not yet been earmarked for the purchaser); and
- Ascertained goods — goods which were unascertained but which have since been identified and unconditionally appropriated to the contract.

The difference between ascertained and unascertained goods and the consequences of classifying goods as one or the other was well illustrated in *Re Wait* [1927] 1 Ch 606. In that case Wait purchased 1000 tons of wheat and resold 500 tons to a buyer who paid him in advance. Before those 500 tons were *isolated, identified and appropriated to the contract* Wait was declared bankrupt (so all of his property vested in the trustee in bankruptcy). The buyer claimed the agreed 500 tons as its true owner. The court held that, because the wheat was still unascertained, property had not passed to him. Accordingly, all he could do was to prove in Wait's bankruptcy with the other creditors.

A money consideration called the price

[6.6]   A contract will not be a contract for sale of goods unless it is supported by a money consideration called the price.[6] Money *must* be involved, as was illustrated in *Esso Petroleum Ltd v Commissioners of Customs and Excise* [1976] 1 All ER 117 in which the Commissioner attempted to levy purchase tax on 'World Cup Coins' given away with every four gallons of petrol purchased. He failed. There was no 'sale' because the consideration, buying four gallons of petrol, was not a 'money consideration'.

However, the price need not be *wholly* in money. For example, in *Commission Car Sales (Hastings) Ltd v Saul* [1957] NZLR 144 a motor car was purchased for £900 cash and a trade-in valued at £300. The transaction was a sale of goods contract.

Ascertaining the price

[6.7]   The price must be specified or, at least, be readily ascertainable or the contract will be void for uncertainty. The price can be ascertained in three ways:[7]

1. it can be fixed by the contract itself (that is, the parties can specify it in dollars and cents in their agreement);
2. it can be left to be fixed in a manner thereby agreed (as in *Foley v Classique Coaches Ltd* [1934] 2 KB 1 where the parties were to agree on the price from time to time. If they could not do so the question was to be referred to arbitration. The reference to arbitration was held to provide a sufficiently certain means of ascertaining the price and the contract was enforceable);
3. it can be determined by a course of dealing between the parties (that is, the price can be implied using the prices that the parties have used previously as a guide).

[6.8]   **Independent valuations**   Under the second of the options discussed above the parties can agree that an independent third person will set the price. If so and if the third person actually makes a determination there is no problem — the purchaser must pay and the seller must accept the amount specified. However, if the third party *cannot* or *does not* set a price then:

*   if the seller still has the goods the contract is void and, if the parties still wish to deal, they must reach a new agreement;
*   if the goods or any part of them have passed to the buyer and if the buyer has appropriated them (that is, dealt with them as if he or she owned them) the buyer must pay a reasonable price;
*   if either party prevents the third party from making a valuation he or she will be liable in damages to the other.[8]

---

6.   ACT s 6(1), NSW s 6(1), NT s 6(1), Qld s 4(1), SA s 1(1), Tas s 6(1), Vic s 6(1), WA s 6(1).
7.   ACT s 13, NSW s 13, NT s 13, Qld s 11, SA s 8, Tas s 13, Vic s 13, WA s 8.
8.   ACT s 14, NSW s 14, NT s 14, Qld s 12, SA s 9, Tas s 14, Vic s 14, WA s 9.

Form of the contract

[6.9]   In most jurisdictions there is no longer any specific format for sale of goods contracts. They are governed solely by the general law of contract and, provided the basic elements are satisfied, they will be enforceable. The Act simply provides that the contract can be in writing (either with or without seal), can be made by word of mouth, or partly in writing and partly by word of mouth or can be implied from the conduct of the parties.[9] Contracts will only be unenforceable if they have been induced by fraud, misrepresentation, duress, coercion, mistake or some other invalidating cause.

The one exception is the old Statute of Frauds requirement that contracts for more than $20 ($50 in the Northern Territory) be in writing to be enforceable (unless the doctrine of part performance applies). The requirement has been abolished in all jurisdictions except Tasmania (s 9), Western Australia (s 4) and the Northern Territory (s 9). Even in those jurisdictions the contracts are not invalid — they are just not enforceable in a court of law.

Passage of property and risk

Risk usually passes with property

[6.10]   The Act provides that, 'unless otherwise agreed', the goods remain at the seller's risk until property (ownership) is transferred to the buyer *but* that once property is transferred so too is the risk, even if the goods have not then been delivered.[10] The 'risk' referred to is the risk of *accidental* loss of, deterioration of or damage to the goods. If the loss, deterioration or damage is due to the wilful or negligent act or omission of any person that person shall, of course, be liable on normal tortious principles and, therefore, he or she 'bears the risk'.

The words, 'unless otherwise agreed' also allow the parties to alter the risk position. Such contrary agreement can occur either expressly (most commonly) or by implication.

Case Example

The seller delivered furs to the buyer 'on approval.' The furs were stolen and the seller alleged that they were at the buyer's risk — even though property had not then passed to the buyer. The court held that, because there was a long-established custom in the fur trade that goods 'on approval' were at the buyer's risk, the buyer was liable. The parties had, by their (implied) contrary agreement, overridden the general rule: *Bevington and Morris v Dale and Co Ltd* (1902) 7 Com Cas 112.

[6.11]   If delivery is delayed through the *fault* of either party the general provision ceases to have effect and the risk attaches to the party through whose fault the delay took place, at least as regards any loss which might not have occurred but for that fault. This comes about because of the first proviso in the section and it was well illustrated in *Allied Mills*

---

9.   ACT s 8, NSW s 8, NT s 8, Qld s 6, SA s 3, Tas s 8, Vic s 8, WA s 3.
10. ACT s 25, NSW s 25, NT s 25, Qld s 23, SA s 20, Tas s 25, Vic s 25, WA s 20.

Ltd v Gwydir Valley Oilseeds Pty Ltd [1978] 2 NSWLR 26. In that case the parties contracted for the sale and purchase of linseed meal. The agreement stipulated that property in the goods was to pass to the buyer on the making of the contract. The seller then deliberately and wrongfully failed to deliver the goods and they were destroyed by fire while they were still in the seller's possession. The seller was liable.

The same result can be expected if delivery is delayed through the buyer's fault though, of course, in that case the buyer will be liable. See, for example, *Demby Hamilton Ltd v Barden* [1949] WN 73, in which the buyer asked the sellers to delay delivery of a consignment of apple juice. The juice went bad. The court held that, although property had not then passed to the buyer that was only because he had asked for delivery to be postponed. Accordingly, he was liable and the seller recovered the price.

Passage of property

[6.12] Determining when property passes from the seller to the buyer is important for a number of reasons:

- risk normally passes at the same time;
- once property has passed the seller can sue for the price. Until then the seller can only sue for damages for non-acceptance: see **[6.81]–[6.85]**;
- if property (but not possession) has passed and the seller resells the goods to a third party the buyer can sue for conversion: see **[16.74]–[16.78]**. If property has not passed the buyer can only sue for damages for non-delivery: see **[6.90]**;
- once property has passed the buyer can pass good title to third parties (whether by sale or otherwise) even though the seller may still have to be paid;
- if either party becomes bankrupt the timing of passage of property may determine whether the goods belong to the non-bankrupt party or to the trustee in bankruptcy; see *Re Wait* [1927] 1 Ch 606; **[6.5]**;
- once title has passed, a breach of condition can only be treated as a breach of warranty.[11] That is, once the buyer has 'accepted the goods' (as that term is defined in the Act[12]) the contract cannot be repudiated and the goods cannot be rejected. After acceptance the buyer's only remedy is damages.

What determines when property passes will usually be the answer to the question — what did the parties' intend? That is, as with most contracts, things happen in sale of goods contracts when and if the parties intend that they happen. However, should their intention not be sufficiently clear, the Act provides a number of 'rules' to assist in determining it.

Rules for passage of property

[6.13] The threshold requirement for passage of property is that the goods must be *ascertained*. Until then (that is, until they have been specifically identified and unconditionally appropriated to the contract) property in them cannot pass to the buyer.[13]

---

11. ACT s 16(3), NSW s 16(3), NT s 16(3), Qld s 14(3), SA s 11(3), Tas s 16(3), Vic s 16(3), WA s 11(3).
12. ACT s 39, NSW s 38, NT s 38, Qld s 37, SA s 35, Tas s 40, Vic s 42, WA s 35.
13. ACT s 21, NSW s 21, NT s 21, Qld s 19, SA s 16, Tas s 21, Vic s 21, WA s 16.

Case Example

> Howlett & Son ordered 20 boxes of fish. Healy sent 190 boxes by rail, instruct-
> ing the railway to deliver 20 of them to Howlett & Son. The train was delayed
> and the fish went off before it was delivered. Howlett & Son refused to accept
> or pay for it. The court held that, because the goods were still unascertained
> when they deteriorated (the *precise* 20 boxes had not then been specifically
> identified and unconditionally appropriated to the contract), property had not
> passed and, therefore, Healy had to bear the loss: *Healy v Howlett & Sons*
> [1917] 1 KB 337.

If the goods in question are specific goods — or if they had been unascertained but have since become ascertained — property will pass when the parties intend it to pass.[14] This does little more than reiterate the rule that applies in all contracts — that what is important in determining rights and liabilities is what the parties intended. The rule for ascertaining that intention also adds little to the general law. It merely says that in ascertaining intention regard is to be had to 'the terms of the contract [and particular note should be made of any term under which the seller reserves title to the goods — as in *Aluminium Industrie Vaassen BV v Romalpa Aluminium Ltd* [1976] 2 All ER 552; [1976] 1 WLR 676 — or a right of disposal[15]], the conduct of the parties and the circumstances of the case'.[16]

[6.14]   Of more importance are the specific rules which apply 'unless a different intention appears'.[17] That is, the parties can expressly override them if they do not reflect what they want. The rules operate as follows:

- **Rule 1** — The effect of Rule 1 is that, where the contract is certain in all its terms (that is, where there is an *'unconditional* contract for the sale of *specific goods* in a *deliverable state'*), property passes *when the contract is made* — and it is immaterial whether the time of payment or the time of delivery, or both, is postponed. This accords with common sense and, in most instances, with what the parties intended, although, occasionally, it can have unfortunate consequences for the seller. See, for example *Bodilingo Pty Ltd v Webb Projects Pty Ltd* (1990) ASC ¶56–001 in which the seller agreed to sell $360,000 worth of office equipment, with the price to be paid in 10 monthly instalments each of $36,000. After five instalments had been paid the buyer defaulted and the seller tried to reclaim the equipment. It failed. The contract had been an 'unconditional contract for the sale of specific goods in a deliverable state', the sellers had not reserved title and, therefore, property had passed to the buyer.

- **Rule 2** — Rule 2 deals with the situation where, under the terms of the contract, the *seller* is bound to do something to the goods to put them in a 'deliverable state'. In that case property does not pass until that thing has been done and the buyer has notice (so that he or she knows that the goods are ready for delivery). Goods are only 'in a deliverable state' when the buyer would be bound, under the contract, to take delivery.[18] 'Deliverable state' therefore need not have its ordinary or literal meaning. The

---

14. ACT s 22(1), NSW s 22(1), NT s 22(1), Qld s 20(1), SA s 17(1), Tas s 22(1), Vic s 22(1), WA s 17(1).
15. ACT s 24, NSW s 24, NT s 24, Qld s 22, SA s 19, Tas s 24, Vic s 24, WA s 19.
16. ACT s 22(2), NSW s 22(2), NT s 22(2), Qld s 20(2), SA s 17(2), Tas s 22(2), Vic s 22(2), WA s 17(2).
17. ACT s 23, NSW s 23, NT s 23, Qld s 21, SA s 18, Tas s 23, Vic s 23, WA s 18.
18. ACT s 5(2), NSW s 5(4), NT s 5(4), Qld s 3(4), SA s 60(4), Tas s 3(4), Vic s 3(4), WA s 60(4).

criterion for deciding is, 'whether the seller has put the goods in the state *demanded by the contract*'.

> **Case Example**
>
> The parties agreed to buy and sell a horizontal condensing machine. It weighed 30 tons and was cemented to the floor of the seller's premises. The contract provided that the seller had to detach the machine *and* load it onto a railway truck. The seller made the necessary arrangements *but* the machine was badly damaged while it was being loaded. The buyer refused to take delivery and the seller sued for the price. Because the machine was not 'in a deliverable state' when it was damaged (because it had not then been loaded onto the railway truck) Rule 2 applied. Property, and therefore the risk, remained with the seller who had to bear the loss: *Underwood Ltd v Burgh Castle Brick and Cement Syndicate* [1922] 1 KB 343.

- **Rule 3** — Rule 3 merely says that where the contract is complete except that the *seller* has to weigh or do something to the goods *to determine the price*, property does not pass until the seller has done that thing *and* the buyer has notice it has been done. This rule (and Rule 2 for that matter) *only* apply when the *seller* has to do what is required. It does not apply if the buyer has to do it. See, for example, *Turley v Bates* (1863) 2 H & C 200; 159 ER 83.
- **Rule 4** — Rule 4 deals with the situations where a seller delivers goods to a buyer on approval or on a 'sale or return' arrangement. In such cases, the rule states that property will pass:
  a. when the buyer expressly or impliedly indicates that he or she has accepted the goods; or
  b. after any fixed time set by the seller has expired or, in the absence of a fixed time, after a reasonable time has expired.

For the first part of this rule *anything* done by the buyer which is inconsistent with a continuation of the seller's title is sufficient to imply acceptance. Therefore, property in the goods will pass to the buyer at that point. So, for example, in *Kirkham v Attenborough* [1897] 1 QB 201 a manufacturing jeweller sent a consignment of jewellery to Winter 'on sale or return'. Winter pledged the jewellery with a pawnbroker and disappeared. The jeweller sued the pawnbroker for return of what he alleged was still his property. The court held that when Winter pledged the jewellery he had 'adopted the transaction' within the meaning of Rule 4 (because pledging it was an act inconsistent with the plaintiff's continuing title). Accordingly, he had acquired property in the jewellery and had passed good title to the pawnbroker. The plaintiff failed.

The operation of the second part of the rule is self-explanatory and the only real question is, what is a 'reasonable time' when the seller has not specified a 'fixed time'. Reasonableness is always a question of fact and it can only be determined by looking at the particular facts of the case. See, for example, *Poole v Smith's Car Sales (Balham) Ltd* [1962] 1 WLR 744. In that case Poole had left his motor car with the defendants to sell it, on the understanding that Poole would receive £325. When the car was not sold three months later Poole demanded that the defendants return it within three days or pay him the £325. It was not returned until some weeks later and it was then in a damaged condition. Poole sued. The contract was clearly one of sale or return and, because the defendants had retained the car for more than a reasonable time (beyond the demanded return date), property in it had passed to them and they were liable for the price.

- **Rule 5** — The first part of Rule 5 essentially says that where the contract is for the sale of unascertained or future goods *by description* and either of the parties, *with the assent of the other* (which assent may be either express or implied and given either before or after the appropriation), unconditionally appropriates goods of that description to the contract, property passes to the buyer at the time of appropriation. The key is clearly the concept of appropriation and the act by which the goods have been so appropriated must be a final one. See, for example, *Carlos Federspiel & Co SA v Charles Twigg & Co Ltd* [1957] 1 Lloyd's Rep 240 in which the parties had contracted for the sale of a number of bicycles 'f.o.b. Liverpool'. The plaintiffs paid for the goods in full and the sellers made a number of preparations for shipment, even marking the boxes with the port of destination and the buyer's name. The goods were never shipped, however, because the sellers went into liquidation. The buyers claimed the goods on the grounds that they had been 'unconditionally appropriated' to the contract and that, therefore, property in them had passed under Rule 5. Their claim failed. Although preparations had been made to ship the goods, that did not amount to an 'unconditional appropriation'. The sellers could have changed their mind and used those goods for some other contract or used some other goods for this contract. Also, because it was an 'f.o.b.' contract (under which the seller bears the risk until the goods are on the ship) the parties had not intended property to pass until shipment.

However, once the goods have been irrevocably appropriated to the contract, property and risk passes to the buyer and, even if the buyer fails to take possession until some time later, he or she will still be responsible for any loss. See, for example, *Pignataro v Gilroy* [1919] 1 KB 459. The defendant agreed to sell the plaintiff 140 bags of rice which were then unascertained. After the plaintiff paid the price the defendant sent him a delivery order allowing him to collect 125 bags from the wharf and a letter saying that the remaining 15 bags were awaiting collection at the defendant's place of business. The plaintiff did nothing for about a month and when he did attempt to take delivery it was discovered that the 15 bags had been stolen. He sued and failed. In advising the plaintiff that the 15 bags were ready the defendant had unconditionally appropriated them to the contract. Hence, property (and risk) had passed to the plaintiff.

A further example of such an appropriation is given in Rule 5(2) — which provides that where a seller unconditionally delivers goods to the buyer or to a carrier for transmission to the buyer the seller is deemed to have unconditionally appropriated the goods to the contract. The reason is simple — the seller can no longer change his or her mind. The goods delivered are those that the contract will cover and the buyer therefore gets property and (usually) assumes the risk from that point.

Case Example

The plaintiffs contracted to purchase 600 cartons of frozen kidneys. When their carrier arrived to pick them up at 8.00 am, he found that they had been placed outside the defendant's cold store. The carrier handed over his delivery note and loading commenced. The loading was completed by noon (at which time some of the cartons had started to defrost). The carrier then signed for them, noting that they were in a soft condition. When the kidneys arrived at the plaintiff's premises the following day they were unfit for human consumption. The buyer claimed damages. Under Rule 5, property in the kidneys, and therefore the risk, had passed when the goods were acknowledged to be the buyer's property. That occurred when the carrier handed over the delivery note and was allowed to commence loading. Since the thawing occurred after that time the goods were at the buyer's risk and his action failed: *Wardar's (Import & Export) Co Ltd v W Norwood & Sons Ltd* [1968] 2 QB 663.

Retention of title and reservation of the right of disposal

[6.15]   The passage of property rules all become academic if the seller reserves the right of disposal. That occurs if, under the contract, the seller retains property in the goods (or the right to dispose of them) until and unless certain conditions are fulfilled. In that case, no property passes to the buyer, regardless of delivery, until the conditions that the seller has imposed are satisfied.[19] See *Aluminium Industrie Vaassen BV v Romalpa Aluminium Ltd* [1976] 2 All ER 552; [1976] 1 WLR 676 and *Chattis Nominees Pty Ltd v Norman Ross Homeworks Pty Ltd (in Liq)* (1992) 28 NSWLR 338.

Transfer of property by a non-owner

The 'nemo dat' rule

[6.16]   In general, property in goods cannot be transferred by anyone except the true owner. This is what is called the 'nemo dat' rule ('nemo dat quod non habet' — no one can give that which they do not have) — a rule which is restated in the Act[20] and which effectively prevents a non-owner from passing good title to a buyer *unless*:

- he or she sells with the true owner's authority; or
- the true owner is guilty of some form of conduct which prevents him or her from denying the seller's authority to sell.

---

19. ACT s 24(1), NSW s 24(1), NT s 24(1), Qld s 22(1), SA s 19(1), Tas s 24(1), Vic s 24(1), WA s 19(1).
20. ACT s 26(1), NSW s 26(1), NT s 26(1), Qld s 24(1), SA s 21(1), Tas s 26(1), Vic s 27, WA s 21(1).

Exceptions to the 'nemo dat' rule

Estoppel

[6.17]   If A, by words or conduct, makes B believe that something is true — and if B alters his or her position *as a result of* that induced belief — A will not subsequently be allowed to retract or deny the accuracy of B's belief if doing so would disadvantage B.

In sale of goods transactions this means that A, the true owner of goods, can be prevented from denying a seller's title (or other authority to sell), if the buyer B's belief in that title or authority was induced by A's words or conduct.

Case Example

Murphy owned a Bedford van and wanted to purchase a Chrysler sedan. He did not have the deposit so the car dealer, Coker, suggested that they tell the finance company that he, Coker, owned both vehicles and that Murphy wanted to buy them. Coker would then sell them to the finance company which would let Murphy take them both on hire–purchase. Unfortunately, the finance company only accepted the proposal for the Bedford but, instead of calling the whole deal off (as he told Murphy he had done), Coker went ahead and completed the sale of the Bedford. The finance company then signed the hire–purchase agreement and, when it did not receive the contracted instalments, tried to repossess the vehicle. Unfortunately, in the interim Murphy had sold his business, including the Bedford, to Goldring. Who had title? Because Murphy had led the finance company to believe that Coker owned the Bedford, he could not deny Coker's authority to sell it. Eastern Distributors had therefore acquired good title and were entitled to the vehicle. When Murphy had purported to sell the van to Goldring, he had no title to give: *Eastern Distributors Ltd v Goldring* [1957] 2 QB 600. See also *Big Rock Pty Ltd v Esanda Finance Corporation Ltd* (1992) 10 WAR 259.

Agency

[6.18]   If a person is appointed as an agent *for the purpose of selling* goods he or she can pass property in those goods on the principal's behalf. This rule is reflected in the words 'under the authority or with the consent of the owner' which appear in the section.

Someone who is appointed as an agent for some other purpose, even though he or she obtains possession of the goods with the principal's consent, cannot pass good title to them unless a reasonable person would believe that the agent had the principal's 'apparent authority' *to sell*.

Disposal by a mercantile agent

[6.19]   At common law mercantile agents can pass title to goods left in their possession even though the owners may not have consented to the sale. That position is preserved in the Sale of Goods Act.[21]

---

21. ACT s 26(2)(a), NSW s 26(2)(a), Qld s 24(2)(a), SA s 21(2)(a), Tas s 26(2)(a), Vic ss 26(a) and 67, WA s 21(2)(a).

A mercantile agent is defined in the Factors Act[22] as someone 'having in the customary course of his business as such agent, authority, either to sell goods or to consign goods for the purpose of sale or to buy goods or to raise money on the security of goods or of documents of title to goods'. Therefore, a mercantile agent is a person who, by the nature of his or her calling, is assumed by the world at large (and therefore also by the law), to have authority to sell and to pass good title to goods left in his or her possession. For a mercantile agent to pass good title, four conditions must be satisfied:

1. he or she must have received possession of the goods in his or her *capacity as a mercantile agent* (so, for example, if the goods were received for repair — say, in the agent's capacity as a mechanic — the agent could not pass good title if he or she sold the goods to a third party);

2. the agent must have obtained possession of the goods with the owner's consent;

3. the sale must be carried out in the ordinary course of the agent's business; and

4. the buyer must not know or suspect that the agent does not have the owner's authority to sell.

The law was well illustrated in *Folkes v King* [1923] 1 KB 282. Folkes had delivered his car to a mercantile agent to sell it for not less than £575. The agent sold it to King for £340 (though King did not know of that breach of authority), and disappeared with the money. Folkes sued for return of his car and failed. He had given the agent possession of the car for sale and, because the sale had been in the ordinary course of the agent's business, King acquired good title. Similar examples can be found in *Lowther v Harris* [1927] 1 KB 393 and *Oppenheimer v Attenborough & Son* [1908] 1 KB 221.

Sale under court order

[6.20]   If a court of competent jurisdiction orders a sale of chattels then, even though the true owner objects to (or fails or refuses to grant permission for) the sale, the buyer will still get good title. Such sales can be ordered, for instance, to satisfy a judgment debt where the debtor either has no cash resources or simply refuses to make payment. In such cases the court can authorise a bailiff to seize and sell the debtor's property under either a warrant of execution or a writ of fieri facias.[23]

Sale under a common law or statutory power

[6.21]   In certain defined cases, people in possession of goods can pass good title to them even though they do not have the owner's express authority to make the sale.[24] Situations in which property can pass under this exception include sales by 'agents of necessity' (for example, carriers in possession of perishable goods can sell them and pass good title under common law authority if the owner cannot be contacted), sales under power contained in bailment contracts, sales under one of the Acts allowing disposal of uncollected goods and sales under the pawnbroking statutes.

---

22. Factors (Mercantile Agents) Act 1923 (NSW), Goods Act 1958 (Vic) Pt II ss 65–81, Factors Act 1892 (Qld), Mercantile Law Act 1936 (SA) ss 4–12, Factors Act 1891 (Tas), Imperial Acts 5 & 6 Vict c. 39 (adopted by Act 7 Vict c. 13) (WA), Mercantile Law Act 1962 (ACT) ss 4–11, Mercantile Law Amendment Act 1861 (SA) applies in NT.
23. ACT s 30, NSW s 29, NT s 29, Qld s 28, SA s 26, Tas s 31, Vic s 82, WA s 26.
24. ACT s 26(2)(b), NSW s 26(2)(b), NT s 26(2), Qld s 24(2)(b), SA s 21(2)(b), Tas s 26(2)(b), Vic ss 26(b), WA s 21(2)(b).

Sale under a voidable title

[6.22]   If a seller has a voidable title to goods the buyer may still get good title to them in certain instances. The rule is that, if the person who could terminate the seller's voidable title has not done so *before* the seller passes it to a bona fide third party who takes the goods for value (that is, providing good consideration) and without notice of the defect in the seller's title, the third party will get good title.[25]

Case Example

A rogue, representing himself as Richard Greene, a well known actor, offered to buy the plaintiff's car, tendering a cheque in payment. The plaintiff asked for identification and was shown a pass to Pinewood Studios with the rogue's photograph on it. The cheque was subsequently dishonoured. Before that, however, the rogue sold the car to the defendant who bought it in good faith and without notice of the fraud. The plaintiff sued to recover it. He failed. The rogue's fraud meant that he had acquired a 'good but voidable' title to the car — as between himself and the plaintiff. However, the plaintiff had not disaffirmed (avoided) that title before the rogue sold the car and, consequently, the defendant had acquired 'good title' to it: *Lewis v Averay* [1971] 3 All ER 907.

Note, however, that if a seller has a voidable title and if the true owner *does* take steps to avoid the contract under which it was obtained then, *thereafter*, the seller's title is *void* and he or she cannot pass property in the goods. See, for example, *Car and Universal Finance Co Ltd v Caldwell* [1965] 1 QB 525 in which the car was not on-sold until *after* the cheque that had been given in payment for it was dishonoured and Caldwell had initiated steps to recover the vehicle. The court held that the rogue's 'good but voidable' title had come to an end so that, when he sold the car to the defendant finance company, he had no title to give. Caldwell recovered his car.

Disposition by a seller in possession

[6.23]   If a buyer leaves goods in the seller's possession and if the seller resells them, logic suggests that the original buyer should bear any resulting loss. After all, he or she could have prevented the second sale by simply taking the goods at the time of his or her purchase and the innocent second buyer should not be made to suffer. The Act provides for precisely that outcome — with some limitations.[26]

What it does is to protect a second buyer *provided* he or she buys the goods in good faith and without notice of the previous sale and also takes delivery of them. The result is that the original buyer runs the risk of losing title if, having bought goods, he or she then leaves them with the seller. If the seller sells them again the second buyer gets good title and the original buyer can only sue the seller in conversion.

---

25. ACT s 27, NSW s 27, NT s 27, Qld s 25, SA s 23, Tas s 28, Vic s 29, WA s 23.
26. ACT s 29(1), NSW s 28(1), NT s 28(1), Qld s 27(1), SA s 25(1), Tas s 30(1), Vic s 30, WA s 25(1).

Case Example

Motordom, a firm of car dealers, financed its stock through a 'floor plan' arrangement with Motor Credits Ltd. Motordom bought cars, 'resold' them to Motor Credits for 90 per cent of cost, but kept them on the shop floor with authority to sell them to the public. When a sale took place Motordom paid Motor Credits the 90 per cent plus interest. Motordom got into financial difficulties and Motor Credits withdrew its blanket authority to sell cars under the arrangement. Despite this, Motordom sold 16 of the cars to Pacific Motor Auctions. Which company had title? The court held that, because Motordom had been the 'seller' of the cars to Motor Credits, because it had 'continued in possession' of them after sale and because Pacific Motor Auctions had bought them in good faith and without notice of the previous sale, Pacific Motor Auctions had acquired good title. Motor Credits Ltd could only sue Motordom in conversion: *Pacific Motor Auctions Pty Ltd v Motor Credits (Hire Finance) Ltd* (1965) 112 CLR 192; [1965] AC 867.

Disposition by a buyer in possession

[6.24]   A seller who gives the buyer possession of goods (or the documents of title to goods) before the sale is finalised (usually by payment of the price) is in precisely the same position as a buyer who leaves goods with the seller after sale. That is, he or she bears the risk if the buyer resells them.[27] See *Gamer's Motor Centre (Newcastle) Pty Ltd v Natwest Wholesale Australia Pty Ltd* (1987) 163 CLR 236.

The major difference between the two situations is that a buyer in possession can only give as good a title as a mercantile agent in possession of the goods could give. Therefore, the third party must be able to show that the buyer in possession obtained the goods in his or her capacity as buyer, that the goods were obtained with the owner's consent, that the sale to the third party was carried out in the ordinary way and that he or she was unaware that the goods were being sold without the true owner's authority.

Sale in a 'market overt'

[6.25]   A 'market overt' is literally an open market and the expression is used to denote recognised markets in which goods are openly displayed for sale. A buyer who buys goods in a market overt acquires good title to them provided he or she buys them in good faith and without notice of the seller's lack of title, they were bought from an open display, the display was of items in which the seller professed to trade and the sale occurred during normal trading hours and in the ordinary course of the seller's business.

The whole idea behind the market overt rule was that if someone sells goods which are not his or her property, the true owner has ample opportunity to find them and retake possession because they are on open display. If the true owner does not do so, third party buyers can acquire good title. In reality it was simply a matter of deciding which of two innocent parties should bear the loss — the original owner (who could have recovered the goods but did not bother) or the third party who had no real means of knowing whether the seller owned the goods. Even then the third party buyer does not get good

---

27. ACT s 29(2), NSW s 28(2), NT s 28(2), Qld s 27(2), SA s 25(2), Tas s 30(2), Vic s 31, WA s 25(2).

title in two instances — when the goods are Crown property, in which case they revert to the Crown and (except in Victoria) if the goods were stolen *and* the true owner has successfully prosecuted the thief to conviction. In that case the property reverts to the true owner and the buyer can only sue the seller.[28]

The concept of the 'market overt' does not apply in Queensland, New South Wales, the Australian Capital Territory or the Northern Territory although it still exists in Victoria (s 28), South Australia (s 22), Western Australia (s 22) and Tasmania (s 22).

Terms of the contract

[6.26]   As with terms in all contracts, the terms of a sale of goods contract can be express or implied. Express terms are those which the parties expressly agree upon and include in their agreement. Implied terms are those which, although not expressly included, were intended by the parties to form part of their contract. Terms may be implied through a particular trade usage or industry custom, through statute or purely because the circumstances of the agreement make it clear that the parties intended to include the term but omitted it through inadvertence, sloppy drafting or some other cause.

Classifying terms

[6.27]   In most cases the terms of a sale of goods contract will be classified as either conditions or warranties. Conditions are terms which go to the root of the contract and a term will be a condition if its non-performance would render the contract *substantially* different from what the parties agreed. Warranties are lesser terms. They are contractual stipulations which do not go to root of the contract. Consequently, while non-performance of a warranty will render the contract different, it does *not* render it *substantially* different. Both parties still get basically what they contracted for. The term 'warranty' is defined in the Act as 'an agreement with reference to goods which are the subject of a contract of sale but collateral to the main purpose of such contract, the breach of which gives rise to a claim for damages but not to a right to reject the goods and treat the contract as repudiated'.[29]

Remedies for breach

[6.28]   As in the general law of contract, a breach of condition in a sale of goods contract entitles the innocent party to elect either to treat the contract as at an end and sue for damages or continue with it and treat the breach simply as a breach of warranty. For breaches of warranty the innocent party can only sue for damages.

Terms and the Sale of Goods Act

[6.29]   The Act essentially restates the common law.[30] It provides that whether a term is a condition or a warranty depends on both the circumstances of the case and the

---

28. ACT s 28(1), Qld s 26(1), SA s 24(1), Tas s 29(1), WA s 24(1).
29. ACT s 5(1), NSW s 5(1), NT s 5(1), Qld s 3(1), SA s 60(1), Tas s 3(1), Vic s 3(1), WA s 60(1).
30. ACT s 16, NSW s 16, NT s 16, Qld s 14, SA s 11, Tas s 16, Vic s 16, WA s 11.

construction of the contract and it acknowledges that a stipulation can be a condition even though the contract calls it a warranty.

The Act also preserves the buyer's right to treat any breach of condition as a mere breach of warranty, to sue for damages and to continue with the contract. Alternatively, the buyer can just ignore the breach altogether ('waive the condition') and recover nothing at all.

The Act also preserves the law with respect to 'frustration of contracts'. If performance becomes impossible (or is otherwise excused by law), the Act prevents an action being taken under the Sale of Goods Act where it would not succeed under the common law. Accordingly, both parties escape further liability under the contract.

There is, however, some departure from the common law in that the Act specifies *two* instances in which a breach of condition *must* be treated as a breach of warranty *unless* the parties, expressly or impliedly, agree otherwise.[31] The two instances are:

1. where the contract is *not severable* and the buyer has *accepted* the goods or any part of them. (The Act says: 'the buyer is deemed to have *accepted* the goods when the buyer intimates to the seller that the buyer has accepted them, or when the goods have been delivered to the buyer, and the buyer does any act in relation to them which is inconsistent with the ownership of the seller, or when after the lapse of a reasonable time, the buyer retains the goods without intimating to the seller that the buyer has rejected them'[32]); and

2. (except in NSW, SA and the ACT where the right has been repealed) where the contract is for the sale of specific goods and property in those goods has passed to the buyer.

In neither case is the buyer entitled to reject the goods and treat the contract as repudiated. He or she can only *recover damages*. However, a condition does not lose its character as a condition just because the Act requires that it be treated as a warranty. It will still be a condition for all other purposes (for example, for construction of exemption clauses and determination of their effect).

Implied terms under the Sale of Goods Act

[6.30] The Act implies certain terms into all sale of goods contracts unless they are lawfully excluded. The terms in question relate to title, correspondence with description, fitness for purpose, merchantability and correspondence with sample.

Implied undertakings as to title

[6.31] The Act provides that unless the circumstances of the contract are such as to show a contrary intention the following terms will be implied into every contract of sale:[33]

- an implied *condition* on the part of the seller that he or she has the right to sell the goods or will have that right at the time that property is to pass;
- an implied *warranty* that the buyer shall have and enjoy quiet possession of the goods after sale; and
- an implied *warranty* that the goods shall be free from any charge or encumbrance in favour of any third party, not declared or known to the buyer before or at the time the contract is made.

---

31. See note 11 above.
32. ACT s 39, NSW s 38, NT s 38, Qld s 37, SA s 35, Tas s 40, Vic s 42, WA s 35.
33. ACT s 17, NSW s 17, NT s 17, Qld s 15, SA s 12, Tas s 17, Vic s 17, WA s 12.

Seller's right to sell

[6.32]   The seller's ability and right to sell the goods is clearly central to the whole contract. Passage of property is the essence of the agreement and the seller must be able to pass title when it is required to pass. If the seller cannot pass title the buyer should be able to treat the contract as at an end and this is the effect of the implied condition.

Case Example

Rowland bought a motor car from Divall, used it for four months and then (when the police took it away) discovered that it had been stolen when he bought it. Neither party had been aware of that when the car was sold. Rowland sued to recover the price. Divall countered arguing that an allowance had to be made for the fact that Rowland had used the car for four months. He also argued that, because Rowland had used the car, he had 'accepted' it within the meaning of the Act and therefore had to treat the breach of the *implied condition* as a breach of warranty — so he was only entitled to damages and not a refund of the price. Both arguments failed. The Court of Appeal held that Rowland had paid for property in the vehicle but had not received it. Therefore there was nothing for him to 'accept' and the Act could not apply. Consequently, he was entitled to a full refund. The fact that he had used the car for four months was irrelevant: *Rowland v Divall* [1923] 2 KB 500.

[6.33]   Feeding title   If the seller does not have the right to sell the goods when property is supposed to pass *but* acquires title subsequently (and *before* the buyer repudiates the contract), title can pass *through* the seller to the buyer and the buyer, having then received title, loses the right to terminate the contract and can only sue for damages. The process is called '*feeding title*'.

Case Example

Ingeborg Persch agreed to buy a car from CAGA Ltd on hire–purchase. She then unlawfully sold it to Clinton Motors and, eventually, the defendants bought it. They sold it to Patten. At that point, CAGA still had title. Two months *after* Patten bought the car, Persch paid CAGA out using money borrowed from Deposit and Investment Co Ltd. She therefore acquired title. The loan with Deposit and Investment was secured by a bill of sale over (inter alia) the car. Two years later Persch defaulted on her payments and Deposit and Investment located and 'repossessed' the car from Patten. Patten sued Thomas Motors for breach of the implied condition as to title. He failed. While Thomas Motors was technically in breach (because it did not have title at the point of sale) it had 'fed title' before Patten repudiated the contract. Persch had perfected her title when she paid CAGA out; that title had then passed immediately down the line of purchasers to Patten. That happened two years before he purported to repudiate. Therefore, the repudiation was ineffective. He had received good title — belated but still good: *Patten v Thomas Motors Pty Ltd* [1965] NSWR 1457.

Title cannot be fed after repudiation. Once a buyer repudiates a contract for breach of the implied condition *nothing* the seller *then* does to perfect title can affect the buyer's right to recover the purchase price. See, for example, *Butterworth v Kingsway Motors Ltd* [1954] 2 All ER 694. In that case Butterworth had purchased a car from Kingsway Motors which, unknown to either party, was still under hire–purchase to a Miss Rudolph. She had sold it, mistakenly believing that she could do so provided she kept up the payments. Nearly a year later the hire–purchase company (the true owner) wrote to Butterworth demanding the car's return. He immediately wrote to Kingsway Motors Ltd demanding repayment of the price. About a week later Miss Rudolph paid the last instalment of the hire–purchase contract and acquired title. Kingsway Motors used this to deny liability arguing that title had been 'fed'. It failed. Butterworth had repudiated the contract before title had been fed and he was, therefore, entitled to a full refund.

[6.34]   'Right to sell' is not co-extensive with 'ownership'   A seller can be in breach of the 'right to sell' condition even though good title can and does pass to the buyer. There may be other limitations on his or her 'right to sell'. In *Niblett Ltd v Confectioners' Materials Co Ltd* [1921] 3 KB 387, for example, the contract was for the sale and purchase of a consignment of imported tinned milk. The wrappings on some of the tins bore the word 'Nissly' which infringed the trademark of the Nestle company. The buyers were forced to remove the offending labels which, of course, reduced the milk's sale value. They sued and succeeded. The sellers had not had the right to sell the goods *in the state* in which they were supplied.

[6.35]   What can be recovered?   If the seller does not have the 'right to sell' the goods (for whatever reason), the buyer can recover both the price and damages for any money properly and reasonably expended on the goods while they were in his or her possession. What is 'proper and reasonable expenditure' depends on the circumstances of each case. For example, in *Mason v Burningham* [1949] 2 KB 545 the plaintiff had bought a typewriter for £20 and had then spend £11/10/- having it repaired. The machine had been stolen and, when the plaintiff was forced to return it, she sued for and recovered the full £31/10/-. The additional expenditure on repairs was both natural and foreseeable and it was, therefore, recoverable.

Quiet possession

[6.36]   The implied warranty of quiet possession protects the buyer's right to possess, use and enjoy the goods without any *lawful* interruption to or disturbance of that possession by or on behalf of the seller. In other words the seller is warranting that, once the goods have been bought, no-one will be *lawfully entitled* to interfere with them, to prevent the buyer using them or to dispute the buyer's title to them.

Case Example

The defendants bought three road-marking machines which, it was later alleged, infringed a patent held by Prismo Universal Ltd. (Prismo had applied for but had not been granted the patent when the sale took place but neither party had known about it.) When the patent was eventually granted Prismo claimed that the defendants had breached it. The buyers refused to pay any further instalments of the purchase price and, when the sellers sued them, they argued that Prismo's claim constituted a breach of the implied warranty of quiet possession.

> They succeeded. The implied warranty of quiet possession extended to any interference with the buyer's possession, whether potentially existing at the time of contract or only becoming apparent later: *Microbeads AG v Vinhurst Road Markings Ltd* [1975] 1 WLR 218.

Freedom from unnotified encumbrance

[6.37]   An owner of goods can always pledge them as security for loans or debts and the resulting encumbrances are not always registered. In such cases, unless the seller specifically brings the encumbrances to the buyer's attention, the buyer may not discover they exist until he or she is confronted by a third party demanding possession. (See, for example, *Patten v Thomas Motors Pty Ltd* [1965] NSWR 1457; **[6.33]**.) In such cases the implied warranty that the goods will be free from any charge or encumbrance will allow the buyer to seek damages from the seller.

Implied conditions in a 'sale by description'

[6.38]   The Act implies into every contract of sale of goods by description a condition that the goods, when delivered, shall correspond with that description.[34] If they do not, the buyer can repudiate the contract and reject them. The term 'sale by description' covers:

- all agreements to sell unascertained goods (for example, 'I will sell you a dozen bottles of scotch'). This is because, being unascertained, the goods can *only* be sold by description — there is no specific (ascertained) item which has been identified and appropriated to the contract at that point;

- all contracts for the sale of specific goods *if* the buyer has not seen them and is relying on the seller's description. If the goods delivered do not conform with that description the buyer can reject them — because they are not what he or she agreed to buy. For example in *Varley v Whipp* [1900] 1 QB 513 Whipp described a reaping machine as 'new last year'. He also said that it had only been used to cut 50 or 60 acres. Varley, who had not seen the machine, agreed to buy it. The machine was in fact much older and in far worse condition than had been described. Varley refused to accept it and Whipp sued. He failed. While the goods were specific goods, Varley had not seen them and had relied on Whipp's description. Therefore the sale was a sale by description and, because the goods did not correspond with their description, Varley could reject them;

- any sale of specific goods which the buyer has seen — provided the goods are sold not as specific goods but as *goods answering a description*. This covers two cases:
  a. where the buyer relies on the seller's (express or implied) description of the goods to ensure that they are what he or she wants. For example, in *Elder Smith Goldsbrough Mort Ltd v McBride* [1976] 2 NSWLR 631 the plaintiffs bought a bull at a 'stud auction'. The bull proved to be infertile and they sued. They succeeded. Even though the sale was of 'specific goods' it was, in the circumstances, also a sale by description. The characteristic described — fertility — was not readily discoverable at the time of sale and the buyers had relied on the seller's description; and

---

34. ACT s 18, NSW s 18, NT s 18, Qld s 16, SA s 13, Tas s 18, Vic s 18, WA s 13.

b. where the goods 'describe themselves' (that is, where the buyer can show that the goods were bought not because he or she wanted the specific items actually purchased — just goods answering their description). For example, in *Beale v Taylor* [1967] 3 All ER 253, Beale bought a car described as a 1961 Herald Convertible. He had inspected it, it had appeared to be a 1961 model but he later discovered that it was in fact the back half of a 1961 model welded to the front half of an earlier model. He sued and succeeded. Even though the sale had been of specific goods (the car he inspected) he *had* relied on the seller's description of it as a 1961 model and, therefore, the sale was a sale by description.

Wide interpretation

[6.39]   The term 'description' has a very wide meaning. It covers not only the description of the specific good itself but also of any peripheral matters (such as ingredients, quantities, packaging or date of consignment) or anything else which might assist in identifying the goods.

Strict liability for breach

[6.40]   Because compliance with description is a 'condition' of the contract, any breach (other than the most absolutely trifling) will allow the buyer to reject the goods and treat the contract as at an end. If the buyer suffers loss as a result of the seller's breach he or she can also sue for damages. The breach need not even be one that adversely affects the goods' fitness for purpose or merchantability (or indeed any other *major* characteristic).

Case Example

Moore & Co Ltd agreed to sell Landauer & Co 3100 cases of canned fruit in boxes each containing thirty 2½lb tins. When the consignment was delivered about half the boxes contained 30 tins, the remainder contained only 24 tins but, overall, the agreed *quantity* was supplied. The buyers refused to accept delivery on a number of grounds — including that the goods, as delivered, did not comply with the contract description. The court held that the contract was a sale of goods by description. Part of that description was the method of packing and the goods supplied did not correspond, at least in part, with it. Therefore, the buyers could reject the entire consignment. It was immaterial that the buyer suffered no actual damage or that the default was merely technical: *Re Moore & Co Ltd and Landauer & Co* [1921] 2 KB 519.

Escaping strict liability

[6.41]   There are at least three ways a seller can escape strict liability:

* *By specific provision*   The parties can always allow a margin for error by inserting appropriate words into the contract. By adding works such as 'a little more or less' the seller may avoid the strictness with which the requirement is enforced. What margin will be allowed will always have to be determined on the facts of each case.
* *Implied terms*   If the trade or industry in which the parties are involved traditionally conducts its dealings in accordance with some unspoken but well-known custom or practice permitting a margin of variation, the correspondence with description

provision will be construed and applied in the light of that custom or practice. However, just as an express term may provide for a margin so too can an express term override an otherwise applicable trade usage or custom. That happened in *Summers v Commonwealth* (1918) 25 CLR 144 where an express stipulation that the marble supplied had to be of a specified size was held to override an industry practice which permitted delivery of blocks which could be *cut down* to produce blocks of the required size.

- *De minimis*   The rigidity with which the provision is construed does not extend to absurd limits. If the breach is so trifling that a reasonable person would disregard it the courts will disregard it too. The reason can be found in the maxim 'de minimis non curat lex' (the law does not concern itself with trifles) the operation of which was illustrated in *Shipton, Anderson & Co v Weil Bros & Co* [1912] 1 KB 574. In that case the sellers had contracted to sell 4500 tons of wheat 'two percent more or less' with an option to tender another eight per cent if they wished. Consequently, they could have supplied a maximum of 4950 tons. They actually delivered 4950 tons 55 lb and, even though they only charged for 4950 tons, the buyers purported to reject the whole consignment. The court held that they could not do so. The difference in weight was so trivial it was insignificant when taken against the consignment as a whole.

The implied conditions of quality and fitness

[6.42]   The onus of ensuring that goods are fit for a particular purpose normally rests with the buyer. The buyer must ascertain *before sale* whether the goods suit his or her needs and if it subsequently turns out that they do not then (barring actions in mistake, misrepresentation, duress, undue influence or unconscionability) he or she is stuck with them. This is simply an application of the 'caveat emptor' (let the buyer beware) rule and it has been carried into the Sale of Goods Act in the opening words of the quality and fitness provision:

> Subject to the provisions of this Act ... there is *no* implied warranty or condition as to the quality or fitness for any particular purpose of goods supplied under a contract of sale, *except as follows*.[35]

The exceptions in the remainder of the section provide protection for a buyer who chooses goods, not in reliance on his or her own skill and judgment, but by relying on the seller in circumstances where it is reasonable to do so. In such cases the section provides implied *conditions* of fitness for purpose[36] and merchantability.[37]

If either (or both) of those implied conditions apply to a particular contract (on the tests set out), they apply to *all* goods *supplied* and not merely those that should have been supplied. That is, the reference to 'goods supplied under a contract of sale' extends the protection. Therefore, if the goods which have to be supplied under the contract are fit for purpose and of merchantable quality but if something supplied with them is not, the buyer can reject the *whole* consignment or, if it has been accepted, can sue for damages.

---

35. ACT s 19, NSW s 19, NT s 19, Qld s 17, SA s 14, Tas s 19, Vic s 19, WA s 14.
36. ACT s 19(2) and (3), NSW s 19(a), NT s 19(a), Qld s 17(a) and (b), SA s 14(I), Tas s 19(a), Vic s 19(a), WA s 14(I).
37. ACT s 19(4), NSW s 19(b), NT s 19(b), Qld s 17(c) and (d), SA s 14(II), Tas s 19(b), Vic s 19(b), WA s 14(II).

Case Example

Mrs Wilson ordered a ton of 'Coalite' from her local coal merchants. Unknown to either party a detonator was mixed in with the delivery and, when it was placed in the fireplace as part of the fuel, it exploded. Mrs Wilson sued, alleging breach of the condition of merchantable quality. The defendants argued that the subject matter of the contract was just the Coalite and that, therefore, only the Coalite was covered by the implied condition. The sellers were liable. The implied condition covered everything actually *supplied* under the contract and, as it (as a whole) was not fit for burning, it was not of merchantable quality: *Wilson v Rickett Cockerell & Co Ltd* [1954] 1 QB 598.

The extension of the implied conditions to all goods actually supplied also allows a buyer to take action if the *container* is defective or dangerous. For example, in *Morelli v Fitch and Gibbons* [1928] 2 KB 636 Morelli was injured when a bottle of 'Stone's Ginger Wine' broke as he opened it. The bottle had been defective. He sued and succeeded. The bottle was clearly not of merchantable quality and, therefore, the 'goods supplied' had not been merchantable.

Nor need there be an actual passage of property — all that is required is passage of possession. For example, in *Geddling v Marsh* [1920] 1 KB 668 Marsh purchased mineral water in bottles with an inscription stating that they remained the manufacturer's property at all times. A bottle exploded, Marsh was injured and she sued. Geddling argued that, as the bottle remained his property, he could not be liable for breach of an implied condition of a contract of *sale*. He was liable. Marsh had bought the mineral water and the bottle had been 'supplied' under that contract. The bottle was unmerchantable and the seller was therefore liable.

Fitness for purpose

[6.43]   The implied condition of fitness for purpose applies when a *knowledgeable* seller warrants the suitability of a product for a buyer's purpose in circumstances showing that the buyer will rely and act upon the seller's advice. There are four required elements:

1. the buyer must make known to the seller the *particular purpose* for which the goods are required;
2. he or she must do so in circumstances showing that he or she *relies on the seller's skill and judgment*;
3. the goods must be of a *description* which it is in the seller's course of business to supply (whether as manufacturer or not); and
4. the sale must not be of a *specified* article under its *patent or trade name*.

If all four elements are present there will be an implied condition that the goods will be fit for the buyer's specified purpose.

Making the purpose known

[6.44]   The buyer can make his or her purpose known either expressly or by implication. Where the purpose is obvious express mention is not needed — it is taken as read. If the goods are not fit for that obvious purpose the seller will be liable.

Case Example

The plaintiff went into the defendant's chemist shop to buy a hot water bottle — something which the chemist sold in the ordinary course of his business. The chemist offered him a rubber model, the plaintiff bought it but the fifth time he used it, it burst and scalded his wife. The plaintiff sued. The chemist argued that he could not be liable because the plaintiff had not made his particular purpose known to him. The court held that, while some goods may have a number of uses, hot water bottles are not among them. The plaintiff had used the hot water bottle for its usual and obvious purpose and, by asking for a hot water bottle, he had put the chemist on notice as to the purpose for which it was to be used. The plaintiff's action succeeded: *Priest v Last* [1903] 2 KB 148. See also *Wallis v Russell* [1902] 2 IR 585 in which the court held that crabs had only one obvious purpose — to be eaten — and if they were 'off' they were not 'fit for purpose'.

A number of 'rules' can be deduced from cases such as these. They include:

- where the buyer's purpose is *obvious,* merely asking for the good is sufficient notification of the purpose for which it is to be used;
- if the goods can be used for several purposes the fitness for purpose condition will only be implied into the contract if the buyer has indicated the purpose or purposes for which they will actually be used; and
- if the buyer has some special condition (medical or otherwise), or if there are circumstances which might affect the fitness of the item for *that* buyer's particular purpose, the buyer must make that condition or those circumstances known to the seller before the condition will be implied. For example, in *Griffiths v Peter Conway Ltd* [1939] 1 All ER 685 the plaintiff (who had an unusually sensitive skin but did not make that fact known to the defendant), purchased a tweed coat. She contracted dermatitis and sued alleging breach of the implied condition of fitness for purpose. She failed. She had not made her 'particular purpose' (wear by an 'abnormal' buyer) known and, therefore, the defendant had had no grounds to suspect that the coat might be unsuitable.

Showing reliance on the seller's skill and judgment

[6.45] The courts have interpreted this requirement fairly liberally. Generally, anything which tends to indicate to the seller that the buyer will rely on his or her skill or judgment will be sufficient. Lord Wright summarised the courts' general attitude in *Grant v Australian Knitting Mills Ltd* [1936] AC 85. He said (at 99):

> It is clear that the reliance must be brought home to the mind of the seller, expressly or by implication. The reliance will seldom be express: it will usually arise by implication from the circumstances: thus to take a case like that in question, of a purchase from a retailer, the reliance will be in general inferred from the fact that a buyer goes to the shop in the confidence that the tradesman has selected his stock with skill and judgement.

[6.46] **Reliance and inherently dangerous goods** The courts seem to have been particularly willing to find the necessary reliance where the goods turn out to have been inherently dangerous or harmful. That is, the courts have been very ready to find that buyers rely on the seller's skill and judgment *not* to sell anything which might cause unwarned-of harm. See, for example, *Grant v Australian Knitting Mills Ltd* (where the sulphite residue in the underpants was not readily detectable) and *Vacwell Engineering Co Ltd v BDH Chemicals Ltd* [1971] 1 QB 88 where a chemical dropped into a sink by one of the plaintiff's employees caused an explosion when it came into contact with water. The plaintiffs sued (inter alia) for breach of the implied condition of fitness for purpose. The defendants argued that they had studied the current texts and other available literature before they put the chemical on the market and had found no mention of its explosive properties. Only subsequently did they discover that earlier textbooks had pointed out the danger. They were still held liable. The plaintiffs had relied on the defendants to warn them of any likely hazards and they had failed to do so.

However, sellers are not under a duty to warn buyers of hazards which should be obvious to a reasonable person. The duty only applies to hazards that are not obvious. For example, in *Todman v Victa Ltd* [1982] VR 849 Todman was injured by something thrown out by the blades of his motor mower. He sued for breach of the implied condition and failed. He should have known that mowers throw out objects over which they pass and, therefore, he could not complain that Victa had not taken special care for his safety.

[6.47]   Partial reliance   Even if the buyer only relies partially on the seller's skill and judgment (perhaps using his or her own knowledge and expertise as well), damages can be recovered if loss occurs — *unless* the defect (and the loss) falls outside the scope of the reliance. The principle was well illustrated in *Christopher Hill Ltd v Ashington Piggeries Ltd* [1972] AC 441 where the defendants were asked to make up food for the plaintiff's mink. The defendants had made up animal foodstuffs generally but they had never before made up food for mink. Knowing this, the plaintiffs gave them a formula. Clearly, there was a split in reliance. The buyers relied on the seller's skill and judgment to ensure that the food was fit for animals generally but they used their own knowledge and expertise to ensure that the food was fit for mink. The food was poisonous, the mink became ill and many died. The plaintiffs sued for breach of (inter alia) the implied condition of fitness for purpose. They succeeded. Although they had not relied on the defendant's skill and judgement with respect to the precise formula, they had relied on them to select proper ingredients of suitable quality. The defendants had not done so. The defect, therefore, fell within the scope of the plaintiff's reliance and the defendants were liable.

Goods of a description which it is in the seller's business to supply

[6.48]   This third required element will be satisfied if the plaintiff proves that the goods supplied belong to the *class* of goods usually sold by that seller; the seller need not actually sell the *particular* goods in question.

Case Example

The sellers dealt in resins, gums and other adhesive substances and they supplied the buyers with glue to manufacture flypaper. It was unsatisfactory and the buyers sued. The defendants argued that they could not be liable because they had never previously supplied that *particular* sort of adhesive and that, therefore, the goods were not 'of a description which it is in the course of the seller's business to supply'. They were liable. The glue came within the *general class* of goods (glue and adhesives) which they sold in the course of their business and they were, therefore, caught by the section: *Spencer Trading Co Ltd v Devon* [1947] 1 All ER 284.

[6.49]   Whether the seller is the manufacturer or not   Retailers cannot escape liability simply because they do not manufacture the goods they sell. For buyers the exclusion of this defence is important for at least two reasons:

- the privity of contract reason. Buyers invariably contract with the retailer not with the manufacturer and, therefore, they would normally have no general contractual remedy against the manufacturer; and
- the manufacturer may not be suable — because of insolvency, overseas domicile or other reason.

The importance of the provision, especially as it relates to latent defects, was well illustrated in *Crotty v Woolworths Ltd* (1943) 43 SR (NSW) 133. Crotty purchased a light bulb from Woolworths. He took it home, fitted it to a socket on the end of an extension cord and hung it in the garage to provide light while he worked on his car. The bulb was defective, it touched and electrified the car's engine and the shock killed him. His mother sued alleging (inter alia) that, in supplying a defective bulb, Woolworths had breached the implied condition of fitness for purpose. The court held that the implied condition had been breached and that Woolworths was liable — even though it was not the manufacturer.

The sale must not be of a specified article under its patent or trade name

[6.50]   This fourth element has also been generously construed in favour of the buyer. A buyer will not be held to have bought an item under its patent or trade name unless the patent or trade name has made such an impression upon his or her mind that the goods are bought because of that impression and not because of anything that the seller says or does. In other words, if there is *any* reliance on the seller's skill and judgment the proviso does not affect the seller's liability.

Case Example

Alexander sold Berliet trucks. Criss was setting up a carrying business and told Alexander that he wanted a truck that could carry five tons and 'hold its own with any other lorry on the road'. Alexander outlined the Berliet's capabilities and Criss agreed to purchase 'a five ton Berliet lorry'. It proved unsatisfactory and Criss sued claiming breach of the implied condition of fitness for purpose. Alexander argued that, because Criss had asked for a Berliet lorry by name, the case came within the proviso and that there was no implied condition as to the lorry's fitness for any particular purpose. The court held that the mere fact that Criss had asked for a Berliet lorry did not automatically invoke the proviso or exclude the implied condition. What had to be determined was whether he had asked for it in a way that showed he made his decision independently or whether he had relied on Alexander's skill and judgment. On the facts it was held that Criss had indeed relied on Alexander's judgment as to the sufficiency of the truck for his purposes and his action succeeded: *Criss v Alexander (No 2)* (1928) 28 SR (NSW) 587.

If all four elements are satisfied

[6.51]   If all four elements are satisfied the seller's liability is *strict*. He or she will be liable to the buyer for all consequential loss or damage even though all possible care was taken and even if no amount of care would have revealed the defect that caused the product to be unfit for the buyer's purpose. For example, in *Frost v Aylesbury Dairy Co Ltd* [1905] 1 KB 608 Frost's wife died after drinking typhoid-infected milk. Frost sued the dairy which argued that, because no amount of skill or judgment could have detected the typhoid, Frost could not have 'relied on their skill and judgment' to ensure that the milk was not contaminated. The court held that latent and undiscoverable defects are not excluded from the operation of the implied condition. Sellers have an *absolute* duty to supply goods which are fit in *all* respects for the buyer's stated purpose and, because the milk was clearly not fit for its obvious purpose (drinking), the dairy was liable.

Merchantable quality

[6.52] Where goods are bought by description from a seller who deals in goods of that description (whether as manufacturer or not) there is an implied condition that the goods will be of merchantable quality subject to the proviso that 'if the buyer has examined the goods, there is no implied condition as regards defects which such examination ought to have revealed'.[38]

The meaning of 'merchantable quality'

[6.53] In very general terms goods will be of merchantable quality if they comply with the description under which they are sold and if they are suitable for the purpose or purposes for which such goods are *ordinarily* used. (Contrast this with the concept of 'fitness for purpose' under which goods must be fit not only for their *ordinary* purpose but also for the seller's *particular* purpose.) A number of 'rules' can be identified from the cases:

- goods will not be unmerchantable merely because they cannot be used for their ordinary purpose in a *particular* place or by a *particular* buyer. For example, in *Sumner Permain and Co v Webb and Co* [1922] 1 KB 55 a consignment of 'Webbs Indian Tonic' was confiscated and destroyed when it arrived in Argentina, because it contained salicylic acid, a substance banned under Argentine law. The goods were not 'unmerchantable'. The defect merely made them unsaleable in one particular place;

- if goods can be used for *several* purposes they will not be unmerchantable merely because they are unfit for the buyer's *particular* purpose (that problem is covered by the 'fitness for purpose' provision). For example, in *Henry Kendall & Sons v William Lillico and Sons Ltd* [1969] 2 AC 31 groundnuts which contained minute traces of a highly poisonous mould were sold to a game-bird farm and fed to its pheasants. Many died. The groundnuts could have been fed, quite safely, to cattle or to other poultry. They were, therefore, 'commercially saleable' and, consequently, they were of 'merchantable quality'. (However, the suppliers were held liable for breach of the 'fitness for purpose' condition);

- whether goods are of merchantable quality depends upon their description and the expectations of a reasonable person. In particular, the characteristics which will affect whether a good is merchantable include, price (if goods are bought at a reduced price the buyer should expect that they will not be of standard quality), any specific description which puts the buyer on notice of possible defects (for example, words such as 'seconds', 'factory rebuilds', 'flawed' and 'imperfect') and the age of the goods (calendar age will not generally affect the goods' merchantability but it could be important with *secondhand goods*. Whether secondhand goods are merchantable

---

38. See note 37 above.

depends on whether they are suitable for the purposes for which such 'secondhand' goods are normally used. See *Bartlett v Sidney Marcus Ltd* [1965] 2 All ER 75, in which Lord Denning indicated that secondhand goods need not be in perfect condition, just in a *usable* condition.)

The goods must be 'bought by description'

[6.54]   As was seen in **[6.38]**, goods can be 'bought by description' even though the buyer has seen and even examined them — provided they are bought *not* as specific goods but as goods answering a description. *Varley v Whipp* [1900] 1 QB 513; **[6.38]** is a good example as is *David Jones v Willis* (1934) 52 CLR 110. In the latter case Mrs Willis had specifically asked the sales assistant for 'comfortable walking shoes'. The resulting sale was held to be a sale by description because she bought the shoes *not* as specific goods but as goods answering that particular description.

The seller must 'deal in goods of that description'

[6.55]   Because the seller must 'deal in goods of that description' the implied condition of merchantable quality only applies when the seller is a 'dealer'. It does not apply to private sales. The question then is 'when is the seller a dealer?' The preferred view is that, if traders hold themselves out as ready, willing and able to supply particular goods in the course of their business, they will deal in goods of that description. As Lord Wilberforce put it in *Christopher Hill Ltd v Ashington Piggeries Ltd* [1972] AC 441 at 495:

> I would have no difficulty in holding that a seller deals in goods 'of that description' if he accepts orders to supply them in the way of business; and this whether or not he has previously accepted orders for goods of that description.

Merchantable quality and partial defects

[6.56]   When a seller supplies a specified quantity of goods, *only part* of which are unmerchantable, the buyer can reject the *entire* consignment *unless*:

- the contract is severable (in which case the buyer will be required to accept and pay for those deliveries where the goods are merchantable but can refuse any deliveries containing goods that are unmerchantable); or
- the defective part is so small that it would be unreasonable not to disregard it (the de minimis rule).

Case Example

Farleigh Estates Sugar Co Ltd was convicted of failing to accept a consignment of cane in breach of an award. The consignment was dead cane (with no sugar content) but it was so intermingled with good cane that the two were, for all practical purposes, inseparable. It argued that, because at least part of the cane had been unmerchantable, it had been entitled to reject the whole consignment. It succeeded. The contract was not severable and the dead cane was not such a small part of the consignment that it could be ignored. The unmerchantable quality of the part had rendered the whole unmerchantable: *Kirwan v Farleigh Estates Sugar Co Ltd* [1918] St R Qd 133.

Merchantable quality and remediable defects

[6.57] As a general principle, where goods are delivered with a defect, even one which can be readily rectified, the goods will be unmerchantable and the buyer will be entitled to reject the entire consignment. This principle was amply illustrated in *Jackson v Rotax Motor & Cycle Co* [1910] 2 KB 937 in which a consignment of motor horns was rejected because many of them were dented, badly polished, badly finished or otherwise poorly manufactured. As Kennedy LJ put it (at 950): 'I do not think we can treat 'merchantable quality' as meaning something which can be made merchantable — it is something which is merchantable at the time when the tender is made by the seller.'

[6.58] The one major exception to this general rule is where both parties expect that the buyer will take any necessary corrective action before he or she uses the 'defective' item. In that case the seller will not be liable if the buyer fails to take the required remedial action and suffers loss or injury as a result. For example, in *Heil v Hedges* [1951] 1 TLR 512 the plaintiff bought pork chops containing a parasitic worm. If the chops had been properly cooked the worm would have been killed but they were not, the plaintiff ate them and she contracted trichinosis. The butcher was not liable. Had the chops been properly cooked (which both parties must have expected), they would have been perfectly safe and of merchantable quality.

However, if it is not reasonable for the buyer to take the necessary remedial action before the goods are first used, the seller may still be liable, as happened in *Grant v Australian Knitting Mills Ltd* [1936] AC 85. In that case Dr Grant purchased a set of long john underwear which, because of an excessive residue of sulphite in the cloth, caused him to break out in dermatitis. The sulphite would have been removed if the goods had been washed but the court found that it was not at all clear that both parties must have intended that the underpants would be washed before they were used. Therefore, the clothing, in the condition in which it was supplied, was unmerchantable.

Goods must remain merchantable for a reasonable period

[6.59] It is not sufficient that the goods be merchantable when they are sold. They must also remain merchantable for a reasonable time thereafter. What is a 'reasonable time' will depend on the nature of the goods (particularly if they are perishable) and on what may be expected of them in relation to other goods of a similar nature.

Case Example

Davids, a wholesale grocer, bought 360 cases of canned beetroot. About 14–16 months later the remaining unsold tins were found unfit for human consumption. Davids sued alleging that the goods had not remained merchantable for a 'reasonable time'. The life of other canned vegetables was a minimum of three years but there was evidence that beetroot canned in vinegar had a shelf life of only one year. Davids' action failed. They could only expect the beetroot to remain merchantable as long as comparable tins of beetroot lasted. It was immaterial that other tinned vegetables lasted longer: *George Wills and Co Ltd v Davids Pty Ltd* (1957) 98 CLR 77

The effect of the proviso

[6.60]   The section provides that 'if the buyer has examined the goods, there is no implied condition as regards defects which such examination ought to have revealed'. The question is: what are 'defects which such examination ought to have revealed'? Do they include defects which a *reasonable* examination ought to have revealed (the 'wide' view) or are they limited to defects which the examination that the buyer *actually conducted* ought to have revealed (the 'narrow' view)? The answer is not entirely clear but the 'wide' view (that all defects which a *reasonable* examination ought to have revealed are excluded from the warranty) seems to be preferred.

Case Example

The plaintiffs agreed to sell the defendants glue. The defendants made a cursory inspection of the casks in which it was supplied but did not ask for them to be opened. Had they done so they would have discovered that the glue was defective. When they did discover it they refused to pay the price arguing that the sellers were in breach of the implied condition of merchantable quality. It was held that the proviso applied and that the buyers could not rely on the fact that their *actual* (inadequate) examination had not revealed the defect. If they had conducted their inspection 'in the ordinary way' (that is, by making a *reasonable* examination), they would have discovered it. Therefore, there was no implied condition that the glue was of merchantable quality and the buyers were liable for the price: *Thornett and Fehr v Beers and Son* [1919] 1 KB 486.

If the defect is such that no ordinary examination of the goods would reveal it, the implied condition of merchantable quality will apply even if the buyer has examined the goods. For example, in *Wren v Holt* [1903] 1 KB 610 the plaintiff was served beer contaminated with arsenic. He sued the publican alleging breaches of (inter alia) the implied condition of merchantable quality. The court held that, even though he could be said to have examined the beer before drinking it, there was no way that the plaintiff could have discovered the arsenic. Consequently, the proviso did not apply and, because the goods were not of merchantable quality, the seller was liable.

Sale by sample

[6.61]   A sale by sample occurs when a sample of the proposed subject matter is produced during negotiations and the seller warrants, expressly or impliedly, that what is delivered will correspond with that sample. The Act implies three *conditions* into contracts of sale by sample:[39]

a) that the bulk shall correspond with the sample in quality;

b) that the buyer shall have a reasonable opportunity of comparing the bulk with the sample; and

---

39. ACT s 20, NSW s 20, NT s 20, Qld s 18, SA s 15, Tas s 20, Vic s 20, WA s 15.

c) that the goods shall be free from any defect, rendering them unmerchantable, which would not be apparent on reasonable examination of the sample.

Producing a sample does not make the sale 'a sale by sample'

[6.62] The section requires that there be '*a term in the contract, express or implied*', to the effect that the sale is a sale by sample. Therefore, merely showing a sample does not necessarily make the contract a sale by sample; there may be other explanations. For example, it could have been used simply to identify the subject matter in a sale by description. Alternatively it could have been used just as a *rough guide* to the type and grade of goods to be supplied or, again, even though a sample was produced, the seller might require the buyer to inspect the bulk and to base his or her purchase decision on that inspection. Further, if the contract is reduced to writing and if the written document does not refer to the sample, the parol evidence rule may stop the sale being classed as a sale by sample.

Case Example

The parties contracted for the sale and purchase of 50 drums of neatsfoot oil. During negotiations a sample of the oil was produced but when the contract was written up it contained no mention of the sample. When the oil was delivered it did not correspond with the sample and the buyer rejected it. It was held that it had not been entitled to do so. There was no term in the contract, express or implied, that the sale was a sale by sample — and a term to that effect could not be added by extrinsic evidence: *L G Thorne & Co Pty Ltd v Thomas Borthwick & Sons (A'asia) Ltd* (1956) 56 SR (NSW) 81.

'Reasonable examination' means a 'normal commercial examination'

[6.63] If the sale is a 'sale by sample' the goods must be 'free from any defect, rendering them unmerchantable, which would not be apparent on reasonable examination of the sample'. The term 'reasonable examination' in this context means an examination that would be 'reasonable in the circumstances'. For example, in *Godley v Perry* [1960] 1 WLR 9 a six-year-old boy lost the sight of one eye when a defective catapult broke into pieces as he used it. He sued the toy shop. The shopkeeper had bought the catapult from a wholesaler and the sale had been by sample. The shopkeeper had inspected the sample but all that he had done was to pull the elastic back once or twice. The retailer sued the wholesaler alleging breach of the implied condition that the goods would be 'free from any defect, rendering them unmerchantable, which would not be apparent on reasonable examination of the sample'. He succeeded. The defect would not have been revealed by a 'reasonable examination' (such as the retailer had made) in the ordinary sense of that phrase. A more detailed examination might have revealed the defect but that more detailed examination was not required for the section to operate.

It is no defence that the goods could be made to correspond with the sample

[6.64] The goods supplied must correspond with the sample when they are delivered. It is not the buyer's responsibility to do anything to them to make them comply. See, for example, *E & S Ruben Ltd v Faire Bros & Co Ltd* [1949] 1 KB 254. The contract there was for the sale of vulcanised rubber, a sample of which had been produced during negotiations. The rubber delivered did not correspond with the sample because it was hard and crinkly and could not be cut on a power press (as the sample could be). The buyer rejected it. The sellers sued for the price, arguing that the faults could have been corrected by simply warming the rubber and pressing out the crinkles. They failed. The court held that, if the goods supplied do not correspond with the sample, the degree or reason is immaterial.

Excluding statutorily implied terms

[6.65] The parties can exclude or vary the implied conditions and warranties in the Sale of Goods Act by including an appropriately worded exemption or limiting clause in their contract. The terms can 'be negatived or varied by express agreement or by a course of dealing between the parties, or by usage, if the usage is such as to bind both parties to the contract'[40] and it is common for contracts, especially standard form contracts, to include clauses to that effect.

However, in consumer transactions (where the parties often have unequal bargaining power), sellers could unfairly use this provision to deprive consumers of the Act's intended protection. To prevent that happening all jurisdictions now have legislation which restricts the seller's ability to exclude or modify the implied terms. The principal provisions appear in Pt V of the Trade Practices Act 1974 (Cth) and in those parts of the various state and territory Fair Trading Acts that were modelled on it. In addition, New South, Victoria and South Australia all have specific legislation dealing with the question. In New South Wales that legislation is in Pt VIII of the Sale of Goods Act 1923, in Victoria it is in Pt IV of the Goods Act 1958 and in South Australia it is dealt with in the Consumer Transactions Act 1972. The relevant provisions of Pt V of the Trade Practices Act (and of the equivalent provisions in the various state and territory Fair Trading Acts) are dealt with in Chapter 9.

Remedies

[6.66] The basic duties of the parties to a sale of goods contract are for the seller to deliver the goods and for the buyer to accept and pay for them in accordance with the contract.[41] If either party fails to do what is expected there is a breach of contract and the innocent party can treat it as at an end and sue for damages. However, especially for the seller, these general law rights can be illusory, particularly if the buyer cannot pay.

40. ACT s 58, NSW s 57, NT s 57, Qld s 56, SA s 54, Tas s 59, Vic s 61, WA s 54.
41. ACT s 31, NSW s 30, NT s 30, Qld s 29, SA s 27, Tas s 32, Vic s 34, WA s 27.

Consequently, the Act sets out a number of remedies which are especially tailored for the particular problems that can arise in sale of goods contracts.

Remedies of the unpaid seller

[6.67] The seller's main cause for complaint will be that the buyer has not paid. If that happens the seller will prefer to get the money or, if that is not possible, he or she will want to recover the goods. The Act gives 'unpaid sellers' rights against both the goods and the buyer.

An 'unpaid seller' in the context of the Act is any seller (including any person standing in the seller's place — such as an agent), who has not yet been paid the *whole* price (or had it tendered) or who, having been paid by bill of exchange or other negotiable instrument as a conditional payment, has not had that condition fulfilled because the bill of exchange or other negotiable instrument was dishonoured on presentation.[42] This accords with what we would commonly understand by the term 'unpaid seller' with, perhaps, some obvious and justifiable extension.

The unpaid seller's rights against the goods

[6.68] The unpaid seller has four specific rights against the goods:[43]

1. a lien (which operates where property has passed to the buyer);
2. a right of stoppage in transitu (which operates where property has passed to the buyer);
3. a right of retention (co-extensive with a and b above) which subsists if the goods still belong to the seller (that is, if property has *not* passed to the buyer); and
4. a right of resale (which is limited by the Act).

The lien

[6.69] The Act provides that, where property in the goods (but not possession of them) has passed to the buyer, the seller can retain them until the price has been paid in full.[44] This 'lien' arises automatically if the buyer becomes insolvent and 'insolvent' in this context does not mean 'bankrupt'. Bankruptcy involves formal acceptance of a debtor's petition by the Registrar in Bankruptcy or the making of a sequestration order by the court. Insolvency merely means that the buyer cannot or will not pay his or her debts as they fall due.[45]

As with all liens the seller's lien under the Sale of Goods Act depends on continuity of possession. If the seller parts with the goods he or she loses the lien — although if possession is lawfully regained the lien may be revived.

A part delivery of the goods does *not* completely destroy the seller's lien.[46] The seller can retain the balance of the goods until the buyer pays for them unless, by releasing the

---

42. ACT s 42, NSW s 41, NT s 41, Qld s 40, SA s 38, Tas s 43, Vic s 45, WA s 38.
43. ACT s 43, NSW s 42, NT s 42, Qld s 41, SA s 39, Tas s 44, Vic s 46, WA s 39.
44. ACT s 44, NSW s 43, NT s 43, Qld s 42, SA s 40, Tas s 45, Vic s 47, WA s 40.
45. ACT s 5(2)(c), NSW s 5(3), NT s 5(3), Qld s 3(3), SA s 60(3), Tas s 3(3), Vic s 3(3), WA s 60(3).
46. ACT s 45, NSW s 44, NT s 44, Qld s 43, SA s 41, Tas s 46, Vic s 48, WA s 41.

part, the seller has waived his or her rights to the lien. That could occur, for instance, where delivery of the part is considered a symbolic delivery of the whole.

[6.70] Effect of the lien Exercising the lien simply allows the seller to retain the goods as security for the price. It does not operate as security for other expenditure (such as storage charges, feed for animals, etc) which are incurred as a result of that retention. Further, if the contract is severable (as is the case with instalment contracts), the lien can only be exercised over instalments which have not then been paid for. Finally, exercising the lien does not terminate the contract and it remains completely enforceable — by both parties.

[6.71] Terminating the lien The seller's lien will terminate in each of six instances:
1. if the seller delivers the goods to a carrier or other bailee, for the purpose of transmitting them to the buyer, without reserving the right of disposal. (Reserving the right of disposal in this context means reserving the right to regain *possession* — because otherwise there will not be the required 'continuity of possession');
2. if the buyer lawfully acquires possession (though, if the buyer acquires possession unlawfully — for example, by fraud or deceit — the lien can be revived if the seller can recover the goods);
3. by waiver (that is, by conduct which indicates that the seller no longer seeks to exercise the lien);
4. if the buyer pays or tenders the price (because then the seller is not an *unpaid* seller and the lien only applies to unpaid sellers);
5. if the seller assents to any sub-sale or other disposition by the buyer.[47] This is effectively an example of waiver because, by assenting, the seller is, at least impliedly, indicating that he or she does not intend to exercise the lien; and
6. if a document of title to goods is lawfully transferred to the buyer and if the buyer transfers it to a bona fide purchaser for value.[48] This again is an example of waiver. By giving the buyer the document of title the seller is, in effect, acknowledging the buyer's right to on-sell the goods and to pass good title to them.

Stoppage in transitu

[6.72] The seller's lien can be lost if the goods are delivered to a carrier for transmission without reserving a right of disposal. However, even then the seller may still be able to stop the goods and recover them under other provisions of the Act. The effect is that possession reverts to the seller, the lien is revived and the goods can be retained until the buyer pays or tenders the price. Exercising the right of stoppage in transitu presupposes that the goods have become the buyer's property. If not, the seller would be able to stop the transit by virtue of his or her ownership and would not have to rely on the statutory power. For the right of stoppage in transit to arise three conditions must be satisfied: the seller must be 'unpaid', the buyer must be 'insolvent' and the goods must be 'in the course of transit'.

What is transit?

[6.73] Transit is defined as the time between the seller delivering the goods to the carrier and the buyer taking delivery of them. In other words, 'from the time the seller's lien terminates until the goods are in the buyer's possession'.[49] Consequently, mere arrival at

---

47. ACT s 50, NSW s 49, NT s 49, Qld s 48, SA s 46, Tas s 51, Vic s 53, WA s 46.
48. See note 47 above.

the destination does not terminate transit unless the goods actually come into the buyer's possession (for example, leaving the goods on a station platform is arrival at the destination but, at that point, the buyer may not have taken delivery of them). Conversely, if the buyer interrupts the transit and takes possession of the goods before they reach their destination the transit comes at an end.

If the goods are delivered to a carrier working for the buyer, that is the same as delivering them to the buyer and the right of stoppage ceases at that point. Effectively, the buyer has taken possession and the period of carriage is no longer 'transit'. Transit may also end if the carrier acknowledges, after the goods have arrived at their destination, that he or she holds them on behalf of the buyer. Again, the buyer has effectively taken possession of the goods even if that possession is through an agent.

How stoppage is effected

[6.74]   Stoppage is effected if the seller takes actual possession of the goods or if he or she gives the person (or the person's principal) who is then in possession of them — usually the carrier — notice that he or she is exercising the right.[50] If notice is given to the principal, the seller must, of course, allow him or her sufficient time to communicate it to the servant or agent who actually has the goods. Once the seller has given notice of stoppage, the carrier or other bailee may not deliver the goods to the buyer — they must be redelivered to the seller — though such redelivery will be at the seller's expense.

Effect of stoppage

[6.75]   Exercising the right of stoppage does not mean that property in the goods (which has, of course, passed to the buyer) *automatically* reverts to the seller. Nor does stoppage automatically cause the contract to be rescinded.[51] All it does is to revive the seller's lien.

Right of retention

[6.76]   The unpaid seller's right to exercise the lien or the right of stoppage in transitu only arises where property in the goods has passed to the buyer. Where property has not passed, the seller does not need the Act's provisions — the goods remain the seller's property and he or she can retain them. The buyer can sue for non-delivery but, invariably, the buyer's breach (which caused the seller to exercise the right of retention) will be a justification and a good defence. The effect of the right of retention is the same as the effect of the rights of lien and stoppage but it applies *in their place*.

Right of resale

[6.77]   The unpaid seller's right to resell the goods affects two sets of contracting parties — the seller and the new buyer and the seller and the original buyer.

The seller and the new buyer

[6.78]   The problem for the new buyer is to establish that he or she gets good title to the goods and that his or her interests are not defeated by the claims of the original buyer. The new buyer will get good title in at least three cases:

---

49. ACT s 48, NSW s 47, NT s 47, Qld s 46, SA s 44, Tas s 49, Vic s 51, WA s 44.
50. ACT s 49, NSW s 48, NT s 48, Qld s 47, SA s 45, Tas s 50, Vic s 52, WA s 45.
51. ACT s 51, NSW s 50, NT s 50, Qld s 49, SA s 47, Tas s 52, Vic s 54, WA s 47.

a) where the seller still owned of the goods at the time of resale (as would be the case, for example, with a resale after the seller had exercised the right of retention);

b) under statutory protection if the seller resells after exercising the lien or right of stoppage.[52] (This applies whether the second buyer knew of the original sale or not); and

c) under statutory protection where a seller in possession sells the goods to the new buyer who takes them in good faith and without notice of the previous sale.[53]

The seller and the original buyer

[6.79]   Where the seller exercises the 'right of resale', questions can arise about the propriety of his or her action and there is at least some potential for the original buyer's rights to be breached. To resolve possible problems the following general principles apply:

- the sale will be lawful if it is authorised by the Act. Consequently the original buyer cannot sue for the seller's failure to perform;
- conversely, because the seller cannot perform, he or she cannot sue for the price;
- if the seller makes a loss on the resale he or she can sue for damages for the original buyer's non-acceptance;
- conversely, if the resale results in a profit, the unpaid seller can keep it; and
- any deposit that the original buyer paid will be forfeit (unless the forfeiture would be a penalty).

Case Example

Ward advertised two motor vehicles which Bignall agreed to buy for £850. He paid a £25 deposit and went to get the balance from his bank. He then had second thoughts and told Ward that he would only pay £800. That 'offer' was refused. Ward subsequently sold the Vanguard for £350 but could not find a buyer for the Zodiac. He sued Bignall for £497/10/- being the agreed price plus £22/10/- additional advertising expenses less the £25 deposit and the £350 received for the Vanguard. The court held that by exercising the right of resale, Ward had rescinded the original contract. This discharged both parties from liability for any further performance, returned title to the cars to Ward and meant that Bignall no longer had to pay the price. Ward could also keep the proceeds of any resale and, if they were less than the agreed price, could seek compensation in damages. Here the parties had agreed that the true value of the Zodiac was £450. Accordingly, damages were assessed at £47/10/- (the agreed price (£850) plus the additional advertising expenses (£22/10/-) less the deposit (£25), the proceeds of sale of the Vanguard (£350) and the agreed value of the Zodiac (£450)): *R V Ward Ltd v Bignall* [1967] 1 QB 534.

---

52. ACT s 51(2), NSW s 50(2), NT s 50(2), Qld s 49(2), SA s 47(2), Tas s 52(2), Vic s 54(2), WA s 47(2).
53. See note 26 above.

Personal remedies of the seller

[6.80]   The unpaid seller has two personal remedies (that is, actions that can be brought against the buyer personally). They are an action for the price and an action for damages for non-acceptance.

Action for the price

[6.81]   The seller can only sue for the price if it is due and payable. This means that the action will only be available if property has passed to the buyer or, if the price was payable on a day certain (irrespective of passage of property) and that day has passed.[54]

> **Case Example**
>
> Shell contracted to sell Elton Cop 1000 tons of oil in monthly instalments. Payment for each instalment was required within 14 days of delivery and Shell could also invoice Elton Cop for any oil it did not take. Elton Cop failed to take delivery of the last 466 tons. Shell sued for the price and failed. Property in the oil had not passed to Elton Cop nor had the contract made provision for payment 'on a day certain.' Consequently, Shell could only sue for damages for non-acceptance: *Shell Mex Ltd v Elton Cop Dyeing Co Ltd* (1928) 34 Com Cas 39.

There are three other occasions on which an unpaid seller cannot sue for the price — when a credit period has been allowed and it has not yet expired, when the buyer has validly rejected the goods and when the seller cannot deliver (or is unwilling to deliver) them.

Damages for non-acceptance

[6.82]   The Act requires the buyer to accept and pay for the goods.[55] If he or she fails to do so and if the seller was ready, willing and able to deliver them, the buyer will be liable for damages for non-acceptance.[56] A similar action is available where the buyer wrongfully fails or refuses to take delivery.[57]

[6.83]   The measure of damages in such cases is determined in accordance with the rule in *Hadley v Baxendale* (1854) 156 ER 145. The Act provides that:

> The measure of damages is the estimated loss directly and naturally resulting, in the ordinary course of events, from the buyer's breach of contract.'[58]

What 'the estimated loss directly and naturally resulting, in the ordinary course of events, from the buyer's breach of contract' is, is also explained. The Act provides that:

> When there is an available market for the goods in question, the measure of damages is prima facie to be ascertained by the difference between the contract price and the market

---

54. ACT s 52, NSW s 51, NT s 51, Qld s 50, SA s 48, Tas s 53, Vic s 55, WA s 48.
55. ACT s 31, NSW s 30, NT s 30, Qld s 29, SA s 27, Tas s 27, Vic s 34, WA s 27.
56. ACT s 53, NSW s 52, NT s 52, Qld s 51, SA s 49, Tas s 54, Vic s 56, WA s 49.
57. ACT s 41, NSW s 40, NT s 40, Qld s 39, SA s 37, Tas s 42, Vic s 44, WA s 37.
58. ACT s 53(2), NSW s 52(2), NT s 52(2), Qld s 51(2), SA s 49(2), Tas s 54(2), Vic s 56(2), WA s 49(2).

or current price at the time or times when the goods ought to have been accepted, or, if no time was fixed for acceptance, then at the time of the refusal to accept.'[59]

[6.84]   The term 'available market' is usually taken to mean a market in which prices are fixed by the economic laws of supply and demand and which is readily available to the seller. Therefore, the effect of the section is to set damages by reference to the price that the same goods would fetch in the market *when* they should have been accepted or, if no time was specified, when the buyer refused to accept them. Therefore, if the market has dropped so that the seller can now only get $80 for goods which the buyer had agreed to buy for $100, the seller is entitled to damages for the difference — in this case, $20. If the market has risen, say, to $120 for the same item the seller suffers no loss — he or she can sell the goods, get what the buyer would have paid and will also get a windfall gain of $20. In such cases the seller cannot seek damages but can keep the windfall gain.

[6.85]   Where there is no 'available market' for the goods the seller will have to prove what, if anything, he or she lost as the direct and natural result of the buyer's breach of contract. In most situations this will mean the amount of profit that the seller would have made on the sale. But even this need not be the case. If the seller has to fight for every sale any profit foregone is profit which he or she will never recover — except through an award of damages. However, if the seller has more potential buyers than he or she can satisfy, the profit that would have been made on the lost sale will be recouped by immediately reselling the goods to a buyer whom he or she would not otherwise have been able to satisfy.

The way in which the question of ready availability of supply can affect the seller's quantum of damages is illustrated by comparing *W L Thompson Ltd v Robinson (Gunmakers) Ltd* [1955] Ch 177 and *Charter v Sullivan* [1957] 2 QB 117. In the former case the contract was for the sale of a Vanguard motor car (which were in plentiful supply). The buyer refused to accept delivery and the seller was awarded damages equal to the profit he would (and should) have made on the sale. In *Charter v Sullivan*, on the other hand, the defendant contracted to buy a Hillman Minx motor car, an extremely popular vehicle which was in short supply. The defendant refused to accept delivery, the seller sued and was awarded nominal damages. His sale to a substitute buyer was not an additional sale he could have made but a 'substitution' sale — he had no other Hillman Minx he could have sold 'as well'.

The buyer's remedies

[6.86]   The buyer's remedies include the right to reject the goods, the right to recover the price, the right to sue for damages for breach of warranty, the right to sue for damages for non-delivery, the right to sue for specific performance and the right to sue in tort (where that is appropriate).

Rejection of the goods

[6.87]   As is the case with all contracts, an aggrieved party can treat a sale of goods contract as discharged if the other party is in breach of a condition. That is a matter for

---

59. ACT s 53(3), NSW s 52(3), NT s 52(3), Qld s 51(3), SA s 49(3), Tas s 54(3), Vic s 56(3), WA s 49(3).

election and under both the general law and the Sale of Goods Act the aggrieved party may elect to be satisfied with damages instead.[60]

The right to repudiate for breach of condition is, however, qualified in sale of goods contracts because the Act provides that, in certain circumstances (notably where the goods have been 'accepted'), the buyer cannot repudiate the contract and can only treat the breach as a breach of warranty and sue for damages: see **[6.29]**.

Recovery of the price

[6.88]   A buyer who has paid for the goods and who is willing to accept the seller's default and terminate the contract can demand a refund of the price.[61] Recovery of the price is a remedy which is in substitution for damages for non-delivery and it is normally used where the buyer can buy similar goods elsewhere at the same or at a lesser price. In fact, where similar goods are readily available at a lesser price it is a preferable remedy because the buyer recovers the full amount he or she paid and not just a sum which would allow him or her to buy equivalent goods. The right may be exercised in a number of situations including where the consideration has failed entirely, where the seller did not have title and where the buyer validly rejected the goods on delivery.

Damages for breach of warranty

[6.89]   Buyers can sue for damages for breaches of warranty.[62] The term 'warranty' covers both those terms of the contract that would normally be regarded as warranties and also any conditions which must be treated as warranties because the goods have been 'accepted'.

The Act confers two rights — the right to set the breach of warranty up as an excuse to diminish or extinguish the price and the right to sue for damages.

If damages are sued for, their quantum is determined in accordance with the Act and, prima facie, will be equivalent to the difference between the value of the goods as delivered and the value that they would have had had they been delivered without breach of the warranty. This, however, is only a prima facie rule and the applicable damages can include additional amounts to compensate the buyer for other, directly and naturally resulting losses. See, for example, *Mason v Burningham* [1949] 2 KB 545; **[6.35]** in which the buyer was entitled to recover not only the purchase price of the typewriter but also the money she had spent having it repaired.

Damages for non-delivery

[6.90]   The right to sue for damages for non-delivery[63] is analogous to the seller's right to damages for non-acceptance: see **[6.82]**–**[6.85]**. The buyer will be entitled to sue the seller for damages for non-delivery if the seller wrongfully neglects or refuses to deliver the goods, if the goods are defective when they are delivered and the buyer validly rejects them (as, for example, in *Cammell Laird & Co v The Manganese Bronze & Brass Co* [1934] AC 402 where a defective ships propellor was rejected) or if delivery is not in accordance with the contract (for example, if the goods are delivered at a later time or in

---

60. ACT s16, NSW s 16, NT s 16, Qld s 14, SA s 11, Tas s 16, Vic s 16, WA s 11.
61. ACT s 57, NSW s 55, NT s 55, Qld s 55, SA s 53, Tas s 58, Vic s 60, WA s 53.
62. ACT s 56, NSW s 54, NT s 54, Qld s 54, SA s 52, Tas s 57, Vic s 59, WA s 52.
63. ACT s 54, NSW s 53, NT s 53, Qld s 52, SA s 50, Tas s 55, Vic s 57, WA s 50.

a different place). In such cases the measure of damages is once again the estimated loss directly and naturally resulting from the seller's breach of contract and the actual quantum will depend on factors such as the available market for the goods.

Specific performance

[6.91]   As in the general law the buyer can apply for an order for specific performance in appropriate circumstances.[64] Specific performance is only available where the contract is for the sale of specific or ascertained goods and it is usually only granted where an award of damages would not be an adequate or appropriate remedy. Accordingly, specific performance will usually only be granted where the goods are unique or of special value to the buyer (because in such cases the buyer cannot merely take the damages and obtain equivalent goods elsewhere). Exceptionally, however, specific performance can be awarded in other cases to ensure that justice is done.

Action in tort

[6.92]   If the buyer is wrongfully denied possession of the goods he or she can sue the seller or any third party who is at fault in either conversion or detinue (see Chapter 16) and will be entitled to damages equal to those he or she would have received in an action for non-delivery.

Auction sales

[6.93]   While auction sales are also dealt with in the Act[65] its provisions are not a code and they can be and often are varied by express agreement. The following rules are important:

*   *Each lot is the subject of a separate contract*   Where the goods to be auctioned are divided into lots, each lot is prima facie deemed to be the subject of a separate contract of sale. This merely allows separate contracts to be formed with the buyers of each lot. This provision is often varied by, for instance, allowing the auctioneer to consolidate or split lots, either at his or her discretion or upon the happening of named events.

*   *The contract is complete on the fall of the hammer*   In providing that the contract is only complete when the auctioneer announces its completion by the fall of the hammer, or in some other customary manner, the Act merely restates the common law. In auction sales the bidder makes the offer and the auctioneer accepts or rejects it. Therefore, no contract arises until the auctioneer accepts the final bid. If the bid is rejected or if the bidder withdraws it before the hammer falls there is no binding contract of sale. The bidder's common law right to withdraw his or her bid at any time prior to acceptance is preserved by the words 'until such announcement is made any bidder may retract his bid'.

*   *Normally sellers may not bid for their own goods*   It was once common for the seller and/or his or her associates (known as 'puffers') to position themselves around the

---

64. ACT s 55, Qld s 53, SA s 51, Tas s 56, Vic s 58, WA s 51.
65. ACT s 60, NSW s 60, NT s 60, Qld s 59, SA s 57, Tas s 62, Vic s 64, WA s 57.

auction room, bid on the items and thus (hopefully) drive up the price. This practice was considered unacceptable, any resulting sale was regarded as fraudulent and the buyer could avoid it. That gave rise to the common law rule that sellers could not bid for their own goods.

There are, however, at least two possibly legitimate reasons for a seller to bid. The first is that the highest bid received is too low and the seller wants to bid to stop the goods being knocked down for less than their true worth. The second is that the seller may have changed his or her mind and may want to keep the goods. This is not really a valid reason because in such cases the seller's proper course of action is to withdraw the goods from sale altogether.

However, because the seller could have a valid reason for bidding, the common law allowed him or her to do so *but* only if he or she had specifically reserved that right and given notice to potential bidders. That position is retained in the Sale of Goods Act but it is subject to further limitations. In summary the statutory position is this:

a. the seller may reserve a right to bid;
b. such reservation must be notified to all potential bidders (usually in the terms of the auction that are read out at its commencement); and
c. if the right to bid is reserved, the seller or any *one* person acting on his or her behalf may bid at the auction. In practice the auctioneer usually exercises this right. If the price fails to reach what the seller will accept, the auctioneer submits a bid on the seller's behalf (usually equal to the minimum price for which the seller is willing to sell) and, if no higher bid is received, the auctioneer will knock the goods down to the seller.

Auctions may be 'subject to reserve'

[6.94] The Act also provides that auctions 'may be notified to be subject to a reserved price'.[66] This allows the seller to set a price below which the item is not to be sold. The reserve price is *not* notified to the bidders. They merely get notice that there is a reserve price (usually in the conditions read out at the auction's commencement).

This means that auction sales fall into three distinct categories: auctions where there is a notified reserve, auctions where there is a reserve price but it is not notified and auctions where there is no reserve.

Notified reserves

[6.95] Where a notified reserve price is set, the auctioneer has no authority to sell the goods *unless* a bid equal to or greater than the reserve is received. If the auctioneer mistakenly knocks the goods down for less than the reserve he or she may (in fact 'must'), refuse to sell them to the buyer once the error is discovered. In such cases the buyer can neither sue for the goods (because he or she knew that no sale would be made below the reserve), nor sue the auctioneer for breaching his or her 'warranty of authority to sell' (because the buyer was aware that that authority was limited).

---

66. ACT s 60(9), NSW s 60(4), NT s 60(d), Qld s 59(1)(d), SA s 57(4), Tas s 62(d), Vic s 64(d), WA s 57(4).

Case Example

The auction was notified to be 'subject to a reserve price'. The plaintiff bid £85 for one lot and it was knocked down to him. The auctioneer later discovered that the lot had had a reserve of £200. He therefore refused to sign the memorandum of sale. The plaintiff sued and lost. The sale was subject to a notified reserve and, as the reserve had not been reached, no sale had occurred. Nor was the auctioneer personally liable: *McManus v Fortescue* [1907] 2 KB 1.

Reserve price not notified

[6.96]   If there is no notified reserve the auction could appear to be without reserve so that the highest bidder should have the goods knocked down to him or her. That, however, is not necessarily what happens. The applicable rules are:

- because there is no sale until the hammer falls the auctioneer can refuse to accept the bid (and therefore refuse to sell the goods). If that happens, the bidder has no grounds to sue the seller because there was no contract of sale;
- in such cases the bidder will have no action against the auctioneer for breach of his or her apparent authority to sell because there has been no sale;
- if the goods are mistakenly knocked down to the buyer he or she has two possible courses of action — to sue the auctioneer for wrongfully warranting his or her *unlimited* authority to sell or (in certain instances) or to sue the auctioneer's principal (the seller) for holding the auctioneer out as having such authority; and
- if the sale is subject to a reserve and the auctioneer actually sells and parts with possession of the goods for less than the reserve price, he or she will be in breach of contract with the seller and liable to him or her in damages. See *Hawke's Bay Farmers' Co-op Assn Ltd v Farquharson* [1916] NZLR 917.

Auctions without reserve

[6.97]   If goods are auctioned without reserve and if the auctioneer refuses to knock them down, the buyer cannot sue on the contract, because there has been no acceptance. However, if the auction was expressly stated to be 'without reserve' the auctioneer may be liable for breach of his or her undertaking that the goods would be sold to the highest bidder: see *Warlow v Harrison* (1859) 1 E&E 309; 120 ER 925. The auctioneer can avoid this danger by stipulating in the 'conditions of the auction' that the highest bid need not be accepted.

Summary and key terms

[6.98]   This chapter has set out to explain the following:

- for there to be a sale of goods contract there must be a contract for the sale of goods for a money consideration called the price;
- property in the goods passes from the seller to the buyer when the parties intend it to pass;
- risk usually passes at the same time;

- as with all contracts the terms of a sale of goods contract can be express or implied;
- the Act implies a number of terms into all sale of goods contracts unless the parties expressly exclude them. They include implied undertakings as to title, correspondence with description and/or sample, fitness for purpose and merchantability;
- an unpaid seller has remedies against both the goods and the buyer;
- the remedies against the goods include a lien, a right of stoppage in transitu, a right of retention and a right of resale;
- the remedies against the buyer include an action for the price and damages for non-acceptance;
- an unsatisfied buyer's remedies include the rights to reject the goods, to recover the price and to sue for damages for either breach of warranty or non-delivery;
- with auction sales the bidder makes the offer and the auctioneer accepts it by the fall of the hammer. There is no enforceable contract until then and the highest bid need not be accepted — though that normally happens only when the auction is 'subject to reserve'.

7
Consumer Protection and Fair Trading

What this chapter does ...

To understand modern consumer protection law it is necessary to take into account the way in which the common law approached the issue. Legislation in the 1960s was necessary to make the law more responsive to modern circumstances and to reflect community expectations.

This chapter outlines the way in which statute law has become a critical part of consumer protection law. It provides the basis for the definition of consumer transaction and expands the reach of the law into areas previously not touched by the common law.

The term 'consumer protection' has given way in many places to the concept of 'fair trading' which probably better expresses the effect of the modern law.

The common law and consumers

[7.1]   It is only relatively recently, since the 1960s, that there has been a body of law that could properly be described as consumer law. The common law — the law developed by judges — reflects the values of earlier centuries and, in the course of its development, was concerned more with the transactions of merchants than of consumers. Until the Sale of Goods Act in 1893 a person who would now be recognised as a consumer had only the law of contract and perhaps tort to rely on in a dispute with a supplier. The decision in *Donoghue v Stevenson* (1932) AC 562 was a breakthrough for consumers because it led to a wider notion of responsibility — beyond contract and into a tortious dimension that recognised a duty of care and a remedy where a breach of that duty led to loss or damage.

The common law believed in the concept of equality of bargaining power, freedom of contract and the rule of *caveat emptor* (let the buyer beware). The lack of realism of the judges who developed these concepts is graphically demonstrated by the way in which they promoted the idea that parties to a contract were equal in bargaining power and were free to set the terms of the transaction. To the modern mind this is a ridiculous idea. Most people who have dealt with a large commercial institution are aware of how unequal they are in negotiating power. How often can an individual traveller who considers that the terms of the contract set out on an airline ticket are not satisfactory negotiate with the airline for a better deal? What chance does the average person have of negotiating terms with a large motor vehicle manufacturer?

Background to the modern law

[7.2]   *Caveat emptor*, translated to mean 'let the buyer beware', imposes a high standard on consumers. In much of modern commerce it would be very difficult to take the precautions necessary to satisfy this rule. In purchasing a sophisticated product such as a computer, a car, video cassette recorder or even a clock radio, the buyer must rely on the manufacturer. Unless a person has skills that combine several disciplines and are above the ordinary, it would be impossible for a defect in a modern electronic device to be detected before the completion of the sale.

The common law rules about privity of contract had the result that a person who purchased a defective product had no rights against the manufacturer — the action was against the seller who was probably not to blame in any case. A person who acquired goods by way of a gift had no rights against either the seller or manufacturer.

The Sale of Goods Act represented a significant step forward in that it provided some rights for consumers. The Act was a summary of common law decisions and represented the laws that were appropriate for transactions between merchants. There were, however, provisions within the Act which assisted consumers and, until the modern consumer law emerged, this was the only statutory intervention available for consumers.

In the 1960s community pressure forced governments to provide legislation that protected consumers by overcoming the unrealistic policies adopted by the common law. In 1974 the Commonwealth entered the field of consumer protection through the Trade Practices Act which, in Pt V, introduced a wide-ranging scheme of regulation of conduct associated with trade and commerce. The Commonwealth has no specific power to make laws with respect to consumer protection but by adapting a range of its constitutional powers it was able to make valid laws on the topic. The High Court decision in the

Concrete Pipes case, *Strickland v Rocla Concrete Pipes Ltd* (1971) CLR 468, demonstrated how the corporations power in the Commonwealth Constitution s 51(xx) could be employed to support valid Commonwealth legislation. The thrust of Pt V of the Trade Practices Act is to penalise unfair conduct and in this way it supplements the competition goals of the Act by promoting fair competition.

Consumer rights

[7.3]   The modern style of consumer protection law recognises that consumers have certain rights — the right to fair treatment, to information, to safe products and to a system of redress. It also aims to overcome the imbalance that the common law had established. To the extent that it promotes honest trading it imposes no extra costs on honest traders and, indeed, protects them from unfair competition. The Trade Practices Act has limited application because of the constitutional limitations; it does not, for example, reach a partnership or sole trader operating entirely within the boundaries of a state. In the 1980s the states introduced largely uniform Fair Trading legislation which mirrored the Trade Practices Act. In this way the law recognised the national dimension of Australian commerce and consumers are treated equally throughout Australia.

The reach of the Trade Practices Act

[7.4]   The Trade Practices Act is Commonwealth legislation and therefore subject to the constitutional limitations imposed by s 51 of the Constitution. There is no power, specifically stated, for the Commonwealth Parliament to make laws with respect to consumer protection and therefore the legislation must rest on several heads of power. By virtue of s 6 of the Trade Practices Act it applies to:

- trading and financial corporations;
- conduct in the course of interstate and international trade and commerce;
- trade and commerce in the Northern Territory and the Australian Capital Territory;
- conduct that involves the use of the postal, telegraphic systems;
- dealings with the Commonwealth and its agencies; and
- conduct which is the subject of an international convention.

The constitutional limitations mean that a family business that was not incorporated operating in Victoria would not be subject to the Act. If, however, that business was in the Australian Capital Territory it would be subject to the Trade Practices Act. If it was in Victoria but carried out television advertising, the Act would apply to that advertising as it would if the business was dealing with an agency of the Commonwealth or was supplying goods from Victoria to an interstate customer.

Where conduct is outside the reach of the Trade Practices Act because, for example, it is carried on by an individual, the relevant legislation is that of the state in which the conduct took place. Thus the Fair Trading Act or more specific consumer legislation such as the Door to Door Sales Act would be appropriate. The combination of the Trade Practices Act and the state Fair Trading legislation means that intra-state activity and businesses other than corporations are subject to the same level of regulation. In respect of the regulation of anti-competitive behaviour, dealt with in Pt IV of the Trade Practices Act, arrangements have been made between the states and the Commonwealth whereby Pt IV applies to all business activity without the previous constitutional limitations.

The modern approach to consumer law

[7.5] Modern consumer law is concerned not only with transactions but also with the way in which disputes arising from those transactions are resolved. The fact that the formal legal system is out of reach of most individuals was recognised when governments introduced small claims jurisdictions. These were in the form of courts or tribunals and provided consumers with a low cost, largely informal forum for resolving disputes. In more recent times industry has recognised the need for dispute resolution arrangements and the first of these was the Banking Ombudsman followed soon after by the General Insurance Claims Review Panel and the Life Insurance Complaints Service. Similar dispute resolution bodies have been established in other industries.

Governments have also paid more attention to the way in which consumer transactions are carried out. The notorious foot in the door uninvited seller, who once having gained entry achieved sales by exhausting the householder into submission, is now under the control of legislation — the customer has a cooling-off period so that a decision made under pressure can be reversed. Some selling techniques are prohibited. Legislation was introduced to prohibit directly false advertising and the making of claims about products that were not true.

Although not referred to as consumer protection legislation, the provisions of Pt IV of the Trade Practices Act which are directed against restrictive trade practices are, in truth, for the benefit of consumers. The aim of Pt IV is to promote competition and, according to orthodox economic thinking and government policy, the beneficiaries of competition are consumers.

What is a consumer transaction?

[7.6] Most people would describe themselves as consumers but that is not exact enough for the law. It is not enough merely to say that one is entering into a transaction as a consumer. That term now has a legal significance but most references to 'consumer' are to be found in the definition of the transactions entered into by or as a consumer. The term is defined in the legislation in a variety of ways. The importance of fitting the description of consumer transaction is that the modern law attaches rights to them which are not available to other commercial transactions. In the modern law a consumer attracts a level of legal protection that was not previously available and is not available to a commercial enterprise. The reason is that consumers are regarded as less able to protect their interests than a commercial concern.

Fair Trading Act 1985 (Vic)

[7.7] Section 6 of the Fair Trading Act 1985 (Vic) refers to 'acquisition as a consumer' and says that:

> For the purposes of this Act, unless the contrary intention appears —
> (a) a person shall be taken to have acquired particular goods as a consumer if, and only if —
> (i) the price of the goods did not exceed the prescribed amount; or

(ii) where that price exceeded the prescribed amount — the goods were of a kind ordinarily acquired for personal, domestic or household use or consumption or the goods consisted of a commercial road vehicle —
and the person did not acquire the goods, or hold out that the person was acquiring the goods, for the purpose of re-supply or for the purpose of using them up or transforming them, in trade or commerce, in the course of a process of production or manufacture or of repairing or treating other goods or fixtures on land; and
[The same test applies in respect of the acquisition of services: s 6 (1)b)]

The critically important 'prescribed amount' is explained as follows in s 6(2):

6(2) [Prescribed amount; price of goods; credit sales] For the purposes of subsection (1) —
(a) the prescribed amount is $40,000 or, if a greater amount is prescribed for the purposes of this paragraph, that greater amount;
(b) subject to paragraph (c), the price of goods or services purchased by a person shall be taken to have been the amount paid or payable by the person for the goods or services;
(c) where a person purchased goods or services together with other property or services, or with both other property and services and a specified price was not allocated to the goods or services in the contract under which they were purchased, the price of the goods or services shall be taken to have been —
(i) the price at which, at the time of acquisition, the person could have purchased from the supplier the goods or services without the other property or services;
(ii) if, at the time of the acquisition, the goods or services were not available for purchase from the supplier except together with the other property or services but, at that time, goods or services of the kind acquired were available for purchase from another supplier without other property or services — the lowest price at which the person could, at that time, reasonably have purchased goods or services of that kind from another supplier; or
(iii) if, at the time of the acquisition, goods or services of the kind acquired were not available for purchase from any supplier except together with other property or services — the value of the goods or services at that time;
(d) where a person acquired goods or services otherwise than by way of purchase, the price of the goods or services shall be taken to have been —
(i) the price at which, at the time of the acquisition, the person could have purchased the goods or services from the supplier;
(ii) if, at the time of the acquisition, the goods or services were not available for purchase from the supplier or were so available only together with other property or services but, at that time, the goods or services of the kind acquired were available for purchase from another supplier — the lowest price at which the person could, at that time, reasonably have purchased goods or services of that kind from another supplier; or
(iii) if goods or services of the kind acquired were not available, at the time of the acquisition, for purchase from any supplier or were not so available except together with other property or services — the value of the goods or services at that time; and
(e) without limiting by implication the meaning of the expression 'services' in section 5(1), the obtaining of credit by a person in connexion with the acquisition of goods or services shall be deemed to be the acquisition of a service and any amount by which the amount paid or payable for the goods or services is increased by reason of so obtaining credit shall be deemed to be paid or payable for that service.

Section 6 (3) provides that 'it shall be presumed, unless the contrary is established, that the person was a consumer in relation to those goods or services'.

Trade Practices Act 1974 (Cth)

[7.8]   A similar concept — acquiring as a consumer — applies under the Trade Practices Act 1974 (Cth) s 4B:

4B**(1)** For the purposes of this Act, unless the contrary intention appears —
(a) a person shall be taken to have acquired particular goods as a consumer if, and only if —
(i)   the price of the goods did not exceed the prescribed amount; or
(ii) where that price exceeded the prescribed amount — the goods were of a kind ordinarily acquired for personal, domestic or household use or consumption, or the goods consisted of a commercial road vehicle,
and the person did not acquire the goods, or hold himself out as acquiring the goods, for the purpose of re-supply or for the purpose of using them up or transforming them, in trade or commerce, in the course of a process or production or manufacture or of repairing or treating other goods or fixtures on land; and
(b) [a similar approach applies in relation to acquiring services.]
(2) For the purposes of sub-section (1) —
(a) the prescribed amount is $40,000 or, if a greater amount is prescribed for the purposes of this paragraph, that greater amount;
(b) subject to paragraph (c), the price of goods or services purchased by a person shall be taken to have been the amount paid or payable by the person for the goods or services;
(c) where a person purchased goods or services together with other property or services [such as credit], or with both other property and services, and a specified price was not allocated to the goods or services in the contract under which they were purchased, the price of the goods or services shall be taken to have been —
(i)   the price at which, at the time of the acquisition, the person could have purchased from the supplier the goods or services without the other property or services;
(ii) if, at the time of the acquisition, the goods or services were not available for purchase from the supplier except together with the other property or services but, at that time, goods or services of the kind acquired were available for purchase from another supplier without other property or services — the lowest price at which the person could, at that time, reasonably have purchased goods or services of that kind from another supplier; or
(iii) if, at the time of the acquisition, goods or services of the kind acquired were not available for purchase from any supplier except together with other property or services — the value of the goods or services at that time;
(d) where a person acquired goods or services otherwise than by way of purchase, the price of the goods or services shall be taken to have been —
(i)   the price at which, at the time of the acquisition, the person could have purchased the goods or services from the supplier;
(ii) if, at the time of the acquisition, the goods or services were not available for purchase from the supplier or were so available only together with other property or services but, at that time, goods or services of the kind acquired were available for purchase from another supplier — the lowest price at which the person could, at that time, reasonably have purchased goods or services of that kind from another supplier; or
(iii) if goods or services of the kind acquired were not available, at the time of the acquisition, for purchase from any supplier or were not so available except together with other property or services — the value of the goods or services at that time; and
(e) without limiting by implication the meaning of the expression 'services' in sub-section 4(1), the obtaining of credit by a person in connexion with the acquisition of goods or services by him shall be deemed to be the acquisition by him of a service and any amount by which the amount paid or payable by him for the goods or services is increased by reason of his so obtaining credit shall be deemed to be paid or payable by him for that service.

---

(3) Where it is alleged in any proceeding under this Act or in any other proceeding in respect of a matter arising under this Act that a person was a consumer in relation to particular goods or services, it shall be presumed, unless the contrary is established, that the person was a consumer in relation to those goods or services.
(4) In this section, 'commercial road vehicle' means a vehicle or trailer acquired for use principally in the transport of goods on public roads.

Fair Trading Act 1987 (NSW)

[7.9] A different definition applies in New South Wales where s 5 of the Fair Trading Act 1987 (NSW) provides that:

5(1) ['Consumer'] In this Act, a reference to a consumer is a reference to a person who —
(a) acquires goods or services from a supplier; or
(b) acquires an interest in land, other than land used, or intended to be used, or apparently intended for use, for industrial or commercial purposes.
5(2) ['Goods or services'] Goods or services referred to in subsection (1) do not include goods or services acquired, or held out as being acquired, for re-supply or, in the case of goods, in the course of a business other than a farming undertaking for the purpose of —
(a) consuming or transforming them by a process of manufacture or production; or
(b) using them for the repair or treatment of other goods or of fixtures on land.

Fair Trading Act 1987 (SA)

[7.10]   In South Australia s 3 of the Fair Trading Act provides that a consumer is a person (other than a body corporate):
- who enters into a consumer contract with a view to purchasing, or acquiring the use or benefit of, goods or services; or
- who enters into a consumer credit contract with a view to obtaining credit, or the use or benefit of, credit; or
- who enters, as mortgagor, into a consumer mortgage.

A consumer contract is one where the person purchases, hires or acquires in some other way goods or services where the consideration is not more than $20,000, but does not include a sale by auction. This definition is not clear — it covers only natural persons and is defined by reference to a monetary limit. It is therefore open to argue that an individual who buys an item for less than $20,000 for use in a business — for example, a computer — would be a consumer. Where goods are acquired for less than $20,000 for resale it is not a consumer transaction, nor where acquisition is by auction sale.

The wide notion of a consumer transaction

[7.11]   What emerges from these definitions is that the idea of a consumer transaction is fairly wide. The acquisition of goods or services, of whatever kind, for less than $40,000, or in some places with no limit, will be a consumer transaction provided that the goods are not intended to be used for re-supply. A transaction which involves a person acquiring an item or services for what is regarded as household use will be treated as a consumer transaction no matter how much the item or service costs. Thus the purchase of a house in which to live would be regarded as a consumer transaction despite it exceeding $40,000 in cost. That is what would normally be understood to be a consumer transaction but the legislation provides a wider meaning. It would be possible for a large company to be involved in a consumer transaction if it were to buy a $30,000 car for use in its fleet.

Relevant legislation

Jurisdiction	Legislation	Section
Commonwealth	Trade Practices Act 1974	s 4B
New South Wales	Fair Trading Act 1987	s 5
Victoria	Fair Trading Act 1985	s 6
Queensland	Fair Trading Act 1989	s 6
South Australia	Fair Trading Act 1987	s 3
Western Australia	Fair Trading Act 1987	s 6
Tasmania	Fair Trading Act 1990	s 5
Australian Capital Territory	Fair Trading Act 1992	s 6
Northern Territory	Consumer Affairs and Fair Trading Act 1990	s 5

Goods or services

[7.12]   In the definitions above, a common thread is that a consumer transaction involves the acquisition of goods or services. This is a significant improvement over the level of protection provided by the Sale of Goods Act which applied only to sales and then only to goods.

Services commonly provided to consumers such as car repairs, hairdressing, house painting, plumbing, and legal services were governed by contract law. Apart from licensing schemes for various professions and occupations, no statutory regulation of transactions for these services was in place. The Trade Practices Act, and later the Fair Trading Acts, changed this approach. That legislation extended to transactions beyond sales of goods and applied to provision of services.

There were often difficulties where a transaction involved a combination of the sale of goods and the provision of a service such as the purchase and installation of an electrical appliance. The wider concept makes it no longer necessary artificially to break the transaction into two — the goods component and the services component. This was the approach of the court in *Collins Trading Co Pty Ltd v Maher* [1969] VR 20 where the consumer was sued for the cost of an oil heater which had been supplied and installed. The transaction involved a contract by the trader to do two things, to supply the heater and to install it. The property in the heater was held to have passed when the heater was delivered to the buyer.

Acquisition

[7.13]   To acquire an item could mean something more than purchasing it — it could be leased, hired, borrowed or obtained by barter which is merely another form of contract. The major distinction is that the very nature of a sale involves the ownership of the item being transferred in exchange for the price. The purchaser, having satisfied the terms of the sale, emerges as the owner of the item — a change of ownership has taken place. In these other forms of acquisition the ownership does not necessarily change at the time of the transaction. The process of the sale and various versions of it are discussed in detail in Chapters 6 and 9.

Summary and key terms

[7.14]   This chapter has explained the significance of consumer protection legislation. In particular it:

- illustrated the shortcomings of the common law as it applied to consumers;
- identified what are regarded as the basic rights of consumers;
- described the 'modern' consumer protection/fair trading law;
- discussed what the legislation regards as a consumer transaction;
- explained how the provision of services can be a consumer transaction;
- drew attention to the significance of the term 'acquisition'.

8

The Consumer Transaction: I

What this chapter does ...

The process leading up to a consumer transaction is important for the consumer and the law takes an interest in it. This is the point at which the decision is made to complete the transaction and it is when that the opportunity to mislead the consumer is greatest.

The chapter examines the legal significance of this stage of the transaction and in particular how the Trade Practices Act, and its counterparts in the states and territories, has overcome the limitations and technicalities of the common law.

It also considers the transaction itself in the variety of forms an acquisition may occur.

Promotion

[8.1]   In a competitive market the supplier of goods and services must first attract the attention of prospective purchasers. This is done by advertising and promoting the commodity or service which is being offered. Once consumers have been attracted, the next step is to convince them to buy or otherwise acquire the item. This often involves a process of negotiation and bargaining. It is only after these steps have been taken that the transaction is consummated into a legally binding relationship. At common law the advertisement was seen as an invitation to treat — it was not part of the contract and was, therefore, of no legal significance. Pre-contractual negotiations were likewise of little significance except where the seller had been fraudulent. The common law approach meant that sellers could engage in conduct that was, if not dishonest, at least sharp and consumers could be induced into transactions for which there was no redress.

Advertising at common law

[8.2]   On the face of it an advertisement is not part of a contract. The advertisement appears in a newspaper or on television and could be indirectly connected to the ultimate transaction. In contractual terms there is a problem as to whether the advertisement is an offer or merely an invitation to treat. Another important question is whether the advertisement amounts to a promise that can be legally enforced. The statements made by an advertiser, although they may have been important in bringing about the transaction, are not necessarily legally significant. One description of advertising is that it is 'puff'. If a pizza shop was to describe its pizzas as 'the tastiest' such a statement would not have any contractual significance, because most people would treat it as meaningless. For one thing, it could not be shown to be true or not true. It might also be said that consumers have come to expect, and make allowances for, exaggerated claims about advertised products. This approach adopts the view that advertising is no more than an expression of opinion.

Advertisements take on legal significance once they include statements of fact. Thus while it would be acceptable for a car dealer to advertise as providing the 'greatest value' or the 'best deal for you' a statement that 'ours are the cheapest cars' would involve contractual consequences. That statement would be a representation rather than puff, one that was regarded as a promise, and if it were not true a seller who had used the advertisement could face action from the buyer. A representation that was deliberately not true — a fraudulent misrepresentation — would enable the buyer to rescind the contract and obtain a refund of any money paid or to sue for damages in the tort of deceit. An innocent misrepresentation — where the advertiser did not intend to mislead — allows the buyer to rescind but only in particular circumstances. The very technical nature of the common law on innocent misrepresentation led to statutory reforms, principally in s 52 of the Trade Practices Act 1974 (Cth) and in s 28 of the Insurance Contracts Act 1984 (Cth).

The line between an opinion and fact is sometimes very hard to find. Until the former Trade Practices Commission (the Australian Competition and Consumer Commission since November 1995) took action about misleading statements in advertising, soap manufacturers would describe their product as providing a wash that was 'whiter than white' or make claims that their product gave the 'cleanest wash'. They would refer to 'university tests' which were said to support these claims. As a matter of strict contract law, these statements had no impact; as a matter of common sense they were meaningless but in terms of persuading people to buy the product they could have been influential. The threat of action from the Commission effectively eliminated this type of advertising.

The common law approach to advertising is not clear and can involve technicalities. Of more significance to advertisers and consumers is Pt V of the Trade Practices Act and its equivalents in the Fair Trading legislation.

Misleading or deceptive conduct

[8.3]   Section 52 of the Trade Practices Act provides that:

(1) A corporation shall not, in trade or commerce, engage in conduct that is misleading or deceptive or is likely to mislead or deceive.
(2) Nothing in the succeeding provisions of this Division shall be taken as limiting by implication the generality of subsection (1)

There are equivalent provisions in the Fair Trading Acts: see [8.6].

Because 'conduct that is misleading or deceptive or is likely to mislead or deceive' is not defined in the Act and is so general and wide, it would be unfair to impose criminal liability for a breach of the section. The Act, appropriately, provides for civil remedies such as damages for those who can prove that they have suffered as a result of misleading or deceptive conduct. Injunctions, corrective advertising or the other ancillary remedies are also available under the Act.

The important components of the section are:

1. *Corporation*   This reflects the constitutional formula necessary to give the Act power to operate in the area of consumer protection. The term has the wide meaning given to it by s 6. The conduct being complained of in an action under s 52 must be that of a corporation as defined in the Act.

2. *Trade or commerce*   The Act's definition of the term explains that it covers trade and commerce in Australia or overseas. The term itself is not helpfully defined by the Act and it has been necessary to rely on the courts to explain its meaning. Following the High Court's decision in *Concrete Constructions (NSW) Pty Ltd v Nelson* (1990) 92 ALR 193 at 197 it is now understood in this light:

What the section is concerned with is the conduct of a corporation towards persons, be they consumers or not, with whom it (or those whose interests it represents or is seeking to promote) has or may have dealings in the course of those activities or transactions which, of their nature, bear a trading or commercial character.

Examples of what amounts to trade and commerce are the normal commercial activities such as selling, distributing goods, advertising, promotion or displaying goods.

The term goes further to include the provision of professional services, the conduct of company directors involved in a takeover, the disposal of the assets of a business, or the showing of a film produced as part of a public debate over forest management. Activities which would not fall into the definition include transactions conducted privately such as the sale of a family house or car. These would be excluded on the ground that they are not part of a business activity and therefore do not bear the trading or commercial character referred to by the High Court.

In *Forbes v Australian Yachting Federation* (1996) ATPR ¶46-158 the plaintiff challenged the federation's nomination of another crew for the Olympic Games. It was argued that the federation's action was misleading or deceptive in that it made representations, in the form of selection criteria, but did not fulfil them. In the New South Wales Supreme Court it was held that the federation was not a trading or financial corporation and that the representations were not made in trade or commerce.

The topic was discussed in *Fasold v Roberts* (1997) ATPR ¶41-561 where Sackville J considered the cases that followed *Concrete Constructions (NSW) Pty Ltd v Nelson*. These were *Tobacco Institute of Australia Ltd v Woodward* (1993) 32 NSWLR 559; (1993) ATPR ¶41-199 and *Prestia v Aknar* (1996) 40 NSWLR 165. It was on the basis of these cases that Sackville J accepted that the term has the same meaning in the Fair Trading legislation as in the Trade Practices Act.

3. *Misleading or deceptive or likely to mislead or deceive* In its simplest form this term means conduct that leads members of the public in their capacity as consumers of goods or services into error or is likely to do so. It appears that 'deceptive' adds nothing. The words 'likely to' have their everyday meaning. They are significant in that it is not necessary that the conduct actually misleads or deceives. The conduct caught by s 52 is what amounts to a misrepresentation.

Another dimension of the term to consider is whether it means the same as confusion. To be confused is not necessarily the same as having been misled. Conduct that leads to confusion in the sense of being bewildered or left wondering cannot be said to be misleading or deceptive. There could be other explanations for that state. Where, however, a person is confused to the extent of not being able to distinguish two products, that can amount to being misled or deceived.

Case Example

The name 'Big Mac' was used by McWilliams Wines as the name of a wine it was marketing. McDonalds who sell 'Big Mac' hamburgers complained that it was misleading for somebody else to use the name. The court said it was not. The difference between wine and hamburgers was clear: *McWilliam's Wines Pty Ltd v McDonalds System of Australia Pty Ltd* (1980) 49 FLR 455.

---

but a different result was reached in:

Case Example

When a corporation opened a Mexican restaurant in Sydney under the name 'Taco Bell', another corporation which had used that name in Sydney over the last five years for its Mexican restaurant was able to succeed under s 52. The confusion created by using the same name became misleading because they sold the same style of food, there was no label to correct the confusion and when consumers went to the restaurant they would not realise their mistake and would thus be misled: *Taco Co of Australia v Taco Bell Pty Ltd* (1982) 42 ALR 177.

In another case involving food the Pizza Ribs chain had been developed over several years in Melbourne. In Seymour, a country town in Victoria, a restaurant was opened under the name Pinky's Pizza and BYO Restaurant. Some time later Pinky's Pizza Ribs opened a store in Seymour and sought to prevent the use of the name Pinky's Pizza and Pasta. In the Victorian Court of Appeal, it was held that the Seymour Pizza business did not contribute to the confusion of the public that arose. It carried on its business in the same way after Pinky's Pizza Ribs had arrived. The s 52 application was lost: *Pinky's Pizza Ribs on the Run Pty Ltd v Pinky's Seymour Pizza and Pasta Pty Ltd* (1997) ATPR ¶41-600.

Specific instances of misleading or deceptive conduct

[8.4]   Examples of what has been held to be misleading or deceptive conduct include:

- Using a photograph of a competitor's cricket helmet on the boxes in which another maker's helmet was sold: *Coonan & Denaly Pty Ltd v Superstar Australia Pty Ltd* (1981) 37 ALR 155.

- A newspaper published articles that were critical of a cruise ship holiday with the result that bookings fell off. This was conduct reached by s 52. There was a consumer connection — consumers bought newspapers and they could be misled by a false description of a product or service: *Australian Ocean Line Ltd v West Australian Newspapers Ltd* (1985) ATPR ¶40-533.

- The use of similar business names: *MIPS Computer Systems Inc v MIPS Computer Resources Pty Ltd* (1990) ATPR ¶41-050.

- False labelling that goods were made in Australia: *Thorp v CA Imports Pty Ltd* (1990) ATPR ¶40-996.

- Failing to tell the whole truth in the case of the sale of a restaurant which had a 2 am licence but undisclosed to the purchaser was the fact that there was, at the time of the sale, a condition requiring that the restaurant closed at 11 pm: *McMahon v Pomersay Pty Ltd* (1991) ATPR ¶41-125.

- Making a false statement to a prospective tenant about the number of tenants in a shopping centre: *Brown v The Jam Factory* (1981) 35 ALR 79.

- Advice provided by a bank in a foreign currency loan transaction: *Mehta v Commonwealth Bank of Australia* (1991) ATPR ¶41-103.

- A persistent statement in a prospectus referring to 'free shares' was held to be misleading because the reference was likely to engender the incorrect notion that the shares being offered in return for members changing their status might be acquired without significant loss or outgoing: *NRMA Holdings Limited v Fraser* (1994) ATPR ¶41-436; (1995) ATPR ¶41-374; (1995) ATPR ¶41-380.

- Wrong advice from a franchisor that a site was suitable for a business when, because of its small population, the site was not suitable: *Thompson v Ice Creameries of Australia Pty Ltd* (1998) ATPR ¶41-611.

Section 52 as a weapon for business

[8.5]   As the Big Mac and Taco Bell examples show, the parties involved in the litigation were commercial enterprises. Although s 52 is part of a consumer protection law, it is often used by commercial competitors against each other. An example is the case of *Colgate Palmolive Pty Ltd v Rexona Pty Ltd* (1981) 37 ALR 391, where the launch of Aim toothpaste was delayed because Colgate Palmolive alleged that Rexona had made claims about its new product which could not be substantiated. In this way it is a useful commercial weapon. Another example is where an accounting firm negligently conducted an audit. The statements made in the audit report were wrong and were thus misrepresentations caught by s 52: see also *Trumpet Software Pty Ltd v OzEmail Pty Ltd* [1996] 560 FCA 1. In *WD & HO Wills (Australia) Pty Ltd v Philip Morris* (1997) ATPR ¶41-590 two rival tobacco companies were in dispute over the use by one of packaging and advertising of its new brand which was very similar to the one already on the market. The Federal Court held that the similarity amounted to misleading and deceptive conduct. The justification for the use of the section for commercial benefit is that a corporation should be able to obtain protection from unfair competition. The section is also attractive for this form of use because, as in a negligent auditor case, the proof requirements are easier. It is not necessary to establish the components of negligence, it is enough to establish that the statement was incorrect.

Conduct which breaches s 52 will often be in breach of s 53. See, for example, *Trade Practices Commission v Optus Communications* (1996) ATPR ¶41-478 where advertising that incorrectly explained the cost of telephone calls was also a breach of s 53(e).

Impact on common law rules

[8.6]   Section 52 has removed some of the technicalities of the common law in respect of misrepresentations. It makes no distinction between fraudulent or innocent misrepresentations. Thus the technical nature of law about innocent misrepresentation is avoided. Likewise there is no requirement that the conduct be intentional and the need to prove fraud is removed. Puff is still treated in the same way — it is acceptable provided it is a self-evident exaggeration or expression of opinion. As with the common law, if a puff statement is not likely to be taken seriously it will be outside the reach of s 52: see *Collier Constructions v Foskett* (1991) ATPR ¶46-071 in this respect.

Many of the s 52 cases have been similar to common law 'passing-off' actions. This is a tort which involves creating the impression, by the use of names or other indicators, that one's product or business is that of, or linked to, another's. Of its very nature the conduct which amounts to passing-off is misleading. The courts have been at pains to make clear that, even though what constitutes passing-off would also breach s 52, it is not correct to say that s 52 is a statutory form of the passing-off action.

Relevant legislation

Jurisdiction	Legislation	Section
Commonwealth	Trade Practices Act 1974	s 52
New South Wales	Fair Trading Act 1987	s 42
Victoria	Fair Trading Act 1985	s 11
Queensland	Fair Trading Act 1989	s 38
South Australia	Fair Trading Act 1987	s 56
Western Australia	Fair Trading Act 1987	s 10
Tasmania	Fair Trading Act 1990	s 14
Australian Capital Territory	Fair Trading Act 1992	s 12
Northern Territory	Consumer Affairs and Fair Trading Act 1990	s 42

Bait advertising

[8.7]   The practice of advertising an item at a bargain price in order to attract people into a store is not of itself unlawful. What is unlawful is such advertising when there is only a small quantity of the item or none at all. The advertised bargain is not genuinely available; the seller does not intend to offer the items for sale as advertised. The bargain price is the bait.

A refinement of this activity is to attract customers with the bargain and then convince them to buy a more expensive item — this is known as switching. For example, a retailer advertises a particular model of a car at a special price and consumers find that the sales staff seek to talk them into buying another, more expensive model.

Where a bargain is advertised the seller must have a sufficient number of the items at that price to meet the demand for a reasonable period or, if not, explain that there is a limited quantity. Some advertisers who find that supplies do not arrive in time for the sale will offer consumers 'rainchecks' so that they can buy the item at the special advertised price. The offering of 'rainchecks' provides a defence to prosecution.

> **Case Example**
>
> Morley Ford advertised Falcon cars at a special price until a certain date. Its sales staff refused to sell at that price and the court found that Morley did not intend to sell at the price: *Reardon v Morley Ford Pty Ltd* (1980) ATPR ¶40–205.

Relevant legislation

Jurisdiction	Legislation	Section
Commonwealth	Trade Practices Act 1974	s 56
New South Wales	Fair Trading Act 1987	s 51
Victoria	Fair Trading Act 1985	s 18
Queensland	Fair Trading Act 1989	s 46
South Australia	Fair Trading Act 1987	s 65
Western Australia	Fair Trading Act 1987	s 19
Tasmania	Fair Trading Act 1990	s 22
Australian Capital Territory	Fair Trading Act 1992	s 21
Northern Territory	Consumer Affairs and Fair Trading Act 1990	s 52

Offering gifts

[8.8]   In all parts of Australia it is forbidden to offer gifts, prizes or free items in the course of trade and commerce without the intention of providing them: Trade Practices Act s 54. Where gifts and prizes are offered it is necessary to ensure that any conditions associated with the offer are made known. If, for example, the offer has a closing date or if there is some catch such as being required to sign up for 40 lessons in order to win 10, these must be disclosed. Similarly, a promotion that offers free overseas air fares must explain if there is a minimum period that the winner must stay overseas or if accommodation must be taken in a particular hotel at a particular price.

An example of how carefully advertising campaigns must be planned came in England in 1993 where an electrical appliance company offered air travel to the United States for anybody who purchased one of its products. The campaign was a great success but more people qualified for the trip to the United States than there were airline seats available then or for the foreseeable future. It was necessary for the company to negotiate alternative prizes for the consumers who missed out.

[8.9]   An illustration of why this legislation was necessary was the claim that a person could win $1 million when the prize being offered was no more than a lottery ticket. It goes without saying that the item described as free or as a gift must be that — it would be a breach of the law if the price of the 'gift' were to be added to the price of the other item.

Relevant legislation

Jurisdiction	Legislation	Section
Commonwealth	Trade Practices Act 1974	s 54
New South Wales	Fair Trading Act 1987	s 48
Victoria	Fair Trading Act 1985	s 15

Jurisdiction	Legislation	Section
Queensland	Fair Trading Act 1989	s 43
South Australia	Fair Trading Act 1987	s 62
Western Australia	Fair Trading Act 1987	s 16
Tasmania	Fair Trading Act 1990	s 19
Australian Capital Territory	Fair Trading Act 1992	s 18
Northern Territory	Consumer Affairs and Fair Trading Act 1990	s 51

Trading stamps

[8.10]   Trading stamps or coupons are sometimes used in sales promotions as an attraction. Consumers are able to obtain trading stamps based on the amount of a certain product or products they purchase. Where the stamp can be redeemed with a retailer or the manufacturer of the goods there is no legislative sanction against them. There is legislation in most parts of Australia which, generally, prohibits stamps of a type where three parties are involved — the consumer, a retailer and a trading stamp company. The main objection to this type of scheme is that consumers are often misled as to the existence of a gift because the price of the product is inflated by the cost of the stamps or the gift is a product of inferior quality.

Trading stamps should be distinguished from loyalty schemes whereby a frequent purchaser is credited with points which can later be redeemed for a gift or a reduced price or a free service such as travel. These schemes may be of dubious value but are not regulated.

Relevant legislation

Jurisdiction	Legislation	Section
Commonwealth	—	—
New South Wales	Fair Trading Act 1987	Pt 5A
Victoria	Consumer Affairs Act 1972	
Queensland	—	—
South Australia	Fair Trading Act 1987	ss 39, 44, 45
Western Australia	Trading Stamp Act 1981	
Tasmania	Trading Stamp Abolition Act 1981	
Australian Capital Territory	Trading Stamp Act 1972	
Northern Territory	Consumer Affairs and Fair Trading Act 1990	ss 123, 124

False representations

[8.11]   Section 53 of the Trade Practices Act prohibits a range of specific forms of false representation by corporations in trade or commerce. Unlike s 52, the terms of s 53 are sufficiently specific to impose criminal liability for a breach even though an intention to mislead has not been established. That is to say, s 53 imposes strict liability. The penalty for a breach is, in the case of a body corporate, a fine of up to $200,000 or, for an individual, a fine of up to $40,000: s 79(1) There is no power to impose a prison sentence under the Act but failure to pay the fine can result in imprisonment: s 79A.

The representations referred to in the section are statements which, according to Franki J in *Given v Prior* (1977) 39 FLR 437 at 440:

> ... may be in any language, including one made by signs that are known and understood by those deaf and dumb people who use them, and one written in shorthand. In the same way I cannot see why pictorial or diagrammatic material should not be included in a statement.

A representation that is 'false' is one contrary to fact. The conduct that amounts to a representation is, as Franki J's explanation shows, very wide. In *Given v Prior* he said that an odometer reading was a representation.

Conduct prohibited by s 53

[8.12]   The protection offered by s 53 applies to consumers and to honest traders. For both groups the prohibited conduct is unfair — they can both suffer as a result of it.

The forms of specific conduct prohibited by s 53 are as follows.

Section 53(a)

[8.13]

> (a) false representations that goods are of a particular standard, quality, value, grade, composition, style or model or have had a particular history or particular previous use.

All of the representations referred to in s 53(a) are of a type which are likely to impress consumers and lead them into a transaction. If the representations are untrue the consumer has been hoodwinked. The supplier has gained an unfair advantage over law-abiding competitors and it is in this context that dishonest conduct of this type should be considered.

Examples include:

- A manufacturer of microwave ovens advertised that its ovens were approved by the Standards Association of Australia. This was false: *Sharp Corp of Australia Pty Ltd v Hartnell* (1975) ATPR ¶40-003 (this was the first prosecution under Pt V of the Trade Practices Act and the company was fined $100,000).
- An advertisement described 'silver rings from teaspoons' when the rings contained no silver at all: *Thompson v Magnamail Pty Ltd (No 2)* (1977) ATPR ¶40–033.
- A shop advertised 'top quality' shoes. They were in fact seconds: *MacFarlane v John Martin & Co Ltd* (1977) ATPR ¶40-034.
- Demonstrator photocopiers were sold without disclosing that history: *Hollis v ABE. Copiers Pty Ltd* (1979) ATPR ¶40-115.
- False odometer readings: *Given v CV Holland (Holdings) Pty Ltd* (1977) 29 FLR 212.
- False statements about the origin of goods: *Barton v Croner Trading Pty Ltd* (1985) ATPR ¶40-525; *Korczynski v Wes Lofts (Aust) Pty Ltd* (1986) ATPR ¶40-707.

- False statements about the quality of wine: *Van Berg v Trade Practices Commission* (1997) ATPR ¶41-545.

Section 53(aa)

[8.14]

> (aa) false representations that services are of a particular standard, quality, value or grade.

A consumer can be misled where the qualities of a service being provided are misleadingly expressed. An example of this is:

- An advertisement for the three-day Rio tennis tournament in Canberra said 'Lendl v McEnroe Nightly at 7.30'. In fact these two players, at that time highly ranked, were scheduled to meet only once: *Kiley v Lysfar Pty Ltd* (1985) ATPR ¶40-614.

Section 53(b)

[8.15]

> (b) false representations that goods are new.

Almost certainly a person will be prepared to pay more for an item that is described as new unless that person was shopping for an antique item. The legitimate expectations of such an item would be much greater than if it were secondhand. The decision to buy new rather than used goods may well have involved the consumer in other arrangements such as financing. To be misled in a matter such as this prevents the consumer from making an informed judgment about value for money. The problem in this area is that the word 'new' has several meanings. In *Annand & Thompson Pty Ltd v Trade Practices Commission* (1979) 25 ALR 91 it was explained that:

> The meaning of the word 'new', particularly in relation to motor vehicles, has been considered several times in the courts. It seems there are at least five possible meanings which the word may bear when used to describe a vehicle. They are:
> (1) That the vehicle has not been previously sold by retail, that is, that it is not a secondhand vehicle.
> (2) That the vehicle is a current and not a superseded model.
> (3) That the vehicle has not suffered significant deterioration or been used to any significant extent.
> (4) That the vehicle is of recent origin.
> (5) That the vehicle is one which has suffered a measure of damage but this damage has been quite effectively repaired, or any damaged part replaced, and the vehicle is otherwise new in every respect.

A breach would occur where a demonstration model, a superseded model or a reconditioned item were represented to be new. Failure to disclose that something had a previous history of use so that the impression was left that it was new would also be a breach of the section.

Section 53(bb)

[8.16]

> (bb) false representations that a particular person has agreed to acquire goods or services.

This was added to the Act to counter the practice of asserting that a person, recently deceased, had ordered goods and then demanding payment for them from relatives. It could also apply to assertions that a living person or a company had ordered goods or services.

Section 53(c)

[8.17]

> (c) representations that goods or services have sponsorship, approval, performance characteristics, accessories, uses or benefits they do not have.

Examples include:

- At the time World Series Cricket was introduced the Australian Cricket Board, the 'official body', used s 53(c) to prevent the World Series matches from being promoted as Test or Super Test matches. The use of the term 'test' suggested sponsorship by the official body: *Parish v World Series Cricket Pty Ltd* (1977) ATPR ¶40-040.
- An advertisement said that a particular type of vehicle was fitted with rear stabiliser bars when some models were not: *Ducret v Nissan Motor Co (Australia) Pty Ltd* (1979) ATPR ¶40-111.
- A claim that by fitting its car burglar alarm a person would qualify for a reduction of insurance premium when this was not so: *Given v Optional Extras* (1976) ATPR ¶40-051.

Section 53(d)

[8.18]

> (d) representations that the corporation has a sponsorship, approval or affiliation it does not have.

Many consumers would be reassured to know that the corporation with whom they are dealing is well thought of by influential organisations. A practical example of this arises from campaigns directed at consumers by trade associations and government advice agencies to deal with traders who are members of a particular trade association. Consumers acting in what they think is a prudent way could suffer damage as a result of false advertising in this regard.

Examples include:

- Where a corporation falsely claimed that it was a member of body such as the Master Builders Association. An affiliation such as this would create the impression that the corporation has satisfied the membership standards of the association and could therefore be trusted.
- If a corporation were falsely to advertise in a way that suggested the approval of the royal family, or that it was associated in some way with the Olympic Games or that it was approved by a prominent and influential personality or organisation it would be in breach of this prohibition.
- A computer company sold computers which were similar to those of a high profile rival and supplied with them the operating manual of that other company's computer, thus creating an unsubstantiated impression that its computers were associated with the more prominent brand: *Apple Computer Inc v Computer Edge Pty Ltd* (1984) ATPR ¶40-453.
- The use of a similar trading name and trade mark were found to amount to a breach of s 53(c) and (d): *Australian Home Loans Ltd (T/A Aussie Home Loans) v Phillips* (1998) ATPR ¶41-626.

Section 53(e)

[8.19]

> (e) false or misleading representations with respect to the price of goods or services.

In the decision about acquiring a particular item or service price is a critical factor. A false representation on such a matter could result in the consumer being misled into an incorrect decision.

- The Trade Practices Act defines 'price' to include a charge of any description: s 4. It would include delivery charges, installation charges, taxes, finance charges, insurance, on-road charges for motor vehicles and any other cost which is added to the basic cost of the goods or services. It follows that a supplier must inform a consumer of the total price. There is no room for hidden extras.
- A price that is described as reduced or discounted or special must be just that. It is a breach of s 53(e) to claim as a discounted price the regular price, or to inflate the regular price and then sell at the normal regular price and claim that it is a discounted price. Where a discount applies only where a certain quantity is purchased that condition must be made known.
- Price comparison is important and when an advertisement is based on comparing the advertiser's price with those of competitors, accuracy is essential. If the price difference were to be exaggerated, even by mistake, it would be a breach of the Act. The safe way to engage in price comparison is to express the price advantage in the form of 'we will guarantee to beat a competitor's price by $X'.
- The advertising of items must leave no wrong impression as to what is available for the price. Barbecue equipment is often advertised in catalogues in a complete setting. If, for example, a gas bottle or umbrella is shown, the advertisement must make it clear if they come at an extra cost.

The provision represents a variation of the common law rule that the advertising or displaying of goods is an invitation to treat. Where a seller makes a representation about the price of goods, even by way of a price label, if the goods are to be sold they must be sold at that price. Where an incorrect price is displayed or otherwise represented, the appropriate way of avoiding liability under s 53(e) is to withdraw them from sale and correct the error.

Examples of breaches of s 53 (e) include:

- The use of dual price tags on clothing where a higher price was crossed out and replaced by a lower price written in. The higher prices were what the consumer would have paid during the particular period if the retailer had not decided to reduce the price. The goods had not previously been offered at the higher price: *TPC v Cue Design Pty Ltd* (1996) ATPR ¶41-475.
- Optus advertised free weekend local calls but failed to mention that the offer did not apply to calls from one mobile telephone to another. The advertisements generated a reasonable expectation that if there are significant exclusions to the offer of free calls an enquirer would be informed by Optus as to the true position. This was not done and thus it was misleading as to price: *TPC v Optus Communication* (1996) ATPR ¶41-478.
- In response to the launch of telephone calls at 20 cents Telstra stated that under its pricing plan local calls would be available at 21 cents. In fact the cost ranged from 21.8 cents to 25 cents: *Australian Competition and Consumer Commission v Telstra* (1997) ATPR ¶41-540.

Section 53(ea)

[8.20]

> (ea) false or misleading representations concerning the availability of facilities for the repair of goods or of spare parts for goods.

A consumer in the process of acquiring goods needs to know as part of the decision-making process whether it will be possible to have them repaired. If this cannot be done the apparent bargain may turn out to be very expensive. This is all the more important where relatively expensive high technology goods are involved. The prohibition is against false or misleading representations about the availability of repair facilities or spare parts; the section does not require the facilities to be made available (that is dealt with elsewhere in the Act: see [9.7]). The important thing is that the consumer is properly informed at the time of making the decision.

Section 53(eb)

[8.21]

> (eb) false or misleading representations concerning the place of origin of goods.

For some consumers it is important to know where items have been made. It may be that goods from a certain country have a high reputation for quality such as Swiss watches or Japanese electronic goods. Other consumers may wish to avoid goods from certain places if, for example, they are involved in a boycott or if a particular place is notorious for poor quality. Made in Australia campaigns directed at persuading consumers to support local industries provide examples of how important the issue of place of origin can become. A problem exists about what level of activity must take place in Australia to enable the supplier to describe them as Australian-made.

Examples include:

* Adhesive tape was imported into Australia from the United States. It was re-packaged in Australia into rolls suitable for retail distribution. Was it correct to say, as the supplier did, that the tape was made in Australia? The court said no: *Korczynski v Wes Lofts (Aust) Pty Ltd* (1986) ATPR ¶40-643.
* Toys were designed in Australia but the manufacture of the outer casing was carried out in South Korea. The material was returned to Australia where it was further processed into the product that went on to the market. More than 50 per cent of the costs of production had been incurred in Australia. The company was held to be in breach of s 53(eb): *Netcomm (Australia) Pty Ltd v Dataplex Pty Ltd* (1988) ATPR ¶40-883.
* Toy koalas were labelled 'Aussie Born' and made in Australia. Another label stated that 'the major component of manufacturing cost' was incurred in Australia. The Australian operation was the most costly part of the process but because a significant part of the manufacture took place outside Australia it was misleading to describe the toys as being Australian: *QDSV Holdings Pty Ltd v TPC* (1995) ATPR ¶41-432.

Case Example

In *Australian Competition and Consumer Commission v Lovelock Luke Pty Ltd* [1997] 1100 FCA; (1997) ATPR ¶41-594 the issue was whether Lovelock Luke Pty Ltd ('Lovelock Luke') contravened s 52(1) or s 53(e)(b) of the Trade Practices Act 1974 by representing for the purposes of sale that various kinds of air conditioners are made in Australia given that the compressors, which are important parts of the air conditioners, are imported.

The packaging of the relevant air conditioners contained the words 'Australian made' and the 'Australian made' logo — the hopping kangaroo — which also appeared on the bodies of the air conditioners. Advertising material described the air conditioners as 'Made in Australia', 'All are Australian made', 'All Australian', 'All of these room air conditioners are Australian-made', 'Australian air conditioners for Australian conditions', 'Australian air conditioning', 'The majority of our air conditioning units are still made in Australia'.

The case was decided by Lockhart J taking into account the following principles:

- There is no absolute meaning of the expression 'Made in Australia' or 'Australian-made'.
- Whether an article is Australian-made must be determined by reference to the facts of each case.
- The word 'origin' in this area of discourse has a purely geographic denotation. Origin directs attention to the beginning of the existence of goods with reference to a source or cause of that existence. To say that goods are made in Australia plainly makes a statement concerning that place of origin.
- Generally the phrase 'Australian-made' is an historical statement suggesting that the goods are substantially, if not wholly, the result of manufacturing processes carried out in Australia.
- Whether a representation that goods are Australian-made constitutes misleading or deceptive conduct must be determined by reference to the effect of the conduct on purchaser or potential purchasers of the relevant goods. In this regard two relevant factors are: (a) the price of the goods because a consumer is likely to devote less care to reading a label where the product is not particularly expensive than where it is an expensive item; and (b) the proportion of purchasers of the product who have only a limited facility of the English language for understanding the label.
- Whether an article of commerce is 'Australian-made' must be determined by reference to the circumstances of each case.

He concluded with the comment that:

> I am content, however, to adopt as the best test in this case for determining the place of origin of the air conditioners namely whether the goods were produced by a manufacturing process which substantially takes place in Australia or whether most of the component parts used in the manufacturing process have themselves been manufactured in Australia.

On that basis Lockhart J decided that the use of the words 'Made in Australia' or 'Australian Made' did not amount to a breach of either s 52 or s 53(eb) of the Act.

This case was applied in *Australian Competition and Consumer Commission v Unilever Australia Limited* (1998) ATPR ¶41-607 where the issue in dispute was a statement that John West brand tuna was 'caught and canned in South Australia' when a considerable proportion of it was produced in Thailand or caught in international waters and freighted to Australia.

Changes to the Trade Practices Act effective from 13 August 1998 provide that 'Product /Produce of Australia' can be used only where the local content is 100 per cent or close to it. To use 'Made in Australia' it is necessary that at least 50 per cent of the cost of producing the product was incurred in Australia: Trade Practices Act Pt V Div 1AA, ss 65AA–65AM enacted by Trade Practices Amendment (Country of Origin Representations) Act 1998.

Section 53(f)

[8.22]

(f) making a false or misleading representations concerning the need for any goods or services.

To force a person into an transaction by falsely claiming that it is necessary is fraudulent. It was common for 'pest exterminators' to tell old age pensioners that their houses were infested with termites and to panic them into having unnecessary work done. Likewise a mechanic could profitably extend a transaction by telling the customer that in the course of a simple repair job it became apparent that more substantial work was necessary.

The 'need' for goods or services can exist when it is only desirable or preferable. It is important to establish that the goods/service were not needed and it may be that the person who reached that conclusion acted reasonably in doing so.

An example of this is:

*   A private health insurance fund told patients that if they wished to be able to choose who should treat them they would be well advised to maintain membership of the fund. This was incorrect: *Keehn v Medical Benefits Fund of Australia Ltd* (1977) ATPR ¶40-047.

Section 53(g)

[8.23]

(g) the making of a false or misleading representation concerning the existence, exclusion or effect of any condition, warranty, guarantee, right or remedy.

Conduct of this nature leads consumers into error about their legal rights arising from the contract. The most common example of such conduct is in the form of signs to the effect that 'We exchange goods but do not give refunds'. The reason such signs are in breach of s 53(g) is that consumers have the right to a refund where goods are defective. The sign not only misleads consumers about their legal rights but in many cases would intimidate them into not asserting those rights.

The prohibition is also relevant where a printed warranty accompanies goods that have been imported and set out the terms of the law applicable in some other country. Importers of such goods must be careful to ensure that the conditions expressed in the warranty are consistent with Australian law.

Examples include:

- Calculators were sold with a pamphlet stating that they carried a one-year warranty when in fact it was only 90 days: *Ballard v Sperry Rand Australia Ltd* (1975) ATPR ¶40-006.
- An insurance agent gave wrong information about the wording of a clause in a disability insurance policy. He said that it applied to the consumer being incapable of carrying out his 'normal occupation' when it, in fact, applied to 'any occupation'. The impression was that the policy operated in a more generous way than the standard type of disability policy. The agent was in breach of the section: *Gates v City Mutual Life Assurance Society* (1982) ATPR ¶40-311.

Sanctions for conduct prohibited by s 53

[8.24] A breach of s 53 amounts to criminal behaviour. It is enforced by way of prosecution. The penalty is a maximum fine of $200,000 for a corporation or $40,000 for a non-corporate person: s 79. Persons who are damaged by a breach of the section are able to obtain damages: s 82. Because of the criminal standard of proof involved in a criminal prosecution it may be easier for conduct in breach of s 53 to be dealt with under s 52. There is no doubt that what is misleading under s 53 is also misleading under s 52 and a sanction such as an injunction or corrective advertising may be more appropriate in the particular circumstances.

Other prohibited conduct

[8.25] Related to s 53 is other conduct which is made illegal:

- False representations and other misleading or offensive conduct in relation to land: s 53A.
- Conduct by a corporation in relation to employment that is to be, or may be, offered that is liable to mislead persons seeking the employment as to the availability, nature, terms or conditions of, or any other matter relating to, the employment: s 53B.

Relevant legislation

Jurisdiction	Legislation	Section
Commonwealth	Trade Practices Act 1974	ss 53, 53A, 53B
New South Wales	Fair Trading Act 1987	ss 44, 45, 46
Victoria	Fair Trading Act 1985	ss 12, 13, 14
Queensland	Fair Trading Act 1989	ss *40, 41
South Australia	Fair Trading Act 1987	ss 58, 59, 60
Western Australia	Fair Trading Act 1987	ss 12, 12, 14
Tasmania	Fair Trading Act 1990	ss 16, 17, 18
Australian Capital Territory	Fair Trading Act 1992	ss 14,15,16
Northern Territory	Consumer Affairs and Fair Trading Act 1990	ss 44,45,46

* Queensland has no equivalent of s 53A of the Trade Practices Act.

Restrictive trade practices

[8.26]   Although regulated under Pt IV of the Trade Practices Act the forms of conduct described in the Trade Practices Act as restrictive trade practices can be no less damaging to consumers than the types of dishonest or unfair conduct that are prohibited under Pt V of the Act. Part IV of the Act deals with conduct that is anti-competitive or has the effect of lessening competition.

Contracts, arrangements or understandings that restrict dealings or affect competition

[8.27]   Section 45(2) provides that a corporation (as defined) shall not make contracts, arrangements or understandings that contain an exclusionary provision or which have the purpose, effect or likely effect of substantially lessening competition.

The term exclusionary provision is defined in the Act in s 4D and, in brief, means an agreement between two or more competitors in which they agree not to supply or acquire goods or services from a particular person or persons. The term is another way of describing a collective boycott. If, for example, wholesalers A and B are supplying C with goods that are discounted an agreement between A and B not to supply C because of that would be an exclusionary provision. It is possible to have such conduct authorised: s 88. See *News Ltd v Australian Rugby League Ltd* (1996) 139 ALR 193 at 347 for a discussion by the Full Federal Court as to whether an exclusionary provision existed.

The term 'arrangement' is not defined in the Act and would take its meaning from *Re British Slag Ltd Agreements* [1963] 2 All ER 807 to mean a meeting of minds with the arousal of certain expectations in the minds of the parties and the acceptance that each party will act in a certain way. An 'understanding' is a meeting of minds where they 'are at one that a proposed transaction [proceeds in a particular way]': see *Top Performance Motors Ltd v Ira Berk (Qld) Pty Ltd* (1975) ATPR ¶40-004.

Critical to the notion of competition is the arena in which it is meant to take place — the market. That term is defined, but unhelpfully, in s 4E. It is necessary to consider 'market' by reference to a number of factors such a product, geographical or level functional — retail or wholesale. The narrower the definition of the relevant market the more likely certain conduct will affect it. Thus it would be important to decide whether potato chips could be said to be in the food market or snack food market. If it were the snack food market then conduct would be likely to have a greater impact because it would be a smaller market.

Competition is referred to but not defined in s 4D(2) and similarly referred to in s 45(3). It denotes a state of rivalry and its level is measured by reference to factors such as the ease of entry of newcomers into a market, the level of activity and rivalry and the number of players in a market.

The term 'lessening of competition' is discussed in s 4G of the Act and is to be 'read as including references to preventing or hindering competition'. The measurement of whether there had been or could be a lessening of competition is largely a matter for expert opinion.

Contracts, arrangements or understandings in relation to prices

[8.28]   Price fixing is probably the most anti-competitive conduct imaginable and is prohibited by s 45A. It is described as anti-competitive per se which means that there is no reference to its effect on competition — it is assumed by the Act to be anti-competitive — but it may be authorised. The critical issue in deciding whether there has been price fixing is to establish that there has been some form of agreement. The fact that competitors may raise their prices almost simultaneously is not necessarily price fixing. It would have to be done in concert to amount to price fixing.

It is not always the case that corporations allegedly in competition formally agree to fix prices. The fixing, controlling or maintaining of prices may be achieved in other ways. For example, an agreement to restrict production or to share pricing information or to use an industry-wide pricing schedule or to have uniform discount rates would have the prohibited effect.

Misuse of market power

[8.29]   Corporations with 'a substantial degree of power in a market' are prohibited from using that power to restrict competition: s 46. The section prohibits the use of power to eliminate or substantially damage a competitor or to prevent a competitor from entering the market or to discourage competitive conduct. The conduct of a monopoly would not, of itself, be a breach of the section. It is not until the power is used in an anti-competitive way that is amounts to a breach: see *Queensland Wire Industries Pty Ltd v Broken Hill Proprietary Co Ltd* (1989) 167 CLR 177; 83 ALR 577.

Exclusive dealing

[8.30]   Exclusive dealing is prohibited where its likely effect is to substantially lessen competition: s 47. It exists in a variety of forms some of which are quite subtle. A crude form is where a supplier of a commodity makes it a condition of supply that the reseller also purchases its brand of another product — a petrol supplier may impose the condition that the reseller also buy its brand of oils. In another form it is where a supplier insists on a minimum order so that the reseller has no physical or economic way of buying from a competitor. A variation of this was a case where an ice cream manufacturer gave the retailer a free refrigerator on condition that it be used only for its brand. That appeared to be reasonable but it was anti-competitive because the refrigerator was so large that another refrigerator could not fit into the shop and therefore no other brand could be sold. The thrust of exclusive dealing is to bind a person in such a way as to exclude or minimise the opportunity for competition.

Prior to the Trade Practices Act exclusive dealing was a way of life in Australia. A common example was that of breweries which bound hotels to take only their brand of beer. Hotels in that relationship were described as tied houses. At the level of consumer transactions, exclusive dealing was rife especially in relation to finance and related transactions. A person who financed the acquisition of a car through a hire–purchase transaction through G Finance Co was required to insure the car with H Insurance, which was a related company. Likewise it was not uncommon for a life insurance company when providing a housing loan to make it conditional upon the borrower arranging insurance cover over the house and contents through a related general insurance company.

Conduct such as this was objectionable because it denied consumers a choice, it forced them into what often were expensive transactions and it denied them the benefit of competition. By virtue of s 47 of the Trade Practices Act, exclusive dealing in these forms is prohibited. Consumers are within their rights to refuse to enter into related transactions with parties nominated by the supplier of another service. It is illegal for a finance provider, for example, to insist as a condition of supply of finance that insurance be taken out with a specified insurer.

Resale price maintenance

[8.31] Section 48 prohibits the practice of resale price maintenance. The practice is defined in s 96 and in summary means that a party at one level of the market seeks to determine the selling price of goods in another level of the market. Thus a manufacturer may attempt to dictate the price at which its goods are sold at retail.

Interference with pricing is inherently anti-competitive and resale price maintenance is an example of conduct where a retailer, for example, is prevented from engaging in competition by discounting the price of a particular product.

Resale price maintenance may take place where a supplier refuses or threatens not to continue to supply unless the retailer ceases the practice of discounting the goods. The objectionable aspect of this conduct is the imposition of a minimum selling price.

There have been many prosecutions over resale price maintenance involving many prominent Australian business enterprises. See *Trade Practices Commission v Sharp Corporation of Australia Pty Ltd* (1975) 8 ALR 255; 1 ATPR ¶40-010; *Trade Practices Commission v Bata Shoe Company of Australia* (1980) 44 FLR 145; (1980) ATPR ¶40-161; *Trade Practices Commission v Dunlop Australia Ltd* (1980) 43 FLR 434; 30 ALR 469; (1980) ATPR ¶40-167; *Trade Practices Commission v Mobil Oil Australia Ltd* (1984) 55 ALR 527; (1984) ATPR ¶40-482; *Trade Practices Commission v Sony (Australia) Pty Ltd* (1990) ATPR ¶41-031.

Prohibition of acquisitions that would result in a substantial lessening of competition

[8.32] The most effective way of removing competition is to take over the competitor. It is therefore not surprising that the Trade Practices Act regulates attempts to control a market by acquiring, directly or indirectly, control of a competitor through the acquisition of shares in 'a body corporate' or the assets of a person if the effect or likely effect of the acquisition is substantially to limit competition. The section provides a list of factors to consider in determining whether the acquisition will have the substantial lessening effect on competition: s 50(3).

In the context of s 50 issues such as 'market' and 'competition' are very important because of the test of substantial lessening of competition.

Authorisation under the Trade Practices Act

[8.33] In order to allow business the opportunity to avoid prosecution the Act provides for a system of authorisation of certain conduct which the business intends to undertake. Authorisations are granted, on application, by the Australian Competition and Consumer Commission: s 88. The procedure is available for conduct that would otherwise breach s 45, s 45 A, s 47, s 48 and s 50. It is not available for a breach of s 46.

In deciding upon the application the Commission is required by s 90 to be satisfied that the benefit that accrues from the proposed conduct outweighs the detriment involved in lessening competition.

In respect of applications for conduct that would be classified as exclusionary provisions, secondary boycotts, forms of exclusive dealing and mergers the Commission must be satisfied that there is sufficient public benefit arising from the conduct that it should be authorised. What is 'public benefit' in respect of a merger is partially explained in s 90(9A) as 'a significant increase in the real value of exports; a significant substitution of domestic products for imported products and all other relevant matters that relate to the international competitiveness of any Australian industry'.

The procedure for determining an application for authorisation is set out in the Act: s 90A.

Notification of exclusive dealing

[8.34]   Interim protection from prosecution can be obtained by notifying the Commission of conduct which amounts to exclusive dealing. The protection remains in place until the Commission decides otherwise and by virtue of notification the conduct is deemed not be have the effect of substantially effecting competition.

Penalties for breaches of Pt IV of the Trade Practices Act

[8.35]   Section 76 of the Trade Practices Act imposes a 'pecuniary penalty' of up to $10 million in respect of a corporation and $500,000 for a person other than a body corporate. An individual may incur liability under the Act because of having aided, abetted, counselled or procured the contravention or by reason of having induced it or by being knowingly concerned in or party to the contravention or conspired with others to effect the contravention: s 75B.

Summary and key terms

[8.36]   This chapter has set to explain:
*   how the law regulates the *methods by which suppliers promote* their goods and services;
*   the *common law approach to advertising*;
*   the operation of *s 52 of the Trade Practices Act*;
*   which specific forms of promotion are subject to the Trade Practices Act; and
*   how s 53 of the Trade Practices Act *prohibits certain forms of unfair conduct*.
*   the range of conduct prohibited by Pt IV of the Trade Practices Act — *restrictive trade practices*.

9

The Consumer Transaction: II

What this chapter does ...

Sales transactions are the most common form of consumer transaction. The law governing sales is that of contract, amended by legislation. Chapter 6 has dealt with the Sale of Goods Act which, however, represents an 'old fashioned' approach to the modern style of consumer transactions.

The emergence of a body of consumer/fair trading legislation has introduced legislation which controls the sale transaction and other aspects of a sale. It also deals with other forms of acquisition of goods and services. The legislation regulates a door-to-door sale, a lay-by sale, and techniques used by sellers such as pyramid selling are subject to legislation to correct abuses or to clarify the legal rules.

Sale and other consumer transactions

[9.1] The law in respect of the sale of goods was discussed in Chapter 6. As that chapter indicated the Sale of Goods Act does not tell the whole story in respect of sales. In fact there is more to the acquisition of goods than a sale. A person is able to obtain goods by hiring them or leasing them or through various techniques which are not accommodated in the Sale of Goods Act. The Act was a creature of the nineteenth century and the ways of doing business and the standards expected by the community have changed a great deal since then. This chapter examines the modern approach to consumer transactions with particular reference to the Trade Practices Act 1974 and its state equivalents.

Shortcomings in the Sale of Goods Act approach

[9.2] The Sale of Goods Act specifically provides that the rules of common law are preserved. In this respect the legislation does not relieve consumers of the technicalities of seeking remedies for misrepresentations or from the impact of the doctrine of privity of contract. From the consumer perspective the Sale of Goods Act is unsatisfactory because it allows for the implied conditions to be excluded. In effect, the contract would be reduced to its most basic common law form. The Act, as its name suggests, deals only with goods and in a contract for services the consumer cannot look to the Act for protection. It should, however, be noted that the courts are prepared to imply into contracts for services terms similar to the statutory terms.

Changes to the Sale of Goods Act approach

[9.3] The limitations of the traditional Sale of Goods Act approach have been resolved to some extent by Div 2 of Pt V of the Trade Practices Act 1974 (Cth). The reform has been achieved by making provision for consumer transactions. In the main the Trade Practices Act has adopted the contractual terms implied under the Sale of Goods Act — as to title: s 69(1)(a); quiet possession: s 69(1)(b); freedom from encumbrances: s 69(1)(c); correspondence with description: s 70(1); merchantable quality: s 71(1); fitness for purpose: s 71(2); and correspondence with sample: s 72, but it is importantly different in the following aspects:

- For constitutional reasons the provisions of this part of the Act apply only where corporations (as defined) are supplying the goods.
- The terms apply not merely to the sale of goods; they apply to other forms of supply such as hiring, exchange, leasing or hire–purchase: s 4.
- The provisions apply to transactions involving goods that are 'of a kind ordinarily acquired for personal domestic or household use or consumption'.
- 'Merchantable quality' is defined by s 66 to mean goods that are:

    ... as fit for the purpose or purposes for which goods of that kind are commonly bought as it is reasonable to expect having regard to any description applied to them, the price (if relevant) and all other relevant circumstances.

Case Example	
Consumers ordered carpet for their house. They specified that it was to blend in with the decor. Soon after installation the carpet developed shading (or permanent pile reversal). They sued for a breach of the implied conditions of fitness for purpose and merchantable quality. The Queensland Supreme Court held in favour of the consumers on the ground that a consumer acquiring new, high quality and expensive carpet could expect it to be fit for floor covering and decoration: *Rasell v Cavalier Marketing (Australia) Pty Ltd* [1991] 2 Qd R 323.	

This imposes a more stringent test — the goods must be fit for *all* of the purposes for which goods of that kind are usually purchased not merely *any*, as the interpretation of the Sale of Goods Acts provides.

- The terms cannot be excluded either directly or indirectly by making a contract subject to another law and nor can they be contracted out of: ss 67, 68.
- A credit provider who is linked with a dealer — regularly operating together by arrangement — is made liable for any breach of the implied terms: s 73.
- Terms are implied into contracts for the supply of services: s 74. The service provider is bound by an implied warranty to provide the service with due skill and care and to ensure that any materials used in the course of supplying the service are reasonably fit for the purpose. 'Service' is defined in s 74(3) in a negative way — it includes all services except those in relation to business transportation or storage of goods and insurance contracts.

Consumers' remedies

[9.4]   Where an implied condition of a transaction under Div 2 has been breached the consumer is entitled to rescind the contract: s 75A. That means that the consumer is able to treat the contract as having come to an end. In order to use this remedy the consumer must either give notice of the breach to the supplier or return the goods to the supplier with details of the breach. Note that this remedy applies only in respect of a breach of condition. If, for example, a piece of clothing is defective — either being not fit for purpose or unmerchantable — a consumer is entitled to a refund. An attempt by the supplier to refuse a refund on the ground that 'our policy is to give credit not refunds' is a breach of the law as is a response that the goods will be repaired. It is for the consumer to say whether they are prepared to accept a lesser solution to their dispute.

Where the breach is of a warranty such as in respect of quiet possession (s 69(1)(a)) or that goods are free of any charge or encumbrance (s 69(1)(c)) the remedy is damages. That is also the case where there has been a breach of the implied conditions under Div 2A of the Act — the consumer is entitled to compensation from the corporations: see s 74B(1), s 74C (1), s 74D(1), s 74E(1).

Manufacturer's warranties

[9.5]   The reality of the modern market place is that the party responsible for most of the defects in goods is the manufacturer. It is, however, the retailer with whom the consumer deals, and under the common law/Sale of Goods approach the consumer has rights against the retailer who, in turn, has rights against the wholesaler and so on. The consumer has no contract with the manufacturer and, because of the common law privity of contract doctrine, can take no action against the manufacturer except by way of a tortious action. The example of a person who receives a gift illustrates the legal problem — there is no contract with the seller (the gift giver made that contract) and none with the manufacturer. If the gift is defective the recipient can either ask the giver to take the matter up with the retailer or else endure the defect. If the recipient was damaged as a result of the defect a tortious action is the only right of redress. That assumes of course that the manufacturer is within the jurisdiction of the Australian legal system.

Manufacturers and the Trade Practices Act

[9.6]   Division 2A of Pt V of the Trade Practices Act 1974 (Cth) is designed to overcome these legal technicalities. It makes a manufacturer liable, not criminally, to compensate a customer for loss or damage where the manufacturer supplies the goods to, say, a retailer for re-supply and the goods are subsequently supplied to a consumer. This means that Div 2A does not apply where a consumer buys direct from the manufacturer; if the goods were defective the action would be against the seller (who happens to be the manufacturer) under Div 2.

The liability arises where the goods supplied to the consumer:

* are not reasonably fit for the purpose — s 74B;
* do not correspond to the description — s 74C;
* are not of merchantable quality — s 74D; and
* do not correspond with a sample: s 74E.

The obligations imposed in respect of the goods are similar in meaning to the terms used in the Sale of Goods Acts and Div 2A of the Trade Practices Act. The protection in respect of fitness for purpose and merchantable quality extends beyond the consumer to 'a person who acquires the goods from, or derives title to the goods through or under, the consumer': ss 74B, 74D. The goods referred to are those 'of a kind ordinarily acquired for personal domestic or household use or consumption': s 74A(2).

Liability also exists

[9.7]   Liability also exists where:

- The manufacturer has failed to provide adequate repair facilities or spare parts. The manufacturer must make a reasonable effort to ensure they exist or otherwise, inform consumers before the transaction that the facilities are not available: s 74F.
- The manufacturer fails to comply with an express warranty in respect of the goods. This means that if the manufacturer of goods gives an undertaking or makes a statement, for example in an advertisement, about some feature of the goods or the availability of parts and fails to live up to the undertaking or statement the consumer has a right of action against the manufacturer: s 74G.

The term 'manufactured' has a wide meaning — it includes grown, extracted, produced, processed and assembled: s 74A(1). The Act also defines 'manufacturer' very broadly: ss 74A(3), (4), (5). It must be a corporation and must be the actual manufacturer or a deemed manufacturer. A deemed manufacturer is:

- a corporation holding itself out to be the manufacturer; or
- a corporation using its own brand name such as a supermarket which has items manufactured and sells them under a house brand; or
- a corporation allowing another person to promote the goods as being manufactured by the corporation. This would apply where, for example, a well known brand of clothing was made under licence; or
- the importer if the manufacturer does not have a place of business in Australia.

Division 2A supplements Div 2 of the Act by providing an alternative defendant. It does not apply where the manufacturer deals direct with the consumer; for Div 2A to apply there must be at least two parties in the chain before the goods reach the consumer. The effect of this part of the Act is to make those who are responsible for the defect accountable to the consumer or to those who acquire the goods through the original purchaser.

Product safety

[9.8]   Product safety is recognised as a fundamental consumer right. As discussed above, the Trade Practices Act implies terms into contracts to give consumers rights should the product not be fit for its purpose or of merchantable quality. That, however, is not the same as being safe.

The more general right to product safety is recognised in Pt V of the Trade Practices Act which sets up the following structure.

Warnings and bans

[9.9]   The Minister responsible for administering the Trade Practices Act has the power to issue a warning notice about specified goods. The notice can state that an investigation is being undertaken to determine whether they will or may injure a person. The notice may warn of the possible risks of using the goods: s 65B(1).

Once the investigation has been undertaken the action available to the Minister is to declare the goods unsafe after a conference with the supplier. If, however, it appears to the Minister that the goods in question create 'an imminent risk of death, serious illness or serious injury' the conference can be dispensed with: s 65L. In such circumstances the

Minister may immediately declare the goods unsafe (s 65C(5)) or ban them permanently: s 65C(7). Once such a declaration is made it is an offence for a corporation to supply those goods: s 65C. If such action is not warranted the Minister is required to publicise the results of the investigation and explain what action is to be taken as a result: s 65B(2).

Consumer product safety standards

[9.10] A corporation is prohibited from supplying goods which do not comply with pre-scribed consumer product safety standards: s 65C(1). These standards are made through the regulations under the Trade Practices Act and are designed to prevent or reduce the risk of injury by specifying requirements in respect of:

(a) performance, composition, contents, methods of manufacture or processing, design, construction, finish or packaging of the goods;
(b) testing of the goods during, or after the completion of, manufacture or processing; and
(c) the form and content of markings, warnings or instructions to accompany the goods,
as are reasonably necessary to prevent or reduce risk of injury to any person.

In order to reduce the amount of time involved in creating a standard the Act allows for standards developed by the Standards Association of Australia and other prescribed bodies to be adopted for the purposes of this part of the Act: s 65E. This has been done in some standards, examples of which include:

- motor vehicle child restraints;
- sunglasses and fashion spectacles;
- trolley jacks;
- portable fire extinguishers;
- bicycle helmets; and
- children's nightclothes.

Product information standards

[9.11] Consumers are entitled to information about the products they intend to buy whether it be for safety reasons or to make a more informed assessment of the product. The Act recognises the need for product information through information standards. Failure to comply with a standard is an offence under the act: s 65D. The process for creating such standards is by way of the regulations and it is also possible to adopt those of the Standards Association.

The only product information standard in force is that of care labelling for clothing, household textiles, furnishings, piece goods and yarns. This standard deals with the important issue of how to look after such items. For example, the label is required to inform about how to wash a garment or whether it is dry clean only. Similarly the ironing instructions are to be specified. Some items are exempted for practical reasons from the need to carry a label — shoelaces, sewing thread, handkerchiefs, bandages and one-use disposable items are some examples.

Product recall

[9.12] While the Act attempts to prevent the supply of unsafe goods it also provides for goods which are already in the market or in use. It does this through a system of compulsory product recall or warnings to the public.

Where it appears to the Minister that:

- goods will or may cause injury; or
- do not comply with a safety standard; or
- have been declared unsafe or permanently banned; and
- the supplier has not taken satisfactory action to prevent injury;

the Minister may require the supplier to:

- recall the goods immediately or within a certain time; or
- publicise the nature of the defect or dangerous characteristic or circumstances where the product is dangerous; or
- advise the public what it intends to do with respect to repairing the goods, replacing them or refunding the price: s 65F.

It is an offence to continue to supply goods that have been recalled or if the defect is not made good: s 65G.

A supplier is of course free to make a voluntary recall of goods. If that is done the Minister must be given written notice: s 65R.

Product safety legislation

[9.13] Product safety is a responsibility of the states and territories and each jurisdiction has its own legislation as follows:

Jurisdiction	Legislation	Section
Commonwealth	Trade Practices Act 1974	Pts V, VA
New South Wales	Fair Trading Act 1987	Pt 3
Victoria	Consumer Affairs Act 1972	Pt IV
Queensland	Fair Trading Act 1989	Pt IV
South Australia	Trade Standards Act 1979	—
Western Australia	Consumer Affairs Act 1971	Pt IIIA
Tasmania	Sale of Hazardous Goods Act 1977	—
Australian Capital Territory	Consumer Affairs Act 1973	Pt IIIA
Northern Territory	Consumer Affairs and Fair Trading Act 1990	Pt IV

Product liability

[9.14] Related to product safety, but a much wider issue, is product liability. There are remedies against a manufacturer in respect of a defective product in contract where one exists, tort and Div 2A of the Trade Practices Act.

Following a report from the Australian Law Reform Commission and the Victorian Law Reform Commission, *Product Liability,* the Trade Practices Act was amended to provide a statutory form of liability. This is set out in Pt VA which took effect on 9 July 1992. The Act imposes liability on manufacturers, which term also embraces importers, in respect of losses suffered and damages sustained, as a result of a defective product. The obligation is not based on any contractual relationship or tort. The statutory action does not dislodge any pre-existing rights of action in common law such as an action in negligence.

Legislative provisions

[9.15]   The Act provides that where goods have a defect, defined to mean 'their safety is not such as persons generally are entitled to expect' (s 75AC) and:

- an individual suffers injury (s 75AD); or
- some other person such as a family member suffers a loss (s 75AE); or
- other goods are damaged (s 75AF); or
- a building is damaged (s 75AG);

the corporation which supplied the goods manufactured by it which were responsible for the loss or damage will be liable to compensate the person who suffered the loss or damage.

The manufacturer has defences against liability: s 75AK. These are:

(a) the defect in the action goods that is alleged to have caused the loss did not exist at the supply time; or

(b) they had that defect only because there was compliance with a mandatory standard for them; or

(c) the state of scientific or technical knowledge at the time when they were supplied by their actual manufacturer was not such as to enable that defect to be discovered; or

(d) if they were comprised in other goods ('finished goods') — that defect is attributable only to:

(i) the design of the finished goods; or

(ii) the markings on or accompanying the finished goods; or

(iii) the instructions or warnings given by the manufacturer of the finished goods.

An example of the type of incident that would be covered is where a person used a dangerous product for a purpose for which it was designed but where, because of inadequate instructions for use on the product label, particularly as to precautions required, the product caused an injury. To the extent that the packaging failed to provide proper instructions as to the use of the product there would be a defect within the statutory meaning of that term.

Auctions

[9.16]   The impact of the Sale of Goods Act on auction sales is discussed in detail in **[6.93]**. It should be noted that, except in relation to title, the rights implied into sales contracts under Divs 2 and 2A of the Trade Practices Act do not apply to auction sales.

The format of auction sales is also regulated as part of the consumer protection/fair trading legislation. One such technique which relies on greed rather than fraud is what the legislation refers to as mock auctions. The style of a mock auction is that the organiser will create the demand for goods and generate bids by either restricting the number of lots on sale to a figure short of the number of bidders or by offering an incentive in the form of a gift or a reduction in the price which was bid. The existence of any one of these circumstances brings the sale within the reach of the legislation which exists in all parts of Australia except the ACT and Northern Territory.

Relevant legislation

Jurisdiction	Legislation	Section
New South Wales	Mock Auctions Act 1973	—
Victoria	Consumer Affairs Act 1972	ss 13B–13F
Queensland	Fair Trading Act 1989	s 56
South Australia	Fair Trading Act 1987	s 28
Western Australia	Auction Sales Act 1973	s 25
Tasmania	Mock Auctions Act 1973	—

Hire

[9.17] The legal classification of a hire transaction is that of bailment: see Chapter 15. The effect of hire is to allow for transfer of possession, usually for an agreed period at an agreed rate for the period. The ownership of the item being hired does not change as a result of the transaction. A common form of hire is that of equipment or of cars. The basis of the transaction is a contract — a hiring agreement which sets out the terms of the transaction. There is no legislation that deals specifically with hiring but the rights of the parties are subject to the Trade Practices Act. In the Trade Practices Act context the hiring amounts to the supply (see s 4 definition) and the acquisition (see s 4 definition) of goods and as a result a hiring could be a consumer transaction and therefore subject to the Act. The effect of the Act in this way would be to imply conditions into the contract. The transaction would, of course, be subject to the usual requirements of the Act in relation to misleading conduct, etc, whether or not it is a consumer transaction.

Credit sales

[9.18] The critical part of the credit transaction is the way in which the purchase of goods is financed. In the former hire–purchase arrangement, where the consumer offered to hire the goods and then paid a rental in a predetermined number of instalments and as part of the agreement exercised the option to purchase at the end of the period of rental, property in the goods did not pass until the final instalment was paid. In a transaction regulated by the credit legislation the emphasis is on the way in which finance is arranged and the respective rights of the parties in respect of the credit component of the transaction. The terms of the sale aspect of the transaction are specified by the Trade Practices Act and the relevant legislation in each of the states and territories. See Chapter 10 for a more detailed discussion of the credit aspect.

Door-to-door sales

[9.19]   It was a recurring nightmare for many consumers to have a persistent seller arrive at the door and, usually by some form of deceit such as asking the householder to participate in a survey, enter the residence and stay there for hours until the sale was completed. Common examples of this technique were sales of encyclopaedia and 'freezer plans' where consumers were sold a domestic freezer and then signed up to purchase food from the same supplier. Usually the goods were overpriced as in the case of the freezer food; they were often inferior — for example, the encyclopaedias were left over from the US market and were only marginally relevant to Australia; the transaction involved a credit component and the consumer had been subjected to high pressure selling which involved a degree of coercion and harassment. Efforts by consumers to withdraw from these unsatisfactory transactions were fruitless. Legislation was first introduced in the 1960s and it regulated the way in which sales away from a seller's place of business could take place. This meant in particular that sales arising from unsolicited visits to a person's home or place of work were subject to the legislation.

The key provision in the legislation is that the consumer has a cooling-off period of 10 days. That means that the consumer is able to withdraw from the transaction during that period.

The legislation in New South Wales and Victoria differs in detail from the uniform legislation elsewhere in Australia. The scheme of the uniform legislation involves the following steps.

The transaction *must*:

- have been unsolicited by the consumer. If a seller arrived uninvited or sought an invitation from the consumer the transaction was unsolicited. The visit by the seller must be to undertake negotiations — not, for example, to provide a quote;
- take place at other than the seller's trade premises;
- be for the supply of goods or services.

Regulation does *not* apply:

- where the contract is made in the course of the consumer's business;
- to a contract for $50 or less;
- to cash sales.

[9.20]   Some general provisions about door-to-door sales are:

- there are certain times when sellers are not permitted to call on a person without first having made an appointment (but sellers are able to telephone);
- the seller must leave the premises at the occupier's request;
- coercion and harassment are prohibited and are subject to a penalty; and
- a seller must carry an identification card and produce it at the first meeting.

If the Act does apply to the transaction then:

- The contract must be in writing and must include the words THIS CONTRACT IS SUBJECT TO A COOLING-OFF PERIOD OF 10 DAYS. This period runs from the day on which the transaction took place.
- The customer must receive a copy of the contract.
- The customer must be given a copy of a notice which sets out the right to rescind the agreement.

The legislation represents a substantial degree of intervention by government into the making of a contract. It means that the formation of the contract is suspended for a period of 10 days because during that period the consumer can effectively retract the offer which formed part of the agreement. The contract cannot be enforced until the cooling-off period has elapsed. A provision in the contract that purports to eliminate the operation of the Act or seeks to make the contract subject to the laws of another place is ineffective. Likewise, the waiver by a consumer of rights under the Act is ineffective as is any attempt by the seller to collect money during the cooling-off period. If a consumer has exercised the right of rescission the seller is prohibited from taking or threatening any debt collection action or having the consumer's name listed as a defaulter.

[9.21]   In New South Wales the Act applies only to credit purchase agreements which are negotiated at the purchaser's place of residence or place of employment and where the attendance of the seller was unsolicited by the purchaser. There is a 10-day cooling-off period and to be enforceable, the credit purchase agreement must be in writing of a specified type size and a copy must be given to the purchaser. Purchasers must also be given a notice setting out their rights under the Act. Failure to satisfy the requirements is also an offence.

In Victoria the legislation applies to credit and cash (above $50) purchase agreements. In order to be enforceable the agreement must be in writing. The purchaser must be given a copy of the advertisement and of a schedule which sets out the rights under the Act. Failure to do these things amounts to an offence. As in other parts of Australia there is a 10-day cooling-off period.

Use of physical force, harassment, coercion in making a sale

[9.22]   The Trade Practices Act does not deal with door-to-door selling as such but in s 60 it prohibits the use of 'physical force or undue harassment or coercion in connection with the supply or possible supply of goods or services to a consumer or the payment for goods or services by a consumer'. This section has not been the subject of litigation but it would be reasonable to say that the type of conduct caught by it would include a seller who refused to leave a person's place of residence. It would probably also include an over-zealous debt collector or a seller who would not take no for an answer.

Relevant legislation

Jurisdiction	Legislation	Section
Commonwealth	Trade Practices Act 1974	s 60
New South Wales	Door to Door Sales Act 1967	
Victoria	Consumer Affairs Act 1972	ss 14–20A
Queensland	Fair Trading Act 1989	ss 57–72
South Australia	Fair Trading Act 1987	ss 13–24; 69
Western Australia	Door to Door Trading Act 1987	
Tasmania	Door to Door Trading Act 1986	
Australian Capital Territory	Door-to-Door Trading Act 1991	
Northern Territory	Consumer Affairs and Fair Trading Act 1990	ss 97–113

Pyramid selling

[9.23]   The technique of pyramid selling is prohibited in all parts of Australia. The unattractive feature of the technique is that what is sold is not so much products as positions in a distribution hierarchy. A person higher in the pyramid makes money from the price paid by new entrants to the scheme. Taken to an extreme, a pyramid selling scheme could absorb the whole population of Australia so that persons at the bottom of the pyramid are unable to generate any income. Everybody in Australia would be in the scheme and the late-comers would have nobody to sell to — either product or positions in the scheme. Pyramid selling is typically marketed in a way that promises a large income which at the lowest level of the pyramid cannot be achieved.

It should not be thought that every form of distributorship of products is part of a pyramid selling scheme. If a person is appointed as an agent of a company, is given a territory in which to operate, has products to sell and is able engage in the normal form of acquiring stock, then it is unlikely that pyramid selling is involved. In Victoria where a scheme may appear to be a pyramid scheme it is possible to seek an exemption from the Act.

[9.24]   Pyramid selling schemes exist in a variety of forms and for that reason the legislation is very complex. The legislation is uniform — based on s 61 of the Trade Practices Act. In summary the section involves the following concepts:

- a corporation — in its extended meaning;
- which promotes or participates in;
- a trading scheme, which is any business arrangement, in writing or otherwise, under which goods and/or services are to be provided by the promoter of the scheme to persons via other persons who are participants but not promoters; and
- holding out the prospect of payments or benefits — a statement by the corporation suggesting the likelihood of some benefit. The statement by the person holding out does not need to create an enforceable right for the person to whom it is made.

The Act prohibits the following conduct in relation to the trading scheme:

- payment to the corporation by a person who has been induced to make it because the prospect was held out that there would be payments or benefits received for introducing other persons to the scheme (s 61(1)); and
- the holding out by the corporation to a person already a participant in the scheme the prospect of receiving payment or benefits for introducing other persons to become participants in the scheme and thus attempts to induce the person to make a payment to a promoter or participant in the scheme: s 61 (2).

[9.25]   The Trade Practices Act merely prohibits and penalises the receipt of payments or the attempt to induce persons to make payments: see *ACCC v Chats House Investment Pty Ltd* (1996) 71 FCR 250; 1119 FCA; *ACCC v Golden Sphere International Inc* (1998) 589 FCA. There is no civil remedy in the sense that a victim of a pyramid selling scheme can seek compensation. The state legislation, however, goes wider and in one form or another allows participants in the schemes to seek recovery of moneys they have paid.

Relevant legislation

Jurisdiction	Legislation	Section
Commonwealth	Trade Practices Act 1974	s 61
New South Wales	Fair Trading Act 1987	s 56
Victoria	Fair Trading Act 1985	ss 23–27
Queensland	Fair Trading Act 1989	ss 55A–D
South Australia	Fair Trading Act 1987	s 70
Western Australia	Fair Trading Act 1987	s 24–27
Tasmania	Fair Trading Act 1990	s 26B
Australian Capital Territory	Fair Trading Act 1992	s 27
Northern Territory	Consumer Affairs and Fair Trading Act 1990	s 56

Referral selling

[9.26]   It was once a common practice for suppliers to offer a 'special deal' to consumers who were prepared to allow their houses to be used as display houses. This was particularly the case where the commodity was an expensive and dubious quality house cladding or some similar treatment of the house. The technique usually involved a substantial over-charging for the service. The 'discount' for displaying the house was earned only if it resulted in another sale. A similar benefit was offered if the consumer introduced a purchaser.

This form of selling, referral selling, has been prohibited for many years and remains so in all jurisdictions except Tasmania. If a corporation was to engage in referral selling in that state the Trade Practices Act would apply.

Relevant legislation

Jurisdiction	Legislation	Section
Commonwealth	Trade Practices Act 1974	s 57
New South Wales	Fair Trading Act 1987	s 52
Victoria	Fair Trading Act 1985	s 19
Queensland	Fair Trading Act 1989	s 47
South Australia	Fair Trading Act 1987	s 66
Western Australia	Fair Trading Act 1987	s 20
Tasmania	Fair Trading Act 1990	s 26A
Australian Capital Territory	Fair Trading Act 1992	s 23
Northern Territory	Consumer Affairs and Fair Trading Act 1990	s 53

Inertia selling

[9.27]   In this form of marketing the supplier relies on the laziness — the inertia — of the person who receives unsolicited goods. Thus a book seller who sent books to a consumer without them being ordered would be hoping that the consumer could not be bothered returning them. This could be a realistic hope given that the books may need to be specially packed or the chances are that the consumer would not get round to returning them.

This form of selling is now unprofitable in that the supplier is prohibited from asserting a right to payment by:

* demanding payment;
* threatening to sue for the 'debt'; and
* having the consumer's name put on a list of defaulters.

Furthermore, after a specified period — one month if the consumer notified the supplier, three months otherwise — the goods become the property of the consumer. The supplier can do no more than ask for the goods but if within the specified period the consumer unreasonably refuses, the property in the goods remains with the supplier.

False directory entries

[9.28]   A variation of inertia selling is the practice of sending an invoice to a business for a directory entry which, if it did appear, was certainly not authorised by the recipient. This practice was often accompanied by threats of suing the business in an overseas court for non-payment of the 'debt' or having it listed as a defaulter with an international credit agency. The success of this form of confidence trick depends entirely on the lax accounting controls of the business.

Relevant legislation

Jurisdiction	Legislation	Section
Commonwealth	Trade Practices Act 1974	ss 64, 65
New South Wales	Fair Trading Act 1987	ss 58, 59
Victoria	Fair Trading Act 1985	ss 29, 30
Queensland	Fair Trading Act 1989	ss 52–55
South Australia	Fair Trading Act 1987	ss 72, 73
Western Australia	Fair Trading Act 1987	ss 29–32
Tasmania	Unordered Goods and Services Act *1973*	
Australian Capital Territory	Fair Trading Act 1992	ss 29, 30
Northern Territory	Consumer Affairs and Fair Trading *Act 1990*	ss 58, 59

Paying for goods and services

[9.29] When examined in contractual terms, the acquisition of property or services involves a promise on the part of the acquirer to pay for whatever was acquired. In many cases, such as buying a newspaper, this part of the transaction — the discharge — is carried out at the time of acquisition and the payment is by way of cash passing from one person to another. In other transactions, although money passes to the person disposing of the goods, it does so indirectly. The supermarket shopping may be paid for through an EFTPOS transaction which involves the debiting of the customer's bank account and the crediting of the supplier's. Another way of paying is by using a credit card. The customer's obligations to the supplier are discharged by the credit card but, in the same transaction, the customer incurs a debt to the credit provider. The same style of transaction takes place with a store account where the customer becomes a debtor of the credit provider which has provided the finance to settle the debt with the store. Where a finance company finances the purchase of a car or a bank finances a house purchase, they pay the money over to the vendor — on behalf of their customer, the borrower. The finance/credit providers are intermediaries in the sense that they are not parties to the original, underlying transaction but they end up in a creditor–debtor relationship with the person acquiring the asset.

Establishing the price

[9.30] The price is a sensitive, if not the most sensitive, part of a consumer transaction. Apart from the very few activities or commodities where government agencies set prices the law takes no interest in the balance of the transaction. It is prepared to intervene where the price has been overlooked and impose one that is reasonable. If, however, a person was prepared to accept a handful of seashells in return for a Rolls Royce car, the attitude of the common law would be that it is interested not in the adequacy of the consideration but in its sufficiency. It would assume that the seashells were valuable to the seller of the car. The lack of interest in the level of the price is based on an assumption that consumers are able to decide whether the price is acceptable. There is also an assumption that the forces of competition are sufficiently robust to ensure that an appropriate price is paid. In this context it is useful to consider the approach of the Trade Practices Act in Pt IV to pricing issues: see Chapter 8. It regards pricing as an important aspect of competition and prohibits several forms of conduct which interfere with the proper setting of prices by the market. The Trade Practices Act regulates price fixing: s 45A (see **[8.28]**); predatory pricing which is a form of abuse of market power: s 46 (see **[8.29]**); and resale price maintenance: s 48; **[8.31]**.

Representations about price

[9.31] The importance of price is further demonstrated by the prohibition in s 53(e) of false or misleading representations about price. Such conduct is a criminal offence. Where goods are promoted on the basis of a price payable in instalments the cash price of the goods must be disclosed: s 53C.

In New South Wales and the Australian Capital Territory where goods carry or are advertised with two or more price labels it is an offence to sell them for more than the lower or lowest price: this is known as dual pricing. A breach can lead to a fine of up to $5000: NSW Fair Trading Act s 40; ACT Fair Trading Act: s 22.

In shops using electronic checkouts where the shelf price is lower than that of the encoded price, the legislation would require the lower price to be charged. There is, however, a code of practice operating in some stores whereby if there is a difference between the shelf price and the computer price the product is supplied free of charge. This goes beyond the requirements of the legislation.

Lay-by

[9.32]   Before credit cards were introduced into Australia a very common method of acquiring goods was by way of lay-by. Under this process the consumer pays a deposit, the retailer puts the goods aside and releases them to the consumer once the agreed number of instalments has been paid. The legal status of lay-by is not clear. For example, what is the nature of the transaction and are the terms always specified? At what stage does property pass? Who bears the risk while the goods are being kept for the consumer? What is the effect of the consumer failing to make the payments? Is the seller able to bring the transaction to an end?

Legislation regulating lay-by has been in existence in New South Wales since 1943. It was amended in 1993 and now forms Pt 5B (ss 60E–60O) of the Fair Trading Act 1987. In summary the requirements for a lay-by transaction in that state are:

*   the terms are to be expressed in writing and given to the consumer;
*   the transaction may be cancelled before the delivery date but subject to a specified cancellation charge which must be a reasonable figure;
*   if the consumer does not maintain instalments the supplier is able to cancel the transaction — the consumer is entitled to a refund of all amounts paid less the cancellation fee; and
*   the cancellation fee cannot be charged where the supplier has failed to provide a correct statement of the terms or has breached the agreement.

Consumers cannot be forced to contract out of the protection provided by the Act.

The other jurisdiction in which there is legislation is Australian Capital Territory: Lay-by Sales Agreement Act 1963.

Summary and key terms

[9.33]   This chapter has set out to explain:

*   *implied terms* in consumer transactions;
*   *consumer remedies* under the Trade Practices Act;
*   manufacturer's warranties;
*   liability of manufacturers;
*   how the Trade Practices Act and other legislation has established a *product safety* regime;

- the system of *warnings and bans*;
- the use of *product safety standards*;
- the *product recall* procedure;
- how legislation has established a statutory form of *product liability*;
- the regulation of certain forms of selling — *auctions, door to door, pyramid selling referral selling, inertia selling, lay-by sales;*
- pricing.

10

Consumer Credit

What this chapter does ...

Credit is a significant factor in consumer transactions. The law that regulates the credit transaction was substantially reformed in the mid 1990s. This chapter examines the principles underlying the legislation and the way in which it affects both consumers and credit providers.

Introduction

[10.1]   The topic of money lending and the often related topic of usury has been controversial since biblical times. Usury in its strictest form is merely the charging of interest for the use of another person's money. The term became synonymous with the charging of high rates of interest. The religious influence which was critical of usury is reflected in the Islamic law which prohibits the charging of interest. The old laws against usury were replaced in the nineteenth century by the Money Lenders Acts which were imported into Australia from England. The twentieth century, in particular the second half, has seen the development of hire–purchase as a major method of financing significant consumer purchases. By the 1950s, an almost uniform regime of legislation to regulate hire–purchase had been established.

What is credit?

[10.2]   Put simply, credit is a process whereby the payment of a debt is deferred. That debt is created by the credit transaction which is separate to the underlying transaction. For example, where a person wishes to acquire a car on credit the sales transaction is the underlying transaction which involves the car; the credit transaction is separate and deals with arrangements for the payment of the price, or the amount yet to be paid, of the car. Through the credit arrangement the finance provider arranges payment to the car seller and the consumer's obligation in respect of the car has been discharged. The relationship that continues is between the credit provider and the consumer who must repay the money paid for the car with the associated costs especially that of interest. The nature of the credit transaction is reflected in the Consumer Credit Code which, in s 4, provides that:

> **'credit'** is provided if under a contract:
> (a) payment of a debt owed by one person (the debtor) to another (the credit provider) is deferred; or
> (b) one person (the debtor) incurs a deferred debt to another (the credit provider).

The legislative background

[10.3]   In 1985 the law in most parts of Australia dealing with consumer credit purchases was reformed. The Hire Purchase Acts were repealed in most states as were the Money Lenders Acts and a new system of almost uniform regulation of credit transactions emerged. The reform of the law had taken almost 20 years to put into effect but, almost as soon as it was introduced, proposals were made for its replacement.

The Credit Acts introduced a system of licensing of credit providers who were not regulated or licensed under any other law. The purpose of the licensing system was to screen persons and companies (and persons associated with companies) seeking to operate as credit providers. Banks, credit unions, building societies and friendly societies, for example, did not require licensing under the credit legislation. Applicants for licences were required to meet legislative standards as to solvency, expertise and conduct in the first instance and were subject to loss of licence should their conduct not continue to meet those standards. Where a credit provider operated without a licence the Act provided that it was unable to recover the amount financed or any credit charges. This 'civil penalty' imposed by the Credit Act was subject to a procedure whereby the credit provider was able to apply for the consumer to be made liable for principal or credit charges as the case may be.

In each of the Credit Act jurisdictions in Australia the Encyclopaedia Brittanica organisation failed to obtain a credit providers licence. It operated in this way for several years and, because the contracts it had made were thus unenforceable, it was forced to go to the Credit Tribunals in each state to seek restoration of liability for principal and interest. In the Victorian Supreme Court decision, *Encyclopaedia Brittanica (Australia) Inc v The Director of Consumer Affairs* (1988) ASC 55–636, Fullagar J explained the background to the application and the policy of the legislation.

[10.4]   Although it had the advantage of being, for the most part, uniform throughout Australia and emphasised consumer rights, the 1985 legislation was unsatisfactory. It was very technical and the complexity of its language and concepts created uncertainty. The requirements for disclosure were demanding and credit providers were exposed to civil penalties for making minor errors such as incorrectly spelling the name of a related company that provided consumer credit insurance. The penalty for such a trivial error was that interest charges could not be enforced unless the court or Credit Tribunal upheld the credit provider's application. Although the error offended the law it was often so trivial that the risk of loss to, or misleading of, the consumer was at the worst very low. Credit providers were put to the task of expensive litigation to regularise their contracts.

The 1985 legislation was subject to a monetary limit which was not uniform and it did not apply to all credit providers or to all forms of credit. Furthermore, it was doubtful whether, in practice, the Credit Act 1985 provided appropriate accessible remedies for consumers.

[10.5]   Under the Uniform Credit Laws Agreement of 1993 between the states a properly uniform credit law was introduced into Australia on 1 November 1996. The agreement provided that Queensland would enact legislation which other states would follow or, at least, maintain consistency with. Western Australia enacted its own laws which maintain consistency with and are very close to the Queensland model. The new legislation encountered several false starts as drafting difficulties delayed its implementation but it eventually came into operation.

The Queensland 'template' legislation is the Consumer Credit (Queensland) Act 1994 which incorporates a Consumer Credit Code (the Code). Supplementing the Code is the Consumer Credit Regulation (sic) 1995 of Queensland. Each state, apart from Western Australia, has incorporated the Queensland Code and Regulation into its own law through the device of using application of laws legislation. Most states have a Consumer Credit Administration Act which provides the mechanism for matters such as licensing of credit providers and which court is to deal with litigation under the Code.

The procedure for amending the legislation is that, if the Ministers of the participating states agree to particular changes, the Queensland law will be changed to reflect those views and the amendments will be binding uniformly.

[10.6]   In considering credit transactions it is necessary to keep in mind that the Credit Code is but one piece of the law that is relevant. The Trade Practices Act and Fair Trading legislation apply in respect of exclusive dealing and misleading conduct. Common law principles also apply except to the extent that they are varied by the Code.

Relevant legislation

Jurisdiction	Legislation
Commonwealth	None
New South Wales	Consumer Credit (New South Wales) Act 1995
Victoria	Consumer Credit (Victoria) Act 1995
Queensland	Consumer Credit (Queensland) Act 1994
South Australia	Consumer Credit (South Australia) Act 1995
Western Australia	Consumer Credit (Western Australia Act 1996
Tasmania	Consumer Credit (Tasmania) Act 1996
Australian Capital Territory	Consumer Credit Act 1995
Northern Territory	Consumer Credit (Northern Territory) Act 1995

Codes of practice

[10.7]   Although they are not formally part of the law, industry codes of practice can be relevant to the provision of credit. The terms of the codes of practice cannot displace the formal law and, to the extent their provisions are inconsistent, the Consumer Credit Code or other relevant legislation will apply. The participants in a code of practice scheme are bound by contract to the terms of the Code and, in that way, the rights under the Code are available to consumers.

If the Consumer Credit Code is silent on a matter the provisions of a code of practice will apply and, no doubt, if the provisions of a code of practice establish higher standards than those of the formal law the code of practice would apply. The codes of practice that are relevant in this context are:

- Building Society Code of Practice
- Code of Banking Practice
- Credit Reporting Code of Conduct
- Credit Union Code of Practice
- Electronic Funds Transfer Code of Practice.

To what transactions does the Code apply?

[10.8]   An important feature of the Code is that it applies without variation to all forms of credit provider — bank, building society, credit union, finance company or private lender. Section 6(1) of the Code provides that:

> This Code applies to the provision of credit (and to the credit contract and related matters) if when the credit contract is entered into or (in the case of pre-contractual obligations) is proposed to be entered into:
>
> (a) the debtor is a natural person ordinarily resident in this jurisdiction or a strata corporation formed in this jurisdiction; and

(b) the credit is provided or intended to be provided wholly or predominantly for personal, domestic or household purposes; and

(c) a charge is or may be made for providing the credit; and

(d) the credit provider provides the credit in the course of a business of providing credit or as part of or incidentally to any other business of the credit provider.

Several features of the section are noteworthy:

- the Code's application to a transaction depends on the purpose of the credit, not on any monetary limit. The purpose is measured at the time of making the credit contract;
- for the Code to apply, more than half of the credit involved in the transaction is to be used for personal, domestic or household purposes. That is how the legislation defines 'predominantly' — s 6(5);
- 'personal, domestic or household purposes' are not defined but, it is submitted, the test for deciding whether the purpose fits that description is what the debtor intended; that is, it is subjective. Similar wording is used in the Trade Practices Act and courts would be guided by the interpretation in that context. Investment by the debtor is not a personal, domestic or household purpose — s 6(4);
- the debtor is to be a natural person and may be a corporation but only where a body corporate was established in respect of the division of land as for example in the ownership of a block of apartments;
- in the case of natural persons there is a residency test. For a body corporate the test is where it was formed. The Code applies only in respect of persons who are ordinarily resident in the jurisdiction. Thus, the Victorian Code would apply only to debtors who normally reside in Victoria or a strata corporation formed in Victoria. Where multiple debtors residing in different jurisdictions are involved s 6(2) provides that the Code that applies is that of where credit is first provided under the contract. If the debtor moves from Victoria to South Australia in the life of the contract the Victorian Code would continue to apply to the transaction: s 6(3)(b).

[10.9] Subject to the qualifications above in respect of credit contracts not predominantly for a personal, domestic or household purpose, the Code regulates five categories of credit transaction. These are:

- *Continuing credit contracts*   As the name suggests, this form of transaction provides credit on a continuing basis. Examples include a store account such as a David Jones, Grace Brothers or Myer card, Bankcard and cards such as Visa, American Express or Mastercard. A bank overdraft is also a form of continuing credit. Common arrangements whereby a person deals with a trader — the milk supplier or the newsagent — on a credit basis are theoretically continuing credit but they are not regulated because in most cases there is no credit charge and it is provided on 30-day terms.

  Continuing credit is probably now the most common form of credit. Each transaction on a card involves a credit sale but it does not require the same level of formality. It is an efficient way of dealing with frequent, multiple credit transactions. A continuing credit contract is not required to be in writing but the debtor must be given, before the first transaction, a copy of 'Things you should know about your credit contract'.

- *Contracts for the sale of goods or services by instalment*
- *Consumer leases*
- *Hire–purchase*   This type of transaction is defined in the s 10 of the Code to mean

  a contract for the hire of goods under which the hirer has a right or obligation to purchase the goods, is to be regarded as a sale of the goods by instalments if the charge that is or may be made for hiring the goods, together with any other amount payable under the contract (including an amount to purchase the goods or to exercise an option to do so) exceeds the cash price of the goods.

- *Other*   Into this category would fall every other form of credit transaction such as a housing loan or personal loan.

Related transactions

[10.10]   A credit transaction may involve an associated transaction such as a mortgage over property to provide security for the debt. Similarly a guarantee could be given to ensure that a debtor's obligations are met by a third party. Since both of these transactions are closely involved with the credit transaction it is appropriate that they be regulated by the Code.

The Code applies to a mortgage if it secures obligations under a credit contract or a related guarantee and the mortgagor is a natural person or a strata corporation: s 8. It applies to guarantees which guarantee obligations under a credit contract and the guarantor is a natural person or a strata corporation: s 9.

Guarantees

[10.11]   Where a credit provider has required another person to guarantee the repayment of the credit provided, that is itself a separate transaction and it is appropriate for that person (the guarantor) to have rights under the Code. The guarantor will, of course, become liable should the debtor default. The liability is limited by the Act to the amount for which the debtor is liable plus any reasonable enforcement charges.

Before the undertaking is made the guarantor must be told what the obligation is and for this reason must be given a copy of the contract which is the subject of the guarantee. The contract establishing the guarantor's undertaking to the credit provider must be in writing and must be signed by the guarantor. The guarantor is entitled to the same statements that are available to a debtor.

Mortgages

[10.12]   A mortgage is a contract whereby the borrower, the mortgagor, transfers title in property (usually real estate) to the lender, the mortgagee, under terms which require that when the debt is repaid ownership will revert to the borrower. Section 8 provides that the Code applies to a mortgage if:

(a) it secures obligations under a credit contract or a related guarantee; and

(b) the mortgagor is a natural person or a strata corporation.

For the purposes of the Code, the term **'mortgage'** includes

(a) any interest in, or power over, property securing obligations of a debtor or guarantor; or

(b) a credit provider's title to land or goods subject to a sale by instalments; or

(c) a mortgage taken to have been entered into under section 10(3): Schedule 1 of the Code

Note, however, that certain arrangements are not mortgages by virtue of the regulations made under the Code. Section 7 refers to exemptions from the Code and provides that it does not apply to the following types of mortgage:

(a) any mortgage relating to perishable goods, livestock, primary produce or foodstuffs
   [but the disclosure requirements of the Code do apply to these];

(b) a banker's right to combine accounts;

(c) a lien or charge arising by operation of any Act or law or by custom.

The mortgage, which if granted in respect of property other than land is better described as a goods mortgage, may be used to secure the obligations of the primary debtor or the guarantor. Where a mortgage is used in conjunction with a guarantee all mortgagors must be guarantors: s 50(2).

The requirements in respect of mortgages are that:

- the mortgage be in writing signed by the mortgagor (s 38(1)) but not in all cases where it is a goods mortgage;
- the mortgagor must be either a debtor or a guarantor (s 44);
- only reasonable enforcement expenses may be imposed (s 45);
- security cannot be taken over property which is to be or may be acquired except where it is to be acquired under the credit transaction (s 41) or employee remuneration or superannuation benefits (s 46(1)) or a negotiable instrument on which the guarantor is liable as an issuer or indorser: s 46(2).

Mortgages are subject to the court's power to re-open transactions under sections of the Code and are subject also to the Code's requirements in respect of enforcement.

Provision of credit to which the Code does not apply

[10.13] Section 7 sets out the circumstances in which the Code does not apply to the provision of credit:

1. *Short term credit* Where the credit is limited to a total period not exceeding 62 days.
2. *Credit without prior agreement* For example, when a cheque account becomes overdrawn but there is no agreed overdraft facility between the bank and the debtor or when a savings account falls into debit.
3. *Credit for which only account charge payable* If the only charge that is or may be made for providing the credit is a periodic or other fixed charge that does not vary according to the amount of credit provided. But, if the charge exceeds the maximum charge (if any) prescribed in the regulations it does apply.
4. *Joint credit and debit facilities* The Code does not apply to any part of a credit contract under which both credit and debit facilities are available to the extent that the contract or any amount payable or other matter arising out of it relates only to the debit facility.
5. *Bill facilities* That is, a facility under which the credit provider provides credit by accepting, drawing, discounting or endorsing a bill of exchange or promissory note. However, the regulations may provide for the application of the Code to the provision of all or any credit arising out of such a facility.
6. *Insurance premiums by instalments* The Code does not apply to the provision of credit by an insurer for the purpose of the payment to the insurer of an insurance premium by instalments, even though payment by instalments is more than what would have been paid in cash.
7. *Pawnbrokers* The Code does not apply to the provision of credit by a pawnbroker in the ordinary course of a pawnbroker's business being a business which is being lawfully conducted by the pawnbroker. However, ss 70–72, which allow the court to re-open unjust transactions, apply to any such provision of credit. Pawnbrokers are regulated by separate legislation in each jurisdiction.

Relevant legislation

Jurisdiction	Legislation
Commonwealth	None
New South Wales	Pawnbrokers and Second-hand Dealers Act 1996
Victoria	Second-hand Dealers and Pawnbrokers Act 1989
Queensland	Pawnbrokers Act 1984
South Australia	Summary Offences Act 1953
Western Australia	Pawnbrokers and Second-hand Dealers Act 1994
Tasmania	Pawnbrokers and Second-hand Dealers Act 1994
Australian Capital Territory	Pawnbrokers Act 1902 (New South Wales)
Northern Territory	Pawnbrokers Act 1980

8. *Trustees of estates* The provision of credit by the trustee of the estate of a deceased person by way of an advance to a beneficiary or prospective beneficiary of the estate is not caught by the Code. Sections 70–72 which allow the court to re-open unjust transactions likewise apply to this form of credit.

9. *Employee loans* The provision of credit by an employer, or a related body corporate within the meaning of the Corporations Law of an employer, to an employee or former employee is not subject to the Code. If, however, the employer provides credit in the course of a business of providing credit, the Code does not apply only where the provision of credit is on terms that are more favourable to the debtor than the normal commercial term.

Under s 7(10) it is envisaged that the regulations may exclude certain forms of credit provision from the application of all or any provisions of the Code. Applications for exemption are first made to the Uniform Consumer Credit Code Management Committee which reports to Ministers and, if they agree to an exemption being granted, an exemption order is enacted through the Queensland Credit Regulation.

Section 11 declaration

[10.14] There is a statutory presumption that a credit contract, mortgage or guarantee is one to which the Code applies unless the credit provider can prove otherwise: s 11(1).That presumption can be conclusively reversed by way of a declaration made by the debtor before entering the contract that the intended purpose of the credit is wholly or predominantly business and/or investment purposes: s 11(2).

A declaration of the type referred to in s 11(2) is ineffective 'if the credit provider (or any other person who obtained the declaration from the debtor) knew, or had reason to believe, at the time the declaration was made that the credit was in fact to be applied wholly or predominantly for personal, domestic or household purposes': s 11(3).

Section 176(5) of the Code sets out the circumstances in which a credit provider is taken to have knowledge of or reason to believe something for the purposes of this Code.

Universal application of the Code

[10.15]   Subject to the specific provisions that it makes in respect of transactions which are not covered, the Code is universal in its reach. In respect of credit transactions entered into prior to the commencement of the Code the applicable law is the relevant Credit Act except for continuing credit contracts that commenced after 1 February 1997: s 43 of the regulations.

A provision of a contract or other instrument by which a person seeks to avoid or modify the effect of this Code is void: s 169(1). Similarly any attempt to have the debtor or guarantor indemnify the credit provider for any loss or liability arising under this Code is void: s 169(2). The Code provides that such conduct exposes a credit provider to a maximum penalty of 100 penalty units — $10,000: s 169(3).

The special provisions made for farm machinery and commercial vehicles in previous forms of credit regulation are not repeated in the Code.

Policy objectives of the Code

[10.16]   The credit legislation serves an important consumer related purpose in that it introduced what was known in the US as 'truth in advertising'. This means that the cost of credit, especially interest rates, is to be expressed in a way that allows consumers to understand better the cost of a particular form of credit and, importantly, to compare what is available from competing credit providers. The Code requires accurate and unambiguous disclosure of information that is important to consumers in making their decision. Such information includes the amount of credit being provided, the percentage rate of interest charges, the rate of calculation of interest, the total amount of interest payable, any credit fees or other fees and default rates of interest. Ideally, under the Code, consumers will be able to make properly informed decisions about credit transactions and, in that way, the goal of a more competitive market place will be achieved. In return for observing the disclosure requirements, credit providers are able to enjoy more freedom in the design of credit products and in the pricing of them.

The Code also prescribes the form and content of contracts and provides consumer protection measures such as in respect to advertising (s 140–143), selling techniques (s 144–146) and unjust contracts: s 70. The Code has its own principles of interpretation set out in Sch 2 which provides, in effect, its own Acts Interpretation Act.

The disclosure regime

[10.17]   Given the philosophy of the Code it is not surprising that debtors and guarantors in a credit transaction are entitled to information at various stages of the transaction — pre-contractually, in the contract documentation and after the contract has been made. The Code requires that notices be easily legible, of a minimum type size (10 pt) and be clearly expressed: s162(1), s 39 of the regulations.

Section 14 prohibits a credit provider from entering into a credit contract unless the debtor has first been given a 'pre-contractual statement' and an 'information statement' in the form required by the regulations. The contents of the pre-contractual statement are made up of what is required to be included in the contract by s 15: see **[10.18]**. It may be the proposed contract or be in a separate document or documents: s 14(5). If it is in more than one document the first document must indicate that it does not contain all of the information required to be given.

The information statement is to be provided in the form of a document entitled *'Things you should know about your credit contract'*. This sets out the debtor's rights and obligations. The details of this document are set out in Form 2 of the regulations.

Disclosure in the contract

[10.18] The contract document must contain the following matters in order to satisfy s 15 of the Code:

(A) Credit provider's name
(B) Amount of credit[a]
(C) Annual percentage rate or rates*
 If there is more then one rate, how each rate applies. If an annual percentage rate under the contract is determined by referring to a reference rate, the name of the rate or a description of it and how to determine or ascertain the rate
(D) Calculation of interest charges*
 The method of calculation of the interest charges payable under the contract and the frequency with which interest charges are to be debited under the contract.
(E) Total amount of interest charges payable*
(F) Repayments
(G) Credit fees and charges*
 A statement of the credit fees and charges that are, or may become, payable under the contract, and when each such fee or charge is payable, if ascertainable.
(H) Changes affecting interest and credit fees and charges*
 If the annual percentage rate or rates or the amount or frequency of payment of a credit fee or charge or instalment payable under the contract may be changed, or a new credit fee or charge may be imposed, a statement or statements to that effect and of the means by which the debtor will be informed of the change or the new fee or charge.
(I) Statements of account
(J) Default rate*
 If the contract is a contract under which a default rate of interest may be charged when payments are in default, a statement to that effect and the default rate and how it is to be applied.
(K) Enforcement expenses
(L) Mortgage or guarantee
 If any mortgage or guarantee is to be or has been taken by the credit provider, a statement to that effect and, where appropriate details of the property subject to the mortgage.
(M) Commission
 Details of any commission to be paid by or to the credit provider for the introduction of credit business or business financed by the contract.
(N) Insurance financed by contract*
 If the credit provider knows that the debtor is to enter into a credit related insurance contract and that the insurance is to be financed under the credit contract details of the insurer, the amount of premium, any commission payable by the insurer.
(O) Other information
 Any information or warning required by the regulations: see Form 3A or 3B of the Regulation.

a. These items are referred to by the Code as *key requirements*: see **[10.19]** and **[10.35]**.

To satisfy the pre-contractual statement requirements this information must be provided before the contract is made.

Key disclosure requirements

[10.19]   The items identified in **[10.35]** as key requirements are so described in s100 of the Code in respect of credit and continuing credit contracts: see s 100 for details of which items apply to each form of contract. The information specified in ss 21(1), 32E and 33 is also designated by s 100 as a key requirement. This is significant because it is only in respect of a breach of a key disclosure requirement that the court can impose a civil penalty: s 102(2).

Level of accuracy required

[10.20]   No doubt as a result of the experience with the Credit Act 1985 where trivial failures to be exact required rectification by the court or Credit Tribunal, the Code allows for tolerances and assumptions in the provision of information about interest charges, repayments, credit fees and charges and names. Section 159 provides that:

> Information disclosed in a pre-contractual statement, contract document, mortgage document or guarantee, statement, notice or consumer lease, or otherwise disclosed for the purposes of this Code, is taken to be correctly disclosed if:
> (a) it is within tolerances allowed by the regulations; and
> (b) the disclosure is made as at a date stated in it.

The details of tolerances are set out in ss 36–38 of the Regulation. For example, in respect of the interest rate, if the rate contains more than four decimal places it is acceptable to express the rate correct to the 4th decimal place.

The section goes on to provide that when disclosures are being made they can be done on certain assumptions. These apply to the disclosure:

- of interest charges (s 159(2));
- of repayments (s 159(3));
- of credit fees and charges (s 159(4));
- in consumer leases (s 159(5));
- of names (s 159(7)); and
- when information is ascertainable: s 159(6).

Disclosure post-contract

[10.21]   The debtor is entitled to a copy of the credit contract within 14 days of its being entered into (s 18(2)) as is the guarantor if one exists. The information to be contained in the statements is set out in s 32.

Section 31 requires that the debtor be provided with periodic statements of account. The timing of those statements is set out in s 31(2):

- credit cards — 40 days;
- other continuing credit contract — 40 days or up to three months if the debtor agrees;
- in any other cases — six months.

There are circumstances where a statement need not be given: s 31(3).

As discussed later, there are circumstances in the relationship between the credit provider and debtor where other notices are to be given; for example, in repossession.

Variation of the credit contract

[10.22] There are several ways by which a credit contract may be varied. Some of these are for the benefit of the credit provider and may be unilateral or by agreement. The debtor is also able to seek the court's assistance in varying a contract by re-opening it.

[10.23] The credit provider is able to vary the contract in several ways but only if the contract allows for the variation to take place. The areas where these changes can be made, referred to as unilateral variations, are as follows:

- s 59 — interest rate changes;
- s 60 — repayment change;
- s 61 — credit fees and charges changes;
- s 62 — credit limit changes in a continuing credit contract.

Where such a change is contemplated by the credit provider it is necessary to give notice to the debtor but if the change works to the advantage of the debtor — for example, by lowering the interest rate — notice is not necessary.

There can be variations made by way of agreement between the parties and where these increase the debtor's obligations notice of the particulars of the change must also be given.

[10.24] A form of variation of the contract is available through provisions of the Code which allow the court to re-open the transaction. This is done by way of an application to the court and is a remedy for debtors, guarantors and mortgagors.

Section 70 of the Code specifies the circumstances in which the court may intervene in this way. In effect the applicant asks the court to re-write the contract where it is alleged the contract is unjust or where, on the grounds of hardship, the debtor seeks relief.

Unjust contracts

[10.25] There is an existing body of law under the Trade Practices Act 1974 s 51A and the Contracts Review Act 1980 (NSW) whereby a contract can be varied because of harshness or unconscionability. The previous legislative regime provided a similar form of relief.

Section 70(1) of the Code allows for a transaction to be re-opened if it is unjust. That term is defined in s 70(7) to include 'unconscionable, harsh or oppressive'. If the court is satisfied that a contract comes within that description it may grant the relief sought by the debtor, guarantor or mortgagor.

In determining whether a term of a particular credit contract, mortgage or guarantee is unjust in the circumstances relating to it at the time it was entered into or changed, the court is to have regard to the public interest and to all the circumstances of the case and may have regard to the following:

- (a) the consequences of compliance, or non-compliance, with all or any of the provisions of the contract, mortgage or guarantee;
- (b) the relative bargaining power of the parties;
- (c) whether or not, at the time the contract, mortgage or guarantee was entered into or changed, its provisions were the subject of negotiation;
- (d) whether or not it was reasonably practicable for the applicant to negotiate for the alteration of, or to reject, any of the provisions of the contract, mortgage or guarantee or the change;
- (e) whether or not any of the provisions of the contract, mortgage or guarantee impose conditions that are unreasonably difficult to comply with, or not reasonably necessary for

the protection of the legitimate interests of a party to the contract, mortgage or guarantee;

(f) whether or not the debtor, mortgagor or guarantor, or a person who represented the debtor, mortgagor or guarantor, was reasonably able to protect the interests of the debtor, mortgagor or guarantor because of his or her age or physical or mental condition;

(g) the form of the contract, mortgage or guarantee and the intelligibility of the language in which it is expressed;

(h) whether or not, and if so when, independent legal or other expert advice was obtained by the debtor, mortgagor or guarantor;

(i) the extent to which the provisions of the contract, mortgage or guarantee or change and their legal and practical effect were accurately explained to the debtor, mortgagor or guarantor and whether or not the debtor, mortgagor or guarantor understood those provisions and their effect;

(j) whether the credit provider or any other person exerted or used unfair pressure, undue influence or unfair tactics on the debtor, mortgagor or guarantor and, if so, the nature and extent of that unfair pressure, undue influence or unfair tactics;

(k) whether the credit provider took measures to ensure that the debtor, mortgagor or guarantor understood the nature and implications of the transaction and, if so, the adequacy of those measures;

(l) whether at the time the contract, mortgage or guarantee was entered into or changed, the credit provider knew, or could have ascertained by reasonable inquiry of the debtor at the time, that the debtor could not pay in accordance with its terms or not without substantial hardship;

(m) whether the terms of the transaction or the conduct of the credit provider is justified in the light of the risks undertaken by the credit provider;

(n) the terms of other comparable transactions involving other credit providers and, if the injustice is alleged to result from excessive interest charges, the annual percentage rate or rates payable in comparable cases;

(o) any other relevant factor.

The court is not required to take into account any injustice arising from circumstances that were not reasonably foreseeable when the transaction, the subject of the application, was entered into: s 70(4).

Under the former legislation the term 'unjust' referred to a contract that was 'unconscionable, harsh or oppressive or had an excessive annual percentage rate'. The Code makes no reference to the interest rate but, making allowance for that change, cases decided under the Credit Act could provide some guidance to the likely outcome of applications under this section. The inclusive nature of the definition of 'unjust' under the Code could lead to a more expansive interpretation of the term. For a discussion of the term under the previous legislation, see *Bava v Carvill Trading Company Pty Limited* (1987) ASC 55-449; *Custom Credit Corporation Ltd v Gray* (1991) ASC 56-096; *Andrews v Westpac Banking Corporation Ltd* (1995) ASC 56-321

Hardship

[10.26]   A debtor is able to seek a change in contractual obligations on account of hardship under s 66(1) of the Code. The grounds are that the debtor is 'unable reasonably, because of illness, unemployment or other reasonable cause, to meet the debtor's obligations under a credit contract and who reasonably expects to be able to discharge the debtor's obligations if the terms of the contract were changed' in a manner set out in s 61(2). It is important to note the qualification that the debtor 'reasonably expects' to be able to meet the obligations if the contract were to be changed.

The ways in which the contract may be changed are set out in s 66(2):

- extending the period of the contract and reducing the amount of each payment due under the contract accordingly (without a change being made to the annual percentage rate or rates);
- postponing during a specified period the dates on which payments are due under the contract (without a change being made to the annual percentage rate or rates);
- extending the period of the contract and postponing during a specified period the dates on which payments are due under the contract (without a change being made to the annual percentage rate or rates).

There is an upper limit of $125,000 on the maximum amount of credit that is or may be provided under the contract.

The remedy is discretionary and the court may combine the changes made in under s 66 with such other orders as it thinks fit: s 68.

Enforcement

[10.27] The credit provider can look for the repayment of the principal, interest and other charges as provided in the contract but subject to the provisions of the Code; for example, where a civil penalty is imposed. The party primarily responsible for meeting the contractual obligations is the debtor but, if the debtor is unable to do so the credit provider has rights against the guarantor if there is one.

The enforcement process

[10.28] The first step in taking action against the debtor is to issue a 'default notice' to the debtor: s 80(3). The debtor has no less than 30 days to make good the default. It is not until these conditions have been satisfied that the credit provider is able to take enforcement action. A similar requirement is imposed in relation to taking action under a mortgage.

There are circumstances where, upon the occurrence or non-occurrence of a specified event, the credit provider is entitled to immediate payment of an amount that under the contract is otherwise not payable: s 84(1). This is where the credit contract includes an acceleration clause. Such a clause can only be used where the debtor or mortgagor remains in default after a default notice has been issued containing details of how the acceleration clause is to operate. Section 85 allows for notice to be dispensed with and the waiting period not observed if:

(a) the credit provider believes on reasonable grounds that it was induced by fraud on the part of the debtor or mortgagor to enter into the contract or mortgage; or

(b) the credit provider has made reasonable attempts to locate the debtor or mortgagor but without success; or

(c) the court authorises the credit provider not to do so; or

(d) the credit provider believes on reasonable grounds that the debtor or mortgagor has removed or disposed of mortgaged goods under a mortgage related to the credit contract or the mortgage concerned, or intends to remove or dispose of mortgaged goods, without the credit provider's permission or that urgent action is necessary to protect the goods.

Action against the guarantor

[10.29] If the guarantee arrangements are associated with a mortgage the credit provider can exercise its rights as a mortgagee, subject of course to the notice requirements of the

Code. In the absence of a mortgage, s 82 restricts the right of enforcing a judgment against a guarantor to the following circumstances:

- the credit provider has obtained a judgment against the debtor for payment of the guaranteed liability and the judgment remains unsatisfied for 30 days after the credit provider has made a written demand for payment of the judgment debt; or
- the court has relieved the credit provider from the obligation to obtain a judgment against the debtor on the ground that recovery from the debtor is unlikely; or
- the credit provider has made reasonable attempts to locate the debtor but without success; or
- the debtor is insolvent.

Failure on the part of the credit provider to observe these requirements can be penalised.

Repossession

[10.30]   A traditional remedy for a credit provider where a debtor is in default is to recover the goods the subject of the financing agreement from the debtor — repossess them. The debtor has also been able, voluntarily, to surrender the goods and this is possible under the Code: s 78. The goods are then sold and the proceeds used to reduce the outstanding debt. In order to assist the credit provider in this regard s 90 provides that the mortgagor can be required to inform the credit provider about the whereabouts of the mortgaged goods. Failure on the part of the mortgagor to provide that information is an offence under the Code.

The repossession remedy is regulated by the Code and the following restrictions apply:

- The amount owing under the contract must not be less than 25 per cent of the amount of credit provided under the contract or $10,000, whichever is the lesser: s 82(1). It is a breach of the Code to ignore this provision but the restriction does not apply:
  - to a continuing credit contract; or
  - where the credit provider believes on reasonable grounds that the debtor has removed or disposed of the mortgaged goods, or intends to remove or dispose of them, without the credit provider's permission or that urgent action is necessary to protect the goods; or
  - where the court has consented.
- The credit provider can enter residential premises in order to recover the goods only if the court has authorised the entry under s 92 or the occupier of the premises has, after being informed in writing of the provisions of this section, consented in writing to the entry: s 91. It is an offence under the Code to enter premises in contravention of s 91.

A credit provider that is entitled to take possession of mortgaged goods may seek a court order to a person who has possession of the goods to deliver them to the credit provider at a specified time or place or within a specified period: s 93.

[10.31]   Once the goods have been repossessed the credit provider must observe further Code requirements:

- *Notice to be given*   Within 14 days of having taken possession of the goods the credit provider must advise the mortgagor in writing of the estimated value of the goods and the enforcement costs so far incurred. This notice must also set out the mortgagor's rights and obligations: s 94.

- *Goods not to be sold immediately* It is not until the elapse of 21 days after that notice has been given that the credit provider can sell the goods, unless the court has authorised the credit provider to do so: s 94(2).
- *Payment during notice period* If the amount in arrears plus enforcement expenses are settled within the 21-day period the credit provider is required to return the goods: s 94(4).

Disposal of repossessed goods

[10.32] It is in keeping with the policy of protecting the debtor's interests that the Code makes specific provision as to the sale of the repossessed goods. They must be sold 'as soon as reasonably practicable (or at such time as the credit provider and mortgagor agree) ... for the best price reasonably obtainable': s 96. It is appropriate to consider this process in similar terms to the duties of a mortgagee exercising a power of sale: see *Pendlebury v Colonial Mutual Life Assurance Society Ltd* (1912) 13 CLR 676.

If the mortgagor introduces a buyer the credit provider is required to offer to sell the goods to that person for the estimated value of the goods or, at any greater amount for which the credit provider has obtained a written offer to buy the goods: s 95.

Accounting for the proceeds of the sale

[10.33] Section 96(2) provides that:

> the credit provider must credit the mortgagor with a payment equivalent to the proceeds of the sale less any amounts which the credit provider is entitled to deduct from those proceeds. On the sale of the goods, the total amount payable under the contract becomes due.

The amounts that the credit provider is entitled to deduct from the sales proceeds are set out in s 97:

- the amount currently secured by the mortgage in relation to the credit contract, not being more than the amount required to discharge the contract;
- the amount payable to discharge any prior mortgage to which the goods were subject;
- the amounts payable in successive discharge of any subsequent mortgages to which the goods were subject and of which the credit provider had notice;
- the credit provider's reasonable enforcement expenses — that is those actually rather than notionally incurred: see s 99.

Civil penalties

[10.34] Under the previous law the credit provider risked losing the right to recover principal and/or charges. This was referred to as a civil penalty which was imposed by the Act as a result of a failure to meet specified requirements. In order to have the rights restored credit providers were required to apply to the court or Credit Tribunal. The restoration of rights for what may have appeared to be a minor mistake in the paperwork — for example, not recording the correct name of an insurance company even though its identity was never in doubt — was a sometimes cumbersome and wasteful process.

The Credit Code has retained the civil penalty system but has adopted a more common sense approach. Civil penalties are imposed only in respect of non-compliance with key requirements as defined in s 100 of the Code. Unlike the former system, the civil penalty does not arise unless applied for — by credit providers or a 'Government Consumer Agency' in respect of a class of contracts or by debtors or guarantors in respect of the particular contracts with which they are involved. The 'Government Consumer Agency' may apply to the court for standing to represent the public interest and the interests of debtors: s 111. Whereas under the old system the penalty could be the loss of the right to recover principal or charges, s 105 of the Code provides a maximum penalty of $500,000 per offence for applications brought in respect of a class of contract and interest only in respect of debtors or guarantors who seek relief for individual contracts.

Key requirements

[10.35]   These are identified in s 100 by reference to a list of provisions of the Code which specify what must be in the contract.
* amount of credit (s 15(B));
* annual percentage rate or rates (s 15(C));
* calculation of interest charges (s 15(D));
* total amount of interest charges payable (s 15(E));
* credit fees and charges (s 15(G));
* changes affecting interest and credit fees and charges (s 15(H));
* default rate (s 15(J));
* insurance financed by contract — the name of the insurer and the amount payable to the insurer (s 15(N)(a) and (b));
* prohibited monetary obligations (s 21(1)) but only at the time the credit contract is entered into;
* interest charges (s 32E) in respect of continuing credit contracts;
* opening balance must not exceed closing balance of previous statement: s 33.

Application for civil penalties

[10.36]   As mentioned earlier, applications may be made to the court by different interests — credit provider or the Government Consumer Agency or debtor or guarantor: s 101(1). An application made under this section by a credit provider or a Government Consumer Agency anywhere in Australia precludes a debtor or guarantor from making an application in respect of that contract: s 101(2).

The court must declare whether or not there was a contravention (s 102(1)) and may order the credit provider to pay a civil penalty. The section provides that in deciding upon a civil penalty the court, at the request of the credit provider, is to have regard primarily to the prudential standing of any credit provider concerned, or of any subsidiary of the credit provider if the credit provider or subsidiary takes deposits or is a borrowing corporation.: s 102(3). There are other matters specified in s 102(4) to be considered by the court:

(a) the conduct of the credit provider and debtor before and after the credit contract was entered into;
(b) whether the contravention was deliberate or otherwise;
(c) the loss or other detriment (if any) suffered by the debtor as a result of the contravention;
(d) when the credit provider first became aware, or ought reasonably to have become aware, of the contravention;
(e) any systems or procedures of the credit provider to prevent or identify contraventions;
(f) whether the contravention could have been prevented by the credit provider;
(g) any action taken by the credit provider to remedy the contravention or compensate the debtor or to prevent further contraventions;

(h) the time taken to make the application and the nature of the application;

(i) any other matter the court considers relevant.

[10.37]   Where the application for a declaration is made by a debtor or guarantor, s 103(1) limits the civil penalty to:

(a) except as provided by paragraphs (b) and (c) — all interest charges payable under the contract from the date it was made; or

(b) in the case of a contravention of a key requirement relating to a statement of account of a continuing credit contract — all interest charges payable under the contract for the period to which the statement of account relates; or

(c) in the case of a contravention of a key requirement relating to prohibited monetary obligations — all interest charges accruing under the contract from the date the contravention occurred.

If, however, the debtor or guarantor satisfies the court that the debtor has suffered a loss as a result of the contravention, s 103(2) allows the court to impose a greater civil penalty, not less than the amount of the loss. The Code also provides that compensation is payable to the debtor or guarantor. Under s 107 on application by a debtor or guarantor the court, if satisfied that there was a loss, may order compensation be paid for a loss arising from contravention of a key requirement. If a civil penalty has already been awarded the court will not make such an order: s 107(3).

The civil penalty imposed by the court on a debtor or guarantor's application may be set off against the amount owed to the credit provider: s 104(1). Where the debt has been paid off, the penalty is payable to the debtor or guarantor. In the case of a penalty imposed following an application by the credit provider or the Government Consumer Agency it must be paid 'into a fund established and operated under another law of this jurisdiction for the purposes of this section or, if no such fund is established, to the Government Consumer Agency': s 106.

[10.38]   In keeping with the emphasis on uniformity of the Credit Code scheme the Code provides protection against the practice of forum shopping by allowing a court to refuse to hear an application on the ground that 'it is more appropriate that the application be determined in another specified jurisdiction': s 109. The section envisages that an objection on this ground would be brought by a credit provider or a Government Consumer Agency. The Code also provides that a civil penalty determined in another jurisdiction may be registered and thus recognised so that the number of applications in respect of a particular contravention by a credit provider is restricted.

Summary and key terms

[10.39]   This chapter has explained:

- how the Consumer Credit Code has established a uniform regime for the regulation of consumer credit in Australia;

- the nature of credit and the transactions that are subject to the Code;

- the key concept of disclosure in the credit transaction;

- how debtors and guarantors are protected;

- how the rights of credit providers in the credit transaction are enforced; and

- the process of imposing civil penalties.

11

Negotiable Instruments and Banking

What this chapter does ...

Commerce revolves around payment — for services, for transfers of land, for goods, for the use of property or for any other benefit. Such payments can be either immediate or postponed (as, for example, where a credit arrangement is involved), can be in kind (as in barter transactions), can be in cash, or can involve using some form of negotiable or non-negotiable instrument or even one of the many forms of 'plastic' that are now in common use. This chapter will look at the non-cash, non-barter forms of payment that are now common in Australia and at the rights, duties and obligations that the law imposes upon those who use them. In particular, it will deal with the general concept of negotiability, with the various types of negotiable instruments and with the relationship between banks and other financial institutions and their customers. Chapter 12 will then deal with the specific rules that govern the day-to-day use of both cheques and credit and debit cards.

Negotiable instruments generally

[11.1]   Before dealing with the specifics of the substantive law it is useful to look briefly at the historical development of 'negotiable instruments' (of which cheques are a modern example), and at the general concept of negotiability itself. In this context, an 'instrument' is simply a document of title to money. As such, it does more than merely represent an obligation to pay the debt that it reflects — it embodies that obligation. Consequently, the 'holder' (the person in possession of the instrument) can usually demand and should receive payment of its face value by simply producing it to the person upon whom the obligation to pay the instrument's face value is imposed.

A 'negotiable instrument' is simply an instrument that can be freely transferred between parties in such a way that title to not only the physical document but also to the payment obligation (including an unrestricted right to enforce that payment obligation in full) is passed from transferor to transferee. Much of the law governing negotiable instruments (and, therefore, also governing cheques) only becomes readily understandable when it is looked at against the background of its historical development.

The historical context

[11.2]   It is generally accepted that the earliest form of trade involved a simple barter system. The parties simply exchanged their goods, giving each other quantities that represented what each would accept as an approximately equal value. This system worked as long as the parties wanted exactly what each other had to offer or if a more complicated multi-party, multi-exchange transfer arrangement could be worked out. It fell down, however, if the 'vendor' or 'vendors' did not want what the 'buyer' or 'buyers' had to offer or did not want the quantity of the 'buyer's' goods that would be equivalent in value to what they had to give in exchange.

This problem with the barter system led to the development of 'money'. Money allowed vendors to sell their goods for a neutral, valuable, transferable medium of exchange which they could take from any buyer and which they could then use to buy whatever they wanted in the quantities they wanted from any vendor who had those things to sell. The introduction of money effectively removed the inflexibility of barter and allowed trade and commerce as we know it to develop.

However, if 'money' was to be universally acceptable as a medium of exchange (or, at least, universally acceptable within particular markets), it had to be durable, portable, preferably divisible into smaller units and, in the eyes of those who traded in the market or markets in which it was to be used, intrinsically valuable. Precious metals clearly fulfilled all these criteria and gold, silver and copper (in particular) ultimately came to be readily accepted as money in most societies.

Unfortunately, using precious metal as the medium of exchange had a number of drawbacks. Chief among these were the difficulties of transporting large sums of money in the form of, especially, gold and silver over long distances and the ever-present dangers of theft or other loss (from, for example, shipwreck) that were inherent in early travel.

[11.3]   To counter these problems the merchants of Europe developed a payment system that was designed to eliminate the need to have large sums of cash always and immediately available to settle individual transactions. In essence, what they did was to establish a system of paper-indebtedness whereby the buyers of goods, instead of sending large sums of money to the sellers, sent documents which contained either a promise of, or an order for, payment. (What we would now regard as either promissory notes or bills of exchange respectively.)

The sellers obtained payment by presenting the documents, either personally or through an agent, at a specified place (usually one of the large trade fairs or one of the buyer's places of business), where the buyer or a duly appointed agent would redeem them for cash. The sellers could then use that cash to redeem their own promissory documents (those that they had used to pay their own suppliers — who were often at the same trade fairs doing the same thing). In this way the need for merchants to carry actual cash was minimised. This was especially so when, as was common, a number of them used the same settling agents. In such cases the only cash that the agents needed to have at the fair was enough to satisfy the difference between the debts that they were collecting and the debts that they were paying.

A logical extension of this system, which evolved soon afterwards, was for sellers to use the documents as a form of money. That is, instead of redeeming them themselves they used the documents with which they had been paid to pay their own debts. They transferred the promissory notes or bills of exchange (and, therefore, the indebtedness that those documents represented) to their own creditors. Those creditors could then either continue using the documents as 'money' or, if they wished, they could obtain cash payment by simply redeeming them.

There were, however, a number of both practical and legal problems associated with this development and, before it could become a widely accepted practice, they had to be overcome.

The practical problems

[11.4]   On the practical side sellers had to convince their creditors that the documents were valuable and that, as 'instruments', they would be redeemed (or honoured) on presentation. This meant, of course, that those instruments that had been originally issued by merchants or trading houses with extensive businesses, a large number of places where their promissory notes or bills of exchange could be presented for redemption and an established reputation for creditworthiness were more readily accepted than equivalent instruments issued by lesser known or even completely unknown merchants.

Even then, potential transferees might still refuse to accept instruments unless the transferor provided some additional guarantee of payment. Such additional guarantees included the transferor accepting a personal liability to pay the debt represented by the instrument if the issuer did not pay it. Transferors accepted that liability by 'indorsing' the note or bill (that is, by signing it, usually on its reverse side). Their indorsement indicated that they had used the instrument to pay their own debts (instead of issuing new notes or bills of their own) and that they accepted a personal liability to pay the instrument's face value if the issuer failed or refused to honour it when it was presented for payment. Consequently, 'indorsers' became potentially liable to everyone to whom the instrument was subsequently transferred. However, as a safeguard, they did retain a right to demand reimbursement from both the person who originally issued the instrument and from all prior indorsers if they were ever called upon to pay it. In other words, the issuer remained *primarily liable* for the debt that the instrument represented — indorsers merely guaranteed subsequent transferees that they would not suffer financially if the instrument was not paid when it was ultimately presented for payment.

The legal problems

[11.5]   On the legal side, transferring debt by transferring the instrument representing it created a significant number of problems. If the transfer was to achieve its desired effect it had to be legally enforceable and, to be legally enforceable, there had to be some mechanism whereby the debt could pass to the transferee in such a way that he or she could personally enforce it against the original debtor. In addition, it had to be possible to transfer the debt without more than minimal checks back through the chain of title. If more than that was required the system could not work. The checks needed to establish title would be too complex and too time-consuming to allow it to work. Unfortunately, the common law, in its then form, was not able to provide the sort of transfer mechanism that the realities of trade and commerce needed.

The common law problem

[11.6]   At common law, debts, even those represented by written acknowledgments and promises of payment, are choses in action — intangible items of personal property: see **[13.17]**. The common law generally regarded choses in action as incapable of being transferred or assigned. The documents representing them (which are, themselves, choses in possession or tangible assets) could be validly transferred but the 'rights' that they represented could not be. Transfers of intangible rights were, however, not illegal — it was just that the law did not recognise them. As a result, transferees or assignees had no means of enforcing the rights that they thought they had 'obtained' through the transfer or assignment. This meant, of course, that if a transferee of a debt had to enforce it he or she could not do so at common law. Consequently, accepting debts represented by promissory notes or bills of exchange was a far less attractive proposition than it might otherwise have been.

The courts of equity did assist to some extent by recognising that such transfers or assignments created equitable rights. However, because enforcing those rights meant enforcing payment of a 'legal' debt — something which only the common law courts could do — equity had no direct means of assisting transferees or assignees. All that it could do was to order the original creditor (the assignor) to lend his or her name to the enforcement action so that the assignee could, indirectly, sue the person who had issued the instrument (that is, the original creditor had to be a party to the proceedings). That, of course, all created unnecessary and unwanted complications.

The problem of notice

[11.7]   A second problem was that, even where an assignment of debt is recognised, the original debtor normally has to be given notice of the assignment before he or she becomes liable to the assignee. With 'normal' debts (those not involving the sort of documented liability involved with promissory notes and bills of exchange) this is quite a reasonable requirement — debtors have to know if their debts have been assigned so that they can make their payments to the right people and ensure that they get a good discharge for those payments. Where a debt is assigned but the debtor is not given notice of the assignment, the assignee cannot demand payment because the debtor cannot be sure that the assignee is properly entitled to it.

However, where debts are represented by promissory notes and bills of exchange this is not as great a problem — the instruments invariably specify the person to be paid with some particularity. Usually, it is the original seller, someone that the seller has 'ordered' the buyer to pay (by indorsing the note or bill of exchange with an appropriate direction) or the 'bearer' of the instrument. That is, the instrument itself indicates that payment is to be made to 'A', to 'A or order' or to 'bearer'. When that is taken into account, along with the fact that the instrument itself has to be presented and surrendered to receive payment, it can be seen that, with debts that are represented by instruments such as promissory notes and bills of exchange, notice of assignment is not really necessary in order to protect the original debtor's interests.

The problem of title

[11.8]   Finally, transferees also had to contend with the fact that all equitable transfers and assignments of choses in action are effected 'subject to equities'. In the present context what that means is that if the transferor's title to the debt was in any way defective (because, for instance, he or she had acquired the instrument acknowledging it by theft, fraud, duress, misrepresentation or other impeachable means) or if there was some 'personal equity' between the transferor and the original debtor (such as a right of set-off which the original debtor might have been able to use to extinguish the debt without further payment), the transferee only got the same rights to recover the debt that the transferor had. Therefore, if the original debtor could have legally paid the original creditor less than the debt's face value, the transferee could only recover the lesser sum. Because transferees and assignees took their transferred or assigned debts subject to pre-existing defects and equities they could lose the right to recover all or a part of those debts. If instruments such as promissory notes and bills of exchange were to be readily acceptable as a means of payment this defect had to be removed. Transferees and assignees had to be able to recover the instrument's full face value irrespective of any defects in title or personal equities which might have affected the instrument's enforceability before the transfer or assignment occurred.

The merchants' solution — negotiability

[11.9]   The merchants solved the problems that the law had created by evolving a concept of 'negotiability'. Negotiability endowed their debt instruments with the three attributes that those instruments needed but which the law could not provide.

The instrument

[11.10]   To begin with, the merchants took the existing system of transferring tangible personal property (choses in possession) and applied it to transfers of debt. Tangibles could be transferred by either deed or delivery (a physical transfer of possession accompanied by an intention to pass ownership). This system was applied to transfers of debt by imbuing the physical manifestation of the debt — the document that contained the promise of or order for payment — with the right to the debt itself. In other words the rights to payment represented by the promissory note or bill of exchange were treated as if they were contained (or locked up) in the note or bill rather than being simply represented by it. In that way, the documents acquired the status of 'instruments' and, as a result, ownership of both the physical document and the rights that it represented could be transferred by either deed or delivery (or, in appropriate cases, by indorsement and delivery).

Notice problem resolved

[11.11]   This adaptation of the common law also removed the need for the person who had issued the document (the original debtor) to be notified of each transfer or assignment. Debtors, when they issued instruments which could be transferred from person to person, knew that title to those instruments and, therefore, to their debts could (and often would) pass and that, consequently, they would usually only find out who they had to pay when the instrument was ultimately presented for payment. They were, however, protected against the risk of paying the wrong person because, when they issued a 'negotiable instrument', the indebtedness that it represented was immediately suspended. Consequently, they could not be forced to pay that debt except on presentation of the instrument (that is, the instrument itself operated as a conditional payment). Further, when that promissory note or bill of exchange, which had to be presented for and surrendered upon payment, was duly paid, the debt that it represented was regarded as having been discharged and extinguished. As a result, once the promissory note or bill of exchange had been paid all the rights that it represented, including the original creditor's contractual right to payment, were deemed to have been satisfied in full and there could be no further demand based on the original debt.

Title problem resolved

[11.12]   Finally, if 'negotiability' was fully to achieve its purpose, it had to override the normal effects that defects in title and personal equities had on transfers of property. As indicated above, the normal position (and the one that still applies to tangible assets) is that transferees take their title 'subject to equities'. Had this rule applied to transfers of 'negotiable instruments', which at common law it did, promissory notes and bills of exchange would have been far less readily transferable than, in fact, they were. Transferees would have refused to accept them unless there was a provable line of good title. Often, good title would have been difficult to establish, even though it existed, particularly if the instrument was simply payable to 'bearer'. ('Bearer' instruments do not have to be indorsed so it is difficult to trace who owned them previously or how those previous owners acquired their title.) Imagine trying to establish your right to the banknotes in your possession (banknotes originated from the 'promissory notes' of medieval commerce and are a species of 'negotiable instrument') if, to do so, you had to verify the title of everyone who had owned them before you.

To get around this problem the principle of 'negotiability' reversed the risk and permitted transferees to take title free of defects and free of equities *provided* they took the instrument in good faith, for value and without notice of any prior defect in title (that is, they must have had no improper motive in taking the instrument, they must have given valuable consideration for it — money, goods, a service or something similar — and they must have been completely unaware at the time of accepting it that there was a problem in the chain of title). If that were the case neither the issuer nor any prior 'holder' of the instrument could challenge or impeach the transferee's title to it.

The concept in practice

[11.13] Consequently, in commercial practice, 'negotiability' came to mean essentially three things:

- debts represented by instruments such as promissory notes and bills of exchange were freely transferable by simple delivery (or, occasionally, by indorsement and delivery), of the instruments in which they were recorded;
- simple ownership of those instruments gave their 'holders' the right to be paid and to enforce the debts that the instruments represented; and
- because the transfer was not affected by any prior defects in title or by any personal equities of which the transferee was not aware, transferees got good title and an unqualified right to be paid. In fact, transferees could even get a better title to the debt (through the transfer) than previous holders of the instrument might have had.

Acceptance of negotiability

[11.14] These aspects of 'negotiability', of course, gave 'negotiable instruments' a preferential status in commerce. However, negotiability was not a *legally* recognised concept and if a debt which had been 'negotiated' was not honoured when the instrument representing it was duly presented, the holder, at least initially, had no formal legal recourse against the issuer. However, this was not as serious a problem as it could have been. The commercial community at that time was relatively small and close-knit and merchants who did not honour their promises of payment (their promissory notes and bills of exchange) were easily and effectively ostracised. In other words, the penalties for not paying were simply too great for most merchants even to consider taking the risk.

If a merchant was reluctant to honour an instrument on presentation because of some valid dispute about his or her actual liability, that problem could also be settled within the 'club'. The merchants had their own system of commercial tribunals and they dealt with commercial disputes according to settled mercantile practice and custom instead of the more inflexible legal rules that applied in the law courts. Eventually, in the eighteenth century, these mercantile tribunals ceded their function to the common law courts but this did not occur before their rules (which were based on international mercantile custom and were collectively known as the 'lex mercatoria' or the 'law merchant') had been absorbed by the common law. The law merchant was well defined by Cockburn CJ in *Goodwin v Robarts* (1875) LR 10 Ex 337 at 346 as:

> neither more nor less than the usages of merchants and traders in the different departments of trade, ratified by the decisions of the Courts of law, which, upon such usages being proved before them, have adopted them as settled law with a view to the interests of trade and the public convenience.

Because the common law adopted the 'law merchant', rules which had originated in commercial practice ultimately became part of the common law and the common law courts came to recognise and enforce negotiable instruments in the same way that those instruments had been recognised and enforced under the law merchant.

That recognition, however, also meant, logically, that if a particular instrument was to be accorded the privileged status of negotiability at common law it must have been recognised as negotiable under the law merchant. Initially, therefore, instruments were only regarded as negotiable at common law if, by pre-existing mercantile usage, they had been transferable by delivery (or by indorsement and delivery) to a bona fide transferee for value who thereby acquired title to the debt that they represented free of all defects and free of all equities.

Statutory recognition of negotiable instruments

[11.15] Eventually, as statutes such as the Promissory Notes Act 1704 (UK) and the Bills of Exchange Act 1882 (UK) were passed, particular instruments had their negotiable status statutorily recognised. Thereafter they did not have to rely upon an established background of commercial usage for negotiable status. However, the influence of mercantile usage has not completely vanished and, as mercantile customs develop to meet developing commercial needs, those customs can be absorbed into the common law. Consequently, particular instruments can still be recognised as 'negotiable' at law if commercial practice accords them that status. However, if they are not generally recognised as 'negotiable' and if statute has not specifically made them negotiable, they remain non-negotiable. Such non-negotiable instruments, when they are transferred, are still transferred under the normal transfer rules for property and the more beneficial treatment accorded negotiable instruments does not apply to them.

Instruments which are recognised as negotiable either because they have traditionally been regarded as negotiable or because they have had negotiability conferred upon them by law include bills of exchange and promissory notes, banknotes, cheques, bearer bonds and debentures, dividend and interest warrants, travellers cheques, bankers' drafts and those share warrants that are payable to bearer.

Non-negotiable instruments include IOUs, money and postal orders, share certificates and debentures, letters of credit, cheques marked 'not negotiable' and all documents of title to goods such as bills of lading. Documents of title to goods (as opposed to money) are not regarded as 'negotiable' because, according to commercial practice, title to goods cannot pass 'free of equities'. Consequently, while documents of title to goods can be 'transferable' they cannot be 'negotiable'; title cannot pass 'free of equities' because the documents lack one of the three essential characteristics of negotiability.

Bills of exchange and cheques

[11.16] The negotiable instruments that are most commonly used in everyday modern commerce are undoubtedly bills of exchange and cheques. Though similar, these documents do have differences and each is now specifically governed by its own Act of Parliament — bills of exchange by the Bills of Exchange Act 1909 (Cth) and cheques by the Cheques Act 1986 (Cth). This was not always the case, however, and until 1987 when the Cheques Act first came into force, cheques and bills of exchange were both governed by the Bills of Exchange Act (BEA). Minor differences between the two forms of instrument were simply catered for by a number of specific provisions in Pt III of the BEA which only applied to cheques. Apart from that, the general provisions of the BEA applied equally to both forms of instrument: see BEA s 78(2).

Bills of exchange

[11.17]   In essence, a bill of exchange is an instrument drawn up by one party (the 'drawer') ordering another party (the 'drawee') to pay a specified sum of money to a nominated person (the 'payee' — who may or may not be the 'drawer') either on demand or at a fixed or determinable future time. If the 'drawee' assents to the drawer's order (that is, if he or she agrees to make the payment specified in the bill) the drawee becomes known as the 'acceptor'. This is because, by that assent (normally signified by writing the word 'accepted' on the face of the bill and then signing it), he or she 'accepts' liability to pay the sum specified in the bill to the person who is in lawful possession of it (the 'holder') when it becomes due: BEA s 59. The 'holder' will be either the original 'payee' or someone to whom he or she has transferred (or 'negotiated') the bill.

If the bill is an 'order bill' (one expressed to be payable to a named payee 'or order': BEA s 13(4)) it is negotiated by indorsement and delivery: BEA s 36(3). If it is a 'bearer bill' (one expressed to be payable to 'bearer' or one on which the only or last indorsement is an 'indorsement in blank': BEA s 13(3)) it is negotiated by simple delivery: BEA s 36(2). If an order bill is negotiated by indorsement and delivery, the holder who negotiates it is referred to as the 'indorser' and the person to whom ownership of the bill is thereby transferred is called the 'indorsee'.

Example of a bill of exchange

[11.18]   A typical bill of exchange would look like this:

Accepted, payable at Commonwealth Bank of Australia, George Street, Brisbane T Jones 1 September 19XX	AUD 100000 Sydney 26 August 19XX 30 days after date pay to Mary Smith or order the sum of Australian dollars One hundred thousand dollars only To: Tom Jones, Queen Street, Brisbane. *Bob Brown*

The 'drawer' of this bill is Bob Brown to whom Tom Jones (the 'drawee') is indebted in the sum of $100,000 (possibly for goods being supplied). Bob has ordered Tom to pay that money to Mary Smith (the 'payee') to whom (presumably) Bob owes money. The bill is intended to satisfy the debt that Bob owes Mary. Bob could, of course, order Tom to pay him instead — in which case Bob would be both the 'drawer' and the 'payee', but that has not occurred here. Tom has 'accepted' the bill (that is, he has accepted the obligation to pay Mary the bill's face value of $100,000) by noting his acceptance on the face of the bill.

The bill is expressed to be payable '30 days after date'. This is the 'usance' (or term) of the bill. This means that the bill will mature and that Tom will have to have the cash to pay its face value 30 days after its date — in this case 26 August 19XX. If Mary wants to use the money that the bill represents before it is due to be paid she can transfer it by negotiation to anyone willing to take it (in exchange for goods, in payment of a debt or even simply for an immediate cash payment).

If Mary exchanges it for an immediate cash payment she is said to 'discount' the bill. In the normal course of events this simply involves Mary taking the bill to her bank, indorsing it in the bank's favour and receiving a credit for the bill's face value less an agreed 'discount'. The 'discount' is the amount that the bank charges Mary for providing her with immediate access to cash. The bank will then collect full payment from either Tom or his agent when the bill matures. Here, that would be the Commonwealth Bank at its George Street, Brisbane branch because that is the agent that Tom nominated when he 'accepted' the bill.

Mary's indorsement of the bill, which is required to negotiate it because it is an 'order' bill, would appear on the bill's reverse side. It could be in the form of either a formal direction, such as 'Pay Commerce Bank or order', followed by her signature or it could be just a signature (in which case Mary is said to have indorsed the bill 'in blank'). If an order bill is indorsed 'in blank' it becomes a 'bearer bill' and it will be payable to 'bearer' instead of to a nominated 'payee' or 'indorsee'.

Bills of exchange in practice

[11.19]   Because bills of exchange can be 'term bills' (that is, bills payable at some fixed or determinable time in the future), which can be negotiated and discounted before they fall due, they are a very popular means of making and receiving payment. That is particularly so in international trading transactions where they may or may not be used in conjunction with 'bankers' documentary letters of credit'. Bankers' documentary letters of credit are, in effect, promises from a bank that its customer's bills of exchange will be honoured when they fall due. That is, the bank guarantees that the bills will be paid at maturity. Therefore, those bills are more readily accepted as a means of payment. Bankers' documentary letters of credit impose a quite separate set of obligations on the parties and they are not discussed any further in this book.

What usually happens when bills of exchange are used in trading transactions is that the seller, who has agreed to accept deferred payment, ships the goods and then sends the buyer the documents of title to them (in particular, the bill of lading) so that the buyer can deal with the goods (on-sell them, mortgage them, etc) while they are still in transit.

However, to give the seller some guarantee of payment, the documents of title will invariably be accompanied by a bill of exchange (which, because it accompanies the documents, is called a 'documentary bill'). The bill will order the buyer (as 'drawee') to pay the seller (the 'drawer') or his or her nominated 'payee' the agreed contract price either immediately ('at sight') or at the end of any agreed credit period (the 'usance' of the bill). The buyer will have to either pay or 'accept' that bill before obtaining access to the documents of title.

The seller normally sends both the documents of title and the accompanying bill of exchange through its bank, instructing the bank not to release the title documents until the bill has been paid (if it is a 'sight bill') or until it has been 'accepted' for payment (if it is a 'term bill'). In this way the buyer cannot get title to, or the physical possession of, the goods until the seller (through its bank) has obtained either payment or an 'accepted' bill of exchange. The entire process is known as a 'documentary collection' and the two release conditions that the seller can impose upon its bank are referred to as 'Documents against Payment' (D/P) or 'Documents against Acceptance' (D/A).

When the seller authorises its bank to release the documents of title against the buyer's 'acceptance' of the bill (instead of against cash payment), the seller gets an immediate accepted bill. That imposes an irrevocable and quite independent obligation on the buyer to pay the bill on maturity and, although that is obviously not as good as cash, especially if the bill has an extended term, there are advantages for both parties. The buyer gets the goods and an extended period of credit within which he or she can raise the cash to pay for them and the seller gets a negotiable bill which can either be kept to maturity or discounted immediately for a marginally reduced cash payment. For these reasons bills of exchange are particularly popular in major commercial transactions.

Cheques

[11.20]   Traditionally, cheques have been regarded as a species of bill of exchange though the origins of the two instruments are quite different. Cheques originated when goldsmiths, who accepted deposits of bullion for safekeeping, agreed to release those deposits to third parties if their depositors gave them written instructions to do so. (Just as, now, banks, building societies and credit unions — collectively called 'financial institutions', see [12.4] — release their customers' funds to third parties upon their customers' written instructions to do so, the instructions found in the customers' cheques.)

Like bills of exchange, cheques have 'drawers' (those who sign them and whose accounts with the financial institution on which they are drawn will eventually be debited), 'drawees' (the financial institutions that will make those payments) and 'payees' (those to whom or in whose favour the payments will be made). Further, unless they are specifically made 'not negotiable', cheques, like bills of exchange, can be freely negotiated by simple delivery or, in the case of 'order cheques', by indorsement and delivery until they are 'discharged'.

However, there are very distinct differences between cheques and 'other' bills of exchange and the two forms of negotiable instrument are used quite differently in commerce. Because cheques are drawn on a 'financial institution' and are payable on demand (usually out of funds which are immediately available from the drawer's account), they are used mainly for simple payments. That is, in the normal course of events the payee will collect the cheque's proceeds personally (by depositing the cheque in his or her own account with one of the 'financial institutions') and there will be no onwards negotiation (and, usually, no 'discounting') of the cheque.

Bills of exchange, on the other hand, are now mainly used in trading transactions or as commercial fundraising instruments. The drawee of a term bill simply 'accepts' it for payment and does not need the cash to pay it until it becomes due. Of course, the bill will ultimately be paid but it may well be negotiated a number of times between its initial acceptance and when it is finally paid. Bills of exchange, therefore, are mainly used to let the drawee defer payment while still giving the payee an opportunity to obtain immediate, if somewhat indirect, access to at least most of the money that the bill represents.

It is this difference between the uses to which the two instruments are put, as well as, in the case of cheques, the presence of a bank or other financial institution as an intermediary holder of the drawer's funds (with all the resulting rights, duties and obligations that that creates), that really distinguishes cheques from 'other' bills of exchange.

Financial institutions and their customers

[11.21]   Cheques are simply unconditional orders in writing addressed to a financial institution requiring it to pay money to a designated payee on demand. The order (and therefore the cheque) will come from one of the financial institution's customers and it will require it to pay a sum of money out of that customer's account. When the cheque is presented for payment the financial institution cannot 'accept' it as drawees can do with other (term) bills of exchange, because cheques must be 'paid' on demand — they cannot be 'accepted' for payment later. Therefore, the financial institution can really only do one of two things — it can either pay the cheque or it can refuse to pay it. Its decision on whether or not to pay will be heavily influenced by its relationship with its customer and, in particular, by any specific instructions that that customer may have given it regarding his or her cheques.

Becoming a customer

[11.22]   Becoming a customer simply involves opening an account. Once the account is open the account holder is automatically a customer and he or she immediately becomes entitled to all the rights, duties and obligations that financial institutions owe their customers. Merely doing business with a financial institution without having an account with it is not enough to confer customer status. Therefore, those who simply use the institution's facilities to cash cheques drawn by others, to change money or to use one of the institution's ancillary services (such as by buying overseas drafts or travellers cheques) are not customers. Lord Dunedin discussed the distinction between customers and non-customers in *Commissioner of Taxation v English, Scottish and Australian Bank Ltd* [1920] AC 683 at 687. He said:

> A person whose money has been accepted by the bank on the footing that they undertake to honour cheques up to the amount standing to his credit is ... a customer of the bank ... irrespective of whether his connection is of short or long standing. The contrast is not between an habitué and a newcomer, but between a person for whom the bank performs a casual service, such as, for instance, cashing a cheque for a person introduced by one of their customers, and a person who has an account of his own at the bank.

The relationship and its obligations

[11.23]   The House of Lords' decision in *Foley v Hill* (1848) 2 HLC 28 determined that the relationship between financial institutions and their customers is essentially that of debtor and creditor. That means that when an institution accepts a deposit from a customer it does so as a borrower rather than as a bailee or trustee. That in turn means that the institution becomes the legal owner of the money deposited with it and that its customers simply get an entitlement to have an *equivalent sum* repaid upon demand. Therefore, financial institutions are not simply custodians of their customers' money; they legally own that money and, as the legal owners, they can use it in their own discretion and for their own purposes. They do not have to keep the money separate from their own funds nor do they have to return the exact same notes and coins that their customers deposited with them — as would be the case if they were mere bailees: see *Brambles Security Services Ltd v Bi-Lo Pty Ltd* [1992] Aust Torts Reports 61,260 and the discussion in [15.1]. All that the financial institutions have to do is to repay the debts that the deposits create, together with any agreed interest, when repayment is due and required.

The relationship between financial institutions and their customers is therefore essentially contractual. The customer contracts to lend money to the institution and it contracts to repay that money either on demand or at some time in the future, together with interest as payment for the right to use it in the meantime. These, however, are not the only terms of the contract. There may also be other express terms (such as that the customer will pay any applicable account fees) and there may also be a number of implied terms. The implied terms can arise under statute (as is the case, for example, with ss 51A, 52 and 74 of the Trade Practices Act 1974 (Cth) and with the equivalent provisions of the various state and territory Fair Trading Acts; and, now, with the provisions of the Consumer Credit Code: see Chapter 10. They can also arise through custom or usage and this is especially relevant to the duties which arise out of the relationship between banks and other financial institutions and their customers. Those duties originated in commercial practice, they were implied because they reflected what those involved in banking transactions could reasonably expect of one another and, by virtue of s 4(3) of the Cheques Act 1986 (Cth), they now apply not only to banks but to all other 'financial institutions' as well. (The term 'financial institutions' is defined in s 3(1) of the Cheques Act: see [12.4].)

The financial institutions' duties

[11.24] The duties that financial institutions owe their customers either generally or under the terms of the contract between them include the following.

To honour their customers' cheques

[11.25] When financial institutions permit their customers to open accounts on which cheques may be drawn they impliedly undertake that they will honour those cheques provided:

- they are duly presented during normal hours at the branch where the customer's account is kept (or at any other branch at which, by arrangement, those cheques may be presented);
- the customer has either a sufficient credit balance in his or her account or an approved overdraft facility; and
- there is no other impediment to payment.

Such 'other impediments' include countermand of payment by the customer before the cheque is presented, the cheque being 'postdated' and not yet due, the cheque having become 'stale', the institution having notice of the customer's mental incapacity, death or bankruptcy, the institution having become aware of a defect in the 'holder's' title to the cheque or having notice of the customer's assignment (that is, transfer to someone else) of his or her rights to the account against which the cheque has been drawn. Each of these impediments is discussed in more detail in [12.51]–[12.62].

To obey their customers' directions

[11.26] While financial institutions have a general duty to pay their customers' cheques, that obligation is subject to one other duty — the duty to obey their customers' directions. Consequently, customers can specifically limit a financial institution's authority to pay their cheques by giving it some express direction to the contrary. Such limitations can be imposed in a number of ways and at a number of times — when the account is opened, when the cheque is drawn or even after the cheque has been drawn but before it is paid.

When an account is opened the customer can, for example, direct the institution not to pay its cheques unless they meet certain criteria — the requirement for signature by two or more authorised co-signatories is a common example. If a financial institution that has been directed not to do so pays a cheque that has not been properly countersigned, it will be in breach of its duty to obey its customer's directions and it may have to re-credit the customer's account with the amount that it paid out without authority: see *Liggett B (Liverpool) Ltd v Barclays Bank Ltd* [1928] 1 KB 48.

Similarly, when a customer draws a cheque he or she can give the institution a number of specific directions. They are given by making the cheque payable to 'bearer' or to 'order', by crossing it or by inscribing it with specific words of direction such as 'not negotiable'. Each of these directions, when written on the face of the cheque, limits or qualifies the financial institution's mandate and authority to pay it. If it then pays the cheque otherwise than in strict accordance with the customer's directions the institution can be liable for any loss that the customer suffers as a result. These limitations are all discussed in further detail in Chapter 12.

Finally, if a customer wants to cancel a cheque to prevent it being paid he or she can do so by simply directing the financial institution not to pay it. This is done by giving notice of countermand. If the customer gives due notice of countermand before the cheque has been paid, the institution's duty and authority to pay that cheque is immediately terminated. Each of these restrictions is discussed in more detail in Chapter 12.

To receive deposits and to collect the proceeds of cheques, etc

[11.27]   Financial institutions have a duty to receive deposits and to collect the proceeds of cheques and other instruments (promissory notes, bills of exchange, etc) that their customers pay into their accounts. When a customer pays a cheque or other instrument into his or her account the institution, by accepting the deposit, undertakes to collect the proceeds of that instrument on the customer's behalf. The collection is done as the customer's agent and, in the absence of any contrary instruction, the proceeds are immediately credited to the customer's account once they are collected. In other words, there is an implied term in the contract between the institution and its customers that, when it acts as a collection agent, it will, immediately after the proceeds have been collected, borrow those proceeds and credit the customer's account accordingly. Therefore, simply by accepting the original deposit the institution does not, then, become liable to its customer for the face value of the instrument — the financial institution's indebtedness only arises after the funds have been collected and when they have been credited to the customer's account. Up to that point the institution only acts as a 'collecting institution'.

To keep the customer's affairs secret

[11.28]   The relationship between financial institutions and their customers is one of confidentiality. In the normal course of events, the institutions cannot reveal details about either their customers or their customers' financial affairs unless they have been specifically authorised to do so.

Case Example

Tournier, whose account with the National Provincial and Union Bank of England was overdrawn by £9.8.6d, agreed to repay the bank £1 per week until the overdraft was cleared. He defaulted in his payments. The bank then discovered that he had received a cheque for £45 and that he had indorsed and paid it over to his bookmaker instead of using it to extinguish his overdraft. The bank manager telephoned his employer to get his private address and, during that conversation, he told the employer that Tournier appeared to be gambling heavily. Tournier was dismissed. He sued the bank alleging slander and breach of its duty of confidentiality. He succeeded. Banks cannot divulge details of their customers' affairs: *Tournier v National Provincial and Union Bank of England* [1924] 1 KB 461.

The court in that case did, however, acknowledge that the duty of confidentiality is not an absolute obligation. In particular, it accepted that banks and other financial institutions can divulge information about their customers in each of the following four instances:

1. Where they are compelled to by law (for example, under the Financial Transactions Reports Act 1988 (Cth) 'cash dealers', which term includes 'financial institutions', are required to report any 'significant cash transactions' of $10,000 or more. Similarly, under s 264 of the Income Tax Assessment Act the Commissioner of Taxation can force a financial institution to disclose details of its customers' financial affairs if the Commissioner believes that those details could have a bearing on some taxpayer's tax liability. Financial institutions can also be required to divulge otherwise confidential information when they are giving evidence before a court of law).

2. Where disclosure is necessary in the public interest (for example, in wartime where a customer's account could indicate transactions with the enemy; where in times of national emergency the operation of the account could indicate treasonous conduct; or when disclosure could prevent or assist with the detection of crime).

3. Where disclosure is required for the financial institution's own protection (as, for example, where the institution is suing or is being sued by a customer or a customer's guarantor and needs to disclose information about that customer to enforce its rights or to protect its interests).

4. Where the customer expressly or impliedly consents to the disclosure. Such consent can be either a general consent (such as when the customer asks the institution to act as a general financial referee), or a more specific and limited consent (such as when the customer authorises it to disclose information to accountants, solicitors or others who are doing work on his or her behalf).

However, unless one of these exceptions applies, financial institutions cannot legally disclose any information about their customers or their affairs. This prohibition applies not only while the customers are still customers but also after that relationship has come to an end (that is, after their accounts have been closed).

To give the customer reasonable notice before closing an account or terminating the relationship

[11.29]   While financial institutions do not normally close customers' accounts unilaterally they can do so. They can simply close the account and repay the amount by which it is then in credit. However, it has long been settled law that financial institutions are 'not at liberty to close an account in credit by payment of the credit balance without giving reasonable notice': per Warrington LJ in *Joachimson v Swiss Bank Corp* [1921] 3 KB 110 at 125. They must give reasonable notice of their intention to close the account so that the customer can find somewhere else to put his or her money and also (and probably more importantly) so that adequate provision can be made for the payment of cheques that the customer has drawn but which have not yet been presented for payment.

To take reasonable care in giving its customers advice or information

[11.30]   Unlike the other duties discussed so far, this duty does not arise directly out of the relationship that exists between financial institutions and their customers. Instead, it comes from a more general duty of care. Just like all other advisers, financial institutions that provide specific advice or information must do so carefully. If they provide information without paying due attention to its accuracy they can be liable in negligence to those (including their customers) who suffer as a result: see Chapter 16.

> ## Case Example
>
> The local branch manager of the Commonwealth Bank gave negligent financial advice to one of the bank's longtime customers in relation to the customer's purchase of a hotel. The vendor was indebted to the bank and the branch manager's advice about the value of the property was influenced by his concern that the price received would allow the vendor to repay that indebtedness. The bank was held liable. The Federal Court found that where a bank gives negligent financial advice the customer has a number of possible causes of action; in negligence, for breach of fiduciary duty or for breach of contract: *Commonwealth Bank of Australia v Smith* (1991) 102 ALR 453.

Other good examples of financial institutions (particularly banks) failing to take reasonable care when giving their customers advice or information can be found in the 'foreign currency loan cases' where banks have been variously found liable in negligence, for breach of s 52 of the Trade Practices Act 1974 (Cth) or for breach of contractual duties to advise and/or monitor the loans they arranged. See, for example, *Foti v Banque Nationale de Paris* (No1) (1989) 54 SASR 354; (No 2) (1989) 54 SASR 433, *Spice v Westpac Bank* (1990) ATPR ¶41-024 and *Chiarabaglio v Westpac* (1991) ATPR (Digest) 46-067.

[11.31]   However, if the customer sues for an alleged breach of the institution's duty of care, it is worth noting that, in most circumstances, the institution only owes its customers a normal duty of care (that is, no more than the duty of care that it would owe any inquirer) to ensure that the information or advice that it gives is accurate. In particular, the relationship between financial institutions and their customers does not ordinarily raise a presumption of undue influence. Therefore, customers cannot generally sue their financial institutions for any loss that they sustain by acting on bad advice when it was clearly imprudent to act on it. See, for example, *National Westminster Bank Plc v Morgan* [1985] 1 AC 686, in which the House of Lords refused to accept a plea of undue influence to overturn an intended foreclosure. The undue influence that was pleaded in that case was alleged to have arisen through the parties' relationship and the bank was accused of abusing that 'influence' for its own benefit. Their Lordships, in rejecting the plaintiff's claims, specifically found that the relationship was not enough, by itself, to raise a presumption of undue influence.

To care for any property that the customer leaves with the institution

[11.32]   Again, this is not a duty that specifically arises out of the relationship. Instead, it arises out of the contract (which may or may not be a contract of bailment — see Chapter 15) under which property is left for safe custody. There is, however, some overlap between this duty and the duty of confidentiality. For example, it has been held that, unless they have some express authority to act to the contrary, financial institutions cannot reveal the contents of safe custody packets or safe deposit boxes that they hold for their customers or in their customers' names to anyone other than those customers. Therefore, in both *O'Reilly v Commissioners of the State Bank of Victoria* (1983) 153 CLR 1 and *Kerrison v Federal Commissioner of Taxation* 86 ATC 4103 it was held that the Commissioner of Taxation was entitled to inspect the contents of the respective customers' safe deposit boxes but, in both cases, that was only because the Income Tax

Assessment Act expressly overrode the bank's right to refuse and gave the Commissioner an absolute right to access.

Duties of customers

[11.33] In the same way that the relationship between financial institutions and their customers imposes a number of duties on the institutions, so too does it impose a number of duties on customers. Those duties are also derived from the implied terms of the parties' contract. If customers breach their duties they may have to compensate the institutions for any resulting losses that they suffer. In addition, the customers may lose any rights that they could otherwise have had to recover amounts erroneously debited to their accounts. The more important of the customers' duties include the following.

To take reasonable precautions to prevent forgeries and fraudulent alterations

[11.34]   Customers must take reasonable steps to ensure that the material parts of their cheques (the amount, the payee, etc) are not filled in or altered without their knowledge or authority. This is sometimes referred to as the 'Macmillan duty' after the decision in *London Joint Stock Bank Ltd v Macmillan and Arthur* [1918] AC 777 especially at 825–6. In normal circumstances, this means that they should not leave gaps before or after the written amounts, that they should clearly and unambiguously specify the payee and that they should not sign cheques in blank leaving others to fill in the details: see *Robarts v Tucker* (1851) 16 QB 560 especially at 580.

If customers fail to take these precautions they may have to indemnify the drawee institutions for any resulting losses.

Case Example

Sydney Wide Stores had drawn a number of cheques in favour of a firm called 'Computer Accounting Services' and had made them payable to 'CAS or order'. An employee then fraudulently added the letter 'H' to the abbreviation 'CAS', so that the cheques appeared to be payable to 'CASH', and presented them for payment. The Commonwealth Bank paid them even though they were for large sums and were marked 'Not Negotiable A/c Payee Only'. When Sydney Wide Stores discovered the fraud it sued the Commonwealth Bank, alleging that the bank had acted negligently. It demanded that the bank re-credit its account with the money that, it said, had been paid out without proper authority. The bank argued that Sydney Wide Stores was at fault because it had drawn its cheques in such a way that they could be fraudulently altered. It said that, as a result, Sydney Wide Stores should bear the loss.

The High Court held that customers have a duty to take all usual and reasonable precautions to prevent their cheques being fraudulently altered if those alterations could cause loss to the bank. The court went on to say that whether a customer has adopted all usual and reasonable precautions in the circumstances is a question of fact which has to be determined on the merits of each case.

In this case it remitted the matter back to the Supreme Court of New South Wales for it to determine whether, in the circumstances, Sydney Wide Stores had been negligent — given that it had made its cheques payable to 'order', had crossed them and had added the words 'Not Negotiable, A/c Payee Only', markings which are not normally found on cash cheques: *Commonwealth Trading Bank of Australia v Sydney Wide Stores Pty Ltd* (1981) 148 CLR 304.

To draw cheques unambiguously and to avoid misleading the institution

[11.35]   Financial institutions have an obligation to pay their customers' cheques and, in the normal course of events, those payments have to be made promptly to avoid damaging their customers' financial reputations. Unfortunately, this also means that they cannot really inspect every cheque exhaustively before paying it. In fact, given the number of cheques used in any one year (an estimated 3 million cheques worth over $17 billion are written *every day* in Australia alone), financial institutions really only refuse payment if there is a very clear and obvious possibility that, if they paid the cheque, they could be acting in a manner inconsistent with their customer's instructions or that the customer could be defrauded. From the customer's point of view, what this means is that, if the authorisation of payment on the face of the cheque is not sufficiently clear, the payment may be refused. That refusal can occur even if the customer's reputation will, thereby, be affected and in most cases the customer will have no recourse against the financial institution at all — its non-payment will have been justified.

Alternatively, if what the customer has written on the cheque is ambiguous and the financial institution adopts what appears to be a reasonable interpretation of it and pays the cheque according to that interpretation, the customer will have no enforceable grounds for complaint if the institution was wrong. A classic example of such ambiguity is where a customer draws a cheque with a discrepancy between the amount written in words and the amount written in figures. Instead of dishonouring the cheque entirely (as it could do), the financial institution might prefer to pay one or other of the amounts (perhaps either the written sum or the lesser of the two specified sums), if that is what it believes its customer wanted. In fact, in such cases, the financial institutions have always had a degree of legislative protection — both the BEA and the Cheques Act contain provisions setting out how much they should pay in such cases. Section 15(2) of the Cheques Act, for instance, expressly authorises payment of the lesser or least of the sums that appear on the cheque's face. It apparently assumes that the customer intended the institution to pay at least that amount.

To advise the institution immediately of any irregularity in the account (the 'Greenwood duty')

[11.36]   Customers must inform their financial institutions immediately they become aware of any real or suspected irregularity in the operation of their accounts. This is so that the institutions can do whatever they can to prevent further loss and, possibly, to recover what has been lost already. If customers become aware of fraudulent transactions but do nothing to tell the institution about them, they will be estopped, at least as against the institution, from denying that those transactions were legitimate and authorised. The obvious consequence of this is that the customers will bear all resulting loss.

Case Example

Greenwood, who had an account with Martins Bank, discovered that his wife had been forging his signature and withdrawing money from it. His wife persuaded him not to inform the bank, telling him that she had taken the money to help her sister, who would repay it in due course. In fact, the wife had used the money herself. When Greenwood discovered this (about eight months later) he finally told the bank about the forgeries and demanded that it re-credit his account with the £410.6s that his wife had taken. The bank refused. Greenwood sued and failed. He should have advised the bank of his wife's forgeries as soon as he became aware of them. Had he done so the bank could have taken steps both to avoid making further payments and to recover the money that it had already paid out. Because Greenwood had not told the bank of his wife's fraud he was the effective cause of much of the loss and, therefore, at least as against the bank, he had lost the right to claim that the cheques were forgeries. Consequently, he could not recover the money that had been debited against his account: *Greenwood v Martins Bank Ltd* [1933] AC 51.

[11.37]   However, while customers have a positive duty to advise their financial institutions of all frauds, forgeries and irregularities that come to their attention, they do not appear to have to take any formal precautions to ensure that those irregularities are discovered. Nor, it seems, do they even have to conduct their day-to-day activities in a reasonable manner where that, by itself, would probably be enough to bring any irregularities to their attention.

Case Example

An employee of the Tai Hing Cotton Mill defrauded it of HK$5.5 million by forging the managing director's signature on about 300 cheques over a period of four years. The fraud occurred because the company's internal control and audit procedures were virtually non-existent. The company had received regular bank statements showing the payments but it had either never checked them or, if it had, had not discovered the forgeries. It was held that, because the cheques were forgeries (which were obviously not a proper mandate for payment), the banks had to re-credit the company's account with the money that they had paid out on them. The banks were liable for the loss. The Privy Council held that the company had not been under any duty to do anything which might have put it on notice that its cheques were being forged — it merely had a duty to advise the banks *if and when* it became aware of any forgeries. In other words, unless there is some express contractual provision requiring a customer to take preventative measures (and the court found that there was no such provision in that case), all that the customer has to do is to avoid drawing cheques in such a way that they are susceptible to forgery or fraud and to advise the banks immediately upon becoming aware of any irregularity: *Tai Hing Cotton Mill Ltd v Liu Chong Hing Bank Ltd* [1986] AC 80.

[11.38]   Consequently, there does not appear to be any duty on customers (as the banks had argued in *Tai Hing* that there was) to take all reasonable care to prevent forgeries being presented for payment. If customers had such a duty they would have to adopt the same level of care towards their financial institutions as the tort of negligence requires of all potential tortfeasors. However, the Privy Council effectively held in *Tai Hing* that the customer's duty is sourced not in tort but in contract.

The Privy Council's decision was subsequently endorsed in Australia in *National Australia Bank v Hokit* (1996) 39 NSWLR 377. In that case Mrs Banno, a bookkeeper employed by several family companies operating hairdressing salons in Sydney, signed some 530 cheques in the name of the companies' controller, Mark Cordony, over four years. Some of those cheques had been drawn for company purposes and Banno had signed them with Mark's knowledge, but she had also signed Mark's name on a number of cheques for her own benefit. The companies eventually discovered the fraud and sued the bank for the amounts debited against their accounts as a result of the latter set of forgeries (the companies accepted that they could not recover for the forgeries of which Mark had been aware). The bank denied liability, arguing that the companies' failure to act with care for their own interests should preclude them from recovering. It was still held liable. The court found that customers' duties are limited to the duties to take usual and reasonable precautions in drawing a cheque to prevent it from being fraudulently altered and to inform the bank of any forgery as soon as the customer becomes aware of it and that those duties should not be extended, either in contract or tort, to require customers to take precautions in the management of their accounts to prevent forgeries being presented. Mahoney P commented (at 392) that the banks could always take appropriate steps to deal with the problem by either setting their fee structure at a level to deal with it or by inserting a term in the contracts with their customers to require them to adopt appropriate prudential standards in the management of their accounts.

Summary and key terms

[11.39]   The main points covered in this chapter were as follows:
- There are a number of *commercially acceptable forms of payment* (other than cash) and the use of each is governed by specific legal rules.
- *Negotiable instruments* are simply documents of title to money that are *freely transferable* between parties in such a way that the rights to payment that the document represents are passed from transferor to transferee.
- The most common negotiable instruments are *bills of exchange* and *cheques*.
- The relationship between *financial institutions and their customers* is that of *debtor and creditor* but it also involves contractual and fiduciary duties on both sides.

12

Cheques and Plastic Money

What this chapter does ...

This chapter follows on from Chapter 11's discussion of negotiability and of the relationship between financial institutions and their customers. It looks in more detail at the specific rights, duties and obligations that are involved in using cheques (in particular) and the various forms of credit and debit cards that are now in common commercial and domestic usage.

Why use cheques?

[12.1] Cheques are mainly used because they offer three advantages — convenience, security and negotiability. The main benefit of negotiability, which was discussed in Chapter 11, is that negotiable instruments are more readily acceptable to transferees and, therefore, are more readily transferable than non-negotiable instruments. The advantages of convenience and security are relatively self-explanatory.

In specifics, cheques are used because:

• They are readily acceptable as a substitute for cash and, therefore, consumers need not carry large sums of money to pay for their transactions. Cheques will be accepted by most businesses, especially when the customer is known to them. Even where that is not the case cheques will usually be accepted if the customer agrees to wait until after the cheque has been cleared before collecting the goods or services.

• Cheques minimise the risks of theft or loss. Cheques are not themselves money, they merely represent a right to be paid a sum of money. If a cheque is lost or stolen the drawer can countermand the financial institution's authority to pay it. Even where blank cheque forms are lost or stolen there is still a degree of protection. Forgeries are not proper directions to a financial institution and they are wholly inoperative as authorities (or mandates) for it to pay money out of a customer's account. If financial institutions pay on forgeries they usually have to re-credit the account with the amount paid out.

• Cheques can be posted or delivered with ease and security.

- They can be drawn for the exact amount owing thereby avoiding the problems, for the person paying, of having to have the exact amount needed for the payment or, for the person being paid, of having to have change available.
- They provide a convenient record of payment. The drawer can and usually does record details of each cheque on the cheque stub which stays in the cheque book as a permanent record. In addition, once a cheque has been cashed, the drawer can obtain it or a facsimile of it from his or her financial institution as proof of payment.
- Should the question ever be litigated, the financial institution's records can be subpoenaed and used as evidence.

Cheques defined

[12.2]   Cheques are defined in s 10(1) of the Cheques Act 1986 (Cth) as follows:

> A cheque is an unconditional order in writing that:
>
> (a) is addressed by a person to another person, being a financial institution; and
> (b) is signed by the person giving it; and
> (c) requires the financial institution to pay on demand a sum certain in money.

Section 10(2) reinforces this definition by providing that, 'an instrument that does not comply with subsection (1), or that orders any act to be done in addition to the payment of money, is not a cheque'.

The remaining sections of Pt II Div 1 (ss 11–18) go on to explain the precise meaning of the various elements of the s 10(1) definition.

Unconditional order

[12.3]   The requirement that a cheque be 'an unconditional order' is really two requirements. First, it must be an 'order'. Section 11 makes it clear that, to be an order, the cheque 'must be more than an authorisation or request to pay'. What is required is a formal *direction* from the customer requiring the financial institution to pay the sum stipulated in the cheque.

Second, the order must be 'unconditional'. This is dealt with in s 12. Subsection 1 provides that 'an order to pay on a contingency is not an unconditional order' — whether or not the contingent event eventually takes place. Therefore, a cheque requiring a financial institution to 'Pay Bill Smith $1000 provided he delivers his goods on time' would not be a cheque because the order to pay is not unconditional. The reason is very simple — financial institutions (and others to whom the 'cheque' might be negotiated before it is eventually paid) do not have the resources to determine whether the condition has been met and an instrument's validity should not be subject to a contingency which cannot be readily checked: see *Carlos v Fancourt* (1794) 101 ER 272 at 273.

However, s 12(2) limits what might be regarded as a conditional order. It provides that an order shall not be taken to be a conditional order simply because it is coupled with either an indication of the particular account that the financial institution is to debit with the payment or a statement of the transaction that gave rise to the order (the cheque).

Consequently, a drawer can (and usually does) indicate the precise account against which his or her cheque is to be debited. This is normally done simply by drawing the cheque on a pre-printed form which contains the name of the branch of the financial institution and the number of the account against which that cheque is to be debited. The provision that the cheque may also contain 'a statement of the transaction giving rise to the order' is rarely used but, if it is, it can help to show that consideration has been given for the cheque, a necessary prerequisite to the right to enforce that cheque: see **[12.28]**.

Addressed to a financial institution

[12.4]   The term 'financial institution' is defined in s 3(1) of the Cheques Act as meaning:

(a) the Reserve Bank of Australia; or

(b) a bank within the meaning of the Banking Act 1959; or

(c) an FIC institution; or

(d) a person who carries on state banking within the meaning of paragraph 51(xiii) of the Constitution; or

(e) a person (other than a person referred to in paragraph (a), (b), (c) or (d)) who carries on the business of banking outside Australia.

Section 3(1) also defines 'FIC institution'. It is 'a body corporate that is, for the purposes of any of the Financial Institution Codes (that is, the Financial Institution Codes of any of the states or territories): a building society, a credit union or a special services provider'.

'Special services providers' (SSPs) are defined in the Australian Financial Institutions Code, s 36(2)(b) of which provides that a body can be registered as a special services provider if it restricts itself to providing treasury management services to societies (building societies, credit unions and any other registered bodies), receiving deposits from societies, investing funds of societies in liquid assets, providing loans or financial accommodation to societies, establishing lines of credit or obtaining financial accommodation or providing other services approved for it by the Australian Financial Institutions Commission.

The definition of 'FIC institution' does not include what s 3(1) defines as 'FCA institutions'. They are corporations registered under the Financial Corporations Act 1974 (but not under the Financial Institutions Codes) which are either building societies or credit unions as defined in that Act or bodies prescribed as FCA institutions for the purposes of the new s 3(1) definition. The effect of not including 'FCA institutions' means that they are not 'financial institutions' for the purposes of the Cheques Act. Therefore, they cannot issue their own cheques. Instead, they have to rely on 'agency cheque' arrangements if they want to provide their customers with a chequing facility: see **[12.71]**.

If the 'unconditional order' is not directed to a 'financial institution' (called the 'drawee institution' because the customer — the 'drawer' — draws the cheque on it), it cannot be a cheque because it is not addressed 'to another person, being a financial institution'.

Section 13(1) also imposes a number of limitations on what constitutes an order addressed to a financial institution. In essence it provides that the order must be addressed to a financial institution and to no other person, that it must be addressed to one financial institution only and that the financial institution must be named or otherwise indicated with reasonable certainty in the instrument containing the order. Because most cheques are drawn on pre-printed forms issued by the financial institutions themselves, the s 13(1) limitations rarely pose any significant problems in practice. The pre-printed forms ensure that the requirements are met.

Signed by the person giving it

[12.5] The customer's signature on a cheque really serves two purposes. First, it creates the cheque. This is because signature is an integral part of any cheque as 'cheques' are defined in s 10(1). Second, the signature authorises the financial institution (or gives it its 'mandate') to debit the customer's account once the cheque has been paid. This second function comes from the terms of the financial institution–customer contract under which the financial institution undertakes to pay the customer's cheques upon receipt of proper authorisation.

The requirement that cheques be signed by the person giving them does not mean that customers must actually sign them in person. Under s 114, a person is taken to sign a cheque or other instrument if his or her signature is written on it by another person acting under his or her authority or, if there is an agreement to that effect, if the customer, or another person acting under his or her authority, places it there using a stamp or other mechanical means. Consequently, cheques can be signed by agents and they can also be validly 'signed' in facsimile form through the use of, for example, rubber stamps.

[12.6] What will never constitute a signature is anything which is written or placed on a cheque without the authority of the person whose signature it purports to be. Section 32(1) (in relation to cheques generally) and s 100A (in relation to 'agency cheques', see **[12.71]**) specifically provide that the 'signature' in such cases is wholly inoperative as that of the relevant person except where that person is estopped from denying either that the signature is genuine or that it was authorised (as was the case in, for example, *Greenwood v Martin's Bank Ltd* [1933] AC 51 — see **[11.36]**), or where that person has ratified or adopted the signature after becoming aware of it. Section 3(6) provides that references in the Act to signatures or indorsements being written or placed on cheques without authority includes references to the forging of those signatures or indorsements.

Signature by agents

[12.7] Where cheques are signed by agents the liability of both the agent and the customer can be limited. Section 33 gives the agent some protection. It provides that where a person signs a cheque for or on behalf of a principal or in some representative capacity *but* adds words which indicate that the document is being signed as a representative and which also adequately identify the principal, the signer (the agent) will not be personally liable on the cheque.

Procuration signatures

[12.8] A procuration signature is one which is placed on a document by an agent who has had his or her actual authority limited by the principal. The principal, therefore, only intends to be liable for those acts that are *actually authorised* and not for anything which might fall within the agent's apparent authority. Consequently, if an agent signs a cheque, indicating clearly that he or she does so by procuration (by either noting the signature with the full phrase 'per procurationem' or with one of the accepted abbreviations such as 'per pro' or 'pp'), the person receiving the cheque is put on notice that he or she is dealing with someone whose authority is limited. Therefore, the principal will only be liable if the agent had actual authority to sign that cheque for that amount. This common law position is confirmed by s 34 which provides that a procuration signature operates as a notice to the payee that the agent has only a limited authority to sign his or her principal's cheques and that the principal is not bound by the signature unless the agent, in signing the cheque, acted within the limits of his or her actual authority.

Requiring the financial institution to pay on demand

[12.9] Section 14(1) provides that an order to pay is an order to pay on demand if either the order is expressed to require payment on demand, at sight or on presentation or if the instrument specifies no time for payment. (If no time is specified, the instrument is assumed to be payable on demand, at sight or on presentation.) From this, it should follow that if an order to pay is expressed to require, or by implication requires, payment otherwise than on demand, at sight or on presentation, or if it specifically requires payment at or before a particular time or if it requires, as a condition of payment, that the instrument containing the order be presented at or before a particular time, it will not be an order to pay on demand — and that is precisely what ss 14(2) and (3) provide.

Post-dated cheques

[12.10] The requirement that cheques be payable on demand obviously creates a problem with post-dated cheques. A post-dated cheque is one which bears a date later than the date on which it was actually drawn. Cheques do not have to be dated (s 16(2)(a)), but if they are, the date that they bear is deemed to be the date on which they were drawn. For a number of reasons, it has always been held that cheques should not be paid until their apparent date has arrived: see *Brien v Dwyer* (1978) 141 CLR 378.

The more important of those reasons all derive from the fact that paying a post-dated cheque before its apparent date can be a breach of the financial institution's duty to obey its customer's directions. By post-dating a cheque the customer effectively directs the financial institution not to pay it until that later date arrives. If the financial institution pays the cheque before its due date and the customer suffers loss the financial institution can be liable in three ways:

- if the cheque is paid before its due date and the customer then cancels it (also before the due date) the financial institution will have to re-credit the customer's account;
- if the financial institution pays the cheque and then dishonours other cheques because the customer's account balance is insufficient to meet them, the financial institution can be liable for damaging the customer's financial reputation; and
- even if the financial institution discovers its error and re-credits the customer's account, holding the post-dated cheque until it falls due, the customer may become bankrupt in the intervening period and the financial institution will have to bear the resulting loss.

[12.11] The problem with post-dated cheques is that, technically, they are not orders to pay on demand. They require, at least by implication, payment otherwise than 'on demand, at sight or on presentation'. Consequently, they seem to fall squarely within s 14(2). However, s 14(2) is specifically made subject to s 16(3) which provides that, 'for the purpose of determining whether a post-dated instrument is a cheque, the fact that the instrument is post-dated shall be disregarded'. That provision is reinforced by both s 16(2)(b) and s 16(4) which provide that cheques are neither invalid nor incomplete nor irregular by reason only that they are post-dated. Therefore, post-dated cheques are valid even though, technically, they are not orders to pay 'on demand'.

The validity of post-dated cheques is further reinforced by s 61(2) which provides that a demand for payment of a cheque before its date arrives does not constitute 'due presentment'. Because a cheque must be duly presented for payment before the drawer or any subsequent indorser becomes liable on it (s 58) no one need pay a post-dated cheque before its apparent date.

A sum certain in money

[12.12]   What constitutes a sum certain in money is dealt with in s 15. It provides that an order 'is not an order to pay a sum certain unless the sum ordered to be paid is specified with reasonable certainty in the instrument.' The 'reasonable certainty' requirement will be met even if the order requires a sum to be paid according to a rate of exchange specified in, or ascertained as directed by, the instrument: s 15(3).

Where there is an element of ambiguity because more than one sum appears to be payable (because, for instance, there is a discrepancy between the amount written in words and the amount written in figures), the lesser or least of those sums is the sum that is to be paid: s 15(2). Similarly, under s 15(4) if an instrument contains an order to pay a specified sum and an order to pay not more than a specified sum (as is often found on cheques which bear notations such as 'not exceeding $1000'), the instrument is presumed to require payment of the lesser of the sums specified.

Types of cheques

[12.13]   All cheques are payable either to 'order' or to 'bearer': s 20.

Order cheques

[12.14]   Order cheques are defined in s 21. It provides that cheques will be payable to order if they are 'expressed, whether originally or by indorsement, to require the drawee financial institution to pay the sum ordered to be paid by the cheque to or to the order of [those who are specified as payees or indorsees]'. (A 'payee' is the person that the customer, the 'drawer', names in the cheque as the person to whom the 'drawee institution' should pay it. The 'payee' can sign the cheque over to someone else and, if he or she does, that other person is called the 'indorsee'.)

Section 3(1A) lists examples of what the words *'to or to the order of'* mean and provides that a cheque will be 'payable to or to the order of a person or persons if:

 (a) it is expressed to be payable:
   (i) to the person or persons; or
   (ii) to the order of the person or persons (or words to that effect); or
   (iii)to the person or persons or to the order of the person or persons (or words to that effect); *and*
 (b) it is *not also expressed* to be payable to bearer' (emphasis added).

Therefore, directions such as, for example, 'Pay A Abel or order' or simply 'Pay A Abel' with the standard 'or bearer' notation that appears on most pre-printed cheque forms struck out, would make the cheque an order cheque.

To be a payee or indorsee the person must be named or otherwise indicated with reasonable certainty in the cheque and must not be a fictitious or non-existing person: s 19(1). If a cheque is payable to a fictitious person it is, in law, a bearer cheque. Where an office-holder, instead of a specific person, is named as the cheque's payee or indorsee (for example, 'pay the Deputy Commissioner of Taxation or order'), the natural person who holds that office for the time being is deemed to be the person named as the payee or indorsee as the case may be: s 19(2).

```
┌─────────────────────────────────────────────────────────────────┐
│                                                                   │
│              COMMERCIAL TRADING BANK                              │
│                  OF AUSTRALIA                                     │
│                                                                   │
│                                        21ˢᵗ MARCH   1977          │
│                                                   or Order        │
│   Pay    B. CARTER                                 orBearer       │
│                                                                   │
│      FIFTY DOLLARS ONLY                      $ 50—                │
│      Amount in Words                                              │
│                                                                   │
│                                                                   │
│                                                 A. Smith          │
│         000001                                                    │
│                                                                   │
└─────────────────────────────────────────────────────────────────┘
```

Figure 12.1: An open order cheque

Significance of an order cheque

[12.15]   If a cheque is an order cheque it is only payable to or to the order of a nominated payee. Should the payee wish to negotiate the cheque he or she must physically indorse it to make it payable to some other party. Payees may indorse their cheques to specific indorsees (as in 'Pay B Bell' accompanied by the payee's signature), or may simply indorse their cheques 'in blank'. That is, the payee simply signs his or her name usually on the back of the cheque. When an order cheque is 'indorsed in blank' it becomes a bearer cheque payable to whomever has it in his or her possession.

Bearer cheques

[12.16]   Cheques that are not payable to order are automatically payable to bearer and the financial institution is required to pay the sum specified 'to bearer': s 22. The term 'bearer' is defined in s 3(1). It means 'the person in possession of a cheque payable to bearer'. Most pre-printed cheque forms have the words 'or bearer' already printed on them so cheques drawn on those forms will automatically be bearer cheques unless a specific person is named as payee or indorsee and the words 'or bearer' have been struck out. Cheques noted 'Pay A Abel or bearer' or 'Pay Cash or bearer' are bearer cheques.

A cheque payable to bearer cannot normally be converted into a cheque payable to order. The sole exception is where an order cheque has been converted to a bearer cheque (which happens if the last indorsement requires the drawee institution to pay it to bearer). In that case the 'holder' may reconvert it into an order cheque by adding to or altering the indorsement so that the drawee institution is required to pay the cheque to or to the order of a nominated indorsee or indorsees instead: s 23(2). Indorsement and its legal consequences are dealt with in **[12.18]**.

```
┌─────────────────────────────────────────────────────────────┐
│        COMMERCIAL TRADING BANK                                │
│             OF AUSTRALIA                                      │
│                                                               │
│                                    22ⁿᵈ March 1999            │
│                                                               │
│  Pay   Cash _____  or Bearer        │
│                                                               │
│  One Hundred Dollars Only _____   $ 100─           │
│  Amount in Words                                              │
│                                                               │
│                                       A. Smith                │
│        000002                                                 │
└─────────────────────────────────────────────────────────────┘
```

Figure 12.2: An open bearer cheque payable to 'Cash'

Negotiability of cheques

Transferability

[12.17]   Section 39(1) makes it clear that 'every cheque may be transferred by negotiation until it is discharged'. Transfer by negotiation is defined in s 40(1) as 'the transfer of the cheque from the holder to another person in such manner as to constitute the other person the holder'. The term 'holder' is defined in s 3(1) as:

(a) in relation to a cheque payable to order — the payee or an indorsee who is in possession of the cheque as payee or indorsee, as the case may be; and

(b) in relation to a cheque payable to bearer — the bearer.

In essence this means that cheques, just like all other negotiable instruments, can be freely transferred from person to person by simple delivery, *free of all prior defects in title and of all personal equities* which could otherwise affect the payment rights that the cheque represents. It also means that simple ownership of the cheque gives its 'holder' the right to be paid the cheque's face value — a right which the holder may enforce in his or her own name and for his or her own benefit: s 49.

Negotiation of order cheques

[12.18]   Order cheques are negotiated by indorsement and delivery: s 40(2). An indorsement can be either a full direction from the indorser, ordering the financial institution to pay some other named person — 'Pay B Bell or order, A Abel' (in which case the cheque will still be payable to order), or it can be just a simple signature. In that case the cheque will be payable to bearer because the financial institution has not been specifically directed who to pay.

'Delivery' is simply 'the transfer of possession of the cheque from one person to another': s 3(1). Physically handing the cheque over, therefore, constitutes delivery.

Consequently, signing and handing over a cheque payable to order is all that is required to transfer it by negotiation. However, the indorsement must be an indorsement of the entire cheque. The indorser must intend to transfer his or her full entitlement to the face value of the cheque and any attempt to transfer only a part of it does not operate as a transfer by negotiation: ss 41(1)(b) and 41(4).

Where a cheque payable to order is payable to two or more persons jointly (either as payees or as indorsees), they must all indorse the cheque in order to transfer it by negotiation *unless* they are partners (in which case any one of them can indorse it on behalf of them all) or unless those who do indorse the cheque have authority to indorse it on behalf of those who do not: s 43.

If a payee or indorsee of an order cheque is wrongly designated on the cheque or has his or her name misspelt that person may indorse the cheque by using the designation or spelling that appears on the cheque's face and he or she *may* also add his or her own 'proper signature'. Adding that 'proper signature' is not, however, necessary and the indorsement will be effective without it: s 44.

An indorsement that purports to be conditional will be good even if the condition is not fulfilled and the financial institution paying the cheque may disregard the condition entirely: s 45. That is, indorsers cannot, by imposing a condition on payment, convert the cheque (an 'unconditional order') into a conditional order. The condition is disregarded and the instrument retains its status as a cheque under s 10(1).

Order cheques transferred without indorsement

[12.19] For order cheques to be negotiated (rather than simply transferred), delivery and indorsement are *both* required. If the holder of an order cheque simply delivers it, for value, to some other person intending to transfer it by negotiation, the transferee, by virtue of the delivery, receives the same title to the cheque that the transferor had and *also* acquires a right to have the transferor indorse it: s 42. If the transferee enforces this right and requires the transferor to indorse the cheque the transfer will be converted into a *transfer by negotiation* and the transferee will get all the rights of a transferee by negotiation, as they are set out in s 49.

Negotiation of bearer cheques

[12.20] Bearer cheques do not have to have a specific payee (they are, in fact, often simply made payable to 'Cash') and they may be paid to whomever has possession of them when payment is demanded. Consequently, negotiation of a bearer cheque simply requires it to be delivered. Indorsement is not required though the transferor can indorse the cheque if he or she so wishes: s 40(3).

Negotiation and crossed cheques

[12.21] Cheques may be either crossed or uncrossed. If they are uncrossed they are referred to as 'open cheques'. Cheques are crossed by simply placing two parallel transverse lines, with or without the words 'not negotiable' between or substantially between them, on the cheque. Nothing else constitutes a recognised crossing under the Cheques Act. Even placing the words 'not negotiable' — by themselves — across the front of the cheque is not a recognised crossing: s 53.

The effect of crossing

[12.22]   Crossing a cheque operates 'as a direction from the drawer to the drawee institution not to pay the cheque otherwise than to a financial institution': s 54. What this means is that the payee or indorsee cannot cash the cheque but must pay it into his or her own account with a financial institution. That institution (the 'collecting institution') must then collect it from the drawee institution. This gives the drawer some additional protection because, if the drawee institution disobeys the direction and pays the cheque over the counter it can be liable (as might be the case, for example, if the cheque had been stolen and was paid to the wrong payee). In such cases the customer's account will have to be re-credited with the amount paid out.

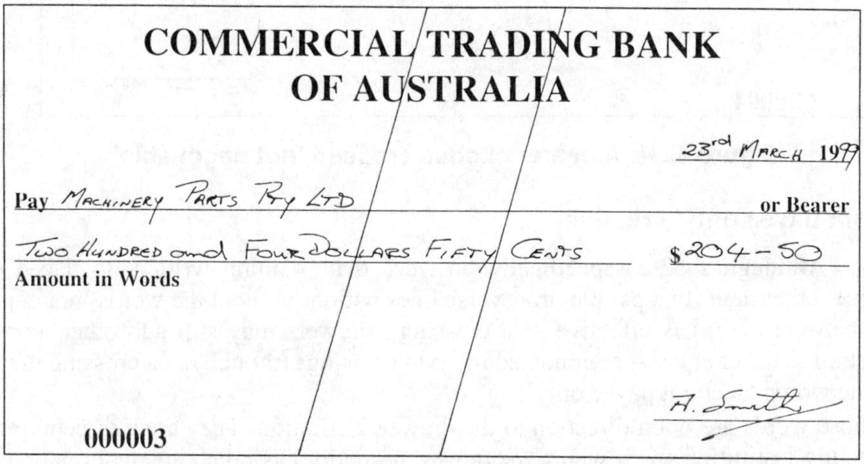

Figure 12.3: A bearer cheque crossed generally

The effect of 'not negotiable' crossings

[12.23]   Where a cheque bears not only two parallel transverse lines but also the words 'not negotiable' between them the cheque can still be transferred but it cannot be 'negotiated'. The transferee does not receive and is not capable of giving a better title to the cheque than the transferor had: s 55. The effect of crossing a cheque 'not negotiable' is to warn the transferee that his or her title is *subject to all prior defects in title and to any personal equities* that may have existed between the drawer, the payee and any prior indorsers. Consequently, if there is some defect, the transferee cannot recover against the drawer or any prior indorsers. He or she can only recover against the person who transferred the cheque to him or her.

```
┌─────────────────────────────────────────────────────────────┐
│          COMMERCIAL TRADING BANK                              │
│              OF AUSTRALIA                                     │
│                                                               │
│                                        24ᵀᴸ MARCH 1979        │
│                                                               │
│   Pay  DEPUTY COMMISSIONER OF TAXATION           or Bearer    │
│                                                               │
│   ONE HUNDRED and FORTY DOLLARS SIXTY CENTS   $140-60         │
│   Amount in Words                                             │
│                                                               │
│              NOT NEGOTIABLE                                   │
│                                                               │
│                                            H. Smith           │
│       000004                                                  │
└─────────────────────────────────────────────────────────────┘
```

Figure 12.4: A bearer cheque crossed 'not negotiable'

'Account payee only' crossings

[12.24]   Although s 53(2) specifically provides that 'nothing written or placed on a cheque, other than [two parallel transverse lines with or without the words 'not negotiable' between them] is effective as a crossing', drawers may still add other words of direction to the cheque. A common addition to crossings (though not a crossing in itself) are the words 'account payee only'.

Those words are not a direction to the drawee institution. They are a direction to the collecting institution (with whom the drawer normally has no contractual relationship) that the cheque is only to be paid into the designated payee's account. In so far as this is an attempt to stop the cheque being transferred (either by negotiation or at all), it fails entirely. Section 39(2) specifically says that cheques may be transferred by negotiation until they are discharged 'notwithstanding anything written or placed on the cheque'.

Therefore, the only real effect of adding the words 'account payee only' is to put the collecting institution on notice that it should make inquiries if it has to collect the cheque for someone other than the named payee. If it collects a cheque for someone other than the named payee without making due inquiry about his or her entitlement to it the collecting institution can be liable if that person did not, in fact, have good title. In such cases its failure to make due inquiry is conclusive evidence of negligence and it loses the statutory protection that it would normally have under s 95: see **[12.66]**.

Who can cross cheques?

[12.25]   A drawer can cross his or her own cheques because crossings are just directions from a customer to his or her financial institution requiring it to pay the cheque in a specified way (that is, to another financial institution). However, under s 56 *any person in possession* of a cheque may add crossings to it — and that applies even if the cheque was already crossed when it came into that person's possession: s 57. In such cases another general crossing can be added to it or the words 'not negotiable' can be added to any pre-existing crossing. This may seem to be inconsistent with the general provision that crossings operate as a direction from the drawer to his or her financial institution but the Act specifically authorises it.

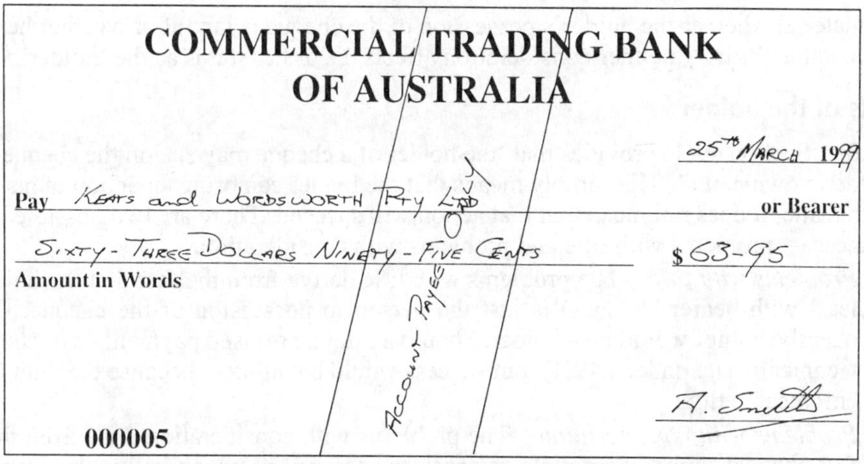

Figure 12.5: An 'account payee only' crossing

Rights of 'holders'

Enforceability of cheques

[12.26] Cheques are independently enforceable. If they are dishonoured when they are presented for payment the drawer and all prior indorsers (all 'prior parties') can be sued for their face value plus interest from the date of dishonour: s 76. It does not matter that there is some dispute over the underlying transaction that gave rise to the cheque — if the cheque is valid it can be enforced.

Therefore, a seller of goods who is paid by cheque can sue the buyer either on the underlying contract of sale or on the cheque if the cheque is dishonoured. Normally, he or she will prefer to sue on the cheque because any defences based on the underlying contract (such as that the goods were unmerchantable or unfit for their specified purpose — see Chapter 6) cannot be pleaded in an action on the cheque. All that the seller has to prove is that the cheque itself is valid and, in the normal course of events, that only requires that the cheque be signed (s 31), that the person signing it have been legally capable (s 30), and that the cheque was delivered: s 25. If all three prerequisites are satisfied the contract arising out of the cheque is complete and the cheque can be enforced.

However, the rights that any specific holder has to sue on and to enforce cheques depend upon whether he or she is a simple holder, a holder for value, a holder in due course or a holder deriving title through a holder in due course.

Holders

[12.27] 'Holders' are defined in s 3(1). With order cheques the holder is a payee or an indorsee who is in possession of the cheque as payee or indorsee. With bearer cheques the holder is simply the bearer. In other words, the holder is always the person who, on the face of the cheque, appears to be entitled to payment (the 'bearer' in the case of bearer cheques and the 'payee' or 'indorsee' in the case of order cheques). It is completely immaterial whether the holder's possession of the cheque is lawful or whether he or she gave value for it — neither consideration affects his or her status as the 'holder'.

Rights of the holder

[12.28] Section 49(1) provides that 'the holder of a cheque may sue on the cheque in the holder's own name'. This simply means that the holder can bring an action in his or her own name; it does not mean that that action will succeed. There are two possible bars to success — problems with title and problems with consideration.

- *Problems with title* The problems with title derive from the fact that the holder (at least with bearer cheques) is just the person in possession of the cheque. Consequently, a thief would be a holder. Should a thief be refused payment he or she could technically sue under s 49(1), but success would be unlikely because the thief has no enforceable title.

- *Problems with consideration* The problems with consideration arise from the fact that cheques embody a simple contract, the essence of which is that the drawer (or some subsequent transferor) will pay money to the payee (or some subsequent transferee). Contractual promises must be supported by consideration. Consequently, the drawer's or the transferor's promise must be supported by consideration and, if there is no consideration, the cheque cannot be enforced, at least as between the two parties affected by the lack of consideration.

  Therefore, someone who receives a cheque as a present or someone who finds a bearer cheque (both of whom would be 'holders' in terms of the Act) could not enforce payment of the cheque because they had not provided consideration for it. A holder who provides consideration (or 'value') for the cheque does not have this problem and 'holders for value' can both sue on and enforce unpaid cheques.

  This does not mean that mere 'holders' have no rights. They can present the cheque for payment and, if it is paid, they can give the drawee institution a good discharge for it. They can also transfer the cheque by negotiation in the manner provided for by s 40 and can defend their title to it against anyone other than the true owner (if they are not, themselves, the true owner — as would be the case with finders).

Holders for value

[12.29] A 'holder for value' is simply a holder who has provided value (or consideration) for the cheque or who is presumed, under s 37, to have taken the cheque for value.

'Value' is defined in s 3(1) as 'valuable consideration as defined by s 35'. Section 35 defines valuable consideration as either 'any consideration sufficient to support a simple contract' or 'an antecedent debt or liability'. Therefore, consideration for the purposes of the Cheques Act is the same as consideration generally — except that antecedent debts and liabilities, which would normally be regarded as past consideration and, therefore, invalid, also qualify. Consequently, debts owed for goods already supplied or for services already rendered can be good consideration even though payment by cheque was not part of the original contractual obligation.

Presumption of consideration

[12.30] There are two other aspects of consideration which differ from the normal contractual treatment. First, s 36 *presumes* drawers and indorsers to have received value for their cheques unless the contrary is proved. This effectively reverses the normal contractual onus of proof under which the promisee must prove that he or she provided consideration for the promisor's promise. In other words, the holder does not have to prove that value was given — the drawer or indorser must prove that consideration was not given in order to prove that the 'holder' was not a 'holder for value'.

Second, under s 37 the holder need not have given value personally in order to be a holder for value. Provided value has *at any time* been given for the cheque the holder is conclusively presumed, at least against the drawer and any indorsers who indorsed the cheque before the value was given, to have taken the cheque for value.

So, therefore, if A draws a cheque in favour of B in payment of a debt, if B then transfers it by negotiation to C (also for value) and if C then gives it to D as a gift (so that D does not actually provide consideration), D will still be a holder for value — at least as against A and B. They are, respectively, the drawer and an indorser who became an indorser before the final transfer for value. Therefore, D could sue A and B if the cheque was not paid when he presented it. However, he could not sue C because, as against C, D is not a holder for value. He did not provide consideration nor is he conclusively presumed, under s 37, to have taken the cheque for value from C.

Rights of a holder for value

[12.31]   A holder for value differs from a mere holder in that the holder for value can both sue on *and enforce* the cheque in the holder's own name. However, the holder for value does not obtain all of the benefits that flow from negotiability and, in particular, he or she takes the cheque *subject to all defects in title and all personal equities* which could permit the drawer or any indorser to avoid liability to pay it. The full benefits of negotiability are reserved for 'holders in due course'.

Holders in due course

[12.32]   A 'holder in due course' is defined in s 50. To be a holder in due course the holder must have had the cheque transferred to him or her by negotiation and, at the time of taking the cheque, it must have been complete and regular on its face, must not have been stale and must not have borne a 'not negotiable' crossing. The holder must also have taken the cheque in good faith, for value and without notice of either any dishonour or any defect in or lack of title. A holder in due course is, therefore, a holder for value with a number of other attributes. Specifically:

1. *He or she must have received the cheque by negotiation*   In other words, the cheque must have been transferred in the manner specified in s 40. This, of course, prevents the original payee from being a holder in due course because he or she receives the cheque from the 'drawer' and not from a 'holder' as that term is defined in s 3(1).

2. *The cheque must have been complete and regular on its face*   'Complete' simply means that the cheque contains all material particulars. If the cheque is an inchoate instrument (one which is signed but which is otherwise wanting in a material particular so that, on its face, it is not complete) the person to whom it is negotiated cannot be a holder in due course because (even though he or she can fill in any blanks to make it a complete instrument — s 18) the cheque was not complete when he or she took it. Material parts of the cheque include the payee (even if the payee is simply 'cash'), the identity of the drawee institution, the sum payable and the drawer's signature. It is arguable that the date is not a material part of the cheque especially as s 16(2)(a) specifically provides that cheques are not invalid by reason only that they are not dated.

'Regular on its face' simply means that the cheque must appear to be in good order and there must be nothing which would 'reasonably give rise to a doubt' about its validity: see Yeldham J in *Heller Factors Pty Ltd v Toy Corp Pty Ltd* [1984] 1 NSWLR 121 at 141. What would give rise to a reasonable doubt is 'a practical question' which must be determined on the facts of each case: see Denning LJ in *Arab Bank Ltd v Ross* [1952] 2 QB 216 at 227 where two promissory notes in the name of 'Fathi and Faysal Nabulsy Co' were indorsed simply, 'Fathi and Faysal Nabulsy'. It was held that, even though the indorsement was valid, the omission of the word 'Co' gave rise to a reasonable doubt about whether the payees and the indorsers were necessarily the same. As a result, the notes were not complete and regular on their face and the bank was, not a 'holder in due course'.

3. *The cheque must not have been a stale cheque*   A 'stale cheque' as defined in s 3(5) is one which appears on its face to have been drawn more than 15 months previously. If a cheque is stale, the drawee institution may refuse to pay it: s 89. Section 46(1) provides that those who accept stale cheques take them *subject to any defect in title* that affected the cheque when it became stale and that they do not receive and *are not capable of giving a better title* to it than the transferor had. Therefore, someone who accepts a stale cheque cannot be a holder in due course because he or she does not acquire the cheque *free from any defect in the title of prior parties [and] from mere personal defences available to prior parties against one another*: s 49(2)(a).

4. *The cheque must not have been crossed 'not negotiable'*   Where a cheque crossed 'not negotiable' is transferred by negotiation the transferee does not receive and is not capable of giving a better title than the title the transferor had: s 55. Consequently, a transferee of a 'not negotiable' cheque cannot be a holder in due course because he or she does not receive the cheque *free from defects in title or personal equities*.

5. *The holder must have taken the cheque in good faith*   Under s 3(2) something is done in good faith if it is done honestly, whether or not it is done negligently. Therefore, if a holder takes a cheque honestly he or she can be a holder in due course. The mere fact that a defect in the transferor's title (or some other problem with the cheque) *could* have been discovered if the holder had exercised more care or pursued more diligent inquiries is irrelevant.

6. *The holder must have taken the cheque for value*   This simply means that the holder must have provided consideration for the cheque (or must be presumed to have provided consideration for it under s 37). That is what gives him or her the right to enforce the cheque in the first place.

7. *The holder must have taken the cheque without notice of any dishonour*   'Dishonour' means that the cheque has been presented for payment and that the drawee institution has refused to pay it. It does not mean that the cheque is worthless and, in fact, both the drawer and subsequent indorsers may be liable to pay its face value: s 76. Cheques that have been dishonoured can be transferred by negotiation but, under s 46(2), anyone who takes them with notice of the dishonour takes them subject to any defect in title that affected them at the time of dishonour. Consequently, a holder who takes a dishonoured cheque does not take it free of defects in title and, therefore, cannot be a holder in due course.

8. *The holder must have taken the cheque without notice of any defect in or lack of title by the transferor*   Those who take cheques knowing that there is something wrong with the transferor's title should not be able, thereafter, to assert that their title is not affected by that defect. Therefore, any transferee who is aware of a defect in the transferor's title cannot be a holder in due course. What constitutes notice of a defect in

title is dealt with (but not exhaustively) in s 50(2). It provides that a holder shall be deemed to have taken the cheque with notice of a defect in title if the holder took the cheque with notice that the person transferred it either in breach of faith or under circumstances amounting to a fraud. Other defects not dealt with in s 50(2) will also fall within the general ambit of s 50(1)(b)(iii)(B).

Presumption that a holder is a holder in due course

[12.33]   Unless the contrary is proved, a holder is normally presumed to be a holder in due course (s 51(1)), and any person who asserts otherwise — usually the drawer or an indorser who is called upon to pay the cheque — must prove that the 'holder' is not a 'holder in due course'. This effectively means that the drawer (or the indorser) must show that one of the s 50(1) elements is absent.

Benefits of being a holder in due course

[12.34]   The benefits of being a holder in due course are set out in ss 49(2) and 49(3). They provide that, in addition to the general right to sue on the cheque conferred by s 49(1), a holder in due course 'holds the cheque free from any defect in the title of prior parties as well as from mere personal defences available to prior parties against one another' and that they 'may enforce payment of the cheque against any person liable on [it]'. In addition, so long as the transfer to a holder in due course was effected *by negotiation*, he or she receives a good and complete title to the cheque, even if the transferor's title was defective.

The drawer of a cheque is also conclusively presumed (at least as regards a holder in due course) to have made an effective delivery of it to complete the contract (s 28(1)), and he or she is estopped from denying to the holder in due course that the cheque was valid when it was issued: s 72. Indorsers are likewise estopped from denying the genuineness and regularity of the signatures and indorsements on the cheque as well as the validity of, and their title to, it at the time it was indorsed: s 74. Strangers to the cheque (dealt with in **[12.40]**) are conclusively presumed to have signed the cheque intending to become liable on it and are, therefore, liable on it as if they had indorsed it: s 75.

Holders deriving title through a holder in due course

[12.35]   Under s 52 a holder who derives title to a cheque through a holder in due course and who is not a party to any fraud, duress or illegality affecting it 'has, as regards the drawer and the indorsers *prior* to the holder in due course, all the rights of the holder in due course'. This means that *if* the transferee is not a holder in due course (as, for example, where the cheque was received with knowledge of some defect in its chain of title), he or she will still get all the rights of a holder in due course.

This protects a holder in due course by letting him or her transfer his or her privileged status and the rights that it confers. Therefore, for example, if a holder in due course becomes aware of a defect in some previous transferor's title, he or she can still negotiate the cheque and the transferee will not be adversely affected by the knowledge of that defect. The transferee should, therefore, be more willing to accept the cheque and the holder in due course will not be disadvantaged by his or her after-acquired knowledge.

Liability on cheques

Who can be liable?

[12.36] Under s 30(1) anyone who has the legal capacity to contract can incur liability on a cheque. Consequently, if they are of full legal capacity, drawers, indorsers and certain 'strangers' can all be liable if a cheque is not honoured when it is presented for payment.

The drawer

[12.37] The drawer is the person who is primarily liable on a cheque. By drawing the cheque, he or she undertakes that, when it is duly presented for payment, it 'will be paid according to its tenor as drawn' and that, if it is dishonoured (or if presentment is dispensed with and the cheque is not paid when it falls due) he or she will compensate either the holder or any indorser who is called upon to pay it: s 71.

In addition, under s 72 'the drawer of the cheque, by issuing the cheque, is estopped from denying to a holder in due course that the cheque was, at the time when it was issued, a valid cheque'. The term 'issue' is defined in s 3(1) to mean 'the first delivery of the cheque to a person who takes the cheque as holder'. Consequently, at least as against a holder in due course, the drawer cannot argue that the cheque should not have been issued in the first place (because, for example, the payee did not deliver the goods or perform the services for which the cheque was given in payment).

When a drawer is liable, the holder may recover damages equal to the cheque's face value, with or without interest: s 76.

The indorser

[12.38] The indorser's liability is similar to the drawer's except that it is secondary in nature and, if an indorser does become liable, he or she can recover from either the drawer or a prior indorser: ss 71(b) and 76(1).

By indorsing a cheque, an indorser undertakes that, when it is duly presented for payment, it will be paid according to its tenor as indorsed and that, if it is dishonoured (or, if presentment is dispensed with and it remains unpaid after its due date has arrived) the indorser will compensate the holder or any subsequent indorser who has to pay it: s 73. As with drawers, indorsers are also subject to a number of estoppels. Specifically, under s 74(1), an indorser is estopped 'from denying to a holder in due course the genuineness and regularity, in all respects, of the drawer's signature and all previous indorsements' and 'from denying to the indorsee ... a subsequent indorsee or to a holder who is not an indorsee ... that the cheque was, at the time when the indorser indorsed it, a valid and undischarged cheque; and ... that the indorser had, at that time, a good title to the cheque'.

[12.39] However, indorsers are subject to two protections which are not available to drawers. First, under s 17(2)(a) the indorser 'may, by an express stipulation written on the cheque, negative or limit his or her liability'. The indorser does this by writing words such as 'without recourse' or 'sans recours' (both of which mean that the indorser accepts no personal liability at all), or some express limitation such as 'only liable up to $100' in which case the limit of the indorser's liability will be the $100 stipulated regardless of the cheque's actual face value. Section 17 allows these limitations as recognition that the liability of indorsers is only secondary.

Second, under s 60(2) an indorser is not liable on a cheque unless it is presented for payment within a reasonable time after indorsement. A similar protection does not apply to drawers who remain liable on the cheque until it is discharged.

'Strangers'

[12.40]   Under s 75, a 'stranger' who signs a cheque is liable as if he or she were an indorser, *if* he or she signed the cheque *intending to become liable on it*. Section 75(2) provides that someone who signs a cheque shall 'as regards a holder in due course — be conclusively presumed to have signed the cheque intending to become liable on [it]' and, 'as regards a holder who is not a holder in due course — be presumed, unless the contrary is proved, to have signed the cheque intending to become liable on [it]' unless it is apparent, on the cheque's face, that there was no such intention.

When someone other than a drawer or indorser signs a cheque intending to become liable on it that person is said to 'back' the cheque. People 'back' cheques to increase their value and acceptability, especially where the drawer's creditworthiness is in some doubt. For example, a payee may be reluctant to take a cheque drawn by a company unless he or she gets an additional guarantee of payment. Accordingly, a director may 'back' the cheque so that, if it is dishonoured, he or she will be liable to pay it in the same way that an indorser would be.

Prerequisites to liability

[12.41]   Even though drawers, indorsers and strangers can all be liable on cheques there are still two prerequisites to liability. First, the cheque must be valid and enforceable in its own right. This basically means that the cheque must have been signed and delivered and that consideration must have been paid for it. Second, before the drawer, indorser or a stranger becomes personally liable, the cheque must have been presented and dishonoured (or presentment must have been dispensed with and the cheque must have remained unpaid after its due date had arrived: ss 71(b)(ii) and 73(b)(ii)).

The requirement for presentment and dishonour comes from ss 58 and 70. Section 58 provides that a 'drawer or an indorser … is not liable on the cheque unless the cheque is duly presented for payment'. Section 70 then provides that a drawer or indorser of a dishonoured cheque is liable whether or not he or she has notice of the dishonour. This leads us to a consideration of what constitutes presentment and dishonour.

Presentment and dishonour

Dishonour

[12.42]   Under s 69 a cheque is dishonoured if three requirements are met:
* the cheque is duly presented for payment;
* the drawee institution refuses to pay it; and
* the drawee institution communicates that refusal to the holder or to the person who presented the cheque on the holder's behalf.

Accordingly, dishonour means any refusal by the drawee institution to pay the cheque according to its tenor after it has been duly presented for payment.

Presentment for payment

[12.43]   Due presentment is defined in s 61. A cheque is duly presented for payment if a demand for payment is made on the drawee institution (on or after the cheque's due date) by or on behalf of the cheque's holder. Cheques may be presented by either the holder personally or by a financial institution (known as the 'collecting institution') acting on the holder's behalf.

Where the holder presents the cheque personally he or she does so by 'exhibiting [it], in person, to the drawee institution at the *proper place in relation to the cheque* at a reasonable hour on a day on which the drawee institution is open for business at the place at which the cheque is exhibited': s 63.

'Exhibiting' a cheque means physically taking it to the financial institution on which it is drawn. (The term is somewhat unhelpfully defined in s 3(7) as *including* the cheque being delivered to the drawee institution.) The requirement that the holder exhibit the cheque to the drawee institution is reinforced by s 68(1) which provides that, once a cheque has been duly presented for payment and paid, the drawee institution has a right to possession of it.

The reference in s 63 to 'the proper place in relation to the cheque' refers to the branch of the drawee institution at which the cheque is payable. This can be either a branch specified in the cheque or, in the absence of any such specification, the branch where the account on which the cheque is drawn is maintained: s 64. The requirement that the cheque be exhibited at a reasonable hour on a day on which the drawee institution is open for business at the place at which the cheque is exhibited is self-explanatory.

Presentment by a collecting institution

[12.44]   Holders do not have to present cheques personally. They can deposit them with their own financial institutions which then collect them and credit the customer's account with the proceeds. In fact, as was noted earlier, if cheques are crossed, the drawee institution should not pay them to anyone other than another financial institution: s 54.

[12.45]   Section 61A provides that financial institutions can present cheques in either of two ways:

- by making an 'external presentment' of the cheque; or
- by making an 'internal presentment' of it.

'External presentments' occur when a financial institution (the 'collecting institution') presents the cheque to *another* financial institution (the 'drawee institution') for payment; 'internal presentments' occur when the 'collecting institution' and the 'drawee institution' are the *same* — so that, when the 'collecting institution' collects the cheque, it makes a demand for payment on itself. That occurs, for example, when one customer deposits a cheque from another customer of the same institution. The deposit institution then has to collect the proceeds of the cheque from itself and both debit the drawer's account and credit the payee's account. It also occurs when the collecting institution acts as a 'collecting agent' for another institution and, on its behalf, collects cheques drawn by its own customers.

In either case the 'collecting institution' is permitted to present (make demand for payment of) the cheque either:

- 'by exhibition'; or
- 'by particulars'.

[12.46] If the 'collecting institution' presents a cheque 'by exhibition', it presents it in essentially the same way that the holder would have presented it (that is, by physically delivering it to the 'drawee institution').

The major difference is that, whereas a holder has to exhibit the cheque at the 'proper place in relation to [it]', the 'collecting institution' has a choice. It can present the cheque by exhibiting it either at the 'proper place in relation to the cheque' or (in the case of external presentments) at a 'designated exhibition place' in relation to it or (in the case of internal presentments) at a 'notified place' in relation to it. Section 65 defines 'designated place' as a place which the financial institution specifies by notice in the *Gazette*, 'as a designated place in relation to cheques for the purposes of this Act'. A 'designated exhibition place' is a designated place which the 'drawee institution' specifies as a place at which its cheques may be presented by exhibition: s 65(2A). 'Notified places' are similarly defined in s 65A. The 'designated place' and 'notified place' provisions are intended to let financial institutions nominate their data processing centres as 'designated places' and/or 'notified places' so they can clear their cheques centrally.

[12.47] With the greater use of electronic processes for handling cheques (both by and between financial institutions), presentment by exhibition (by other than individual holders) has become rare. Most cheques are now presented 'by particulars' as is allowed under ss 62(1)(c) (for external presentments) and s 62A(1)(b)(ii) (for internal presentments). That is, most cheques are now presented by electronic 'truncation' — the communication of the cheques' particulars (or details) from the collecting institution to the drawee institution instead of the collecting institution physically producing (or 'exhibiting') the cheques. The particulars must identify the cheque with reasonable certainty, they must also be communicated to the drawee institution in an intelligible or readily decipherable form and they must be forwarded to either a 'designated place' in relation to the cheque (in the case of external presentments) or to the 'proper place in relation to the cheque' or to a 'notified place' in relation to it (in the case of internal presentments).

If a cheque is presented by particulars the drawee institution may still want to sight it (or a copy of it) to ensure that it is a proper direction from its customer. Alternatively, it may simply need further particulars before it finally decides to pay it. In either case it can request the 'collecting institution' either to exhibit the cheque (or a copy) to it or to provide it with specified further particulars: ss 62(5) and 62A(2). If it does the 'collecting institution' must either exhibit the cheque (or a copy of it) or provide the 'drawee institution' with the further particulars: ss 62(9) and 62A(7).

Statutory duties and liabilities of financial institutions

[12.48] In addition to their contractual duties and liabilities (discussed in Chapter 11) financial institutions have a number of statutory duties and liabilities. They also have a number of statutory protections. The main statutory duties and liabilities are as follows.

The drawee (paying) financial institution

[12.49] Drawee institutions have a general contractual duty to pay their customers' cheques when those cheques are presented for payment. This common law duty is augmented by a statutory duty, under s 67(1), to 'either pay or dishonour the cheque as soon as is reasonably practicable' after it has been duly presented. If the drawee institution does not do so then, unless it has become aware of a defect in the holder's title or that the holder has no title at all, it 'may not dishonour the cheque' and it 'is liable to pay [it] to the holder', though this 'does not prejudice any rights that the drawee institution may have to debit the drawer's account with the amount of the cheque': s 67(3).

Section 67(2) lists a number of considerations which are taken into account in determining whether the drawee institution has paid or dishonoured the cheque *as soon as was reasonably practicable*. Those considerations include:

*   the fact that the cheque is a cheque and that it is reasonable to expect that it will be paid or dishonoured promptly;
*   how and where the cheque was presented;
*   the means that the drawee institution had for paying or dishonouring the cheque;
*   the relative speed, reliability and cost of those means;
*   the institutions' common practice in relation to the payment and dishonour of cheques;
*   if the cheque was presented by particulars and if the drawee institution then requested either further particulars or exhibition of the cheque, that fact and any delay that resulted from the making of the request, waiting for a response or both; and
*   any other facts that may be relevant in the particular case.

The right to dishonour

[12.50]   If there are no funds in the customer's account and no overdraft arrangements in place the drawee institution can refuse to honour the customer's cheques when they are presented for payment. However, even if funds are available the drawee institution can still refuse payment in certain circumstances — because s 88 provides that 'the drawing of a cheque does not, of itself, operate as an assignment of the funds that are available, in the hands of the drawee institution, for the payment of the cheque'.

In other words, when a customer draws a cheque, the cheque operates only as an order to his or her financial institution to pay the payee (or some transferee or assignee). It does not operate as an *immediate* transfer or assignment of funds to the payee (or to the transferee or assignee). Therefore, neither the payee nor any transferee or assignee has any independent right to demand payment and the drawee institution can refuse payment secure in the knowledge that its only liability, if any, will be to its own customer. Even then, there are a number of reasons why a financial institution may be entitled (or even obliged) to dishonour a cheque that has been presented for payment. They include the following.

[12.51]   Post-dated cheques   While post-dated cheques are valid and enforceable (s 16), it is clear that the customer did not intend them to be paid (and, therefore, did not authorise the drawee institution to pay them) until on or after the cheques' apparent date. Section 61(2) reinforces this by providing that, if a demand is made for payment of a post-dated cheque before its due date, that demand shall not be regarded as due presentment. Under s 69, a cheque must have been duly presented for payment before it can be dishonoured. Consequently, the drawee institution is entitled (in fact it is obliged) to refuse to pay post-dated cheques before their apparent date — and such refusal does not constitute dishonour.

[12.52]   Stale cheques   A stale cheque is one which appears on its face to have been drawn more than 15 months previously: s 3(5). Under s 89(1) a 'drawee institution *may refuse* payment of a stale cheque' (emphasis added). However, that discretion does not apply if, under s 89(2), the drawee institution has an agreement with the drawer to pay it or if the drawer directs it to do so (in which case the cheque must be paid) or if, under s 89(3), the drawee institution has an agreement with, or has been directed by, the drawer, *not* to pay the cheque (in which case it cannot be paid).

If a drawee institution does refuse to pay a stale cheque that does not discharge the drawer's liability to pay it under s 71. That terminates only when the cheque is discharged which, in this case, will usually be when the six-year Statute of Limitations period expires.

[12.53] **Countermand of payment** Under s 90(1)(a) a drawee institution's duty and authority to pay a cheque are terminated by countermand of payment. Countermand is simply a direction from the customer ordering the drawee institution not to pay the cheque. To be effective, the countermand must be clear and unambiguous and it must be communicated to a responsible officer in the appropriate branch. If either prerequisite is not fulfilled the drawee institution may not be liable if it pays the cheque by mistake.

For a countermand to be clear and unambiguous the customer normally has to provide the drawee institution with sufficient details for the cheque to be accurately identified. Details such as the cheque's number, the branch on which it was drawn, the date on which it was drawn, the identity of the payee and the amount would all be expected. If the customer makes a mistake in describing the cheque he or she may not be able to recover if the cheque is paid despite the countermand.

Case Example

Hilton sent the Westminster Bank a telegram ordering it to stop payment of one of his cheques. By error, he gave the number of the cheque as 117283 instead of 117285. When cheque no. 117285 was presented for payment the bank paid it believing that it had been given in substitution for cheque no. 117283 which had been cancelled. Hilton sued the bank and failed. The House of Lords held that a cheque's number is the one certain way in which it can be positively identified and, since Hilton had given the bank the wrong number, the bank was not liable: *Westminster Bank v Hilton* (1926) 43 TLR 124.

[12.54] Similarly, it is not sufficient that the customer advise 'someone' in the drawee institution that the cheque should be stopped.

Case Example

Gossler, a Commonwealth Bank customer, paid a deposit on a car by cheque and then changed his mind about the purchase. His wife rang the bank and told a typist that her husband wanted the cheque held until he came in to cancel it. The typist failed to pass the message on and, when the cheque was presented, it was paid. The bank was held not liable because there had been no effective countermand. Countermand meant notifying a relevant person in the bank who could be expected to either make or supervise payment: *Commonwealth Trading Bank v Reno Auto Sales Pty Ltd* [1967] VR 790.

For the same reason, a countermand which is communicated to one branch of a financial institution is not effective, of itself, to stop payment of a cheque drawn on another branch.

Finally, financial institutions are reluctant to act on verbal notices of countermand. While it may be prudent for a customer to telephone the drawee institution immediately he or she decides to countermand payment, the institution will invariably require the customer to confirm that direction in writing. This is to protect both the drawee institution and the customer because the drawee institution cannot be certain, over the telephone, whether the person countermanding payment is in fact its customer. If the drawee institution were to accept mere verbal directions and stop payment of the cheque, it could be liable to the customer if the countermand was not authentic. Consequently, drawee institutions will not normally act only on verbal instructions. However, they do not generally pay cheques when they have received verbal countermands; instead they tend to return them noted 'payment deferred pending instructions from drawer' to indicate that the cheque has not been dishonoured, simply that they are awaiting further instructions before they decide whether to pay or dishonour it.

[12.55]   Where a drawee institution does pay a cheque despite its customer's countermand, it cannot debit the customer's account. That is because, in paying the cheque, the drawee institution disobeyed its customer's instructions and, therefore, it had no mandate to pay it. However, it can usually recover the money from the person to whom it was paid, as money paid under a mistake — at least where it can show that the payment would not have been made but for the mistake: see *Barclays Bank Ltd v WJ Simms, Sons & Cooke (Southern) Ltd* [1980] QB 677, which the High Court cited with approval in *David Securities Pty Ltd v Commonwealth Bank of Australia* (1992) 175 CLR 353. However, if the payee, in good faith, has changed his or her position — or is deemed in law to have done so — the drawee institution may be estopped from recovering.

Case Example

The Bank of New South Wales had, by mistake, paid a cheque for $1000 to Murphett, even though it had received notice of countermand. It was held that it could recover the money unless Murphett could show that he had changed his position in good faith, or was deemed in law to have done so. Murphett could not show any such change in position and, therefore, he was ordered to repay the bank: *Bank of New South Wales v Murphett* [1983] VR 489.

[12.56]   **Notice of mental incapacity**   Under s 90(1)(b) a drawee institution's duty and authority to pay a cheque are terminated by notice of the drawer's mental incapacity. Under s 30(1) capacity to incur liability on a cheque is co-extensive with capacity to contract. Therefore, drawee institutions have no duty or authority to pay cheques drawn by their insane customers, at least while they are insane, provided the institutions have proper notice of the insanity. The problem, for drawee institutions, is that the mentally incapable can have periods of lucidity. Further, mental incapacity does not necessarily mean insanity; it can be derived, at least temporarily, from things such as intoxication. The critical question for financial institutions, therefore, is not so much whether the customer was incapable but whether they had reasonable (and reliable) notice of the nature and effect of the incapacity when the cheque was drawn.

[12.57]   **Notice of the drawer's death**   Under s 90(1)(c) a drawee institution's duty and authority to pay a cheque are terminated by notice of the drawer's death. Again, the termination of authority dates from the notice rather than from the death. Even then s 90(2) allows the deceased's cheques to be paid provided they are presented not more than 10 days after the drawee institution received notice of the death and provided there has been no countermand of payment from the deceased's personal representative or from a beneficiary. This allows those who received cheques from the deceased to be paid without having to prove for payment against the estate — an often protracted and cumbersome process.

[12.58]   **Notice of bankruptcy or winding up**   While the Cheques Act does not specifically prevent drawee institutions paying cheques drawn by bankrupts or by companies being wound up, the drawee institutions' authority to pay those cheques is effectively terminated by the Bankruptcy Act 1966 (Cth) and, through it, the winding up provisions of the Corporations Law. Under the Bankruptcy Act, a bankrupt's property automatically ceases to be his or hers and vests, instead, in the trustee. Nothing in the Cheques Act, in any way, affects the application of the Bankruptcy Act to cheques: s 4(1).

[12.59]   **Notice of assignment of the customer's balance**   If a customer assigns the balance in his or her account to some third party, the third party becomes the owner of that balance and the drawee institution cannot, at least after it is has notice of the assignment, pay out any part of it without authority from the assignee.

[12.60]   **Notice of the presenter's defective title**   Under s 67(1) drawee institutions are required either to pay or to dishonour cheques as soon as is reasonably practicable *unless they have become aware of a defect in the holder's title or that the holder has no title to the cheque*. Consequently, a drawee institution need not pay or dishonour a cheque where it has notice of a defect in the presenter's title — it simply refuses to pay the cheque. This right is reinforced by s 79 which provides that a cheque is only 'paid in due course if the cheque is paid to the holder in good faith and without notice of any defect in the holder's title or that the holder had no title to the cheque'. If a drawee institution pays a cheque when it has notice of a defect in the presenter's title the cheque is not paid 'in due course' and, therefore, will not be discharged under s 78(1)(a).

[12.61]   **Drawer's signature forged**   Section 32(1) provides that signatures placed on cheques without authority are, normally, wholly inoperative (s 100A contains a similar provision for agency cheques). Consequently, drawee institutions may not pay cheques on which the drawer's signature has been forged or placed without authority. If they do, they will be liable to re-credit the customer's account with the unauthorised payment.

[12.62]   **Where the cheque has been discharged**   Where a cheque has been 'discharged' all rights on it are extinguished: s 82(1). That includes the right to present the cheque and to be paid its face value. Cheques can be discharged in a number of ways — most of which are set out in s 78.

Section 78(1)(a) provides that a cheque is discharged if it 'is paid in due course by the drawee institution'. In fact, payment is the most common means by which a cheque is discharged. However, if the cheque is paid by the drawer or an indorser instead of by the drawee institution it is not discharged: s 87. Consequently, indorsers who have had to pay the cheque under s 73 can be reimbursed by either the drawer or a prior indorser. If their payment discharged the cheque they would lose that right.

Under s 78(1)(b), if 'the holder, at any time, absolutely and unconditionally renounces [his or her] rights against the drawer or all persons liable on the cheque' the cheque is discharged. However, the discharge is only effective if the cheque is delivered to the drawer to give effect to the renunciation: s 80.

Under s 78(1)(c), if 'the holder intentionally cancels the cheque or the drawer's signature and the cancellation is apparent from the cheque', the cheque is discharged. The holder is *presumed* to have made the cancellation intentionally and not to have made it under a mistake of fact unless the contrary is proved: s 81(2). However, if the holder can prove that the cancellation was made under a mistake of fact, the cancellation does not discharge the cheque: s 81(1).

The cheque will also be discharged under s 78(2) if it has been fraudulently or materially altered by the holder. An alteration is 'material' if it changes a right, duty or liability of the drawer, an indorser or the drawee institution: s 3(8). Therefore, any alteration of the date, the payee (or any indorsee), the amount payable or the signature or description of the person who signed the cheque (or who subsequently indorsed it), would be a material alteration — because those changes all affect the legal nature of and, therefore, the legal liability of the parties to, the cheque.

The collecting (deposit) financial institution

[12.63]   Financial institutions have a duty to receive deposits and to collect the proceeds of cheques and other instruments for their customers. This duty is reinforced by s 66 which provides that 'deposit institutions' must present their customers' cheques for payment, or ensure that they are duly presented for payment, as soon as is reasonably practicable. If they do not they are liable for any resulting loss. What is 'as soon as is reasonably practicable' is dealt with in s 66(3) which, in all material respects, mirrors the provisions of s 67(2) (the subsection that defined the same words in the context of drawee institutions paying or dishonouring cheques).

Protections for financial institutions

Protections for the drawee (paying) institution

[12.64]   The drawee institution's primary duty is to pay its customers' cheques when they are duly presented for payment. However, it is often very difficult for drawee institutions to be certain that those cheques are valid, enforceable and not affected by some defect such as fraud or theft. This would not be a critical problem if the institutions could thoroughly investigate the provenance of each cheque before paying it. However, they do not have that luxury because, under s 67(1), they must pay or dishonour cheques 'as soon as is reasonably practicable'. Consequently, unless there is something about a cheque that should reasonably put them on inquiry, drawee institutions tend to pay without carrying out any real checks. If they make a mistake and pay a cheque that should not have been paid, or pay the proceeds to a person who was not entitled to them, the drawee institutions can be liable to either the customer or the cheque's true owner.

This imposes an, arguably, unfair onus on drawee institutions and, for this reason, the Act sets out a number of statutory protections in ss 91–94. Those protections *only* apply where the drawee institution pays the cheque in good faith and without negligence.

[12.65]   Therefore, under s 91, if a cheque has been fraudulently altered to increase its amount (and if that is the only material alteration that has been made fraudulently) then, provided the drawee institution pays the holder in good faith and without negligence, it can debit the drawer's account with the amount for which the cheque was *actually drawn*

— even though it exceeded its mandate by paying the full, altered, amount. It may also be able to recover the difference between the two amounts, if it can show that the over-payment was caused by the customer breaching his or her duty to take reasonable precautions to prevent forgeries and fraudulent alterations: see **[11.34]**.

Similarly, if the drawee institution pays a crossed cheque to another financial institution it is deemed to have paid the cheque in due course, provided it acted in good faith and without negligence. Conversely, if it pays a crossed cheque *otherwise* than to another financial institution (that is, if it pays it across its own counter), it will be liable to the true owner for any resulting loss: s 93(1). However, if a crossed cheque is presented for payment but does not appear on its face to be, or at any time to have been, crossed, the drawee institution will not be liable simply because it pays it. It will be deemed to have the paid the cheque in due course, provided it paid it in good faith and without negligence: s 93(2).

Finally, if a drawee institution pays a cheque which should be indorsed but which is not indorsed at all, which is irregularly indorsed or which contains a fraudulent or unauthorised indorsement, the drawee institution (which probably has no way of checking the identity or signature of the indorser anyway) may not be liable. In the case of unauthorised and false indorsements, the drawee institution will not be liable if it pays the cheque *in any way* and, with cheques that are either not indorsed at all or which are irregularly indorsed, it will not be liable if it pays them *to another financial institution*. In both cases, however, the drawee institution must also pay the cheques *in good faith and without negligence*. If it does it will be safe because it will be deemed to have paid them *in due course*: s 94.

These protections only apply to forged *indorsements*. They do not apply to forgeries of the drawer's signature. This is because ss 92–94 are all 'subject to s 32(1)' which provides that, if the drawer's signature is forged, it is wholly inoperative.

Protections for the collecting institution

[12.66]   If a financial institution collects the proceeds of cheques (either as a 'collecting institution' or as a 'collecting agent') for someone other than the true customer it is technically guilty of the tort of conversion and liable, even though it acted in good faith and without negligence and even though it had no real way to check for theft or to scrutinise indorsements for possible forgery.

Consequently, the Act provides that, if financial institutions collect the proceeds of cheques (either as 'collecting institutions' or as 'collecting agents') in good faith and without negligence, they will not be liable, by reason only that they received payment of a cheque when they should not have: s 95.

'In good faith and without negligence'

[12.67]   The statutory protections for both paying and collecting institutions depend upon them acting in good faith and without negligence. 'Good faith' is defined in s 3(2) as something 'being done honestly, whether or not [it] is done negligently'. Consequently, all that is required is that the institution pay or collect the cheques in the honest belief that it is entitled to do so. There are no reported cases where lack of good faith has resulted in financial institutions being denied the statutory protections.

[12.68]   **Without negligence**   The Act does not define negligence but there are a significant number of cases which do. Essentially, a financial institution will act negligently if

311

it pays or collects a cheque without due inquiry in circumstances where it *knows or ought to know* that something could be wrong with it.

The test was succinctly stated by the House of Lords in *The Commissioners of Taxation v E, S & A Bank Ltd* [1920] AC 683 at 688 in terms the High Court subsequently adopted in *London Bank of Australia v Kendall* (1920) 28 CLR 401 at 410. Their Lordships' view (as modified slightly by the High Court) was that 'the test of negligence is whether the transaction of paying in any given cheque, coupled with the circumstances antecedent and present, was so out of the ordinary course that it ought to have aroused doubts in the bankers' mind, and caused them to make inquiry'.

The House of Lords acknowledged that the question is necessarily a question of fact and that each case has to be determined on its own merits. Consequently, whether a financial institution has acted negligently will always depend on whether it has done what might reasonably be expected of it in the circumstances.

Financial institutions have been held negligent where they have permitted employees to pay cheques that were drawn by their employers payable to others (or drawn by others payable to their employers) into their own accounts, where directors have been allowed to pay cheques payable to their companies into their own accounts, where agents with authority to sign cheques on behalf of a principal have drawn cheques and paid them into their own accounts and where cheques clearly marked 'Account payee only' have been accepted and credited to accounts other than those of the named payee — without, in each case, checking the customers' title to those cheques.

However, 'negligence' need not be confined simply to the physical act of collecting or paying cheques. As the House of Lords pointed out in *Commissioners of Taxation v E, S & A Bank Ltd*, the court must also take into account all the antecedent and present circumstances. One of the things that can be relevant, particular if the cheques turn out to have been stolen, is whether the financial institution exercised sufficient care, when it opened the account, to establish its new customer's bona fides. If it allowed the customer to open an account without making the usual and proper inquiries it could be held that, in subsequently collecting cheques for that customer, it may have acted negligently.

Case Example

The London Bank of Australia allowed a new customer to open an account even though he was not known to it, had no credentials, disclosed no information about himself and was depositing mainly cheques which, on their face, may or may not have been his property. Immediately thereafter he deposited Kendall's cheque (which had been stolen) and the bank collected it on his behalf. Taking all the circumstances into account, the court held that the bank had been negligent because it should not have collected cheques for such a suspicious new customer without making inquiries to satisfy itself of his bona fides: *London Bank of Australia Ltd v Kendall* (1920) 28 CLR 401.

However, the negligence that is required is not negligence in opening the account but negligence in collecting. The circumstances surrounding the opening of the account are only relevant to the extent that they shed light on the question of whether there was negligence in collecting the cheque.

So, for example, in *Commissioners of Taxation v E, S & A Bank Ltd* [1920] AC 683, on facts similar to those in *Kendall's* case, the E, S & A Bank was held not to have been negligent. There, even though the bank had allowed a rogue to open a false account, it had followed standard procedures and there was nothing innately suspicious about any of the rogue's deposits. (The stolen cheque in that case was an open bearer cheque — quite different in effect to the crossed cheques that had been deposited and collected in *Kendall's* case.) In other words, the bank had done all that any reasonable bank would have done in the circumstances. There was nothing 'of an unusual character calculated to arouse suspicion and provoke inquiry'. Therefore, the bank had not been negligent.

Cheques a financial institution draws on itself

[12.69] Cheques that a financial institution draws on itself (what were previously called 'bank cheques') are normally used because payees know that they will not be dishonoured for lack of funds. For this reason they are often stipulated as the required method of payment in large property transactions.

Section 5(1) of the Cheques Act makes it clear that cheques that a financial institution draws on itself — even though they are not 'addressed by a person *to another person*' — are still to be treated like all other cheques. (Though some of the Act's other provisions do not apply to them, either because they are specifically excluded under s 5(2) or because they are inapplicable because of their context.) Section 5(4) reinforces s 5(1) by providing that references to such cheques are to be taken as references to 'an instrument that *would be a cheque* if the drawer and the drawee were not the same person'.

The fact that such cheques are to be treated just like all other cheques means, of course, that they can be dishonoured if the financial institution is aware that the holder has a defective title, or if they are forged or not supported by consideration.

Case Example

The plaintiff company was paid with a bank cheque that had been stolen and on which a signature, purporting to be that of a bank officer, had been forged. When the cheque was dishonoured the plaintiff sued the bank and failed. Because the cheque was a forgery the bank was not liable: *Johns Period Furniture Pty Ltd v Commonwealth Savings Bank of Australia* (1980) 24 SASR 224.

Similarly, in *Sidney Raper Pty Ltd v Commonwealth Trading Bank of Australia* [1975] 2 NSWLR 227 (a case followed and applied in *Justin Seward Pty Ltd v Commissioners of Rural and Industries Bank* (1982) 60 FLR 51) the bank dishonoured its own cheque when the cheque with which its customer paid for it was itself dishonoured. It was held that the bank could dishonour the cheque in those circumstances, because it had not received consideration for it. Therefore, it was not liable.

Circumstances where a financial institution's own cheques will be dishonoured

[12.70] The decision in the *Sidney Raper* case caused concern in the commercial community because, until then, bank cheques had been thought of as being as good as cash. Following discussions with, in particular, the Australian law societies, the Australian Bankers' Association announced in 1985 that bank cheques would not be dishonoured except in five specific situations, where:

313

- the cheque has been forged;
- it has been materially altered;
- it has been reported stolen or lost;
- there is a court order restraining the bank from honouring it; or
- the bank has not received consideration for it.

It is likely that the 'non-bank' financial institutions will adopt the same rules for cheques that they draw on themselves, especially if they want them to have the same level of commercial and legal acceptance that bank cheques and bank drafts have.

Agency cheques

Definition

[12.71]   Section 3(1) defines 'agency cheques', very unhelpfully, as cheques 'to which subsection 100(2) applies'. Agency cheques have their origins in the inability of what were previously called 'non-bank financial institutions' ('NBFIs') — essentially building societies and credit unions — to issue cheques of their own. Instead, they had arrangements with their banks whereby the banks allowed them to issue cheques to the NBFIs' own customers which those customers would write against their accounts with the NBFIs *but* which were drawn against the NBFIs' accounts with the 'drawee banks'. Those arrangements got around the old rule that only banks could issue cheques but they meant that the resulting 'agency cheques' contained the names of two institutions — the NBFI that issued them and the bank against which they were actually drawn.

[12.72]   Agency cheques are still permitted and *both* 'FIC institutions' and 'FCA institutions' (see **[12.4]**) can issue them (in which case they are referred to as 'issuing institutions'). Therefore, even though FIC institutions, as 'financial institutions', can issue their own cheques, the Act allows them — together with FCA institutions (which cannot issue them and which, therefore, have to rely on agency cheque arrangements) — to issue agency cheques (drawn against any financial institution that is prepared to act as the 'drawee institution').

The treatment of agency cheques

[12.73]   If a customer signs an agency cheque under an arrangement with an 'issuing institution' the issuing institution has the same duties and liabilities and the same rights that it would have had if the customer had drawn the cheque addressed to it instead. That is, the issuing institution must ensure that the cheque is paid (unless there is some valid reason why it should not be) and, once it has been paid, it can debit the customer's account. Under s 68(2A) it is entitled to possession of the paid cheque (in case of a dispute) and it must retain it (or a copy of it) for seven years: s 68(3AA). Failure to do so is an offence punishable by a fine not exceeding $10,000: s 68(7).

[12.74]   Unauthorised signatures on agency cheques are dealt with under s 100A which parallels s 32(1) (dealing with unauthorised signatures on cheques generally). It provides that a signature written or placed on an agency cheque without the customer's authority only operates as the customer's signature (for the purposes of s 100 liability) if the customer is estopped from denying its genuineness or the existence of authority (as could occur, for example, if the customer breaching the 'Greenwood duty' referred to in Chapter 11) or if the customer ratifies or adopts it.

There is no provision equivalent to s 32(2) — which deals with unauthorised signatures of persons other than the drawer (effectively 'indorsers') — though, unlike s 32(1), it is not specifically precluded from applying to agency cheques. Therefore, it seems that s 32(2) applies to agency cheques just as it applies to cheques generally.

Credit and debit cards

[12.75]   One of the major developments in Australian banking since the early 1970s has been a rapid expansion in the use of credit and debit cards. However, unlike cheques and other bills of exchange, plastic cards are not closely regulated by their own statutes, although a number of consumer protection provisions — including, in particular, the mandatory disclosure requirements of the uniform state and territory Consumer Credit Codes — apply to them. The cards are mainly regulated by contracts between those who issue them and those who use them.

Credit cards

[12.76]   Credit cards are simply a practical means whereby consumers can pay for goods and services (and, with some of the cards, can obtain cash advances) on prearranged credit terms. Credit cards can either be two-party cards or three-party cards. Two-party cards are those which are issued, normally, by major retailers and which can only be used within their own stores. The Myer and David Jones cards are examples. The three-party cards are cards issued by a credit provider (usually a financial institution, though they are also issued by specialist issuers such as American Express and Diners Club, in which case they are more accurately referred to as 'charge cards'). Unlike two-party cards they can be used to purchase goods and services from a wide range of providers rather than from a single provider. The use of three-party cards grew rapidly from 1974 when the Australian banks established Bankcard. Today, most Australian adults have at least one credit card and plastic cards have largely usurped the payment function that, until the mid-1970s, was mainly the preserve of cheques and cash.

The legal position

[12.77]   Unlike cheques and other bills of exchange, credit cards are not instruments. They are not an embodiment of money but merely the physical manifestation of a contractual credit arrangement between the cards' issuer and the cardholder. The legal position, therefore, depends upon the parties' individual contractual arrangements rather than upon any laid down set of rights and obligations. The contracts and their terms are, however, fairly standard.

With most three-party cards there are at least three contractual relationships: the contract between the card's issuer and the cardholder; the contract between the issuer and the merchant who agrees to accept the card as a means of payment; and the contract between the cardholder and the merchant that arises when goods or services are purchased.

The issuer/cardholder contract

[12.78] The issuer/cardholder contract authorises the cardholder to use the credit represented by the card to make purchases from authorised merchants on terms usually dictated by the issuer. Those terms are normally set out in a standard form contract which is headed simply 'conditions of use'.

Typically, the conditions of use will require the cardholder to accept liability for all transactions in which the card is used unless the card has been stolen and the issuer has been notified of that fact (in which case the cardholder's liability may be reduced or eliminated altogether), and to reimburse the issuer for all payments made to merchants with whom the cardholder uses the card. The agreement also commonly provides for payment of interest on overdue amounts and/or an annual fee.

The conditions of use usually require the cardholder to notify the issuer if the card is either lost or stolen and prohibits the cardholder from raising against the issuer any defence or counterclaim that the cardholder might have been able to raise against the merchant. So, for example, if goods bought using a credit card turn out to be unmerchantable the cardholder cannot use that fact to escape paying the issuer. The cardholder's sole recourse is against the merchant from whom the goods were bought. Merchants can raise debit notes cancelling out the transaction and, if they do, the card's issuer will take them into account when calculating the cardholder's periodic indebtedness.

The issuer/merchant contract

[12.79] The contracts that the various card issuers enter into with individual merchants — either directly or through the merchant's own financial institution — vary but, again, there are a number of standard inclusions. In exchange for the issuer agreeing to reimburse the merchant for transactions paid for by credit card, the merchant agrees to accept the card as payment and to seek payment from the issuer. In addition, the merchant agrees to adopt a number of security measures to, at least, minimise the possibility of credit card fraud and loss to the issuer. These include verifying the signature on and currency of cards presented for payment, checking cards against a 'hot list' of stolen or lost cards and obtaining express authority for transactions where the sum involved exceeds the merchant's 'floor limit' (a maximum monetary amount set by the card's issuer for which the merchant is authorised to accept card payment without specific authority).

The merchant/cardholder contract

[12.80] Normally, the contract between the merchant and the cardholder is simply the contract under which the goods are sold or the services are supplied. The only real difference is that there is at least an implied term that the merchant will accept the credit card in payment and that payment by credit card will discharge the debt. This means that the merchant must look for physical payment to the issuer of the card rather than to the cardholder. See, for example, *Re Charge Card Services Ltd* [1987] Ch 150 (affirmed on appeal at [1989] Ch 497), where it was held that the sale contract contained a term that tender of payment by credit card discharged the debt between the merchant and the cardholder and that, thereafter, the merchant could only seek payment from the card's issuer. The issuer is the only person who can demand cash payment from the cardholder.

Debit cards

[12.81] Debit cards are simply cards which allow customers of financial institutions to obtain electronic access to the funds in their accounts. Keycards, Flexicards,

Handycards, and Redicards are all examples of debit cards. They incorporate information which is encoded on a magnetic strip on the card which can be read electronically by a terminal. Customers are issued with an electronic signature (PIN number) which allows them to conduct transactions through computer-linked terminals. The terminals include automatic teller machines, cash dispensers and EFTPOS (electronic funds transfer point of sale) terminals. Some credit cards can be used as either debit or credit cards (as is the case with some financial institution issued credit cards) if the financial institution issues a PIN number that can be used when they are used as debit cards.

As with credit cards there is no specific legislation regulating the use of debit cards and the rights and liabilities of the parties are governed by the terms of the contract under which the financial institution issues and the customer accepts the card. Those terms are based on and reflect the provisions of the 'EFT Code of Conduct', sponsored by the federal government and supervised by the Australian Payments System Council. They are usually issued to customers in a pamphlet entitled simply 'conditions of use': see **[12.83]**.

Debit and credit cards distinguished

[12.82]   The one major difference between debit and credit cards is that debit cards usually involve only one contractual relationship — that between the issuer of the card and the cardholder, at least where the card is only used to deposit and withdraw money from the cardholder's account. Additional contractual relationships can arise if the cardholder uses the card to pay for commercial transactions (as has become increasingly popular, particularly with the proliferation of EFTPOS terminals in major retail stores, automated fuel dispensers, card telephones and so on).

EFT code of conduct

[12.83]   The main conditions of use affecting debit card issuers and their customers (all of which comply with the federal and state governments' 'Electronic Funds Transfer — Code of Conduct') include the following:

- On the part of the cardholder:
  - to accept general liability (subject to a number of specific exclusions) for any transactions completed using the card when the cardholder's PIN number authenticates the transaction;
  - to sign the card immediately upon receiving it;
  - to provide reasonable protection to prevent the card being stolen;
  - not to permit any other person to use the card;
  - not to disclose the PIN number to any other person;
  - not to record the PIN number on the card or on any article carried with the card;
  - to destroy expired cards;
  - to advise the issuer of any change of address;
  - to use the card strictly in accordance with the conditions of use; and
  - to advise the financial institution as soon as possible upon becoming aware that the card has been lost or stolen or that the PIN number has been divulged or that the card has been misused.
- On the part of the card's issuer:
  - to accept deposits into and to make payments out of the cardholder's account when the card is used at any of the card issuer's own or affiliated automatic teller

machines, cash machines or EFTPOS terminals and to issue terminal transaction slips to verify each transaction if the cardholder so requires;

- to issue periodic statements;
- not to make the cardholder liable for any unauthorised transactions that occur prior to the cardholder receiving his or her card and PIN number;
- to accept a reduced level of cardholder liability when the cardholder had not contributed to an unauthorised transaction by voluntarily disclosing the PIN number, indicating the PIN number on the card (or keeping a record of it with the card), or by delaying unreasonably in notifying the issuer of any loss, theft or misuse of the card, or of someone else becoming aware of the PIN number (that limited liability is normally the lesser of $50 or the balance in the cardholder's account or the actual loss incurred up to the time when the financial institution is notified of the card's loss or theft or of the existence of an unauthorised transaction); and
- to investigate all complaints about apparent errors or instances of unauthorised transactions.

The financial institutions also normally reserve the right to impose daily or weekly limits on the amounts that customers can withdraw using their electronic funds transfer facilities. It is also normal for them to reserve the right to alter the 'conditions of use' unilaterally.

Summary and key terms

[12.84]   This chapter has set out to explain the following:
- Cheques are simply unconditional orders in writing, addressed to a financial institution requiring it to pay money to a designated payee on demand.
- Cheques can be drawn payable to either bearer or to order.
- Cheques may be crossed, in which case they should not be paid otherwise than to another financial institution. A 'not negotiable' crossing is a warning to transferees that they cannot get a better title than their transferor had.
- A 'holder's' rights depend upon whether he or she is a 'holder', a 'holder for value', a 'holder in due course' or a 'holder deriving title through a holder in due course'.
- In general, financial institutions are not liable for paying or collecting a cheque if the payment or collection was 'in good faith and without negligence'.
- Agency cheques are a device used by institutions that either cannot or elect not to issue their own cheques to provide their customers with a cheque drawing facility.
- Credit and debit cards are not negotiable instruments and they are governed by a series of contractual arrangements between the cards' issuers, those who use them and the merchants who honour them.

13

Property

What this chapter does ...

Property is the basic ingredient of almost all commercial transactions. Whether the parties are renting premises, leasing equipment, buying or selling goods, issuing or transferring cheques or just providing services, they will be dealing with property. Therefore, an understanding of what property is and what rights its owners or possessors have is fundamental to much of the law governing business transactions. This chapter will deal with the concept of property generally rather than with specific transactions involving it. It will attempt to explain some of the major rights, duties and liabilities that attach to the ownership or possession of property.

The concept of property

What is 'property'?

[13.1]   In law, the word 'property' has two distinct meanings. It can mean both 'objects of ownership' (things such as land, books, shares and debentures, and even those more ephemeral possessions such as interests in a trust) and 'rights of ownership'. This dual nature of property is reflected in the way in which it is referred to. When people say, 'that book is my property', they are saying that the book, as an 'object of ownership', belongs to them. A lawyer, on the other hand, may refer to somebody 'having property in the book'. By this the lawyer means that that person enjoys all the proprietary rights (the 'rights of ownership') that flow from owning the book. These rights of ownership, to an extent, depend upon the nature of the 'object' that is owned and, in particular, whether it is land or non-land property.

Classifying 'objects of ownership'

[13.2]   Property, in its 'objects of ownership' sense, can be classified as either 'real property' or 'personal property'. Real property consists of land and all those things attached to or forming part of the land. Personal property consists of everything else.

  The distinction between these two is largely historic in origin and the reason for classifying property as either real or personal is no longer as important as it was. However, the distinction does still exist, the rights attached to real property are slightly different from those attached to personal property, some legislation applies to one form of property and not to the other (for example, the Sale of Goods Acts only apply to personal property — see Chapter 6) and the distinction may also be important in some personal documents (for example, a testator may leave his or her 'real property' to one beneficiary and his or her 'personal property' to another).

The origins of the distinction

[13.3]   In feudal times wealth (and, therefore, property) consisted of basically two things: land and various types of moveable property (the moveable property generally being referred to as 'chattels' — from the Latin 'catalla' meaning 'cattle'). When owners of land were unlawfully dispossessed of it they could sue to recover the land itself (the very 'thing' of which they had been deprived) because it was still there. The Latin for 'thing' is 'res' and the action taken to recover possession of land was called an action 'in rem'. This was subsequently referred to as a 'real' action and the land that was recovered using it came to called 'real property' or 'realty'.

With non-land property (cattle, sheep, household implements and so on) actions 'in rem' were not really possible because, by the time the action was heard, the property that had been taken or interfered with could have been killed or destroyed, taken out of the court's jurisdiction or otherwise disposed of so that the court could not effectively order its return. For this reason, the owner of such property was allowed to sue the person who had deprived him or her of it for damages rather than for the property itself. As a result, the action was referred to as an action 'in personam' or a 'personal' action because recovery was against the defendant personally. In time, the property affected by such actions came to be called 'personal property' or 'personalty'.

The slightly different rights and liabilities that attach to real and personal property are largely derived from this distinction between the actions that the owners of particular property could institute to protect their rights to it when someone unlawfully interfered with those rights.

Real property

Tenure

[13.4]   In essence, the Australian system of land tenure is based on the system that William the Conqueror introduced into England after the Norman Conquest in 1066. That is, as a starting point, all land belongs to the Crown (subject now to the decisions in *Mabo v Queensland [No 2]* (1992) 175 CLR 1 and *Wik Peoples v Queensland* (1996) 187 CLR 1 and to the Native Title Act 1993 (Cth), which recognise a form of native title to what would otherwise be Crown Land). The Crown grants the right to use and enjoy parts of that land, on an exclusive basis, to individual subjects whom we loosely refer to as the land's 'owners'. In fact there is no such thing as absolute ownership of land in either Australia or England for reasons that are largely historical.

In feudal times, as now, land could only be held 'of the Crown' — no one owned land outright — and the various forms of land tenure all involved the 'tenant' performing some form of military, personal or agricultural service for his or her immediate lord, on a continuing basis, in exchange for the right to occupy and use particular land. Accordingly, the tenant's 'interest' or 'estate' in the land was dependent on the tenant remaining willing and able to perform his or her 'tenant's' duties. This system of conditional tenure of land in exchange for specified feudal services gradually fell into disuse and it was finally abolished by the Tenures Abolition Act 1660. However, it does still have some residual effect on our system of land ownership in that, technically, all land is still owned by the Crown and, therefore, it is merely held 'of the Crown' by those who are nominally regarded as its 'owners'. This can and does have some impact on the actual extent of an 'owner's' control over his or her land because the Crown, either by express reservation contained in the original 'Deed of Grant' or otherwise, does still have some rights to deal with it. This is discussed further in [13.15] and [13.27].

Fixtures

[13.5]   In law, land consists of not only the soil but also of all things that form part of or that are attached to the soil. Consequently, things growing on the land such as trees or crops, and other things which have been added to the land such as houses, swimming pools, fences and any other chattels that have been permanently affixed to it are part of the land. Things that have been attached to the land (as opposed to things that are growing on the land) are called 'fixtures'.

A fixture is a chattel which has become so attached to land that it has become part of the land. Whether something has become a fixture really depends on two tests — the *degree* to which the chattel is attached and the *purpose* for which it was attached.

Degree of annexation

[13.6]   The degree of annexation refers to the extent to which the chattel is physically attached to the land and whether it can be readily removed without substantial damage either to itself or to the thing (the 'land') to which it is attached.

The courts use a number of presumptions to help determine whether a chattel has become affixed to such a degree that it has become a fixture. First, if the chattel is actually fixed to the land by means other than its own weight there is a strong presumption that it was intended to be a fixture. On the other hand, if a chattel is held in position only by its own weight, the presumption is that it was not intended to be a fixture. Finally, if the thing has been attached in such a way that it cannot be removed without substantial damage either to itself or to the thing to which it is attached — either the land or to some other acknowledged fixture (the test of 'injurious removal') — it is again presumed that the person who attached it intended it to be a fixture: see *APA Co Ltd v Coroneo* (1938) 38 SR (NSW) 700 at 712–13.

Purpose of annexation

[13.7]   It should therefore be clear that the degree of attachment is not, by itself, a final test and that what is critical is whether the chattel was *intended* to form part of the realty when it was attached. Blackburn J illustrated the problem very nicely in *Holland v Hodgson* (1872) LR 7 CP 328 at 335 when he said:

> Thus blocks of stone placed one on the top of another without any mortar or cement for the purpose of forming a dry stone wall would become part of the land, though the same stones, if deposited in a builder's yard and for convenience sake stacked on the top of each other in the form of a wall would remain chattels. On the other hand, an article may be very firmly fixed to the land, and yet the circumstances may be such as to show that it was never intended to be part of the land, and then it does not become part of the land. The anchor of a large ship must be very firmly fixed in the ground in order to bear the strain of the cable, yet no one could suppose that it became part of the land ... An anchor similarly fixed in the soil for the purpose of bearing the strain of the chain of a suspension bridge would be part of the land.

One test that has been suggested is to ask whether the chattel was attached to the land so that it could be better used or enjoyed as a chattel (in which case it will not have become a fixture) or whether it was affixed for the better enjoyment or permanent improvement of the land — or the building — to which it was attached (in which case it will have become a fixture). MacGregor J put the point clearly in *Johnston v International Harvester Co of New Zealand* [1925] NZLR 529 at 539, saying that what had to be looked at was whether the attachment was 'for the permanent and substantial improvement of the building, or merely for a temporary purpose and the more complete enjoyment of it as a chattel'.

Therefore, in *D'Eyncourt v Gregory* (1866) LR 3 Eq 382 a number of statues, figures, vases and stone garden seats surrounding a house were held to be fixtures even though they were only attached to the land by their own weight. They were essentially part of the house or of the architectural design of the building or grounds. Again, in *North West Trust Co v Rezyn Developments Inc* (1991) 81 DLR (4th) 751, 10 prefabricated bowling lanes, which were simply screwed to the building, were held to be fixtures because the purpose of their annexation was for the better use of the building. Similarly, in *Belgrave Nominees Pty Ltd v Barlin-Scott Airconditioning (Aust) Pty Ltd* [1984] VR 947 it was held that air conditioners which were not physically attached to the buildings that they serviced (because they stood on a number of pads designed to reduce vibration and noise) were still fixtures because they were intended to be permanently affixed — they formed an essential part of the buildings which were being used as office premises.

On the other hand, some chattels which have been physically attached to either land or to other fixtures have been held not to be fixtures themselves because they were not attached for permanence but simply to enable their owners to better use or enjoy them. So, for example, in *Thomas v Beck* (1983) ANZ Conv R 200 a clothes drier attached to a laundry wall was held not to be a fixture because it had only been put there to facilitate its use. (On the other hand, in the same case, an electric dishwasher which was housed in a *purpose-built recess* in the kitchen bench and which was *permanently affixed* to the household plumbing was held to be a fixture because it was clear that that had been the installer's intention.) In *Attorney-General of the Commonwealth of Australia v R T Co Pty Ltd [No 2]* (1957) 97 CLR 146 printing presses weighing about 45 tons each were held not to be fixtures even though they were securely attached to the land by means of bolts set in concrete. Again, the court accepted that their attachment was not intended to make them a permanent part of the building but to allow them to be more efficiently used as printing presses. Similar reasoning can also be found in *Canadian Imperial Bank of Commerce v Alberta Assessment Appeal Board* (1992) 89 DLR (4th) 20 in which automatic teller machines enclosed in separate lockable areas within the bank and connected to the building by electrical cables were held not to be fixtures because they were attached to allow customers to use them and not to enhance the buildings to which they were connected.

[13.8]   Houses are invariably treated as fixtures whether they are physically annexed to the soil on which they are erected (through their foundations) or simply resting by their own weight on concrete, brick or wooden stumps. O'Connor J, for example, commented in *Reid v Smith* (1905) 3 CLR 656 at 679 that:

> It would I think be stretching the rules of the common law to a point at which they cease to be rules of common sense, if it were to be laid down as a general rule that, except in very exceptional cases, wooden houses, resting by their own weight on land, could ever be regarded as mere chattels, removable at the will of the owner of the timber of which they are built.

That thinking was recently applied in *Elitestone Ltd v Morris* [1997] 2 All ER 513, where the House of Lords held that a bungalow resting on concrete blocks was part of the land and not a mere chattel. Critical to their Lordships' decision was their finding (at 516) that the bungalow 'could not be taken down and re-erected elsewhere. It could only be removed by a process of demolition'. This, they said, created 'a strong inference that the *purpose* of placing the structure on the original site was that it should form part of the realty at that site, and therefore cease to be a chattel'.

That is not to say that buildings will always be regarded as fixtures. As O'Connor J indicated in *Reid v Smith*, there may be exceptional circumstances where that was not the intention. Site huts on building projects are good examples. They are clearly not intended to be fixtures. Similarly, in *H E Dibble Ltd v Moore* [1970] 2 QB 181, a greenhouse was held not to be a fixture because there was evidence that 'it was customary to move such greenhouses every few years to a fresh site': per Megaw LJ at 187. Likewise, in

Yallingup Beach Caravan Park v Valuer-General (1994) 11 SR (WA) 355, it was held that park homes permanently on site in a caravan park were still chattels because the clear intention was that they would be moved on a regular (even if infrequent basis) and that they would not constitute part of the land.

Tenants' fixtures

[13.9]   Generally, when tenants affix chattels to leased premises the chattels become part of the premises (and therefore the landlord's property), unless the degree of annexation is not sufficient to make them fixtures or the landlord agrees to allow the 'fixtures' to be severed and removed when the tenant leaves.

However, where chattels have been attached as trade fixtures or for ornamental or domestic purposes (called collectively 'tenants' fixtures') this general rule has been relaxed and, unless the lease contains a specific term to the contrary, the tenant may remove the affixed items — if that can be done without substantial damage to the leased property. Therefore, in *Webb v Frank Bevis Ltd* [1940] 1 All ER 247 the tenant was allowed to remove a shed which was 135 feet long and 50 feet wide and attached to a concrete floor by iron straps. The shed had clearly become part of the realty but because it was in the nature of a tenant's fixture — having been erected by him for use in his trade — he could remove it at the end of his tenancy. Similarly, in *Spyer v Phillipson* [1931] 2 Ch 183 the personal representatives of a deceased tenant were allowed to remove oak panelling which the tenant had installed in the premises — for ornamental or domestic purposes — during the tenancy.

Where the tenancy is for a fixed term (one year, three years, five years, etc) the tenant must remove the fixtures before the fixed term expires but, where the tenancy is for an uncertain period (such as where the tenancy is at will) the tenant has a 'reasonable period' after the lease ends to remove them: see *D'Arcy v Burelli Investments Pty Ltd* (1987) 8 NSWLR 317 at 323. In some jurisdictions the tenant's right to remove tenants' fixtures — especially agricultural fixtures — is governed, at least in part, by statute. Examples include s 155 of the Queensland Property Law Act 1974; s 28 of the Victorian Landlord and Tenant Act 1958; s 21 of the New South Wales Agricultural Holdings Act 1941; and s 26 of the Tasmanian Landlord and Tenant Act 1935 — as well as provisions in the various state Residential Tenancies Acts.

If a tenant tries to remove fixtures which are not 'tenants; fixtures' the landlord can seek an injunction to prevent them being removed and, if the fixtures have already been removed, the landlord can sue the tenant for damages under the doctrine of 'waste': see **[13.31]**.

Emblements

[13.10]   Emblements are similar to tenants' fixtures. They are the produce of a year's crop and, while things growing on land are normally regarded as the property of the land-owner, if a crop has been sown by an outgoing tenant whose tenancy terminates before the crop can be harvested, the tenant can still claim it. However, again, this right only arises where the tenancy was for an undefined time so that the tenant was not at fault in failing to have the crop harvested before the tenancy terminated.

The extent of land (up and down)

[13.11]   Land consists of not only the soil and the things attached to or forming part of it but also everything above and below the surface — at least in theory. As Windeyer J said in *Bursill Enterprises Pty Ltd v Berger Bros Trading Co Pty Ltd* (1971) 124 CLR 73 at 91: 'At common law a freeholder is the owner not only of the surface of his land, but also of everything above it up to the sky and of everything below it to the centre of the earth'. This theory is based on the Latin maxim *'cuius est solum eius est usque ad coleum et ad inferos'* (to whomever belongs the soil, his it is to heaven and to the middle of the earth).

In practical terms, however, the interests of landowners are a little less than the maxim might indicate and there are a number of constraints on what they can do to enforce their rights to both the sub-stratum of their land and to the air space above it. As Lord Wilberforce said in *Commissioner for Railways v Valuer-General* [1974] AC 328 at 351–2 '[there is no] authoritative pronouncement that "land" means the whole of the space from the centre of the earth to the heavens: so sweeping, unscientific and unpractical a doctrine is unlikely to appeal to the common law mind'.

Rights to air space

[13.12]   A correct view of the rights that a landowner has to the air space above his or her land is probably that which was laid down in *Bernstein v Skyviews and General Ltd* [1978] 1 QB 479. In that case the defendants had flown over the plaintiff's land to take photographs which they intended to sell him. The plaintiff objected and demanded that the negatives and prints be handed over or destroyed. When the defendants failed to do either Bernstein sued them alleging that, by entering the air space above his property, they had been guilty of trespass. His action failed. The court held that an owner's rights to the air space above his or her land are not unlimited. Instead, they are restricted 'to such height as is necessary for the ordinary use and enjoyment of his land and the structures upon it and ... above that height he has no greater rights in the air space than any other member of the public'.

This obviously leaves open the question of what height is 'reasonable' and what incursions can be prevented. In *Bernstein's* case Griffiths J gave a number of examples of the sorts of rights that would be enforced in favour of a landowner. He said that landowners were entitled to lop the branches of trees overhanging their boundary (while acknowledging that this right seemed to be founded in the tort of nuisance rather than in the tort of trespass), to cut wire strung over their land (though this would now be subject to the statutory and other rights that authorities such as the electricity and telephone authorities have to erect transmission lines over private property), and to require that signs projecting into their air space be removed: *Kelsen v Imperial Tobacco Co Ltd* [1957] 2 QB 334.

[13.13]   In addition, it has also been held that landowners are entitled to prevent trespass to their air space by things such as building equipment and scaffolding or even cranes on adjoining land (see, for example, *Bendal Pty Ltd v Mirvac Project Pty Ltd* (1991) 23 NSWLR 464 and *Graham v K D Morris & Sons Pty Ltd* [1974] Qd R 1 respectively). The test in such cases, as it was enunciated in *LJP Investments Pty Ltd v Howard Chia Investments Pty Ltd* [1989] Aust Torts Reports 80–269 and applied in *Bendal Pty Ltd v Mirvac Project Pty Ltd* (above), appears to be, as Hodgson J put it at 68,871:

> not whether the incursion actually interferes with the occupier's actual use of the land at the time, but rather whether it is of a nature and at a height which may interfere with any *ordinary uses* of the land which the occupier may see fit to undertake. [emphasis added]

So, in *Bendal Pty Ltd v Mirvac Project Pty Ltd*, an injunction was granted to stop the defendant, which was building a multi-storey office building on land adjoining the plaintiff's property, from having its safety screens encroach into the plaintiff's air space. This was even though they posed no immediate danger to the plaintiff and did not interfere with its actual use of the property. Bryson J recognised that the plaintiff could use the space (or could license others to use it) for building work (such as was being undertaken by the defendant) and that it was therefore entitled to protect that right and to force the defendant to negotiate for and to pay for using its air space.

It should also be noted that statute can limit a landowner's complete freedom to enjoy his or her air space. The statutory rights of authorities, such as the electricity and telephone authorities, to erect transmission cables across private land have already been noted. In addition, most countries have Civil Aviation legislation which gives statutory protection to aircraft overflying private land provided the flights are at a reasonable height and provided they comply with all statutory requirements.

Rights to the sub-stratum

[13.14]   As regards a landowner's right 'to the centre of the earth' it appears that that right applies at least, as with air space, to such extent as is necessary for the ordinary use and enjoyment of the land and the structures upon it and that any interference with that right will constitute an actionable trespass which may either be prevented by injunction or compensated for in damages.

Case Example

The plaintiff sued to restrain the defendant from entering a cellar beneath his house. Their two houses had originally been owned by a butcher who used one as business premises and the other as a residence. The houses had separate entrances but had been connected by doors on the ground floor and on an upper floor. In addition, there were steps leading from the business premises to a cellar beneath the residence. There was no access to the cellar from the residence itself. After the butcher's death the doors were sealed and the buildings were sold. The plaintiff, who had acquired the residence, objected to the defendant, who had acquired the business premises, using the cellar which lay beneath his (the plaintiff's) house. The court held that, because there was no contrary provision in the conveyancing documents, the land that the plaintiff had bought included not only everything on the surface but everything beneath it. Therefore, the cellar belonged to him and he could prevent the defendant using it: *Grigsby v Melville* [1973] 3 All ER 455.

How much of the sub-stratum?

[13.15]   Whether a landowner's rights actually extend all the way to the centre of the earth is debatable — especially given the general reasoning underlying the decision in *Bernstein's* case. It is clear that those rights do extend down at least as far as the landowner is capable of exercising 'dominion' over the sub-stratum, but it is doubtful whether they extend to areas that the landowner cannot access and use. As Logan J commented in his dissenting judgment in *Edwards v Sims* 24 SW 2d 619 (1929) (an American decision involving a landowner's claim to share in profits made by conducting tours of a cave, part of which ran 350 feet below his land, even though there was no access to it from his property), 'No man can bring up from the depth of the earth the Stygian darkness and make it serve his purposes, unless he has the entrance to it'.

However, in the end result, the question of how far down a landowner's rights extend probably does not matter in any real practical sense. Most Deeds of Grant issued in Australia are subject to a number of 'reservations' by which the Crown reserves to itself the rights to things such as the minerals under the surface. (This is the basis upon which the Crown can still issue mining leases over land, 'ownership' of which has already been granted to others.) In addition, a landowner's rights to his or her subsoil are effectively limited by the rights that the various public authorities (acting through the Crown) have to lay, for example, drains, water pipes and underground power and telephone cables into and through private land.

Personal property

Personal and real property: the difference

[13.16]   The main distinction between real and personal property is that items of personal property cannot be specifically recovered in a 'real' action. Instead, their owners may have to be satisfied with a remedy in damages should they be deprived of their property. Therefore, because real actions can only be brought in cases involving ownership of land, personal property is basically anything other than land.

Forms of personal property

[13.17]   Personal property consists of two classes of chattel, chattels personal (or 'pure personalty') and chattels real. Chattels personal consist of most tangible and intangible items of non-land property and chattels real consist of interests in land that fall short of freehold title (that is, the term 'chattels real' refers mainly to leasehold interests in land). Leaseholds are regarded as personal property because, originally, lessees who were dispossessed of their land could not recover the land itself. They could only sue for damages for loss of its use. However, the fact that leaseholds are classified as chattels real indicates that, while a lessee's interest in the land is 'personal', he or she does still have a proprietary interest of sorts in it which can be enforced not only against the landlord but also against anyone else who interferes with it.

Chattels personal (pure personalty)

[13.18]   Chattels personal are sub-classified into 'choses in possession' and 'choses in action'. The word 'chose' is simply French for 'thing', and a chose in possession is, therefore, a thing which is capable of physical possession — in other words a tangible, moveable object.

Choses in action are the intangibles. They were described by Channel J in *Torkington v Magee* [1902] 2 KB 427 at 430 as 'all personal rights of property which can only be claimed or enforced by action, and not by taking physical possession'. This definition may be a little misleading in that some choses in action are a little more physically possessable than others. These are those intangibles which are 'represented' by some sort of document. Examples include the rights to be paid a sum of money that are embodied in a cheque, the rights to physical possession of goods that are embodied in a Bill of Lading, the rights to insurance cover that are embodied in a policy of insurance and so on. In each of these cases the 'object' being possessed is not the document as such but the rights that it represents. Therefore, when we speak about ownership of shares, for example, we are really talking about ownership of the rights that the shares represent and not the intrinsically worthless piece of paper on which that ownership is recorded. Other choses in action (for example, most contractual rights) which are not represented or 'locked up' in a document in the same way that, say, the rights to be paid a sum of money are locked up in a cheque, may be referred to as 'pure intangibles' as opposed to the 'documentary intangibles', of which cheques, bills of lading and so on are examples.

[13.19]   The significance of the distinction between 'pure' and 'documentary' intangibles really lies in the fact that documents which represent intangible rights are, to a very large extent, equated with the rights that they represent. Consequently, they allow those rights to be more readily transferred or assigned because the documents (and therefore the rights that they represent) can be enforced using actions for, for example, conversion and detinue: see Chapter 16. At common law, 'pure intangibles' were not assignable (though this defect was subsequently, to an extent, remedied in equity — see Chapter 11) and clearly they, as pure intangibles, cannot be recovered using actions in conversion or detinue because there is no physical asset to recover.

Chattels attached to chattels

[13.20]   When one chattel is attached to another or when chattels have become so intermingled that they are no longer separately identifiable, there is a potential question about whether ownership of the attached chattel stays with the original owner or whether it passes to the owner of the principal chattel in the same way as, for example, chattels become a landowner's property when they become fixtures.

The basic principle is that the chattels retain their separate ownership *unless* the parties intended otherwise. For example, a standard inclusion in most hire–purchase contracts is a statement to the effect that 'any accessories or other goods attached to the goods (those being hired) shall become a part thereof'. Accordingly, because of the agreement, if someone buys a motor vehicle on hire–purchase and installs a radio in it, the radio will thereafter belong to the hire–purchase company. Consequently, if the car is repossessed, the hirer can only remove the radio if he or she gets the hire–purchase company's permission to do so first.

[13.21]   However, there is no general legal principle that an attached chattel will automatically become the property of the owner of the principal chattel, unless that finding is necessary. That could be the case, for instance, where the attached chattel can no longer be separately identified or where it cannot be readily detached from the principal item without substantial damage to either itself or to the principal item (the test of 'injurious removal'). For example, in *Rendell v Associated Finance Pty Ltd* [1957] VR 604 the court had to determine whether a short motor owned by Rendell that had been installed in a truck owned by Associated Finance had become Associated Finance's property or whether it was still Rendell's. It was clear that Rendell had intended to retain property in the engine and, because there was also no evidence to show that it could not be removed without damage either to itself or to the truck, the court held that it was still his.

Intermingling (confusion of goods)

[13.22]   Who owns chattels that have been so intermingled that they are no longer separately identifiable depends on why they were intermingled. If they were intermingled by consent it is presumed that the original owners intended to share in the new 'whole' in the proportions in which they contributed to it. So, therefore, if A's two tonnes of grain is consensually intermingled with B's eight tonnes of grain it would be presumed that they would have, respectively, a 20 per cent and an 80 per cent share in the entire intermingled mass. The same applies where the intermingling occurs by accident. However, if the intermingling was done purposely and without the consent of one of the parties, that party can demand back the same quantity of goods that he or she owned previously, will have any dispute as to quantity resolved in his or her favour and may be entitled to recover damages for any loss suffered as a result of a diminution in the overall quality of the goods that are recovered after the intermingling. See *Indian Oil Corp Ltd v Greenstone Shipping SA* [1988] 1 QB 345, a case involving the unauthorised intermingling of two cargoes of crude oil. Whether the same rule applies when the goods are not of substantially the same nature and quality is still to be determined: see Staughton J's judgment at 370–1.

Conversion of property from one form to another

[13.23] Personal property can be converted to realty by the simple act of affixing it to land in such a way that it becomes a fixture. Similarly, real property can become personal property by a process known as 'severing'. Severing simply involves something which is attached to or which forms part of the land being detached from it with the intention that it will become a separate item of property. So, for example, trees when they are cut or gravel when it is removed from a gravel pit, cease to be part of the land and become separate chattels. In the same way, air conditioners and other fixtures that are removed from buildings, either by the owner or with the owner's consent, cease to be part of the real property and become, instead, separate items of personal property.

Property as 'rights of ownership'

Property rights

[13.24] A person who owns property has basically two rights: those that flow from ownership and those that flow from possession. Ownership and possession can co-exist but they need not. They can be separated and it is this aspect of property that makes many commercial dealings possible. For example, it is only because one person can own property and another can have the legal right to possession of it that hiring and lease arrangements and other forms of bailment can take place. ('Bailment' is simply a delivery of goods from one person, called the bailor, to another person, called the bailee, under an arrangement whereby the bailee is required, after the purpose for which the goods were bailed has been fulfilled, to return those goods to the bailor, to otherwise deal with them according to the bailor's directions or to keep them until the bailor reclaims them: see Chapter 15.)

The separation of ownership and possession can be either lawful or unlawful. For example, all contracts of bailment involve a lawful separation because the true owner of the goods *voluntarily* delivers possession of them to the bailee for a specific, and usually known, purpose. On the other hand, the separation may be unlawful as, for instance, where goods are stolen. In that case, the true owner retains ownership of the goods but, clearly, the thief, at least for the time being, has possession of them.

The concept of ownership

Who is the owner?

[13.25]   The owner of property is the person who has all the legal rights to that property. The owner has rights of enjoyment against the entire world and may freely part with those rights either in their entirety (by, for example, selling or giving or bequeathing the property to others) or in part (by, for example, lending or hiring it to others).

Ownership can be either 'original' or 'derivative'. Most ownership is derivative because most owners acquire their property from others through purchase, gift or inheritance. Ownership is original where the owner creates the property or is the first acquirer of it. Examples of the former include the ownership that authors and inventors have in their copyrights and patents (and a good illustration can be found in *Breen v Williams* (1996) 186 CLR 71 in which the High Court unanimously held that a patient's medical records, as chattels, belonged to the doctor who created them and not to the patient). Examples of the latter include the ownership that anglers and hunters have in the fish and animals that they take.

Ownership of land

[13.26]   As was seen earlier, landholders in Australia do not 'own' their property absolutely. Our system of land tenure, which is based on the English system, presupposes that all land is owned by the Crown and that lesser interests (or 'estates') in it have simply been granted to individual subjects so that they can use and enjoy it. Consequently, in a technical sense, no one other than the Crown really 'owns' land. Those who are usually called 'owners' merely own interests in the land rather than the land itself and they are still strictly 'tenants' of the Crown because they 'hold' their interests, directly or indirectly from the Crown by virtue of a Crown grant.

The Crown's interest in land

[13.27]   This aspect of land ownership has a number of practical ramifications for what 'owners' can do with their land. First, as was seen earlier, the Crown can (and usually does) grant land subject to conditions and reservations. Consequently, the Crown has, for example, reserved to itself the rights to most minerals so that it, and not the individual land holders, can exploit those minerals and the rights to them, for its own purposes and advantage. Second, the Crown's paramount right to land also entitles it to use land for Crown purposes even when that land has been alienated by grant and when the Crown's use of it might be inconsistent with the ongoing use and occupation of the 'owners'. In extreme circumstances this can even involve the Crown resuming control of the land (through full or partial resumptions), thereby denying the owners any further use of it. (Resumptions are now closely regulated by statute and, where they occur, the landowners are entitled to fair compensation for the loss of their interests in, and continuing use of, the land that is being resumed.) Finally, if a landowner dies intestate and without heirs, his or her land can be deemed to be *bona vacantia* (property without an owner) and, in that case, it can revert to the Crown.

Forms of land tenure

[13.28]   There are two main forms of land tenure in Australia — freehold and leasehold.

Freehold

[13.29]   Freehold estates, for all practical purposes, involve what would normally be referred to as 'ownership' of the land. Someone with a freehold interest holds the land directly from the Crown so that no-one is interposed between him or her and the Crown. Original grantees of land and all those who derive title through them (by sale, gift, will, on intestacy or by operation of law), have a freehold interest in it.

There are a number of freehold estates but the most important of them are 'estates in fee simple' and 'life estates'.

[13.30]   Estates in fee simple   An estate in fee simple is an estate of unlimited duration and those who have estates in fee simple in land have an almost absolute ownership of that land. Consequently, the holder of an estate in fee simple can basically deal with the land in any way in which he or she chooses, can dispose of it by sale, gift, will or on intestacy and can create subordinate estates (such as leaseholds), over it. Most land holdings in Australia are held in fee simple.

[13.31]   Life estate   The other major form of freehold tenure is the 'life estate'. As its name implies, a 'life estate' simply means that the 'owner' owns the property only for the duration of a particular life in being. A life estate can subsist during either the life of the person with the life estate (the 'life tenant') or during the life of someone else — in which case the life tenant is said to have an estate *pur autre vie* ('for another life'). After the death of the person upon whose continued life the life estate depends, the property reverts to whomever has what is called the 'reversionary interest'. That person is called the 'remainderman' because his or her interest in the property is what remains after the life tenant's interest terminates.

Life estates (and their accompanying reversionary interests) are often created by will (for example, 'I leave my house to my mother for life and then to my brother in fee simple'), but they can also be created inter vivos (during life) by either sale or gift. However, irrespective of how they are created, the life tenant only gets a limited interest in the land which, although it is greater than a leasehold interest, is significantly less than a fee simple. For example, although he or she can dispose of the life estate (by selling it or by giving it away) and can also create subordinate interests (for example, leaseholds) in it, a life tenant cannot transfer it on his or her death (unless it is an estate *pur autre vie*), because, once he or she dies, there is nothing left to transfer. Nor can he or she transfer or create an interest that will survive his or her death. So, for example, anyone who buys a life estate from a life tenant or who takes a lease from a life tenant will have his or her interest in the land automatically terminated when the person on whose life the life estate depends dies.

Life tenants are also somewhat restricted in what they can do with property during their 'ownership' of it. Specifically, they are generally prohibited from committing acts of 'waste'. That is, they cannot do anything that would have the effect of reducing the property's value while it is in their 'ownership'. The reason is simple. If a life tenant could commit waste by, for example, tearing down the buildings on the land, that would affect not only his or her interest in the land, it would also affect the interests of the remainderman. Therefore, unless waste is specifically permitted by the terms of the instrument by which the life estate was created, the life tenant must try to maintain the property in its original condition so that it reverts to the remainderman in that same condition once the life tenant's life estate terminates. The holder of an estate in fee simple is not subject to any such restrictions because his or her 'ownership' is not affected by any equivalent co-existing reversionary interest.

Leasehold

[13.32]   Leasehold interests are all those interests in land that are less than freehold. They usually involve the interposition of someone (that is, a landlord) between the leaseholder and the Crown and they can often be distinguished from freehold interests because they usually last for a defined time (the period of the lease). At the end of that time the lease-holder's interest terminates and the possession and right to use the land reverts to the landlord. Leases of fixed duration as well as tenancies at will (those that continue as long as both parties want them to continue) and tenancies at sufferance (those that continue as long as the landlord is prepared to suffer them to continue) are all examples of leasehold interests. Their particular importance lies in the fact that they give the tenants rights to the land which can be enforced not only against the landlords but also against the rest of the world (so, a tenant can sue anyone who interferes with his or her possession of the property). However, those rights are still clearly less than the full rights of 'ownership' that accompany a freehold interest.

Co-ownership

[13.33]   In the same way that individuals can own property personally, two or more people can co-own property as either joint tenants or tenants in common. In both cases each co-owner owns an undivided share of the whole property rather than simply a separate and specific part of it. All co-owners may, therefore, exercise their rights of ownership over the entire co-owned asset and they are not restricted to using just a part of it.

Joint tenancy

[13.34]   It is very common in our society for married couples, in particular, to own property as joint tenants. This is because joint tenancy carries with it the 'right of survivorship'. This means that when one of the joint tenants dies his or her interest in the joint property automatically passes to the surviving joint tenant or tenants. The deceased cannot leave his or her interest to some other person because that interest passes automatically to the surviving joint tenant or tenants.

To establish a joint tenancy it is necessary to show that the alleged joint tenants have 'unities' of interest, possession, time and title. This means that:

- each of them must have the same type of interest in the property (freehold, life estate, leasehold, etc) and have the same size interest in that property (that is, each will have, for example, an undivided one-half or one-quarter interest, etc);
- each of them must be entitled to possession of the *whole* of the property and none of them must have exclusive rights to any part of it;
- their interests must have arisen at the same time; and
- their interests must have arisen by virtue of the same legal transaction (that is, under the same conveyance, deed or act of adverse possession).

If a joint tenancy does exist an individual joint tenant cannot dispose of his or her interest in the property by will but he or she can dispose of it in other ways during life. A joint tenant can sell or give away his or her interest in jointly owned property (in which the case the joint tenancy is said to be 'severed'), and the new owner of that interest in the property will then hold it as a tenant in common with the other former joint tenants: *Gibbons v Wright* (1954) 91 CLR 423.

Tenancy in common

[13.35] A tenancy in common occurs when two or more people own distinct shares in property (usually land). That is, each tenant in common owns a distinct and separate (though 'undivided') share in the property which need not be equal and which may have come into existence at different times and as a result of different legal transactions. (This would be the case, for example, if a joint tenant sells his or her interest in jointly owned property to two or more buyers who, as discussed earlier, acquire that interest as tenants in common with the seller's former joint tenants). Consequently, the only 'unity' that applies to tenancy in common is the unity of possession. In other words, each tenant in common has a right to use and enjoy the *entire* asset and is not restricted to using only some portion of it. That right co-exists with the equivalent right enjoyed by all of his or her fellow tenants in common.

The concept of possession

Meaning of possession

[13.36] Possession, like ownership, is very difficult to define precisely. However, it is generally accepted that possession, in law, means the physical *control* of a thing coupled with *an intention* to exercise continuing control over it. In this context, physical control does not necessarily mean *actual* possession. Possession can be 'constructive' because all that is required is control of either the asset itself or of some larger object in which it is contained or of land in or beneath which it is located — whether that control is direct or indirect.

> **Case Example**
>
> An ancient boat was discovered buried on Elwes' property when the defendant gas company, to whom Elwes had leased the property for 99 years, excavated the land to erect a gas holder. It was held that, as Elwes was in possession of the land (including all the subsoil), he was also in possession of the boat even though he was unaware of its existence. He was, therefore, entitled to claim it: *Elwes v Brigg Gas Co* (1886) 33 Ch D 562.

Similarly, in *South Staffordshire Water Co v Sharman* [1896] 2 QB 44 it was held that the appellant water company was entitled to two gold rings which Sharman had found in the mud at the bottom of a pool on its property even though it had not known of their existence. The court found that, because the company was in possession of the land with the clear intention of exercising control over it, it was also in lawful (if not actual), possession of the rings.

Rights of the possessor

[13.37] It is often said that 'possession is nine-tenths of the law'. What this means is that the person in possession of property has greater rights to it than anyone in the world other than the true owner. Consequently, someone in possession of property can defend his or her rights to it against anyone other than the true owner or someone deriving title through the true owner. ('Someone deriving title through the true owner' includes people such as lessees or bailees of property. If they lose that property and someone else finds it, they still retain a superior right to it and can demand that the finder — the new 'possessor' — return it to them.)

What this means is that those who are in lawful possession of property (that is, those who have control of the property and an intention of continuing in control of it) can lawfully defend their possession (and, possibly, their claim to possessory ownership) against nearly all comers. No one can deprive them of the property by simply pleading that it appears to have no true owner — though if it has no true owner the legal possessor is entitled to it. This was well illustrated in both *Elwes v Brigg Gas Co* and *South Staffordshire Water Co v Sharman* discussed above. In *Elwes'* case the landowner, as the legal possessor of the land and, therefore, also of the boat, was able to defeat the gas company's claim to it because his rights, as the possessor of something which had obviously been abandoned by its, now long-dead owners, gave him property in it. In *Sharman's* case the water company, as possessor of the land, was also held to be in legal possession of the rings and, therefore, they were able to defeat Sharman's claim to them.

[13.38] The classic illustration of the rights of a possessor against the rest of the world is the decision in *Armory v Delamirie* (1722) 1 Strange 505; 93 ER 664. In that case, the plaintiff, a chimney sweep, found a piece of jewellery, took it to the defendant's shop and gave it to an apprentice to find out what it was and whether it was worth anything. The apprentice removed the stone from the setting and tried to return the setting by itself. The plaintiff objected and sued to recover the stone or its value. The defendant argued that the plaintiff did not own the jewellery but was only a finder and that his physical possession was not sufficient to give him a cause of action. The court held that possession was, in fact, some evidence of ownership and that, as such, the possessor of property was entitled to keep it unless it was claimed by the rightful owner. As a result, the sweep had sufficient grounds upon which to bring his action.

It should, therefore, be clear that the possessor of property has rights to it which are subservient only to the rights of the true owner. In fact, in some cases the possessor's rights might even take priority over the rights of the true owner. This occurs, for example, under some legal arrangements such as hire–purchase contracts, lease contracts or contracts under which property has been pawned or pledged or has had a lien created over it (generally entitling those who have done work on property to retain it until the work has been paid for). In such cases the possessor has possession with the owner's consent and under an arrangement which precludes the owner from recovering possession until the contract has expired or the debt for which it was given as security has been discharged. Consequently, the possessor's rights — at least to continue in possession — are greater than those of the property's true owner.

Finders

[13.39] Finding does not, of itself, give the finder ownership of the property found. Nor, as should be clear from the above, does it necessarily give the finder legal possession. Whether a finder is entitled to the goods depends upon whether the true owner can be found and, if not, whether the finder has validly acquired legal possession. A finder will not acquire legal possession in two instances:

- where the item was found on someone else's property in circumstances where the owner (or occupier) of the land was already in constructive possession of it; and
- where the item was found in the course of the finder's employment.

Things found on another's property

[13.40] The legal position of someone who finds something on someone else's property depends, at least initially, on whether the thing was found *attached to or under* the land or *on* it. The cases all seem to use as their start point the following quote from Pollock and Wright's *Essay on Possession in the Common Law* (1888), p 41:

> The possession of land carries with it in general, by our law, possession of everything which is *attached to or under* that land, and, in the absence of a better title elsewhere, the right to possess it also. And it makes no difference that the possessor is not aware of the thing's existence. [emphasis added]

This is, of course, entirely consistent with the principle underlying the law governing fixtures (see **[13.5]**–**[13.8]**) and with the decisions in both *Elwes v Brigg Gas Co* and *South Staffordshire Water Co v Sharman*. It also means that if something is found in or under land the landowner will have a better title to it than anyone other than the true owner — including the finder.

Case Example

While he was fossicking with a metal detector in a public park owned by the Waverley Borough Council, Ian Fletcher found a medieval gold brooch buried about nine inches under the ground. After he dug it out and reported the find the Council claimed the brooch, arguing that, as it owned the park, it also owned the brooch. The Council's claim succeeded. The court held that, in the absence of a claim by the true owner, the Council, as the lawful possessor of the land on which it had been found, had a better claim to it than the finder: *Waverley Borough Council v Fletcher* [1996] QB 334.

Similar reasoning can be found in *City of London Corporation v Appleyard* [1963] 1 WLR 982 where the Council, as the owner of a building which was being demolished, was held to be entitled to the contents of a safe which the demolition crew found recessed into the building's wall. It was also the basis of the decision in *Ranger v Giffin* (1968) 87 WN (Pt 1) (NSW) 531 where workmen excavating soil from under a house owned by the Schindlers to extend their garage found a tin containing £8500 in notes. It was held that, because the money's true owners could not be found, the Schindlers, as owners of the freehold, had the best claim to it. Likewise, in *Webb v Ireland* [1988] IR 353, where a hoard of treasure was found in the land of a ruined abbey, it was held that the owner of the land was entitled to any chattel found in it even if the finder was excavating it with the owner's consent.

[13.41] When something is found *on* someone else's property (as opposed to in, under or attached to it) the answer to the question 'who has the greater possessory rights' depends on whether the owner of the land (or its lawful possessor) intended to exercise control over not only the land but also whatever was on it. The rule is that if something is found on land the landowner (or its lawful possessor) will *only* have a better title than the finder 'if he exercised such *manifest control* over the land as to indicate an intention to control the land and everything that might be found on it' (emphasis added): per Auld LJ in *Waverley Borough Council v Fletcher* [1996] QB 334 at 346. Whether a property owner has exercised the necessary 'manifest control' or 'dominion' over his or her property is on it is, in all cases, a question of fact and degree.

> ### Case Example
>
> Bridges found a small parcel of banknotes on the floor of Hawkesworth's shop. He handed the parcel to Hawkesworth and asked him to keep the notes until the owner claimed them. They were not claimed and, three years later, Bridges asked for the money. Hawkesworth refused to hand it over. It was held that, as the finder, Bridges had the better claim to the notes. Hawkesworth had not known that the parcel had been dropped and, therefore, he had not in any sense exercised control over it — the banknotes had never been in his custody or 'within the protection of his house'. As Donaldson LJ subsequently explained (in *Parker v British Airways Board* [1982] 1 QB 1004 at 1012), 'the unknown presence of the notes on the premises occupied by Mr Hawkesworth could not, without more, give him any rights or impose any duty upon him in relation to the notes'. Bridges was entitled to the money: *Bridges v Hawkesworth* (1851) 21 LJQB 75; 18 LT 154.

> ### Case Example
>
> Parker found a gold bracelet in British Airways' executive lounge. He handed it to the airline which, when the bracelet was not claimed, sold it. Parker demanded the proceeds of sale. British Airways refused to give them to him. The court held that Parker had the better title to the bracelet (and, therefore, a better right to receive the money). British Airways had not established that it had 'a manifest intention to exercise control over the lounge and all things which might be in it' and, therefore, had never been in legal possession of the bracelet. British Airways' control over its lounge was really limited to the lounge itself and did not extend to things which were in it from time to time: *Parker v British Airways Board* [1982] 1 QB 1004.

The court in *Parker v British Airways Board* indicated that the decision would have been quite different if the gold bracelet had been found, say, on the floor of a private home. In that case, it said, the 'manifest intention' of the owner (or lawful possessor) of the house to control not only the premises but also any chattels found in or on them would have been clear.

Employees as finders

[13.42]   Where employees (or agents) find something in the course of their employment (or agency), they must account for it to their employers (or principals) and, if the true owner cannot be found, the employer (or principal) generally has the best claim to it. So, for example, in *Willey v Synan* (1937) 57 CLR 200, a boatswain who found a bag of coins while searching his ship for stowaways could not keep them because they had never been legally in his possession. At best, they may have been in his 'custody' because, as an employee who had found them in the course of doing what he was employed to do (searching the ship), Willey had to account for them to his employer. The court relied heavily on the decision in *M'Dowell v Ulster Bank* (1899) 33 Ir L T Jo 223, in which it was held that a bank porter, who found a roll of banknotes near the tables on which customers wrote out their cheques, could not keep them. Because he had found the notes in the course of his employment (his duties involved picking up lost property and handing it over to the bank), the bank was the legal possessor and, as his employer, it was the 'person' entitled to them.

[13.43]   The critical determinant in both of those cases was the fact that the finding had occurred 'in the course of the employee's employment'. If that had not been the case the employees would have been able to keep, respectively, the coins and the banknotes. That is, if the employment or agency is merely *incidental* to the finding and not its *effective cause*, the employee or agent will be the legal possessor and, therefore, can keep whatever has been found.

Case Example

A police constable performing special duty directing traffic at a drive-in theatre found a gold ingot near the theatre's exit. The Crown claimed the ingot, arguing that the plaintiff had found it in the course of his employment. It was held that merely being on duty at the theatre was not the real cause of his find, it simply afforded him the opportunity to make it. He had not acquired possession of the ingot *by reason of* the fact that he was a constable or in the performance of his duties (he was not required to look for lost property). The fact that he was on duty when he found it was merely coincidental. Consequently, he could keep it. As Gibbs J put it at 148, 'To give the master a right to a chattel found by his servant, it is clearly not enough that the servant happened to be going about his duties when he found it, for the fact that he was performing his duties may have been accidental, and not the cause of the finding': *Byrne v Hoare* [1965] Qd R 135.

Rights and obligations of finders and occupiers

[13.44]   Donaldson LJ summarised what he saw as the rights and obligations of a finder and the rights and liabilities of an occupier of premises in *Parker v British Airways Board* [1982] 1 QB 1004 at 1017–18 in words subsequently accepted and endorsed in *Waverley Borough Council v Fletcher* [1996] QB 334. He said:

Rights and Obligations of the Finder
1.   The finder of a chattel acquires no rights over it unless (a) it has been abandoned or lost and (b) he takes it into his care and control.
2.   The finder of a chattel acquires very limited rights over it if he takes it into his care and control with dishonest intent or in the course of trespassing.
3.   … a finder of a chattel, whilst not acquiring any absolute property or ownership in the chattel, acquires a right to keep it against all but the true owner or those in a position to claim through the true owner or one who can assert a prior right to keep the chattel which was subsisting at the time when the finder took the chattel into his care and control.
4.   Unless otherwise agreed, any servant or agent who finds a chattel in the course of his employment or agency and not wholly incidentally or collaterally thereto and who takes it into his care and control does so on behalf of his employer or principal who acquires a finder's rights to the exclusion of those of the actual finder.

5. A person having a finder's rights has an obligation to take such measures as in all the circumstances are reasonable to acquaint the true owner of the finding and present whereabouts of the chattel and to care for it meanwhile.

Rights and Liabilities of an Occupier

1. An occupier of land has rights superior to those of a finder over chattels in or attached to that land and an occupier of a building has similar rights in respect of chattels attached to that building, whether in either case the occupier is aware of the presence of the chattel.

2. An occupier of a building has rights superior to those of a finder over chattels upon or in, but not attached to, that building if, but only if, before the chattel is found, he has manifested an intention to exercise control over the building and the things which may be upon it or in it.

3. An occupier who manifests an intention to exercise control over a building and the things which may be upon or in it so as to acquire rights superior to those of a finder is under a obligation to take such measures as in all circumstances are reasonable to ensure that lost chattels are found and, upon their being found, whether by him or by a third party, to acquaint the true owner of the finding and to care for the chattels meanwhile ...

4. An 'occupier' of a chattel, for example, a ship, motor car, caravan or aircraft, is to be treated as if he were the occupier of a building for the purposes of the foregoing rules.

Summary and key terms

[13.45]   This chapter has set out to explain the following:
- The term 'property' refers to both '*items of property*' and '*property rights*'.
- Property can be classified as either *real* or *personal property*.
- Real property consists not only of the land but of everything attached to or forming part of it.
- Fixtures are things permanently affixed to land — whether something has become a fixture depends on the *purpose* and the *degree of its annexation*.
- The tenant can usually remove tenants' fixtures at the end of the lease.
- Personal property divides into *chattels real* and *chattels personal*. Chattels personal divide into *choses in possession* and *choses in action*.
- The rights of *ownership and of possession* are separate and distinct and the owner of property can alienate one without necessarily alienating the other.
- Property can be *co-owned*. The most common forms of co-ownership are *joint tenancy* and *tenancy in common*.
- Possessors of property have better rights than anyone except the true owners.
- Finders *acquire possessory ownership* unless their find is in the course of employment or on property over which someone else exercises a complete dominion.

14

Intellectual Property

What this chapter does ...

As was seen in Chapter 13, ownership of property can be either original or derivative. Most property is derived from others by purchase, gift or inheritance. Some, however, can be acquired originally as, for example, when an angler catches a fish, an author writes a book or an inventor creates a new invention. Just as the law protects the angler's ownership and possession of his or her fish so too does it protect the rights of authors and inventors over their creations. However, authors and inventors have a particular problem in that their creation is susceptible not only to theft but also to unauthorised copying and use. Accordingly, to protect their rights fully, they must be able either to prevent any unauthorised copying or use or, if it has occurred, to take action for just compensation.

The interests that need that sort of protection are referred to, in law, as intellectual property (or, occasionally, industrial property), and, in Australia, they are protected by a number of Commonwealth statutes. The more important forms of intellectual property and the Acts that protect them are:

- copyright (protected by the Copyright Act 1968 (Cth));
- designs (protected by the Designs Act 1906 (Cth));
- patents (protected by the Patents Act 1990 (Cth)); and
- trade marks (protected by the Trade Marks Act 1995 (Cth)).

These forms of intellectual property and the statutory provisions that affect them are dealt with in this chapter.

Copyright

What is copyright?

[14.1]   As its name suggests, copyright is simply the right to reproduce or copy something and the Copyright Act is designed to ensure that the owner of a copyright has, as s 31(1) puts it (at least in relation to 'works') the exclusive right (inter alia)

> (a) in the case of a literary, dramatic or musical work, to do all or any of the following acts:—
> (i) to reproduce the work in a material form;
> (ii) to publish the work;
> (iii)to perform the work in public;
> (iv)to broadcast the work;
> (v) to cause the work to be transmitted to subscribers to a diffusion service;
> (vi)to make an adaptation of the work;

(vii)to do, in relation to a work that is an adaptation of the first-mentioned work, any of the acts specified in relation to the first-mentioned work in sub-paragraphs (i) to (v), inclusive, of this paragraph; and

(b) in the case of an artistic work, to do all or any of the following acts:-

(i) to reproduce the work in a material form;

(ii) to publish the work;

(iii)to include the work in a television broadcast;

(iv)to cause a television programme that includes the work to be transmitted to subscribers to a diffusion service.

Of necessity, giving the copyright owner the exclusive right to do all or any of those things means that he or she must also have the right to prevent others from doing them, at least without proper authority or permission.

[14.2]   Section 196 of the Copyright Act provides that 'copyright is personal property'. It is an incorporeal right (a personal right or interest which is not of a tangible nature — a species of chose in action: see **[13.8]**).

However, a work that is subject to copyright and the copyright in that work are quite separate assets. They may belong to different people and they may be protected in different ways. An illustration of the difference can be found in *Re Dickens; Dickens v Hawksley* [1935] Ch 267. That case concerned a life of Christ that Charles Dickens had written for his family's use and which was not published during his life. When he died Dickens left all of his private papers (which included the manuscript to the life of Christ) to his sister-in-law and all of his remaining property to his children. While the manuscript itself clearly belonged to his sister-in-law, it was held that the copyright in that manuscript, as a separate incorporeal chattel in its own right, belonged to his children. The same reasoning was applied in *Moorhouse v Angus and Robertson (No 1)* [1981] 1 NSWLR 700 in which an author was held to be entitled to demand the return of a manuscript which he had sent to his publishers even though he had granted them the exclusive right to print, publish and sell the work that it contained in Australia and elsewhere. As a separate item of property the manuscript, as a document, still belonged to him.

What is protected?

[14.3]   Copyright only extends to something that has been given physical form. Copyright does not protect ideas as such. Therefore, if someone gives an author an idea for a book or a songwriter an idea for a song, he or she gets no copyright in the book or song when it is completed.

Case Example

The plaintiff, a jockey, claimed copyright in a number of articles which had been written by a journalist to whom he had recounted his experiences and which had been published in the defendant's newspaper. He failed. The court held that what he had given the journalist was simply an idea for a story and that the story itself was the journalist's creation. Consequently, because he had 'clothed the idea in form', the journalist owned the copyright in the finished articles: *Donoghue v Allied Newspapers Ltd* [1938] 1 Ch 106.

This restriction on what can be protected has a number of ramifications. First, as was the case in *Donoghue v Allied Newspapers Ltd*, those who merely pass on ideas have no rights in the finished product unless there is some agreement to the contrary. Second, two or more people can have the same or a similar idea, can produce similar works, can both have copyright in their own work and neither will have infringed the other's copyright. Mere similarity, without copying, does not constitute an infringement of copyright.

Copyright Act 1968 (Cth)

[14.4]   The Copyright Act 1968 (Cth) extends its protection to two broad categories of intellectual property — original literary, dramatic, musical and artistic *works* (Pt III of the Act), and 'subject-matter *other than works*' including sound recordings, films, television and sound broadcasts and published editions of works (that is, the way in which a particular edition of a work is set out as opposed to the already copyright material that it contains — Pt IV of the Act). In neither case are there any registration requirements. Once something protected by the Act comes into existence copyright arises and, thereafter, the copyright in it will be protected. (In Australia something will, normally, only be covered by copyright if it falls within the scope of the Copyright Act because s 8 provides that, generally, copyright subsists only by virtue of the Act.)

Copyright in works

[14.5]   Part III of the Act deals with the protections accorded 'original literary, dramatic, musical and artistic works' whether published or unpublished: s 32. Therefore, whether something is protected by Pt III depends upon whether it is 'original' and, if so, whether it can be properly classified as a 'literary, dramatic, musical or artistic work'.

Originality

[14.6]   The requirement for originality simply means that the final product for which copyright is claimed must, itself, be original. Because there is no copyright in ideas, the idea upon which it is based can be borrowed but what is produced using that idea must be original. This simply means that the end product must be the author's own work in the sense that it results from his or her own skill and effort and that it is not copied from somewhere else. It has been held that, in copyright law, the word 'copy' is construed strictly and that it refers to 'literal transcription'. Consequently, in *John Fairfax & Sons Pty Ltd v Consolidated Press Ltd* [1960] SR (NSW) 413 the *Sydney Daily Telegraph* was held not to have infringed the *Sydney Morning Herald's* copyright when it republished Birth and Death Notices that had appeared in earlier editions of the *Herald* because, before republishing them, the *Telegraph* had altered them in various ways. The *Herald* only had copyright in the form in which the announcements had appeared in its newspaper and, as this form had not been copied exactly when the announcements appeared in the *Telegraph*, the *Telegraph* had not infringed the *Herald's* copyright.

Literary works

[14.7]   Essentially, a literary work is something which is intended to provide information, instruction or literary enjoyment. Therefore, books (both educational and others), short stories, anthologies and similar works all qualify though things that might be thought to have no literary merit at all, such as catalogues and examination papers, have also been held to be literary works and, therefore, within the protection of the Copyright Act.

The term 'literary work' is not exhaustively defined and s 10 merely provides that:

literary work includes:

(a) a table or compilation, expressed in words, figures or symbols (whether or not in a visible form); and

(b) a computer program or compilation of computer programs.

Consequently, the term is wide enough to include things such as racing programs (*Mander v O'Brien* [1934] SASR 87) and lists of a newspaper's promotional bingo numbers: *Mirror Newspapers Ltd v Queensland Newspapers Pty Ltd* [1982] Qd R 305. The specific inclusion of computer programs and compilations of computer programs was inserted in 1984 to overcome perceived problems arising out of the Federal Court's decision in *Apple Computer Inc v Computer Edge Pty Ltd* (1984) 53 ALR 225 in which it was held that copyright did not subsist in certain kinds of computer programs. Under those amendments copyright in computer programs is now protected even where the programs have no physical manifestation and are simply stored on microchips. See *Autodesk Inc v Dyason* (1992) 173 CLR 330 where the High Court held (at 335) that the term 'computer program' included not only written programs but also 'the stored set of instructions in a non-sensate form such as electrical impulses'.

However, to be a literary work the 'work' must have real substance. For example, in *Victoria Park Racing and Recreation Grounds Co Ltd v Taylor* (1937) 58 CLR 479 the High Court held that there was no copyright in a series of numbers signifying race results because the list was not the result of any original work. It was merely a statement of knowledge already in the public domain. Similarly, to be a literary work the work must actually provide some form of information, instruction or literary pleasure. Consequently, mere names and titles do not normally qualify and, therefore, are not protected by copyright. For example, in *Exxon Corp v Exxon Insurance Consultants International Ltd* [1982] Ch 119 the Exxon Corp failed, in a copyright action, to restrain the defendant company from using the word 'Exxon' as part of its name. Because the name 'Exxon' was not a 'literary work' (in the sense that it did not afford information, instruction or literary enjoyment) and was, instead, simply an artificial combination of letters used for identification purposes, it was not protected. (Though it would have been protected if it had been registered as a trade mark: see [14.33]. Alternatively, in Australia, Exxon could have taken action under the misleading and deceptive conduct provisions of the Trade Practices Act or brought an action for passing off: see [16.82]ff.)

Dramatic works

[14.8]   Dramatic works are those which are intended to be publicly presented or performed. Therefore, plays and monologues are dramatic works. Section 10 also includes choreographic and other dumb shows within the definition, provided they are described in writing in the form in which the show is to be presented (so ballets and mime shows could qualify). It also includes scenarios or scripts for films (though not the film itself — because films are separately protected under Pt IV of the Act).

Musical works

[14.9]   Musical works are not defined in the Act and, therefore, they have their ordinary meaning. Musical scores and lyrics are both included.

Artistic works

[14.10]   Section 10 defines an 'artistic work' as meaning paintings, sculptures, drawings, engravings or photographs as well as buildings or models of buildings (in all cases with the qualification 'whether the work is of artistic quality or not') and works of 'artistic craftsmanship' which are not covered by any of those specific inclusions. The section also provides specific, though not exhaustive, definitions of the terms 'sculpture', 'drawing', 'engraving', 'photograph' and 'building'.

From s 10 it is clear that whether something is or is not an artistic work depends not so much on its artistic merit as on whether it qualifies as a painting, sculpture, drawing, engraving, photograph, building or model of a building. If it does, it is an artistic work; if it does not, it is not. The sole exception to the lack of any requirement for artistic merit is in relation to 'works of artistic craftsmanship' which do not fall within the specific inclusions. Whether something is a work of 'artistic craftsmanship' is difficult to define given the fairly nebulous nature of what might be regarded as artistic. However, in *Cuisenaire v Reed* [1963] VR 719, Pape J used as his test, whether the person who made the article applied skill and taste to its production with the main object of creating something with substantial aesthetic appeal even though it may also have been intended to be intrinsically useful. In that case the Cuisenaire rods (a set of multi-coloured rods of different sizes designed to help primary school students learn mathematics) were held not to be works of artistic craftsmanship because there was neither any real skill involved in their production nor were they designed to appeal to the aesthetic sense of purchasers.

Subject matter other than works

[14.11]   Part IV of the Act provides for copyright in sound recordings, films, broadcasts and published editions. The protection which Pt IV provides is slightly different to that which s 31 provides for 'works'. Instead of a general protection, the Pt IV rights depend upon the specific subject matter under consideration. For example, copyright in relation to a sound recording is the exclusive right to make a record embodying the recording, to cause the recording to be heard in public, to broadcast the recording or to enter into a commercial rental agreement in respect of the recording: s 85. For films, copyright is the exclusive right to make a copy of the film, to cause the film to be seen or heard in public, to broadcast the film or to cause it to be transmitted to subscribers to a diffusion service: s 86. For television and sound broadcasts, copyright is the exclusive right to make films or sound recordings of a broadcast (or copies of such films or records embodying such a recording) and to re-broadcast any such broadcast: s 87. With published editions of works copyright is the exclusive right to make, by a means that includes a photographic process, a reproduction of the edition: s 88.

Who is protected?

[14.12]   The person protected by copyright is the person in whom copyright in the work (or the subject matter other than a work) subsists.

For 'works', s 35(2) provides that generally 'the author of a literary, dramatic, musical or artistic work is the owner of any copyright subsisting in [it]'. To this there are three exceptions.

- When journalists produce a literary, dramatic or artistic work as part of their employment for a newspaper, magazine or similar periodical they retain copyright but only insofar as it relates to reproducing the work in a book or photocopying if after publication. For all other purposes the proprietor of the newspaper, magazine or periodical is the owner of the copyright.

- Similarly, under s 35(5) copyright in photographs taken for a private or domestic purpose and portraits and engravings that have been made under a specific commission normally subsists in the person who commissioned the photograph, portrait or engraving, provided the person who took the photograph, painted the portrait or engraved the engraving was paid to do it.
- Apart from these instances, where a literary, dramatic or artistic work (other than those discussed above) is created in the course of employment, the creator's employer, rather than the creator, owns the copyright in that work: s 35(6).

With 'subject matter other than works' copyright is generally owned by the person who made the sound recording, the film, the television or sound broadcast or who published the edition. However, as with the Pt III provisions, if a sound recording or film is made for valuable consideration, for someone other than its creator, then that other party will, normally, own any copyright in the recording or film: ss 97–100.

How long does copyright subsist?

[14.13]   With literary, dramatic and musical works and artistic works other than photographs, copyright continues for the duration of the author's lifetime and for 50 years thereafter if the work was 'published' during the author's lifetime. Where the work was not published during the author's lifetime, copyright subsists for 50 years from the calendar year in which it is first published: s 33. 'Publication' in this context simply means to make public something which was not previously public and 'making something public' simply means supplying it to the public whether by sale or otherwise, in sufficient quantities to satisfy the public's reasonable requirements: s 29.

Where the author's identity is unknown because the work was produced either anonymously or under a pseudonym, copyright continues for 50 years after the calendar year in which the work was first published: s 34(1). If, however, the identity of the author can be ascertained the work ceases to be regarded as anonymous or pseudonymous and the standard 50 years calculated from the year of the author's death, instead of from first publication, will apply. Where works are the subject of joint authorship and the duration of copyright is dependent on the life of an author, the copyright protection runs from the death of the last surviving joint author: s 80.

With photographs and engravings copyright continues until 50 years after the end of the calendar year in which the photograph or engraving was first published. With sound recordings, films and broadcasts copyright subsists for a period of 50 years from the date on which the recording or the film was first published, or the broadcast was first made: ss 93–95. Copyright in published editions of a work continues for 25 years after the end of the calendar year in which the edition was first published: s 96.

Infringements

[14.14]   Section 36(1) provides that 'the copyright in a literary, dramatic, musical or artistic work is infringed by a person who, not being the owner of the copyright, and without the licence of the owner of the copyright, does in Australia, or authorises the doing in Australia of, any act comprised in the copyright'. The acts comprised in the copyright of such works are, of course, those set out in s 31: see **[14.1]**. Therefore, for example, in *Australasian Performing Right Association v Telstra* (1995) IPR 289, Telstra was held to have infringed copyright when it supplied music to callers 'on hold'. The Federal

345

Court held that it had infringed the copyright owner's exclusive rights 'to broadcast the work' and/or 'to cause the work to be transmitted to subscribers to a diffusion service'.

In addition, copyright in 'works' will be infringed if someone, without the licence of the owner of the copyright, imports an article into Australia for the purpose of selling, hiring, distributing or exhibiting it when the importer was aware that, had the article been made in Australia, it would have infringed the copyright owner's copyright: s 37. Copyright will also be infringed if someone sells or hires or, by way of trade, exhibits an article in public where he or she knew that making the article constituted an infringement of copyright or, if it was imported, that making it would have constituted an infringement of copyright: s 38. These provisions prevent 'parallel importation' and protect the owners of the *Australian copyright* in works from infringement by the owners of the *overseas copyright* in the same works.

Case Example

Time-Life had an exclusive licence from the American publisher of a series of cookery books to publish them everywhere in the world — except in the United States. Time-Life retailed the books in Australia for $16.95. Angus & Robertson, a retail bookseller owned by the appellants, purchased copies of the same books from a Californian wholesaler (at prices well below those for which they were available in Australia), intending to sell them in its Sydney bookshops for $8.95. The High Court held that, because the appellants had not imported the books under licence, they had infringed the respondent's Australian copyright: *Interstate Parcel Express Co Pty Ltd v Time-Life International (Nederlands) BV* (1977) 138 CLR 534.

Under s 44A 'non-infringing books' (books which were legitimately published in their country of origin) which were *first published overseas* can now be imported into Australia without restriction. However, to protect the local publishing industry, the restriction on parallel importation of books which were *first published in Australia* has been only partly relaxed so that importation of commercial quantities are still effectively prohibited — unless the book cannot be supplied from Australian sources within 90 days of it being ordering. Section 44A does not apply to musical scores, computer software manuals or periodicals.

Similarly, ss 44D and 112D permit imports of 'non-infringing copies of sound recordings'. Consequently parallel importation of legitimately copyrighted (that is, not pirated copies of) CDs and other sound recordings is now legal and the previous monopoly on the import of CDs which was held by a number of multinational record companies no longer applies. In line with this change the Act has also been amended to increase penalties for importation of pirated CDs and a number of other measures have been introduced to protect legitimate importations and the Australian music industry.

[14.15] Copyright in a literary, dramatic or musical work is infringed by anyone who *permits* a place of public entertainment to be used for the performance in public of the work where the performance constitutes an infringement of copyright, unless that person can show that he or she was not aware and had no reasonable grounds for suspecting that the performance would be an infringement or that he or she gave the permission gratuitously, for a nominal consideration or for a consideration representing cost recovery: s 39.

This means, for example, that theatre owners as well as theatre companies can be liable if a copyright owner's consent is not obtained before a play or musical is performed.

With 'subject matter other than works' copyright will be infringed if someone who is not the owner of the copyright does or authorises any act comprised in the copyright without the licence of the holder. Acts comprised in the copyright are those set out in ss 85–88: see **[14.11]**. In addition, as with the infringement provisions relating to 'works', it is also an infringement to knowingly import infringing copies for sale or hire or to sell, hire or, by way of trade, exhibit infringing articles in public: ss 102–103.

Non-infringing dealings

[14.16]   Clearly, it is not an infringement of copyright to do something with the consent (or licence) of the copyright owner. In addition, there are a number of public interest defences. Specifically, the Act provides that fair dealing — for the purposes of research and study, or for criticism or review, or for reporting of news in the media or for the purposes of judicial proceedings or for giving professional advice — is not an infringement of copyright. 'Fair dealing' is not defined, though the various fair dealing sections (ss 40–43) do provide some individual guidance for specific categories of 'fair dealing'. Under these provisions copying a 'reasonable portion' of a copyright work, any copying by educational institutions for educational purposes, any library photocopying and any copying done under statutory licence are normally not infringements of copyright. Public readings, performances at home, copying of artistic works in public places, depictions of buildings and incidental inclusions of artistic works in films or television broadcasts as well as a number of other specific inclusions are also covered in the statutory exceptions.

Remedies for infringement

[14.17]   Section 115 specifically provides that 'the owner of a copyright may bring an action for an infringement of the copyright'. However, s 134 limits this right by providing that actions cannot be brought 'after the expiration of six years from the time when the infringement took place'.

A number of specific statutory remedies for infringement are laid down in s 115 which provides that the court may grant a copyright owner an injunction and either damages or an account of profits as well as, in the case of flagrant infringements, 'such additional damages as it considers appropriate in the circumstances'. Under s 116, a copyright owner may also bring an action for conversion or detention to recover any infringing copies of the copyright material (or the device used for making them). Relief granted under s 116 is *in addition* to any relief granted under s 115 — though the Act specifically provides that relief *is not* to be granted under s 116 *if* relief under s 115 would be a sufficient remedy.

The only real protection that an infringer of copyright has under ss 115 and 116 is the provision, in both sections, that, where the infringement was essentially innocent, the damages that can be awarded are restricted, under s 115, to an account of profits and, under s 116, to costs.

In addition to the statutory remedies, a copyright owner may also be able to obtain an Anton Piller order (named after *Anton Piller KG v Manufacturing Processes Ltd* [1976] 1 Ch 55 in which the order was first granted). An Anton Piller order is an order from the court authorising the plaintiff or his or her representatives to enter the defendant's premises to search for and take into custody both documents relating to any possible infringement and any infringing copies of works or other subject matter to prevent those documents or infringing copies being destroyed or disposed of before a normal copyright action can be heard.

Penal sanctions under the Act

[14.18]   Finally, in addition to the civil sanctions, the Copyright Act also provides for a number of penal sanctions. Some infringements of copyright are also offences which are punishable, normally by a fine but, in some cases, by imprisonment. Examples of illegal infringing activity include making articles for sale or hire, selling, hiring or offering articles for sale or hire, exhibiting articles in public, distributing articles for any purpose that prejudicially affects the rights of the owner of the copyright, importing articles for illegal purposes and being in possession of articles for illegal purposes — where the person doing any of those acts knows or ought reasonably to know that he or she is infringing another person's copyright. It is also an offence to cause a literary, dramatic or musical work to be performed in public or a sound recording to be heard in public or a film to be seen in public at a place of public entertainment if the person showing it knows or ought reasonably to know that copyright is, thereby, going to be infringed.

Assignments and licences

[14.19]   Because copyright is personal property it can be dealt with in the same way as all other forms of personal property and, in particular, s 196(1) specifically makes it 'transmissible by assignment, by will and by devolution by operation of law'.

An 'assignment' is simply a transfer of the copyright from the copyright owner to someone else. To be effective it must be in writing and must be signed by or on behalf of the assignor. The assignment may be limited (so that, for example, the rights are restricted to a specific geographic area or to one of the exclusive rights comprised in the copyright — see s 31(1)) or it may be unlimited.

'Licences' are not transfers of the copyright itself but merely authorisations which permit the licensee to do something which, without the licence, would be an infringement of copyright. Licences may be either exclusive or non-exclusive. An exclusive licence, as defined in s 10, is 'a licence in writing, signed by or on behalf of the owner ... of copyright, authorising the licensee, to the exclusion of all other persons, to do an act that, by virtue of this Act, the owner of the copyright would, but for the licence, have the exclusive right to do'. An exclusive licensee has all the rights of enforcement of his or her interest that the copyright owner would otherwise have had.

Designs

Protection of designs

[14.20]   How particular products look may make them more attractive to consumers than rival products and, therefore, more saleable. Consequently, their 'design' has a commercial value which should be protectable. In Australia, design rights are currently protected under the Designs Act 1906 (Cth). (The Australian Law Reform Commission completed a comprehensive review of the designs legislation in 1995 and recommended substantial changes, focusing on the need to develop a new system to better meet the needs of Australian industry; the government's response to that report is being coordinated by IP Australia but, as yet, there have been no firm proposals for replacement legislation. For the time being, therefore, designs are still governed by the Designs Act 1906).

'Design' defined

[14.21]   Section 4(1) of the Designs Act defines the word 'design' to mean 'features of shape, configuration, pattern or ornamentation applicable to an article, being features that, in the finished article, can be judged by the eye, but does not include a method or principle of construction'. What is being therefore is not the article itself, nor the idea behind it nor its 'method or principle of construction' (those matters can be protected under the Patents Act 1990), but its external appearance — that which 'can be judged by the eye'. In other words, designs are concerned with how an article *looks*, not with how it *works*.

Even then, designs of a primarily literary or artistic character will not be registered because they are more appropriately protected under the Copyright Act 1968 (Cth). Examples (which are listed in reg 11) include book jackets, calendars, certificates, forms or other documents, dressmaking patterns, greeting cards, leaflets, maps, plans, post-cards, stamps, transfers and medals.

Designs can be either two-dimensional (in which case they will usually be registered as 'features of ... pattern or ornamentation') or three-dimensional (in which case they will usually be registered as 'features of shape [and/or] configuration'). Consequently, designs that appear on fabric, paper or other two-dimensional surfaces — which are used to make the material more visually attractive — can be protected under the Act but so too can designs of, for example, furniture, appliances and other three-dimensional objects.

Registrable designs

[14.22]   Only designs which comply with the s 4 definition and which are also 'new or original' (s 17) are registrable. What constitutes newness or originality sufficient to jus-tify registration is difficult to define and each case is necessarily viewed on its own merits. However, as a minimum the design must not have been previously registered, published, used or sold in Australia. Substantial novelty and individuality of appearance is also normally required — having regard to the nature of the article, the design of which is being submitted for registration.

Designs will not have the necessary novelty if they differ from another design that is already registered, published or used in Australia in respect of the *same article* only in immaterial details, or in features commonly used in the relevant trade, or if they are obvi-ous adaptations of a design that is registered, published or used in Australia in respect of any other article: s 17.

The registration process

[14.23]   The owner of an unregistered design can apply to register it. The 'owner' is usu-ally the person who created the design except where the design was commissioned, created under a contract of employment or where it has been assigned to someone else. In each of those cases the design is owned not by the creator but by, respectively, the per-son who commissioned it, the creator's employer or the design's assignee: s 19.

The owner applies for registration by lodging an application form, together with 'rep-resentations' (drawings, sketches, specimens, photographs, etc of the design sufficient to clearly identity it) at the Designs Office. The owner may supply, or the Registrar of Designs may require, a 'statement of novelty' (identifying the features for which 'nov-elty or originality is claimed') and a 'statement of monopoly' (indicating the features of the design over which the owner seeks monopoly). Separate applications are required for each article or set of similar articles to which the design is to be applied: s 20.

The Registrar may then either register or refuse to register the design. If the Registrar intends to refuse registration the applicant must be given an opportunity to be heard and if, after that hearing, registration is still refused, the applicant can appeal to a court. Registration, if it occurs, takes effect from the date on which the application was lodged (called the 'priority date'). Thereafter, the design is protected unless the registration is later invalidated because, for example, the design was not 'new or original' after all.

If a design is registered it is entered in the Register of Designs and a Certificate of Registration is issued. The Register is open to public inspection and, if members of the public believe that the design lacks novelty or originality, they can bring that belief to the Registrar's attention within 11 months of the 'priority date' and the Registrar will take it into account when determining whether to extend the period of registration. The initial registration comes into effect on the 'priority date' and ceases 12 months thereafter. However, the Registrar may, on application, extend the registration for a period of six years from the 'priority date' and, thereafter, may grant two further extensions each of five years (giving a maximum total possible registration period of 16 years): s 27A.

If an owner fails to seek an extension of registration before it lapses he or she can apply for 'restoration' of the design provided the application is made without undue delay and the Registrar is satisfied that the failure was unintentional. Registration cannot be extended beyond the 16 year total period and, once the 16 years have expired, the design is in the public domain and may be freely used by anyone.

Effect of registration

[14.24]   Once a design has been registered its owner has a monopoly in it, as long as it remains registered. That is, the owner has the exclusive right to use the design when making any article in respect of which that design is registered and may also take action to prevent, or be compensated for, any infringement of his or her rights by others.

Infringements

[14.25]   A registered design is infringed if someone, without its owner's licence or authority, applies it (or any fraudulent or obvious imitation of it) to articles in respect of which the design is registered, imports any article in respect of which the design is registered and to which the design (or any fraudulent or obvious imitation of it) has been applied, or sells or hires, or offers or keeps for sale or hire, any article to which the design (or any fraudulent or obvious imitation of it), has been applied in infringement of the monopoly in the design in Australia or elsewhere: s 30.

Remedies for infringement

[14.26]   Under s 30(2) the owner of a registered design may bring an action for infringement and the available remedies include an injunction and, at the option of the plaintiff, either damages or an account of profits: s 32B. The injunction is always available but damages or an account of profits may be refused if the defendant can satisfy the court that, at the time of the infringement, he or she was not aware the design was registered and that all reasonable steps to ascertain whether there was a monopoly in the design were taken. The courts can also order that any infringing articles and items such as moulds and dies from which infringing articles could be manufactured be either delivered up or destroyed.

Patents

Protection of inventions

[14.27]   New inventions clearly have a value to those who invent them and to those who want to exploit them. To protect that value, inventors (like authors and designers) need some means of controlling the use that others make of their work. In Australia, the rights of inventors are protected by the Patents Act 1990 (Cth).

What is a patent?

[14.28]   In essence, a patent is simply a monopoly granted by the Crown to an inventor, giving the inventor an exclusive right to exploit his or her invention for a specified period (the term of the patent), in exchange for detailed particulars of the invention being placed on the public record. There are two forms of patent available in Australia — the 'standard patent' and the 'petty patent'. (In 1997 the Minister for Science and Technology announced that petty patents would be replaced by a new 'Innovation Patent System' but legislation to effect that change has yet to be introduced into parliament).

Standard patents and petty patents differ in the degree of disclosure that is required before they will be granted, in the time it takes for them to be granted and in the term during which they subsist once they have been granted.

What can be patented?

[14.29]   Essentially, inventions can be patented but, to be patentable, the invention must fall within the ambit of s 18(1). The essential requirements are that the invention must be a 'manner of manufacture', it must be novel, it must involve an inventive step, it must be useful and it must not have been secretly used previously.

The requirement that the invention be a 'manner of manufacture' means it must be either a new product or a new process by which something can be manufactured. This prevents new ideas or discoveries, by themselves (that is, as opposed to the methods or apparatus for putting them into practice), being patented. It also prevents non-functional details of shape, configuration, pattern or ornamentation being patented (though they can and should be protected under the Designs Act 1906: see **[14.20]**.

Similarly, because an invention must be a 'method of manufacture', new developments not involving a new product or a new process such as, for example, new strains of crops cannot be patented (though, in appropriate circumstances they can be protected under other legislation, such as the Plant Variety Rights Act 1987 or the Circuit Layouts Act 1990). Section 18(2) also specifically provides that 'human beings, and the biological processes for their generation, are not patentable inventions'. So, for example, a process for cloning human beings would not be patentable.

Whether the invention is 'novel' and involves 'an inventive step' is determined by looking at it in the context of 'the prior art base'. Novelty essentially means that the 'invention' must never have been disclosed to the public in any form anywhere in the world before the patent application was filed. Inventions which are already known through publication or use are said to be 'in the public domain' and patents are not granted for 'inventions' in the public domain.

The requirement for an 'inventive step' simply means that the advance from the 'prior art base' must have involved an element of original thought and that it must not have been simply a step that would have been 'obvious to a person skilled in the relevant art in the light of the common general knowledge as it existed in the patent area before the priority date of the relevant claim'. The 'common general knowledge' is normally taken to mean that body of knowledge which is known or used by all those in the field of expertise in which the alleged 'invention' was developed.

The requirement that the invention be 'useful' simply means that it must be capable of doing what the inventor claims it can do in the way in which he or she claims it can do it. It does not mean that it must fulfil some worthwhile function in society or that it be commercially exploitable.

The prohibition on 'previous secret use' simply means that the inventor must not have used the invention and deliberately concealed that use from the public before applying for the patent (that is, the invention must still be 'new' in every sense of the word when the patent is applied for). The prohibition does not prevent the invention being used for reasonable trial and experiment or pursuant to a confidential disclosure or for a purpose other than trade or commerce before the inventor applies to patent it: s 9. What the prohibition is designed to do is to encourage registration of inventions and to discourage inventors from trying to extend their period of monopoly use by deliberately delaying patent applications until their de facto monopoly is threatened.

Obtaining a patent

[14.30]   Patents are obtained by filing a patent request, together with all the prescribed documents, with the Patent Office. The documents that must accompany the patent request will depend upon whether the patent being applied for is a 'standard patent' or a 'petty patent' and whether the application is a provisional application or a complete application. The specifics of the variables are beyond the scope of this chapter but there is a useful summary in IP Australia's 'Patent Application Kit' (available through IP Australia's homepage at http://www.ipaustralia.gov.au).

The next step is normally an examination of the patent application by a patent examiner to determine whether the 'specification' complies with the requirements of the Act and whether the invention is a 'patentable invention' in terms of s 18(1). The examination will also determine whether a patent should be refused for other reasons set out in the Act. If the examination reveals no lawful ground on which the application should be rejected, the request and specification must be accepted. Once that happens the applicant is notified and a notice of acceptance is published. If the general public has not already become aware of the invention the notice of acceptance will act as notification and will advise the public that the patent request and complete specification are open for inspection. Members of the public can then inspect the application and, if they wish, oppose the patent being granted on the grounds laid down in s 59. They include:

* that the invention is not a patentable invention;
* that the specification does not comply with the requirements of the Act; or
* that the nominated person is not entitled to the grant.

If the grant of a patent is opposed, the opposition is dealt with by the Commissioner (subject to an appeal to the Federal Court). If the opposition is unsuccessful or if there is no opposition, a patent will be granted. Petty patent applications are subjected to a much less strenuous process than applications for a standard patent and petty patents are usually granted within six months of application instead of the years that it can take to obtain a standard patent.

Patent rights

[14.31]   A patent gives the patentee the 'exclusive rights, during the term of the patent, to exploit the invention': s 13(1). This means that he or she has the exclusive rights to make, hire, sell or otherwise dispose of the patented product or to use the patented method or process for the purpose of making, hiring, selling or otherwise disposing of the product.

   The patentee can either exercise those rights personally or can license others to exercise them. In addition, because the patent is a species of personal property, he or she can sell, assign or otherwise dispose of those rights in total. The rights subsist, in the case of standard patents, for 20 years from the date on which the patent was sealed. With petty patents the patent rights exist, initially, for only 12 months from the date that the patent was sealed but, during the first 11 of those months (the time within which other parties can try to show why the petty patent should not be extended) the patentee can apply for a once-only extension of up to six years.

Infringements and remedies

[14.32]   A patent will be infringed if someone exercises any of the patentee's exclusive rights without the patentee's consent. Both the patentee and any exclusive licensee can sue anyone infringing patent rights. If they do, the court can grant an injunction and can also award either damages or an account of profits: s 122(1). As was the case with designs, however, a court can refuse to award damages or an account of profits if it is satisfied that, at the date of the infringement, the defendant was not aware, and had no reason to believe, that a patent existed: s 123.

Trade marks

[14.33]   Manufacturers of goods and providers of services try to gain and maintain market share by differentiating their products and/or services from their competitors' in all sorts of ways. One way of generating product recognition and brand identification is by using something which is readily distinguishable and which induces customers to remember and buy not only *a* version of the product but *your* version of that product. Therefore, for instance, the Coca-Cola and Pepsi-Cola companies devote a lot of time and energy to creating a clear public distinction between their respective products — Coke and Pepsi — so that people do not simply order 'a Cola' but a 'Coke' or a 'Pepsi'.

Definition of a trade mark

[14.34]   Section 17 of the Trade Marks Act defines a 'trade mark' as:

> a sign used, or intended to be used, to distinguish goods or services dealt with or provided in the course of trade by a person from goods or services so dealt with or provided by any other person.

   Therefore there are three features of a trade mark: it will be a 'sign', it will be used (or will be 'intended to be used') in relation to goods or services and it will be used to distinguish its registered owner's goods or services from goods or services dealt with or provided by any other person.

Sign

[14.35]   Section 6 defines the word 'sign' to include 'the following or any combination of the following, namely, any letter, word, name, signature, numeral, device, brand, heading, label, ticket, aspect of packaging, shape, colour, sound or scent'. Therefore, especially as the definition does not purport to be exhaustive, virtually any identifying symbol can be a 'sign' for trade mark purposes — provided it makes the public connect a particular product with a particular manufacturer or supplier.

In other words anything which promotes product recognition or brand identification can be a trade mark. Those things can include logos consisting of a letter (such as the stylised 'M' in McDonalds' 'Golden Arches'), a made-up word such as 'Kodak' or 'Aspro', the manufacturer's name or signature (such as those used on 'designer label' clothing), numerals (such as the distinctive 7 and 9 used as station identifiers by the two television networks), devices (such as Mercedes Benz's three pointed star), as well as other equally identifiable characteristics such as the product's packaging (David Jones' distinctive houndstooth), its shape (Coca-Cola's bottle), a colour (the shade of purple used in Cadbury chocolate wrappers), a sound (the ABC's news bulletin call sign, the distinctive burble of an MG's engine and even jingles, slogans and musical themes used in advertising, such as Toyota's 'Oh, what a feeling') or a scent (the distinctive beer smell registered by Unicorn Products in respect of its darts).

Used or intended to be used

[14.36]   The mark must be actively used or the applicant for registration must intend to use it to distinguish his or her goods or services. Trade marks cannot be registered just to prevent other people using them nor can they be registered to create a 'stock' of trade marks which the person registering them intends to sell rather than to use. If a registered trade mark is not being used it can be removed from the Register. The one exception is 'defensive trade marks' which are discussed in [14.43].

To distinguish goods or services

[14.37]   Because a trade mark is 'used to distinguish goods or services', applications for registration (and, therefore for protection) must specify the goods or services in respect of which the trade mark is going to be used and, therefore, for which registration is sought. The regulations provide 34 separate classes of goods and eight separate classes of services and applications for registration must specify the class (or classes) of goods or services to which the trade mark will be applied. That is, because registration gives the applicant an *exclusive* right to use the mark, he or she is only permitted to register it in relation to those goods on services in respect of which it is actually going to be used.

Registration

[14.38]   *Unregistered* trade marks can be used to promote goods and services but they are not protected by the Act. Therefore, if an *unregistered* trade mark is infringed its owner can only sue in 'passing off' (a tort discussed in [16.82]) or under the misleading and deceptive conduct provisions of the Trade Practices Act 1974 (Cth) (or the equivalent provisions of the various state and territory Fair Trading Acts). Both remedies can be involved and it is far easier to register the mark and use the protection mechanisms of the Trade Marks Act 1995 (Cth) instead.

The benefits of registration

[14.39] Under the Act the owners of registered trade marks have the exclusive right to use them (and to authorise others to use them) in respect of the goods and/or services for which they were registered: s 20(1). The owners can prevent the marks being used in respect of the same or substantially similar goods; they can also prevent infringing goods being imported (by giving the Australian Customs Service a notice objecting to their importation — s 132) and, if their trade mark is infringed, they can sue for either damages or an account of profits (s 126). The protection afforded by the Act applies throughout Australia and the trade mark does not have to be separately registered in each jurisdiction. Finally, because the trade mark is personal property, it can be transmitted by assignment, by will or otherwise by operation of law: ss 21 and 22. It can, therefore, be sold or disposed of either separately or as part of a sale of the owner's business.

The registration process

[14.40] Registration begins with the person claiming to be the trade mark's owner lodging an application with the Trade Marks Office within IP Australia: s 27. The owner can be an individual, a company, an unincorporated club, an association, a firm or a partnership. If more than one person claims to own the trade mark the application can be lodged jointly. The application has to be in the required form, it must include a graphical representation of the trade mark (applications must be rejected if the trade mark cannot be represented graphically — s 40) and it must specify the goods and/or services in respect of which the owner seeks to register the trade mark.

The application will then be examined to ensure that it has been made in accordance with the Act and that there are no grounds for rejecting it: s 31. A major ground for rejection is that the trade mark does not adequately distinguish the applicant's goods and/or services: s 41. For example, applications for the registration of a proposed trade mark that simply describes some aspect of the goods and/or services — such as 'safety matches' or 'delicious chocolate cake' or which are common surnames or geographical names will not normally be registered — because those words could describe the goods or services of every other supplier and, if they were registered, no one else would be able to use them. Applications will also be rejected if the proposed trade mark is likely to deceive or cause confusion (s 43), if it is substantially identical with or deceptively similar to an existing registered trade mark (s 44), if it is scandalous or if its use would be contrary to law: s 42.

If the application has been made in accordance with the Act and if there are no grounds for rejecting it, the Registrar must accept it (s 33(1)), the applicant will be notified and the acceptance will be advertised in the *Official Journal of Trade Marks*: s 34. That allows others to oppose registration. Notices of opposition may be lodged on any of the grounds on which the Registrar could have rejected the application (normally that the trade mark is substantially identical with or deceptively similar to an existing trade mark or that it is otherwise likely to deceive or cause confusion — see Div 2 of Pt V). If there is no opposition the trade mark is registered, details are recorded in the Register of Trade Marks and the registered owner is given a Certificate of Registration.

If the examination reveals a problem (the application may not be in accordance with the Act or there may be grounds for rejecting it) the Registrar will send the applicant a report detailing the matters that have to be addressed. If the applicant addresses those matters the application proceeds. If there is still a problem (or if there is opposition) the Registrar must give the applicant an opportunity to be heard and, following that hearing, must either accept (and ultimately register) the application or reject it. If the application is rejected the applicant can appeal to the Federal Court: ss 35 and 56.

If the trade mark is registered the initial period of registration is 10 years from the date of filing (s 72) but registration can be renewed indefinitely for further periods each of an additional 10 years: s 77.

Removal of the trade mark

[14.41]   If a trade mark is not being used it can be removed from the Register. That occurs if someone 'aggrieved by the fact that the trade mark is or may be registered' applies to the Registrar to remove it under s 92. That usually happens when that person has applied to use an identical or sufficiently similar trade mark and the application is being held up by the existence of the registered (but unused) trade mark. The application to remove the trade mark can be to remove it entirely or just in respect of some of the goods and/or services in respect of which it was registered. In either case the person applying for the removal must show either that the registered trade mark has not been used for three continuous years before the application to remove it was lodged or that, when the original application was filed, there was no bona fide intention to use it in relation to the goods and/or services to which the non-use application relates, and that it has not been so used.

The application is advertised in the *Official Journal of Trade Marks* and the trade mark's owner is notified. If he or she does not oppose the application the trade mark will be removed: s 97. If a notice of opposition is filed (s 96) the Registrar may either remove the trade mark from the Register (in respect of any or all of the goods and/or services to which the application relates), decide that the trade mark should not be removed (s 101) or, in certain circumstances, make its continued registration subject to conditions or limitations so that it cannot be used on goods or services dealt with or provided in a specified place or which are to be exported to a specified market: s 102.

Certification, defensive and collective trade marks

Certification trade marks

[14.42]   Certification trade marks are marks which indicate that the goods or services on which they appear comply with certain specified standards. They are designed to distinguish goods which have been certified by the owner of the certification trade mark 'in relation to their quality, accuracy or some other characteristic, including (in the case of goods) origin, material or mode of manufacture from other goods or services dealt with or provided in the course of trade but not so certified': s 169. The trade mark used by the Standards Association of Australia (which denotes that particular goods have met its minimum standards) is a good example of a certification mark.

As with all trade marks, certification marks must be distinctive before they will be registered and applicants for registration of a certification mark (who can now include individual traders) must be competent to certify the specified characteristics of the goods or the services being certified. Policing this is the responsibility of the Australian Competition and Consumer Commission: s 175. Once a certification mark has been registered, its registered proprietor has the exclusive right to use and to allow others to use it in relation to the goods and services in respect of which it is registered.

Defensive trade marks

[14.43]   As already seen, when the owner of a trade mark applies to register it, he or she must specify the class of goods and/or services in respect of which the trade mark is going to be used. Registration is then only granted in respect of those goods and/or services. The problem is that a well-known trade mark can still have appeal if it is applied to other goods and/or services (those in respect of which it is not registered and, therefore, in respect of which it is not protected). Consequently, if a registered trade mark has been used to such an extent, in relation to the goods or services in respect of which it has been registered, that it is *likely* that 'its use in relation to other goods or services would be taken to indicate that there is a connection between those other goods or services and the registered owner of the trade mark', it can be registered as a defensive trade mark in respect of those other goods and services — even though the owner of the trade mark does not intend to use it in respect of them: s 185. This allows the owner of a registered trade mark to prevent others from 'pirating' it for use on *other* goods or services. The Coca Cola, Levi's, Kelloggs and Holden trade marks (among others) have all been registered as defensive trade marks in Australia so, therefore, they cannot be used in respect of *any* goods or services — not just soft drinks, jeans, breakfast cereals or motor vehicles.

Collective trade marks

[14.44] A collective trade mark is 'a sign used, or intended to be used in relation to goods or services dealt with or provided in the course of trade by members of an association to distinguish those goods or services from goods or services so dealt with or provided by persons who are not members of the association': s 162. Trade marks used by members of the Motor Trades Industry Association (MTIA), by chains of independent retailers and by associations of real estate agents are good examples of collective trade marks.

Infringement and remedies

[14.45] Once a trade mark has been registered the registered proprietor has the exclusive right to use it in relation to the goods or services in respect of which it has been registered and to seek relief if that exclusive use is infringed.

A trade mark is infringed if someone other than the registered proprietor or a person acting with the registered proprietor's consent (s 123) uses the mark (or another mark which is substantially identical with or deceptively similar to the trade mark) in relation to goods or services (or similar goods and services) in respect of which the trade mark is registered: s 120. However, it is not an infringement if all that is being used is that person's own name (or that of a predecessor in his or her business), or the name of his or her place of business, or a bona fide description of the character or quality of his or her goods or services *if* that use is made in ignorance of the fact that it is an infringement of a registered trade mark: s 122. Infringement also occurs if someone imports and sells goods bearing a trade mark which is identical to, substantially identical to or deceptively similar to, an Australian registered trade mark.

Any actual or intended infringement of a registered trade mark may be prevented by injunction and the court can also award either damages or an account of profits: s 126. In addition, anyone who falsifies or unlawfully removes a registered trade mark (s 145), falsely applies one to goods (s 146), makes or possesses a die or block to be used to falsify a registered trade mark (s 147) or sells, possesses or imports goods to which a falsified mark has been applied (s 148) with the intent to defraud, is guilty of an offence and liable to a fine and/or imprisonment not exceeding two years. Aiding or abetting the commission of any of the above offences is also an offence: s 150.

Summary and key terms

[14.46]   This chapter has set out to explain:
- The four principal forms of intellectual property are copyright, designs, patents and trade marks.
- *Copyright* is the right to reproduce or copy something. It attaches to 'works' and to specified 'subject matter other than works'. It is normally owned by the person who produced the work or by someone to whom the copyright has been assigned and it normally subsists for the 'author's' life plus 50 years. Infringements can be dealt with by injunction, damages, an account of profits, orders for delivery of infringing copies and, criminally, by fines or imprisonment.
- *Designs* are features applicable to an article that can be judged by the eye. They are protected by registration, the result of which is that the owner of the design gets a monopoly over its use. He or she can protect that monopoly by means of injunctions, awards of damages, accounts of profits and orders for delivery or destruction of infringing copies.
- A *patent* is a monopoly granted by the Crown giving an inventor an exclusive right to exploit his or her invention for a specified time. Only 'inventions' which involve a manner of manufacture, which are novel, which involve an inventive step and which have not been secretly used before may be patented. Two types of patent are available — standard patents and petty patents. Both are obtained by filing a patent request with the required supporting documents. A patent holder can prevent infringements of his or her patent by injunction, or where an infringement has occurred, can sue for an award of damages or an account of profits.
- *Trade marks* are marks used to delineate the affiliation of particular goods or services. They are protected by registration and infringements are dealt with by injunctions, awards of damages (or accounts of profits), by orders for deletion of offending marks and by a number of criminal sanctions.

15

Bailment

What this chapter does ...

Chapter 13 dealt with the concept of property as the basic ingredient of almost all commercial transactions. It showed that it is possible for one person to own property while another has a lawful right to possession of it. This chapter will deal with one situation where ownership and possession of property is separated — where goods are 'bailed' from one person to another. It will discuss how bailments arise and how they terminate, what the respective rights, duties and liabilities of the bailor and the bailee are, and will look at the rules that apply to two special types of bailments — common carriers and common innkeepers.

What is bailment?

[15.1] 'Bailment' is simply a delivery of goods from one person (called the bailor) to another person (called the bailee) under an arrangement whereby, when the purpose for which the goods were bailed has been fulfilled, the bailee must either return them to the bailor, deal with them according to the bailor's directions or keep them until the bailor reclaims them.

All that passes in a bailment is possession — property in the goods remains with the bailor. That is what distinguishes a bailment from a sale or other transfer of ownership, such as an assignment or a gift. It is also what allows retention of title clauses to work: see **[6.15]**. Further, because the critical element in all bailments is the transfer of possession, traditional bailments only exist over tangible items of personal property.

Therefore, depositing money in a bank account is not a bailment (the bank does not have to return the *exact same* notes and coins to its customer — see **[11.23]**) but delivering it to a security firm to take it to the bank is. The difference is that in the latter case both parties intend that the security firm will deal with the bailor's *particular* notes and coins — of which it has possession — as the bailor directs. Therefore, the security firm, as bailee, is obliged to keep the customer's cash separate from other money in its possession and has to deliver it in accordance with the bailor's instructions: see *Brambles Security Services Ltd v Bi-Lo Pty Ltd* [1992] Aust Torts Reports 61,260.

Bailments can arise as the result of a contract, such as where the bailor hires a chattel (for example, a video or a dinner suit or a car) to the bailee or leaves a chattel so the bailee can work on it (as in contracts for repair) or simply leaves something for safekeeping where the bailee charges a fee (as might be the case when goods are left in a cloakroom or in a bank's safe custody vault). They can also arise independently of contract, such as where you simply lend a chattel to someone else without a fee, where you leave something with someone for safekeeping, again without fee, where a merchant sends you goods 'on approval' hoping you might buy them or where you simply find goods belonging to someone else.

Bailment and licences

[15.2] Because bailment involves possession and control of the goods passing to the bailee, bailments can be distinguished from mere licences. With licences possession and control does not pass and, therefore, the other person is not subject to the duties and liabilities of a bailee. A finding of bailment means (as will be seen in the discussion of bailee's duties below) that the bailee assumes responsibility for safeguarding the goods from loss, damage or destruction while they are (or should be) under his or her control.

In the absence of some specific contractual or other duty to take that level of care a mere licence does not involve that responsibility or potential liability.

Case Example

Greenwood went swimming at Bondi Beach. He changed in sheds owned and operated by the council and left his clothes in a locker provided by them for a fee which he paid. When he returned his clothes were missing. He sued the council alleging that it was in breach of its duties as a bailee. He failed. The Court held that merely placing clothes in a locker owned by the council did not make the council a bailee. It had never acquired possession or control of Greenwood's clothes either in fact or in intention. What had happened was that the council had hired him a locker. What he did with it was his business. In law, there was no bailment — there was merely a *licence* by the council allowing Greenwood to use its property for a specific purpose: *Greenwood v Municipal Council of Waverley* (1928) 28 SR (NSW) 219.

Whether leaving goods as Greenwood did constitutes a bailment or just a licence depends very much on the individual circumstances of each case and, in particular, on whether the alleged bailee assumed sufficient *possession of and control over* the goods to justify the inference that he or she had also undertaken a responsibility to safeguard them. The considerations that the courts take into account to make the determination include the nature of the goods and the circumstances in which they were left, any expectations or assumptions about the nature of the relationship that might reasonably have arisen from anything said between the parties or from their prior dealings and the alleged bailee's ability to secure and to control access to and redelivery of the goods.

The problem is well illustrated in the 'car-parking' cases — where cars left in car parks are stolen and the owners seek to make the facilities' operators liable for the loss. The critical question is whether the owners relinquished 'exclusive possession and control' of their cars. If so, the operators are likely to be bailees (and, therefore, at least potentially liable). If not, they are usually not responsible. Where a facility is open and the cars' owners are free to collect their cars and drive them away without going through a checkpoint or barrier the tendency has been to hold that there is no bailment — because there is no effective passage of exclusive possession and control. On the other hand, if the cars are physically parked by one of the car park's attendants or if the cars' owners have to leave the keys or if they have to produce a ticket before they can collect their cars the tendency has been to find that there is a bailment.

So, for example, in *Ashby v Tolhurst* [1937] 2 KB 242; **[16.77]**, where the plaintiff was simply allowed to park his car on the defendant's land for an up-front payment of one shilling, the court held that there was no bailment — because possession and control of the car had not passed. Similarly, in *Tinsley v Dudley* [1951] 1 All ER 252 a hotel keeper was held not to be the bailee of a motorbike which one of the hotel's patrons parked in the hotel car park while he was inside having a drink. On the other hand, the operators of the car parks in both *Sydney City Council v West* (1965) 114 CLR 481 and *Waltons Stores Ltd v Sydney City Council* (1968) 70 SR (NSW) 244 were held to be bailees because, in both cases, the cars' owners had to produce a ticket to reclaim possession of their vehicles and could not simply drive them away.

Bailed goods containing other goods

[15.3]   Determining whether possession and control has passed becomes more difficult if the goods bailed contained other goods. For instance, if I hand you a locked briefcase containing important papers, do you become bailee of the briefcase alone or are you also bailee of the papers? If I lend you my car do you also become bailee of the fur coat in the boot? The answers to questions like these are in two parts:

* If it was reasonable to assume that the item handed over contained goods of the same *type* that it did in fact contain, the bailment extends to the contents. Therefore, in the illustrations above the bailment would probably extend to the papers in the briefcase as well as to the briefcase itself. See, for example, *Moukataff v BOAC* [1967] 1 Lloyd's Rep 396 where £20,000 in banknotes being sent by registered mail from London to Kuwait were stolen by a baggage handler when the mailbags were being loaded onto the aeroplane. BOAC denied liability arguing that (inter alia), while it might have been a bailee of the mailbags, it was not a bailee of their contents. That argument failed. The court held that because BOAC knew that the mailbags contained mail and, in particular, that the red-labelled registered mailbags contained valuables, it had become a bailee of both the bags and their contents.

* If it was *not* reasonable to assume that the item actually delivered contained goods of the same *type* that it did in fact contain the *only* way in which the bailment can extend to the contents is if the bailor made specific mention of them *at the time of delivery*. See, for example, *Mendelssohn v Normand* [1969] 2 All ER 1215 where Mendelssohn was prevented from locking his car by a car park attendant. He informed the attendant that the car contained valuables and asked him to ensure that it was locked after it had been parked. When he returned he found the car unlocked and the valuables gone. The company was held liable. It had been a bailee of both the car and its contents *because* it had been put on notice that the car contained valuables.

Types of bailment

[15.4]   As indicated in **[15.1]**, bailments can arise in many ways, including simply leaving the chattel with someone to look after it, either with or without reward; leaving goods with someone to work on them, again either with or without reward; leaving them with a bailee so that he or she can use them, again either with or without reward; or simply leaving them as security for a loan (as is the case where goods are pledged or pawned): see *Coggs v Bernard* (1703) 2 Ld Raym 909; 92 ER 107.

This traditional classification of bailments once had a very real significance because the duties and liabilities of the parties (especially of the bailee) varied considerably according to the type of bailment and, in particular, according to the benefits that the respective parties gained from it. The old distinctions have now largely disappeared and the question of liability is now resolved mainly by asking whether the parties took reasonable care to carry out their respective duties *in the circumstances*.

A more useful distinction is between gratuitous bailments and bailments for reward. Gratuitous bailments differ from bailments for reward in that a lesser standard of care is normally required of gratuitous bailees (because of the different circumstances of the bailment), the bailment (not being for good consideration) is normally terminable at the will of the bailor and, because continued possession of the goods by gratuitous bailees is not assured, their ability to take action against third parties can be limited: see **[15.19]**.

The distinction between bailments and non-contractual bailments (including sub-bailments, gratuitous bailments and involuntary bailments — those which arise by finding goods or receiving unsolicited goods) can also be important. Contractual bailments are governed not only by the law of bailment (with the rights, duties and liabilities that it imposes) but also by the specific provisions of the parties' own contract.

Duties of the bailee

Generally

[15.5] The law of bailment imposes a number of duties on all bailees independent of contract. These include the duties to take due care of the goods, to retain possession of them, not to make unauthorised use of them and to return them in due course. If the bailment is contractual there may also be other duties — such as to pay any hire charges or, if work is to be done on the goods, to carry it out in a careful and competent manner.

To take due care of the goods

[15.6] While a bailee is not an insurer of the goods (and therefore not under a duty to take every possible care for them) he or she must take *reasonable care* to safeguard them from loss, damage or destruction. Failure to do so makes the bailee liable for negligence as a bailee. The care required is the care that 'a man of ordinary prudence would take for the preservation of his own property' (per Lord Diplock in *China Pacific SA v Food Corp of India, The Winston* [1982] AC 939 at 960) or the 'care and diligence ... which a careful and vigilant man would exercise in respect of goods of his own of the same kind in similar circumstances': per Windeyer J in *Hobbs v Petersham Transport Co Pty Ltd* (1971) 124 CLR 220 at 238.

The duty includes (inter alia) ensuring that adequate security measures are taken. So, for example, in *Pitt Son & Badgery Ltd v Proulefco SA* (1984) 153 CLR 644 a wool broker was held liable when an intruder gained access to a wool store, lit a fire and destroyed the wool. The broker had failed to take appropriate steps to ensure that the fence surrounding the store was adequate to keep intruders out. On the other hand, in *Nibali v Sweeting & Denny* [1989] Aust Torts Reports ¶80-258, where a motor being reconditioned for use in a drag racer was stolen from the repairers' premises, the repairer was held not liable. The court found that its premises were adequately secured and that it had taken all reasonable care for the security and safety of the motor. In other words, it had exercised 'the care and diligence which a careful and vigilant man would exercise in respect of his own motor in similar circumstances'.

In determining whether a bailee has done what was required in the circumstances the courts take into account considerations such as the value of the bailed goods, the location of the place of bailment (leaving a barn unlocked in the country might be reasonable, leaving a warehouse unlocked on an industrial estate in the city would not be), any fees paid by the bailor, the bailor's knowledge of the circumstances and situation in which the goods would be held for safekeeping, the practicality of adopting the required security measures and any history of thefts in the neighbourhood.

> **Case Example**
>
> The defendant was held liable when thieves entered its premises through a skylight and stole the plaintiff's motor vehicle, the keys of which had been left in the ignition. The court held that, even though the premises were located in a well-lit street adjacent to a busy bus depot and had not been the subject of break-ins or thefts for 15 years, the defendant had failed to exercise the standard of care that would have been expected of a careful and vigilant person in like circumstances. The fact that security bars, an alarm system and warning signs were all installed at minimal expense after the theft was held to be evidence that all those precautions were practicable and that they could and should have been taken before it: *Tottenham Investments Pty Ltd v Carburettor Services Pty Ltd* [1994] Aust Torts Reports ¶81-292.

The onus of proof in such cases lies mainly with the bailee — because he or she had possession of the goods and was in the better position to know what happened to them: see *Jackson v Cochrane* [1989] Qd R 23; **[15.10]**. The bailor has to show that the goods were lost, damaged or destroyed while they were in the bailee's care but it is then up to the bailee, if he or she wants to avoid liability, to show that the loss, damage or destruction was not due to negligence or default on his or her part: *Westpac Banking Corporation v Royal Tongan Airlines* [1996] Aust Torts Reports ¶81-403. The bailee can do this in two ways: by proving that he or she took reasonable care of the goods or, if that was not the case, that his or her failure to take reasonable care did not contribute to the loss — that is, by proving that the loss 'was not due to his fault': per Menzies J in *Hobbs v Petersham Transport Co Pty Ltd* [1971] 124 CLR 220 at 234.

To retain possession of the goods

[15.7] When goods are bailed it is assumed that they will (generally) remain in the bailee's possession unless the bailor consents (expressly or impliedly) to them being delivered to someone else. If that consent cannot be shown and if the goods are lost or damaged while they are outside the bailee's possession the bailee will be responsible not for breach of his or her duty of care but for breach of his or her duty to retain possession.

Sub-bailments

[15.8] The most common situation in which bailees give up possession (with or without the bailor's consent) is when a sub-bailment is created. Sub-bailments arise where a bailor (the head bailor) delivers his or her goods to a bailee who in turn delivers them to another person (called a sub-bailee) usually for a limited time or for a specific purpose. Such arrangements happen daily. For example, if you borrow a book from the library and then lend it to someone else or if you leave your car with a mechanic who sends it to an auto-electrician or if you give your goods to a carrier who engages someone else to store them, the subsidiary transfers of possession create sub-bailments.

In such cases, if the goods are lost, stolen, damaged or destroyed the sub-bailee may be liable — but so too may the bailee. The questions in each case are, who is liable — the bailee, the sub-bailee or both — and, if the sub-bailee is liable, to whom is he or she liable — just the bailee, just the bailor or both?

> ## Case Example
>
> Mrs Morris sent her mink stole to a furrier to be cleaned. The furrier did not do cleaning work and with Morris' consent he sent the mink to CW Martin & Sons Ltd, a well-known and reputable firm of cleaners. The mink was stolen by one of its employees. Mrs Morris sued. There was clearly no contractual relationship between Mrs Morris and CW Martin & Sons Ltd nor was there evidence that the company had been tortiously negligent in failing to take adequate steps to safeguard the mink. However, it was held liable on the grounds that it had failed to take reasonable care of the fur in its capacity as a sub-bailee for reward: *Morris v CW Martin & Sons Ltd* [1966] 1 QB 716.

The general rules governing the liability of bailees and sub-bailees (emanating from cases such as *Morris v CW Martin & Sons Ltd* [1966] 1 QB 716) are:

* if the bailee sub-bails with the knowledge and authority of the bailor then, unless the bailee was negligent in choosing the sub-bailee, the only person liable if the goods are lost or damaged will be the sub-bailee (see *Morris v CW Martin & Sons Ltd* [1966] 1 QB 716 and *KH Enterprise v Pioneer Container* [1994] 2 All ER 250);

* if the bailee sub-bails without the bailor's authority he or she will usually be liable to the bailor, not because the loss or damage has occurred, but because he or she is in breach of the duty to retain possession of the goods (see *Edwards v Newland & Co* [1950] 2 KB 534 especially at 539 and 542);

* in either case the sub-bailee will be liable to the bailee for any loss or damage attributable to his or her breach of duty or (if the bailment is contractual) breach of contract (see, again, *Edwards v Newland & Co* [1950] 2 KB 534 especially at 539–40); and

* the sub-bailee will also be directly liable to the head bailor, at least if he or she knows that the goods are the head bailor's property or that they are the property of someone other than the person from whom he or she received them (the bailee): see *Gilchrist Watt & Sanderson Pty Ltd v York Products Pty Ltd* [1970] 44 ALJR 269 where the defendant sub-bailees, stevedores and ships' agents to whom a case of clocks were entrusted by a shipping company (the bailee) for storage and delivery, were held liable to the bailor when the clocks were lost from their shed. See also *Lee Cooper Ltd v CH Jenkins & Sons Ltd* [1967] 2 QB 1 especially at 8–9.

Not to make unauthorised use of the goods

[15.9]   The purpose for which and the extent to which the bailee is permitted to use the goods depends on the nature of the bailment and, if there is one, on the terms of the contract under which the bailment arose. The goods may not lawfully be used for any other purposes (that is, purposes to which the bailor has not expressly or impliedly consented) — unless the unauthorised use is necessary to preserve them. If they are, the bailee will be liable for any resulting loss or damage. So, if a car is lent or hired to a bailee, the bailee will be entitled to drive it and otherwise deal with it as is necessary or reasonable to fully effect that use. However, if the same car is bailed to a mechanic for repair the mechanic is not permitted to use it otherwise than is necessary to do (and test) the repairs.

Any unauthorised use (or misuse) of the goods also terminates the bailment (see *Penfolds Wines Pty Ltd v Elliott* (1946) 74 CLR 204 and *Milk Bottles Recovery Ltd v Camillo*

[1948] VLR 344; **[15.20]**) and the right to possession reverts to the bailor — if he or she wishes to exercise it. If the bailment was contractual, the unauthorised use may also constitute a breach of contract for which the bailor can sue.

To return the goods in due course

[15.10]   The bailee must return the *exact same* goods to the bailor (or in accordance with his or her directions) once the bailment terminates. This duty applies to all bailees but, in particular, it is the primary legal duty of a *bailee for reward*: see *Jackson v Cochrane* [1989] 2 Qd R 23. In that case a dealer with whom the owner of a caravan had left it 'on consignment' handed it over to three people whom he incorrectly but honestly believed had the owner's authority to take it. He was held liable because 'misdelivery stands on a different plane from mere failure to take reasonable care in the custody of the goods'. If a bailee for reward cannot return the goods because he or she no longer has them the question of care is irrelevant; the bailee will be liable.

With *gratuitous bailees* the rule is slightly more liberal. A gratuitous bailee will be liable for failure to redeliver the goods unless he or she can show that the goods had been lost without negligence or default on his or her part. See *Graham v Voight* (1989) 95 FLR 146, where a landlady with whom a tenant had left a number of stamp albums and who was unable to account for them when he demanded their return was held liable — because she could not prove that their loss was not caused by negligence or other default on her part. On the other hand, in *WGH Nominees Pty Ltd v Tomblin* (1985) 39 SASR 117 a bailee of a ring who had unwillingly had it pressed on him by its owner was held not liable when it was stolen from his pocket in a hotel. The court held that, in the circumstances, he had shown that there was no negligence or default on his part.

If the bailment is a bailment *at will*, the goods must be returned on demand. If it is a bailment for a *fixed term* the goods must be returned either without demand at the end of that fixed term or without demand if the bailee breaches the terms of the bailment. Should a bailee fail or refuse to return the goods when he or she is required to do so the bailor can sue in the torts of detinue, conversion or negligence (see Chapter 16) or, if the bailment is contractual, for breach of contract.

Duties of the bailor

[15.11]   As with bailees, the law of bailment imposes a number of duties on bailors which arise independent of any contractual relationship. These include the duties to deliver the goods and, thereafter, not to interfere with the bailee's lawful possession of them, to inform the bailee if they are dangerous and, where the bailment involves the hiring of goods for reward, to ensure that the goods hired are merchantable and fit for the bailee's purposes: see Chapter 6. If the bailment is contractual there may be other duties, such as to pay the bailee's reasonable charges for work done on the goods during the bailment, perhaps to keep them insured or, if the bailor has agreed to keep them in good repair (as happened in *Wicks Farming Pty Ltd v Waraluck Mining Pty Ltd* [1996] 1 Qd R 99), to ensure that any required repair work is done in a timely and competent manner.

Not to interfere with the bailee's lawful possession of the goods

[15.12]   It is implicit in all bailments that the bailor has (or will have) the right to deliver possession of the goods when they are due to be delivered and, at least in contractual bailments for a fixed term, that the bailee will have quiet possession of them until the bailment expires — unless that possession is lawfully disturbed by the bailor (such as might occur if the bailee defaults) or by some third party entitled to the goods under a charge or encumbrance which was disclosed to the bailee at the time of the bailment: see *Warman v Southern Counties Car Finance Corporation Ltd* [1949] 2 KB 576. If a bailor in a bailment for reward for a fixed term wrongfully tries to interfere with the bailee's lawful possession he or she can be restrained by injunction and may also be liable for damages in trespass, conversion and/or breach of contract.

With bailments at will the bailor's duties are not so onerous and he or she can retake possession of the goods at any time provided doing so does not involve a breach of the peace: see *Parastatidis v Kotaridis* [1978] VR 449.

To inform the bailee if the goods are of a dangerous nature

[15.13]   The bailor is under a positive duty to inform the bailee if the goods are of a dangerous nature — whether the bailment is gratuitous or for reward. Failure to do so renders the bailor liable for any resulting injury: *Coughlin v Gillison* [1899] 1 QB 145 at 149. The corollary, of course, is that, if the bailor does inform the bailee, he or she will not be liable if the bailee ignores the warning and suffers injury as a result.

Case Example

Schirillo, a market gardener, lent an onion sorting machine to Chernabaeff. He had earlier removed the safety guard with which the machine had originally been fitted and he warned Chernabaeff not to let children near it when it was operating. Chernabaeff ignored the advice and used it with the help of a 13-year-old boy, Pivovaroff. Pivovaroff's hand was crushed and badly injured. Schirillo was held not liable. He had been under a duty to warn Chernabaeff of the potential dangers but he had discharged that duty by informing him of the risks and of the proper procedures to employ in using the machine: *Pivovaroff v Chernabaeff* (1978) 21 SASR 1.

To ensure that the goods are of merchantable quality and fit for purpose

[15.14]   When goods are hired (or otherwise supplied for good consideration) the common law imposes a duty on the supplier to ensure that the goods are both merchantable (fit for their normal purpose) and, if the bailee makes his or her particular purpose known, fit for that purpose as well: *Gemmell Power Farming Co Ltd v Nies* (1935) 35 SR (NSW) 469 at 475. So, for example, in *Derbyshire Building Co Pty Ltd v Becker* (1962) 107 CLR 633 the bailor was held liable for injuries which the plaintiff sustained because the electric saw which the bailor provided him had a safety guard which stuck — making the saw unsafe to use. Similar reasoning can also be found in *Cottee v Franklins Self-Serve Pty*

Ltd [1997] 1 Qd R 469 where Franklins was held liable for injuries that Mrs Cottee sustained while trying to prevent a loaded shopping trolley — which Franklins had supplied and which had a defective front wheel — from capsizing.

The difficulty with this duty is that because it mainly arises in hire contracts it can be subject to exemption clauses. Consumers now have some additional protection under the Trade Practices Act 1974 (Cth) and the various state and territory statutes (including the Consumer Credit Code — see Chapter 10) which reinforce the common law duty and which, in many cases, limit the bailor's ability to exclude or limit their liability.

Exemption clauses

[15.15] By definition, exemption clauses most often apply to contractual bailments — because the clauses appear in the contracts. They are also most commonly imposed by the bailee — usually a bailee who has taken possession of the goods to work on them. Irrespective of how they arise the same rules that apply to exemption clauses generally apply to exemption clauses in bailment contracts. That is, in particular, the proferens must give notice of the clause and, even then, the effect of the clause will be construed narrowly, if that is possible. It all depends on whether the clause, on its proper construction, is wide enough to cover the bailee's breach of duty. See *Nissho Iwai Australia Ltd v Malaysian International Shipping Corp, Berhad* (1989) 167 CLR 219 especially at 227. Exemption clauses and their effect are discussed in more detail in Chapter 3.

Rights of the bailee

[15.16] All bailees have a right to use the goods in accordance with the terms of the bailment and to quiet possession of them until the bailment comes to an end. There are also a number of other rights that apply to bailees for reward, which are designed to help them ensure that they do get paid. Some of these arise in contract (as, for example, the right to sue for damages or a quantum meruit) and they are governed by normal contractual principles, but damages may also be recovered for any tort or other breach of duty. See, for example, *Frank Davies Pty Ltd v Container Haulage Group Pty Ltd [No 1]* (1989) 98 FLR 289, where the court held that a liquidated damages clause in the lease did not prevent the lessor claiming rent up to the date of termination in addition to the liquidated damages nor for damages in respect of an accident where the claim was fully accrued before the termination of the lease nor for damages for the lessee's failure to return the truck and for its associated deterioration.

Bailees for reward are also entitled to exercise a lien over the goods on which they have worked until they have been paid for that work.

Bailee's lien

[15.17] A lien is an involuntary bailment arising by operation of law. Liens can be classified in a number of ways but in the general law of bailment the one that is important is the 'possessory lien'. A possessory lien is a right of one person to retain possession of another person's goods until an indebtedness has been satisfied. For example, if you leave your car with a mechanic to be repaired, the mechanic will have a lien over it that will entitle him or her to retain possession of it until you have paid the account.

The key to liens is 'possession'. For a valid possessory lien to exist, the person claiming the lien must have possession, must have acquired it legally and the possession must be unbroken. The lien will be lost if the bailee loses possession of the goods, if he or she does anything that amounts to a waiver or abandonment of the lien or if the goods are allowed to become intermingled or confused with other chattels belonging to someone else: see **[13.22]**. The lien also only entitles the unpaid bailee to retain the goods until he or she has been paid; it does not entitle him or her to sell the goods to satisfy the indebtedness. That can only be done if there is a contractual (or possibly statutory) right to do so (as is provided for, for example, in the various state and territory Disposal of Uncollected Goods Acts).

Possessory liens can be divided into particular possessory liens and general possessory liens.

Particular possessory liens are the more common of the two. They relate only to the particular goods on which the work was done. General possessory liens extend to *all property* of the debtor in the bailee's possession and not just the particular item on which the work giving rise to the lien was done.

General liens can only arise in two ways:

- by specific agreement between the parties (for example, in *George Baker (Transport) Ltd v Eynon* [1974] 1 WLR 462, the agreement specifically provided that 'The carrier shall have a *general lien* against the owner of any goods for any money due from such owner to the carrier'); or
- by custom or trade usage (for example, a general lien is presumed in the case of mercantile agents, bankers, stockbrokers and solicitors in respect of chattels or securities left with them; so they can retain them not only as security for the particular indebtedness associated with those chattels or securities but also for *all debts* the bailor owes them, however those debts arose).

Remedies

[15.18]   Because bailment involves its own rights, duties and obligations and because it can be either contractual or non-contractual, the innocent party may be able to pursue three separate sets of remedies in the event of a breach — those available for breach of the duties associated with bailment, those available in tort (if the breach involved a tort such as conversion, detinue or negligence) and — if the bailment was contractual — those available for breaches of contract: see *Sydney City Council v West* (1965) 114 CLR 481 at 496–7.

Remedies against third parties

[15.19]   In addition to the remedies that the parties have against one another they can also take action against any third party who interferes with either the goods or the bailee's possession of them. The only question is — who takes the action?

With bailments *at will* the bailor generally has the best right to take action because he or she is the person with an immediate right to possession (he or she can demand that the goods be returned at any time). Being able to prove an immediate right to possession, rather than mere ownership, is crucial: see *Kahler v Midland Bank Ltd* [1950] AC 24 at 33–4. In some circumstances a bailee may also be able to take action on the grounds that, as a lawful possessor, his or her rights are superior to those of any third party. However, in such cases only one action will succeed.

Case Example

O'Sullivan, a bailee, sued for damages for the lost use of her boyfriend's car. The boyfriend had already successfully sued the defendant for both the value of the car and for damages for loss of its use. O'Sullivan's action failed. The damages the boyfriend (the bailor) obtained had finalised the matter because the damages he received for loss of use included loss of the use he allowed O'Sullivan to make of it: *O'Sullivan v Williams* [1992] 3 All ER 385.

Where the bailment is for a *fixed term* the bailee has the primary right to take action because he or she is the person entitled to immediate possession. Exceptionally the bailor may also be able to take action if the third party's interference with the goods is likely to adversely affect the bailor's reversionary interest (as would be the case, for example, if the third party was attempting to damage, destroy or steal the goods: see *Mears v London & South Western Railway Co* (1862) 11 CBNS 850).

Termination of the bailment

[15.20]   Bailments can terminate in any of the following ways:
- *By natural expiry*   Bailments are usually for a defined time or for a defined purpose. Therefore once the time has expired or the purpose has been achieved the bailment comes to an end and the goods should be returned without further demand.
- *By agreement or by the unilateral act of either party*   Any bailment can be terminated by agreement and gratuitous bailments at will can also be terminated either by the bailor giving the bailee notice of termination — requiring the bailee to return the goods — or by the bailee simply returning them of his or her own volition.
- *By the bailee's wrongful act*   If a bailee deals with goods for purposes other than those for which they were bailed or if he or she otherwise acts in a way that is inconsistent with the bailor's ongoing ownership (as, for example, by damaging the goods or by trying to sell them), the bailment terminates and the owner gets an immediate right to regain possession. So, for example, in *Penfolds Wines Pty Ltd v Elliott* (1946) 74 CLR 204, the court held that delivering Penfolds' wine bottles to the defendant so that he could fill them with another brand of wine was sufficiently repugnant to the terms of the bailment to justify it being terminated. Penfolds therefore had an immediate right to retake possession of the bottles and could sue in detinue to recover them or damages for their wrongful detention. Similar reasoning was used in *Milk Bottles Recovery Ltd v Camillo* [1948] VLR 344 (involving the conversion of the plaintiff's milk bottles by a dairyman to whom they had been bailed). However, the bailment is not automatically terminated in such cases; the bailor merely gets the *right* to terminate it.

- *By the destruction of the subject matter* A bailment is terminated when the subject matter of the bailment is lost or destroyed or changed to such a degree that it becomes impossible to use it for the purposes for which it was bailed.

Special bailments

[15.21] While bailees are not normally regarded as 'insurers' of the goods (see [15.6]) there are two classes of bailee — common carriers and innkeepers, on whom the common law does impose an absolute duty of care. Accordingly, if goods in their care are lost or (in the case of common carriers) damaged they are liable to the owners. In most jurisdictions this regime of strict liability has been modified to some extent by statute.

Common carriers

[15.22] A common carrier is someone who holds himself or herself out as willing to carry goods for anyone prepared to engage his or her services and to pay a reasonable price for them. Common carriers must accept and carry all goods of the kind (or kinds) that they hold themselves out as prepared to carry and can only refuse to carry them if they already have a full load, if they do not carry to the desired destination, if the consignor refuses to pay the carrier's reasonable charges in advance or if the goods are not properly packed. A wrongful refusal to carry goods offered to them for carriage makes them liable to the goods' owners for any consequent loss or damage: *Crouch v London & North Western Railway Co* (1854) 14 CB 255; 139 ER 105.

At common law common carriers are also under an absolute duty to deliver the goods in good condition and without undue delay and they are liable for any loss of or damage to those goods whether or not it is caused through their negligence or default. Their liability arises independently of contract (so the owner of the goods does not have to prove the existence of a contract in order to recover) and it has its origins in the fact that they are in possession of another's goods. The only exceptions are for losses 'arising solely from act of God or the Queen's enemies or inherent vice in the goods carried or from the fault of the consignor': per Menzies J in *Hobbs v Petersham Transport Co Pty Ltd* (1971) 124 CLR 220 at 234. In other words, common carriers are liable unless the loss or damage was due to something *completely* outside their control, even in instances where the goods were stolen with overwhelming and irresistible force: see *Coggs v Bernard* (1703) 2 Ld Raym 909; 92 ER 107. Their liability commences immediately they accept the goods for carriage — either personally or through a duly authorised agent or employee — and it ends only when the goods have been safely delivered at the agreed destination.

Common carriers differ from private carriers in that private carriers do not hold themselves out as willing to carry goods for anyone: they overtly reserve the right to 'pick and choose' (even if, in practice, they rarely if ever refuse a consignment). Like other bailees for reward, private carriers are only liable for loss of or damage to goods in their custody if they cannot show that the effective cause of the loss or damage was not their negligence or default. The onus of proof in such cases is on the private carrier.

It is now rare to find common carriers because most carriers expressly disavow that status in disclaimers inserted into their contracts of carriage (words such as 'We are not common carriers' are sufficient to make them private carriers). However, if a carrier is a common carrier he or she can exclude or limit his or her common law liability by inserting an appropriately worded exemption clause into the contract of carriage: see *Ludditt v Ginger Coote Airways Ltd* [1947] AC 233.

Most jurisdictions also have legislation which limits the liability of common carriers in certain circumstances. Those statutes include the Common Carriers Act 1902 (NSW) — applicable in NSW and the ACT; the Carriers and Innkeepers Act 1958 (Vic); the Carriers Act 1891 (SA) — applicable in SA and NT; the Carriers Act 1920 (WA) and the Common Carriers Act 1874 (Tas). The equivalent Queensland statute, the Carriage of Goods by Land (Carriers Liability) Act 1967, was repealed in 1993 and the liability of common carriers in that state is now entirely governed by the common law. Where a statute does apply it usually provides that the common carrier is not liable for any loss of valuable goods, such as gold, silver, money, silks, furs, jewellery, watches, paintings, etc, if the value exceeds a stated maximum monetary amount (usually $20) per package unless, when the goods were delivered to the carrier, the consignor declared the value and nature of the goods to the carrier and paid the special rate charged for those goods — a rate which carriers wanting to take advantage of the statutes are required to have conspicuously displayed on their premises.

Innkeepers

[15.23]   Common innkeepers are those who hold themselves out as ready and willing to provide accommodation and/or food for travellers in the course of their journeys — provided they are willing to pay a reasonable price for it. That is, like common carriers, they cannot 'pick and choose' and they are liable if they refuse to receive and lodge a traveller unless they have some reasonable ground for the refusal: see *Medawar v Grand Hotel Co* [1891] 2 QB 11 at 20. 'Reasonable grounds' include that there is no available bedroom accommodation or that the traveller is drunk, is in an otherwise objectionable condition or is behaving improperly. In Australia both hotels providing accommodation and motels are regarded as inns (see *Turner v Queensland Motels Ltd* [1968] Qd R 189), but private or residential hotels where apartments or single rooms are let to lodgers are generally not.

At common law innkeepers are absolutely liable for the *loss* of (though not for damage to) their guests' goods, whether or not the loss was due to negligence or default on their part: *Williams v Linnett* [1951] 1 KB 565. The only restriction is that the goods must have been within the 'hospitium' of the inn at the time of loss (the 'hospitium' includes the inn buildings and any precincts that are so intimately related to the inn as to be treated as part of it; for example, in *Williams v Linnett* the hotel's car park was regarded as part of its 'hospitium'). In other words, innkeepers are the 'insurers' of their guests' goods and their liability is independent of both contract and tort. The only exceptions are where the losses result from an act of God, an act of the Queen's enemies, seizure by public authorities or the guest's own negligence. Common innkeepers are only liable for *damage* to a guest's goods if it results from their negligence or other default: per Swift J in *Winkworth v Raven* [1931] 1 KB 652 at 657. In that case the innkeeper was held not liable for damage sustained by a guest's car when its radiator froze because it was left parked in a partially open garage at the defendant's inn during unusually cold weather. The innkeeper had not been negligent nor was he otherwise at fault.

The innkeeper's liability is also restricted to liability for the loss of goods belonging to 'guests'. Guests are those who arrive at the inn — as travellers — without any previous contract or arrangement and who request food and/or lodging. They must be distinguished from 'lodgers' or 'boarders' who are not in the inn as ordinary wayfarers but as the result of some prior arrangement with the innkeeper which is normally intended to last for some considerable time. The innkeeper is only liable to lodgers when the loss of or damage to their goods is due to the innkeeper's negligence or other default amounting to a failure to take reasonable care of them.

As with common carriers the liability of innkeepers is now governed to a large extent by legislation. In New South Wales the Innkeepers Act 1968 limits the innkeeper's liability for loss of or damage to a guest's property to $100 unless the loss or damage was caused by some default, neglect or wilful act of the innkeeper (or an employee) or if the property had been deposited with the innkeeper for safekeeping. This limitation of liability only applies if the innkeeper displays a notice near reception and in the guest's room advising the guest of it. There are similar provisions in the Carriers and Innkeepers Act 1958 (Vic), the Liquor Licensing Act 1988 (WA), the Innkeepers Liability Act 1902 (NSW) — applicable in the ACT, and the Hotel-keepers Act 1981 (NT). There was similar legislation in Queensland, South Australia and Tasmania but it has been repealed and has not been replaced — with the result that innkeepers in those jurisdictions are subject to the common law rule of strict liability.

Summary and key terms

[15.24]   This chapter has set out to explain:
- Bailments involve the delivery of possession of goods to someone else usually for a defined time or for a specific purpose.
- Both bailees and bailors have a number of duties which arise independent of contract.
- Bailments may terminate in any of a number of ways including by natural expiry, by agreement between the parties, by the unilateral act or either party (at least in gratuitous bailments), by the bailee's wrongful act or by the destruction of the subject matter.
- Special rules apply to both common carriers and common innkeepers who, at least at common law, are regarded as 'insurers' of goods in their care.

16

Torts

What this chapter does ...

Torts are civil wrongs. They are acts or omissions by one party (called the 'tortfeasor'), which are not authorised by law and which infringe someone else's private or public rights. This chapter looks at torts generally, at the distinctions between torts and crimes and torts and breaches of contract and deals with the elements of a number of specific torts with direct relevance to commerce — negligence, the torts that involve unlawful interference with goods (trespass to chattels, conversion and detinue), and the torts that involve an unlawful interference with business — passing off, procuring breach of contract, intimidation and conspiracy. It will end with a consideration of vicarious liability — the means whereby one person can be made liable for torts committed by someone else.

Definition of tort

[16.1]   The word 'tort' comes from the Latin 'tortus' meaning twisted or crooked (note the similarity to our word 'tortuous'). Accordingly, a tort is any form of twisted or crooked behaviour that causes loss, damage or injury to someone else. In short, torts are civil wrongs. They are acts or omissions by one party (called the 'tortfeasor') which are not authorised by law and which infringe someone else's private or public rights, giving that other person a right of action. Such actions arise quite separately from actions that could otherwise arise through breach of contract, breach of trust or breach of fiduciary duty.

Unfortunately, torts do not lend themselves to a more precise definition than that because, really, there is no such thing as a law of torts in any general sense. Instead, there is a wide variety of torts, each having its own specific elements, because each developed in response to a particular form of wrongdoing.

Further, the class of torts is not closed. As new civil wrongs arise they can be recognised as torts and those who suffer loss, damage or injury can be afforded a remedy. This is an application of the old maxim *'ubi jus, ibi remedium'* (where there is a right there is a remedy), which simply means that a right is not really a right unless it can be enforced with some form of legal recourse if others unlawfully interfere with it. The rationale behind this fairly open-ended approach to torts can be found in Holt CJ's judgment in *Ashby v White* (1703) 92 ER 126 where he said, 'If men will multiply injuries, actions must be multiplied too; for every man that is injured ought to have recompense'.

In that case a Returning Officer had refused to allow the plaintiff to vote in a parliamentary election. The plaintiff sued. The House of Lords held that he had the right to vote and that the defendant had violated that right by refusing to allow him to vote. Accordingly, even though there was no specifically recognised tort covering the situation, he was awarded damages on the basis of the wrong itself.

There are, however, two qualifications to this general principle: there can be loss, damage or injury for which the law provides no remedy because such loss, damage or injury does not arise through what the law considers to be a wrong (a *'damnum absque injuria'* — a loss or damage without wrong), and there can be instances where a wrong (an infringement of a right) will provide a right of action (and will, therefore, allow the plaintiff to recover some form of remedy), even though the wrong complained of did not cause any actual loss, damage or injury (*'injuria sine damno'* — a wrong without damage).

Losses or damage not caused by a legal wrong

[16.2]   Torts are founded on 'illegitimate' acts or omissions. That is, only acts or omissions that are *not authorised* by law give rise to a cause of action in tort. Where the act or omission complained of was authorised, or where it was simply a legitimate means of achieving a legitimate end, there can be no action against the alleged 'tortfeasor' for the simple reason that what he or she has done is not, in law, a 'wrong'.

Lawful business conduct

[16.3]   Good examples of such acts and omissions can be found in the area of business competition. A trader's actions will clearly have an effect upon his or her competitors and, often, that effect will be detrimental. However, provided the trader's actions are lawful, there will be no tort and the competitors will have no grounds upon which they can bring an action if they do suffer loss.

Case Example

The defendants, a group of shipowners who wanted to monopolise the tea trade between China and England set their freight rates to undercut their competitors and threatened to boycott shipping agents who acted for them. The plaintiff company was driven out of the market and sued. Its action failed. The defendants had done no more than pursue their legitimate trade interests and, as they had done so in a lawful way (there was no fraud, intimidation or interference with the plaintiff's contractual rights), and for the lawful purpose of extending their trade and increasing their profits, they had committed no recognised 'wrong'. (This case was, of course, decided before the statutes regulating anti-competitive behaviour were passed. Had it arisen today the plaintiff may have been able to use, for example, the anti-competitive provisions of the Trade Practices Act 1974 (Cth) to prevent the cartel forcing it out of business): *Mogul Steamship Co Ltd v McGregor, Gow & Co* [1892] AC 25.

Other examples of loss arising out of what the law does not regard as a wrong can be found in situations where harm is caused by someone simply exercising rights over his or her own property. For example, in *Mayor of Bradford v Pickles* [1895] AC 587, Pickles, who wanted to force the local council to buy his land as part of its water supply scheme, intercepted the underground water which percolated through his property in undefined channels and pumped it out so that it did not seep down to land that the council owned. The council sued and failed. What Pickles had done was simply a lawful use of his own property and, consequently, his actions were not tortious.

Malice

[16.4]   However, although Pickles' motive was clearly mercenary, what he did was legal and it was probably not malicious. An otherwise lawful use of one's own property can become unlawful if that use is for an unlawful purpose and motivated by malice.

Case Example

Christie and his family were musically inclined and made a lot of noise singing and playing musical instruments. This annoyed Davey, who retaliated by hammering and banging metal trays on the party wall separating their residences. Christie sued for an injunction and succeeded. Although the noise would not normally have warranted an injunction, the fact that Davey had intended to cause annoyance converted what might have been a lawful act (a simple use of his own property) into an unlawful act. The court held that Davey was not entitled to use his property as he pleased if his *dominant purpose* was to annoy the Christies: *Christie v Davey* [1893] 1 Ch 316.

Legal wrongs not resulting in actual loss or damage

[16.5]   Some wrongs are actionable 'per se'. That is, there are cases where a person whose rights have been infringed can sue even though there has been no loss, damage or injury and even though, on occasion, the tortfeasor may not have even been aware that he or she was committing an infringement. Such torts are necessarily limited. They have their origins in history and they are usually attached only to those 'rights' which the law regards as fundamental and paramount. Such rights include the right to dominion over one's land, safety of one's person and protection of one's reputation.

Accordingly, a trespass to land can be actionable even though no actual loss is suffered and even where the tortfeasor did not realise that he or she was trespassing (provided that lack of realisation was due to his or her negligence so that there is some element of fault). Similarly, both assault and battery can be actionable even though the plaintiff does not sustain any actual harm (a battery can involve only the slightest brush, push or laying on of a hand and an assault is merely any threat of battery which puts the other person in actual fear). Also, where the difference between libel (a written defamation) and slander (a spoken defamation) is maintained, a libel can be actionable even though it was inadvertent or accidental and even though it caused the plaintiff no real harm.

Of course, in such cases, the law tries to maintain a balance between doing justice and ensuring that justice is seen to be done by allowing the action (thus recognising the technical infringement of the right), but awarding only nominal damages (thus recognising the lack of culpability, where appropriate, and the lack of any actual loss or damage).

Torts and crime

[16.6]   It should therefore be apparent that there can be a considerable overlap between torts and crime. Both are species of 'wrong' and both can arise out of the same facts. For example, murder is a crime but it can also be a tort to the person killed and to his or her dependants. The same thing can be said about manslaughter and assault. Theft (or stealing) is a crime but the same acts can also constitute the tort of 'conversion'. Similar overlaps can be found in many areas of criminal behaviour especially where the 'crime' involves interference with the plaintiff's person or property.

Crimes but not torts

[16.7]   However, it is also clear that there can be occasions where a crime will be committed but there will be no corresponding tort. In particular, actions that constitute a crime will not normally also give rise to an action in tort if the plaintiff does not suffer any actual loss, damage or injury. Good examples can be found in the law of attempts. If someone attempts to commit an offence that attempt is, in itself, an offence. However, unless there is some accompanying loss, damage or injury it will not also be a tort. Consequently, especially where the intended victim remains unaware of the attempt, there will be no tort and no cause of action.

Similarly, some crimes are crimes against society as a whole, and they do not specifically affect any particular individual. In those cases there is a criminal offence but there is no tort because no individual suffers harm. Good examples are treason and sedition and it has even been held that perjury falls into this category (though, with perjury, the reasoning seems to be that public policy considerations require that witnesses be immune from civil action arising out of evidence which, because of subpoenas, they cannot avoid giving). For example, in *Hargreaves v Bretherton* [1959] 1 QB 45 the plaintiff, who had been convicted of fraud on the defendant's evidence, tried unsuccessfully to sue him alleging that he had 'falsely and maliciously and without just occasion or excuse committed perjury' at the plaintiff's trial.

Torts but not crime

[16.8]   There can also be instances where a tort has been committed but the facts are not sufficient to prove commission of a crime. The classic illustration is trespass to land. Trespass can be both a civil and a criminal wrong. However, to be a crime the trespass must be committed with the intention of committing some other offence. Where there is no such intent, there is no criminal trespass. The difference between civil and criminal trespass was amply illustrated when Michael Fagan entered the Queen's apartments in Buckingham Palace in 1982 and sat chatting to her until palace security officials could be summoned. The authorities could not charge him with criminal trespass because they could not prove that he had entered the palace intending to commit an offence.

The difference between torts and crimes

[16.9]   The major difference between torts and crimes is in the policy that underlies them as two separate means of dealing with two separate types of wrongdoing. The aim of the criminal law is, quite simply, to protect society as a whole by imposing deterrents to what society sees as criminal behaviour. That is, the criminal law tries to prevent criminal behaviour by using threats of punishment. Where criminal behaviour occurs anyway, the punishment that the courts mete out is also aimed at protecting society either:

- by attempting to reform or rehabilitate the offender (for example, through probation orders, community service orders or short periods in rehabilitation facilities); or
- by preventative detention (that is, locking the offender away so that he or she does not have the opportunity to re-offend).

On the other hand, the law of torts is principally aimed at compensating an injured party for any loss, damage or injury that results from the other person's wrongful act or omission. The possibility of having to pay damages may, incidentally, act as a deterrent and it may, therefore, prevent a potential tortfeasor from behaving in a tortious manner. However, the law of torts is not really aimed at deterrence; it is aimed at compensating the injured party.

The overlap between torts and crimes

[16.10]   When a single act is both criminal and tortious the perpetrator can be both prosecuted for the crime and sued for the tort. There are, however, a number of qualifications to this, the most important of which is that statute can remove the right to sue for the tort. That is, an Act of Parliament can provide that the criminal prosecution is final and that civil proceedings arising out of the same fact situation cannot be taken against the offender. For example, in some Australian states such provisions apply in respect of criminal assaults, offences analogous to stealing and some offences against property where those offences are dealt with summarily (that is, by a magistrate instead of in some higher court before a jury). Consequently, the victims cannot sue for compensation for the effects of the offender's wrongful actions. However, in the absence of some such statutory prohibition, anyone who has been convicted of a criminal offence can also be sued in tort if his or her actions are, in fact, both criminal and tortious.

Where some statute does prevent a victim suing in tort the magistrate or judge is often empowered to order the offender to pay either compensation or restitution because, otherwise, the victim could neither be compensated nor recover his or her property. If there is no such restitutionary power or if it is restricted to particular classes of offence, there is no 'right' to compensation as such. However, in such cases, all jurisdictions now have a Criminal Injuries Compensation Scheme under which the victim of (usually violent) crime can be given an ex gratia payment from the government. The problems with such ex gratia payments are that they cannot be obtained as of right, they are usually of a fixed and limited amount and they can bear little or no relationship to the claimant's actual loss, damage or injury. They are, however, something and, given that offenders often have no financial substance, victims may in fact recover more from the scheme (little though it may be) than they would by suing the offender in tort.

Tort and contract

[16.11]   The main difference between tort and contract is that the law of contract essentially deals with the enforcement of rights that the parties have created for themselves through their agreement while the law of torts deals with the enforcement of rights that have been conferred by law irrespective of agreement.

Both branches of the law deal with types of 'civil wrong' and both are aimed at providing remedies for those who suffer loss, damage or injury as the result of someone else's wrongdoing. However, the real differences lie in the bases on which the respective actions can be taken (to succeed in contract you must prove that some promise or undertaking has been breached whereas in tort there need be no such promise or undertaking), and in the rationale behind and the nature of the remedies available for the various 'breaches' of either contractual or tortious duty.

Overlap between tort and contract

[16.12]   As with tort and crime, there is a measure of overlap between tort and contract and the same fact situation may give rise to actions both in tort and for breach of contract.

For example, if you engage a solicitor to conduct investigations on your behalf before you buy a business and if those investigations are carried out in such a way that the advice you receive is wrong, you may be able to sue the solicitor both in the tort of negligence and for breach of contract. (Although, in *Hawkins v Clayton* (1988) 164 CLR 539, a case dealing with a solicitor's negligent conduct when dealing with a client's will, Deane J suggested that, in cases of professional negligence the plaintiff, in the absence of any express contractual term, should generally sue in tort alone.) Of course, if you do sue in both tort and contract, you cannot recover double damages — you can recover only what you have actually lost. However, you can still ground your action in either plea and, if you are unsure which is most likely to succeed, you can even plead both causes of action in the hope that you will succeed under one of them.

Your decision might also be influenced by the remedy you hope to receive, especially if it could involve an award of damages. Damages in tort are generally awarded to restore the injured party to the position that he or she occupied *before* the breach. Damages in contract are awarded to place the injured party in the position that he or she would have occupied *but for* the breach (that is, the position that he or she would have been in if the contract been performed as it should have been). This can obviously include a component for 'loss of expectation' including loss of expected profit. This difference between the two bases upon which damages are calculated can be extremely important.

For example, assume that someone sells you a vase misrepresenting it as a genuine Ming. You pay $20,000, intending to resell it privately for $25,000. In fact, the vase is a cheap copy worth no more than $100. If you sue in tort (that is, in the torts of either deceit or negligence), and succeed, you should be awarded damages of $19,900. That is the amount that will put you in the position you would have been in but for the tortious act (that is, in possession of property worth $20,000). If, however, the misrepresentation was also incorporated into the contract you could recover $24,900 — the amount that would put you in the position that you would have been in but for the breach (that is, in possession of property worth, on sale, $25,000).

Differences between tort and contract

[16.13]   There are other significant differences between actions in tort and actions in contract. Some of the more important include:

- *The effect of contributory negligence*   In tort, if an injured party is partly to blame for the loss, damage or injury, the damages are reduced. In contract there is no similar provision. If loss is caused by a breach of contract the party in breach is completely liable. So, for example, in *Harper v Ashtons Circus* [1972] 2 NSWLR 395 the plaintiff, who was injured when he fell from seating provided by the defendant circus, sued it for breach of contract and negligence. He then withdrew his claim in negligence to frustrate the defendant's defence of contributory negligence. The court held that contributory negligence had no role to play in breach of contract actions; liability depends simply upon whether there has been a breach and whether the damage complained of is a natural and foreseeable consequence of that breach.

- *The position of third parties*   In general, third parties who suffer as a result of a breach of contract have no rights at all. There are exceptions to this but generally it holds true. In contrast, third parties who suffer because of some tortious action (especially third parties who are dependants of whomever has been directly affected by the tort) may be able to sue in their own right. Such actions are usually only limited by the question of whether the third party's (indirect) loss, damage or injury was reasonably foreseeable and whether the relationship between the third party and the tortfeasor was sufficiently 'proximate' to warrant a finding of liability.

- *Limitation of actions*   All actions are subject to statutory limitation. That is, actions may be brought for a particular time after the tort has been committed or the contract has been breached but, thereafter, all rights to sue lapse. However, there is a difference in the way in which the period of limitation is calculated. In contract, the period runs from the point of the breach whereas, in tort, it runs from the point at which the loss or damage is suffered. This distinction may sometimes be critically important, especially if the damage complained of does not occur until some time after the act or omission that caused it was committed (as could be the case where faulty foundations subsequently cause the walls of a building to crack).

- *The liability of minors and lunatics*   Minors and lunatics are not generally liable for breaches of their contractual obligations except in certain clearly defined situations. In contrast (though there is still some dispute about it), both minors and lunatics are responsible for their tortious acts. The sole qualification to this general principle appears to be that, if the tort is one that requires an element of intent, a minor or lunatic will not be liable if he or she was not capable of forming the requisite intent when the act or omission complained of was committed.

Negligence

[16.14]   The remainder of this chapter will examine a number of specific torts included because of either their overall importance or their particular relevance to business transactions. Of the torts discussed, by far the most important is the tort of negligence.

Negligence defined

[16.15]   To a layman, negligence probably means no more than careless behaviour. However, in its tortious sense, negligence is a more complex concept and it can involve both advertent and inadvertent acts and omissions. Broadly speaking, someone will be negligent in a legal sense if he or she fails to take reasonable care to prevent loss, damage or injury to others whom he or she could reasonably have foreseen might have been injured if that care was not taken. Lord Wright described the concept in *Lochgelly Iron and Coal Co Ltd v M'Mullen* [1934] AC 1 at 25 saying:

> In strict legal analysis negligence means more than heedless or careless conduct, whether in omission or commission: it properly connotes the complex concept of duty, breach, and damage thereby suffered by the person to whom the duty was owing.

Consequently, to establish that a defendant has been negligent, in a legal sense, a plaintiff must prove three things:

- that the tortfeasor owed him or her a 'duty of care';
- that there has been a 'breach' of that duty of care; and
- that he or she has suffered loss, damage or injury as a result of that breach.

The duty of care

[16.16]   The modern doctrine of negligence is derived from the House of Lord's decision in *Donoghue v Stevenson* [1932] AC 562. In that case the old idea that a duty of care could only exist in contractual and other specifically defined relationships (such as those between occupiers of premises and their invitees) was finally discarded. In its place the court accepted that a duty of care could exist in *any situation* provided loss, damage or injury to one party was 'reasonably foreseeable' and the relationship between the parties was 'sufficiently proximate' to require one to take care not to put the other at risk. The appellant in *Donoghue v Stevenson* had had a bottle of ginger beer bought for her by a friend. The bottle was of dark opaque glass and the condition of its contents could not be ascertained by inspection. After she had drunk some of the ginger beer she poured the remainder onto a dish of ice cream and the decomposed remains of a snail floated out of the bottle. She suffered shock and, later, severe gastroenteritis. She sued the ginger beer's manufacturer and succeeded. The court held that manufacturers have a general duty *to the entire consuming public* to ensure that their products do not contain potentially dangerous defects which cannot be discovered on a reasonable inspection. This finding clearly expanded the category of people to whom the courts were willing to find that a duty of care was owed. Explaining what he saw as the nature and extent of the duty of care, Lord Atkin said (at 580):

> You must take reasonable care to avoid acts or omissions which you can reasonably foresee would be likely to injure your neighbour. Who, then, in law is my neighbour? The answer seems to be — persons who are so closely and directly affected by my act that I ought reasonably to have them in contemplation as being so affected when I am directing my mind to the acts or omissions which are called in question.

[16.17]   Over the ensuing years the courts have tried to develop a universal test which could be used to determine whether a duty of care exists in any given fact situation. However, they seem to have recently accepted that it is not possible to find what Lord Bridge of Harwich described in *Caparo Industries plc v Dickman* [1990] 2 AC 605 at 617, as 'any single general principle to provide a practical test which can be applied to every situation to determine whether a duty of care is owed'. In Australia, Kirby J came to a similar conclusion in *Pyrenees Shire Council v Day* (1998) 151 ALR 147, saying at 215:

> the search in this court for exact precision and sure predictability by the use of concepts such as 'foreseeability', 'proximity' and 'reliance' should, I think, be taken to have failed. In these circumstances, it is preferable to adopt an approach which accepts honestly that exact precision and certainty are ultimately unattainable in this area of the law.

The approach which Kirby J adopted (which involved the same three-stage test that the House of Lords used in *Caparo Industries plc v Dickman* [1990] 2 AC 605) asks three questions:

1. Was it reasonably foreseeable to the alleged wrongdoer that his or her acts or omissions would be likely to cause harm to the person who suffered the loss, damage or injury (or to a person in the same position)?

2. Was there a relationship between the parties which the law characterises as one of 'proximity' or 'neighbourhood' (so that the harm was not only foreseeable but the wrongdoer was also under a positive duty to avoid the risk of that reasonably foreseeable injury to the other)?

3. If so, is it fair, just and reasonable that the law should impose a duty of a given scope upon the wrongdoer for the benefit of the other person?

These questions operate in what may perhaps be best described as an 'inverted pyramid' structure, with each qualifying and limiting the 'liability' effect of a positive answer to the previous question. What this means is that you only have to answer the second question if your answer to the first question was 'Yes' and you only have to answer the third question if your answers to both the first and second questions was 'Yes'. If, at any time, your answer to any of the questions is 'No' there will be no liability in negligence, regardless of whether you answered 'Yes' to any of the earlier questions. And in every case the onus of showing that the question should be answered in the positive rests with the person alleging that the wrongdoer owed him or her a legal duty of care.

Reasonable foreseeability

[16.18]   Before a duty of care can exist it must have been reasonably foreseeable to the wrongdoer that others could be injured as the result of his or her acts or omissions — unless care was taken to ensure that injury did not occur. Therefore, before plaintiffs can succeed in a negligence action they must be able to show that they belonged to that class of people whom the defendant should have regarded as being 'at risk'. The precise loss, damage or injury that they actually suffered need not have been reasonably foreseeable — all that is required is that it must have been reasonably foreseeable that the *class* of people, of whom the plaintiff is one, could have suffered *some* loss, damage or injury as a direct, consequential result of the defendant's acts or omissions.

'Proximity' or 'neighbourhood'

[16.19]   Unfortunately, the 'reasonable foreseeability' test, by itself, is unacceptably wide, especially in cases other than those simply involving personal injury or physical damage to property. For example, if you make an off-the-cuff remark to a friend in a public place, it is reasonably foreseeable that that remark could be overheard and, possibly, passed on. However, it would be quite unreasonable if your 'duty of care' to ensure that that remark was not actively misleading extended to everyone who subsequently became aware of it, whether directly or indirectly.

Consequently, the law limits a defendant's legal duty of care to those with whom he or she is in a 'sufficiently proximate relationship' or, to use Lord Atkin's words, to those, 'who are so closely and directly affected by my act that I ought reasonably to have them in contemplation ... when I am directing my mind to the acts or omissions which are called in question'. Otherwise, a single tortfeasor could find himself or herself liable, directly or indirectly, to everyone in the world who suffers loss, damage or injury which can, in some way, be linked to his or her negligent acts or omissions.

Who is proximate?

[16.20]   The question then is, who is in a sufficiently 'proximate relationship' because, as Deane J put it in *Sutherland Shire Council v Heyman* (1985) 157 CLR 424 at 495:

> The common law imposes no general duty to avoid loss or injury to another merely because it is reasonably foreseeable that one's actions or omissions are likely to cause it ... Such a duty arises ... only if there be the requisite element of proximity in the relationship between the parties with respect to the relevant act or omission.

What proximity involves in any specific case is simply, as Deane J explained it in *Jaensch v Coffey* (1984) 155 CLR 549 at 584, 'the notion of nearness or closeness'. He went on (at 584–5) to say that that nearness or closeness could be established in any of three ways:

- by 'physical proximity' (in the sense of space or time) between the person or property of the plaintiff and the person or property of the defendant;
- by 'circumstantial proximity' — that which exists in particular circumstances (such as between employers and employees or between professionals and their clients); and
- by 'causal proximity' in the sense of the closeness of directness of the relationship between the defendant's particular act or omission and the injury that the plaintiff sustained.

Establishing proximity

[16.21] In *Pyrenees Shire Council v Day* (1998) 151 ALR 147 at 216 Kirby J said that being able to establish the necessary proximity will always 'depend upon an analysis of the spectrum of "proximity factors" advanced to define the relationship between the parties out of which a duty is said to arise'. Therefore, whether the necessary proximity can be established will always be a question of fact and degree. However, the necessary relationship can normally be shown in any of the following three ways:

- by showing that injury to the plaintiff was reasonably foreseeable. As Deane J said in *Sutherland Shire Council v Heyman* at 495, 'Reasonable foreseeability of loss or injury to another is an indication and, in the more settled areas of the law of negligence … commonly an adequate indication that the requirement of proximity is satisfied';
- by showing that the plaintiff relied or depended on the defendant (particularly in cases of negligent advice); or
- by showing that the relationship fell within one of the established duties of care (what Deane J would have referred to as instances of 'circumstantial proximity').

In each of those instances, it can normally be shown that there is not only a connection between the tortfeasor and his or her victim but that it is so 'close or direct' that any reasonable person should have realised that the act or omission complained of could have affected that victim.

[16.22] Reasonably foreseeable injury Reasonable foreseeability is not only itself an element of the duty of care, it can also help to establish the element of 'proximity' or 'neighbourhood'. That is, if injury to a particular defendant was reasonably foreseeable because of either his or her physical proximity (such as might be the case, for example, when a defendant detonates explosives without checking that the surrounding area is clear first) or his or her circumstantial proximity (such as when an employer fails to take adequate care to safeguard his or her employees), the required 'proximate relationship' will have been established in the sense that the tortfeasor should have had the person who has been affected in mind when 'directing [his or her] mind to the acts or omissions which are called in question'. Therefore, manufacturers of foodstuffs should have consumers in mind when they develop their production or packaging processes, those who manufacture equipment should have those who will use or come in contact with it in mind when they make it and motorists should have all other road users, whether they be drivers, passengers or pedestrians, in mind when they venture out onto the highway. In each of those cases the identified persons clearly fall within the general class of those whom the tortfeasor should have had in mind as potential victims of any possibly negligent behaviour.

In recent years the concept of reasonable foreseeability of injury (and, therefore, the relationships that can fall within the necessary proximity) has been extended to include those suffering nervous shock as the result of seeing or hearing about injuries to those close to them (*Jaensch v Coffey* (1984) 155 CLR 549), and those suffering pure economic loss (loss which occurs independently of any personal injury to the plaintiff or damage to his or her property) either as the result of negligent misstatements (*Hedley Byrne and Co Ltd v Heller* [1964] AC 465), or the tortfeasor's other negligent acts: *Caltex Oil v The Dredge 'Willemstad'* (1976) 136 CLR 529.

[16.23] Reliance or dependence   Where the relationship between the parties is such that one of them is clearly relying or depending upon the other's knowledge, ability or skill and that is, or should be, apparent to the other, the relationship between them will be sufficiently proximate. Consequently, the person being relied upon will be liable if, through his or her negligence, the other party does suffer loss, damage or injury. Examples can be found in cases where professionals, tradespeople or other workers who hold themselves out as having particular skill fail to exercise it appropriately.

Reliance and dependence has become especially important in the negligent misstatement cases. If someone gives advice or information knowing that he or she is being trusted to give it accurately and in circumstances in which it is reasonable for the person who receives it to rely upon it, the relationship between the adviser and the advisee has been held to involve the necessary proximity. Consequently, if the advice is given negligently, the adviser can be liable: see **[16.59]–[16.66]**.

[16.24] A relationship within the established duties of care   In many ways the law regarding relationships within an established duty of care is simply an application of the doctrine of precedent. Certain relationships have already been examined by the courts in other cases and have been found to involve a duty of care. As a result, plaintiffs in similar positions do not have to prove the existence of the duty in their own cases — that will be presumed because the courts have already accepted that such a duty exists in equivalent relationships. Relationships that have been examined and which have been found to involve a duty of care include (inter alia) those between professionals and their clients, employers and their employees (at least as regards safety matters), teachers and their students (at least as regards supervision and safety matters), highway users and other highway users, occupiers of premises and their invitees, suppliers and consumers, bailees and bailors, and even prison warders and police officers and the inmates in their care.

The 'fair, just and reasonable' requirement

[16.25]   In *Pyrenees Shire Council v Day* (1998) 151 ALR 147 at 216 Kirby J explained the third requirement, that it be 'fair, just and reasonable to impose a duty of care of a given scope on the alleged wrong-doer', as simply a means of weighing' any competing considerations of legal policy in order to determine whether, notwithstanding the proof of foreseeability and proximity, the law should not impose a duty at all or a duty of a scope which the injured party needs in order to succeed'. In other words, it is a means whereby the wrongdoer can be 'let off the hook' if there are good reasons for doing so. The sorts of situation that would be covered by this test include those where, economically, it would be unreasonable to demand that the defendant should have taken the required preventative steps.

> ### Case Example
>
> Stovin was injured when his motorcycle collided with a car at a dangerous (though not abnormally hazardous) road junction. The defendant council knew that the junction was dangerous and intended to remove part of an adjoining embankment which impeded motorists' view, work which was not carried out before the accident happened. It was held not liable. Whether it did the required work was within its discretion and, on policy grounds, the court felt that it was not up to it to interfere. As Lord Hoffmann said (at 958):
>
> > In my view the creation of a duty of care upon a highway authority, even on grounds of irrationality in failing to exercise a power, would inevitably expose the authority's budgetary decisions to judicial inquiry. This would distort the priorities of local authorities, which would be bound to try to play safe by increasing their spending on road improvements rather than risk enormous liabilities for personal injury accidents. They will spend less on education or social services. I think that it is important, before extending the duty of care owed by public authorities, to consider the cost to the community of the defensive measures which they are likely to take in order to avoid liability.
>
> *Stovin v Wise* [1996] AC 923.

[16.26]   Therefore, questions of resource allocation and their possible diversion as well as other budgetary considerations can be taken into account but so too can other policy considerations involving the dangers of interfering (usually with the benefit of hindsight) in the exercise of properly conferred or delegated powers or discretions.

> ### Case Example
>
> The mother of the last of the Yorkshire Ripper's victims sued the Chief Constable arguing that, because he had not caught the Ripper earlier, he was liable for her death. The court — heavily influenced by policy considerations — decided in the Chief Constable's favour. It felt that to find that he had been negligent would have imposed unacceptable limits on the police discretion to investigate and prosecute crimes as they see fit, would not have taken their limited resources into account and would have detracted from the overall concept of compensation by making it, at least in part, dependent on where one fell in the sequence of a series of crimes. Consequently, the court held that, while police could be liable if people were injured as a direct result of their acts or omissions, they owed no general duty of care to the public at large to identify or apprehend unknown criminals, or even to individuals — unless their failure to act created an exceptional, additional risk which was greater than the risk to the public generally: *Hill v Chief Constable of West Yorkshire* [1989] 1 AC 53.

Breaching the duty of care

[16.27] To succeed in an action in negligence, a plaintiff must not only prove that the defendant owed him or her a duty of care, but also that that duty has been breached. To prove that the duty has been breached a plaintiff must prove two things:

- that he or she was owed a particular 'standard of care' (this might be referred to as the 'scope of the duty of care' and its extent is a question of *law*); and
- that the defendant failed to meet that required standard (a question of *fact*).

The 'standard of care'

[16.28] The 'standard of care' that is owed in any situation varies and the standard that is expected always depends on 'what a reasonable man would do by way of response to the risk'. In other words, there are no rigid rules and the appropriate standard of care will depend upon the circumstances and on what the courts consider to have been reasonable in those circumstances. As Kirby J put it in *Romeo v Conservation Commission of the Northern Territory* (1998) 151 ALR 263 at 300 there are:

> practical considerations which must be 'balanced out' before a breach of the duty of care may be found … [and] … courts have both the authority and responsibility to introduce *practical and sensible notions of reasonableness* that will put a break on the more extreme and unrealistic claims. [emphasis added]

What is considered reasonable, therefore, can depend upon a number of factors including, as Mason J listed them in *Wyong Shire Council v Shirt* (1980) 146 CLR 40 at 47–8 (in a passage cited with approval in *Romeo*), 'the magnitude of the risk and the degree of the probability of its occurrence, along with the expense, difficulty and inconvenience of taking alleviating action and any other conflicting responsibilities which the defendant may have'. Perhaps these considerations can be put more simply as:

- the probability of danger;
- the likelihood of resulting damage; and
- the options that were open to the defendant.

The probability of danger

[16.29] The impact that the probability of danger has on what should be the required standard of care was well illustrated by Lord Neaves in *Mackintosh v Mackintosh* (1864) 2 Macph 1357 at 1362–3. He said: 'no prudent man in carrying a lighted candle through a powder magazine would fail to take more care than if he was going through a damp cellar'. The High Court made the same point in somewhat less evocative terms in *Swinton v The China Mutual Steam Navigation Co Ltd* (1951) 83 CLR 553 at 566–7, saying: 'The measure of care increases in proportion with the danger involved'.

Therefore, if the risk of something happening is remote and the eventual occurrence unlikely, the 'tortfeasor' will probably not be liable if loss, damage or injury does occur. As Miles CJ said in *Gillespie v Commonwealth* (1991) 105 FLR 196 at 203:

> A life-threatening event (for example, the collapse of a factory roof in Canberra by an earthquake) might be so unlikely that reasonable care would require little or nothing to be done to avoid it.

What this means is that no one is expected to adopt a standard of care which involves guarding against remote possibilities of unlikely or improbable events. If the improbable does occur, the tortfeasor will not be liable because he or she will not be in breach of the 'reasonable' standard of care that the law requires.

Similarly, even where a duty of care is clearly owed to the person actually injured, the 'tortfeasor' will not be liable just because he or she failed to take steps to counter the possibility of injury arising out of totally unexpected or unforeseen circumstances.

Case Example

The council allowed a church picnic party to take its tea in its public tea rooms. While the urn was being carried in it was dropped and children at the counter were scalded. The court held the council not liable. In normal circumstances, merely carrying a tea urn would not have created any unusual danger and the injury to the children was, therefore, not reasonably foreseeable. As Lord Wright put it (at 464–6):

the present case ... was not, in my opinion, per se dangerous ... That the men should be negligent in so simple an operation ... was a mere possibility, not a reasonable probability. [Accordingly], there was no reasonably foreseeable danger to the children from the use of the premises which the appellants permitted to be made.

Glasgow Corp v Muir [1943] AC 448.

[16.30] Dangerous activity   On the other hand, if any activity that does result in injury is inherently dangerous, or if there is an above normal risk of danger, the potential tortfeasor is expected to exercise a proportionately higher standard of care.

Case Example

Workers employed by the Dominion Natural Gas Co installed a gas regulator in a building with the safety valve discharging excess gas into the building instead of into the open air. The gas inside the building ignited and exploded, killing Perkins and injuring Collins. The company was held liable. The nature of its equipment and the abnormal danger that it posed to those who came near it demanded that it should have exercised a greater standard of care than would normally be required. As Lord Dunedin put it (at 646):

... in the case of articles dangerous in themselves, such as loaded firearms, poisons, explosives and other things ejusdem generis, there is a peculiar duty to take precaution imposed upon those who send forth or install such articles when it is necessarily the case that other parties will come within their proximity.

Dominion Natural Gas Co Ltd v Collins and Perkins [1909] AC 640.

[16.31]   The reasoning behind this requirement was subsequently explained by Starke J in *Adelaide Chemical & Fertiliser Co Ltd v Carlyle* (1940) 64 CLR 514 at 523. He said:

A reasonably prudent man would, no doubt, in the cases of such things exercise a 'keener foresight' or 'a degree of diligence so stringent as to amount practically to a guarantee of safety', or 'a high degree of care amounting in effect to an insurance against risk', or 'the greatest care' or 'consummate care'. The duty is 'more imperious' when things dangerous in themselves are being handled.

In that case the plaintiff's husband had been splashed with sulphuric acid when the earthenware jar in which it was contained came apart in his hands. He was badly burnt, developed streptococcal septicaemia and died. The defendant company, which had sold the acid in the (breakable) jar, was held liable because it had supplied an inherently dangerous substance in a container that was generally unsafe and dangerous and which a reasonably prudent person would not have used for that purpose.

[16.32] Therefore, using dangerous substances or engaging in inherently dangerous activities carries with it an obligation to exercise a proportionately higher standard of care than would otherwise be required, because there is a greater risk that something unfortunate might happen. If something unfortunate does happen and if the added precautions that should have been taken were not, the person who should have taken them will be liable, a consequence confirmed by the High Court in *Burnie Port Authority v General Jones* (1994) 179 CLR 520; 120 ALR 42. In that case the Port Authority, which had allowed some especially flammable insulating material to be stored on its premises in close proximity to where welding was being done, was held liable when the material ignited, set fire to the building and destroyed three coldrooms full of the plaintiff's frozen vegetables. Given the real and foreseeable risk of fire that having such highly flammable material on the premises posed, the Authority should have taken *special* precautions to ensure that it was not ignited. It had not taken those special precautions and, therefore, it had not exercised the standard of care that was required of it in the circumstances.

[16.33] Children A greater standard of care is also required if children are among those who might be injured if the heightened degree of care is not taken. It has been accepted since at least 1841 (when *Lynch v Nurdin* (1841) 1 QB 30; 113 ER 1041 was decided) that children are of an abnormally inquisitive and mischievous nature, that they are prone to meddle with whatever happens to come within their reach and that, on impulse, they can and will do things that no 'reasonable' person would dream of doing. Given that, those who know — and those who should be able to anticipate — that children might place themselves in danger have a duty to take special care to ensure that they are not unavoidably injured.

> **Case Example**
>
> Thompson, a 13-year-old boy, was electrocuted and seriously injured while climbing a power pole to retrieve a bird's nest. The High Court found that, given the serious consequences of electrocution and the likelihood that 'inquisitive, meddlesome and adventurous boys' could be in the vicinity of the pole, the defendant corporation, which controlled the electricity supply, should have taken special care to ensure that the earth wire attached to the pole (which had caused the electrocution) did not become electrically charged. It had not done so and, therefore, it was liable: *Thompson v Bankstown Corp* (1953) 87 CLR 619.

The likelihood of resulting damage

[16.34] When determining the appropriate standard of care that should be adopted in any particular situation a potential tortfeasor must not only guard against dangers to which the public might be exposed generally, he or she must also exercise special care to guard against particular dangers to which those with specific disabilities might be exposed because of their disabilities. This does not mean that a potential tortfeasor must take special preventative measures 'just in case' someone with a particular disability happens

along; he or she need only take those special precautions where it is clear that those with
disabilities (or someone with a disability), could be affected.

Case Example

The plaintiff, a mechanic who had lost the sight of his left eye in World War II,
lost the sight of his right eye when a chip of metal sheared off a bolt and struck
it. His employers were held liable because they had not supplied him with safety
goggles. The court accepted that supplying safety goggles was not a standard
practice in the industry but said that, in this case, the defendants had owed the
plaintiff a higher than normal standard of care because of the greater risk to him,
not of an accident occurring but of serious injury if an accident involving possible eye damage did happen: *Paris v Stepney Borough Council* [1951] AC 367.

However, 'knowledge of the risk' can work both ways. For example, in *Cook v Cook*
(1986) 162 CLR 376 the plaintiff invited the defendant, who was neither licensed nor
competent to drive a motor car, to drive her vehicle to the local fish and chip shop. The
defendant negligently ran the car into a pole and the plaintiff was injured. The High Court
held that the plaintiff's knowledge of the defendant's incompetence as a driver took their
relationship out of the ordinary driver/passenger relationship and put it into a separate
category with a different and lower standard of care. (The defendant's negligence in driving the motor car was, however, so great that the High Court finally held that she had
failed to live up to even that lower standard of care and the plaintiff was, therefore,
awarded damages.) Similar reasoning was applied in *Gala v Preston* (1991) 172 CLR
243 where the High Court held that the (drunken) driver of a stolen car owed no duty of
care to a passenger who was involved in the illegal activity and who was clearly aware
of the driver's intoxication.

The options open to the defendant

[16.35]   If, *despite all reasonable precautions* that could have been taken in the circumstances, some unavoidable risk still remains, the defendant will not be liable just because
someone does sustain an injury. All that the law demands is that defendants take those
preventative measures that can reasonably be expected in the circumstances.

Case Example

The plaintiff, who had a history of dermatitis, sued her employer arguing that it
should not have allowed her to do work which involved a risk of causing or ag-
gravating the disease. The employer pointed out that the plaintiff had been
given the driest work available, that she had requested and accepted that work
without protest and that the only other alternative open to it would have been
to have dismissed her. The company was held not liable. It had done all that
could reasonably be expected of it short of refusing to employ the plaintiff at all
and, therefore, had met the required standard of care vis-à-vis the plaintiff. The
court would not accept that the company should have been put in the position
of having either to dismiss her or pay her damages when the inevitable happened: *Withers v Perry Chain Co Ltd* [1961] 3 All ER 676.

Failure to meet the required standard

[16.36]   Failure to meet the required standard of care simply means a failure to do that which a 'reasonable man' would have done in the circumstances. Therefore, each case will depend on its own facts. However, matters that may be relevant in determining what was reasonable in the circumstances may include:

- the risk that was actually involved in the defendant's act or omission;
- the need for the defendant to accept an element of risk in the circumstances (otherwise known as the defence of 'emergency');
- the practicality of requiring the defendant to adopt the sort of preventative measures that would have been required to eliminate the risk; and
- any established community standards governing the type of activity that caused the loss, damage or injury and the precautions expected of those engaged in that activity.

The risk involved

[16.37]   Clearly, the standard of care that should be demanded in any situation should bear some direct relationship to the risk that the defendant's acts or omissions might actually result in loss, damage or injury to others. As Mason J put it in *Wyong Shire Council v Shirt* (1979) 146 CLR 40 at 47:

> In deciding whether there has been a breach of the duty of care the tribunal of fact must first ask itself whether a reasonable man in the defendant's position would have foreseen that his conduct involved a risk of injury to the plaintiff or to a class of persons including the plaintiff. If the answer be in the affirmative, it is then for the tribunal of fact to determine what a reasonable man would do by way of response to the risk.

Therefore, if the risk of danger is minimal and the preventative measures that the defendant has taken are appropriate, he or she should not be liable if something completely unexpected happens.

Case Example

The plaintiff was injured when she was struck by a cricket ball that had been hit out of the defendant's cricket ground. The ball had been hit nearly 100 yards and it had cleared a protective fence which was approximately 17 feet above the level of the cricket pitch and located about 78 yards from the batsman. The court held that, although there was a risk that balls would be hit out of the ground (six had been hit out of the ground in the previous 28 years), that risk — and the risk that someone would be struck — was so minimal (no -one had ever been hit before), that the steps the defendants had taken to avoid the danger were 'reasonable in the circumstances'. They were not liable: *Bolton v Stone* [1951] AC 850.

[16.38]   On the other hand, if there is a real risk and if the defendant fails to take proper steps to counter it, he or she will be liable for any resulting loss, damage or injury. For example, in *Hilder v Associated Portland Cement Manufacturers Ltd* [1961] 3 All ER 709 the defendant company allowed children to play football on land which was screened from the highway by a fence which was only a metre high. The company was aware that the ball periodically went over the fence and onto the roadway. On this occasion a ball passed over the wall and caused the plaintiff's husband to fall off his motor bike. He sustained injuries from which he later died. The company was held liable. A 'reasonable man' would have appreciated that there was a risk to highway users and the company had failed to take steps to guard against the sort of danger that it should have foreseen.

The High Court applied the same principle in *Nagle v Rottnest Island Authority* (1993) 177 CLR 423. In that case the defendant authority was held liable for failing to warn the plaintiff of the very real dangers of diving in an area where there were a number of submerged and not readily visible rocks. The Authority had actively promoted the area for recreational purposes, was aware of the presence of the rocks but had not erected signs to warn visitors of the dangers. The court found that the Authority had a duty to take reasonable care to avoid foreseeable risks to visitors, that there was a very real and foreseeable risk that divers in that area could be injured (even though diving there might reasonably have been regarded as foolhardy or unlikely), that the Authority should have considered the possibility that at least some of its visitors might not take proper care for their own safety and that it should have erected warning signs as an appropriate means of discharging its duty. By failing to erect those signs it had not met the standard of care required of it in the circumstances.

On the other hand, in *Romeo v Conservation Commission of the Northern Territory* (1998) 151 ALR 263 the Conservation Commission was held not liable for failing to fence off a cliff top to prevent visitors falling. Unlike the situation in *Nagle's* case, the danger of falling was, or should have been, obvious to all. Consequently, while the Commission had to take into account the possibility of inadvertent or negligent conduct by people visiting the site, it was also entitled to assume that most of them would take reasonable care for their own safety. As a result (and in the circumstances) its failure to provide a barrier fence as protection against the risk that occurred (the plaintiff falling off the cliff while affected by alcohol) was not unreasonable.

The need to accept an element of risk

[16.39]   Occasionally, defendants may have to accept an element of risk to the general population or even just to those with whom they are in close contact because of some greater or more pressing need. The need to take risks in such cases is justified on the grounds of either 'emergency' or 'necessity' and, if injury does result, the defendant will not normally be liable because, under situations of emergency or necessity, exceptional risks may be acceptable. Therefore, provided the risk taken is no greater than was warranted in the circumstances, the defendant will probably be held to have met the required standard of care. The defence of 'emergency' is only accepted where it is clear that the risk taken was completely warranted.

Case Example

Watt, a fireman, was injured when an inadequately secured jack rolled onto his leg. It was being transported (using the only available means) to free a woman trapped under a heavy vehicle 300 yards from the fire station. He sued the Fire Authority and failed. In the circumstances, the officer in charge had been justified in accepting the risk to those stabilising the jack on the back of the truck because the woman's life could have been in grave danger had those measures not been taken: *Watt v Hertfordshire County Council* [1954] 2 All ER 368.

The practicality of adopting preventative measures

[16.40]   It is probably possible to adopt preventative measures which will avoid any but the most outrageously unexpected injuries occurring to any person. However, the law does not demand that level of precaution. All that it requires is that defendants adopt those measures which a 'reasonable man' would take in the circumstances. If a particular measure is not practical or if it would be an unwarranted or unnecessary safeguard it will not be demanded. So, for example, in *Bolton v Stone* a higher fence could have been erected but it was not really a practical solution given the nature of the risk that the cricket club faced.

Similarly, in *Latimer v AEC Ltd* [1953] AC 643 the defendant factory owners were held not liable for injuries that the plaintiff sustained when he slipped on an oil patch on the factory floor. An abnormally heavy storm had caused a flood of water through the factory and a thin film of oil remained on the floor when the water subsided. The company spread a layer of sawdust over the affected areas but it did not have enough to cover the entire space. The plaintiff slipped in one of the untreated areas. He sued arguing, inter alia, that the factory should have been closed. The House of Lords held that the company had done all that could reasonably have been expected of it in the circumstances. It would have been unreasonable to have expected it to close the factory given that the floor area had been made as safe as it could be in those circumstances.

Whether the same result would be reached today is a problematical question. In recent years the courts have increasingly required a standard of care that takes into account the possibility that people can and will do silly things and that they will not always take the sort of care for their own safety that they should take. So, in *Nagle v Rottnest Island Authority* the Authority was held liable even though the court found that diving in the area in question was foolhardy and that it was reasonably unlikely that anyone would attempt it. The essential question that the court asked itself was, 'Was the risk so unlikely as to be far-fetched or fanciful?' Clearly, in that case it was not and, on that basis, the Authority was held liable. Similar reasoning was used in *Bus v Sydney City Council* (1989) 167 CLR 78 where the defendant council was held liable for the death of an electrician electrocuted when he touched live terminals in a service cabinet which a council employee had left uncovered. The electrician had known that the terminals were 'live' but that did not affect the council's liability. Its employee should have recognised the possibility that the plaintiff might have acted negligently or might have inadvertently touched the terminals and should have guarded against that possibility (which was neither far-fetched nor fanciful) by simply replacing the protective cover before he left the area. (The same reasoning was referred to with approval but was held not to be applicable on the particular facts of *Romeo v Conservation Commission of the Northern Territory* (1998) 151 ALR 263.)

[16.41]   Therefore, if there is a real risk and if the preventative measures that were not taken could have been taken without undue effort or cost (as, for example, in *Miletic v Capital Territory Health Commission* (1995) 130 ALR 591, where the cause of the plaintiff's injuries — castors jamming on a hospital bed — could have been eliminated by the simple and inexpensive expedient of oiling them periodically with a lubricating spray), the tortfeasor may be held liable for any resulting loss, damage or injury. The critical questions in such cases are always: could the measures have been taken and would the 'reasonable man' have taken them?

> ## Case Example
>
> Haley, who was blind, tripped over a long-handled hammer which the London Electricity Board's workmen had leaned against a rail to warn pedestrians away from a hole which they had excavated in the pavement. Haley had not seen nor felt the hammer until he tripped over it. The board was held liable because its employees had failed to take those precautionary measures (which they could have taken without undue effort) to avoid endangering people (including blind people) whom they might reasonably have expected to use the pavement before proper barriers were erected: *Haley v London Electricity Board* [1965] AC 778.

Obviously, similar principles were applied in both *Nagle v Rottnest Island Authority* and *Bus v Sydney City Council* but were not relevant on the facts in *Romeo v Conservation Commission of the Northern Territory*.

Established and accepted community standards

[16.42] Community standards can operate both for and against a defendant. If there is an accepted community standard (as in, for example, the workplace health and safety standards) and the defendant fails to comply with what might be considered 'the usual practice', that failure can clearly be a failure to adopt the standard of care required in the circumstances. Worse, the defendant will not be able to argue that the measures that should have been taken were not practicable because, obviously, others in similar circumstances (those who had adopted and implemented them) had found them to be practicable. However, merely failing to follow a statutory standard may not be proof of negligence. A defendant may well have valid reasons for not doing what a particular statute seems to require and, in any case, failure by one party to follow a statutory standard does not necessarily excuse the other party from his or her duty to take reasonable care.

> ## Case Example
>
> The defendant had breached the traffic regulations by failing to give way to a car on his right. It was held that that was not enough to establish that he had acted negligently or that his negligence had been the sole cause of the accident. The court accepted that the other driver also had a duty to act reasonably and that he could not simply say that, because the defendant had failed to perform his statutory duties, he (the plaintiff), was completely free of blame: *Sibley v Kais* (1967) 118 CLR 424.

[16.43] Accepted practice as a defence Even where a defendant does conform to accepted practice that conformity may still not operate as an absolute defence. In particular, adherence to community standards will not be a defence to an allegation of negligence where the circumstances warranted a higher than normal standard of care. This was the case, for example, in *Paris v Stepney Borough Council* [1951] AC 367 where the court found that the employer had owed the plaintiff a higher standard of care than normal because he had already lost the sight of one eye.

Similarly, the mere fact that a community standard applies to a particular practice does not necessarily mean that that standard is all the law will require. If the community's 'usual practice' involves unnecessary risk, the standard itself might be negligent. What the law requires is that the 'tortfeasor' adhere to a standard of what *ought* to be done rather than what is usually done. So, for example, in *Mercer v Commissioner for Road Transport and Tramways (NSW)* (1937) 56 CLR 580 the Commission was held liable for failing to fit a 'dead man's handle' to its trams to guard against the possibility that one of its driver's could collapse at the wheel and cause injury to passengers or other road users, even though those devices were not used as standard in other tramway systems. The High Court simply pointed out (at 593) that 'the general practice itself may not conform to the standard of care required of a reasonably prudent man. In such a case it is not a good defence that the defendant acted in accordance with the general practice'.

Proving the breach of duty

[16.44]   In any litigation, the general rule of thumb is that 'he or she who alleges must prove'. This simply means that it is always up to the plaintiff to convince the court that there is at least a prima facie case for the defendant to answer. If the plaintiff cannot establish a prima facie case, his or her action must fail. In negligence actions this means that the plaintiff must prove not only that the defendant owed him or her a duty of care but also that the defendant breached that duty and, thereby, caused loss, damage or injury. In the normal course of events this means that the plaintiff must be able to identify the person whose acts or omissions are alleged to have been negligent and must then show that that person failed to exercise the standard of care that was required of him or her in the circumstances.

Res ipsa loquitur

[16.45]   Occasionally, the plaintiff's job is made a little easier if the identity of the alleged tortfeasor and the negligence of his or her acts or omissions are relatively clear. In those cases, the plaintiff may be able to plead *'res ipsa loquitur'* and, thereby, avoid some of the problems of proving his or her case. *Res ipsa loquitur* means 'the thing speaks for itself'. In other words, something has happened, it does not 'normally' happen unless someone has been negligent and, therefore, negligence can be assumed.

Res ipsa loquitur is a rule of *evidence* rather that a rule of substantive law and, as such, it allows negligence to be inferred. That is, it does not mean that negligence will necessarily be found. The onus of proving negligence still rests with the plaintiff and, although, strictly, a defendant need not *disprove* negligence, if a plaintiff relies on a plea of *res ipsa loquitur*, the defendant should try to adduce evidence to show that his or her actions were not negligent or that they were not the effective cause of the plaintiff's injury.

Pleas of *res ipsa loquitur* were successful in:

- *Byrne v Boadle* (1863) 2 H&C 722, in which the plaintiff was struck by a barrel of flour that fell from an upper window of the defendant's premises;
- *Scott v London & St. Katherine Docks Co* (1865) 3 H&C 596, where a customs officer was injured when he was struck by six bags of sugar falling from a jigger hoist being used to lower them from the upper levels of the defendant's warehouse; and
- *Chaproniere v Mason* (1905) 21 TLR 633, in which the plaintiff broke a tooth on a stone contained in a Bath bun he had bought from the defendant bakers.

In each of those cases the facts were such that negligence could be inferred (because accidents of those kinds do not normally occur without negligence) and, in addition, there was a reasonable inference that the person who had been negligent was the defendant because, in each case, the defendant had had the exclusive control of the thing which caused the injury.

Limitations of *res ipsa loquitur*

[16.46]   A plea of *res ipsa loquitur* is not necessarily proof of negligence. A defendant can argue, for example, that the facts simply indicate that *someone* has been negligent, not that he or she was that someone (in which case the plaintiff's action must fail because the plaintiff bears the onus of establishing the tortfeasor's identity). Alternatively, a defendant can argue that, although his or her acts or omissions resulted in the injury and the facts are such that a plea of *res ipsa loquitur* could establish a prima facie case of negligence, he or she had actually done all that was reasonable to prevent injury occurring and, therefore, had met the required standard of care.

Case Example

The plaintiff's home was destroyed and her husband was killed when a gas main fractured, gas escaped and exploded. The Gas Board showed that the main had broken because of a very severe frost, that there were really no reasonable steps that it could have taken to safeguard the public against the consequences of such occurrences but that it had had work crews standing by to deal with problems as they were discovered. Essentially, their defence was that no amount of care would or could have prevented the particular leak or the explosion that followed it. The board was held not liable because it had done all that could reasonably be expected of it in the circumstances: *Pearson v North Western Gas Board* [1968] 2 All ER 669.

Similarly, a defendant may be able to defeat a plea of *res ipsa loquitur* by showing that the plaintiff has not established a sufficient causal link between the alleged breach and the injury.

Case Example

The plaintiff, who was injured when he slipped on a grape in the haberdashery department of the defendant's shop, failed to recover because the presence of the grape could not be linked to the defendant. The plaintiff had also failed to establish how long the grape had been on the floor and whether it was reasonable for the defendant to have cleared it away during that time. The court held that, in the absence of such evidence, the action had to fail because there was nothing to show that the defendant had breached its duty of care: *Dulhunty v J B Young Ltd* (1975) 7 ALR 409.

Proving 'damage'

[16.47]   The third element required in any action in negligence is proof that the plaintiff suffered loss, damage or injury as a result of the defendant's negligent acts or omissions. Without proof of damage there is no action because negligence is not actionable per se. To establish the necessary damage a plaintiff must prove three things:

- that the loss, damage or injury that he or she suffered is loss, damage or injury which the law is prepared to recognise;
- that the loss, damage or injury was actually caused by the defendant's negligence; and
- that the loss, damage or injury is not too 'remote' in law to be recoverable.

Damage recognised by the law

[16.48]   The requirement that the plaintiff's damage be damage that the law is prepared to recognise simply means that the plaintiff's loss, damage or injury must be loss, damage or injury that the law is prepared to compensate. There are at least three instances in which the law will not recognise damage in that sense:

- Where the damage suffered is the termination of some benefit flowing from criminal or fraudulent activity. For example, in *Burns v Edman* [1970] 2 QB 541 the plaintiff sought compensation for the death of her husband, a thief killed in a car accident. Her claim for deprivation of support failed because what she might reasonably have expected her husband to provide (and, therefore, what she had lost as a result of his death) was really only the proceeds of his future criminal activities.
- Where the damage is too vague to be legally recognised. This simply means that if the loss, damage or injury cannot be quantified in money terms the plaintiff cannot recover. For example, in *Roberts v Roberts* (1864) 122 ER 874 the plaintiff's action for slander failed because the damage she alleged (expulsion from her church) was too vague and unquantifiable to be recoverable.
- Where the plaintiff cannot prove that any loss, damage or injury has been suffered at all. In such cases damages cannot be awarded because there is no proven loss, damage or injury to justify compensation.

The causal link between the breach and the damage

[16.49]   A plaintiff must also be able to show that the loss, damage or injury that he or she suffered was effectively caused by the defendant's negligent acts or omissions. A test that is often used to establish the required causal link is the 'but for' test. It works by asking the question, '*but for* the acts or omissions complained of, would the plaintiff have sustained the loss, damage or injury actually suffered?' If the loss, damage or injury would not have been sustained 'but for' the defendant's acts or omissions, it is reasonably safe to say that the required causal link between the defendant's breach of duty and the plaintiff's loss, damage or injury has been established.

Unfortunately, the 'but for' test cannot be applied in every instance, particularly if the defendant's negligent acts or omissions were only part of what caused the plaintiff's loss, damage or injury.

Case Example

The plaintiff's husband was killed when he had an epileptic fit and fell from a painting platform 20 feet above the ground. The platform was unsafe, because it did not comply with the statutory safety regulations, but the plaintiff's husband had also been negligent in not informing his employer that his doctor had forbidden him to work at heights because he could suffer a fit and fall. Clearly, in that case, the 'but for' test was of little real use because the husband's death was really caused, in equal measure, by the deceased's negligence in not informing his employer of his medical condition and the employer's negligence in not complying with the required safety standards: *Cork v Kirby Maclean Ltd* [1952] 2 All ER 402.

[16.50] A preferable test is probably to ask whether, on the balance of probabilities, the defendant's acts or omissions *caused or materially contributed to* the plaintiff's loss, damage or injury. The operation of this test was well illustrated in *Bonnington Castings Ltd v Wardlaw* [1956] AC 613 in which the plaintiff, a steel dresser, contracted pneumoconiosis by inhaling silica dust at his place of work. Inhalation of some of the dust was inevitable given the technological standards of the time but some of the danger could have been prevented had his employers kept the dust extraction ducts on their swing grinders free from obstruction, as the relevant safety regulations required. The House of Lords held that the employers were liable because, on the balance of probabilities, inhaling the dust from the swing grinders had caused or had materially contributed to the plaintiff contracting the disease.

One instance in which a plaintiff will not be able to establish the necessary causal link is where his or her loss, damage or injury was inevitable and was not materially caused or contributed to by the defendant's acts or omissions.

Case Example

The plaintiff's husband presented at the defendant's hospital complaining of vomiting. He was sent home and told to see his own doctor the next day. A few hours later he died of arsenic poisoning. The plaintiff sued the hospital alleging that her husband's death had been caused by the negligence of its medical staff. She failed. Although the doctor on duty had not met the required standard of care (had been negligent) in refusing to examine him, her husband's death was not the result of that negligence. Even if he had been seen and treated, he would still have died because the effects of the poison could not have been reversed: *Barnett v Chelsea & Kensington Hospital Management Committee* [1969] 1 QB 428.

The damage must not have been 'too remote'

[16.51] A defendant is not liable for all possible consequences of his or her negligent acts or omissions; he or she is only liable for such consequential damage as was 'reasonably foreseeable'. In other words, there must be a causal link between the defendant's negligent acts or omissions and the plaintiff's loss, damage or injury not only in fact but also in law. The test of 'reasonable foreseeability' (could the defendant have reasonably foreseen the *kind* of loss, damage or injury that the plaintiff suffered?) was laid down in *Overseas Tankship (UK) Ltd v Morts Dock & Engineering Co Ltd (The Wagon Mound No 1)* [1961] AC 388 and whether something will or will not be 'reasonably foreseeable' in any particular circumstance was discussed in *Overseas Tankship (UK) Ltd v Miller Steamship Co Pty Ltd (The Wagon Mound No 2)* [1967] AC 617.

Case Example

The appellants carelessly allowed a large quantity of bunkering oil to escape into Sydney Harbour where it drifted to a wharf where two of the respondent's ships were undergoing repairs. Hot metal from some oxy-acetylene welding and cutting work fell onto cotton waste floating in the oil, the waste ignited, the oil was set alight and the respondent's ships were damaged.

The court found that a reasonable man having the knowledge and experience of a ship's chief engineer should have known that there was a real risk that the oil would catch fire and should have taken steps to prevent that happening. It held that 'something will be reasonably foreseeable if a reasonable man in the defendant's position would recognise it as a real possibility and not brush it aside as too far-fetched'. In other words, damage will be 'reasonably foreseeable' if there is a real risk that it could occur: *Overseas Tankship (UK) Ltd v Miller Steamship Co Pty Ltd (The Wagon Mound No 2)* [1967] AC 617.

The 'egg shell skull' rule

[16.52]   One major qualification to the general requirement that the plaintiff's damage must have been reasonably foreseeable before the defendant will be liable for it, is what is described as the 'egg shell skull' rule. In essence, this rule simply says that you must take your victim as you find him or her. If the victim has some affliction which means that a particular injury might have more serious consequences than normal, the defendant cannot use that fact alone to limit or escape liability. In law, if the injury actually inflicted was foreseeable, the tortfeasor will be liable for all of its consequences whether they were foreseeable or not. For example, in *Smith v Leech Brain & Co Ltd* [1962] 2 QB 405 the plaintiff's husband was burnt when he was accidentally splashed with molten metal while carrying out some galvanising. The burn caused cancerous tissues to turn malignant and he eventually died. The court found that because the burn was a foreseeable consequence of the defendant's negligence and because the husband's death was a direct consequential result of the burn, the defendant was liable even though the death, in itself, was not a reasonably foreseeable consequence of the failure to prevent the original burn.

Novus actus interveniens

[16.53]   A plea of *'novus actus interveniens'* (literally a 'new intervening act') allows a defendant to escape liability if his or her negligence was not, in fact, the 'proximate cause' of the plaintiff's loss, damage or injury. That is, the defendant escapes liability because the loss, damage or injury was effectively caused by something which happened *after* the defendant's negligent act or omission.

Case Example

A police constable sent to close a traffic tunnel in which the defendant had over-turned his car was injured when he collided with an oncoming motor vehicle. He sued, alleging that his injuries were a direct result of the defendant's negligence in overturning his car. He failed. The orders that his inspector had given him (to close the tunnel), and the route that he taken to carry those orders out (riding against the one-way flow of traffic), constituted a *novus actus interveniens* with-out which he would have not have been injured. In other words, neither his orders nor his chosen method of carrying them out could be characterised as a *natural and probable consequence* of the defendant's negligence. Nor were they reasonably foreseeable. Consequently, although there was some causal link *in fact* between the defendant's negligence and his injury, there was no causal link *in law*. The defendant was not liable. (The inspector was, however, found liable because he had failed to take steps to ensure that the plaintiff was not exposed to unwarranted risk.): *Knightley v Johns* [1982] 1 All ER 851.

[16.54]   Not all intervening acts 'break the chain of causation' and allow the defendant to escape liability for the 'indirect' consequences of his or her negligent behaviour. To have that effect, the intervening act itself must not have been reasonably foreseeable. For example, in *Stansbie v Troman* [1948] 2 KB 48 the defendant, a decorator who knew that he was alone in the plaintiff's house left it to get some wallpaper. He closed the door behind him but did not lock it. A thief entered the house and stole the plaintiff's property. The decorator was held liable. He had been negligent in leaving the house unlocked and, although he was not the direct cause of the plaintiff's loss, the chain of causation had not been broken by the intervening event (the entry of the thief), because that was a *likely and unforeseeable consequence* of his negligent omission.

Defences open to a defendant

[16.55]   A defendant can always defend an allegation of negligence on the grounds that the plaintiff has failed to prove the necessary elements. That is, the defendant can try to show that, in the circumstances, the plaintiff was not owed a duty of care at all, or that the defendant's acts or omissions were not a breach of any such duty or that, if they were, the plaintiff's loss, damage or injury was not properly compensable for any of the reasons discussed above. Defendants can also limit or even eliminate their liability by pleading either contributory negligence or *'volenti non fit injuria'*.

Contributory negligence

[16.56]   Originally, if a plaintiff was in any way responsible for his or her own loss, dam-age or injury the defendant escaped liability entirely. This could be very unfair and that rule has now been statutorily altered in all Australian jurisdictions. The relevant provi-sions, except in the case of Western Australia, are modelled on s 1(1) of the United Kingdom Law Reform (Contributory Negligence) Act 1945, which provides that:

Where any person suffers damage as a result partly of his own fault and partly of the fault of any other person or persons, a claim in respect of that damage shall not be defeated by reason of the fault of the person suffering the damage, but the damages recoverable in respect thereof shall be reduced to such extent as the court thinks just and equitable having regard to the claimant's share in the responsibility for the damage.

Consequently, to establish contributory negligence a defendant must prove that the plaintiff was at least partially at fault and that that fault effectively contributed to the loss, damage or injury.

A defendant can show that the plaintiff was at fault in essentially two ways — by showing that the plaintiff breached some duty that he or she owed the defendant, or by showing that the plaintiff failed to exercise reasonable care for his or her own safety. An example of the former occurs when a job applicant tells the employer that he or she has particular skills which he or she does not have. If the employee is then injured performing tasks that he or she should have been competent to perform, the employee will be guilty of, at least, contributory negligence and his or her damages will be reduced accordingly. For example, in *Kerry v Carter* [1969] 3 All ER 723 the plaintiff, an 18-year-old apprentice whose hand was injured by a circular saw he was using to cut up firewood, had his damages reduced by two-thirds because (a) he had put his hand across the blade of the saw and, (b) he had deliberately misled his employer about his previous experience with and competence to use circular saws.

[16.57]   Contributory negligence arising out of a failure to take care for one's own safety is a little more complex. Generally, if people act in total disregard for their own safety and are injured they must bear at least a proportion of the blame *unless* they can plead 'justification'.

Case Example

The plaintiff was trapped in a cubicle in a public toilet because its internal door handle was missing. She attempted to climb out placing her right foot on the toilet roll. When it rotated, she fell and was injured. Her action against the council succeeded but her damages were reduced by 25 per cent because of contributory negligence. In relying on the toilet roll for support, she had not taken reasonable care for her own safety and that failure could not, at least in this case, be excused on the grounds of 'justification': *Sayers v Harlow Urban District Council* [1958] 2 All ER 342.

On the other hand, in *Caterson v Commissioner for Railways* (1973) 128 CLR 99, the plaintiff, who was injured when he leapt from a slowly moving train, was held not to have been guilty of contributory negligence because, in the circumstances, his actions were justified. The train had started moving without warning and, because he knew that the next stop was 80 miles away, because the train was moving slowly and because his young son was waiting for him on the platform, he decided to jump. When weighed against the degree of inconvenience to which he would have been subjected had he not jumped, the risk he had taken was 'justified'.

Volenti non fit injuria

[16.58]   *'Volenti non fit injuria'* means 'the willing cannot be injured'. The defence of *'volenti'* essentially operates by asserting that the plaintiff freely and voluntarily assumed the risk that gave rise to his or her injury. Consequently, having assumed that risk, the plaintiff should not be allowed to lay the blame on someone else. Unlike contributory negligence, *volenti* is a total defence. That is, if it succeeds the plaintiff gets nothing at all. However, to make out a defence of *volenti* the defendant must show that the plaintiff consented to the actual risk to which he or she was exposed. Such consent can be either express or inferred. Defences based on express consent are relatively rare (probably because those who could be plaintiffs in such cases realise that they have no chance of succeeding and do not sue), but they do occur. For example, in *Bennett v Tugwell* [1971] 2 QB 267, the plaintiff was denied compensation for injuries he suffered when the defendant drove the vehicle into the back of a parked car — because he had accepted a ride in a motor vehicle in which a sign clearly warned passengers that they travelled 'at their own risk'.

Where the plaintiff's consent to undertake the risk is to be inferred, the defendant must show both that the plaintiff was aware of the risk and that he or she freely consented to it. The mere fact that a plaintiff participates in something which he or she knows to be *generally* dangerous is not enough to establish that he or she willingly undertook the *particular risks* that gave rise to the injury actually suffered.

Case Example

The plaintiff was injured while waterskiing when he collided with a boat moored in the water. He alleged that the defendant had been negligent in steering the ski boat too close and in not warning him of the other boat's presence. The defendant argued that the plaintiff had voluntarily assumed the risks of water-skiing and that, therefore, he was not liable. The High Court accepted that the plaintiff had voluntarily assumed the *normal* risks associated with waterskiing, including the risk of colliding with obstructions in the water, but it did not accept that he had voluntarily undertaken the risk that the defendant would negligently fail to warn him of obstructions or fail to exercise due care in steering the ski boat. It held the defendant liable: *Rootes v Shelton* (1967) 116 CLR 383.

Negligent misstatement

[16.59]   Liability for negligent misstatement is simply a variation of liability for negligence generally. Therefore plaintiffs must still show that the defendant owed them a duty of care, that he or she breached that duty, that there was a resulting loss and that there was a sufficiently 'proximate' relationship to warrant a finding of liability. The real difficulty in negligent misstatement is ascertaining whether, on the facts, there was the required 'proximate' relationship between the parties.

The early position

[16.60]   The early common law position was that a mere negligent misstatement did not, of itself, allow an injured party to recover against the person who had made it. The plaintiff had to show that the defendant had been bound to supply correct information (or at least information which he or she believed on reasonable grounds to be correct) under an obligation founded in either contract or fiduciary duty.

Even after *Donoghue v Stevenson* established the general principles of negligence in 1932 the courts showed a marked reluctance to extend those principles to allow a plaintiff to recover pure economic loss suffered as a result of relying on a defendant's negligent misstatement. That reluctance was based on a concern that many individuals could suffer loss as the result of a single negligent misstatement and all might be able to satisfy the test of 'reasonable foreseeability'. In effect, the courts thought that allowing people to sue for economic loss resulting from a negligent misstatement would open up a whole new Pandora's box of potential litigation.

[16.61]   The first judicial recognition that there might be a *general* right of recovery where a plaintiff suffered loss or damage as a result of receiving and acting on negligent advice was in Lord Denning's dissenting judgment in *Candler v Crane, Christmas & Co* [1951] 2 KB 16, a case dealing with the liability of accountants for false and misleading accounts which had been given to potential investors by the company for which they had been prepared. Lord Denning took the view that the duty of care in such cases was not owed to *everyone* who might possibly use the information (the 'neighbour' principle from *Donoghue v Stevenson*). Instead, it was restricted to those for whom, or for whose specific purposes, the information was actually provided. To the question, 'to whom do advisers owe a duty of care?' Lord Denning provided the answer (at 180):

> They owe the duty, of course, to their employer or client, and also, I think, to any third person to whom they themselves show the accounts, or to whom they know their employer is going to show the accounts so as to induce him to invest money or take some other action on them. I do not think, however, the duty can be extended still further so as to include strangers of whom they have heard nothing and to whom their employer without their knowledge may choose to show their accounts.'

[16.62]   It was not, however, until 1964 that there was a *general* recognition that a limited duty of care existed in situations where loss resulted from receiving and acting on negligent advice or information. The case was *Hedley Byrne & Co Ltd v Heller & Partners Ltd* [1964] AC 465 and the general principle it established was that if a person who possesses special skill undertakes, irrespective of contract, to apply that skill in circumstances where it will be relied on, a duty of care will arise. The basis of liability in such cases, it was said, was to be found in the existence of a 'special relationship' between the adviser and the advised. That 'special relationship' arose out of the special knowledge, skill or ability and the assumption of responsibility (on the part of the adviser) and reliance (on the part of the advised). The decision, therefore, demanded that the defendant have 'special knowledge' and that the plaintiff have reasonably relied on it. In practice, therefore, liability for negligent misstatement was effectively limited to professional advisors and those who held themselves out as having a special skill or expertise on which others were entitled to rely.

Case Example

Before Hedley Byrne organised advertising for Easipower Ltd, it did a credit check. Easipower's bank, Heller & Partners Ltd, replied that Easipower Ltd was a 'respectably constituted company, considered good for its ordinary business engagements'. However, it *specifically* gave that information 'without responsibility'. When Easipower went into liquidation, Hedley Byrne suffered loss. It sued Heller & Partners arguing that it had given its assurance negligently. The House of Lords held that a defendant *could* be liable for negligent misstatements in the absence of a contractual or fiduciary relationship — if there was a 'special relationship' between the parties. As Lord Morris put it:

> if someone possessed of a special skill undertakes, quite irrespective of contract, to apply that skill for the assistance of another person who relies on such skill, a duty of care will arise. Furthermore, if ... a person takes it upon himself to give information or advice to, or allows his information or advice to be passed on to, another person who, as he knows, or should know, will place reliance upon it, then a duty of care will arise.

Despite this the appellants were unsuccessful — the disclaimer prevented them recovering: *Hedley Byrne & Co Ltd v Heller & Partners Ltd* [1964] AC 465.

'Assumption of responsibility' and 'reliance'

[16.63]   When the question came before the High Court of Australia in *MLC v Evatt* (1968) 122 CLR 556 the court treated *Hedley Byrne v Heller* as a guide rather than as establishing definitive principles and the majority judges applied a less restrictive test. In particular, Barwick CJ specifically refused to limit liability to situations where advice was given by a professional or by someone holding himself or herself out as having special skill. He believed that there were only three questions to be satisfied to establish a duty of care:

a) was the advice given in respect of a serious or business matter;

b) were the circumstances such that the adviser should have realised that he or she was being trusted to give correct advice; and

c) in the circumstances, was it reasonable for the advised to have relied on the advice?

This more liberal view was overruled on appeal to the Privy Council but the High Court has since reinstated it (appeals to the Privy Council were abolished in 1975). Therefore, in Australia the critical point is not the expertise of the adviser, but the dual requirements of *assumption of responsibility* by the adviser and (reasonable) *reliance* upon that advice by the advised.

The advice must still be in respect of some serious or business matter and the only person who can sue for any resulting loss is still the person for whom it was intended. But *anyone* giving advice can now be liable and liability can result from even 'off-the-cuff' advice if it was given in circumstances in which the adviser could reasonably have foreseen that the other person would rely and act on it.

Case Example

The Parramatta City Council was asked by a developer whether land that he intended to acquire was affected by a road-widening proposal. It advised him that it was not when in fact it was. The council was held liable. The court held that a special relationship had arisen between the parties when the council gave the developer information or advice in circumstances in which it should have realised that it was being trusted to give the information or advice accurately. That relationship was sufficient to create the necessary proximity: *Shaddock and Associates v Parramatta City Council* (1981) 150 CLR 225.

[16.64] The critical importance of both *assumption of responsibility* and *reasonable reliance* was well illustrated by the High Court's later decision in *San Sebastian Pty Ltd v Minister Administering the Environmental Planning and Assessment Act 1979* (1986) 162 CLR 340. The court made it clear that, without those two elements, the parties will not be in a sufficiently 'proximate' relationship to warrant a finding of liability.

Case Example

The NSW State Planning Authority developed a number of 'study documents' for redeveloping Woolloomooloo which the council accepted and placed on public exhibition. The plan was later abandoned when it was discovered that the public transport system would not cope but, in the interim, the plaintiff — allegedly relying on the plan — purchased land in the area. It suffered economic loss and sued the government on the grounds that it had been negligent in publicising the plan. It failed. The 'study documents' were not a firm representation that redevelopment *would* occur — they were only a guide to what *might* occur, 'an expression of present intention and future expectation ... the function of [which was] to provide a general and flexible planning framework within which developers and businessmen are expected to make their own judgments': *San Sebastian Pty Ltd v Minister Administering the Environmental Planning and Assessment Act 1979* (1986) 162 CLR 340.

[16.65] The critical part of the judgment in that case was the court's discussion of the principles used to determine liability for negligent misstatement. It singled out and emphasised the element of *reliance*. Special skill and knowledge on the part of the representor formed no real part of the court's consideration at all — what was critical was *assumption of responsibility* by the representor and *reliance* by the representee. As Gibbs CJ, Mason, Wilson and Dawson JJ said (at 355):

> When the economic loss results from negligent misstatement, the *element of reliance* plays a prominent part in the ascertainment of a relationship of proximity between the plaintiff and the defendant, and therefore in the ascertainment of a duty of care ... In cases of negligent misstatement, reliance plays an important role, particularly so when the defendant directs his statement to a class of persons with the intention of inducing members of the class to act or refrain from acting, in reliance on the statement, in circumstances where he should realise that they may thereby suffer economic loss if the statement is not true.

The court also recognised that there is no real reason why an action for negligent mis-statement cannot be brought even where, as in that case, there is no antecedent request for information, saying (at 356–7):

> But there is no convincing reason for confining the liability to instances of negligent mis-statement made by way of response to a request by the plaintiff for information or advice. The existence of an antecedent request for information or advice certainly assists in demonstrating reliance, which is a cornerstone of liability for negligent misstatement. However, such a request is by no means essential, though it has been suggested that instances of liability for misstatement volunteered negligently will be rare.

[16.66]   That reasoning was recently confirmed in *Esanda Finance Corporation Ltd v Peat Marwick Hungerfords* (1997) 188 CLR 241 where the High Court held that the respondent auditors (Peats) were not liable for losses that Esanda suffered when Excel, a company to which it had lent money (allegedly relying on the published accounts and Peat's audit report), could not repay the loans. Esanda had argued that Peats were bound to comply with the Australian Accounting Standards, that those standards required audi-tors to recognise that loan providers and creditors were likely to be the prime users of their financial statements and that, as Esanda fell within the class of persons who might reasonably rely on the accounts, Peats owed them a duty to ensure that the accounts and the report were reasonably based and reliable.

Relying on the principles established in *MLC v Evatt* and *San Sebastian*, the High Court held that, to establish liability for economic loss, a plaintiff has so show that there was a relationship of 'proximity' between himself or herself and the defendant — some-thing which can only be established in 'special cases'. The mere fact that it was reasonably foreseeable that someone (such as creditors) *might* rely on a statement and suffer loss was not enough. The plaintiff also had to show that the defendant assumed responsibility for providing the information or advice in circumstances in which he or she knew or ought to have known that the plaintiff *would* access the information, that he or she *would* act upon it for a serious purpose and that he or she could suffer loss if it proved to be inaccurate. Here, the mere fact that Peats should reasonably have foreseen that members of a particular class (creditors) *might* rely on the audited accounts was not enough. As Brennan CJ put it (at 252):

> But, in every case, it is necessary for the plaintiff to allege and prove that the defendant knew or ought reasonably to have known that the information or advice would be commu-nicated to the plaintiff, either individually or as a member of an identified class, that the information or advice would be so communicated for a purpose that would be very likely to lead the plaintiff to enter into a transaction of the kind that the plaintiff does enter into and that it would be very likely that the plaintiff would enter into such a transaction in reli-ance on the information or advice and thereby risk the incurring of economic loss if the statement should be untrue or the advice should be unsound. If any of these elements be wanting, the plaintiff fails to establish that the defendant owed the plaintiff a duty to use reasonable care in making the statement or giving the advice.

Therefore, to establish liability for negligent misstatement there must be an 'assump-tion of responsibility' by the defendant (in the knowledge or expectation that the advice or information will be acted on) and 'reliance' by the plaintiff (in the reasonable expec-tation that the plaintiff will take due care in providing *him or her* with that information or advice).

Torts involving unlawful interference with goods

[16.67]   The law regards a person's right to possess and enjoy his or her property without others interfering with it as fundamental. Accordingly, if someone does interfere with it, the law provides a number of remedies aimed at either stopping the interference or compensating the affected party for the consequences of it. Most of these remedies are found in specific torts all of which have their origins in 'trespass', a tort involving some form of direct interference with someone else's property or person.

Trespass to goods

[16.68]   Trespass, as a general cause of action, is the oldest tort and, in broad terms, it simply provides plaintiffs with a remedy for any direct interference with either their land, their person, or their goods. Trespass to land occurs whenever one person directly and unlawfully interferes with another person's lawful possession of land. Usually, it involves the defendant entering or remaining on the plaintiff's land without permission though more indirect interferences can also constitute trespass if they are intentional or, at least, negligent. Therefore, placing, throwing or deliberately letting something (such as a tree) fall onto another person's land will constitute trespass. So will tunnelling under the surface of the land (*Bulli Coal Mining Co v Osbourne* [1899] AC 351), or passing or causing something to pass through the air space above it: *Graham v K D Morris & Sons Pty Ltd* [1974] Qd R 1 and *Bendal Pty Ltd v Mirvac Pty Ltd* (1991) 23 NSWLR 464.

Trespass to the person involves a number of specific torts of which the most important are assault (a direct threat of physical violence), battery (any direct act which results in bodily contact with the plaintiff without his or her consent) and false imprisonment (any direct act by which the plaintiff is wholly deprived of his or her liberty without lawful justification).

Trespass to goods occurs whenever one party directly and unlawfully interferes with someone else's personal property (as opposed to their land). Like trespass to the person it involves a number of specific torts. The more important of these are trespass to chattels, conversion and detinue. All three are dealt with below.

Trespass to chattels

[16.69]   A trespass to chattels is any direct and unjustified physical interference with another's *possession* of goods. There are a number of critical aspects of the tort. First, the tort is committed against a person's possession of goods rather than against his or her ownership of them. Therefore, only the possessor of goods can bring an action in trespass to chattels. The owner (unless he or she is also the possessor) has no legal standing and, therefore, cannot sue.

Case Example

Penfolds sold wine in bottles which passed into the possession of its customers. The bottles were, however, clearly marked with the words, 'This bottle always remains the property of Penfolds Wines Limited'. The defendant, a hotel keeper, obtained empty bottles from his customers (including bottles still owned by Penfolds), refilled them with bulk wine, and then resold them.

> The High Court held that his actions did not constitute a trespass to Penfolds' chattels because he had not interfered with their possession. When he refilled and resold the bottles, they were not, and for some time had not been, in Penfolds' possession: *Penfolds Wines Pty Ltd v Elliott* (1946) 74 CLR 204.

To be in possession of chattels a plaintiff must generally be in actual possession. However, if he or she has an *immediate* right to possession that will suffice. Therefore, if, as Dixon J noted in *Penfolds Wines Pty Ltd v Elliott* (at 227), the goods are in the possession of a servant, an agent or a bailee under a revocable bailment, the master, principal or bailor will be able to bring an action because, at the time of the interference, he or she had an immediate right to possession of the goods.

[16.70]   Second, there must be a *recognised* interference with the goods. Such recognised interferences include damaging or destroying the goods, removing them from the plaintiff's possession, using them without consent or just moving them from one place to another without permission. That is, unless the 'interference' involves damage, dispossession or asportation (moving something from one position to another), it will not constitute a trespass to chattels. In other words, trespass to chattels generally requires something more than simply touching or handling a chattel without permission (though there is some dispute as to whether that will always be the case).

That does not mean that a defendant need necessarily come into direct bodily contact with the plaintiff's goods in order to commit a trespass to chattels. All that is required is that the defendant interfere with those goods in some way. Such interference could involve not only coming into personal contact with them, it could also involve causing something else (a motor car, a projectile or something similar) to come into contact with them or, where the goods are capable of moving by themselves, by doing anything calculated to cause the necessary interference with the plaintiff's possession of them. So, for example, driving a plaintiff's farm animals away by using loud noises or gestures instead of direct physical contact would still constitute 'direct interference' and would, therefore, be a trespass to chattels.

[16.71]   Third, the interference must cause direct (as opposed to consequential) harm to the goods. So, for example, in *Hutchins v Maughan* [1947] VLR 131 the court held that merely throwing baits onto unfenced land where dogs could find them was not a trespass to the plaintiff's dogs (which subsequently took the baits and died) because the harm (the deaths) that resulted from the physical act of throwing the baits was consequential and not direct. Presumably, throwing the baits to the dogs instead of just throwing them onto land where they could find them would have been a sufficiently direct interference to constitute trespass to chattels. See Herring CJ's comments (at 135) and the decision in *Hamps v Darby* [1948] 2 KB 311 where the defendant, who deliberately shot the plaintiff's homing pigeons, was held to have committed trespass to chattels.

[16.72]   Finally, the defendant must have been at fault in committing the trespass. That is, he or she must have either intended to commit the act that resulted in the interference or must have committed it negligently. Therefore, simply bumping into goods and damaging them would not necessarily be a trespass unless the bumping was either deliberate or the result of negligence. So, for example, in *National Coal Board v Evans* [1951] 2 KB 861 the court held that the defendants, who accidentally damaged the plaintiff's underground electricity cable, were not liable in trespass to chattels. They had not known of the cable's presence and had neither acted intentionally nor been negligent when they accidentally damaged it.

Remedy for trespass to chattels

[16.73]   If trespass to chattels can be established, the plaintiff will be entitled to recover damages equal to either the value of the goods (if they have been destroyed or if they are otherwise irrecoverable), or to an amount equal to the reduction in their value or the costs of repairing them, whichever is the more appropriate (if they have simply been damaged).

Conversion

[16.74]   Dixon J defined the essence of conversion in *Penfolds Wines Pty Ltd v Elliott* (1946) 74 CLR 204 at 229 as 'dealing with a chattel in a manner repugnant to the immediate right of possession of the person who has the property or special property in the chattel'. Therefore, conversion involves an interference with the plaintiff's immediate right to possession of a chattel in such a way that the plaintiff is either physically deprived of it or, if his or her physical possession is not affected, the chattel is so damaged or altered that it becomes useless for the plaintiff's purposes. It differs from trespass to chattels in that trespass to chattels is mainly concerned with interference to the physical state of the goods, whereas conversion is more concerned with interference to the plaintiff's continuing rights to possess or control them.

Who may sue?

[16.75]   Because conversion is a tort affecting the *possession* of goods, only those who were in possession of, or who had an immediate right to possession of, the goods before they were converted can sue in conversion. Consequently, those who can sue include the owner of the goods (provided he or she was in possession or was entitled to possession when the goods were converted), others in possession of the goods with the owner's consent (for example, bailees) and, as was seen in Chapter 13, finders: see, again, *Armory v Delamirie* (1722) 1 Strange 505; 93 ER 664 in which the chimney sweep brought his action against the jeweller in 'trover', a forerunner of the current tort of conversion.

What amounts to conversion?

[16.76]   Because conversion is dealing with a chattel in a manner repugnant to someone else's immediate right to possess it a number of things can constitute the tort. Dixon J enumerated some of them in *Penfolds Wines Pty Ltd v Elliott* (1946) 74 CLR 204 at 229, saying that it could take:

> the form of a disposal of the goods by way of sale, or pledge or other intended transfer of an interest followed by delivery, of the destruction or change of the nature or character of the thing ... or of an appropriation evidenced by refusal to deliver or other denial of title.

Consequently, any wrongful taking, keeping, use, abuse, destruction, alteration, transfer, sale, pledge or other disposal of chattels can constitute a conversion if those actions affect the plaintiff's immediate right to possession of the goods by either dispossessing him or her of them entirely or by adversely affecting his or her immediate right to possession in some other way.

The element of intent

[16.77] There is, however, an additional requirement of *intent*. Before any action can constitute conversion it must be shown that the defendant intended the act that resulted in the deprivation of or the impairment of the plaintiff's immediate right to possess the goods allegedly converted.

Case Example

The defendants owned a car park. One of their employees mistakenly allowed a thief, who had misrepresented himself as the plaintiff's friend, to drive the plaintiff's motor vehicle away. The defendants were not liable in conversion. While they may have dealt with the car in a manner inconsistent with the plaintiff's rights to immediate possession of it, they had not done so intentionally: *Ashby v Tolhurst* [1937] 2 KB 242.

On the other hand, if a defendant has deliberately done something which is clearly and directly inconsistent with the plaintiff's continuing rights to possession, those intentional acts can constitute conversion. So, defendants who sell goods that they have no right to sell will be guilty of conversion even though they may have honestly believed that they were entitled to sell them. The critical requirement is that the defendant must have intended the *act* that deprived the plaintiff of possession (or impaired that possession); he or she need not also have intended that the act would deprive the plaintiff of possession (or impair that possession). In fact, the defendant may not even have known that the plaintiff had an interest in the goods. For example, anyone who acquires stolen goods in good faith and without notice of the theft and then sells them will be guilty of conversion even though he or she is unaware that they were stolen.

Remedies for conversion

[16.78] Where goods have been converted, the plaintiff's usual remedy is in damages. However, unlike the situation with trespass to chattels, the damages that are awarded are normally the full value of the goods that have been converted (plus, in appropriate cases, additional compensation for any special loss that the plaintiff may have suffered as a result of the conversion). Because of this, title to those goods passes to the defendant. Consequently, where the plaintiff is not the owner of the goods but merely, for example, a bailee, he or she will have to account to the true owner for that part of the damages that represents the goods' value and will only be able to retain so much as was awarded as compensation for the loss of the use and possession of the goods.

Detinue

[16.79] Detinue is the wrongful detention of goods or the wrongful refusal to return them to the person entitled to possession of them after their return has been demanded. Consequently, unlike both trespass to chattels and conversion, there is no need for unlawful interference or wrongful dealing with the goods — all that is required is a refusal to return them and it is immaterial whether that refusal is because the defendant cannot (as would be the case where the goods have been lost or destroyed) or will not return them.

As with both trespass to chattels and conversion, detinue deals with unlawful impediments to a plaintiff's *possession*, or right to possession, of goods. Consequently, a person with an immediate right to possession can bring an action in detinue even though he or she is not the owner of the goods that are being unlawfully detained. To succeed in an action in detinue a plaintiff normally has to prove that he or she has a right to immediate possession of goods and that the defendant has unlawfully refused to return them. Refusal to return is shown by proving that a specific demand has been made and that the defendant has refused to comply with it. Unless 'demand and refusal' can be shown, an action in detinue cannot succeed. The demand must be 'specific' in the sense that it must indicate both a time and a place at which the goods are to be returned. The refusal need not be unequivocal — mere inaction on the part of the defendant will suffice, provided the facts make it clear that the defendant had no intention of complying with the plaintiff's request. However, if the 'refusal' is not absolute (as, for example, where the defendant simply requests additional time to comply with the request) it will not be a refusal for the purposes of the tort.

Remedies for detinue

[16.80] Where detinue can be established, the courts can order a defendant either to return the goods that have been unlawfully detained or to pay the plaintiff damages equal to their value. The plaintiff can also be awarded damages to compensate him or her for any other losses suffered as a result of the unlawful detention.

Torts involving an unlawful interference with business

[16.81] In addition to the torts outlined above, all of which can affect business as well as the public generally, there are a number of torts which specifically involve some form of direct interference with business. These include the torts of passing off, interference with contractual relationships, intimidation and conspiracy.

Passing off

[16.82] The tort of 'passing off' involves selling goods, providing services or carrying on a business in a manner calculated to mislead others into believing that the goods being sold, the services being provided or the business being conducted has some connection with another established business operation. Consequently, passing off is a particular form of misrepresentation which involves unlawful interference with someone else's business interests in a way that can adversely affect the other person's goodwill or business reputation. If passing off can be established, the courts can and will prevent the misleading or deceptive behaviour continuing and can also award damages for any actual loss that the plaintiff has suffered.

Elements of passing off

[16.83] For a defendant to be guilty of passing off, a plaintiff must prove five things (per Lord Diplock in *Warnink v Townend & Sons (Hull) Ltd* [1979] AC 731 at 742):
- that there has been a misrepresentation;

- that it was made by a trader in the course of trade;
- that it was made to his or her customers or to those who would ultimately consume the goods or services that he or she supplied;
- that it was calculated to injure the business or goodwill or another trader (in the sense that the injury must have been a reasonably foreseeable consequence of the defendant's misrepresentation); and
- that it caused, or will probably cause, actual harm to the other trader's business or goodwill.

Essentially, this means that, to be guilty of passing off, a defendant must engage in behaviour that is likely to mislead the public (or a reasonable portion of it) into believing that the defendant's goods or services, or his or her business, is in some way connected with the plaintiff, with the plaintiff's goods or services or with his or her business. The sort of behaviour that can have this effect includes using business or product names that are the same as or similar to the plaintiff's business or product names or using similar or identical packaging, identifying marks, trade marks, logos, slogans or visual images.

Case Example

The South Australian Brewery Co introduced a product which it marketed as 'Duff' beer — a brand associated with the fictional television character, Homer Simpson. While there was no overt mention of 'The Simpsons' in its promotional material the brewery clearly intended to 'cash-in' on the goodwill associated with the show and hoped that customers would associate its product with it. Tamberlin J held that using the name 'Duff' made it 'more probable than not that a large and substantial section of the consuming public will be misled into believing that the beer ... is sanctioned or permitted by the producers or proprietors of 'The Simpsons'. He therefore found the brewery liable in passing off: *Twentieth Century Fox v SA Brewery* (1996) 66 FCR 451.

[16.84]   However, even such intentionally misleading behaviour will not, by itself, constitute passing off unless the public is thereby deceived into believing that, when it deals with the defendant, it is getting the quality, reliability, reputation, backing or other characteristics of the plaintiff's goods or services. Therefore, to mount an action in passing off, the plaintiff must be able to show that his or her products or services have an established reputation (or that there is a certain goodwill attached to them), that that reputation or goodwill is ultimately tied up with some identifier (such as a name or a trade mark), that the defendant has used, or is using, the same or a similar identifier to mislead the public and that the public has been or is likely to be deceived by the defendant's behaviour. The mere fact that the defendant has used, or is using, something associated with the plaintiff's products is not sufficient; there must be such a public perception that the identifier being misused is associated with the plaintiff (or with his or her products) that the public would be deceived into believing that the defendant's activities were, in some formal way, associated with the plaintiff or with his or her products or services.

Case Example

The defendants produced and marketed a Spanish sparkling wine as 'Spanish Champagne'. They were ordered to stop on the grounds that, in the public's mind, the word 'champagne' was intimately connected with wine produced in the Champagne district of France — wine which had an established reputation and following. When the defendants used the word to describe their wine they did so to benefit from that reputation and in the hope that the public would not understand the difference. As Danckwerts J put it (at 567):

> persons whose life or education has not taught them much about the nature and production of wine, but who from time to time want to purchase 'Champagne', as the wine with the great reputation are likely to be misled.

Bollinger v Costa Brava Wine Co (No 2) [1961] 1 WLR 277.

[16.85] On the other hand, if the public is unlikely to be misled by a defendant's conduct there will be no passing off. So, for example, in *Francesco Cinzano & Cia (Aust) Pty Ltd v Ruggiero (No 2)* [1980] 25 SASR 341, the defendants, who had applied to use the word 'Cinzano' in the name of their restaurant, were held not to be guilty of passing off because the difference in the nature and magnitude of their restaurant business and the plaintiff's wines and spirits business was so great that the general public would not be misled into believing that one was linked to the other simply because they both used the same name.

Remedies for passing off

[16.86] Where passing off can be established, the plaintiff can seek a number of possible remedies. He or she can seek damages (which, at common law, are said to be 'at large') for any loss actually suffered as a result of the passing off, including damages for loss of goodwill or damage to business reputation. In addition, exemplary or punitive damages can be awarded in appropriate cases. Alternatively, the plaintiff can sue for an account of the profits the defendant made by passing his or her goods or services off as the plaintiff's. Injunctions to prevent both actual and threatened passing off can also be sought.

Alternatives to actions for passing off

[16.87] If a plaintiff does not want to sue in passing off, he or she can instead bring an action under one of the specific statutes, such as the Trade Marks Act or the Designs Act (see Chapter 14) that provide protection for 'industrial property' or, alternatively, under either the 'misleading and deceptive conduct' or the 'false or misleading representations' provisions (ss 52 and 53) of the Trade Practices Act 1974 (Cth). The remedies available under those sections include both injunctions to prevent further infringing conduct and damages for losses that the plaintiff has suffered as a result of it. The specific provisions are dealt with in more detail in Chapter 8.

Procuring breach of contract

[16.88] All that has to be shown to establish the tort of 'procuring breach of contract' is that someone has induced one party to a contract to breach his or her obligations under it. If that happens, the other party can sue the interloper for either an injunction (if the breach has not yet occurred) or for damages (if the breach has occurred). Wightman J set out the basic principle upon which the tort rests in *Lumley v Gye* (1853) 118 ER 749. In that case, a Miss Wagner had been contracted to appear exclusively in the plaintiff's theatre but was induced to breach her contract and to appear in another theatre. The plaintiff sued alleging that the defendant had maliciously interfered with the original contract and had induced Miss Wagner to breach it. He succeeded. As Wightman J put it (at 757):

> It was undoubtedly prima facie an unlawful act on the part of Miss Wagner to break her contract, and therefore a tortious act of the defendant maliciously to procure her to do so; and, if damage to the plaintiff followed in consequence of the tortious act ... an action on the case is maintainable.

Elements

[16.89]　　It is not enough to show that, simply because of some action by the defendant, the contract has been breached. There must be an element of fault on the defendant's part and, specifically, the plaintiff must be able to show six things:

* that there was a valid contract on foot;
* that the defendant was aware of its existence (though knowledge of its precise terms is not necessary);
* that the defendant intended to cause the breach that actually resulted from of his or her actions;
* that the interference was wrongful or unlawful (in the sense that it was not justified on either general legal principles or under some statutory provision);
* that a breach of contract did in fact result from the defendant's interference; and
* that the plaintiff suffered damage as a result of that breach.

Remedies for the tort of procuring breach of contract

[16.90]　　Where the tort has been committed, a plaintiff can recover damages (which, again, are said to be 'at large') for any loss that he or she actually suffers as well as, in appropriate circumstances, exemplary or punitive damages for, among other things, injured feelings. In appropriate cases injunctions may also be available to prevent prospective behaviour that could result in a breach of contract. Injunctions may also be sought under the secondary boycott provisions of the Trade Practices Act 1974 (Cth).

Intimidation

[16.91]　　The tort of intimidation arises when one person is coerced by threats of violence or other unlawful acts as a result of which he, she or some third party suffers loss. The critical aspects of the tort are:

1. An *unlawful act* which may be either criminal or tortious. That is, it is not intimidation to threaten someone with a lawful act. So, in *Allen v Flood* [1898] AC 1 the House of Lords held that threats by an Iron-workers' Union delegate to allow his members to go out on strike unless the plaintiffs, shipwrights to whose presence the iron-workers objected, were dismissed, was not intimidation because strike action was lawful. Therefore, no unlawful means had been used to have the plaintiffs' employment terminated. The sort of activity that has been held to constitute 'unlawful means' has included threats of violence and breaches of contract, restrictive trade practices, unlawful picketing and any acts in contempt of court.
2. An *intention* on the part of the defendant that his or her unlawful act would result in the plaintiff being injured.
3. No *lawful justification* for the unlawful act.

Remedies for intimidation

[16.92] Where intimidation has occurred the plaintiff is entitled to damages (which, again, are said to be 'at large') for any loss, damage or injury that he or she can specifically prove. In addition, he or she may be entitled to exemplary or aggravated damages to compensate for matters such as inconvenience, unhappiness or injured feelings. In appropriate circumstances, where the intimidation has not yet had the desired effect, an injunction may be available to prevent the intimidatory behaviour continuing.

Conspiracy

[16.93] Conspiracy can be either a criminal offence or a tort. In either case, it is unlawful and those who suffer loss, damage or injury as a result of it can take action either to prevent it or to terminate it and, where appropriate, to recover damages. Lord Brampton described conspiracy in *Quinn v Leathem* [1901] AC 495 at 528 as:

> an unlawful combination of two or more persons to do that which is contrary to law, or to do that which is wrongful and harmful towards another person … It may also consist of an unlawful combination to carry out an object not in itself unlawful by unlawful means.

Elements of conspiracy

[16.94] The elements of civil conspiracy are:

- an unlawful combination of two or more persons;
- having, as its predominant purpose, injuring the plaintiff's business interests;
- the combination must actually cause damage; and
- the actions involved must not have been legally justified.

Of these, the critical aspects of the tort are an *unlawful* combination of persons intended to and actually inflicting harm upon a plaintiff. As Viscount Cave LC said in *Sorrell v Smith* [1925] AC 700 at 712:

> from [the] authorities … I deduce … two propositions of law, which may be stated as follows: —
>
> (1) A combination of two or more persons wilfully to injure a man in his trade is unlawful and, if it results in damage to him, is actionable.
>
> (2) If the real purpose of the combination is, not to injure another, but to forward or defend the trade of those who enter into it, then no wrong is committed and no action will lie, although damage to another ensues.
>
> The distinction between the two classes of case is sometimes expressed by saying that in cases of the former class there is not, while in cases of the latter class there is, just cause or excuse for the action taken.

In *Sorrell v Smith* an association of newspaper proprietors had threatened to discontinue supplying newspapers to the plaintiff, a wholesale newsagent, who was, in turn, supplying newspapers to members of a renegade union of retail newsagents who were trying to prevent new retail newsagents entering the industry. The association was held not to have been guilty of conspiracy because its members had not specifically intended to injure the plaintiff; they were simply attempting to protect their own trade interests by encouraging an increase in the number of retail outlets from which their newspapers could be sold.

Conspiracy and motive

[16.95] A critical consideration with conspiracy is whether the 'conspiracy' is for the predominant motive of harming the plaintiff or whether it is, instead, aimed mainly at advancing the defendant's own legitimate interests. The defendant's own legitimate interests include not only those which can be described in financial terms but also anything else which might be of legitimate concern to him or her.

Case Example

The Musicians' Union 'blacked' the plaintiff's ballroom in protest at its policy of refusing to admit 'coloureds'. The plaintiff sought an injunction and failed. The court held that, if the union honestly believed that its members wanted to pursue a policy against racial discrimination then, in pursuing that policy, it was advancing its members' interests — even though those interests could not be positively translated into or reflected in financial terms: *Scala Ballroom (Wolverhampton) Ltd v Ratcliffe* [1958] 3 All ER 220.

Compensation for conspiracy

[16.96] Where civil conspiracy has occurred, the plaintiff can obtain damages to compensate him or her for any actual pecuniary loss, damage or injury suffered, though damages are, once again, 'at large' and, in appropriate cases, exemplary damages may also be awarded. So, in *Pratt v British Medical Association* [1919] 1 KB 244, the plaintiffs, against whom members of the defendant association were held to have conspired, were awarded damages for (inter alia) the humiliation that they had suffered as a result of the defendants' activities. If the conspiracy has not yet had the desired effect on the plaintiff or on his or her business, injunctions may also be sought to prevent the conspiracy continuing.

Vicarious liability

[16.97] 'Vicarious liability' refers to one person's liability for torts that were actually committed by someone else. That is, a person can be liable for a tort even though he or she was not personally at fault (in the sense that he or she did not personally commit the tortious act or omission that gave rise to the action). Vicarious liability arises out of the relationship between the actual tortfeasor and the person being made vicariously liable. It usually arises in, but is not confined to, cases of negligence and it can occur in relationships between employers and employees, principals and agents and, in rare cases, between those who engage independent contractors and the contractors that they engage. In each case, if the employee, the agent or the independent contractor commits a tort, the employer, the principal or the person who engaged the contractor can be made vicariously liable for it.

The employer–employee relationship

[16.98] The employer–employee relationship is the relationship in which most actions involving vicarious liability are brought. Employers are liable for the tortious acts and omissions of their employees provided:

- the 'employee' was, in fact, an employee; and
- the tortious act was committed 'in the course of his or her employment'.

Establishing the employment relationship

[16.99]   Whether someone is, in fact, an employee depends upon whether, using the common law tests, he or she is regarded as an employee. Usually this simply means that the person alleged to be the 'employer' must have the right to exercise *control* over not only what the 'employee' does but also the *manner* in which the employee does it. This is what is referred to as the 'control' test. It is, however, not foolproof and the courts can and do use a number of other tests to ascertain whether an employment relationship exists. These include a modified control test under which the courts accept that the 'employer' need only have *power* to control the employee's work 'to the extent to which there is scope for such control'. This allows, for example, professionals such as doctors working in hospitals, ships' captains and airline pilots to be classified as employees even though, clearly, their employers do not tell them, in any but the most general way, how they are to carry out their specific day-to-day duties. Even this more liberal test is sometimes insufficient to identify, with any real certainty, the true status of those who could be 'independent contractors' instead of employees. In such cases (often involving 'employees' such as commission agents to whom very detailed instructions on how they are to carry out their work have been given) the courts use what is called the 'integration' test. This essentially looks at how closely the 'employee' is integrated into the employer's business. The more closely the 'employee' has been integrated into — and the more intimately involved he or she is in — that business the more likely he or she is to be regarded as an employee for whose actions the employer can be vicariously liable.

In the course of employment

[16.100]   An employer is only liable for an employee's tortious acts or omissions if they are committed 'in the course of the employee's employment'. If the tortious acts are not committed in the course of the employee's employment the employer will not be vicariously liable for them.

The meaning of 'in the course of employment' is, therefore, critical to a determination of whether an employer is or is not vicariously liable. The term has a very wide meaning. Essentially, an employee will be acting in the course of his or her employment whenever he or she does anything that he or she is employed to do, is authorised to do or which is reasonably incidental to his or her employment.

Case Example

The driver of a petrol tanker employed to deliver petrol to service stations lit a cigarette and negligently threw the lighted match away. A fire started, there was an explosion and the petrol tanker, a car and some surrounding houses were either substantially damaged or destroyed. The employer was held vicariously liable because, even though smoking cigarettes was not part of the employee's job, the smoking had occurred in the course of his work — in the sense that it was an accepted part of his daily routine while at work. It was, therefore, 'reasonably incidental' to the way in which the work was performed: *Century Insurance Co Ltd v Northern Ireland Road Transport Board* [1942] AC 509.

An employee can even be acting within the course of employment when he or she intentionally commits some wrongful act. This can occur in either of two ways:

- If the employee commits the wrongful act to further or to protect what he or she sees as the employer's interests. For example, in *Poland v John Parr & Sons* [1927] 1 KB 236 the employee struck a small boy whom he had seen with his hands on bags of his employer's sugar that were being transported in a wagon. The boy fell under the wagon's wheel and was injured. Because the employee had believed that the boy was stealing the sugar and because he had done what he had done to stop what he believed was an act of theft, he was held to be acting in the course of his employment. Consequently, the employer was liable.

- Where the wrongful act is simply an unauthorised mode of doing what the employee is employed to do. For example, in *Lloyd v Grace, Smith & Co* [1912] AC 716 a solicitor's managing clerk who was authorised to receive deeds for safe custody and who carried out the firm's conveyancing work without supervision fraudulently persuaded the plaintiff, one of the firm's clients, to transfer some of her property to him. It was held that his fraud was committed in the course of his employment because what he had done was simply a wrongful means of carrying out the duties that he was employed to perform. The fact that he was carrying them out for his own benefit was irrelevant.

Defences

[16.101] An employer will not be vicariously liable for an employee's torts if what the employee has done can be regarded as a 'frolic of his or her own'. Frolics can occur where the tortious act is done outside working hours (as, for example, where an employee, without authority, comes back to work after hours) or where what is done is not connected with the employee's employment and is done to advance or to protect the employee's own interests. For example, in *Deatons Pty Ltd v Flew* (1949) 79 CLR 370 a barmaid to whom insulting language had been used tossed a glass of beer over her tormentor. Unfortunately the glass 'slipped' from her hand, struck the plaintiff in the face and injured him. Because her actions were an independent personal act not connected with nor incidental to the work she was authorised to do, the employer was not vicariously liable. Similarly, in *Daniels v Whetstone Entertainments* [1962] 2 Lloyds Rep 1, a dance hall bouncer struck a customer in the mistaken belief that the customer was about to assault him. Later, after the fracas had ended, he struck him again outside the hall. The employer was held vicariously liable for the first assault but not liable for the second. The bouncer's job involved using appropriate force to stop disturbances but his authority did not extend to taking personal revenge.

Other instances in which an employer will not be held vicariously liable include those where the employee commits the tort during an unauthorised deviation. An employee will not be acting 'in the course of employment' if, even while doing what he or she is employed to do, he or she deviates unnecessarily from what might be regarded as the 'normal' means of doing the job. For example, if a delivery driver deviates from his or her set route in order to visit friends and, in the course of that deviation, negligently collides with another vehicle, the employer will not be liable for the results of the collision. It occurred outside the course of the employee's employment. However, to remove an employee's actions from the course of his or her employment, the deviation must be clearly unauthorised. Minor deviations involving actions which could be regarded as reasonably incidental to the employee's employment are not enough. For example, in *Chaplin v Dunstan Ltd* (1938) SASR 245 the employee, a truck driver who had been working for about nine hours and who still had about an hour's driving to do before he finished for the day, made a short detour from his route to get a drink at a nearby hotel. He collided with and injured a motor cyclist. His employer was held to be vicariously liable because the deviation was reasonably incidental to the driver's employment.

Finally, an employee will be engaged in a frolic of his or her own if he or she does something which the employer has expressly prohibited.

Case Example

Bean's Express had expressly forbidden its drivers to allow unauthorised persons to travel in the company's vehicles. Despite that, one of its drivers gave Twine a lift. The vehicle was involved in a collision and Twine was killed. Bean's Express was held not liable because, in defying the express prohibition, the employee had acted outside the course of his employment: *Twine v Bean's Express Ltd* [1946] 1 All ER 202.

However, the prohibition in such cases must be absolute. If all that is forbidden is a particular means of carrying out a specific act rather than the act itself, the employer can still be liable if the employee does the authorised act in the forbidden manner.

Case Example

An employee, who had been told to cook his midday meal in a hut in which there was a frying pan chose, instead, to cook it in the open — something which his employer had forbidden. The fire escaped and a neighbour's property was damaged. The employer was held vicariously liable because he had not forbidden the employee to light a fire; he had simply forbidden him to light it outside the hut. Consequently, what the employee had done was an authorised act performed in an unauthorised way and, therefore, it was still 'within the course of his employment': *Bugge v Brown* (1919) 26 CLR 110.

The consequences of vicarious liability

[16.102]   Where an employer is found vicariously liable for the acts or omissions of his or her employees, he or she is responsible for the consequences of those acts or omissions and liable to compensate third parties for any foreseeable loss, damage or injury.

Recovering from an employee

[16.103]   An employer who suffers loss as the result of an employee's torts can seek an indemnity from the employee if he or she can show that the loss was caused by the employee breaching an express or implied term of his or her contract of employment. For example, in *Lister v Romford Ice and Cold Storage Co* [1957] AC 555 the employer, which had been successfully sued for personal injuries caused by an employee who reversed a truck over his offsider, recovered the full amount of the judgment from the employee. The driver had been under a contractual duty to carry out his driving tasks with care and skill and, because he had failed in that duty, he was liable to his employer for the natural and foreseeable consequences of that failure.

Restrictions on the right to recover from an employee

[16.104] Employers have two major restrictions on their right to recover an indemnity from an employee. First, the employer can only recover if the employee committed the tort while performing duties that he or she was employed to perform. This is because otherwise the tortious acts would not be a result of the employee failing or refusing to do something which he or she had warranted that he or she was capable and competent to do.

Case Example

A storekeeper who from time to time used his own motor cycle to carry out errands for his employer was held not liable to indemnify the employer for damages paid to a fellow employee who was injured as a result of the storekeeper's negligent driving. The storekeeper had not expressly or impliedly warranted that he was skilful in the management of a motor cycle and it was not part of his duties, as a storekeeper, to be competent or careful in riding one. Consequently, he was not in breach of the terms of his contract of employment and was not liable to the employer: *Harvey v O'Dell* [1958] 2 QB 78.

Second, in some jurisdictions (New South Wales, South Australia and the Northern Territory) the employer's right to indemnity has been abolished by legislation. Insurers throughout Australia have also lost the right to enforce their right of subrogation because s 66 of the Insurance Contracts Act 1984 (Cth) provides that, unless the employee has been guilty of 'serious or wilful misconduct', an insurer 'does not have the right to be subrogated to the rights of the insured against the employee'. Consequently, an employer's insurer who has indemnified the employer in respect of loss caused through an employee's torts cannot recover against the employee even though the employer might have been able to do so.

Summary and key terms

[16.105] This chapter has set out to explain:

- Torts are civil wrongs that result in loss, damage or injury to others.
- There can be considerable areas of overlap between tortious and criminal behaviour and between torts and breaches of contract.
- The tort of negligence requires proof of three elements: duty, breach and damage.
- To establish that one person owes another a duty of care it must be shown that loss, damage or injury to the latter was 'reasonably foreseeable' and that there was a sufficiently proximate relationship between the parties.
- To prove a breach of the duty of care a plaintiff must show that he or she was owed a particular 'standard of care' (a question of *law*) and that the defendant's behaviour failed to meet that required standard (a question of *fact*).
- Even if there has been a breach of the duty of care the defendant will not be liable unless the plaintiff has suffered damage that the law is prepared to recognise, which

was caused by the defendant's negligence and which is not too *remote* to be recoverable.

- The three main defences to an action in negligence are that the plaintiff has not established the three elements of the tort, that the plaintiff was partly to blame for his or her own loss or injury (contributory negligence) and that the plaintiff voluntarily undertook the risk that resulted in the injury (*volenti non fit injuria*).
- Negligent misstatement is simply an example of negligence generally and all the same elements have to be proved. The major difference is that 'proximity' is established using the twin requirements of 'assumption of risk' and 'reasonable reliance'.
- The torts involving an unlawful interference with goods include trespass to chattels, conversion and detinue.
- The torts involving an unlawful interference with business are passing off, procuring breach of contract, intimidation and conspiracy.
- Vicarious liability refers to those instances in which one person can be made liable for torts committed by someone else.

17

Insurance

What this chapter does ...

It explains what insurance is and the various forms it takes.

For such an important part of the economy it is necessary to have a series of laws which protect the public interest and the interests of both parties to the transaction. This chapter explains what those rules are and how they were developed.

It illustrates how a contract of insurance works and what the important concepts of an insurance transaction are. You will see practical examples of how the law of insurance applies and some of the documents involved in an insurance contract.

Insurance is an important feature of commercial and domestic life. The institutions which provide it represent a significant component of the financial services sector. Not only do they provide a socially and commercially important service by compensating the amount of loss but the scale and management of their investments can be influential in the economy.

The role of insurance

[17.1]   Insurance is about risks. The insurer says, in effect, that in return for a premium it will cover the insured against loss or damage caused by a risk. or risks it is prepared to underwrite. The premiums form a pool which is supplemented by investment income and in this way the cost of the claims for loss or damage is financed. The insurer fixes the premium after an actuarial assessment of the physical risk. In this respect, matters such as the location of a property, the suburb in which a car is kept, the type of construction and the occupation of the person seeking cover could be important. Thus it would charge a higher premium for cover against cyclone damage in northern Australia than it would for similar cover in Victoria where the risk of a cyclone is much less likely. There is also a moral hazard to consider in respect of the proposed insured. An underwriter would attach weight to the fact, for example, that a person seeking fire cover had been convicted of arson. The fact that a person had been convicted of dangerous driving may not be relevant in a consumer credit policy but it would be relevant in a motor vehicle policy. Convictions for crimes of dishonesty would be influential in assessing the risk for a house contents policy.

The nature of the transaction involves uncertainty — either as to the occurrence of the specified event or, if like death it is bound to happen, about when it will occur. Where the event is bound to occur the term 'assurance' is often used. That term is not used in the Australian Constitution which is the source of the power of the Commonwealth to make laws and 'insurance' and 'insured' are the more common practical terms in Australia.

The nature of an insurance transaction

[17.2]   On the face of it, insurance appears to be a form of gambling. According to this view the insured in effect bets, with a premium of, say, $500, that a particular event will occur, for example, a house will be destroyed by fire and the insurer accepts the bet by promising to pay $50,000 if that occurs. As will be discussed later there was an element of gambling in the early history of insurance but the law was changed to require that an insured had an existing interest to protect at the time of entering the insurance transaction. The insured was required to show that if a certain event took place it would be prejudicial in the sense that a financial loss would be suffered. This was a significant difference because, in the case of a bet, the risk of loss is created by making it.

Classification of insurance

[17.3]   The main categories of insurance are general, life and marine. Another major area is that of reinsurance which is internal to the insurance industry and is the process by which the risks are spread between a number of insurers. Compulsory forms of insurance such as workers compensation, health and motor vehicle third party are imposed by legislation and have their rules which are quite distinct in detail and principle from those governing general, life and marine insurance. Specialist forms of insurance such as voluntary health insurance and insurance of exports also exist. For present purposes the significant distinction is between general, life and marine.

General insurance

[17.4]   The Insurance Contracts Act 1984 defines a contract of general insurance as one that is not a contract of life insurance: s 11(6). The basic feature of this form of insurance is that with only a few exceptions it is indemnity based. That is to say that the insured is compensated for the loss suffered as a result of a peril covered by the contract. In some cases the indemnity principle does not apply. An example is a new-for-old policy where, say, a five-year-old carpet is replaced by a new one without any allowance for depreciation. This style of policy which applies to home content policies is the result not of any legal requirement but of market pressure. Companies seeking a larger part of the insurance market developed a new product which was more attractive than the traditional indemnity policy. Indemnity does not apply in sickness or personal accident policies which are 'valued' contracts and are also classified as 'contingency'.

Other classifications

[17.5]   Another classification is 'property' which is self-descriptive — it provides insurance of a person's interest in property. Liability insurance is another classification. It is defined in the Insurance Contracts Act as insurance which provides cover 'in respect of the insured's liability for loss or damage caused to a person who is not the insured': s 11(7). Examples of this form of insurance include third party property insurance where a car owner is covered for any liability incurred as a result of damage to a third person's property. Professional indemnity insurance covers the liability of a person such as a lawyer or accountant who has been negligent in providing a service to a client. A more common form of this style of insurance is the occupiers liability insurance component of a householder policy. If a person visiting the insured's property were to be injured by a carelessly discarded garden tool or a passer-by by an overhanging tree branch it would be under this part of the policy that the insured would be indemnified for any claim made by the passer-by.

Most commonly, general insurance is classified into specific types of cover. Thus there is insurance of motor vehicles, home building, home contents, sickness and accident, consumer credit and travel. These are the categories described in the Insurance Contracts Regulations which specify the 'standard cover' for this range of insurance contracts: see regs 5–28. Some policies are marketed under brand names or in packages which combine several forms of cover. General insurance can also be described in its traditional forms — fire, accident or all risks.

The range of cover is almost limitless. If a person seeks to protect an investment or to avoid a loss or damage, insurance cover is usually available. Show business personalities are often reported as being covered for large sums against injury to themselves or particular parts of their body. Promoters of a sporting event often insure against the losses likely if there is rain beyond a certain level. A hole-in-one competition in a golf tournament is often insured. Instead of paying $100,000 in prize money the sponsor of the event pays a much smaller premium and the insurer provides the prize. If there are no 'off-the-shelf' policies the insurer may be prepared to underwrite the risk or it may be placed through a broker at Lloyd's of London. The risk in that case would be underwritten by a syndicate of members of Lloyd's.

Life insurance

[17.6]   The Insurance Contracts Act in s 11(3) defines a contract of life insurance as:

(a) a contract that provides for payment of money on the death of a person (not being death by accident or specified sickness only) or on the happening of a contingency dependent on the termination or continuance of human life;

(b) a continuous disability insurance contract; or

(c) a contract that provides for payment of an annuity for a term dependent on the continuation of human life.

The modern development of life insurance has been towards investment rather than as a solely prudential form of death cover. Superannuation, which is becoming significant as a result of government policy, includes a life insurance component. The more traditional forms of life insurance are:

- *Whole of life*   The benefits under this policy are paid on the death of the insured.
- *Endowment*   The benefits are paid upon death or at a particular time, for example, on the insured's 45th birthday. This type of policy has an investment flavour.
- *Term*   Cover is provided for a specified period of time such as one year. The uncertainty aspect of this policy is whether the insured will die in the period covered. The sum insured is payable only if the insured dies within the period.

The definition in the Act refers to the payment of an annuity. This is in effect a pension financed by the payment of a lump sum to an insurer who then pays a pension to the person on that person's reaching a certain age, for example, 65. This has been a traditional type of arrangement but has been made more important as a result of government policy on retirement income and taxation.

Marine insurance

[17.7]   The earliest forms of insurance were based on marine adventures and marine insurance has a deep history. Many of the fundamental principles of insurance grew out of marine insurance and it is now governed by the Marine Insurance Act 1909 (Cth). As the name suggests, this insurance is related to things marine — ships and cargoes. While it covers ocean-going ships it also deals with pleasure craft that put to sea. A marine policy would also cover the inland transport of a cargo to or from a ship. The legislation makes it clear that marine insurance is that which covers losses 'incident to marine adventure': s 7. A marine adventure exists where a ship or cargo is exposed to maritime perils. Likewise where the earning of freight, passage money, commission, profit or other pecuniary benefit is exposed to maritime perils there is a marine adventure taking place. The essential issue in a marine policy is whether or not there is exposure to a maritime peril. That term is defined in s 9 of the Marine Insurance Act as:

> the perils consequent on, or incidental to, the navigation of the sea, that is to say, perils of the seas, fire, war perils, pirates, rovers, thieves, captures, seizures, restraints and detainments of princes and peoples, jettisons, barratry, and any other perils, either of the like kind, or which may be designated by the policy.

Because a substantial volume of goods is transported by road in Australia the term 'marine insurance' in practice embraces inland transport as well as shipments by sea. It also applies to shipments by air.

A person who owns a pleasure craft could find that the insurance policy is governed by the Marine Insurance Act. That legislation does not reflect the modern, more consumer-friendly principles of the Insurance Contracts Act.

Regulation of insurance

Constitutional position

[17.8]   In Australia regulation of insurance is, for the most part, under the control of the Commonwealth. This follows as a result of s 51(xiv) of the Constitution which says that the Commonwealth Parliament has power to make laws with respect to, 'Insurance, other than State insurance; also State insurance extending beyond the limits of the State concerned'.

The law governing the insurance institutions is made by the Commonwealth Parliament and the most significant statute affecting the insurance transaction is also Commonwealth. There is some state legislation but it is does not have the same impact as the Commonwealth law. Insurance can also be affected by laws of general application such as the anti-discrimination laws.

A recent development has been the emergence of codes of practice. The General Insurance Code of Practice which came fully into effect in July 1996 is a voluntary, in the sense of being not imposed by government, code drawn up by the industry. The life insurance Code of Practice for Advising, Selling and Complaints Handling in the Life Insurance Industry is not voluntary. It was developed by government, the industry and consumers to overcome some unsatisfactory industry practices and took effect in August 1995 as an attachment to an Insurance and Superannuation Commission circular. There is also a General Insurance Brokers code of practice.

The 1984 reforms

[17.9] Until 1 January 1986 the most significant influence on the insurance transaction was the common law. This reflected the contractual basis of insurance. The significance of 1 January 1986 was that it was the commencement date of the Insurance Contracts Act 1984 and parts of the Insurance (Agents and Brokers) Act 1984. This legislation was enacted following the recommendations of the Australian Law Reform Commission which conducted a reference into insurance law with a view to overcoming the unsatisfactory common law approach to insurance. So significant was the reform of the law that it is unsafe to rely on textbooks published before the new law and cases decided under the 'old law' should be approached cautiously. In short, the common law paid insufficient attention to the imbalance between the parties to the transaction. A classical example of the lack of realism can be seen in *Jumna Khan v Bankers and Traders Insurance Co Ltd* (1925) 37 CLR 451 where an illiterate person insured his house through an insurance agent. The proposal form was completed by the agent without his insurance history having been accurately disclosed. The insured had not been asked any questions and the form contained only what the agent had provided. On the strength of that failure to disclose, and without making allowance for the circumstances and the insured's disability, the Supreme Court of New South Wales, and ultimately the High Court of Australia, held that there was no cover.

While the legislation did much to overcome the shortcomings of the common law, it did not erase its influence and much of the Insurance Contracts Act preserves common law principles. In some cases, for example the doctrine of disclosure, courts have tended to revert to the common law.

There are two dimensions of regulation. One is the regulation of the institutions which provide insurance; the other is the regulation of the transaction and the relationships it creates.

Regulation of the institutions

[17.10] The Commonwealth is the major regulator in this area and has divided insurance into two categories — life and general. As it becomes more important, the superannuation industry (which involves a high component of insurance) will no doubt be regulated by specific legislation. The Commonwealth introduced laws governing the prudential regulation of superannuation funds in 1992. The importance of the funds, their size and the catastrophe that would result if one collapsed made it essential that there be control over the way in which they were managed. Prudential regulation is a term commonly used in relation to institutions that are entrusted with large sums of money by the public, for example, banks and other financial institutions. The regulatory body for insurance is the Insurance and Superannuation Commission established by the Insurance and Superannuation Commissioner Act 1987.

Life Insurance Act 1995

[17.11]   To carry on the business of life insurance, companies must be registered under the Act: s 17. Registration is achieved by application to the Insurance and Superannuation Commissioner who can refuse to register but then only with the approval of the Treasurer: s 21. The policy behind the restricted entry into the industry recognises that large sums of money are at stake and the companies in whom the public has placed its trust must be financially viable and secure enough to meet their obligations. As part of the scheme of prudential regulation, the Act requires all companies carrying on life insurance business to maintain a statutory fund: ss 29–47. The way in which this fund can be used is closely regulated and the Act imposes duties and liabilities on directors in relation to the fund: s 48.

The company is required to meet a solvency standard (s 67) and a capital adequacy standard: s 72. In Pt 6 the Act provides for the financial management of the company. It specifies the accounting treatment of income and outgoings and for the annual lodgment of financial statements. The Act requires that there be an annual audit (s 83) and the auditor is to report to the company and the government agency responsible for the prudential standards of insurance companies. In s 90 the Act specifies that there be an audit committee and in s 91 sets out the composition of the committee. The powers and functions of the audit committee are set out in s 92.

The company is required to appoint an actuary who is to investigate and report on the financial condition of the company as at the end of every financial year: s 113. These requirements emphasise the prudential controls over life companies — they must be in a position to know what obligations they may be required to meet and have the financial capacity to do so. It follows from this level of regulation that companies must disclose information to the government agency responsible for the prudential standards of insurance companies which is empowered to investigate the affairs of the company: s 134. After investigation, the Commissioner may direct the company as to how to carry on its operations (s 150) or can apply to the Federal Court for an order that the company be put under judicial management (s 157) or be wound up: s 181.

Insurance Act 1973

[17.12]   This legislation regulates the providers of most forms of non-life insurance. There are some exceptions which are set out in s 3 of the Act. Some institutions — state insurance enterprises, Commonwealth insurers and specified insurers — are not regulated.

General insurance business can only be carried on by a body corporate (s 21) or by a Lloyd's underwriter and it is necessary to obtain authorisation from the Commissioner: s 21.

As with the life companies, the policy of the Act is to require insurers to maintain the capacity to meet their obligations. In this respect the body corporate must maintain a solvency margin — that is, a surplus of assets over liabilities: s 29. In determining this margin the Act specifies that certain assets are not to be taken into account: s30. These include loans to directors or related parties; unsecured loans to employees of more than $1000; the encumbered proportion of assets subject to a charge; guarantees and intangible assets. The basis of valuation of assets is prescribed: s 33.

Another requirement to enhance the insurer's ability to meet its obligations is that of reinsurance: s 34. Reinsurance is the process by which the insurer shares part of its risk with another insurer or insurers. Thus, where an insurer has provided cover for a catastrophic event and its potential liability could be greater than its capacity to pay, it is able to go into the reinsurance market and arrange for part of its exposure to be covered by other insurers. The insurer's normal reinsurance arrangements, which are bound by a contract (referred to as a treaty) between the two parties, must be approved by the Insurance Commissioner.

The Commissioner has power to investigate and, in circumstances where there is some doubt about the insurer's ability to meet its liabilities or where a breach of the Act is suspected, the Commissioner is able to demand information about the insurer's affairs: s 51. The Commissioner acts in this context by appointing an inspector: s 52. If an insurer is, or is about to become, unable to meet its obligations the Treasurer has power under the Act to direct it as to the carrying on of its business.

Agents and brokers

[17.13]   While the ultimate providers of insurance services are the insurance companies, the actual contract of insurance is made with an intermediary — either an agent (which would include an employee) or a broker. Prior to the Insurance (Agents and Brokers) Act 1984 intermediaries were free of regulation and there was doubt about the status of their relationship with clients. There were instances where clients arranged insurance through brokers and paid premiums to them but the brokers did not pass the premiums on to the insurers.

[17.14]   **Registration of brokers**   The Insurance (Agents and Brokers) Act established a scheme of registration of brokers. Without registration a person is not permitted to carry on the business of insurance broking (s 19) and can be fined or imprisoned for doing so. Applications for registration are made to the Commissioner for Insurance and Superannuation.

The registration of a broker may be suspended or cancelled if the broker has been convicted of a breach of the law relating to insurance or a crime of dishonesty and if the Commissioner is of the opinion that the person is thus unfit to carry on business as an insurance broker: s 25. The broker is required to maintain an insurance broking account into which money paid by or payable to an insured must be paid: s 26. The section also prescribes the way in which the money can be handled.

Premiums paid to the broker must be paid over to the insurer within 90 days of the commencement of the cover. Money paid by the insurer through the broker must be paid to the insured within seven days of receipt: s 27. The Act further protects the broker's client by providing that in the event of insolvency the money held in the insurance broking account is not available to creditors: s 28. It must be applied to insureds, for example, in payment of claims and then to insurers. The provisions of s 28 override the Bankruptcy Act and the insolvency provisions of the Corporations Law. Brokers are also required by s 19 of the Act and s 3 of the Regulations to have professional indemnity insurance cover. In this way the legislation seeks to protect the client should a loss arise from the broker's negligence. Whether this is effective is not clear, especially where the broker, for example, gave advice on a retirement benefit product that would not mature for, say, 30 years.

Agents are not subject to this level of regulation but foreign insurance agents — those who are agents for insurers not authorised by the Act — must be registered and must observe the same style of requirements as registered brokers.

Regulation of the transaction

At common law

[17.15] The basis of insurance is a contract. In return for the payment, or promise of payment, of a premium, the insurer promises to provide cover to an insured against loss or damage suffered as a result of the occurrence of a particular event.

The resolution of disputes over the existence of a contract of insurance, the interpretation of its terms or their application to particular events is undertaken by the courts and, over a period of more than 200 years, a considerable body of principles has emerged. The courts were initially disposed to regard insurance contracts as a form of gambling or wagering and it was necessary in the eighteenth century to introduce the concept of insurable interest. From then on the courts were able to deal with insurance without the shadow of illegality.

As well as the contract itself, the courts were involved in the determining issues about agency — a lively issue was on whose behalf did an insurance agent act? Similarly, the relationship between brokers and their clients was considered by the courts.

The common law is not a flexible instrument and, as a result, its capacity to reflect changed contemporary values is limited. The uneven relationship between an insurance company and an individual consumer is not relevant to the common law. Principles developed in the eighteenth and nineteenth centuries are not necessarily appropriate to changed commercial and social conditions but the common law is unable to adjust quickly. It became clear that the common law principles and approach were unsatisfactory, especially for insureds.

Statute law

[17.16] As mentioned earlier, the Australian Law Reform Commission was given a reference in 1976 to report on insurance law in Australia. Specifically it reported on the insurance transaction itself and on the relationship between the insurer, the insured and the intermediaries involved in the transaction. The two reports of the Law Reform Commission led to the enactment of the Insurance Contracts Act 1984 and the Insurance (Agents and Brokers) Act 1984. The Insurance Contracts Act commenced on 1 January 1986 and the latter Act between 1 January 1986 and March 1987. The impact of both Acts was significant. Although it did not dislodge the common law the Insurance Contracts Act amended it, clarified it and generally modernised it so that the principles of insurance law were, where necessary, adjusted to achieve a just result. It would not be an exaggeration to say that the Act made insurance law more responsive to the position of the consumer.

Relationship between agents and insured

[17.17] The Insurance (Agents and Brokers) Act brought significant changes to the law governing the relationship between insureds and the intermediaries with whom they deal.

The role of agents which had previously been confused and complex was simplified — persons who act as agents bind the insurer and are not the agents of the insured.

Marine Insurance Act 1909

[17.18]   As mentioned earlier, marine insurance was one of the earliest forms of insurance and its principles influenced the development of insurance law. For example, it was through the Marine Insurance Act (UK) of 1745 that the concept of insurable interest was introduced. In Australia the relevant legislation is the Marine Insurance Act 1909. No doubt reflecting its historical background, marine insurance is defined in that Act to be 'a contract whereby the insurer undertakes to indemnify the assured ... against marine loss, that is to say, the losses incident to marine adventure'.

The Marine Insurance Act operates to the exclusion of the Insurance Contracts Act. The principles which it incorporates were developed through the common law and in some respects it is the common law of 1909 expressed in an Act.

State regulation of insurance

[17.19]   The constitutional powers of the Commonwealth in relation to insurance have largely excluded state regulation of insurance. State government insurance offices, where they exist, are not subject to regulation by the Commonwealth because of the Constitution but they are governed by legislation within their own state. Compulsory third party insurance which applies to motor vehicles is regulated in all states and territories by local rather than Commonwealth legislation. Similarly, workers compensation insurance is a state and territory matter.

The insurance contract

[17.20]   The relationship of an insurer and insured is governed by a contract. Although there are special qualities of the contract, its formation involves the same process as other contracts.

Formation

[17.21]   The offer and acceptance phase takes place at the proposal stage. The offer is made by the intending insured — the proponent — who completes and submits a proposal to the insurer either directly or through an agent of the insurer. In this document, the proponent supplies the type of information which is necessary to support a contract — the identity of the intended insured, the subject matter of the insurance, the amount of insurance cover required and the duration of the cover. The usual method of supplying the information is by answering a series of questions on the form. The insured is, however, also under a duty to disclose information even if not asked specifically: see [17.76].

Identity of the parties

[17.22]   The identity of the parties is basic to the existence of any contract but in an insurance contract the identity of the insured can be especially important. The proponent must be clearly identified since it is only the person who has an interest in the property who can seek to have it insured. Another important practical consideration is that there may

431

be some special characteristics of the proponent which are relevant to the insurer. These include matters such as the person's insurance history or those which go to the moral hazard. An example of the latter is where the person is a convicted arsonist and is seeking fire cover. The subject matter of the policy will be identified. In one respect this will occur because the form will describe the type of policy but more particular details are required. The identity of the life to be insured or the nature of the property to be insured can be essential issues for the insurer. An expensive, attractive car could be excluded from cover because the insurer's underwriting guidelines so specify. The guidelines may say that a particular model of a car is not to be insured or that cars with modifications such as wide wheels are not to be accepted or that such cars owned by persons under a certain age will not be insured. They might also say that before the contents of a house can be insured specified precautions such as the fitting of deadlocks must be followed. It is also necessary to establish clearly the identity of the property so that if it becomes necessary to make a claim there is no dispute about whether the property was insured.

Consideration — the premium

[17.23]   The amount of insurance cover sought will be a major factor in determining the cost of the insurance — the premium. Assuming all other hazards are equal, the larger the sum insured the higher the premium. It is not as simple in practice, however, because the insurer must assess the risk of loss or damage before setting the premium. The greater the risk the higher the premium. One method of keeping the premium to a lower figure is by setting an excess on the policy. In a conventional motor vehicle policy the 'basic excess' is in the order of $300 but the policy could also include a 'special excess' of, say, $2000 where the car owner had a bad driving record. This means that, in return for a lower premium or as a condition of being insured, the driver is required to meet the first $2300 of the claim. The insurer may impose non-financial conditions such as that certain persons are not to drive the vehicle.

Sum insured

[17.24]   The sum insured becomes critical at the time of making a claim and policies often express it in different ways. An agreed value policy sets a value for the property and, if it is totally destroyed, the insurer will pay that value. Alternatively, the policy could be a market value policy, which means that in the case of a total loss the insurer will pay the market value of the property at the time of the loss. Considerable confusion exists with these policies because the property might be insured for $20,000 and premium has been paid for that cover but nine months later when it is destroyed the insurer pays only $14,000. The significance of the $20,000 figure is that it represents the maximum cover; if the market value happened to be $25,000 the insurer would pay only $20,000. It is not uncommon for houses to be over-insured through ignorance. The householder insures under an indemnity policy for a large amount, say $350,000, and when a claim is made for total loss the payment is $200,000 which is the market value of the house. The insured has wasted premium by purchasing a policy which was to pay a maximum figure of $350,000 only if that was the market value. In one sense, however, this over-insurance is preferable because, if the house was to be under-insured and a partial loss occurred, the claim could be subject to an average clause which means that the insured must bear part of the loss.

Period of the policy

[17.25]   The duration of the contract is critically important because it determines the time at which the insurer is 'on risk' and thus whether the property was covered. In a general insurance policy the duration is usually for one year but it may be longer as in a consumer credit policy which runs for as long as the insured has obligations under the finance contract. In a life policy the duration can be for a specified term, for example, five years or for the person's lifetime or, as in an endowment policy, up to a certain age.

Renewal of policies

[17.26]   The short duration of a general insurance policy means that at the end of the period it is necessary to renew it. In the renewal process a new contract is created and if the details that were originally supplied have changed it is necessary for those changes to be notified to the insurer. In marine insurance the duration of the policy is usually the length of the voyage. Cover might commence once the goods are on board and terminate when they are delivered into store. The period of cover will vary depending on the specific terms of the policy.

Acceptance

[17.27]   Once the proposal has been completed it is submitted to the insurer who decides whether or not to accept the risk and, if so, on what terms. The insurer's decision about whether or not to accept a proposal will be determined by its underwriting guidelines. They, ultimately, set out the matters that a person is required by the Insurance Contracts Act s 21 to disclose. The insurer is able, quite legitimately, to establish its own underwriting criteria which reflect its values and commercial judgment. They are relevant to the insurer's assessment of risk. For example, an insurer assesses the driving risk of persons between 16 and 19 years of age on their driving history over the past five years. The underwriting decision — which risk to accept — is one that can be made only by the insurer. There is no law that requires an insurer to accept a proposal from a person who presents the type of risk it does not wish to underwrite. For that reason it is necessary for proposals to be accurate. In the example above, the insurer might say that had it known the facts its decision would have been to deny cover because the driver failed to disclose an 'at fault' accident within the past five years. On that basis the insurer would be entitled to deny liability.

When the insurer accepts the offer from the proponent the contract comes into existence at that point. If the insurer does not accept the proposal there is no policy.

Interim insurance — the cover note

[17.28]   In practice it is not uncommon for insurers to provide interim insurance by way of a cover note. This provides cover until the insurer has made the decision about accepting a proposal. During the life of the cover note, which is usually two to four weeks, the property is covered and the insurer would be required to provide benefits to the insured should loss or damage occur. The cover note may, however, run for more than the period it is stated to run. Under the Insurance Contracts Act s 38 the insurer remains liable under what the Act refers to as an interim contract in certain circumstances. These are where the insured has been given a cover note and, before it expired, has submitted a proposal for insurance to replace the cover note. The insurer remains liable until the earliest of:

433

- when a replacement policy is issued — either another interim policy or the proposal has been accepted;
- the time the interim policy is cancelled; or
- the time of withdrawal of the proposal.

The intention of the Act is clear — it does not wish to see a person left uninsured. A person whose proposal for a policy has been declined remains covered until it is possible to arrange another policy.

Policy terms

[17.29] The contract is formed in the proposal process and the consideration element comes from the insured in the form of a premium. The insurer promises to provide cover in return for the payment of the premium or the promise to pay it.

At the proposal stage the insured will very often not have seen the terms of the policy. In such cases the proposal will include a declaration by which the insured agrees to accept the insurer's usual terms and conditions. The policy terms are those chosen by the insurer and, realistically, there is little the insured can do to influence the terms. For the most part, however, non-industrial policies are standard products which are mass marketed like any other financial product. In some cases where special circumstances exist a broker would be able to place the risk or it might be necessary to obtain cover through an underwriter at Lloyd's of London.

The policy

[17.30] What is referred to as the policy is, more accurately, part of the contract in writing. As stated above, the policy is usually a standard set of terms. The specific features of the particular contract — the name of the insured, the subject matter, the sum insured — are often set out in a schedule which of course is also part of the contract.

The policy document typically begins with the promise by the insurer:

Our Agreement

Provided You have paid or agreed to pay the premium to Us, then subject to the terms, conditions and exclusions contained in or endorsed on this Policy or Schedule, **We will insure you against loss, damage or liability as described in this Policy** occurring during the Period of Insurance stated in the Schedule and any future period for which We may accept payment of premium.

You are covered for each Section or Part where a Sum Insured appears in the Schedule or which is indicated as being operative in the Schedule.

The Policy, Schedule and Endorsements together form the Agreement.

Most policies include a definition section which explains what certain terms mean in the context of that policy. In many policies the terms which are defined or have a particular meaning are printed in block letters or are otherwise highlighted. In the extract above, the policy defines 'You', 'Us', 'We', 'Policy' and 'Schedule'. The definitions are of great importance in deciding whether a particular event is covered. In one policy 'illness' means any sickness or disease while 'injury' has a quite specific meaning: '... bodily injury resulting from an accident and caused by violent, external and visible means but does not include any condition which is also an illness'.

Defined events

[17.31]   The policy then usually sets out the defined events or specified perils. These are very important because the policy will apply only if the loss or damage was caused by such events or perils. Sometimes it is critical to pay attention to the way in which the specified perils are expressed. For example, a man who was cleaning the eaves of his house accidentally spilt water from a bucket on to the motor that drove the garage door. The water damaged the mechanism beyond economic repair but the claim for the cost of its replacement was refused because the policy was a defined event policy and accidental damage was not one of the defined events.

The cover

[17.32]   The extent of the cover will also be specified in the policy.

For example, in the NRMA policy some of the defined events and the cover provided for them are described as follows:

Accidental damage
If your vehicle suffers accidental damage, we may decide to:
* repair your vehicle
* pay you the cost of repairing your vehicle, or
* pay you the agreed value.
For each of the above you must pay an excess if the accidental damage is your fault. If we agree that it was not your fault but you cannot give us the name and address of the other driver, you must still pay the excess.
Theft
If your vehicle is stolen and not found, we will pay you the agreed value less the excess. If your vehicle is stolen and found damaged, we may decide to:
* repair your vehicle
* pay you the cost of repairing your vehicle, or
* pay you the agreed value.
For each of the above you must pay an excess.
Depreciation
We may make an allowance for depreciation (based on the age and condition of your vehicle), except when we pay you the agreed value.

[17.33]   Most policies include a general exclusions section which sets out those events or consequences of a defined event for which cover is not provided by the policy. Thus a claim would not normally be successful where the loss or damage arose from 'mechanical, structural or electrical failures'; 'destruction, loss of or damage to or liability incurred where at the relevant time the vehicle is being used for an unlawful purpose'; or 'any loss or expenditure incurred solely in remedying a fault in design'.

In many modern policies there is a series of sections which offer different types of cover. An example of this 'modular' form is a policy where there are sections providing insurance cover for house, contents, personal injury, public liability, farm property, farm machinery, road transit and motor vehicle. The insured is able to specify the type of cover being sought.

Plain English

[17.34] Another feature of modern policies is the attempt to make them more comprehensible by the use of 'plain English'. A pioneer in this field is NRMA Insurance Ltd whose comprehensive motor vehicle policy begins:

> Your Comprehensive Insurance policy is a contract between you (the insured) and us (NRMA Insurance Ltd).

> It is an agreed value policy. This means that, in return for your premium, we will cover your vehicle up to the amount we have agreed upon.

> We will also cover you for damage your vehicle causes to someone else's property as a result of an accident ...

This is a far cry from the old style of policy which was expressed in legalese and was almost incomprehensible. The policy is also written in a style that makes it easy to read. This is the modern trend, in contrast to the old-fashioned policies which were in small print and not at all user-friendly. In this way, if the insured can be made to read the policy, there is a much better chance that it can be understood.

Standard cover

[17.35] As part of the consumer protection thrust of the reforms in the Insurance Contracts Act attention was paid to the ability of consumers to inform themselves about the details of policies on the market. The legislation attempted to overcome the confusion created by the variety of policies by introducing standard cover. This is, in effect, minimum cover and is dealt with in roundabout language in ss 34–36 of the Act. The Insurance Contract Regulations establish standard cover through 'prescribed contracts' which exist for motor vehicles, home buildings, home contents, sickness and accident, consumer credit and travel insurance. Insurers are not required to draft policies to conform to the standard cover, but they are required to advise of any derogation from standard cover prior to entering into the contract. One way of doing this is to provide the insured with a copy of the policy wording prior to entering the contract. This is regarded as sufficient notification to the intending insured of any variation from standard cover. In this way insurers are able to avoid the Act's provisions about standard cover and the insured is no better off.

The regulations set out the contents of the 'prescribed contracts' and specify what would otherwise be the defined events and the exclusions.

Consistent with the process of informing consumers, s 37 of the Act requires of insurers that they notify the insured of any unusual terms in policies — other than those that come under the standard cover provisions.

The parties

[17.36] If the proposal is accepted, the proponent becomes the insured and the other party to the contract is the insurer. They are the principal parties. There are policies sold by a travel agent, for example, under the agent's name but underwritten by an insurance company. The contract of insurance in such a case is between the insured and the travel agent. There is, however, a variation of the usual rule that only parties to the contract may recover. That is provided by s 48 which allows a person who is not a party to the contract, but who is specified in the contract as a person to whom cover extends, to recover any loss sustained.

It is possible that at various stages in the life of the policy other persons become involved. They will, however, be acting as agents of one or other of the principal parties.

Where two parties who, say, own a house in a joint tenancy relationship insure the house they are regarded as joint insureds. A policy covering the separate interests of two or more parties is described as 'composite'.

Agents

[17.37]   The fact that insurers are companies means that they must act through agents — either employees or persons appointed by the insurer to sell its products or to act on its behalf. The law of agency is well established and the relationship of principal and agent has been developed through the cases. In the insurance context the significance of agency arose in a negative way. A question often litigated was — who was the principal of a particular agent? Did the agent act for the insurer or the insured? Flowing from this was the real issue of whether the agent's conduct bound the insurer. The problem in the common law position was based on authority — to what extent was the agent authorised to carry out acts which bound the insurer?

Insurance (Agents and Brokers) Act 1984

[17.38]   The unsatisfactory nature of the law as illustrated in the *Jumna Khan* decision (see [17.9]) led to the reference to the Australian Law Reform Commission and ultimately to the enactment of the Insurance (Agents and Brokers) Act 1984. The Act has clarified the law so that the role of agents and the significance of their conduct can now be better understood. A person is an agent of an insurer who, while acting as an insurance intermediary, is not a broker: s 12. The term 'insurance intermediary' is defined to mean a person who acts for reward as an agent or broker in arranging insurance contracts: s 9. This means that anyone who arranges insurance but is not a registered insurance broker will be treated as an agent and in this way much of the common law difficulty has been overcome.

Insurer's responsibility for agent

[17.39]   Once it is established that a person is an agent or employee of an insurer s 11 of the Act sets out the scope of the insurer's responsibility. It provides that:

11(1) This section applies to any conduct of an employee or agent of an insurer:

(a) on which a person in the circumstances of the insured or intending insured could reasonably be expected to rely; and

(b) on which the insured or intending insured in fact relied in good faith.

(1a) An insurer is responsible, as between the insurer and the insured or intending insured, for the conduct of an employee of the insurer in relation to any matter relating to insurance, whether or not the employee acted within the scope of his or her employment.

(1b) If a person is the agent of one insurer only, the insurer is responsible, as between the insurer and the insured or intending insured, for the conduct of the agent in relation to any matter relating to insurance, whether or not the agent acted within the scope of the authority granted by the insurer.

...

(2) The responsibility of an insurer under subsections (1a), (1b) ... extends so as to make the insurer liable to an insured or intending insured in respect of any loss or damage suffered by the insured or intending insured as a result of the conduct of the agent or employee.

---

(3) Subsections (1a), (1b) ... and (2) do not affect any liability of an agent or employee of an insurer to an insured or intending insured.
(4) An agreement, in so far as it purports to alter or restrict the operation of subsection (1a), (1b), ... or (2), is void.
(5) An insurer shall not make, or offer to make, an agreement that is, or would be, void by reason of the operation of subsection (4).
Penalty: 150 penalty units.

The section also explains where responsibility lies when an agent acts for more than one insurer: s 11(1C)–(1J).

Agent of the insurer

[17.40] The effect of the Act is to remove the issue of authority as a ground of dispute. It is no longer necessary to argue over whether the agent acted within the scope of authority from the insurer. The insurer is now bound by what the agent does in relation to any matter relating to insurance. If an agent completes a proposal form but does not correctly record the insured's answer to a question, the insured, on being able to prove the mistake, is able to argue that the insurer was given the information and any decision by the insurer based on the failure to supply the information is of no effect. An insured who has been incorrectly advised about the benefits of the policy (for example, that it covers flood damage) would be able to insist that the insurer paid a claim for such damage. The width of s 11 is very significant for insurers, especially in view of the way in which insurance is marketed. A travel agent who sells a travel policy and mistakenly accepts the insured's valuation of goods without proper verification would bind the insurer, notwithstanding that this was in breach of the insurer's procedures. Similarly, a credit provider who arranges consumer credit insurance could, by failing to record an answer, deny the insurer the opportunity to reject a proposal which, if the facts were known, would have failed the underwriting guidelines. In the case of life insurance, which often has a substantial investment component, an insurer would be liable because of s 11 for incorrect advice given by the agent on any aspect of the transaction (for example, the taxation implications of the policy). Although the advice might have been given on specific, non-insurance issues it would be 'conduct ... in relation to any matter relating to insurance' and s 11(1) would apply.

Agent's authority to act

[17.41] The Act, in s 10, requires that persons who hold themselves out to be insurance agents must have a written authority from the insurer. If, however, a contract is arranged by a person who is not so authorised the validity of the contract is not affected: s 10(6).

Payments of premium to agent

[17.42] Payments by an insured or intending insured to an agent are treated by the Act as payments to the insurer: ss 14(1), (2). Where the insurer makes payments to the insured through an agent the insurer is not relieved of liability until the money has been passed on: s 14(3). Payments made to the agent by the insured, or intending insured, are held in trust for the insurer and are not available for the agent's creditors: s 37(1). The money must be paid to the insurer as soon as is reasonably possible: s 37(3).

The legislation means that insurers are now in a position where they might have considerable obligations arising from the activity of agents. The shortcomings of the agents do not affect the insured but could give rise to litigation between the insurer and the agent for breach of contract or negligence.

Case Example

Metrot owned premises in Newcastle which it insured in June 1987 with Manufacturers' Mutual Insurance Ltd (MMI). The policy was renewed for the period 27 May 1988 to 27 May 1989. Before the expiry of the renewed policy, MMI sent to John H Boardman Insurance Brokers Pty Ltd (the broker) a renewal notice for the policy. On or about 22 May 1989, Metrot instructed the broker to arrange for the renewal of the policy and forwarded a cheque for $2892.35, consisting of a premium of $2692.35 and a commission to the broker of $200. On 28 December 1989, the premises were damaged as the result of the Newcastle earthquake. Metrot's claim on MMI was rejected on the basis that the insurance policy had lapsed on 27 May 1989, following the failure of the broker or Metrot to renew the policy or pay the premium.

[The parties agreed that either MMI or the broker is liable to indemnify Metrot. The question in this case was which of those parties should bear the burden of that liability.]

A majority of the High Court held that:

> ... no contract of insurance came into being for the period of 27 May 1989 to 27 May 1990 by virtue of the common law ...

> It remains to be considered whether the operation of s 14(2) of the Act alters the common law position in relation to the making of an insurance contract. Section 14(2) of the Act provides as follows:

> 'Payment to an insurance intermediary by or on behalf of an intending insured of moneys in respect of a contract of insurance to be arranged or effected by the intermediary, whether the payment is in respect of a premium or otherwise, is a discharge, as between the insured and the insurer, of any liability of the insured under or in respect of the contract, to the extent of the amount of the payment.'

> ... [t]he renewal of a contract of insurance renewable by mutual consent results in a fresh contract, rather than an extension of an existing contract. Thus, when moneys are paid to a broker in respect of a renewal of a contract of insurance to be effected by the broker, such payment will fall within the operation of s14(2). It is accepted in this case that the broker was an insurance intermediary as defined in s 9 of the Act. Accordingly, the question is: how does s 14(2) operate in the circumstances of this case?

> In our view ... s 14(2) can only operate to make the payment of the premium to [the broker] the discharge of a liability under a contract effected as contemplated by the offer of renewal. It does not operate to make the payment the acceptance of the offer ...

The broker was thus liable to Metrot: *Manufacturers' Mutual Insurance Ltd v John H Boardman Insurance Brokers Pty Ltd* (1994) 179 CLR 650; 120 ALR 401; (1994) 68 ALJR 385.

Brokers

[17.43] The traditional role of brokers has been to act for the insured in obtaining appropriate insurance cover. The regulation of the way in which they conduct their business was discussed earlier: see **[17.14]**. The relationship between a broker and a client is, for the most part, governed by the common law, in particular contract law and the law of torts.

If a client seeks the services of a broker, there is an expectation that the broker will arrange the appropriate cover; failure to do so could amount to a breach of contract. The broker must be careful to ensure that the client observes the duty of disclosure when completing a proposal. If the broker fails in this respect, and if as a result the insurer is able to avoid the contract, the insured would have an action for breach of contract. Where notice or information or some other communication is required to be given to the insured under the Insurance Contracts Act, for example, advice as to the duty of disclosure, that requirement does not apply where the contract has been arranged through a broker: s 71(1).

Brokers acting under binder

[17.44] The agency role between broker and client is well established but there is one situation where the broker will be an agent of the insurer. This is where the broker is 'acting under a binder' which means that the broker is authorised by the insurer to act as its agent in arranging insurance or dealing with a claim. In such circumstances the broker is the agent of the insurer, not of the insured: s 15. A broker acting in that capacity must advise the client of that fact: ss 16, 17.

Brokers are not limited in the way in which they are able to earn income, but as agents of the insured, there is a prima facie conflict when they receive a fee or commission from the other party to the transaction. The insured is able to request information about the benefits a broker earns from the insurer: s 32(1).

Other parties in insurance

[17.45] At the claim stage of an insurance transaction two other parties, each of whom is an agent of the insurer, appear. One is the loss adjuster whose role is to advise the insurer on the claim. It is not uncommon for insurers to rely on the advice of an adjuster in making the decision about admitting liability. The loss adjuster is usually a technical expert and a firm of adjusters would provide a range of technical skills. The adjuster can also be involved in the determination of quantum, that is, the amount to be paid under the claim. The loss adjuster, especially when advising on the liability issue, necessarily interprets the policy. In some cases the adjuster is the only person the claimant deals with and the agency dimension of the adjuster's role becomes more pronounced.

Investigators

[17.46] In some cases the insurer, or the adjuster, will engage an investigator to report on a particular claim. This would most likely be when there are suspicions about the bona fides of the claim. The conduct of the adjuster or investigator is imputed to the insurer so that if either of them had acted improperly the insurer would be held to have acted in the same way and its position could be jeopardised. An example of what would be unacceptable conduct on the part of an investigator is where, by threats and harassment, an insured is made to withdraw a claim. Conduct such as that is contrary to the standard of good faith expected of parties to an insurance contract and would go against an insurer which was attempting to deny liability on the grounds that the claim was withdrawn.

Marketing/agency

[17.47]   Where an insurer markets its policies through outlets such as a bank or travel agent there is an agency relationship. The insured generally believes for all intents and purposes that the contract is with the BDP Bank, and it is, but the underwriter of the policy will be a registered insurer. What the insured tells the bank and what the bank tells the insured will be treated as if the information was communicated to or from the insurer.

The claim

[17.48]   The promise made by the insurer 'we will insure you against loss, damage or liability' means that if, as a result of a defined event the insured suffers any of those consequences, the insurer has an obligation to compensate the insured in accordance with the terms of the contract. For the promise to be made good the insured must first suffer a loss or damage from an insured peril and then lodge a claim. If the claim is accepted it will be settled and in the process the insured will sign a release which will bring the matter to an end.

Burden of proof

[17.49]   It is a fundamental rule of insurance that the insured must prove that there has been loss, damage suffered or liability incurred and that it was brought about by a peril insured against — the defined event. The insured must prove that the claim satisfies the insurance contract.

The procedure for making the claim is usually specified in the policy. It involves the completion of a form where details of the loss and the property involved are set out. In the case of theft the insured is required to report the matter to the police though, in most jurisdictions, the police rarely investigate.

There are normally only two periods of intense interest in an insurance transaction. One is the formation stage and the other is when a claim is made. It is at this time that it is necessary to consider the doctrine of proximate cause and the interpretation of the contract becomes important.

Proximate cause

[17.50]   This doctrine is, in a sense, a very straightforward proposition. It means no more than that an insured, in order to make a claim under a policy, having proved that there was loss, damage or liability suffered must also prove that the cause was an event covered by the policy. It must have been a defined event or a specified peril.

It is, therefore, necessary to establish the proximate cause of the loss damage or liability. If there were two proximate causes and one of them was an event excluded by the policy then the claim will fail.

Case Example

A ship, damaged by a torpedo, was towed into harbour. Because of the state of the weather and the danger the ship presented, it was moved out of harbour and thereupon sank. The owners claimed under a policy which covered perils of the sea but excluded liability for war damage.

The issue in the case became one of identifying the proximate cause — what caused the ship to sink? Was it the torpedo damage or the weather. Lord Shaw said:

> The true and the over-ruling principle is to look at the contract as a whole and to ascertain what the parties to it really meant. What was it that brought about the loss, the event, the calamity, the accident? And this not in an artificial sense, but in that real sense which parties to a contract must have had in their minds when they spoke of cause at all.

The court took the view that the ship was more likely to sink in its torpedoed condition. It said that the sinking of the ship was a natural consequence of the torpedo attack: *Leyland Shipping Co Ltd v Norwich Union Fire Insurance Society Ltd* [1918] AC 350.

Proximate cause in Australia

[17.51]   In an Australian case, *Judd v Suncorp Insurance and Finance* (1988) 5 ANZ Ins Cas 60-832 at 75,186, Carter J explained that passage by saying that 'One therefore looks to see what was the real cause, the proximate cause, the efficient cause of the loss and puts to one side the somewhat enticing subtleties of distinctions which are drawn in metaphysics'. That approach reflects the view that what has to be established is the direct, real or common sense, dominant operative or efficient cause of the damage. Since the *Leyland Shipping* case, the courts have moved away from saying that the proximate cause is the one last in time.

Case Example

The insured had stored cartons of Easter eggs in its factory in Lismore. Rainwater entered the factory and had collected under the pallets on which the cartons were stored. The insured argued that the damage to the Easter eggs was '... caused by or as a direct consequence of ... storm and/or tempest ...' and was therefore covered by the insurance policy. In his decision, Kirby P (at 78,762) applied the following analysis to the facts to establish the cause of the damage:

(i) The storm, tempest or rainwater caused water to enter and collect in Stargift's factory.

(ii) That water evaporated.

(iii) The evaporated water attached to the confectionery under the cellophane and collected there.

(iv) There it caused the damage.

The cause of the damage was a specified peril under the policy and the insured was able to recover: *Manufacturers' Mutual Insurance Ltd v Stargift Pty Ltd* (1985) 3 ANZ Ins Cas 60-615

[17.52]   The proximate cause issue could also arise in a personal accident policy where a person who had been standing on the deck of a yacht had fallen into the sea and whose body was later recovered from the sea. A personal accident policy applies only where there has been death or injury arising from an accident. In this example, it would become important to know whether the person fell into the sea and died from drowning or whether the person had died on the deck and had then fallen into the sea dead. The cause of death in such a case would be critical in determining whether the personal accident policy would respond to the claim.

Establishing the cause of the loss, damage or liability is the responsibility of the insured. It is very important but as the examples above show, it is more likely to be achieved by the application of common sense than by a complex discussion of causation.

Interpretation of the policy

[17.53]   The insurance transaction is contractual and, in theory, the parties have agreed on its terms. As with any other contract, if there are disputes as to the meaning of a particular clause the court is required to interpret the contract. The court seeks to determine what the parties intended in their transaction. It is no exaggeration to say that some insurance policies present legal jargon at its worst and, having been drafted by the insurer, are excessively protective of the insurer's position. Those policies which have not incorporated plain English are very often incomprehensible to all but the most experienced lawyers. Unfortunately that does not become apparent until after a loss has occurred and the insured discovers when the claim is denied that the policy was not what it seemed.

Meaning of the words

[17.54]   The importance of the way in which a contract is interpreted can be seen from the number of cases where the courts have been asked to establish the meaning of particular words or phrases. Very often the wording of a policy will be amended to take into account the decision of a court — for the benefit of the insurer. In a significant High Court decision *Australian Casualty Company Ltd v Federico* (1986) 160 CLR 513; 66 ALR 99 the dispute was about the meaning of 'bodily injury caused by an accident'.

The High Court's interpretation was important because on it turned the decision as to whether the insured could recover under the policy. The case was also important for what was said about the interpretation of insurance contracts.

Case Example

Mr Domenico Federico was born in Italy and, for practical purposes, he was illiterate in the English language. In 1976, Mr Federico entered into the policy with Australian Casualty Co Ltd (Australian Casualty). The policy was in force in April 1978 when he suffered a *cauda equina* lesion caused by a central disc prolapse while he was working as a tiler in the construction of a home at Keilor in Victoria. It was conceded that, for the purposes of the policy, he became and remains totally unable to 'perform' any 'gainful occupation'. It was Mr Federico's task, as a tiler, to prepare the bed on which the tiles were to be laid to form the kitchen floor. To do that, he used a straight edge or scrimmer. The task of drawing the straight edge towards the operator required the exertion of considerable force while the operator was in a squatting or bending position.

On the occasion in question, Mr Federico, who had never previously had any illness and was a fit and strong man, felt pain in his back when levelling the mixture of sand and cement.

He had sustained a massive central disc prolapse and consequential damage to the nerves within the spinal canal. It was common ground that the cause of the central disc prolapse was not any prior injury or pre-existing degenerative condition. The cause of the prolapse was what the treating surgeon described as 'a significant traumatic event', adding the explanation that Federico's action in moving the sand and cement mixture while his spine was bent involved 'tremendous pressure ... through the lumbar disc system'.

The primary benefit for which the policy provided was the payment of a 'monthly indemnity' in respect of 'total disability' resulting from 'injury ... or ... sickness'. The period during which the indemnity was payable varied according to whether the 'total disability' resulted from 'injury' or from 'sickness'. If it resulted from 'injury', the liability to pay the indemnity continued for so long as total disability continued.

The issue for the High Court to decide was whether Mr Federico's condition was an injury or a sickness. In their joint decision, Wilson, Deane and Dawson JJ said:

> ... The policy is a standard document used by Australian Casualty in the course of its insurance business. It is apparently offered in different States of the Commonwealth to ordinary working people, such as Federico, who are unlikely to have the advantage of the advice of a commercial lawyer when they purchase from an insurance company protection against the contingency of sustaining disability from earning as a result of injury or sickness. It contains nothing which would be likely to suggest to those to whom it is proffered that its terms are to be construed in any special technical sense or as conveying other than what they convey as a matter of ordinary language read in the context of the whole policy. That being so, the starting point of a consideration of whether Federico's central disc prolapse and its consequences were an 'injury' for the purposes of the policy must be a consideration of what the words of the policy convey, as a matter of contemporary language read in the context of the whole policy, to a reasonable non-expert in this country. If that meaning is plain, it can be of but limited significance if, at other times and in other places, other courts, however eminent, have held that similar words in other policies were to be construed as having had some different meaning ...

> For present purposes, the critical provisions of the policy are to be found in the introductory section, in the definitions of 'Injury', 'Sickness' and 'Total Disability'. ... They read as follows:

> '"Injury" means bodily injury of the Insured caused by an accident occurring [sic] while this Policy is in force and resulting directly and independently of all other causes in loss covered by this Policy. "Sickness" means sickness or disease of the Insured contracted and commencing after this Policy has been in force for not less than thirty days after its Effective Date and resulting in loss covered by this Policy.

> "Total Disability" wherever used in this Policy means the inability of the Insured by reason of injury or sickness to perform each and every gainful occupation for which he is reasonably suited by education, training or experience ...'

> ...

What is here in issue is the requirement that the 'injury' be 'caused by an accident occurring [sic] while [the] Policy is in force'. It is not disputed that, if Federico's central disc prolapse and its consequences were caused by an accident, the accident occurred while the policy was in force. The question in issue is whether they were caused by an accident at all.

As a matter of ordinary language in this country, an 'accident' ... is something which happens without intention or design. When used with reference to something which causes injury, it means an unexpected and unintended mishap ...

In the present case, Federico intentionally performed the acts involved in levelling the mixture of damp sand and cement with his straight edge. He did not, however, intend to create internal pressure to an extent which his disc system could not withstand ... Federico's injuries were not the result of any pre-existing degenerative condition. They were the result of the pressure through the disc system being more than his body could withstand without serious injury while he was in a bending or squatting position. That excessive pressure caused the central disc prolapse, forcing disc substance into the spinal canal where the nerves were compressed and damaged. The creation of pressure of a kind which his body could not withstand without serious injury was an unintended and unexpected incident of the acts which he intended to perform. As a matter of ordinary language it was an accident or mishap.

Rules of interpretation

[17.55]   In the same case Gibbs CJ made it clear that the usual rules used by courts to interpret contracts will apply. He said:

The ordinary rules of interpretation apply to a policy of insurance. As in the case of any other commercial contract, a court may depart from the strictly literal meaning of a particular expression to place upon it an alternative construction which is more reasonable and more in accord with the probable intention of the parties if the words will bear that construction: *McCowan v Baine* [1891] AC 401 at 403; see also MacGillivray & Parkington, ... and Sutton: *Insurance Law in Australia and New Zealand* ... Further, the trend is, if anything, to adopt a liberal interpretation in favour of the assured, so far as the ordinary and natural meaning of the words used by the insurers permits this to be done': Halsbury, 4th ed, vol 25, para 594, note 1, cited in *Mount Albert City Council v New Zealand Municipalities Co-operative Insurance Co Ltd* [17983] NZLR 190 at 193.

Notwithstanding that approach to interpretation, Gibbs CJ said that '... with all respect I find it impossible to agree that the words "bodily injury ... caused by an accident" in the policy simply mean "accidental injury"'.

Special meaning of words

[17.56]   There are circumstances where it would not be appropriate to apply the ordinary and natural meaning of words. One such circumstance is where the word or phrase has a particular meaning within the policy, set out in the definition section. An example of the difference between everyday language and that of a policy can be seen in a case where a newspaper report referred to 230 homes 'as having suffered damage during the floods'. The insured was, however, required to show that the circumstances of the case came within the policy definition which said 'flood means the covering of land which is normally dry by water which has overflowed the banks of a natural water course or lake (whether changed by man or not) or of any reservoir, canal or dam'.

Another time when it is not appropriate to use the ordinary meaning of the words is where the term has a technical meaning developed in an earlier decision of a court or within a particular trade or profession. It is necessary to keep in mind that a contract is meant to express the intentions of the parties and it would be far-fetched to argue that a highly technical engineering term is to be given its specialised meaning when it appears in a householder's policy. Perhaps the technical meaning would be applied if the insured has an engineering background but the courts are more inclined to interpret words as they are understood by ordinary people.

Exclusion clauses

[17.57]   Insurance policies almost invariably contain exclusion clauses. They reduce the scope of the cover. For example, an all risks policy might contain an exclusion stating that:

> The Company shall not be liable for loss or destruction or damage
> (i) from wear or tear;
> (ii) from or attributable to the action of light or atmosphere moths parasites or vermin; or
> (iii)to any machine or apparatus arising from mechanical or electrical breakdown or derangement

The insurer bears the onus of proving that the loss (which had first been established by the insured) was the result of wear and tear for example.

Another example of an exclusion clause

[17.58]   Another example of an exclusion clause is one which states:

> We may refuse a claim or cancel this policy or do both if at the time of the incident which results in a claim your car:
> (i) was being driven by a person who was under the influence of intoxicating liquor ...

In this case the insurer must prove that the driver was under the influence of intoxicating liquor. It is not enough to show merely that the insured had a blood alcohol reading above the legal limit: see *Government Insurance Office of New South Wales v Nowalinski* (1983) 3 ANZ Ins Cas 60-629. The insurer would need to show that the driver was under the influence of intoxicating liquor within the meaning given to that term by the courts. Indeed in some states there is legislation to the effect that it is not permitted for an insurer to say that because a person recorded above the prescribed concentration of alcohol that person was under the influence of intoxicating liquor. In practice it is not always easy for an insurer to prove that a person was in this state.

The onus of proof in exclusion clauses

[17.59]   The attitude of the courts in requiring the insurer to prove that the insured's case is caught by an exception is no more than the general rule that the party which asserts something must prove it. It also reflects the *contra proferentem* rule. This is a conventional rule of interpretation which when applied to insurance means that the party who drafted the contract — the insurer — has the opportunity to express it clearly and if there are any ambiguities they are to be applied against the insurer.

Observing the commercial purpose of insurance

[17.60]   The decision of the New South Wales Court of Appeal in *Legal & General Insurance Australia Ltd v Eather* (1986) 6 NSWLR 390; 4 ANZ Ins Cas 60-749, especially the judgment of McHugh JA, emphasised a practical approach to interpreting a term of a policy. The insured owned jewellery which he decided to leave in a bank during the period he was to be overseas. He put it in a bag on the back seat of his car, covered it with a towel and set off for the bank. He parked the car and, having arrived before the bank opened, went shopping; he found on his return that the jewellery was missing. His claim was denied on the ground that the policy said 'You are to take all reasonable precautions to avoid or minimise injury ...'. McHugh JA said:

> ... insurance policies will be construed in their commercial setting and social setting having regard to their purposes. If one construction strikes fundamentally at the purpose of the policy, which is to spread the risk insured against, whilst another construction that is reasonably available would effect that purpose, the latter will be preferred: See *Albion Insurance Co Ltd v Body Corporate Strata Plan No 4303* (1983) 2 ANZ Ins Cas 60-511 ...

> ...

> Obviously the word 'all' in the condition must be read down by reference to two considerations. The first is the companion adjective 'reasonable'. It is only 'all reasonable' precautions that must be taken. The second consideration is the purpose of the policy, in which the condition appears. Clearly, its purpose is to permit the insured, whilst maintaining possession of his personal property, such a jewellery here in question, to pass the risk of loss to the insurer.

> If the insurer wished to insist that items generally, or items of a particular value, must be deposited before it is at risk it should say so. Likewise, if it wished only to be at risk when the property was in a locked safe or other secure receptacle, it should make provision to that effect in its policy. Were it to do so, it would make its condition clearer to the insured. But it might also forfeit the market because many insureds might consider such conditions unacceptable. ...It is this recognition, that the insured will retain and use possession of the property the subject of the insurance, that undermines the insurer's argument that a rigorous obligation was imposed by the condition. Such an obligation would be contrary to the normal expectations of persons insured under such a policy. It would undermine the commercial utility of the insurance policy ...

Wrongly answered questions

[17.61]   The consequences of a wrong answer to a question on a proposal form will depend on the circumstances.

If the question could reasonably have been understood to have the meaning the insured apparently gave to it, that is, if it was ambiguous, the Act provides in s 23 that the meaning understood by the insured is the meaning the question has. In other words, if the question is ambiguous and the answer was given according to one meaning, it will not be construed as a misrepresentation. Section 23 was considered in the New South Wales Supreme Court case of *Fruehauf Finance Corp Pty Ltd v Zurich Australian Insurance Ltd* (1990) 20 NSWLR 359; 6 ANZ Ins Cas 61-014.

It was once the case that if an insured wrongly answered a question in a proposal which included a clause — a basis clause — that warranted the truth of the answers and stated that the truth of the answer was the basis of the contract, the insurer was able to terminate the contract even if the answer was not relevant to the risk. An extreme example may be where the insured was asked for details of a distant relative. Clauses such as this are still used but are no longer as devastating as they once were. Section 24 of the Insurance Contracts Act states that wrongly answered questions are to be treated as misrepresentations. The Act, in s 28, sets out the consequences of making a misrepresentation according to whether it is innocent or fraudulent.

Where a person makes a statement that is wrong but was believed to be true and a reasonable person in the same circumstances would have held the same belief, s 26 provides that the statement is not to be treated as a misrepresentation. This section was considered in the *Fruehauf Finance Corp* case and in *Plasteel Windows Australia Pty Ltd v C E Heath Underwriting Agencies Pty Ltd* (1990) 95 ALR 305; 6 ANZ Ins Cas 60-964.

Significance of breach of conditions

[17.62]   Section 54 of the Act reformed the common law in an important way. It removes from insurers the power to deny liability for a mere breach of a term of the contract. An insurer could previously deny liability for a claim for a stolen car by relying on a condition of the policy that required the car to be kept roadworthy and by showing that the car was unroadworthy. The section was recommended by the Law Reform Commission to overcome that situation. It would be reasonable to rely on the condition of the contract where the state of the car contributed to its loss but if it was stolen, the roadworthiness would be irrelevant. Under s 54 the insured must prove that the type of act relied on by the insurer could not have caused or contributed to the loss. If the insured's conduct prejudiced the insurer, the claim may be reduced.

If the car was damaged because it was unroadworthy, the insurer would be able to rely on the terms of the contract and deny liability. If it was damaged, while in an unroadworthy condition, because another party collided with it while it was parked, s 54 would prevent the insurer from relying on the terms of the contract to deny liability. If the car was unroadworthy and there was an accident for which another person was partly responsible the insurer would be able to reduce the claim to pay only the proportion of the other party's contribution to the damage. For an explanation from the High Court on the operation of s 54 see *Ferrcom Pty Ltd v Commercial Union Assurance Co of Australia Pty Ltd* (1993) 176 CLR 332; 111 ALR 339.

Settlement of the claim

[17.63]   The claim is often administered on behalf of the insurer by a loss adjuster and it is not uncommon for the whole process to be conducted by the adjuster. If the insurer admits liability it will pay the insured, or in some cases replace stolen or damaged goods with equivalent goods it has arranged to purchase (at a discount in order to minimise the cost), or in other cases pay for repairs. The insurer usually reserves an option in the contract as to how it will settle a matter. Once the claim has been settled the insurer requires the insured to sign a release to acknowledge that it is a full and final settlement and that the claim is discharged. Although such a release is a legally significant document there are circumstances where a court would set it aside, for example, where it has been obtained under duress. An issue at the time of settlement is that of salvage — who will keep the wreck of the car. Unless otherwise agreed it is the insurer.

If the claim relates to a total loss, for example, where a house is burned to the ground or a car is damaged beyond repair the settlement of that claim usually brings the policy to an end even if it occurred early in the life of the policy. Sometimes, however, there are circumstances where, for example, only the public liability cover has been exhausted but the other elements of the policy remain.

The concepts

[17.64] The foregoing introduction to the insurance transaction has emphasised its contractual basis and has outlined the process from the formation of the contract to performance by way of settlement of a claim. The insurance contract has the features of a conventional contract but it also has additional, special characteristics which are fundamental to the insurance transaction. These characteristics which are imposed by common law and by statute are discussed below.

Utmost good faith

[17.65] At the heart of every insurance transaction is a requirement that both parties exercise utmost good faith towards each other. The reason for this is well illustrated in *Carter v Boehm* (1766) 3 Burr 1905; 97 ER 1162 where the judge explained:

> Insurance is a contract upon speculation. The special facts, upon which the contingent chance is to be computed, lie more commonly in the knowledge of the insured only: the underwriter trusts to his representation, and proceeds upon confidence that he does not keep back any circumstance in his knowledge, to mislead the underwriter into a belief that the circumstance does not exist, and to induce him to estimate the risqué as if it did not exist. The keeping back of such a circumstance is a fraud, and, therefore, the policy is void … Good faith forbids either party by concealing what he privately knows, to draw the other into a bargain, from his ignorance of that fact, and his believing the contrary …

The principle is the creation of the common law and is sometimes expressed by saying that insurance contracts are contracts uberrimae fidei. The Insurance Contracts Act has incorporated the duty of utmost good faith in s 13 which states:

> A contract of insurance is a contract based on the utmost good faith and there is implied in such a contract a provision requiring each party to it to act towards the other party, in respect of any matter arising under or in relation to it, with the utmost good faith.

and in s 14(1) it provides:

> If reliance by a party to a contract of insurance would be to fail to act with the utmost good faith, the party may not rely on that provision.

A similar provision exists in the Marine Insurance Act 1909.

Extent of duty of utmost good faith

[17.66] Parties to an insurance contract are required to act with utmost good faith at all stages of the transaction — during its negotiation, during its life and in the process of making a claim. It is important to note that the duty is imposed on each party. There is a tendency to think that it applies only to the insured but that reflects the attitudes of a period before the rights of consumers were as well recognised by the law as they are now. There is good reason to think that in the light of the imbalance between a large insurance company and an individual the duty falls more heavily on the insurer.

What is expected when exercising utmost good faith

[17.67] The extract from *Carter v Boehm* provides a good example of what is expected from an insured. Indeed, the requirement of disclosure developed from the principle of utmost good faith. An insurer would be in breach of the duty if it attempted to cancel a contract because after a policy had been issued a catastrophic loss became inevitable, for example, advising householders in the path of a bushfire that their policies were cancelled. Such conduct would, however, be ineffective because of the cancellation procedures laid down in s 59 of the Act. In *Australian Associated Motor Insurers Ltd v Ellis* (1990) 54 SASR 61; 11 MVR 143; 6 ANZ Ins Cas 60-957 the court held that to meet its duty under the Act the insurer was required to give the insured adequate warning of the general nature and effect of a policy condition dealing with modifications to the car that was being insured.

The duty of utmost good faith involves the notion of honesty and fair dealing. In *Kelly v New Zealand Insurance Company Ltd* (1996) 9 ANZ Ins Cas 61-317 it was alleged that the insurer had breached its duty. In the course of his judgment Owen J rejected that allegation with the words '[t]here was no dishonest, capricious or unreasonable conduct' on the part of the insurer. He referred to 'the essential element of honesty that is at the heart of the good faith principle'.

Much of what would be regarded as the duty of utmost good faith has been absorbed into specific sections of the Act. A more realistic possibility of a breach of the duty would be at the claim stage. An inordinate delay in settling a claim; a perverse interpretation of the policy; a refusal to explain why a claim was being refused or an unsupported allegation of fraud could all amount to a lack of good faith. The insurer's agents could also create a breach, for example, where an investigator appointed by the insurer in relation to a claim threatened or harassed a claimant.

Fraud

[17.68]   The form of conduct that is most contrary to the notion of good faith is fraud. At any stage of the transaction, fraudulent conduct which is conduct carried out with an intention to deceive or recklessly as to its truth will have serious consequences. A fraudulent misrepresentation or failure to disclose allows the insurer to avoid the contract: s 28(2). Where a fraudulent claim has been made, the insurer is entitled under the Insurance Contracts Act to refuse to pay the claim: s 56. In many policies a fraudulent claim or a failure by the insured to be 'truthful and frank' in relation to a claim would provide grounds to refuse a claim or cancel the contract.

It is a serious matter for an insurer to allege fraud and the conduct said to be fraudulent must involve more than making a mistake. In making the allegation the insurer bears the onus of proving that the insured acted with the necessary intention to defraud. The task of proving fraud very often involves circumstantial rather than direct evidence, for example, the insured was in financial difficulty; the car needed expensive repairs; the insured was attempting to sell the house; the house was insured for more than its market value or the insured had a history of similar claims. The action of the insurer in a fraud case can, however, create a risk of breaching the duty of good faith. If the insurer does not have any more than a suspicion of fraud but refuses a claim on that ground it leaves the insured in a position where the only thing to do is to litigate. In effect the insurer can say 'we are not meeting the claim, sue us'. For the average individual, litigation against an insurance company is not economically feasible and if the insurer were to exploit that situation it would be a clear breach of the duty of utmost good faith.

Paramount nature of the duty

[17.69]   The importance that the Act attaches to the duty of utmost good faith is emphasised by s 12 which says that no other law, including the Act itself, can limit or restrict the Act's provisions about the duty. If there is any conflict between what the Act says about utmost good faith and any other law, the duty of utmost good faith prevails.

Section 14 of the Act means that the application of the terms of the insurance contract is subject to the duty of utmost good faith. If to apply the terms of the contract would amount to a breach of the duty, s 14 says that the terms cannot be relied upon. The interpretation of the contract must undertaken in good faith.

Exclusion of other statutory provisions

[17.70]   The weight attached to the duty of utmost good faith by the Act can be seen in s 15 which provides that certain legislative relief does not apply to insurance contracts. The legislation, which includes the Trade Practices Act 1974 (Cth), the Fair Trading Acts of the states and the Contracts Review Act (NSW), provides relief in respect of 'harsh, oppressive, unconscionable, unjust, unfair or inequitable' contracts. Other legislation which relieves a person from the common law consequences of misrepresentations is also excluded. This does not however mean that relief for damages under ss 52 or 53 of the Trade Practices Act (or its Fair Trading Act equivalent) could not be sought.

The rationale of s 15 appears to be that adherence to the duty of utmost good faith should remove the need for the relief offered by the legislation referred to. Amendments to s 15 in 1994 provide that a person is able to seek compensatory damages: s 15(2). The section identifies some forms of conduct which would offend the notion of utmost good faith. Essentially, to exercise utmost good faith a person should act fairly and not exercise any advantage that may exist by virtue of a more powerful bargaining position.

Effect of breach of good faith

[17.71]   Where the insured commits a breach of the duty, s 60(1)(a) of the Insurance Contracts Act allows the insurer to cancel the contract. This is the only section that specifically applies to a breach but other sections in the Act offer remedies for conduct that amounts to a breach, for example, s 28 for failure to disclose and s 56 for a fraudulent claim. Where the insurer commits the breach the insured would be able to resist a term of the contract that has been applied with a lack of utmost good faith: s 14. The insured would also have the right to sue for breach of the term implied into the contract by s 13 of the Insurance Contracts Act.

Insurable interest

[17.72]   In the area of general insurance the common law notion of an insurable interest is that the insured should have a pecuniary interest in the subject matter of the contract. This means that the insured should benefit by the property continuing to exist or remaining undamaged or, alternatively, that prejudice would be suffered if either of those events occurred. In this way the basic concept of insurance can be honoured — that is, on the occasion of a loss the insurer compensates the insured. Although the common law rules about insurable interest have been changed by the Insurance Contracts Act the principle remains.

It was applied in the House of Lords in *Macaura v Northern Assurance Co Ltd* [1925] AC 619 where M had sold his business to a company of which he was a major shareholder. The property which was transferred to the company had been and remained insured in M's name. It was destroyed by fire and when M claimed under his policy he was met with the argument that the company was now the owner of the property and, even though he was a major shareholder, he had no interest in the property recognised by the law. The court held that M had not suffered any loss or prejudice as a result of the fire. His interest in the company property was indirect at best and at common law it was insufficient to sustain his claim. The property was not insured in the name of the company and as a result it was forced to bear the loss.

Life policies — insurable interest

[17.73]   In a life policy everybody has an insurable interest in his or her own life. At common law if one wished to insure the life of another it was necessary to demonstrate a pecuniary interest in that life. The common law view about insurable interests in life insurance has been supplemented by s 19 of the Insurance Contracts Act which sets out the range of insurable interests. These are:

* persons in their own lives;
* spouses in each other's life;
* a parent or guardian in the life of a person who is under the age of 18 years;
* persons who will suffer a pecuniary or economic loss on the death of another have an interest in that other person's life, for example, parties to long-running litigation would have an interest in the judge's life because if the judge were to die there would be extra costs;
* a body corporate in the life of an officer or employee;
* an employer and employee in each other's life; and
* a person has an insurable interest in the life of a person who provides maintenance and support.

The Act provides that the amount of the interest is unlimited.

Statutory amendment of the requirement

[17.74]   The Insurance Contracts Act provides that the absence of an insurable interest at the time of entering a contract of general insurance does not make the contract void: s 16. It is enough that at the time of the loss the insured suffered a 'pecuniary or economic' loss as a result of the event: s 17. The two sections have relaxed the common law which required an insurable interest, measured as a recognised legal interest, at both the time of entering into the contract and at the time of the loss. The effect of the Act is not to remove the need for an insurable interest but to relieve the strictness of the common law. Had the *Macaura* case been decided under the Act, s 17 would have allowed the shareholder to recover because, even though he had no recognised interest in the company property, he could have demonstrated that as a result of the fire his interest in the company was reduced in value.

The Insurance Contracts Act provides that the insurable interest in a life policy must exist at the time of entering into the policy, otherwise the contract is void: s 18.

Disclosure

[17.75]   Insurance companies are not benevolent institutions. They need to generate the funds to provide the benefits and as commercial enterprises they have a profit goal. The nature of insurance is that the insurer is asked to provide cover against a certain peril. To do so it must assess the risk so that it can first decide whether or not to accept the risk and, if so, at what premium. Insurers have a great deal of actuarial information about risks. They know the probability of a house fire and they can set their premium at a rate that covers their obligations and makes a profit. What they do not know, without being told, is the history of the insured and they need that information in order to assess their risk. A 21-year-old person seeking life cover after having been diagnosed as suffering a terminal illness knows something that the insurer could not possibly know and which would influence the insurer's decision. It would be necessary for that information to be disclosed to the insurer.

Achieving disclosure: questions and duty

[17.76]   Disclosure of information is achieved by the insurer asking questions on the proposal form. The insured must answer those questions correctly, otherwise there has been a misrepresentation. However, the disclosure process goes further. As a matter of common law, as part of the duty of utmost good faith, the insured is expected to disclose information which would influence the insurer's decision to accept the proposal. The insured must correctly answer the questions asked, otherwise there is a misrepresentation but the duty of disclosure goes further. It involves, in effect, answering the questions that were not asked.

As the early case of *Carter v Boehm* (1766) 3 Burr 1905; 97 ER 1162 explained:

... The special facts, upon which the contingent chance is to be computed, lie more commonly in the knowledge of the insured only: the underwriter trusts to his representation, and proceeds upon confidence that he does not keep back any circumstance in his knowledge, to mislead the underwriter into a belief that the circumstance does not exist, and to induce him to estimate the risqué as if it did not exist ...

The Insurance Contracts Act replaces the common law rules about disclosure by an insured to an insurer; the common law remains in relation to the insurer's duty of disclosure. The critical provision is s 21(1) which states that:

(1) Subject to this Act, an insured has a duty to disclose to the insurer, before the relevant contract of insurance is entered into, every matter that is known to the insured, being a matter that —

(a) the insured knows to be a matter relevant to the decision of the insurer whether to accept the risk and, if so, on what terms; or

(b) a reasonable person in the circumstances could be expected to know to be a matter so relevant.

A problem with the statutory duty of disclosure is that assumes that the insured knows enough about insurance underwriting to know what information is relevant to the insurer. For many reasons this is unrealistic. It has been argued that insurance companies have been in business long enough to know what it is they need to know and should ask all that they wish to know on the proposal forms. Thus the insured would be expected to meet a standard of honesty rather than something far more technical. In order to meet this objection the Act was amended with the addition of s 21A which, according to the Explanatory Memorandum, is

designed to redress [the] imbalance and improve the capacity of an insured to comply with the duty of disclosure by requiring insurers to ask specific questions in respect to a proposed contract of insurance, in default of which the insurer is deemed to have waived the duty of disclosure.

The effect of the new section is that if the insurer does not ask a question on the proposal form about a particular matter it cannot later plead a breach of the duty of disclosure if the insured did not provide the information it regards as significant to its decision to underwrite the risk. Section 21A applies to domestic and personal forms of insurance but is not, however, intended to apply to renewal contracts. As mentioned earlier, the duty of disclosure in renewable contracts arises annually or each time the contract is renewed. The Explanatory Memorandum sheds no light on why this distinction exists. Perhaps it is expected that the General Insurance Code of Practice will assist insureds in that they will be given better documentation. There will thus be two standards of disclosure — one at the time of first entering into a contract of insurance and another at each periodical renewal under the current s 21 rules.

Significance of misrepresentation

[17.77] The requirement that the insured will answer questions correctly is hardly surprising. It would be inconsistent with the duty of utmost good faith if a person were to fail deliberately to tell the truth and it would prejudice the insurer's position if wrong answers were given to matters which are critical in the assessment of risk. A misrepresentation will be significant under the Insurance Contracts Act only where it affected the insurer's decision to enter the contract: s 28(1). Thus, if the insurer would have accepted the risk even if the intending insured had not given incorrect information then the misrepresentation makes no difference.

Statutory adjustment to misrepresentations

[17.78] A misrepresentation is no more than an incorrect statement but, if one is made on the basis of the person's belief, that being a reasonable thing to believe in the circumstances, it is not a misrepresentation for the purposes of the Insurance Contracts Act: s 26. If person who was asked 'Are you in good health?' and answered 'yes' was later found to be suffering from a rare disease those are circumstances which would be within the reach of s 26. The incorrect answer about the state of health is a misrepresentation but if the disease was rare and not obvious it would be reasonable for the person to answer yes and, by reason of s 26, the answer would not be regarded as a misrepresentation.

The failure to answer a question or an obviously incomplete or irrelevant answer does not amount to a misrepresentation: s 27. In s 23 the Act says that if a reasonable person would have understood the question in the way the insured did then it has that meaning even if it was not intended by the insurer. An example of this is a question that is often asked on consumer credit proposal forms — 'Are you in good health?' That is an imprecise question and a reasonable person could answer 'yes' when meaning to say 'I am in good health for a 56-year-old man all things considered'. If it turned out that the person was suffering from, but not restricted by a disease, the answer could not be treated as a misrepresentation.

Effect of misrepresentation

[17.79] A misrepresentation can be innocent or fraudulent. It is innocent where there was no intention to mislead. Although the two categories are quite different, each can have serious consequences for an insured. For example, a misrepresentation provides a ground for cancellation of the contract: s 60. Where there has been an innocent misrepresentation in the course of completing the proposal, the insurer is able to rely on s 28(3) which allows it to take action to be put into the position it would have been in had the correct information been given. An example of this section's operation is where an insured has failed to inform the insurer of two driving licence cancellations. If the insurer could prove that such information is critical to its decision about accepting the risk and that it refuses proposals from intending insureds with such a record, it would be able to rely on s 28(3) to say that it would not have issued the policy. It could then deny liability in respect of that claim. Alternatively, it might say that for persons with such a record it charges a premium of double the normal figure or that it imposes an excess of $1000. In these cases it would be required to pay under the policy but it would reduce the amount paid in accordance with its practice. The information about how it would react to a particular client is to be found in the internal underwriting guidelines which lay down the philosophy of each insurance company.

Disclosure in a marine policy

[17.80] In a marine insurance policy the failure to 'disclose every material circumstance which is known to the assured' allows the insurer to avoid the contract: Marine Insurance Act s 24. Fraud is not an issue and in this respect the common law approach to disclosure is applied. A person whose pleasure craft was insured and who failed to disclose a matter would find that the consumer orientation of the Insurance Contracts Act 1984 does not apply to such a situation.

Fraudulent misrepresentation

[17.81] A fraudulent misrepresentation occurs where the insured makes a statement knowing it to be untrue or reckless as to whether it is true. It is intentionally deceitful. The effect of such a statement in a proposal is that the insurer is able to treat the contract as never having been in existence. In the words of the Act, the insurer 'may avoid the contract': s 28(2). If the insurer avoids the contract it says, in effect, that the contract never existed and consequently it was never exposed to the risk. The insurer's action brings to an end a relationship that as a matter of law had never been formed. It must refund the premium because it was never on risk.

Alternatively, it can choose not to avoid but to rely on s 28(3) and treat it in the same way as an innocent misrepresentation. The effect of a fraudulent misrepresentation can be reduced by applying s 31. This section gives to the court a discretion to disregard the fraudulent conduct if it would be harsh and unfair not to do so and if the court is satisfied that the insurer has not been prejudiced by the fraudulent misrepresentation. Although the section appears on its face to tolerate fraud, the critical consideration is whether there had been any prejudice to the insurer and in this respect the onus of proving a lack of prejudice rests on the insured.

Misrepresentations in life insurance

[17.82] The expectation that an intending insured will provide relevant information is the same for a life policy. There can be no doubt that an insurer would need to know the state of health of a person before providing life cover. The law as to what amounts to a misrepresentation is the same for life as it is for general insurance. The effect of a misrepresentation in a life policy is dealt with by s 29 of the Act. The misrepresentation is of no significance if the insurer would have entered the contract despite it or if the misrepresentation is about the age of the intended insured. The insurer may avoid the contract if the misrepresentation was fraudulent. If it was not fraudulent and the insurer would not have entered the contract at all, the insurer has three years in which to avoid the contract: s 29(3). If the right of avoidance is not exercised, the insurer may, within three years of entering the contract, vary it to what it would have been had the misrepresentation not been made. Thus if the misrepresentation led to a lower premium the insurer can vary the contract so that it provides the sum insured that the lower premium would have obtained had the insurer been properly informed: s 29(4).

Misrepresentation of age

[17.83] The age of an insured is an important consideration in a life policy. It follows that an older person represents a greater risk and should command a higher premium than a younger person. If there has been a misstatement of age the Act provides a formula which allows the insurer to vary the contract so that if a person's age has been understated the sum insured is reduced to what the premium set under those circumstances would have bought. Similarly if a person's age has been overstated and the resultant premium has been set higher than necessary, the insurer may increase the sum insured or reduce the premium and repay with the interest the premiums overpaid: s 30.

Statutory duty of disclosure

[17.84]   As mentioned earlier, the process by which the insurer is informed about the risk it is being asked to cover involves more than merely supplying answers to questions. Section 21 of the Act makes it clear that the insured must disclose certain matters. The duty of disclosure could perhaps be summarised as the requirement on the insured to inform the insurer of the matters not asked on the proposal. The duty established by s 21 has removed several difficulties that were associated with the common law. No longer is it necessary to consider what is material; nor is it necessary to take account of a 'prudent insurer'. There has, however, been a tendency for some judges to rely on the old concepts: see Samuel JA in *Toikan International Insurance Broking Pty Ltd v Plasteel Windows Australia Pty Ltd* (1989) 15 NSWLR 641; 94 ALR 485; 5 ANZ Ins Cas 60-903 and Rogers CJ in *Ayoub v Lombard Insurance Co (Aust) Pty Ltd* (1989) 5 ANZ Ins Cas 60-933. The duty is, however, an onerous one because a failure to observe it is treated in the same way as a misrepresentation. The failure can be treated as fraudulent or as innocent and the consequences for the insured and the remedies for the insurer are the same as discussed above in the context of misrepresentations.

The components of Section 21

[17.85]   Section 21 lays down that:
1. *An insured has a duty*   According to the High Court decision in *Advance (NSW) Insurance Agencies Pty Ltd v Matthews* (1989) 166 CLR 606; 85 ALR 161 the duty applies to each insured if there are more than one. In the case of a joint policy the failure by one insured affects the others so that the others who are completely free of blame can lose cover because of the breach of duty by that person. In a *Matthews* situation if a husband and wife are co-insureds and the husband, say, fails fraudulently to disclose a matter which would have resulted in the proposal not being accepted, the wife who is completely innocent of any non-disclosure is treated as if she had failed to make the disclosure. The same result applies where the policy was a composite one, that is, where the parties were insuring different interests: see *Zurich Australian Insurance Limited v Contour Mobel Pty Ltd* [1991] 2 VR 146; (1990) 6 ANZ Ins Cas 60-984.
2. The *duty arises 'before the relevant contract is entered into'*   There is no duty to disclose matters that arise after the contract has been made. Thus, if a person whose proposal for life cover has been accepted subsequently contracts a terminal illness, there is no duty to disclose that matter to the insurer. In a general policy there may, however, be a condition requiring the insured to notify the insurer of any change in circumstances which develops during the currency of the policy. It is also necessary to note that in general insurance, where policies are renewed annually, a new contract is made on renewal: s 11(9). This means that the duty of disclosure is revived at each renewal and if anything has changed in the past year it must be disclosed. A practical example of how the duty applies on renewal is in the case of a motor vehicle. If the condition of the motor vehicle has deteriorated in the past year, say, because of rust, that fact must be disclosed to the insurer. Similarly, if the driver has been fined during

the year for speeding that must be disclosed. Failure to do so, whether innocent or deliberate, could result in the insurer denying liability when a claim is made.

3. The insured is required to disclose *'every matter that is known to the insured'* This is reasonable in that an insured cannot be expected to disclose something that is unknown. The insured is not required to disclose matters that ought to have been known by the insurer.

4. What must be disclosed are matters the insured knows, or a reasonable person in the circumstances could be expected to know, are relevant to the insurer's decision whether to accept the risk and if so on what terms. This goes to the heart of the duty — the reason for it is to provide the insurer with information it needs to take into account in order to assess the risk — that is, information it does not have and which of course is relevant to the risk being considered. The insured's history of driving accidents would not be relevant in considering a proposal for fire insurance and it would therefore not be necessary to disclose it (unless of course it was a question on the proposal). The duty of disclosure would be activated where, for example, a person seeking fire cover had stored at the premises a large quantity of flammable material. That fact would be known to the insured, it would certainly be 'relevant to the insurer' in deciding whether or not to accept the risk and, if so, at what premium and/or with what conditions such as special storage arrangements. This was the issue in *Prime Forme Cutting Pty Ltd v Baltica General Insurance Co Ltd* (1990) 6 ANZ Ins Cas 61-028, at 76,879.

Materiality test no longer relevant

[17.86] Section 21 has replaced the common law test of materiality. The issue is now whether the matter was relevant to the insurer in the decision-making process. That does not require the person to have the same knowledge of insurance practices as an insurer. If the insured does not know it was relevant, the next question is whether a reasonable person in the circumstances could be expected to know that the matter was relevant. In the example above a reasonable person could be expected to know that the presence on the premises of flammable material would be relevant to the insurer who is assessing the risk in a fire policy. The fact that the insured did not know or had not thought about it is of no consequence — the reasonable person test would result in the failure to advise about the material being classified as a breach of the duty of disclosure. See the discussion by Brooking J in *Twenty-first Maylux Pty Ltd v Mercantile Mutual Insurance (Aust) Ltd* [1990] VR 919; 92 ALR 661; (1990) 6 ANZ Ins Cas 60-954.

Duty of disclosure excused

[17.87] There are circumstances where the insured is excused from the duty of disclosure. These are set out in s 21(2) and are matters that:

* *Diminish the risk* It would be unnecessary for an insured to tell the insurer that a house was protected by extra security measures. The insurer would not be prejudiced by not knowing that.

* *Are of common knowledge in the sense that both parties know* For example, if the insured had disclosed that a car was used for business purposes it would not be necessary to repeat that information on renewal of the policy since the insurer already knew it.

* *The insurer knows or should know in the course of business as an insurer* If the insured's business generated a toxic form of waste the insurer would be expected to

know that and need not be told. If, for example, the insured had previously made a claim on this insurer it would not be necessary to disclose that fact.

Waiver of compliance with duty

[17.88]   The duty also does not apply where the insurer has waived compliance in relation to the matter: s 21(3). This occurs where there has been a failure to answer a question or an answer has been given that is obviously incomplete or irrelevant and the insurer has not sought clarification of the way in which the question was answered.

Pre-existing conditions — relief from disclosure

[17.89]   An important exception to the need to disclose is to be found in ss 46 and 47. These sections do not so much eliminate the need to disclose as reduce the effect of failing to disclose. Both sections refer to pre-existing defects. In the case of s 46, where a policy allows for limiting or exclusion of liability in respect of the defective condition of a 'thing' prior to entering into the contract, the insurer cannot rely on the limitation or exclusion where the insured was not aware of the defect and a reasonable person would not have been aware either. Thus, if a person purchased a car and later, because of a serious defect in its design, the car was damaged s 46 would prevent the insurer from relying on a term of the policy which excluded liability for design faults. The section applies to domestic policies but not to certain policies prescribed in reg 30 of the Insurance Contracts Regulations. In s 47 the same principle applies in respect of a person who is, at the time of purchasing a policy, unaware of a disease or disability which is the subject of a limitation or exclusion under the policy. A person who purchased a consumer credit policy — to provide benefits in case of unemployment due to illness — and subsequently fell ill with a pre-existing but undiagnosed disease would be protected by s 47 and would not be denied benefits.

Disclosure not necessary in some forms of insurance

[17.90]   The difference between 'discretionary' insurance and the types that are imposed by law — for example, health or motor vehicle third party — is well illustrated by the fact that in most of the compulsory forms there is no need for disclosure. Persons are admitted into these schemes without any consideration of underwriting issues; no attention is paid to their health history or records as drivers.

  The duty of disclosure is an important feature of forming an insurance contract. If there was non-disclosure the consequences are the same as for misrepresentation. Section 28(2) allows the insurer to avoid the contract if the non-disclosure was fraudulent and s 28(3) applies where it was innocent. The application of either of those provisions could see the 'insured' person left without cover.

Notifying insured of duty to disclose

[17.91]   The importance of the duty is recognised by s 22 of the Act which requires insurers 'to clearly inform the insured in writing' of the general nature and effect of the duty of disclosure. The way in which the information may be conveyed is set out in the Schedule to the Insurance Contracts Regulations.

Indemnity

[17.92]   In most general insurance policies, even if not in as many words, there is a promise from the insurer to 'indemnify the insured against losses caused by an event covered by the policy'. Life policies are not based on the indemnity principle because it is not possible to assess in money terms the loss on death. Sickness and personal accident policies are not indemnity policies either. It is quite possible to take out several of these policies.

The *Macquarie Dictionary* meaning of indemnify is 'to compensate for damage or loss sustained, expense incurred etc; to engage to make good or secure against anticipated loss; give security against (future damage or liability)'. The basis of an indemnity policy is that the insured is entitled, as a matter of contract, to have a loss made good. Flowing from that proposition it can be said that a person cannot profit from the occurrence of an insured peril. The way in which the insurer makes good is a matter for the contract — there is no principle that prevents an insurer from paying cash or providing substitute goods (reinstatement) or repairing the goods. If, for example, the insured lost a five-year-old camera, the insurer usually reserves the option of paying the insured in cash the depreciated value of the camera or of arranging to supply a camera of the same age.

The principle of indemnity reinforces the need for an insurable interest. It follows that a person cannot seek to be protected from a loss arising from a particular peril unless there is an interest to protect.

Extent of indemnity

[17.93]   The level of compensation that is available in an indemnity policy will depend on the amount specified in the contract. A person whose house is insured for $100,000 could not complain if the insurer paid $80,000 being the amount necessary to build the same style of house because the extent of the loss was $80,000. Likewise, if the house was valued at $125,000 the insured could expect to receive no more than $100,000. The sum insured in an indemnity policy is a maximum figure. The insurer promises to indemnify 'up to' that figure. That is why a person whose car is insured under a market value policy for $20,000 may receive only $17,000 which is the market value at the time of the loss. Where there has been a partial loss the policy will compensate for that loss (subject to averaging). In travel policies where medical cover is provided the insurer will pay the cost of the medical expenses less whatever amount was recovered under health insurance. Where there has been a cancellation of travel the policy indemnifies the insured against the pre-paid cost of travel that is not recoverable from the travel operator. In both examples the insurer pays the loss suffered by the insured and in this way satisfies the notion of indemnity.

Market value

[17.94]   The valuation of the loss is an essential feature of indemnity. In a partial loss the insured is entitled to the difference between the value before the partial loss and the value after it. Policies are more likely, however, to provide for repairs to be carried out or for replacement of the damaged item. Where there has been a total loss the prima facie measure of value is market value. This can create confusion about which market is referred to. Is it the retail market or the wholesale market? The Court of Appeal in New South Wales has said that where jewellery is involved, the market price is what the insured could have bought or sold the item for — not the wholesale market value. If the item is special in that it appeals to a limited number of persons, for example, a modified car, the market value of a modified car would be what collectors of such items would pay: see *Gold Star Insurance v O'Brien* (1984) 3 ANZ Ins Cas 60-605. Where there is no available market for the goods as occurred where oaten hay was destroyed by fire and the insured was entitled to be paid the value of the hay, the court held that because there was no available market from which to replace the hay the proper method to ascertain its value was to establish the gross proceeds had the insured been able to sell the hay and from that figure deduct the selling expenses: see *Whybrow v Royal Insurance Australia* (1984) 3 ANZ Ins Cas 60-565.

Agreed value

[17.95] A variation of the market value indemnity style of policy is one described as 'agreed value' or 'valued'. In such a policy, according to the High Court in *British Traders' Insurance Co Ltd v Monson* (1964) 111 CLR 86; [1964] ALR 845 the parties agree '... as to the value of the subject-matter, not the amount of the loss ...'. Thus if there is a total loss of a car insured under an agreed value for $25,000, that is the figure which is paid to the insured. Had that been a conventional policy the insured would have been paid the market value of the car which might have been $20,000. An agreed value policy is an indemnity policy where the insured is indemnified for the agreed loss suffered. Once the figure has been set, and absent fraud, the parties are bound for better or worse to the sum agreed upon. It could happen that the insured appears to have recovered more under an agreed value policy than the market value but that difference does not offend the indemnity principle: it reflects the fact that the value of the subject matter was agreed at too high a figure.

Replacement policies

[17.96] A departure from the indemnity approach can be seen in replacement policies or, as they are sometimes referred to, 'new for old'. Under this type of policy the insured pays a higher premium and is entitled to a level of cover that will allow for a house to be 'rebuilt to a condition equal to but not better than or more extensive than when new'. The insurer does not provide open-ended cover — there is a maximum figure but many policies, as an additional benefit, will absorb the impact of inflation. There is usually an allowance for the type of problem that could arise with an old house — it may not be possible to replicate a house built in the nineteenth century because modern building standards are higher and the replacement house will, to that extent, be better. The insured pays for cover to replace the asset, not merely to indemnify against the loss.

Maximum cover

[17.97] The Insurance Contracts Act in s 42 has introduced the requirement that an insured is entitled to receive the maximum cover that the premium charged for the policy will provide. Thus if a person paid $100 to insure goods and if that level of premium purchased $7500 worth of cover the maximum cover will be $7500 rather than any lower figure negotiated by the parties.

Double insurance

[17.98] Whereas under-insurance can create problems for an insured, over-insurance is often no more than a waste of money. One form of over-insurance that is significant, however, is where the same risk is insured against under more than one policy — double insurance. A person could take out insurance cover with more than one insurer or could be in the process of changing from one to another and during that period have overlapping policies or have luggage covered under the temporary removal benefit of a household policy and also under a travel policy. Double insurance means that a person is in the position of being able to recover twice for the same loss from different insurers. It does not, however, exist where the risk has been spread between a number of insurers. Double recovery is offensive to the notion of indemnity and many insurers seek information about other insurance on the proposal or provide in the policy that non-disclosure of other insurance amounts to a breach of the contract. The Insurance Contracts Act, in s 76, provides that where there is double insurance in a general insurance context the insured is able to be indemnified by one or more of the insurers who are then able to adjust the matter according to common law rules so that each contributes to the settlement. It is not possible to be over-insured in life, personal accident and sickness policies, nor does double insurance arise in those contexts.

Average

[17.99]   Also associated with indemnity is the concept of averaging.

If a person insures a house valued at $150,000 for $105,000 the effect of the under-insurance is that the person has accepted part of the risk of the house being destroyed. Should the house be totally destroyed the insured will receive only $105,000 and will have borne part of the risk. In effect, the insured by under-insuring the property was a co-insurer. Insurance practice and the idea of what is fair has developed a rule to deal with the situation where there is under-insurance at the time of a partial loss. Assume that damage to the extent of $72,000 was sustained to the house. This is well inside the maximum sum insured. Should the insured be able to recover all of the $72,000 loss? The insurer would argue that if a person is able to recover 100 per cent of a loss by paying a premium for 70 per cent cover then there is an element of inequity.

The answer is that it depends on two things. The first is whether an average (or co-insurance) clause appears in the policy. A general insurance policy that does not provide for averaging will not be subject to average; marine policies are always subject to average and do not need a clause. In practice average clauses appear in fire and householder policies.

The average clause provides that, if at the time of the loss the property was under-insured, the insured will bear part of the loss in accordance with the proportion that has been self-insured. Using the example above the value of the property at the time of loss was $150,000 but it was insured for 70 per cent of that value. Thus the insured was insuring 30 per cent of the property and, in the case of a partial loss of $72,000, would be required to meet $21,600 of loss.

Statutory modification of average

[17.100]   The second qualification reflects the impact of s 44 of the Insurance Contracts Act. This section limits the operation of the average clause so that:
- it will not apply unless before the contract was entered into, the insurer had clearly informed the insured, in writing, of the nature and effect of an average clause;
- in respect of a house and/or contents policy, the clause will apply only where the sum insured is less than 80 per cent of the value of the property; and
- if it does apply, the value on which it is calculated is 80 per cent rather than 100 per cent of the value of the property.

Another alteration achieved by the Act is that the comparison of values takes place at the time of entering the contract, not the time of the loss.

Example of average

[17.101]   By way of illustration, using the figures above, and assuming that:
- the policy contains an average clause;
- the insured was clearly informed in writing of the nature and effect of averaging; and

- the house was used 'primarily and principally' to house the insured's family or those with whom the insured had a personal relationship.

averaging would apply because at the time of the contract being formed the sum insured ($105,000) was less than 80 per cent of the value of the property ($150,000). Thus the insured is required to bear part of the loss which is $72,000. The proportion of that loss borne by the insurer is calculated as follows:

Value at time of loss 150,000

80% of that value 120,000

Sum insured 105,000

Loss 72,000

$$72,000 \times \frac{105,000}{120,000} = 63,000 \ (87.5\%)$$

The insured would be required to bear $9000 (12.5%) of the cost.

Subrogation

[17.102]   When a person has been indemnified, the insurer has compensated that person for any losses or damage. The loss or damage may have been the result of the negligence of a third party in respect of which the insured has a right to recover through litigation. It would appear to be wrong as a matter of principle that a person, having recovered from the insurer, could recover again — in effect to obtain double compensation. It is also wrong that the party at fault should be able to escape liability. The law accommodates this situation through the principle of subrogation which means that once the insured has been indemnified the insurer stands in the shoes of the insured. The legal rights of the insured will be enforced in the insured's name by the insurer who is thus able to recover what it was required to pay to its insured as a result of the conduct of the third party.

In *Castellain v Preston* (1883) 11 QBD 380; [1881–85] All ER Rep 493 the principle was explained in this way:

> As between the underwriter and the assured the underwriter is entitled to the advantage of every right of the assured, whether such right consists in contract, fulfilled or unfulfilled, or in remedy for tort capable of being insisted on or already insisted on, or in any other right whether by way of condition or otherwise, legal or equitable.

Knock-for-knock agreements

[17.103]   The right of subrogation is an integral part of any policy of indemnity but it will not apply where the insurer has a 'knock-for-knock' agreement with another insurer. Insurers may agree among themselves that they will indemnify their insureds having waived their right to subrogation. The insured has no interest in that arrangement unless there has not been full indemnification. Thus if X, who is insured by Company A, has a right of action against Y, who is insured by Company B, the knock-for-knock agreement would mean that Company A would not exercise its subrogation rights to sue, in the name of X, Company B, who would be required to defend Y.

A practical aspect of the doctrine is that it is a term of most insurance policies that insureds will not admit liability or compromise or settle any actions. To do so could jeopardise the insurer's capacity to exercise its subrogation rights and it is not uncommon for insurers to deny liability because of the conduct of the insured in this regard. It is the doctrine of subrogation which allows insurers to pursue the 'at fault' party in a vehicle accident.

Salvage

[17.104]   Also related to the subrogation principle is the question of salvage once a claim has been paid out. If, for example, a car has been so badly damaged as to be a constructive total loss or trading stock has been in a fire the question arises as to who owns the wreck or the damaged stock. As they are able to reduce their liability through subrogation so are insurers also able to assert ownership of the subject matter of a claim. This is achieved through a term of the policy or in the final settlement document once a claim has been paid.

Termination of the contract

[17.105]   There are several circumstances where an insurance contract comes to an end. An obvious example is where a general insurance policy expires or where a life endowment policy matures. Where a renewable policy is about to expire, the Insurance Contracts Act provides that at least 14 days' notice of the impending expiry must given to the insured: s 58(2). Failure to give that notice means that the policy continues to run, for a long as 12 months, even though it may have passed its expiry date and was not renewed: s 58(3). Another example is where there has been total destruction of the subject matter of the policy — it follows that there is nothing left to insure and the insurer, having indemnified the insured, has discharged its obligations under the policy. Other methods of bringing the transaction to an end raise legal issues.

Cancellation

[17.106]   In a general insurance contract the only circumstances in which an insurer can cancel the contract are if the contract provides for it or as specified by s 60 of the Act, and the procedure in s 59 has been followed. That procedure requires at least three days' written notice of the proposed cancellation. Section 60 allows for cancellation in the following circumstances:

(1) Where, in relation to a contract of general insurance —
(a) a person who is or was at any time the insured failed to comply with the duty of utmost good faith;
(b) the person who was the insured at the time when the contract was entered into failed to comply with the duty of disclosure;
(c) the person who was insured at the time when the contract was entered into made a misrepresentation to the insurer during the negotiations for the contract but before it was entered into;
(d) a person who is or was at any time the insured failed to comply with a provision of the contract, including a provision with respect to payment of the premium; or
(e) the insured has made a fraudulent claim under the contract or — under some other contract of insurance (whether with the insurer concerned or with some other insurer) that provides insurance cover during any part of the period during which the first-mentioned contract provided insurance cover, the insurer may cancel the contract.

(2) Where —
(a) a contract of general insurance includes a provision that requires the insured to notify the insurer of a specified act or omission of the insured; or
(b) the effect of the contract is to authorise the insurer to refuse to pay a claim, either in whole or in part. by reason of an act or omission of the insured or some other person, and, after the contract was entered into, such an act or omission has occurred, the insurer may cancel the contract.
(3) A reference in sub-section (2) to an act or omission of the insured includes a reference to an act or omission of the insured that has the effect of altering the state or condition of the subject-matter of the contract or of allowing the state or condition of that subject-matter to alter;
(4) Where a contract of insurance is —
(a) a contract that is in force by virtue of section 58; or
(b) an interim contract of general insurance, the insurer may at any time cancel the contract.

Cancellation in life policies

[17.107]   In the case of life insurance, the period of notice under s 59 is 20 days but the cancellation procedure for a life policy involves a further consideration. If premiums have been paid for at least three years and the surrender value of the policy exceeds the amount outstanding the insurer must give the insured 28 days' notice that the policy will be forfeited. An insured may cancel a life policy provided it is done within 14 days of receiving the policy: s 64(1). This is known as the 'free-look' period. The insured is able to cancel a general insurance policy only if the contract allows for it.

If a policy has been cancelled the insured is entitled to request from the insurer a written statement of reasons for the cancellation: s 75.

Non-formation of the policy

[17.108]   Although this is not a form of termination of the policy the timing could create the impression that there had been a cancellation. There are circumstances where a person, having completed a proposal and for all intents and purposes being insured, finds that there was in fact no policy. This situation arises where the policy has been avoided by the insurer. If the insured had fraudulently breached the duty of disclosure or made a fraudulent misrepresentation s 28(2) of the Insurance Contracts Act allows the insurer to avoid the contract. In a life policy s 29 allows the insurer to avoid a policy for similar reasons.

Avoidance is quite different to cancellation because it amounts to saying that this contract never existed (it is often referred to as avoidance *ab initio*) whereas cancellation brings to an end an existing contract. Under the Insurance Contracts Act retrospective cancellation is not possible. Once the policy has been avoided the insurer is able to deny liability on the ground that it was never under any obligation to indemnify. For that reason, the premium must be refunded since the insurer did nothing to earn it, not having been exposed to risk.

[17.109]   If the insurer is unable to, or elects not to, avoid the contract the remedy under s 28(3) could result in the insured being unable to claim under the policy. That, however, is not cancellation or avoidance. It is the result of the insurer exercising its right to be put into the position it would have been had there been no misrepresentation or failure to disclose. Significantly, the s 28(3) remedy applies only to a particular claim, the contract continues but the grounds which trigger s 28(3) would also justify the cancellation of the policy under s 60(1)(b) or (c).

Other ways of terminating the contract

[17.110]   One of the grounds for cancellation in s 60 is the non-payment of the premium. The payment of, or promise to pay, the premium is the consideration moving from the insured in the insurance contract. Failure to pay amounts to a breach of the contract. The problem of unpaid premiums is more common at the time of renewal of the policy. Late payment could result in the contract not having been renewed and a loss after the expiry date would not be covered. The resolution of disputes about non-payment or late payment of premium depends upon the terms of the contract. It is also important to establish whether as a matter of contract or practice the insurer has extended credit to the insured for payment of premium.

Where the premium for a general policy is payable by instalments, s 62 of the Insurance Contracts Act provides that the policy cannot be cancelled for non-payment unless at least one instalment has been outstanding for at least one month and the insurer has 'clearly informed' the insured about the cancellation clause in the contract.

Surrender of life policy

[17.111]   In a life policy the insured is able to surrender the policy provided that premiums have been paid for at least three years: Life Insurance Act 1995 s 207. This process allows the insured to recover the surrender value of the policy which is calculated in accordance with a formula in that Act. A less terminal process is that of conversion which allows an insured who has paid premiums for three years to cease payment and have the policy converted into a paid-up policy: Life Insurance Act s 209.

Refusal to renew

[17.112]   There is no obligation on either party to a renewable policy such as a car insurance policy to renew it. For the insured the procedure is simply a matter of not completing the renewal notice. The insurer is able to refuse to renew the policy, or decide not to renew it, and if this is done the insured must be given at least 14 days' notice of the insurer's intention. Refusal to renew can have serious consequences for an insured because in a subsequent proposal a question will almost invariably be asked such as 'Have you ever been refused renewal of a policy?' The refusal to renew or the advice that 'we will not be inviting renewal' could be based on a number of reasons. It could be because that line of business is no longer profitable and the insurer is vacating the particular field of insurance or it may be on underwriting grounds such as the insured's driving record or claims history or that the insured lives in a locality where the insurer no longer wishes to insure properties. As with cancellation, the insured is able to request written reasons from the insurer as to why the policy is not being renewed.

Summary and key terms

[17.113]   This chapter has set out to explain:

- The *nature* of insurance and, in particular the fact that it is a transaction which is based on *risk*. The insurer decides whether it is prepared to provide cover against the happening of an event which would have *adverse consequences* for the insured.
- The various *types* of insurance.
- How, because of the importance of insurance to the economy and to those who are insured, the government has *regulated* the industry.
- The role of the *intermediary parties* within the insurance transaction.
- The *contractual basis* of insurance:
    - The *offer* is made by way of a *proposal* for insurance.
    - That offer is *accepted* or not by the insurer.
    - The *consideration* is provided by
        - the *insurer* in the form of the *promise to indemnify*; and
        - the *insured* in the payment of, or promise to pay the *premium*.
- The special feature of the contract:
    - Insurance is one of those transactions or relationships where the law requires the exercise of utmost good faith by both parties.
- The *concepts* fundamental to insurance:
    - utmost good faith;
    - insurable interest;
    - disclosure;
    - indemnity; and
    - subrogation.
- Other *important aspects* of the insurance transaction:
    - defined events;
    - proximate cause; and
    - average clauses.
- The *degree of intervention* in the transaction in the form of legislation which covers the main types of insurance:
    - Insurance Contracts Act 1984;
    - Life Insurance Act 1995; and
    - Marine Insurance Act 1909.
- The extent of *reform* in Australian insurance law brought about by legislation. The role of common law in general and life insurance has been significantly diminished by the impact of the Insurance Contracts Act 1984. The position of consumers in insurance transactions has been recognised and improved. Difficult legal issues such as the respective roles of agents and brokers have now been resolved by the Insurance (Agents and Brokers) Act 1984.
- The way in which the *terms* of an insurance contract are *interpreted*.
- The *settlement* process — the *performance* of the contract by the insurer and the final stage of the transaction.

18

Debt Recovery, Bankruptcy and Insolvency

What this chapter does ...

It is a fact of commercial life that suppliers of goods and services to others sometimes have difficulty in being paid. This chapter examines the methods of ensuring payment either through self-help methods or by court action for recovering small claims. The following matters are discussed:

- *what is a debt;*
- *forms of security and other precautions;*
- *launching a court action and enforcing the decision;*
- *filing a defence — set-off and counterclaim;*
- *executing a judgment — garnishees and warrants of execution;*
- *what happens when a debt remains unpaid after debt recovery litigation;*
- *the forms of bankruptcy and creditors' options to seek settlement of their debts in this process.*

Nature of a debt

[18.1] A debt exists when one person owes money to another. The debt is created by a transaction such as a contract which may be oral or written or a mixture of both. In contractual terms a person who fails to pay for goods or services has broken the agreement which the contract represents — 'I promise to pay if you undertake to supply me with those goods'. The person who is owed the money is called the creditor and the person who owes the money is called the debtor. Debts may arise in several ways and the method of recovery of the money owed will vary accordingly. If the debt is owed under an ordinary contract for the sale or supply of good or services, it is most likely unsecured and while self-help is possible many such debts will be recovered through court action. If the debt is secured, for instance by mortgage which is another contractual transaction, then the mortgagee may sell the property to recover the money owed. That is a form of non-court debt collection where the creditor has taken the precaution of creating a right to use a self-help remedy.

Unsecured debt

[18.2] Any person who is owed money may recover that money by civil court action, provided that a legal debt can be proved. These debts will most often arise due to refusal, inability or neglect to pay by one party to the contract. While the contract may take many forms it will often be the case that the person suing to recover money has, in performance of contract, provided the debtor with goods or services. These contracts may be partly in writing as in order forms, invoices and delivery dockets, but are rarely supported by security.

The person who owes the money may refuse to pay for no particular reason or there may be a number of reasons for non-payment of the money promised in return for the goods or services. There may be a complaint as to the quality of the goods or services, there may be an argument as to the amount of money owed or the debtor may be in the position of having no money available to pay the debt.

Self-help remedies

[18.3] Litigation may not be the most efficient way of recovering or settling a debt or obtaining payment. It may be a time-consuming and expensive option. Worse still, the debtor may be a 'man of straw', in the sense of not having sufficient resources to be worth suing.

There are alternative methods of seeking payment or to recover from a debtor:
- lien;
- guarantee;
- reservation of title;
- secured debt; and
- repossession.

Lien

[18.4] A lien is not so much a security but more of an incentive to have a debtor pay for services provided by the creditor. It is a common law remedy for creditors and can also be contractual. Thus in certain circumstances it arises because the common law says that in such circumstances the creditor has the right to retain goods until payment has been made. It is also possible for a contract to specify that, for example, goods that have been repaired will be retained by the repairer until the repairs have been paid for.

Essentially a lien operates in this fashion — a person to whom money is owed for work done to goods retains possession of the goods until the debt is paid. Thus the mechanic who has repaired a car is able to refuse to surrender the car until the work has been paid for. This is known as a *possessory lien* to distinguish it from equitable and maritime liens which do not require possession.

The possession which is the critical factor in a lien must be uninterrupted. The mechanic referred could not have released the car and sought to regain possession of it when the debt was not paid. There is no common law right to take possession of another's property and to do so could invoke a legal action from the owner of the property and perhaps criminal action. In the standard mechanic–customer relationship the possession of the car is lawfully with the mechanic and can be uninterrupted if the mechanic detains the car. Even if the contract for the repairs was not express about a lien the right would be implied.

The mechanic's lien is further described as *particular* because it applies to goods over which a particular liability exists. The essence of such a lien is that work has been done on the goods which are the subject of the lien.

Another form of lien is the *general possessory* lien in which possession is a key factor. The difference is that the goods being retained need not be those over which there is a liability. If, for example, the mechanic had repaired another of the debtor's cars and had not been paid for it there is a right to retain the car currently being repaired pending payment of the earlier debt. Whereas a particular lien will be implied a general lien needs to be authorised by a contractual term or by the custom within a trade before it can be invoked.

A lien will come to an end when the debt has been paid or some arrangement made to secure payment or where the creditor loses possession lawfully. If the debt has not been paid the person exercising the lien does not have a right to sell the goods unless it is given by statute: Disposal of Uncollected Goods Acts in each state and territory.

Relevant legislation

Jurisdiction	Legislation
New South Wales	Disposal of Uncollected Goods Act 1966
Victoria	Disposal of Uncollected Goods Act 1961
Queensland	Disposal of Uncollected Goods Act 1967
Western Australia	Disposal of Uncollected Goods Act 1970
Tasmania	Disposal of Uncollected Goods Act 1968
Northern Territory	Disposal of Uncollected Goods Act 1976
Australian Capital Territory	Uncollected Goods Act 1996

An *equitable* lien does not require possession but will be used to ensure payment of a debt. An example is where a company is owed money for calls on shares; it can exercise a lien over the shares involved. A person who acquired the shares with notice of the lien does so at the risk of losing them if the company exercises its rights under the articles to forfeit them.

In the case of a *maritime* lien the person exercising it has a claim against the ship or its cargo or its owners. The exercise of this form of lien is somewhat more formal than with a possessory lien because it is necessary to issue a writ in a court exercising admiralty jurisdiction. Notice of the lien is given by fixing the writ to the mast of the ship.

Guarantees

[18.5]   Without going to the extent of setting up a security, a creditor might seek reassurance by asking a third party to *guarantee* the repayment of the debt. In this process a person who is not a party to the underlying transaction is asked to pay should the *primary debtor* default. The creditor and the third party make this arrangement in the form of a contract. The agreement between the debtor and the guarantor as to the legal consequences of default is a matter between them. The guarantee is a useful device where a minor is the debtor because if there was difficulty in enforcing the contract against the minor it could be enforced against the guarantor.

Guarantees are common in consumer credit transactions. The guarantor has rights and obligations similar to those of the debtor. See **[10.11]** for more detail.

Reservation of title (Romalpa clause)

[18.6]   In order to avoid the legal problem which arise when a business collapses a creditor may supply goods on the basis that property in them does not pass until the goods are paid for. Another version provides that property in the goods does not pass until the buyer has paid for all goods supplied — not just this shipment. Such a clause in the contract of sale is often referred to as a Romalpa clause after the case in which it was considered, *Aluminium Industrie Vaassen BV v Romalpa Aluminium Ltd* [1976] 2 All ER 552. The clause in that case was as follows:

> The ownership of the material to be delivered by A.I.V. will only be transferred to purchaser when he has met all that is owing to A.I.V., no matter on what grounds.

> Until the date of payment, purchaser, if A.I.V. so desires, is required to store this material in such a way that it is clearly the property of A.I.V. A.I.V. and purchaser agree that, if purchaser should make (a) new object(s) from the material, mixes this material with (an) other object(s) or if this material in any way whatsoever becomes a constituent of (an) other object(s) A.I.V. will be given the ownership of this (these) new object(s) as surety of the full payment of what purchaser owes A.I.V. To this end A.I.V. and purchaser now agree that the ownership of the article(s) in question, whether finished or not, are to be transferred to A.I.V. and that this transfer of ownership will be considered to have taken place through and at the moment of the single operation or event by which the material is converted into (a) new object(s), or is mixed with or becomes a constituent of (an) other object(s). Until the moment of full payment of what purchaser owes A.I.V. purchaser shall keep the object(s) in question for A.I.V. in his capacity of fiduciary owner and, if required, shall store this (these) object(s) in such a way that it (they) can be recognized as such. Nevertheless, purchaser will be entitled to sell these objects to a third party within the framework of the normal carrying on of his business and to deliver them on condition that — if A.I.V. so requires — purchaser, as long as he has not fully discharged his debt to A.I.V. shall hand over to A.I.V. the claims he has against his buyer emanating from this transaction.

[18.7]   A Romalpa clause can also provide that property does not pass until payment but risk does on delivery. These provisions exploit the scope in the Sales of Goods Act for parties to determine such matters for themselves.

The Romalpa clause is used to protect the supplier's interest ahead of those of other creditors. The goods supplied cannot be the subject of a security such as a bill of sale or charge and are not available for distribution amongst creditors in a bankruptcy because they do not belong to the debtor/bankrupt. The courts have tended to interpret Romalpa clauses (or their derivatives) narrowly. One objection to them is that they are a de facto charge over the goods but are not registered and therefore other creditors are not aware of them. Another is that the effect of the clause is not always clear. For example:

*   To what extent can the creditor exercise rights when the goods are partly paid for?
*   How does the clause operate when the goods are consumed in the course of manufacture of another product such as the leather used in making bags or the flour in bread?
*   What are the respective rights of creditors when several goods are used in a finished product and each has used a Romalpa clause?
*   What is the significance of the buyer/debtor selling a product which includes components that are the property of another?
*   Is the buyer/debtor an agent for the supplier/creditor of the goods or a bailee?

Secured debt

[18.8]   Another form of self-help for creditors is to obtain a *security* from the debtor. The security works in this way — the debtor's property is *legally encumbered* so that if there is a default in repayment of the debt the creditor becomes the owner of the property and uses it to satisfy the debt.

Perhaps the most common form of security is the mortgage over real estate such as the family home. When the loan is made the debtor promises in the loan contract to repay it with interest. The lender, say a bank, will require a more tangible assurance of repayment or, at least, of not being out of pocket as a result of the loan. The bank therefore will require the borrower to mortgage the property, or another property, to provide security for the loan. This is a separate transaction under which the bank as lender obtains an interest in the property which can be enforced as a matter of law. Once the mortgage has been completed the bank registers it with the land titles office or equivalent. This has the effect of noting on the title to the land that the bank has a mortgage — that the land is subject to a debt owed by the owner to the bank. The registration process makes it theoretically impossible for the borrower to dispose of the house and land without first repaying the debt to the bank. Any buyer with the faintest sense of caution would search the title to establish if there are other interests. The title would reveal the bank's interest and the buyer would know that the vendor is selling an encumbered property. Should the transaction proceed, the bank's interest remains and will not be extinguished until the debt owing to it has been discharged. The new owner will not obtain a complete title until that is done.

Mortgagee's power of sale

[18.9]   The mortgage agreement usually gives the *mortgagee* (lender) a power of sale over the property. Thus if a *mortgagor* (borrower) defaults on a housing loan the lender could sell the property in order to recover the money owing to it. A mortgagee exercising a *power of sale* must act to ensure that the best possible price is obtained. If the proceeds of the sale are greater than the amount outstanding the excess is repaid to the mortgagor.

If the proceeds are less than the outstanding amount the shortfall remains as a debt and the lender is an unsecured creditor for that amount. Reduced property values or exaggerated valuation of the security by a lender could see this happen frequently as it did in the 1980s. The registration process acts as a valuable warning procedure for subsequent lenders because they can see that the property being offered as a security is not as valuable as it might otherwise appear to be.

Case Example

The debtor buys a house valued at $150,000 and borrows $100,000 from Bank A to finance the transaction. Bank A is the mortgagee with its loan of $100,000 secured by a mortgage over a house and land with a value of $150,000. That interest would be registered on the title. If Bank B were to be asked to lend say $40,000 secured by a mortgage over the property it would know of Bank A's interest from searching the title. It would be a matter of judgment for Bank B to decide whether it was prepared to accept the encumbered interest as security. Bank A having registered first would have priority over the proceeds of the sale of the property.

Other securities

[18.10]   Mortgages are used by individuals and companies. Other similar forms of security are:
- *Bills of sale* over non-real estate assets (*chattels*)   The bill of sale is registered with the appropriate official registry and acts in the same way as a mortgage. It is commonly used to secure debts for items such as motor vehicles and trading stock.
- *Charges*   These are securities over the assets of a company. They must be registered to be enforceable. Charges can be *fixed* which means that they attach to a specific asset such as a factory. They can also be *floating* which is a charge over all or over a particular class of the assets of a company. When the debtor defaults the floating charge *crystallises* and becomes a fixed charge attached to a specific asset or assets.

Repossession

[18.11]   Under the Consumer Credit Code a traditional remedy for a credit provider where a debtor is in default is to recover the goods the subject of the financing agreement from the debtor; in other words, repossess them. The goods are then sold and the proceeds used to reduce the outstanding debt. In order to assist the credit provider in this regard s 90 of the Code provides that the mortgagor can be required to inform the credit provider about the whereabouts of the mortgaged goods. Failure on the part of the mortgagor to provide that information is an offence under the Code. See **[10.30]** for a more detailed discussion.

A letter of demand

[18.12]   A creditor will usually make several demands for payment, and may write a letter of demand before beginning court action. Threats of legal action are often effective and many unsecured debts are collected without recourse to court action. The first step taken by either a debt collection agency or a solicitor will usually be to send a letter of demand;

creditors can of course send a letter of demand on their own behalf. The receipt of a letter of demand may often prompt payment by the debtor as the letter conveys the message that the creditor is serious and will pursue the debt until recovery. If this is successful the creditor is saved the often substantial costs of litigation.

There is no special form of words or phrases which must be used in a letter of demand but the letter, even though it is not a formal part of the litigation process, is the first step towards what could be a court case or even more significant, a bankruptcy or insolvency proceeding. The letter of demand will be the basis of the statement of claim. The creditor should keep a copy of the letter and the original should either be personally delivered or sent by registered mail.

The letter of demand should clearly and precisely set out the following information:
- the name and address of both the creditor and debtor;
- the transaction, contract or conduct which gives rise to the debt; and
- the amount claimed.

[18.13]   The creditor should then demand payment of the debt, set a deadline for payment and state what will happen if the amount is not paid by that deadline — this may be to put the matter in the hands of a debt collection agency or a solicitor or to commence proceedings to recover the debt in court.

If the letter of demand does not prompt the debtor to pay the debt, then the creditor may decide to abandon the claim or to carry out the action specified in the letter of demand. In these circumstances litigation is often the next step.

Going to court

Time limit for court action to recover debts

[18.14]   The period within which legal action may be taken to recover a debt or enforce a right arising from a contract is limited by legislation. Its aim is not to defeat a debt but to make the debt unenforceable after a certain period of time. The object of this legislation is to relieve a person from having to defend a claim for an indefinite period of time; it recognises that with the passing of time it will be increasingly difficult to obtain evidence and for witnesses to remember facts and events clearly.

In most parts of Australia a creditor has six years from the date on which the debt arises to make a claim against the debtor to recover the money owing: see, for example, the Limitation Act 1985 (ACT) s 12. The exception is the Northern Territory where the period of limitation is three years: Limitation Act 1981. The legislation does not extinguish the debt but takes away the right to sue on it after the six-year period. If the debtor confirms the debt before the end of those six years the time will begin to run again from the moment of the confirmation. If the debtor either acknowledges the debt in writing or makes a payment under the debt that will amount to confirmation.

Whom to sue?

[18.15]   Many businesses are conducted by corporations or partnerships trading under the banner of a business name. It is important that all documents correctly identify the parties to the action, and that all notices and other documents to be served are properly addressed to the corporation or partnership.

Preserving the assets of the debtor: Mareva injunctions

[18.16]   Where the debt claimed is substantial the creditor may fear that the debtor will, in order to avoid enforcement of any judgment, remove assets from the jurisdiction. The courts have developed the Mareva injunction to prevent this, and will, where it is just and convenient, make an order prohibiting the transfer of any property or assets of the debtor from the jurisdiction. At first these injunctions were granted only to prevent foreign defendants transferring assets out of the jurisdiction. They take their name from the case *Mareva Compania Naviera SA v International Bulkcarriers SA* [1975] 2 Lloyd's Rep 509. The power to grant a Mareva injunction comes from the courts' inherent equitable jurisdiction to prevent the frustration of the enforcement of their judgments and from the courts' power to prevent an abuse of their process.

Usually the creditor applies for a Mareva injunction in the absence of the other party, ex parte. An interim order will be granted with a return date for a hearing to give the defendant an opportunity to raise objections and put arguments to the court. The creditor must satisfy the court of the debtor's intention to transfer assets in order to avoid execution of any later judgment. The injunction will not be granted merely to prevent the dissipation of assets through the usual business activities of the defendant.

The Mareva injunction must be specific and cannot go beyond preventing an abuse of process by transferring assets out of the jurisdiction. The court can, for instance, make an order for the preservation of specific assets or that the defendant give security for a certain amount from a specified fund. This injunction does not create new property rights nor will it have the effect of converting an unsecured creditor to a secured creditor. The purpose of the injunction is to preserve property where there is a likelihood that it would be disposed of in order to frustrate the plaintiff in the execution of any judgment.

The creditor will be required to give an undertaking as to damages. This means that should the creditor fail in the action for debt, the creditor will be liable to pay compensation for any loss or damages caused to the debtor by the freezing of the assets.

Which court?

[18.17]   If the demand for payment does not succeed then the creditor may take an action against the debtor in a court which hears civil claims. These are the state Supreme Courts, intermediate courts such as the District Court, magistrate or local courts and, in some jurisdictions, the small claims courts. The person seeking to recover a debt will have to decide whether to take action in the Supreme Court or the lower courts in the appropriate jurisdiction. Creditors have the right to take their action in the Supreme Court, but they are discouraged from doing so if the claim could have been made in a lower court. If there is a complex question of law to be decided, it may be desirable to commence an action in the Supreme Court. A creditor cannot recover the solicitor's fees and other costs involved in the court action if the action could have been taken in a lower court.

The choice of court in which to take action to recover the debt will primarily depend on the amount of the debt. In the Australian Capital Territory the Small Claims Court can hear claims of up to $5000 — Small Claims Act 1974 s 4(2); the Magistrates Court may hear claims for amounts up to $50,000 — Magistrates Court (Civil Jurisdiction) Act 1982 s 5(1)) and the Supreme Court can hear claims of any amount. All other Australian jurisdictions have similar limits.

The amount owed

[18.18]   Civil courts may hear claims for damages arising from breach of contract, or acts of negligence, as well as claims for debts owed. It is important to understand the difference between the two. Damages will be claimed to recover an amount of money to compensate a person for loss suffered as a result of the action of the other. It will often be the case that the plaintiff is not able to specify the exact amount to be paid. Where the court is asked to determine the amount to be paid by the defendant the claim is said to be for an unliquidated amount. A claim for a debt, where the amount of money owing by the debtor to the creditor can be precisely stated, is said to be a liquidated amount. Typical examples of liquidated claims are goods sold and delivered, work done where the amount was agreed, money lent, money paid, rent or professional services rendered. In such instances the amount of the judgment will be for the amount of the debt claimed by the creditor.

The distinction between liquidated and unliquidated amounts is important because it has practical implications, as it will determine the process that is available to the creditor. Only where the sum claimed is a liquidated amount can the speedy default judgment process be used. This chapter deals with debt collection through the Magistrates Court in the Australian Capital Territory. The Magistrates Court (Civil Jurisdiction) Act 1982 applies; this is similar but not identical to the rules and acts applying to the lower and Supreme Courts in all Australian jurisdictions.

Originating process

[18.19]   In proceedings to recover a debt the creditor may begin proceedings by making an application to the court as a special claim or an ordinary claim. In the case of action to recover a debt for a specified amount a special claim is most often used, because it will be faster: it allows the creditor to proceed to final judgment if the debtor has not filed a defence within 21 days. This is known as default judgment.

[18.20]   The creditor will begin the court process by lodging a special claim with the court, and if the Registrar is satisfied that the claim complies with the requirements of the Act the claim will be filed, and a file number allotted to that claim. The creditor will be the plaintiff and the debtor the defendant in the court action. A special claim must be in the form set out in the Schedule to the Act.

Service on the defendant

[18.21]   When the plaintiff lodges the claim with the Registrar, duplicate copies plus one copy for every defendant must also be lodged. These will be numbered and stamped by the Registrar; each defendant must then be served with an official notice of the claim being made. Service may be achieved by delivering a copy of the claim to the defendant personally or by leaving a copy of the claim at the last known place of residence or business of the defendant. Where the defendant has a solicitor, service may be achieved by delivering a copy of the claim to the defendant's solicitor and having that solicitor endorse a copy of the claim to show that service has been accepted on behalf of the defendant.

Some debtors may attempt to avoid service, by not answering the door or by sending children to say they are not known at that address. In this case the plaintiff may apply to the court to bring the claim to the debtor's attention in another way. This is called an order for substituted service. The plaintiff may, for instance, apply to the court for postal service and the Registrar will then serve the claim on the defendant by posting a copy to the defendant's address.

The plaintiff will have to prove to the court that the defendant has been served with the special claim. This satisfies the court that the defendant knows of the claim, of the steps available to defend the action, and of the consequences of inaction. Service of documents may be proved by the oath of the person who served the document, by affidavit or by production of the postal certificate.

The debtor's choices

If the debt is admitted

[18.22]   The defendant or debtor has 21 days in which to respond to the claim served. If the debtor admits that the debt as claimed is owed to the plaintiff then there are three choices available — to pay the full amount, to confess to the amount claimed by the plaintiff or to do nothing.

If the defendant pays the amount claimed to the plaintiff that will bring the matter to an end. The plaintiff is not required to do anything further and after 12 months the action lapses. The defendant may pay the full amount claimed or a lesser amount into court. This is not an admission of liability to pay, but may be a speedy way to settle the matter between the parties and so avoid a full defended hearing. The court will give the plaintiff notice of payment into court and the plaintiff may accept the amount paid in satisfaction of one or all the causes of action pleaded. Where the plaintiff accepts money paid into court in satisfaction of a cause of action any further proceedings in relation to that action are stayed. This will be so even if the amount was not the full amount originally claimed.

If the defendant confesses the full amount of the claim then a statement of confession must be filed at the court. This will often be accompanied with an application to pay by instalments. The Registrar will then serve a notice of confession on the plaintiff and enter judgment in favour of the plaintiff for the amount claimed.

Default judgment

[18.23]   If the defendant takes no action in response to the claim, then the plaintiff may, once service has been proved and a period of 21 days has expired from the date of service, make an application to the court for the Registrar to enter final judgment against the defendant for the amount claimed and costs. A default judgment is not an automatic process: the plaintiff must apply to the court to have judgment entered and must do so within one year of the date of service of the claim.

The court has the discretion to order the parties to pay, or to divide, the party-to-party costs which will not necessarily be all the costs incurred by the successful party, but are limited to those costs which the successful party must incur to obtain justice and must be reasonable and not incurred through excessive caution. It may also order the payment of incidental costs as it sees fit. If the court makes no order as to costs then the costs of the proceedings shall follow the event of the proceedings. Where the plaintiff has obtained a default judgment, the defendant will be required to pay the costs.

Interest

[18.24]   Interest on the debt from the date on which the cause of action arose can be awarded, but must be requested. Where either a default judgment or a judgment following confession or agreement is entered for the plaintiff the interest for the period between the time the cause of action arose and the date of judgment shall be deemed to be part of the amount claimed and included in the amount for which judgment is entered. If the defendant does not pay the judgment debt within 21 days of the date of judgment then interest is payable on the balance of the debt from time to time and is regarded as part of the judgment debt.

If the debt is disputed

[18.25]   The defendant may admit that a debt is owed to the plaintiff but dispute the amount of that debt. Then the defendant may pay a lesser amount into court, confess to a part of the claim or enter a defence to the claim. If the defendant does not intend to enter a defence to the claim it may nevertheless be in his or her interest to make an offer to the plaintiff and to reach an agreement with the plaintiff before the plaintiff has judgment entered. The debtor will be liable for the creditor's legal costs if judgment is entered in favour of the plaintiff; these costs will be less if judgment follows confession to the whole or part of the claim, or an agreement between the parties.

Confession to a part of the claim

[18.26]   A matter may be settled by the plaintiff's acceptance of a lesser amount paid into court by the defendant. So too the defendant may confess to a part of the amount claimed by the plaintiff by filing a statement of confession with the court within 21 days of service of the claim. The Registrar will then serve on the plaintiff a notice of confession which will set out the amount the defendant has confessed to and give the plaintiff 14 days in which to file a notice refusing to accept that amount. If the plaintiff does not refuse the amount then the Registrar will enter judgment in favour of the plaintiff for the amount confessed to plus costs.

Defending a claim

[18.27]   The confession of a part of the amount claimed, or the payment into court of an amount less than that claimed is, practically speaking, the making of an offer to settle by the debtor to the creditor. The creditor must take action to reject that offer, and then move to obtain a default judgment. The settlement of the matter for a lesser amount may often be attractive to the creditor for that settlement will avoid the costs and time of a full hearing.

If the defendant wishes to negotiate further after the court process has been started by the service of a claim, then the defendant should file a notice of defence within 21 days of the date of the service of the claim. This will give the defendant time to obtain legal advice and to make a formal offer of settlement. The creditor may be willing to negotiate a settlement to avoid the time and costs of proving the case in a hearing.

Filing a defence

[18.28]   A defendant in these proceedings may at any time before final judgment is entered file a notice of the grounds of defence. Usually this would be within 21 days from the date of receiving the claim. The notice must set out the reasons for denying the claim, and plead facts in support of any cross claim. It is filed at the court by the defendant and the Registrar will serve it on the plaintiff.

The plaintiff has 21 days from the date the notice of defence is served to file a reply. Each party may ask the other for further and better particulars of any or all causes of action pleaded. The defendant may ask whether the contract was written or oral, or how the figure claimed was reached. At the end of the exchange of pleadings a certificate of readiness is filed by the parties and the matter will be given a date for hearing by the court. When the court has completed the hearing it may give judgment and make such orders as it thinks just.

Types of defences

[18.29]   A defence is a response to the plaintiff's claim which denies, answers or disputes the claim and alleges that the defendant is not liable to the plaintiff. The defendant in a statement of defence may admit, not admit or deny the plaintiff's allegations as well as set out any facts in support of a positive case in answer to the claim.

A complete denial of liability may be based on an assertion that there never was an agreement or contract between the parties. Suppose an insulation supplier had agreed to pump foam insulation into the wall cavity of the house at 16 Smith Street, but in error insulates the house at number 14. When the insulation firm claims the contract price from the owners of number 14 the defence would be to deny the existence of a contract.

Cross-claims, counterclaims and set-offs

[18.30]   If the defendant does not have a direct answer to the plaintiff's claim, there may be a cross-claim against the plaintiff which may either reduce or extinguish the plaintiff's claim. The legislation relating to actions for debt allows defendants to raise by way of defence claims or actions they may have against the plaintiff. These may arise from the same transaction as the plaintiff's claim or they may be quite independent of it. For instance, there may be a claim for damages relating to defective goods, the payment for which is the subject of the plaintiff's claim or there may be a claim relating to a supply of defective goods prior to that which is the subject of the plaintiff's claim. This would be common where parties deal with each other on a regular basis.

In the Australian Capital Territory, the Magistrates Court (Civil Jurisdiction) Act 1982 s 48 provides:

> [A] defendant in proceedings may, in her or his notice of grounds of defence, plead a cross-claim founded on any cause of action in respect of which she or he might have instituted proceedings in the court against the plaintiff, being a cross-claim for an amount that does not exceed the maximum amount for which the court has jurisdiction under this Act.

A cross-claim is defined to mean 'a claim (whether by way of counterclaim, cross action, set-off or otherwise) pleaded in a notice of grounds of defence filed by a defendant in proceedings'.

The aim of this provision is to prevent repetitious or circuitous litigation: all matters in dispute between the parties should be settled in the one procedure. It is possible to counterclaim against both the plaintiff and third parties, provided that there is sufficient connection between all of the parties and the relief sought in the counterclaim.

Cross-claim

[18.31]   The defendant would argue that the nature of the cross-claim is such that the plaintiff should not be paid until the court has made a decision on the cross-claim. A cross-claim may be either a counterclaim or a set-off, and must be pleaded as a separate action, as if the defendant had sued the plaintiff in other proceedings. Although a cross-claim allows the defendant to plead either a set-off or a counterclaim (or both), they are different in some aspects.

Counterclaim

[18.32]   The defendant may plead any matter against the plaintiff as a counterclaim, and is not limited to a claim for a liquidated amount. A counterclaim is a claim asserted against the plaintiff by the defendant, and although part of the original action it is treated for procedural purposes as a separate action. Since it is a separate action, the counterclaim against the plaintiff need not relate to the subject of the original claim. However, if the defendant asserts the counterclaim against a third party as well as the plaintiff, then there must be a common question relating to the defendant, the plaintiff and the third party. A plaintiff may, of course, counterclaim against the defendant's counterclaim.

A counterclaim, therefore, is not linked to the fate of the original claim, so if the plaintiff discontinues the original action the counterclaim remains on foot and continues to be tried. Judgment of a counterclaim is not limited to payment of debt or damages and the court may award other relief, such as an injunction. The court will make orders which reflect the balance between the parties at the end of the matter; for example, if the successful counterclaim is for an amount greater than that successfully claimed by the plaintiff then the court will enter judgment for the defendant to the amount of the excess.

Set-off

[18.33]   A set-off is a claim by the defendant against the plaintiff arising out of an independent cause of action. It will usually be a claim for a liquidated amount but equity allows a set-off to be an unliquidated amount, such as damages arising from another transaction. A set-off may be raised as a defence where there are mutual debts or where it would be inequitable to allow the plaintiff to proceed until the defendant has raised the matters showing the inequity. To maintain an equitable set-off the defendant must show either a debt or damages which is so related to the plaintiff's claim that it would be unjust for the plaintiff to recover the full amount of the claim without deduction for the defendant's damages.

The defence of a set-off does not deny the debt, but impliedly acknowledges it, while saying that there are reasons why the plaintiff is not entitled to be paid. There must be mutual indebtedness, that is, the parties must owe each other a debt, but these debts need not arise at the same time and need not be related to each other. The set-off must be capable of being brought as a separate action; however, the mutual debt is not pleaded for its own sake but to resist the demands of the plaintiff. A set-off is used as a shield against the plaintiff's claim, not as a sword. Once a set-off is established the plaintiff's claim is extinguished at least to the extent of the set-off. Therefore the set-off follows the pattern of the original claim. If the plaintiff discontinues the claim, then the set-off will come to an end.

Setting aside a default judgment

[18.34]   The power of the court to set aside a judgment refers to all judgments and orders. The defendant could apply to have a judgment set aside where he or she had defended the claim. The plaintiff can apply to set aside a judgment or order, for example, an order for payment by instalments.

The default judgment process aims to balance the rights of the defendant to have a chance to put any favourable arguments by way of defence or cross-claim to the court and the right of the plaintiff to a speedy trial. It will often be that the defendant had no knowledge of the action, or had a good defence to the claim or believes that the plaintiff could not prove the case in a full hearing. A judgment which has been given irregularly, illegally or against good faith may also be set aside. The defendant who wishes to have the default judgment set aside must show sufficient cause to the court. The defendant will need to show that there were good reasons for not responding to the claim, and that there is a proper defence to be put.

A court will not often set aside a judgment unconditionally as this would leave both parties in a state of uncertainty. The court will impose some conditions on the parties, usually that the defendant file a defence within a certain time. If these conditions are not met the plaintiff may apply to the court to have the judgment re-entered.

The defendant can apply at any time for an order setting aside the judgment, even if the plaintiff has commenced proceedings to execute the judgment. The setting aside of a judgment does not prevent the plaintiff from enforcing the judgment, and will not affect the title to property already sold under a warrant of execution before the making of the order setting aside the judgment. A defendant should therefore also make an application to the court for an order setting aside any enforcement procedures, warrant issued or order made pursuant to the judgment. The defendant can apply to set aside the orders for enforcement of the judgment even where there is no application to set aside the judgment itself.

Appeal

[18.35]   An appeal from the magistrates or lower courts is taken to the Supreme Court in the relevant jurisdiction. An appeal to the Supreme Court is, however, not an automatic right. For example, in New South Wales the only appeal from a Court of Petty Sessions judgment is on the ground that the magistrate has made an error of law. In the Australian Capital Territory an appeal cannot be brought unless the Supreme Court gives leave, and is not available in relation to judgment for amounts of less than $2000. An application for leave to appeal must be made within 21 days of the date of the judgment.

Enforcing a judgment debt

[18.36]   When a creditor obtains judgment against a debtor the amount ordered to be paid is called the judgment debt, and is payable immediately. In the usual case the debtor will be required to pay the amount of the debt, the creditor's legal costs, court costs and interest, so it is to the debtor's benefit to pay the debt as soon as possible. If the debtor does not pay the judgment debt to the creditor, the creditor can use further court procedures to recover the money from the debtor.

Each Australian jurisdiction has procedures for the enforcement of a judgment debt. Many are now contained in legislation such as the Magistrates Court Act 1930 (ACT) or the Supreme Court Rules in each jurisdiction: see **[18.42]**. Most of these procedures for recovery of a judgment debt have their origin in the common law, for example, writs of *fieri facias*. Some common procedures in the recovery of a judgment debt are payment by instalments, oral examination, garnishees and warrants of execution. In this chapter the Magistrates Court Act 1930 and the Magistrates Court (Civil Jurisdiction) Act 1982 of the Australian Capital Territory will be referred to.

Payment by instalments

[18.37]   If the claim is defended then the debtor or the creditor can ask the magistrate for an order that the debt be paid by instalments, or the magistrate may on his or her own volition makes such an order. After a judgment has been entered either party may apply to the court for an order for payment by instalments. This is usually done by the debtor, and must be done without delay. There are benefits to the debtor in the obtaining of an order to pay by instalments:

- The debtor controls the method of satisfying the judgment debt, otherwise the creditor chooses the means of enforcement, such as attachment or sale of the debtor's property.
- So long as the instalments are made in accordance with the court's order, the creditor cannot enforce the payment by any other means. The creditor may make an application to the court to vary the order for payment by instalments, if for instance the debtor's financial circumstances improve. If the debtor does not make the instalments as ordered then the creditor may ask the court to revoke the order. The order for payment by instalments acts as a stay of enforcement by other means and prevents the creditor from seeking an examination order, a garnishee order or a warrant of execution.
- Payment by instalments avoids the embarrassment which often accompanies enforcement by other methods of recovery, such as an order to garnishee the debtor's wages.

Oral examination

[18.38]   Before applying for an order for payment by instalments the creditor must first conduct an oral examination of the debtor. An examination summons is issued by the Registrar of the court and is served on the debtor in the same way as a special claim. The examination summons directs the judgment debtor to attend court to be examined as to financial means and assets. If the judgment debtor is a corporation the summons may be issued calling upon the manager or secretary to appear to be examined on behalf of the company. The debtor may also be directed to produce documents or things in the possession of control of the debtor, which show the financial circumstances of the debtor. Specific documents such as bank books and titles to property may be requested. If the judgment debtor fails to appear the judgment creditor may ask for a warrant of apprehension to be issued.

The examination can be conducted in open court but is usually done by the Registrar. Many debts are settled in this process either because the debtor decides to pay the full amount rather than be examined, or because the parties are able to discuss the matter and reach an agreement, often for payment by instalments. The oral examination serves two purposes; first, to inform the Registrar about the debtor's financial position, to assist in the decision as to whether to make an order for payment by instalments; second, to give the creditor information about the assets of the debtor in order to choose another method of enforcement. The creditor may. for example. examine the debtor about bank accounts and wages so that they can be garnisheed, instead of asking for payment by instalments.

[18.39] The following are some of the questions a debtor may be asked in an oral examination:

- Are you the judgment debtor?
- What is your occupation?
- Is the judgment debt still owing?
- How many dependants do you have?
- Do you own or are you purchasing any real property?
- Do you own or are you purchasing a motor vehicle?
- Does any person owe you money?
- Do you have any bank accounts?
- What is the source of your income?
- What regular household expenses do you have and from whose money are they paid?
- What debts and liabilities do you have?

It is not necessary to go through the process of an oral examination before the creditor attaches or realises property of the debtor to satisfy the judgment debt. The answers to questions such as those above would, however, enable the creditor to determine whether or not the debtor has property available for attachment or realisation.

Warrant of execution

[18.40] If the judgment debtor has property, whether real or personal, the creditor can apply to the magistrates or lower court for a warrant of execution. This empowers the bailiff to seize property and sell it unless the debt is paid — the proceeds are used to pay the amount of the judgment The bailiff may continue to seize property until sufficient funds are raised to cover the debt. The creditor may apply for such a warrant at any time up to 12 years after judgment.

One purpose of a warrant of execution is to frighten a debtor into paying or coming to some arrangement with the creditor. The bailiff goes to the debtor's house, shows the debtor the notice of a warrant of execution and explains that if the debtor does not pay the amount of the judgment debt the bailiff will seize the goods and auction them to pay it off. The debtor can pay the debt at any time up to the sale of the goods.

The powers of the bailiff

[18.41] The bailiff is an officer of the court whose duties include enforcing the judgments of the court. The powers of the bailiff are, however, subject to the following restraints:

- Only goods and chattels belonging to the debtor can be seized on a warrant of execution. If another person claims to own or have an interest in the goods seized by the bailiff then the special procedure of interpleader can be used. The person claiming the goods must make a claim against property. The court will decide who is in fact the owner of the goods in dispute. The bailiff cannot seize wearing apparel, bedding, tools and implements of trade which are worth less than $100 and being used by the debtor or family.
- The bailiff cannot forcibly enter the debtor's house but can enter through an unlocked door. The debtor can refuse to let the bailiff in and is entitled to use reasonable force

to prevent the bailiff from entering. The bailiff is entitled to forcibly enter any buildings other than the dwelling house.

- The bailiff will usually seize goods without taking them away. It may be practicable to leave the goods in the debtor's house while the sale is arranged, and the debtor may make arrangements to pay the debt after the visit by the bailiff. The bailiff may make a list of the goods so seized and places a notice of seizure on the goods. Any person who removes the goods so identified or the notice of seizure from the goods is guilty of an offence. Once the goods have been so seized the bailiff can use forcible entry to collect them.
- A warrant of execution may only be executed by the bailiff between sunrise and sunset.

Originally the bailiff could only seize and sell goods but legislation now provides that land may also be seized and sold. The bailiff cannot, however, seize the land unless the goods seized are not sufficient to pay the debt. If that occurs in the Australian Capital Territory, the bailiff will inform the court that the warrant of execution is returned unsatisfied.

The creditor will then return to the Magistrates Court and apply for a certificate of judgment for filing in the Supreme Court.

This certificate will be then filed in the Supreme Court and final judgment for the amount outstanding may be entered in the Supreme Court in favour of the creditor. Once final judgment is entered for the creditor that judgment may be enforced as if it had been a final judgment entered in an action of like nature in the Supreme Court. This means that the creditor can then apply for a writ of *fieri facias* to be issued. This writ empowers the bailiff to seize and sell any real property belonging to the debtor. The costs incurred by the plaintiff in preparing and filing the application for a writ are added to the judgment debt.

Garnishee

[18.42] Not all the property of the debtor can easily be seized and realised to satisfy the judgment debt. For example, a debt owed by another person to the debtor is the property of the debtor and can be taken in execution of a judgment. The garnishee is the method by which the creditor can seize this property. A garnishee is an order to a person who owes money to the debtor to pay the money to the creditor instead of to the debtor in payment of the judgment debt. The most common garnishee orders are against the employer of the debtor for payment from the debtor's wages, and against the bank of the debtor for payment from accounts held by the debtor.

Relevant legislation

Jurisdiction	Legislation
New South Wales	Supreme Court Rules Supreme Court Act District Court Act 1973 District Court Rules 1973 Judgment Creditors Remedies Act 1901 Local Courts (Civil Claims) Act 1970 Local Courts (Civil Claims) Amendment Act 1990 Local Courts (Civil Claims) Rules 1988

Jurisdiction	Legislation
Victoria	Supreme Court Rules County Court Rules Judgment Debt Recovery Act 1984
Queensland	Rules of the Supreme Court District Court Rules
South Australia	Supreme Court Rules Debtors Act 1936
Western Australia	Supreme Court Rules Debtors Act 1871 District Court of Western Australia Act 1969 Restraint of Debtors Act 1984
Tasmania	Rules of the Supreme Court Debtors Act 1870
Australian Capital Territory	Rules of the Supreme Court of the Australian Capital Territory Magistrates Court (Civil Jurisdiction) Act 1982 Magistrates Court Act
Northern Territory	Supreme Court Rules 1970 Local Courts Act 1941

Bankruptcy

[18.43] The final and most serious option for a creditor is to take action under the bankruptcy law for an individual debtor or the insolvency law for a corporate debtor. This process does, however, involve formal legal steps and does not ensure that the creditor will recover all that is outstanding.

When a creditor has successfully sued a debtor but has not been able to recover the debt which a court says exists, an option is to institute bankruptcy proceedings. This is also an appropriate option where there are other indications that the debtor is either unable or unwilling to pay debts.

Bankruptcy is the modern substitute for the imprisonment of debtors. It is designed to assist unsecured creditors in obtaining access to a debtor's property and to ensure that they are treated equally. From the debtor's perspective bankruptcy exists to assist in financial rehabilitation. It is a serious process with profound consequences for a debtor. It is subject to the Bankruptcy Act 1966 (and the Bankruptcy Rules made under that Act) which is a Commonwealth statute made under its constitutional power in this area: Constitution s 51(xvii).

The bankruptcy process can be initiated by a creditor or by a debtor. It involves another party, the trustee, taking control of a debtor's affairs and property and administering them for the benefit of creditors who must be treated equally without any particular creditor or class of creditor being treated preferentially. There is a limit on the period for which a person remains in a state of bankruptcy.

Participants in the bankruptcy process

[18.44]   The main participants in the bankruptcy process are:

- *The debtor*   Without a person being unable or unwilling to pay debts as they fall due there is no need for bankruptcy. Section 7 of the Bankruptcy Act makes it clear that the legislation applies to debtors who are not Australian citizens and that age is not a relevant issue. Neither a corporation nor partnership can be the subject of bankruptcy proceedings

- *The creditors*   There must be debts owed to unsecured creditors or to secured creditors who have waived their security. The creditor is the party for whose benefit bankruptcy proceedings exist.

- *The trustee*   When a person becomes bankrupt the affairs of that person and the interest of the creditors become the responsibility of a trustee: Bankruptcy Act s 58. The trustee in bankruptcy administers the estate of the bankrupt for the benefit of the creditors. The trustee can be a private practitioner — a registered trustee — who has satisfied the Inspector-General of compliance with the criteria in s 155A as to qualifications, experience, ability, insurance cover arrangements and good character. Where a registered trustee is not appointed the *Official Trustee* becomes responsible. The duties of the trustee are set out in s 19 of the Act. They include to make known that the person has become bankrupt, to establish the bankrupt's assets and liabilities, to hold meetings of creditors, recover property for the benefit of the estate, take action to ensure the bankrupt complies with the Act and advise law enforcement authorities of any evidence of an offence by the bankrupt. The trustee must administer the estate as 'efficiently as possible by avoiding unnecessary expense' and must operate in 'a commercially sound way'.

- *The court*   The Federal Court has exclusive jurisdiction in bankruptcy matters but, by virtue of cross-vesting arrangements the Supreme Courts of the states and territories are able to deal with bankruptcy.

  Others who play a role in the process are:

- *The Official Receiver*   This is a formal office. There is one in each bankruptcy district which, under s 13, equate to the states of Australia. The Official Receiver may exercise the powers of the Official Trustee in the district: s 18(8). Persons in this capacity are under the control of the court and subordinate to the Official Trustee: s 15.

- *The Inspector-General of Bankruptcy*   The Inspector-General is a statutory office holder who is, in effect, the overseer of the bankruptcy system: s 11. The Inspector-General is empowered to undertake inquiries and investigations about the administration by or conduct of a trustee's duties and can be asked to review certain decisions of the trustee: s 12.

Grounds for bankruptcy

[18.45]   The court may make a *sequestration order* against a debtor's estate on the petition of a creditor: s 43. A creditor cannot lodge a petition unless the *indebtedness* of the debtor is $2000; this figure can represent a single debt or several or be the value of debts owed to several creditors: s 44. Where a *judgment debt* is for less than $2000 a bankruptcy notice can be issued and the debtor's failure to comply with it amounts to an act of bankruptcy but that debt is not sufficient to sustain a *creditor's petition*.

The critical requirement is that the debtor must have committed an *act of bankruptcy*. This is the trigger for the process. No matter how large the debt, if there is no act of bankruptcy the petition cannot proceed.

Acts of bankruptcy

[18.46]   What amounts to an act of bankruptcy is specified in the Act: s 40(1)(a)–(n). That section identifies 19 major classifications. They are:

(a) *Conveyances and assignments of property for the benefit of creditors:*

This requires that the debtor has dealt with property by disposing of it for the benefit of all creditors. It is an indication of the debtor's incapacity to pay debts.

(b) *Dealings with property that would be void against the trustee:*

In this situation the debtor has dealt with property with a view to giving preference to a creditor or to defrauding creditors. This form of conduct is contrary to the philosophy of equal and fair treatment of creditors and in a bankruptcy the transaction would be ineffectual against the trustee who is able to act as if the transaction did not occur.

(c) *The debtor's departing Australia, going absent or keeping house with intention of defeating or delaying creditors:*

The critical aspect of this act of bankruptcy is the intention of the debtor. A creditor must prove that the debtor did any of those things with the intention to defeat or delay creditors. The act of keeping house means no more than that access to the debtor is denied to creditors because the debtor is in hiding at home.

(d) *Where execution has been issued against the debtor:*

This arises where a creditor has obtained judgment against a debtor and action has been taken to enforce that judgment. The significance of this act of bankruptcy is that the fact of the debtor's indebtedness has been established in a court. This becomes significant when the petition is presented.

(da) *The debtor has presented a declaration under s 54A:*

Section 54A deals with debtors' petitions and as a step in that process the debtor must present to the Official Receiver a declaration of intention to present a debtor's petition

(e) *Where the debtor has failed to take action for voluntary submission to bankruptcy or to the Pt X process:*

A meeting of creditors may make a resolution that the debtor present a debtor's petition or institute action under Pt X. If the debtor fails to do so it amounts to an act of bankruptcy. If the debtor does obey the creditors' resolution each step is an act of bankruptcy.

(f) *Where the debtor makes an admission of insolvency to creditors and fails to observe their requirement to present a debtor's petition or institute Pt X proceedings:*

Insolvency is not the same thing as bankruptcy. It means that a person does not have the money or quickly realisable assets to pay debts as they fall due. Bankruptcy involves the inability or unwillingness to pay debts (which is demonstrated by the act of bankruptcy) and a formal legal process to manage that state of affairs. Under this ground the insolvent debtor has been given the opportunity to submit voluntarily to the Act's processes but has failed to do so.

(g) *Failure to comply with a bankruptcy notice:*

This is the most common act of bankruptcy. The debtor in such a case has been found liable in debt by a court and the creditor has obtained a bankruptcy notice from the Official Receiver. In order to obtain such a notice the creditor must be able to convince the Official Receiver that there is a final judgment or order by a court against the debtor. Details of the form of the notice are set out in reg 4.02.

The notice must be served personally on the debtor who is given time to comply with the notice — usually 21 days — and has the opportunity to settle the debt owed to the judgment creditor or of satisfying a court that there is a counterclaim, set-off or cross demand against the creditor of at least equal value to the judgment debt.

It is the failure of the debtor to comply with the notice — to settle the debt within the stated period — that amounts to the act of bankruptcy. The notice is a significant document; it is more than a debt-collecting ploy. It can have profound consequences for the debtor. If the debtor wishes to mount a counterclaim the time limit on the notice needs to be extended. The debtor may seek to prove in a court that the notice is defective.

The bankruptcy notice has a life of six months and if it is not presented it has no further significance. If a debtor does not comply with the notice but later settles with the debtor the non-compliance amounts to an act of bankruptcy which is irreversible.

(h) Giving notice of suspension or impending suspension of payment of debts:

If the debtor gives such notice in a formal way to any creditor that amounts to an act of bankruptcy. The suspension must be in respect of all of the debtor's debts, not in respect of an individual debt. Conduct such as this speaks for itself as an indication that the debtor is unable or unwilling to pay debts.

The 1996 amendments to the Bankruptcy Act introduced the Pt IX procedure which allows a debtor to make a debt agreement proposal with creditors. These agreements allow a debtor to avoid sequestration. To initiate the procedure the debtor advises the Official Trustee who then seeks the views of the creditors.

(ha) Once giving the Official Trustee the proposal the debtor has committed an act of bankruptcy.

(hb) acceptance of the proposal is an act of bankruptcy.

(hc) a breach of an agreement is an act of bankruptcy.

(hd) termination of the agreement under ss 185P or 185Q amounts to an act of bankruptcy.

The acts of bankruptcy specified in s 40(1)(i)–(n) are steps in carrying out Pt IV compositions or schemes or Pt X arrangements.

(i) The debtor signs an authority under s 188 of the Act:

This is the first step in a Pt X procedure and is clear evidence of the debtor's financial position.

(j) Calling of a meeting of creditors following a s 188 authority:

After signing the authority the next step is for the trustee or solicitor to call a meeting of creditors. This is part of the Pt X procedure.

(k) Failing to attend the meeting of creditors called in consequence of a s 188 notice:

Unless the debtor is prevented by some good cause such as an illness this amounts to an act of bankruptcy. The court is empowered to make a sequestration order in these circumstances.

(l) Failure of the debtor to execute a deed of assignment or arrangement or to present a debtor's petition:

The meeting of creditors under Pt X will make a resolution about what is expected of the debtor. Failure by the debtor to carry it out is an act of bankruptcy.

(m) Where a deed of assignment or of arrangement or a composition under Pt X is declared void:

The court has power to terminate or declare an arrangement under Pt X void.

(n) Annulment by the court of a composition or scheme of arrangement:

This can occur where the debtor has failed to honour the terms of the Pt X undertaking or to implement it would be unjust or create delay for the creditors or debtors.

Debtor's petition

[18.47]   A debtor is able to present a petition for bankruptcy to the Registrar: s 55. It is not necessary to prove insolvency. It will not be accepted if a creditor's petition has been presented. The petition is presented in the form prescribed under the Rules.

The debtor is bankrupt immediately upon the petition being accepted by the Official Receiver. Before that occurs an extra procedure is to be followed which requires the debtor to lodge a declaration of intention to present a debtor's petition: s 54A. The purpose of this additional procedure is to allow the debtor the opportunity to explore alternatives to bankruptcy but not all debtors are entitled to use it. To ensure that debtors do not use the procedure to defeat creditors it is not available to debtors whose affairs are being administered under the Act. If, however, the debtor is able to use the procedure and the Official Receiver is satisfied that the debtor has been directed to the sources of assistance, the Official Receiver accepts and endorses the declaration — assuming it has been correctly completed — and gives a copy of the declaration to the debtor. This stamped declaration can be used by the debtor to prevent creditors from enforcing their judgments: s 54E. The debt is frozen for a maximum period of seven days from the date upon which the declaration was accepted by the Registrar. During this period there is a moratorium.

Part IX

[18.48]   A debtor is given the opportunity of being released from debt without being the subject of a sequestration order under the procedures in Pt IX of the Act.

Section 185C provides that a debtor may give the Official Trustee a written proposal for a debt agreement. The proposal must identify the debtor's property to be dealt with, how it is to be dealt with and authorise the Official Trustee or a registered trustee or other person to deal with the property.

The Official Trustee then contacts the 'affected creditors' either by way of a meeting or by mail in order to canvass their opinion about the proposal: s 185A. If the creditors at a meeting pass a special resolution or a majority of them with at least three-quarters of value of the debts agree the proposal is accepted: s 185B.

Once the proposal is accepted and recorded in the National Personal Insolvency Index all action in respect of enforcing the debts is prevented: ss 185F, 185K. The debtor is released from provable debts — as if having been discharged from bankruptcy — when the details are entered in the Index: s 185J.

The Act provides for varying an agreement (s 185M), ending it (s 185N) and terminating it: ss 185P, 185Q, 185R.

Part X

[18.49]   Bankruptcy is a serious legal procedure for both debtors and creditors. It can be expensive in that, after the costs of administration have been met, the creditors may receive a smaller proportion of the debt. From the debtor's point of view bankruptcy involves a period of legal disability and the debtor could become captive to a formal legal process. The Act recognises that there may be circumstances where it is in the interests of all concerned to avoid bankruptcy. That does not mean that the debtor is forgiven outstanding liabilities. The Act provides a procedure under Pt X whereby the debtor makes an offer to creditors as to the future conduct of their relationship and, if a majority of creditors agree, a trustee is appointed to administer the debtor's affairs in accordance with the arrangement.

[18.50] The basis of the Pt X procedure is that the debtor offers creditors a way of resolving the indebtedness in one of the following forms:

- *Deed of assignment* The debtor acts in a way that approximates bankruptcy by assigning for the benefit of creditors all of the property that would have been available had bankruptcy taken place. The difference between this and bankruptcy is that property acquired after the assignment is not available for creditors as it would have been in a bankruptcy.
- *Composition* The creditors agree to accept a proposal that their debts be paid in instalments or that they be paid less than what is owed in full satisfaction of the debt. Thus, they may accept payment of 20 cents in the dollar immediately with subsequent payments of 40 cents in the dollar over the next two years. The alternative form of composition is to offer to pay, say, 34 cents for each dollar of debt as full settlement.
- *Deed of arrangement* The debtor offers a proposal which is neither of the above. For example, the creditors may be asked to accept a proposal under which all of the debtor's property is to be assigned for their benefit and they are to be paid from the income generated in the debtor's business. The provision about the further payment goes beyond a deed of assignment and the proposal would this be classified a deed of arrangement.

Procedure for Pt X

[18.51] Part X is invoked when an insolvent debtor authorises a registered trustee or a solicitor or the Official Trustee to call a meeting of creditors and, in the case of the trustee, to take control of property. This is formally done by the debtor signing an authority under s 188. Within 14 days prior to the meeting the debtor must provide to the trustee or solicitor a statement of affairs and a proposal for how Pt X is to be applied: s 188A. The meeting of creditors must be held within 35 days of the authority being given and after 14 days notice being given to creditors identified in the debtor's statement of affairs: s 194. The debtor must attend the meeting: s 195.

The outcome of a creditor's meeting will be expressed in a special resolution — one passed by a majority in number and at least 75 per cent of the value of those present — in which they resolve that:

- the debtor's property no longer be subject to the trustee's control; or
- the debtor be required to execute a deed of assignment or a deed of arrangement; or
- the composition be accepted; or
- the debtor be required to lodge a debtor's petition within seven days.

The process of instituting Pt X involves or can involve several acts of bankruptcy. Signing the authority, calling the meeting, not attending the meeting, failing to carry out the terms of the resolution are all acts of bankruptcy under s 40(1). A creditor could use the fact of instituting the Pt X procedure as a ground for presenting a petition but it would be successfully resisted if the court was satisfied that a special resolution had been passed:

s 206. Once the deeds are executed all of the creditors are bound and no debt recovery action can be undertaken: ss 228 and 233. Similarly in the case of the composition: s 238.

[18.52]   The debtor is released from all *provable debt* where a deed of assignment has been executed (s 230) or a composition has been accepted: s 240. A deed of arrangement will release the debtor from debt only if it expressly provides: s 234. There are circumstances where the Pt X arrangements can be set aside:

- if the debtor failed to carry out the terms of the creditors' resolution;
- if the arrangement cannot be implemented without delay or injustice to the debtor or creditor;
- where the debtor had been misleading or acted fraudulently; or
- the procedural requirements have not been met.

Presenting the creditor's petition

[18.53]   Once there is a debt of at least $2000 and an act of bankruptcy within the past six months a creditor's petition can be presented against the debtor: s 44. The court needs to have proof of the matters set out in the petition and that the debtor has been served with the petition: s 52(1). The debt on which the petition is based must still exist.

Making the sequestration order

[18.54]   In hearing a petition the court will require proof of what is stated in the petition such as the existence of the debt (unless it is a judgment debt where that has already been established) and the commission of an act of bankruptcy. The court will wish to be satisfied that the petition was served on the debtor and that there is still a debt of at least $2000. The court will, if satisfied, make a sequestration order the effect of which is to strip away the debtor's property and vest it in the trustee. The property is then used to satisfy the creditors.

[18.55]   The debtor is entitled to contest matters in the court and it is the creditor who has the burden of proving the matters in the petition. If solvency is at issue the debtor must establish it. Because of the serious nature of the process the court will treat the proceeding as more than a civil action involving a dispute between a debtor and a creditor.

The consequences of a sequestration order

[18.56]   Once the order is made the debtor is bankrupt. There is no declaration of bankruptcy as such. The Act defines a bankrupt as a person against whom a sequestration order has been made: s 5. Sequestration means that property is diverted into the control of another. In the context of bankruptcy it means that the debtor's property vests in the trustee (s 58) and is then realised for the benefit of creditors.

The immediate impact of the sequestration order on the debtor is to create the status of bankrupt and also to require the bankrupt to submit to the trustee. The bankrupt is no longer liable for the debts to the creditors. The bankrupt is required to lodge a statement of affairs to the trustee. It may also be necessary to attend meetings, to provide financial information, to supply documents or to be examined before the court or a Registrar. It may be the case that upon bankruptcy the bankrupt is affected — for example, as a member of parliament, as a member of a profession or as a partner where bankruptcy is a disqualifying condition.

The role of the trustee

[18.57] The ultimate task of the trustee is to ensure that creditors are able to recover as much of what is owed to them by the bankrupt as quickly and as fairly as possible. The trustee must manage the bankrupt's estate with this in mind. The basic requirement is to establish how much is owed and what resources are available from within the bankrupt estate to repay the amounts owed. The trustee may find it necessary to examine transactions entered into by the bankrupt and set them aside on the ground that, for example, they were fraudulent. A commonly held view is that a person can obtain protection from the effect of bankruptcy by moving property into the name of others, in particular into the name of a spouse or child. In some circumstances transactions such as that can be undone and a trustee would look to doing so in order to recover more assets for realisation and distribution of the proceeds to creditors. The trustee makes a decision about whether to disclaim property or contracts which are not worthwhile.

The relationship with the bankrupt is to ensure that the maximum benefit is obtained for creditors and in this respect a trustee may find it useful to undertake a public examination of a less than cooperative bankrupt: s 81. The statement of affairs prepared by the bankrupt is a starting point for establishing the extent of the trustee's task.

The trustee is an agent for the creditors but has ultimate responsibility for administering the bankruptcy. It would be inefficient if creditors were able to deal individually with the bankrupt. The Act makes provision for the trustee to call meetings of creditors and there is also provision for creditors to require a meeting to be called: s 64. Where the facilities exist it is possible to hold telephone conferences: s 64C. The meetings allow for consultation and communication with creditors

The trustee is able to seek directions from the court where an issue arises in the course of the bankruptcy which cannot be resolved by a meeting of creditors or which is identified by a legal adviser as a serious legal issue: s 134.

Establishing the level of indebtedness

[18.58] The trustee must ascertain the amounts owing by the bankrupt, and to whom. In the language of the Act the trustee must know the provable debts — which are those from which the bankrupt is discharged as a result of the bankruptcy. What is a provable debt is set out in s 82 and essentially it is a debt or liability existing at the date of the bankruptcy. Making a claim for such a debt is referred to as submitting a proof of debt.

In order to be included in the process the debt/liability must be expressed in money and must be legally enforceable. Some claims are made not provable by s 82. They are:
- unliquidated damages (where the amount claimed is not specified) arising other than by reason of a contract, promise or breach of trust. A claim for unliquidated damages in tort would thus not be provable;
- penalties and fines imposed by a court;
- interest accruing after the date of bankruptcy; and
- debts/liabilities incapable of being fairly estimated by a court.

Secured creditors are able to rely on their security for settlement of the debt. In one sense they are not touched by the bankruptcy. If the value of the asset on realisation exceeds the debt, the secured creditor is able to recover what is owing and has no need to submit a proof. The excess must be paid to the trustee. If the asset realises less than the debt the creditor ranks as an unsecured creditor for the shortfall: s 90. A secured creditor is permitted to surrender the security to the trustee and prove for the whole of the debt as if unsecured: s 90. This could happen where the realisation of the asset would involve more trouble than it is worth.

Proving the debt

[18.59]   Bankruptcy has the effect of converting a creditor's right to sue for recovery of the amount owing to a right to participate in the distribution of the bankrupt's estate. The creditors must prove the debt and do so by satisfying the trustee that the amount they are claiming is a genuine debt. The first step is to lodge a proof of debt.

The trustee after having examined the proof must advise creditors whether it has been admitted and how much of it has been admitted as a provable debt. Where a proof is rejected creditors may ask the trustee to reconsider or seek a court review of the decision: s 82.

Priority payments

[18.60]   The policy of bankruptcy administration is that all debts that are proved rank equally and, if there are insufficient funds, creditors are to be paid proportionately: s108. This goes to the heart of the matter of avoiding a law of the jungle approach to settling debts. There are, however, some payments which are given priority ahead of the general body of debts. Priority is established by s 109 in the following circumstances and in the order set out:

- costs of the petitioner and of the administration of the bankruptcy including remuneration of the trustee;
- costs of administering Pt X proceedings;
- liabilities incurred under a previous insolvency administration since terminated, annulled, declared void or set aside;
- funeral and testamentary expenses of a person who died insolvent;
- payment of salaries and wages to employees in respect of services rendered, subject to a maximum payment of $1500 to any one employee;
- workers compensation payments in respect of liabilities arising before the date of bankruptcy;
- payments due to employees in respect of long service leave, extended leave, annual leave, recreation leave or sick leave accrued before the date of bankruptcy;
- prepayment of any premium paid by an apprentice or articled clerk to the bankrupt; and
- priority payments to creditors approved by a meeting of creditors.

Property available for payment of debts

[18.61]   The categories of property which is divisible amongst the creditors of the bankrupt are set out in s 116(1). It is property which belonged to or was vested in the bankrupt at the commencement of the bankruptcy or was acquired by the bankrupt after that date and before discharge. It also includes the bankrupt's enforceable rights over property. The Act defines property to include real or personal property located in Australia or elsewhere.

There are exceptions, set out in s 116(2):

(a) Property held on trust by the bankrupt for another. Even though the legal title is vested in the bankrupt the beneficial owner is the other person and it is not the bankrupt's property.

(b) Household property: see reg 6.03.

(c) Tools of trade, equipment, professional instruments and reference books to a value of $2600.

(ca) A motor vehicle or other means of transport up to a value of $5000.

(d)–(fa) Certain life or endowment assurance policies and annuities.

(g) Rights of the bankrupt to recover damages in tort.

(h) Repealed.

(k)–(mb)[1] amount paid to the bankrupt under various rural adjustment schemes.

(n) Property acquired through protected monies — from sources referred to in (d)–(mb).

(o) Repealed.

(p) Certain amounts paid to the bankrupt by the trustee under s 166(2) or s 116(4).

Doctrine of relation back

[18.62]   An important qualification in discussing what property is available to the creditor is the *doctrine of relation back*: s 115(2). This doctrine influences the commencement of the bankruptcy. Its effect is that dealings with a person's property within the six months after committing an act of bankruptcy are to be treated as if the bankruptcy took place at the time of the act of bankruptcy. Once a debtor has committed an act of bankruptcy, and even if a petition has not been presented, dealings by the debtor in that property can be set aside. A creditor who takes property during that period with the knowledge of the act of bankruptcy does so at the risk of not obtaining a good title. The significance of relation back is that the significant starting point of the bankruptcy relates back to the act of bankruptcy. The commencement date of bankruptcy is post-dated.

After-acquired property

[18.63]   When the bankrupt acquires property after becoming bankrupt it vests, as soon as the bankrupt obtains it, in the trustee: s 58(1)(b). Property in this context means property divisible amongst the creditors and the exemptions which apply in s 116(2) as to what can be divided amongst the creditors also apply to after acquired property.

Income of the bankrupt

[18.64]   One of the objects of Div 4B of Pt VI of the Act is 'to require a bankrupt who derives income during the bankruptcy to pay contributions towards the bankrupt's estate': s 139J.

The Act gives 'income' its common law meaning — any amount derived that is income according to ordinary usages and concepts: s 139L. The term's meaning is, however, expanded to include other receipts of the bankrupt such as payments from superannuation and related funds; payment in respect of termination of employment; proceeds of a life assurance policy; distributions of an income nature from a trust; and money received by another for work done by the bankrupt: s 139L(a)–(e). There is also a deeming provision where the bankrupt who has not received money but has directed how it is to be dealt with is deemed to have earned income.

The reason for defining income so widely is because the Act has introduced a scheme whereby the bankrupt is liable to pay contributions from income to the creditors. The scheme involves the trustee making an assessment of the bankrupt's income (s 139S) at the beginning of *a contribution assessment period.* This is compared to the bankrupt's

---

1. no (l).

actual income threshold amount (s 139K) and any excess is divided by two: s 139S. The contribution is reviewed each year during the bankruptcy. If the bankrupt reports a level of income that is below what is reasonable the trustee is able to deem that the bankrupt earns a *reasonable remuneration*: ss 139Y, 139Z. Failure by the bankrupt to cooperate in providing the information necessary to make the assessment allows the trustee to make a default assessment: s 139ZI.

The assessment by the trustee maybe challenged by the bankrupt who may request the Inspector-General to review the decision: s 139ZA. That decision can, in turn, be reviewed by the Administrative Appeals Tribunal: s 139ZF.

[18.65]   Once the state of the bankrupt's affairs has been established the trustee must take action to realise the assets in the estate and distribute the proceeds to creditors.

The trustee must be satisfied that all of the bankrupt's property has been accounted for. In this respect the trustee or creditor or Official Receiver is able to seek a public examination of the bankrupt or of a third party who may have knowledge of the bankrupt's affairs: s 81. This allows the trustee to reconstruct the bankrupt's financial history and in that process the trustee could identify certain transactions involving the bankrupt's property which can be upset.

Preferential treatment of creditors

[18.66]   If a creditor has been treated *preferentially* by the debtor the trustee can recover the property transferred. That term includes a payment of money: s 120(7). The preference is voidable: s 122. This is not so much a part of establishing the amount owing but more a matter of treating the creditors equally. The money recovered becomes part of the property available for distribution and the preferred creditors become part of the pool of creditors.

An avoidable preference arises where an insolvent debtor who later becomes bankrupt makes a preferential payment to an existing creditor who knows of the debtor's insolvency. If the bankrupt were to pay cash for an item or open a new debtor–creditor relationship there is no voidable preference. A preferential payment is one where the existing creditor is owed less as a result of the payment. The rule about preferential payments can create practical difficulties. Consider an overdrawn bank account where the bank is thus a creditor. As the debtor's receipts are banked the indebtedness is reduced. The overdraft is an example of a *running account*. In such cases the payment does not necessarily terminate the relationship of debtor–creditor — it usually allows it to be maintained. A similar situation is where the debtor pays a creditor for goods supplied. If the payments do no more than provide for continuation of supplies there is no preference. If, however, in both examples, part of the payment is devoted to reducing overall indebtedness over a period then the extra amount will be treated as a preferential payment.

Transactions void against the trustee

[18.67]   Where property is transferred by a person who later becomes bankrupt the transfer is void against the trustee if:

- the transfer took place in the period within five years of the commencement of the bankruptcy up to the end of the bankruptcy; *and*
- the person who took the property gave no consideration or a value less than market value: s 120 (1).

The transfer is not void if it took place more than two years before the commencement of the bankruptcy and the transferor was solvent at the time: s 120(3).

Section 120(2) sets out transactions which are not caught by s 120(1) — payment of taxes; transfers under maintenance arrangements; transfers under debt agreements; and transfers that would cost more to recover than 'the value of the creditors of the property': see reg 6.09.

The rights of a person who acquired property in good faith and for at least market value are not affected by the section: s 120(6).

Fraudulent transactions

[18.68] Section 121 declares void any disposition of property made with the intention of *defrauding creditors* and following which the person who made it becomes bankrupt. The title of person who acquires property in good faith and for valuable consideration is not affected. This applies to a person who acquired the property in a subsequent transaction.

The critical requirement under s 121 is to establish an intention to defraud creditors and it need be only one of the existing creditors. If the main purpose can 'reasonably be inferred from all the circumstances' then it satisfies the section: s 121(2). To defraud creditors means to prevent them from obtaining access to property which could settle the debt owed to them.

The policy of the Act in respect of property is clear — all possible forms of property must be made available for the creditors' benefit.

Administration of the property

[18.69] The trustee is required to take possession of property 'capable of manual delivery' and is able to have the court enforce possession (s 129) or to apply for a warrant for seizure of property: s 130.

The trustee is able to disclaim property which is unsaleable, not readily saleable or which could be realised only at a loss: s 133. Persons who claim to have an interest in the property may seek a vesting order from the court. If nobody seeks such an order presumably the property is forfeited to the Crown or, as in the case of shares, would be treated by the company as forfeited in accordance with its articles.

In the administration of the estate the trustee has a range of discretionary powers: s 134. These are supplemented by s 135 which allows the trustee, with permission of the creditors or the court, to carry out transactions involving the property. It is possible if permission is obtained from creditors to settle creditors' claims by transferring property rather than realising it where it could not be sold advantageously. These powers assist the trustee in realising the assets in the estate at the best possible price.

Realisation and distribution of estate

[18.70] Once the property has been realised the trustee 'shall ... with all convenient speed, declare and distribute dividends amongst the creditors who have proved their debts': s 140(1).

Effect of bankruptcy on creditors

[18.71]   The bankruptcy process exists for the benefit of creditors in that it provides for the orderly distribution of the property of the bankrupt. The creditor might not receive the full value of the debt but could be paid more than if bankruptcy had not been instituted. The immediate effect on creditors is that they cannot commence legal proceedings or enforce remedies in respect of a provable debt (s 58(3)) but a secured creditor is able to realise property that is the subject of a security: s 58(5).

Effect of bankruptcy on the debtor

[18.72]   Bankruptcy means in effect that another party, the trustee, takes over the management of the bankrupt's financial affairs. As noted earlier the bankrupt's property is transferred to the trustee (s 58) and with only some exceptions is used to pay the debts that brought about the bankrupt's condition. The bankrupt is no longer subject to legal actions in respect of the debts — the trustee is responsible for settling them.

A person upon becoming bankrupt is subject to obligations imposed by the Act. These include being required to attend meetings of creditors, being publicly examined, being required to provide documents and information about property. The bankrupt's passport must be surrendered to the trustee (s 77(a)(ii)) and permission from the court is needed before the bankrupt can travel overseas: s 139ZU. Failure to cooperate in the administration of the bankruptcy has criminal consequences.

The bankrupt may be employed by the trustee and be paid an allowance: ss 134(1)(m), 135(1)(j). Income derived by the bankrupt can be used to provide a contribution to creditors: s 139P.

The bankrupt is limited in obtaining credit because it is necessary to disclose the bankruptcy when seeking credit of $3000 or more: s 269. Another limitation is that the bankrupt cannot be a company director: Corporations Law s 229(1). In a partnership, unless the agreement specifies otherwise, bankruptcy has the effect of bringing it to an end. The fact of bankruptcy prevents a person from being elected or from sitting as a member of the Federal Parliament: Constitution s 44. Bankruptcy must also be notified or can be a disqualifying condition in some professional occupations.

Discharge

[18.73]   One object of bankruptcy is to provide a mechanism for the rehabilitation of bankrupt debtors. This is achieved by providing that the bankrupt is to be discharged from bankruptcy: s 149. The period of bankruptcy is three years from the date on which the bankrupt's statement of affairs was lodged. This is referred to as *automatic discharge* but it is possible for the trustee of Official Receiver to object: s 149D. If an objection is not challenged it can result in the bankrupt's discharge being delayed for a further five years.

Early discharge can be sought by the bankrupt from the trustee (s 149S) but not within six months of the filing of the statement of affairs. The grounds to be satisfied for an early discharge are set out in s 149T and apply where there is no chance of a dividend being paid. The grant of an early discharge does not follow merely from the application; the Act sets out grounds which will prevent it from being granted: ss 149X–149ZE.

Once discharged the bankrupt is required to provide assistance to the trustee in respect of the realisation of the property: s 152. The discharge 'operates to discharge [the bankrupt] from all ... debts (including secured debts) provable in bankruptcy ...': s 153.

Annulment

[18.74]   If the court is satisfied that a sequestration order should not have been made or a debtor's petition it accepted it may annul the bankruptcy: s 153B.

Dealing with corporate debtors

[18.75]   The procedure for recovering a debt from a company is largely the same as for an individual. A creditor is able to secure a debt or to exercise a lien or to take the company to court. Bankruptcy is not, however, an option when the debtor is a company. See Chapter 22 for discussion of the process of dealing with an insolvent corporate debtor.

Summary and key terms

[18.76]   This chapter has set out to explain:
- The types of debt — *secured* and *unsecured*
- What a creditor can do to ensure payment. The remedies include — a *lien*; a *guarantee*; *reservation of title*; *securing* the debt; *repossession*.
- The key steps in suing to recover money owing — the *letter of demand*; the *court* process; the *documents* used.
- The avenues available to enforce a *judgment debt* — in particular, payment by *instalments*; *warrant of execution*; the role of the *bailiff*; *garnishee* orders.
- The process of *bankruptcy* where a debtor is unwilling or unable to pay debts.
  - The parties involved in bankruptcy — *creditors*, *debtors*, *trustee*.
  - The *grounds* for bankruptcy.
  - A *creditor's petition*.
  - A *debtor's petition*.
  - The *Pts IX* and *X* procedures.
  - The *sequestration order* and its effect.
  - *Proving* the debt.
  - *Preferential* payments.
  - *Property available* to divide between creditors.
  - The *effect of bankruptcy* on the *debtor* and on *creditors*.
  - *Discharge* from bankruptcy.

19
Agency

What this chapter does ...

The sheer scale of modern commercial life makes it necessary for business to be undertaken through intermediaries. Individuals are often in circumstances where they must transact their affairs through others. The law recognises that this happens and has developed a set of rules dealing with the relationship of principals and agents and the parties who deal with them.

This chapter looks at how the agency arrangement comes into being, it discusses the nature of the relationship between the principal and agent, the significance of what is done between the agent and third parties and how the third party is brought into a relationship with the principal.

The fiduciary nature of the principal–agent relationship is emphasised, with a discussion of its significance including the criminal consequences of breaching the important duties.

Common agency situations are identified and discussed, especially where they involve special features or departures from the common law. Included in this area are partnerships, companies, stockbrokers, insurance agents and brokers.

The termination of the relationship and its consequences are also discussed.

Introduction

[19.1]   The law has long recognised that most of what a person can do personally can be done by another. The exceptions to that rule are the obvious ones — marriage requires a personal commitment, as does voting and the performance of contracts where the person has a unique skill such as a performing artist. In other activities the person acts through another but is deemed to have acted in person. This is possible through the operation of the relationship of principal and agent. Much activity of everyday life is undertaken through agents — houses are bought and sold through real estate agents; insurance is arranged through insurance agents; travel is arranged through travel agents; a trader may be the exclusive agent for a product; stock and station agents provide services to the rural industries.

The nature of a principal and agent relationship

[19.2]   The notion of an agent suggests one person acting on behalf of another but in legal terms it goes somewhat further. The principal can be deemed to act in person because the person who is acting has the authority of the principal. It is this which marks out the difference between a mere representative and an agent. The agent is a representative authorised to act on behalf of the principal and able to enter into transactions which bind the principal. The benefits of such transactions go to the principal. The agency arrangement is sometimes described as an exception to the doctrine of privity of contract under which a stranger to the contract is not able to enforce it. In the case of agency the principal is a party to the contract because the agent has acted in a way to create a state of privity between the principal and the other party.

The agent has a relationship with the principal but also has a relationship with third parties. It is the work of the agent that brings the principal into a legal relationship with the third parties. While an agent is transacting with the third party on behalf of the principal there is no legal relationship between the agent and the third party.

The agent is limited to the extent of the principal's capacity. Thus an agent of an infant can bind the infant principal only to the extent that the infant could personally be bound. Dealing through an agent does not expand a person's contractual capacity and therefore the limitations on enforcing a contract against an infant would apply when the infant is acting through an agent.

The fiduciary dimension

[19.3]   An important feature of an agent's relationship with a principal is that it is fiduciary: see *Hospital Products Ltd v United States Surgical Corporation* (1984) 156 CLR 41; 55 ALR 417. It is not difficult to imagine circumstances where an agent is entrusted with matters of great significance to the principal. It could also happen that the agent has access to information about the principal's affairs which could be exploited profitably for the agent's benefit. The contract between agent and principal is therefore special in the sense that because it is fiduciary there are special, onerous duties imposed on the agent. These obligations exist even if the contract is silent. They may be varied but to do so it would be necessary to make the variation expressly so that no doubt existed that it had been agreed to by the principal.

The agent must:

- always act in the principal's interests;
- never accept payment from another party;
- give personal attention to the principal;
- follow the principal's instructions;
- exercise due care, skill and diligence; and
- account for all transactions.

Agent must always act in the principal's interests

[19.4]   The nature of a fiduciary relationship is that the agent must never allow the duty to the principal and personal interest to conflict. An example of how conflict could arise is where a stockbroker is also a share trader. The stockbroker's interests conflict with the interests of the client — because the stockbroker, as a trader, could benefit from the client's share transaction. The Corporations Law provides that a stockbroker shall not deal as a principal with a client without first disclosing that fact to the client: s 843(2). Where the stockbroker does deal as a principal it is not possible to charge a fee for the transaction: s 843(4). Under the Corporations Law the client has 14 days in which to rescind the contract provided the shares have not subsequently been disposed of: s 843(7). If, however, the principal trading does not come to light until later, the client has the common law remedy and could sue for breach of the duty. It is a matter of basic commercial morality that a person should trade for the client, not in competition with the client.

A related requirement under the Corporations Law which illustrates the fiduciary dimension is that a stockbroker cannot trade as a principal while there are any unfulfilled orders from clients. Priority must be given to clients' orders: s 844.

Agent must not accept payment from another party

[19.5]   In order to protect the principal the agent is not permitted to accept payment from another party except with the principal's consent. The ultimate breach of the fiduciary duty would be for the agent to accept a secret commission. A secret commission is a benefit received by the agent from the third party with whom the agent is dealing. The third party provides the benefit knowing that the person receiving it is an agent of the principal in the transaction. It is a benefit which is given without the principal's knowledge or consent: *Industries & General Mortgage Co Ltd v Lewis* [1949] 2 All ER 573. The benefit need not be in cash — it can be by way of services provided to the agent.

The secret commission is not necessarily a bribe but the law presumes that it was paid with a view to influencing the agent. It is not relevant whether or not the agent was influenced.

Receiving a secret commission is contrary to the principal's interests and to the good faith and straight dealing which should be the characteristics of a fiduciary relationship. Where it occurs the principal has the right to terminate the relationship and not pay commissions. The principal can also choose whether to continue with the transaction or to treat it as if it was void from the very beginning. If it is too late to terminate the transaction the agent is required to pay an amount equivalent to the secret commission to the principal. If the conduct of the agent and the third party has resulted in an inflated price the principal can sue them.

In addition to these civil sanctions, the receipt or offering of a secret commission leaves the agent and the third party liable to criminal punishment. This conduct is criminal in all jurisdictions within Australia. At the Commonwealth level it is restricted by constitutional limitation to conduct in the course of interstate and international trade and transactions with the Commonwealth or its agencies. The state and territory legislation would, however, apply to secret commissions paid in other circumstances.

Relevant legislation

Jurisdiction	Legislation	Section
Commonwealth	Secret Commissions Act 1905	—
New South Wales	Crimes Act 1900	Pt 4A
Victoria	Crimes Act 1958	s 176
Queensland	Criminal Code Act 1989	Ch 42A
South Australia	Secret Commissions Prohibitions Act 1920	—
Western Australia	Criminal Code	s 530
Tasmania	Criminal Code	s 266
Australian Capital Territory	Agents Act 1968	s 72
Northern Territory	Crimes Act 1973	s 236

Agent must give personal attention to the principal

[19.6] The appointment of an agent is personal and the principal is entitled to the agent's personal attention. From that follows the limitation that the agent cannot delegate responsibility and must act on behalf of the principal in person. In a practical sense, however, it may be impossible for an agent to deal personally with a principal's affairs. It is acceptable for the agent to have an employee undertake the work but the important thing is that the agent does not delegate responsibility to the employee. The agent would, ultimately, be responsible to the principal.

Agent must follow the principal's instructions

[19.7]   This is related to the matter of authority. If an agent is appointed to buy something at no more than a certain price the authority is thus limited and the agent cannot bind the principal beyond that limit. An application of this rule can be seen in the case of a stockbroker who must obey the instructions of the client. Failure to do so will leave the stockbroker exposed to personal liability unless the client ratifies the unauthorised transaction.

Agent must exercise due care, skill and diligence

[19.8]   The agent is not under any special duties in respect of care, skill and diligence. The usual standards of care, skill and diligence apply. An exception to this is where the agent professes special skills and is engaged for that purpose. The fiduciary nature of the relationship requires the agent to meet the most stringent standards of honesty and good faith as demonstrated above in respect of the conflict of interest issue.

Agent must account for all transactions

[19.9]   The agent must be able to account for all transactions to the principal. In effect this means that the agent must maintain separate accounts. This was a problem in a period when stockbrokers were not as regulated as they are now and they mixed their funds with those of clients with the inevitable result that the financial affairs became hopelessly muddled. Where legislation regulates agency relationships, as with stockbrokers, it is mandatory that proper accounts are kept.

The emergence of a relationship of principal and agent

[19.10]   The relationship can be created by or emerge as a result of:

- agreement;
- ratification;
- legal presumption;
- necessity; and
- estoppel.

Creation by agreement

[19.11]   The relationship is formed by a contract and in that respect is the only way in which an agency arises by a positive act. The key aspect of the contract is the investing of the agent with authority to bind the principal. It also sets out the terms of the relationship such as the arrangements for commission or payment, the period for which it runs and, if appropriate, the types of transactions to which the agency will apply. The agreement may be express or, in respect of some aspect of the relationship, implied. It is more accurate to say that what is implied is authority to act in a certain way. When an agent is appointed the principal invests the other person with authority. This is referred to as actual authority.

The agreement may be oral or in writing. Prudence requires that, like any other contract, it be in writing to ensure that the terms of the agreement are properly recorded. If the agent is to be empowered to make contracts or execute documents under seal the agreement must be in the form of a deed.

A common method of appointing an agent is by way of a power of attorney. For example, a person who is ill or one who is leaving Australia for an extended period, might have affairs that need to be dealt with and would appoint a person under a power of attorney.

Relevant legislation

Jurisdiction	Legislation
New South Wales	Conveyancing Act 1919
Victoria	Instruments Act 1958
Queensland	Property Law Act 1974
South Australia	Powers of Attorney and Agency Act 1984
Western Australia	Property Law Act 1969
Tasmania	Powers of Attorney Act 1934
Australian Capital Territory	Powers of Attorney Act 1956
Northern Territory	Powers of Attorney Act 1980

Implied authority

[19.12]   The implied agreement creates an implied authority for the agent to act in a certain way. It arises where the express agreement is silent on a matter. It may be stated as a general rule that every agent has implied authority to act in accordance with the customs and usages of the sphere in which the relationship applies.

Case Example

The agent of an overseas principal paid cheques which had been drawn in favour of the principal into its own account. When the agent went into liquidation it became apparent that the agent had not transferred to the principal all of the money that had been received on its behalf. The principal sued on the basis that the agent had no authority to pay cheques made out to the principal into its own account. The Privy Council held that in view of all of the circumstances — the principal was based in Belgium, it had no bank account in Australia and foreign exchange restrictions were an obstacle — the agent did have authority to bank the cheques. It was necessary to imply that authority to give business efficacy to the relationship: *Australia & New Zealand Bank Ltd v Ateliers de Constructions Electriques de Charleroi* (1967) AC 86; (1966) 39 ALJR 414.

Ratification of an agent's conduct

[19.13]   Ratification involves the retrospective authorisation of conduct. An example is where the agent has exceeded the existing limits of authority in a transaction and the principal later takes the benefit of the transaction. Thus the principal adopts the contract as if it had been properly authorised. The principal, by ratifying the agent's unauthorised conduct, puts the transaction into the state it would have been had the agent been fully authorised at the time of the transaction.

In order for ratification to occur there must have been a relationship in existence at the time of the contract. An example of the common law approach to this issue is to be seen with the conduct of company promoters in the period before the company is incorporated. At that time there is no company and therefore no principal and therefore no agency relationship could exist. There was certainly no authority for the promoters to bind the company even if it was absolutely certain the company would come into existence. Contracts entered into by promoters before incorporation are incapable of ratification at common law. This created a difficult position for promoters of companies and the problem was not overcome until the enactment of legislation: Corporations Law s 183. Because there was no company in existence at incorporation there could be no agency relationship but the Act allows the company to authorise contracts entered into prior to its coming into existence, thus relieving the promoters of personal liability. The company is, however, under no obligation to do so.

As well as the need for the existence of an agency it is also necessary that the agent was acting as an agent and not personally. If the contract had been made for the agent's benefit then it is not capable of ratification because the principal has no interest in the transaction.

Ratification is the making good of an agent's lack of authority. It follows that if there is to be ratification the principal must ratify the whole of the agent's conduct. There is no intermediate position, no partial ratification. The act of ratification must be positive in the sense of being conduct by the principal which indicates not only knowledge of the agent's exceeding authority but also adoption. It can occur either expressly or by implication arising from the principal's taking advantage of what the agent did. If an agent purchased goods on behalf of a principal but purchased more than the authorised quantity the principal, knowing of the breach, would ratify the agent's conduct by accepting the goods.

Legal presumption of agency in the case of cohabitation

[19.14]   Without considering the question of a principal's authority, the law (except in South Australia) presumes that a cohabiting wife, including a de facto, is able to bind her husband in certain circumstances. The fact of living together is important because if the parties are not doing so the third party is required to prove the existence of some authority.

The cohabiting wife is able to pledge her husband's credit for goods necessary for the household taking into account the number of members of the household and what is reasonable according to their standard of living.

The presumption means in effect that a wife has implied authority in these matters but it is only a presumption of fact which means that it can be rebutted — that is, shown to be inappropriate in the circumstances. The husband can rebut the presumption and thus avoid liability by showing that:

- he has expressly warned the third party not to supply goods on credit;
- he has expressly forbidden his wife to pledge his credit — this will be effective even if third parties are not aware of it; and
- his wife is sufficiently supplied with money to buy articles without pledging his credit.

This presumption was clearly the product of an earlier era when a wife was invariably financially dependant upon her husband. It is probably now easier for a husband to rebut the presumption.

Necessity

[19.15]   This situation, as the name entails, does not arise from any agreement or appointment but rather from a presumption that in certain circumstances a person has an assumed authority. The exercise of that assumed authority, to act on behalf of another, binds the other person.

An agency of necessity may arise in two circumstances.

1.   An emergency:
   - where it is necessary for a person to take action to preserve the property or safeguard the interests of another person; and
   - where it was not possible to obtain from that other person authority to do whatever needed to be done; *and*
   - the action was taken in good faith on behalf of the other person.

   It is probably the case that an agency of necessity relationship will develop from an existing relationship, not necessarily an agency. It would be unlikely that a passer-by would come into the relationship. An example of how it could emerge is where a person has gone away, is out of reach and has entrusted another with looking after a house. If the house lost its roof and was in imminent danger of being inundated, the person looking after it would have the authority to commit the owner to a liability in order to save the house from that damage. Where these circumstances apply the person who has taken action binds the other party. If the action involved the agent in spending money the principal is liable to reimburse or indemnify the agency in respect of money spent or costs incurred.

2.   A deserted wife or one who is living apart from her husband through no fault of hers is an agent of the husband to buy necessaries. This applies where she is not receiving maintenance from the husband or has not sufficient financial resources of her own. This form of agency works quite differently from the presumption arising from cohabitation. It springs from the fact that the parties are married. It does not apply in South Australia.

Estoppel

[19.16]   Where a person's conduct creates the impression that there is an agency the principle of estoppel applies. This means that a person, having created an impression, cannot later deny that a certain state of affairs applies. Thus, if one expressly or impliedly represents that another has authority to act as agent and a third party relies on the representation and deals with the 'agent' in that capacity, the person who made the representation will be held liable as if the agent did in fact have the authority. The representation that there was authority will create the authority. The person who made the representation will be estopped from denying the existence of the authority and thus the agency relationship. The authority is not, as in an agency created by express agreement, actual; it is described as apparent or ostensible because it involves the appearance of authority. Examples of apparent authority occur where members of a partnership hold out that a person is a partner or where a former agent's termination is not notified to those who are accustomed to dealing with that person as an agent. This form of authority has arisen in company cases as indicated in the following example.

Case Example

The articles of a company operating as a property developer provided power to appoint a managing director. Kapoor was acting as the managing director with the knowledge and approval of the board but had not been formally appointed to the position. He engaged architects on behalf of the company but it disclaimed liability arguing that Kapoor had no authority to act on its behalf.

The court held that Kapoor had no *actual* authority but the company, by permitting him to act as managing director, had created apparent authority and any act done within the ambit of that authority was binding on the company. The conduct of Kapoor fell within the ordinary scope of a managing director of a property developer: *Freeman & Lockeyer v Buckhurst Park Properties (Mangal) Ltd* [1964] 2 QB 480.

Brennan J in the High Court's decision in *Northside Developments Pty Ltd v Registrar-General* (1990) 170 CLR 146; 93 ALR 385 discussed, and confirmed, this decision and quoted (at 403) the following passage from the judgment of Diplock LJ:

> [W]here the agent upon whose 'apparent' authority the contractor relies has no 'actual' authority from the corporation to enter into a particular kind of contract with the contractor on behalf of the corporation, the contractor cannot rely upon the agent's own representation as to his actual authority. He can rely only upon a representation by a person or persons who have actual authority to manage or conduct that part of the business of the corporation to which the contract relates.

Rights and duties of the principal and agent

[19.17]   As mentioned in **[19.3]** the relationship between principal and agent is fiduciary and the rights of the principal are influenced by that. As well, the underlying contract which established the agency could specify rights which the agent is obliged to observe.

The agent also is entitled to rights specified in the contract but, as well, there are implied rights.

- *Remuneration*   Because the relationship is fiduciary the strict legal position is that the agent cannot be paid unless the contract specifically so provides. There is, however, a presumption that where a professional agent is engaged there is a right to remuneration once having carried out the duties. Where remuneration is by way of commission the agent is entitled to the commission only when the event on which it depends has occurred. This is a matter where the contract should be clear.

An agent is entitled to be reimbursed for expenses even if the agency is gratuitous. This could arise in an emergency where the agency arose out of necessity and the agent incurred expenditure in the interests of the principal.

* *Indemnity*   Where an agent, acting in the course of an authorised transaction, has incurred liabilities on behalf of the principal there is a right to be indemnified, that is, to be relieved of the liability or, if the agent has discharged it, to have it made good by payment.

* *Lien*   Where an agent has possession of goods belonging to the principal those goods can be the subject of a lien. They will form a security for any outstanding debts of the principal to the agent. The agent cannot create this right by seizing the goods, they must have been obtained in the course of the agency transaction.

Relations with third parties

[19.18]   When an agent has undertaken a properly authorised transaction the principal is brought into a contractual relationship with the third party. The agent, having played the role of bringing the parties together in a legal sense, is no longer associated with the transaction. Likewise, if a transaction is ratified or there is an agency of necessity or by estoppel, the agent who has participated in bringing about the transaction bows out. There will be occasions where there is a dispute with the third party asserting that the principal is bound by the conduct of the agent. In such a case the third party must prove that there is an agency relationship in existence.

In this respect there are several factors to consider:

* *Did the agent disclose the existence of and the name of the principal?*   If the agent makes it clear that there is an agency and identifies the principal then the agent cannot be liable and the third party must take action against the principal. The agent should at all times make it known that the conduct is being carried out in the capacity as an agent.

* *Did the agent reveal the existence but not the identity of the principal?*   If so, and the agent acted in all other respects with authority, then there is no personal liability on the agent. So long as the third party is aware that the other person is an agent, the agent will not be liable.

* *What if the existence of a principal is not disclosed?*   This is known as the undisclosed principal situation. The third party has entered into a contract with the agent oblivious of an agency relationship. The third party believes that the agent, the other party to the transaction, is dealing as a principal. Should the third party later discover the existence of a principal, and should there be a need for legal action, there is an option. The third party can choose which of the two parties to sue, if necessary. The logic is that the third party is entitled to hold liable the person who appears to be the other party to the transaction. In a case like this the agent remains liable until the third party has made it clear who is to be treated as the other party to the contract. The agent will also escape liability if the principal emerges and takes action against the third party.

Aspects of the relationship with third parties

[19.19]   Where the agency runs smoothly, the agent observes the limits of authority and there is no problem about the existence and identity of the principal, the result is that the principal and the third party conclude a transaction without any difficulty. If, however, the agent were to make a misrepresentation in the course of making the contract, the third party has the same remedy as if the misrepresentation had been made by the principal. Where fraud is involved and the principal sanctioned the fraudulent conduct the principal will be liable in an action in deceit. If it was only the agent who was fraudulent then the third party has an action against the agent. The principal is able to argue that the agent's authority did not extend to acting fraudulently and therefore was not within the scope of the relationship. If the agent was also an employee the principal will be vicariously liable for the agent's action.

Agent's misrepresentation

[19.20]　If the agent had made a misrepresentation in breach of s 52 or s 53 of the Trade Practices Act 1974 (Cth) the principal will be liable also. This is provided for by s 84(2) of that Act which states:

> **(2)** Any conduct engaged in on behalf of a body corporate —
> (a) by a director, servant or agent of the body corporate within the scope of the person's actual or apparent authority; or
> (b) by any other person at the direction or with the consent or agreement (whether express or implied) of a director, servant or agent of the body corporate, where the giving of the direction, consent or agreement is within the scope of the actual or apparent authority of the director, servant or agent, shall be deemed, for the purposes of this Act, to have been engaged in also by the body corporate.

That section applied in *Guthrie v Metro Ford Pty Ltd* (1977) ATPR ¶40-030 in the following circumstances.

Case Example

In 1975, in an effort to stimulate the economy, the Commonwealth Treasurer, Dr Jim Cairns, announced a reduction in sales tax on motor vehicles. The reduction was to take effect in stages so that after 30 April 1975 the rate of tax would return to normal in stages of 2.5%. Thus at 30 April the rate of tax would be at its lowest, 15%, and it would return to the normal rate of 27.5% by September 1975. Metro Ford was a dealer in Brisbane and it had a television advertisement prepared by its advertising agency, Doyle Dane & Bernbach Pty Ltd. The advertisement included the following passage:

> Dr Jim's lovely tax cuts are guaranteed till only April 30, so if you haven't been out to Metro Ford by then you could be a deadset April Fool. Metro Ford offer immediate delivery of automatic Falcon 500 sedans that save you $335.00. If you don't take delivery by April 30 you're up for an extra 335 bucks in tax.

The words 'Dr Jim's lovely tax cuts are guaranteed till only April 30' were found to be misleading. The court found that the advertising agents acted in accordance with their contract with the client and that it was a clear case for the application of s 84(2). The principal, Metro Ford Pty Ltd, was found guilty of a breach of s 53(e): see also *Guthrie v Doyle Dane Bernbach* (1977) ATPR ¶40-037 in which the agent was found guilty of a breach of s 53(e) as a result of the advertisement.

Agent fails to pay money over

[19.21]   An issue to consider when dealing with an agent is what happens if the agent fails to pay the money over to the principal either because the money is lost or stolen or the agent has become bankrupt. Is the third party required to pay the money again to the principal? If the money was paid with the intention that it be paid to the principal the third party will be discharged from further liability to pay if the agent had been authorised to collect the money. More than likely it would be argued that the agent, even if not specifically authorised to accept payment, had apparent authority to do so and in such circumstances the third party's obligation to pay would be discharged. If the money was to be paid to the third party and is given to the agent by the principal for that purpose, the agent's failure to pay does not excuse the principal from liability. There were examples of payments to insurance agents and brokers going astray and not reaching their intended destination. This created the problem of whether the third party was insured despite having paid a premium or whether a claim had been properly settled by the insurer. In s 14(1) and (2) of the Insurance (Agents and Brokers) Act 1986 (Cth) it is provided that payment to an insurance intermediary, such as a broker or agent, of moneys payable by an insured or intending insured is a discharge as between the insured/intending insured and the insurer. In that setting the insurance broker is regarded as the agent for the insured while the insurance agent is agent for the insurer. In *Manufacturer's Mutual Insurance Ltd v John H Boardman Insurance Brokers Pty Ltd* (1994) 179 CLR 650;120 ALR 401, a majority of the High Court held that s 14(2) applies only where a contract is in existence. Payment of a renewal premium to a broker did not satisfy s 14(2). Failure by the broker to pay the money to the insurer meant that the policy was not renewed

Types of agency arrangements and some comparisons

[19.22]   There are several ways of categorising agency arrangements. They can be:

- *Universal*   The agent has unrestricted authority to act on behalf of the principal. An example of this situation is a power of attorney which states:

  … I Edward Mannix Flynn of 110 Rennie St Moonee Ponds APPOINT Honorah Rose Lang of 80 Kenna St Queanbeyan my attorney for me and in my name or otherwise on my behalf to do and execute all or any of the following acts deeds and things …

- *General*   A general agent does not have the same degree of authority as the universal agent. The authority runs to a particular aspect of the principal's activities. In contrast to a universal agency which extends to personal matters, a general agency might cover only the business affairs of the principal and then perhaps only some. A third party dealing with a general agent would be entitled to assume that the agent has wider powers than had been actually given. In such a case apparent authority would exist.

- *Special*   This applies where the agent has authority only in respect of a particular transaction such as the real estate agent selling a house or a broker arranging insurance. In these cases a third party could rely on apparent authority but only to the extent of what a real estate agent or insurance broker would normally do.

- *Del credere agents* An agent of this type is authorised to receive payment on behalf of the principal. The special feature of such an agent is that in return for a higher commission the agent undertakes that the goods will be paid for, if not by the buyer then by the agent.
- *Mercantile agents* This class of agent is special because a person will obtain a good title to goods purchased in good faith from a mercantile agent even if the agent has only limited authority. The normal rule is that a purchaser cannot obtain a better title than the seller has.

The transaction is made special only where the agent has been 'entrusted as such with the possession of goods or the documents of title to goods'. This status is granted by the legislation which governs mercantile agents.

Relevant legislation

Jurisdiction	Legislation
New South Wales	Factors (Mercantile Agents) Act 1973
Victoria	Goods Act 1958
Queensland	Factors Act 1892
South Australia	Mercantile Law Act 1936
Western Australia	Law of Merchants Act Amendment Act 1842
Tasmania	Factors Act 1891
Australian Capital Territory	Mercantile Law Act 1962
Northern Territory	Mercantile Law Amendment Act 1861

- *Employees* It is not necessarily the case that an employee is an agent but it is possible to combine both capacities. The key issue is whether it is within the scope of the person's employment to bring the employer into a relationship with third parties. A good example of an employee who is also an agent is a shop assistant who is an agent to sell goods. The extent of an employee's authority would be measured with regard to apparent authority. Clearly, a junior clerk could not be assumed to have authority to bind the employer in a significant contract. It should be noted, however, that an employer will be responsible vicariously for the conduct of an employee.
- *Independent contractors* When a person engages another to perform work under a contract of services such as a painter or a solicitor the relationship is not that of employer–employee but client–independent contractor. It could be the case that in this relationship there is an agency component. A real estate agent is engaged on this basis with authority to act as an agent. The house painter would most likely have no authority from the client. Whether agency exists depends on the nature of the service and the circumstances.
- *Trustees* A trustee has in common with an agent a fiduciary duty. In the case of a trustee the duty is owed to the beneficiaries. The trustee's authority is granted by the person who sets up the trust, the settlor, but it is not the settlor for whose benefit the trustee works. Thus the similarity with agency is limited.

Specific examples of agency relationships

[19.23]   In many of the agency arrangements encountered in everyday life, such as travel agents, the party described as the agent acts with the authority of the supplier of the goods or services. The consumer who deals with a travel agent, for example, is a third party in such a transaction. A farmer who sells livestock through a stock and station agent would, however, be a principal. Agencies apply in other common relationships and arrangements.

Partnership

[19.24]   This is an example *par excellence* of where an agency applies. The partners have a fiduciary relationship between each other and according to the Partnership Act:

> **9(1)** A partner in a firm is the agent of the firm, and of the other partners in the firm, for the purposes of the business of the firm.
>
> **(2)** An act done by a partner in a firm for carrying on in the usual way business of the kind carried on by the firm binds the firm and the other partners in the firm unless —
>
> (a) the partner who does the act has in fact no authority to act for the firm in the particular matter; and
>
> (b) the person with whom he is dealing either knows that he has no authority or does not know or believe him to be a partner in the firm.
>
> **10(1)** Subject to the next succeeding sub-section, an act or instrument relating to the business of the firm done or executed —
>
> (a) in the firm-name; or
>
> (b) in any other manner showing an intention to bind the firm,
>
> by a person authorised to do the act or execute the instrument, whether a partner in the firm or not, is binding on the firm and all the partners in the firm.
>
> ...
>
> **11(1)** Where a partner in a firm pledges the credit of the firm for a purpose apparently not connected with the ordinary course of business of the firm, the firm is not bound unless the partner is in fact specially authorised by the other partners in the firm.
>
> ...

Other sections of the Act reinforce the notion of agency. In the following three sections the Partnership Act incorporates aspects of the fiduciary relationship. A partner in a firm is bound to render true accounts and full information of all things affecting the firm to another partner, or to the legal personal representatives of another partner, in the firm: s 33. A partner who, without the consent of other partners, uses the firm's connections or name for a personal benefit is bound to account to the firm for that benefit: s 34. Similarly if a partner, without the consent of other partners, competes with the firm the Act requires that any profit made from that activity be paid to the firm: s 35.

Relevant legislation

Jurisdiction	Legislation
New South Wales	Partnership Act 1892
Victoria	Partnership Act 1958
Queensland	Partnership Act 1891
South Australia	Partnership Act 1891

Jurisdiction	Legislation
Western Australia	Partnership Act 1895
Tasmania	Partnership Act 1891
Australian Capital Territory	Partnership Act 1963
Northern Territory	Partnership Act 1891(SA)

Companies

[19.25] A company is a legal person but its physical form is no more than a collection of documents. It can perform only through the agency of humans — the officers and employees of the company. Persons who have dealings with a company are now, by virtue of s 164 of the Corporations Law, in the absence of actual knowledge to the contrary entitled to assume that a person who is held out by the company as an agent has the authority to carry out the duties of a person in that position. This upholds the concept of apparent authority and a third party dealing with a managing director would be able to assume that the managing director has the authority that managing directors normally have.

Tax agents

[19.26] A person who prepares income tax returns, objections or transacts income tax business on behalf of a taxpayer must be registered in order to charge a fee: Income Tax Assessment Act 1936 (Cth) s 251L. In the language of the Act the preparer of the return is a tax agent. A client of a tax agent is the principal in a relationship where the tax agent (the agent) is required to undertake income tax related work. If the agent is slipshod, for example, failing to advise the client about the effect of a change in the law, the client could sue for a breach of the contractual duty to apply skill and care: *EVBJ Pty Ltd v Greenwood* 88 ATC 4977. The Act in s 251M provides that if an agent negligently causes a client to be penalised or fined the agent is liable to pay that amount to the client. This is in addition to the client's common law rights under contract. A tax agent who is unregistered is not permitted to charge a fee, nor to sue for the fee or otherwise seek to recover it: s 251L(5).

Insurance intermediaries

[19.27] Most insurance business is transacted through an insurance intermediary. This term is defined in s 9 of the Insurance (Agents and Brokers) Act 1984 (Cth) to mean:

> a person who —
> (a) for reward; and
> (b) as an agent for one or more insurers or as an agent for intending insureds,
> arranges contracts of insurance in Australia or elsewhere, and includes an insurance broker
> ...

Prior to the Act there was considerable confusion as to the principal for whom an insurance agent acted. Decisions of the courts described the agent as that of the insured. The Act, however, makes it clear that an agent of the insurer is just that. Section 11(1a) provides:

> An insurer is responsible, as between the insurer and the insured or intending insured, for the conduct of his agent or employee, being conduct —

(a) upon which a person in the circumstances of the insured or intending insured could reasonably be expected to rely; and

(b) upon which the insured or intending insured in fact relied in good faith,

in relation to any matter relating to insurance and is so responsible notwithstanding that the agent or employee did not act within the scope of his authority or employment, as the case may be ...

Section 12 says in a roundabout way that a broker is not an agent of the insured.

The Act follows the Income Tax Assessment Act model by requiring a broker to be registered. If an insurer deals with an unregistered broker it will be responsible for the conduct of the broker. A broker will be regarded as an agent of the insurer when acting under a binder: s 15. A binder is an authority given by the insurer to another person 'to enter into, as agent for the insurer, contracts of insurance on behalf of the insurer': s 9.

Auctioneers

[19.28]   The role of the auctioneer is to act as agent for the sale of property at an auction sale. The auctioneer's authority could be limited by being told of a reserve price. If the property is sold at below that price the principal is not bound but if the auctioneer was not aware of the reserve then the principal would be bound. Auctioneers are subject to legislation in all states and territories.

Relevant legislation

Jurisdiction	Legislation
New South Wales	Property, Stock and Business Agents Act 1941
Victoria	Auction Sales Act 1958
Queensland	Auctioneers and Agents Act 1971
South Australia	Auctioneers Act 1934
Western Australia	Auction Sales Act 1973
Tasmania	Auctioneers and Real Estate Agents Act 1991
Australian Capital Territory	Auctioneers Act 1959
Northern Territory	Auctioneers, Dealers and Travel Agents Act 1935

Real estate agents

[19.29]   In the process of buying or selling land, including a house built on the land, a person may engage what is described as a 'real estate agent'. The relationship between the parties is usually defined in an agreement. Problems sometimes occur as to when the agent is due to be paid the commission. Where a person who is a buyer deals through the agent it is rare for an agency relationship to exist. More likely, the buyer is dealing with an agent of the vendor. If the buyer engages the agent to buy property a contract to that effect would be needed. Real estate agents are regulated in each state and territory.

Relevant legislation

Jurisdiction	Legislation
New South Wales	Property, Stock and Business Agents Act 1941
Victoria	Estate Agents Act 1980
Queensland	Auctioneers and Agents Act 1971
South Australia	Land Agents, Brokers and Valuers Act 1973
Western Australia	Real Estate and Business Agents Act 1978
Tasmania	Auctioneers and Real Estate Agents Act 1991
Australian Capital Territory	Agents Act 1968
Northern Territory	Agents Licensing Act 1979

Stockbroker

[19.30]   Persons wishing to buy or sell shares on the Australian Stock Exchange must deal through a stockbroker. The relationship is contractual. The stockbroker is the client's agent and would be authorised by the client in respect of each transaction. As discussed earlier, the relationship between a stockbroker and client is one where the fiduciary aspect comes into play. The stockbroker is required to make the best bargain possible for the client. Thus, if the stockbroker was instructed to sell for $1.50 and it was possible to sell for $1.75, the client could complain if the $1.75 price was not obtained. Stockbrokers are regulated not only by their contract with the client but also by Business Rules of the Australian Stock Exchange and the Corporations Law. They are technically referred to as dealers in the Corporations Law and, to comply, they must:

- be licensed (s 780);
- maintain proper accounting records (s 856);
- maintain trust accounts for their clients' money (s 866);
- bank money received on clients' behalf within one day (s 868); and
- not withdraw funds from the trust account for other than specified purposes: s 869.

Termination of the relationship

[19.31]   To the extent that an agency relationship was the product of an agreement it can come to an end through:

- another agreement to bring the relationship to an end where, for example, the parties wish to part company;
- the expiration of the period for which the relationship was set up such as a one-year exclusive agency;
- completion of the transaction for which the agent was appointed as with the real estate agent who was engaged for the sale of a house.

Where the agency arose from an emergency, the passing of that emergency and the settlement of the principal's liability to the agent closes the relationship. In the case of a deserted wife her capacity to bind her husband would cease upon divorce or upon her being able to provide either through maintenance payments from her husband or from her own resources. The agency arising from cohabitation would cease when the parties no longer live together.

Ratification is a once-only process in the sense that it authorises conduct of the agent. It does not set a period or apply prospectively — it applies retrospectively. The conduct which led to the agency has passed and the ratification is no more than the formalising of what the agent did without authority.

Where a person has been estopped from denying the existence of agency nothing can be done about what happened in the past. The principal is bound in that respect by the representations made. In respect of the future, the risk of an agency relationship could be removed by the discontinuance of the representations and by notifying those dealing with the 'agent' that there is no authority. An agent could bring the relationship to an end by renouncing the authority but in doing so could be in breach of the contract.

Revocation of authority

[19.32]   Without authority either actual, implied or apparent, there can be no agency relationship. The person who claims to be an agent but lacks the essential authority cannot bind anyone. Subject to the following qualifications, when a principal revokes an agent's authority, the agency is terminated:

* the revocation does not have retrospective effect and transactions entered into while the agent had authority would not be affected;
* the revocation could not operate in such a way as to leave the agent exposed to liability for 'work-in-progress'; and
* in a relationship created by a power of attorney for valuable consideration and expressed to be irrevocable the principal cannot revoke the authority without the agent's consent.

Other means of termination

[19.33]   Other means of termination include the following:

* *Death*   On the death of the principal the authority comes to an end. If the agent was not aware of the principal's death, any transactions after the time of death are binding on the agent unless the executor of the principal's estate ratifies contracts made on behalf of the deceased principal.

  When the agent dies it is no longer possible to provide the personal service that is fundamental to the agency relationship. The agency is thereby terminated.
* *Bankruptcy*   The principal's capacity to make contracts is limited and from the date of the bankruptcy the principal cannot sustain an agency relationship. Similarly, the bankruptcy of the agent terminates the relationship.
* *Insanity*   The relationship comes to an end.
* *Frustration or subsequent illegality*   Where the agency was entered into in order to carry out a particular transaction, and performance of the contract is frustrated, for example by the destruction of a house which the agent was due to sell, the agency terminates.

If the transaction for which the agency was set up becomes illegal to perform, the agency is terminated.

* *Receiving a secret commission* The principal is able to revoke the agent's authority where the agent receives a secret commission.

Summary and key terms

[19.34] This chapter has set out to explain:

* How an *agent* is more than an intermediary or representative.
* The importance of *authority* — the special feature that allows an agent to *bind* a *principal*.
* How an agency relationship can come about — by *agreement, ratification, legal presumption, necessity, estoppel*.
* That the agent has a relationship with the principal and carries out transactions which *create a relationship between the principal and third parties*.
* The extent of the duties of an agent and, in particular, those which arise from the *fiduciary nature* of the relationship.
* The various forms of authority — *actual, implied* and *apparent*.
* The effect of an agency in *dealings with a third party* in particular where the principal is *undisclosed*.
* The way in which agencies are *classified*.
* How common arrangements such as *partnerships, companies, stockbrokers, insurance agents and brokers*, and *auctioneers* involve agency and how in some ways they are affected by legislation.
* The methods by which an agency is *terminated*.

20

Non-corporate Business Arrangements

What this chapter does ...

There are several forms of organisation for operating a business enterprise which are alternatives to forming a company. They include:

- *sole traders;*
- *partnerships;*
- *joint ventures;*
- *trading trusts; and*
- *syndicates and associations.*

In this chapter each of those arrangements is discussed with special reference to their legal significance. Partnerships are the most regulated form of arrangement within that group and this chapter examines the legislation which affects partnerships and partners.

Sole traders

[20.1]   The sole trader, sometimes referred to as a sole tradership, is the simplest and most basic of enterprise organisations. It means that the business is owned by an individual natural person. In the evolution of a business to that of a large scale enterprise, it is possible for the organisation to have begun its life as a sole tradership, and to have later developed into a large public company.

Definition of sole trader

[20.2]   A sole trader is an individual natural person who owns a business enterprise as principal. That individual is solely responsible for the provision of capital and all risks involved and has total control of the business. As a matter of law there is no separation between the sole trader's individual and business affairs. The sole trader is often the day-to-day manager of the business, although it is possible to delegate part of this role to employees.

Examples of the type of business operated by a sole trader are small businesses such as a milk bar, a retailer or perhaps a garage. Some single person businesses may be within the trades such as a plumber, or a professional practice such as an accountant or lawyer. Some people must operate as a sole trader by law, for instance a barrister must practice alone.

There is no simple way of distinguishing a sole trader and other types of business organisation, other than by an examination of the facts. The distinction between the form of a sole trader, a partnership, joint venture or employment of an independent contractor can be blurred. For instance, where a sole trader has a number of employees, particularly those with a degree of independence or who work for commission, then the classification of the business organisation may be unclear. An independent contractor may be a sole trader (or some other independent business form) in his or her own right. Where the sole trader has a number of persons working with, and for him or her, then it is important to distinguish whether these persons are partners, employees or sole traders in their own right, since there are different legal implications for each. Whether the business is controlled by a sole trader, or another type of business, is assessed by the degree of control over other individuals and an assessment of who pays tax, insurance and other employment expenses. Whether a sole trader is in fact a sole trader is a question of fact, and will be determined irrespective of what the business calls itself. A business enterprise may operate as D Park & Co, yet not be a company since the facts show only one person operating within the business. Likewise XYZ Pty Ltd, an incorporated company, may conduct a business operation as David Park — its business name.

The law governing sole traders

[20.3] There are very few formalities involved in setting up a business as a sole trader. There may be particular regulations which affect an individual enterprise, such as the need for a hawker's licence if selling in public, or professional qualifications if providing some regulated professional service such as a medical practitioner or solicitor does. Formalities and regulations applying to sole traders are universal to all businesses and involve complying with laws regulating: the registration of the commercial name of the business, the premises at which business is being conducted, environmental matters, occupational health and safety, workers compensation, local government and taxes of various types. Recently, in 1996, the Trade Practices Act provisions were extended by agreement with the states to cover the competitive behaviour of individuals and unincorporated bodies, and hence sole traders.

If an operator of a business conducts a business in a name other than his or her own, that name must be registered as a business name under the appropriate Business Names Act of the state. This protects the business against another party attempting to take advantage of the reputation of the business and it gives protection to a valuable business name which could be a considerable asset of the business.

The legal significance of operating as a sole trader

[20.4] Operating as a sole trader involves some important legal aspects:
* The business has no separate entity from the owner. That means that the sole trader is indistinguishable from the business and therefore has unlimited liability for all debts, crimes and civil liabilities arising from the conduct of the business. The for-

tunes of the business affect the personal affairs of the sole trader. There is no buffer between personal and business affairs as there can be when operating a business in the form of an incorporated company.

- Unlimited liability means that the owner is personally liable for all debts of the business. Sole traders should, where appropriate, take out indemnity insurance to guard against potential claims. There are various forms of insurance to protect a sole trader's solvency should there be litigation. Some professional bodies will not register an operator unless he or she has insurance. During the late 1980s and early 1990s there was an increase in litigation for negligent advice by professionals. A common example was that of companies suing their auditors for allegedly carrying out audits in a negligent fashion.
- Taxation is personal as the business has no separate entity from the owner. Thus the income of the business and the personal income of the trader are the same.
- The business may have a limited life if it cannot be sold or there is no one to take it over. Continuity is always difficult for a sole tradership, particularly where it provides personal services which may be individual to the business owner. However, it may still possible to sell the business as a going concern if it is managed properly so that stock, equipment and customer lists can be transferred.

Advantages and disadvantages of operating as a sole trader

[20.5] One advantage of this business style is that it is easy to set up and start trading, since there is less government regulation compared to other business forms. It is often easier to protect privacy because there is no need to make public disclosures. Accounting is simple and only necessary for statutory taxation such as income tax and sales tax, unlike the strict requirements of corporations. Once the business grows, however, the sole trader is faced with the problem of raising more capital. Personal taxation for a successful enterprise may exceed the lower corporate rate. Similarly, the greater the size of the business, the greater the risks for the owner because of unlimited liability associated with business as a sole trader. Most sole traders therefore have to consider incorporating once their business and risk has grown.

Partnerships

[20.6] Before the arrival of the modern company, most businesses were operated as sole tradership or partnerships. Some of the forerunners of modern partnerships were found in the early societies. These were groups of traders who shared resources and risks, their activities regulated by the rules of the law merchant which was a body of customary law developed by the merchants of Europe.

In 1890 the United Kingdom passed the first Partnership Act. It gathered all the common law and equitable law into a useable and understandable piece of legislation. The Partnership Act of the United Kingdom was a direct model for the Australian colonies which passed similar legislation.

There is a largely uniform Partnership Act in each state and territory in Australia but there is no Commonwealth partnership legislation. There is also a large body of case law which complements the Act. The Act does not abolish equity and common law provided that body of law is not inconsistent with the Act.

Partnership defined

[20.7]   The Partnership Act[1] defines a partnership in the following terms:

> Partnership is the relation which subsists between persons carrying on a business in common with a view of profit.

A partnership is basically a relationship between persons who conduct business together with the view of making a profit. This definition excludes people who are conducting business and making profits for an incorporated company, or some other body. A club or association is also not a partnership, even it raises funds and makes profits. This is because a club is not making a profit for distribution to its members but is making money for the use of the organisation in achieving its goals.

The tests for determining if a partnership exists are whether:

- a commercial relationship exists between the parties;
- a common business is conducted by the parties; and
- a business is conducted with a view to profit.

The definition of a partnership is important, since it determines whether a partnership exists in the light of each business relationship. A partnership may exist in law, even though the persons involved did not set out to create one. This happened in *Canny Gabriel Castle Jackson Advertising Pty Ltd v Volume Sales (Finance) Pty Ltd* (1974) 131 CLR 321, where the parties believed they were in a joint venture but the court found them to be a partnership. A partnership created by a formal agreement would readily satisfy the above tests. Some people operating a business may not realise that they are in fact a partnership, since they have no written agreement. If, however, one of the steps for establishing a partnership is missing, for example an intention to make a profit, there is no partnership.

A commercial relationship

[20.8]   Whether a commercial relationship exists between parties can be decided according to any agreement they have. There may be a formal document which has been signed, or, indirectly, the behaviour of the parties may indicate an agreement. Evidence may be gathered to show that the parties were acting in some mutual way which amounted to more than mere friendship. The facts may further indicate what kind of relationship exists.

Case Example

A company promoted tours of Australia by the then popular British singers, Cilla Black and Elton John. To finance the tour, the company borrowed from Volume Sales (Finance) Pty Ltd. The agreement between the promoters and Volume Sales described their relationship as joint venturers. Volume Sales later entered into an agreement with Canny Gabriel, an advertising agency which provided further finance for the tour and held as security a claim on the box office receipts.

---

1. NSW s 1, Vic s 5(1), Qld s 5, SA s 1 (and NT), WA ss 4, 7, Tas s 6, ACT s 6.

This meant that both Volume Sales and Canny Gabriel had a claim to the box office receipts. When money was received at the box office it was taken by Volume Sales. There was a dispute between Canny Gabriel and Volume Sales over who should get the money first, because there did not appear to be enough for both parties.

The High Court decided that Volume Sales and the concert promoters were a partnership, even though they called themselves joint venturers.

The High Court decided there was a partnership because of the following factors:

- the parties had joined in a commercial enterprise with a view to profit;
- they had agreed to share profits;
- disputes were to be decided by arbitration; and
- there was to be mutual agreement on the particular enterprise.

Canny Gabriel Castle Jackson Advertising Pty Ltd v Volume Sales (Finance) Pty Ltd (1974) 131 CLR 321.

Does a business exist?

[20.9]   Whether there is a business being carried on is first determined by the Act which defines a business as including 'every trade, occupation or profession'.[2]

A business can be defined as a systematic commercial enterprise conducted by the parties. It is an active occupation or activity continuously carried on, not an isolated act but a number of activities making it a going concern.

Sometimes, however, a single transaction may be taken to be a business. The courts may come to this conclusion because a single exchange may have been the first of many transactions.

Case Example

Turnbull supplied rice to Ah Mouy who was to pay Turnbull a commission for any rice he sold. Ah Mouy made a loss on his sales and refused to pay the commission. Ah Mouy claimed there was a partnership and hence he could not be sued by a partner under contract. The court found there was no partnership because there was one single venture which did not amount to the carrying on of a business. There was only a contract for sale of goods: *Turnbull v Ah Mouy* (1871) 2 AJR 40.

Whether a business is being carried on is an important question in taxation law. It may determine whether certain receipts are income or expenses which are to be allowed as deductions. In determining whether a partnership is being carried on the court will look for the following characteristics.

---

2.   NSW s 45, Vic s 3, Qld s 3, SA s 45 (and NT), WA s 3, Tas s 4, ACT s 4.

A business in common?

[20.10]   For a partnership to exist there must be some relationship between the parties, where they carry on a business on behalf of each other, or all together. However, because a person is active in a business does not necessarily make that person a partner. It is necessary to distinguish a variety of relationships and situations which do not amount to the creation of a partnership.

An active person working with an enterprise may be an agent of the undertaking, either as a co-owner, trustee or perhaps as a contracted independent operator. In the case of *French v Styring* (1857) 140 ER 455 two owners of a racehorse agreed to share the costs and race winnings of their horse. The court decided that despite the agreement to share the returns it was not a business in common — despite the common ownership, one party cared for and raced the horse while the other was like an investor.

In the case of *Checker Taxicab Ltd v Stone* [1930] NZLR 169 a taxi driver rented a cab from the owner by paying him a commission from the takings. The court found there were in fact two separate businesses and therefore no business in common. A business in common means there are shared rights and duties between the parties, more than just agent and principal. For instance, in *Keith Spicer Ltd v Mansell* [1970] 1 WLR 333 a person ordered goods for a business he hoped to commence with a friend. He did not pay for the goods and the business did not start. The creditor attempted to sue claiming there was a partnership. The court found there was not a business in common, no sharing of rights and liabilities, merely a preparation for business.

In the case of *Smith v Anderson* (1880) 15 Ch D 247 a court found that a unit trust did not amount to a partnership, the unit holders had no mutual relationship and were mere contributors to the enterprise. Hence there was no business in common.

Alternatively, a person may still be a business partner even though not active in the business. A non-active partner might include a person who lends capital as a business owner, even though not participating in the management of the business.

A view of profit?

[20.11]   A business has a view of profit since the objective of a commercial enterprise is to achieve some gains. A partnership conducts a business so that it can distribute any profit amongst its members. A charity, club or society is therefore distinguished from a partnership since it may trade through fund raising activities, but makes a profit for the purposes of its organisation and not for the members. Of course, once an organisation begins to distribute profits to its members, it probably falls within the definition of a partnership.

Statutory rules for deciding the existence of a partnership

[20.12]   The Act[3] adds to the basic definition of partnership specific rules about whether a partnership exists. These rules provide a number of exceptions for situations which might otherwise be seen as business arrangements.

The rules can be summarised as follows.

1.   *Joint ownership of property*   The Act states that:

> joint tenancy tenancy in common joint property, or part ownership does not of itself create a partnership as to anything so held or owned, whether the tenants or owners do or do not share any profits made by the use thereof.

---

3.   NSW s 2, Vic s 6, Qld s 6, SA s 2 (and NT), WA s 8, Tas s 7, ACT s 7.

This exception covers people who jointly inherit or buy property. The ownership of property together does not of itself make a partnership.

Case Example

Two sons inherited their father's business and property. There was no formal agreement between them, but the sons managed the business and property of two houses. When one of the brothers died intestate a court had to determine what was owned individually and what was in a partnership. The court found that co-ownership was only one element of a partnership. Because the brothers had regular drawings from the business, they had gone beyond mere co-ownership to partners in the business, while the property inherited was individually owned. The brothers appeared to have some agreement between them indicating a business in common: *Davis v Davis* [1894] 1 Ch 393.

---

2. *Sharing of gross returns*   The Act states that:

Sharing of Gross Returns does not of itself create a partnership whether the persons sharing such returns have or have not a joint or common right or interest in any property from which or from the use of which the returns are derived.

This means that where there is sharing of a return via the rent of a house, or interest on an account or dividends from shares, the persons sharing are not by that very fact partners. This allows for the possibility of sharing being on account of a joint venture, a syndicate, inheritance or two separate businesses. It is relevant to note that gross returns is a very different concept to profits. Profits are gross returns from which all costs have been deducted.

Case Example

The owner of a farm leased part of his land to a tenant who worked the land and paid rent as a share of returns to the owner. The tenant employed a worker who was injured. The worker tried to sue both his employer and the owner of the land as partners. The court found, however, that the tenant and the landowner had separate businesses. They were merely sharing in gross returns of the farms as a form of rent and this did not form a partnership: *Cribb v Korn* (1911) 12 CLR 205.

---

3. Receipt of a share of profits: The Act provides that where a person receives a share of the profits of a business this is:

… prima facie evidence that that person is a partner in the business.

but,

… the receipt of such a share or of a payment contingent on or varying with the profits of a business does not of itself make that person a partner in the business …

This means that a person may be receiving profits from a business for reasons other than being a partner. The Act gives particular instances where a share of profits does not of itself amount to a partnership:

a) where a person receives repayment of a debt as a share of profits;

b) where an agent or employee receives a share of profits as a form of salary;

c) where a widow or child of a deceased partner receives a share of profits as an annual payment;

d) where a person makes a loan to a business and receives a rate of interest which varies with profits, as long as the contract is signed by all the parties; and

e) where a person receives an annual payment or share of profits in return for the sale of a business.

[20.13]   These rules mean that a person is not a partner merely by receiving profits from a business. In the case of *Walker v Hirsch* (1884) 27 Ch D 460 a clerk in a tea company lent money to his employers. Instead of receiving interest he was to receive a share of profits. The firm dismissed him and the clerk, on the basis of his profit share, tried to show he was a partner who could not be dismissed. The court found that he was not a partner, his share of profits was for reasons other than being a partner.

Similarly, in *Cox v Hickman* (1860) 11 ER 431 creditors managed a company as trustees in an effort to retrieve money owed to them by the company. The trustees were to receive a share of the profits as a repayment of what they were owed. When the company failed to pay a particular debt to a different creditor, that creditor tried to show that the trustees were partners with the company they managed. The court found, however, that the share of profits was for reasons other than for a partnership.

Where persons do share profits on a business basis, then they will be held to be partners, unless they fall into one of the exceptions. In *Canny Gabriel* (1974) 131 CLR 321 a promoter of a series of concerts who shared the profits was found to be a partner, even though the parties were not to share losses in a similar fashion: see [20.8].

The existence of a partnership

[20.14]   Litigation over partnerships usually arises in disputes about the existence of the partnership, the rights and liabilities of the partners and their obligations to third parties.

The existence of a partnership involves an agreement which can be express or implied. An express agreement can be written or oral, though an oral agreement is sometimes difficult to prove. Prudence dictates that agreements be in writing.

As discussed above, a partnership is defined by the Partnership Act, with clarification of the definition and the relationship provided by case law. The fact that parties may refer to themselves as partners, or believe they are in a partnership, may be evidence of the existence of a partnership but it is not conclusive. In fact, it is possible to be in a partnership without the parties calling themselves partners, or even being aware of the existence of a partnership since it can be implied from the relationship.

A partnership can be a formal arrangement whereby the parties actually construct a partnership agreement and determine the rights, liabilities and contributions of each partner. This is an express agreement, which is best put in writing. A written agreement is preferred because disputes may arise in the future about the terms of the partnership. These problems can be overcome with a formal agreement — in fact, standard forms can be obtained from the Law Society of each state. The existence of a written agreement is important in a taxation context. The conduct of partners in accordance with a written agreement will provide evidence to the Australian Taxation Office that the partnership is genuine.

An express agreement is a contract between the members: it modifies certain presumptions made about the relations of partners to each other in the Partnership Act. In the absence of an agreement the Partnership Act will determine the rights and duties between parties. If no formal agreement is constructed it is possible that an implied agreement can be construed based on the rules of partnership law and the conduct of the parties.

The legal significance of a partnership

[20.15]   The partnership has no separate existence from that of the partners. The partners are bound by a contract. They are both agents and principals of their partnership. For example, partner A and partner B can both separately bind AB partnership by their individual actions. This means that the partners have unlimited liability for partnership debts and obligations, each partner's personal assets being potentially liable to partnership creditors.

Other consequences of the partnership entity are that a partner cannot contract with the partnership, or sue the partnership, since there is no distinction between the personality of the members and the partnership. This means, for instance, that partners cannot be employed by the partnership, because partners would then be employing themselves.

The law recognises in a limited way a separate partnership entity, for instance, it is named as a firm in the Partnership Act.[4] Similarly, under the rules of court, the partnership is recognised as an entity for litigation purposes. As well, the fact that a registered name of a partnership allows for partners to enter and leave suggests a type of entity. Further, a partnership can make contracts, sue and be sued in its own name as an entity. A firm can have 'Co' attached to its business name, but not 'Ltd' which is a term that can be used only in the name of a company with limited liability.

A partnership does not have to be composed of human persons; it may consist of a number of diverse organisations such as individuals, trusts or companies.

The regulation of partnerships

[20.16]   At first instance the regulation of partnerships is by way of the partners' agreement. The Partnership Act, however, determines relations between the partnership and outsiders such as creditors. It also fills any gaps in the partnership agreement, where, for example, the partners have overlooked some aspect of the relationship. The legislation provides for the application of common law and equity where it is not inconsistent with the Partnership Act.[5]

The partnership must be for a legal purpose, must not be contrary to public policy, must not have a member who is an enemy alien, and must satisfy the requirements of professional groups which have the power to regulate their profession, such as by prohibiting a partnership between a lawyer and non-lawyer.

Partnerships are between two to 20 people. Once a partnership is greater than 20 people it normally must incorporate: Corporations Law s 115. There are certain exceptions whereby firms of stockbrokers, actuaries and medical practitioners can have up to 50 members; architects, pharmaceutical chemists and veterinary surgeons can have up to 100 partners; and accounting and legal firms up to 400. These are designated 'outsized' partnerships.

---

4.   NSW s 4, Vic s 8, Qld s 3, SA s 4 (and NT), WA s 10, Tas s 9, ACT s 8.
5.   NSW s 46, Vic s 4, Qld s 48, SA s 46 (and NT), WA s 6, Tas s 5, ACT s 5.

Other regulations governing partnerships include the usual occupational health and safety requirements, licences and statutory provisions. One important form of regulation is under the Uniform Business Names legislation whereby partners who are operating under a different name to their own should register it. This deters any other business from using a particular business name, and allows partners to enter and leave the business without having to change the firm name each time. It also provides a public record so that an outsider dealing with a business operating under a business name can establish the persons behind the name. It is particularly pertinent where the firm name is a non-personal one such as 'Zippy Cleaners'. The Trade Practices Act now applies to the competitive practices of unincorporated bodies such as partnerships.

Relevant legislation

Jurisdiction	Legislation
New South Wales	Business Names Act 1962
Victoria	Business Names Act 1962
Queensland	Business Names Act 1962
South Australia	Business Names Act 1963
Western Australia	Business Names Act 1962
Tasmania	Business Names Act 1962
ACT	Business Names Act 1963
Northern Territory	Business Names Act 1963

Limited liability partnerships

[20.17]   In all states, except South Australia, there is legislation which allows for limited liability partnerships. A limited liability partnership is a partnership which has non-participating partners and working or general partners. This type of partnership must have at least one general partner with unlimited liability. A limited liability partnership offers a simpler means of limiting personal liability, without the expense of incorporating. Incorporated bodies have the onerous tasks of reporting annually to the Australian Securities and Investments Commission (ASIC) and keeping records. A limited partnership allows for more confidentiality than a company. As a result of an amendment to the Income Tax Assessment Act 1936 (Cth) in 1992, limited liability partnerships are now treated as companies for the purposes of taxation. Losses sustained by the partnership are treated differently to those of a 'standard' partnership in that they are not distributed to the individual partners. Limited liability partnerships have therefore lost some of their attraction, though they might be used instead of a joint venture.

The main advantage of limited liability partnerships is that silent non-participating partners who do not take part in the management can be designated as 'limited partners' and are liable only for what they have already contributed to the partnership.

Relevant legislation

Jurisdiction	Legislation
New South Wales	Partnership Act 1892 (as amended)
Victoria	Partnership Act 1958 (as amended)
Queensland	Partnership (Limited Liability) Act 1988
Western Australia	Limited Partnerships Act 1909
Tasmania	Limited Partnerships Act 1908

Partners' dealings with non-partners

[20.18]   While partners may make the rules about their relationship, the Partnership Act imposes rules regarding the liability of partners to outsiders dealing with the firm. Partners are both principals of the firm and agents as well.

The Partnership Act[6] states that:

> Every partner is an agent of the firm and his other partners for the purpose of the business of the partnership and the acts of every partner who does any act for carrying on in the usual way business of the kind carried on by the firm of which he is a member bind the firm and his partners, unless the partner so acting has in fact no authority to act for the firm in the particular matter and the person with whom he is dealing either knows that he has no authority or does not know or believe him to be a partner.

Persons dealing with the partnership are able to hold the firm liable for any of the actions of its agents, which includes the partners, employees and other authorised individuals. To show a partner has acted as an agent on behalf of the business, and not for himself or herself personally, the action must satisfy the criteria laid down in the Partnership Act of being business in the usual way, within the business of the firm and the outsider believed the partner had authority.

Business in the usual way

[20.19]   Carrying on business in the usual way is one criterion. Where the business of the firm is conducted in an unusual way, the person dealing with the partner is suspicious of whether it is actually partnership business, or whether the partner has authority, then the particular transaction might not be enforceable against the partnership. This is because the party dealing with the partner should have made further inquiries. Unusual transactions might be in the manner of payment, for example, payment in cash instead of a cheque, or paying for something at an unusual location or outside business hours. In the case of *Goldberg v Jenkins* (1889) 15 VLR 36 one partner borrowed money at 60 per cent interest when the interest rate was normally 6–10 per cent. The court found that the lender should have been aware that there was a lack of authority in such an unusual deal, or at least should have made inquiries and, therefore, the firm was not liable.

---

6.   NSW s 5, Vic s 9, Qld s 8, SA s 5 (and NT), WA s 26, Tas s 10, ACT s 9.

The business of the firm

[20.20]   A partnership will be liable for the partners' conduct only where it is in the course of business which is related to or comes within the scope of the firm's normal activities. If the business appears to be outside the normal transactions of the firm, the person dealing with the partnership should make further inquiries to see if the partner has authority. In *Mercantile Credit Co v Garrod* [1962] 3 All ER 1103 two partners had a garage business. One of them sold a car to a finance company without permission of the owner, and without informing the other partner. The finance company sued both partners and the transaction was held to be within the normal course of business, despite the fact that the partners rarely sold cars. The court found that selling cars was not unusual in that form of business. The courts will consider the facts of each case when determining whether the transaction was within the normal scope of the business.

Knowledge of a partner's authority

[20.21]   The outsider's knowledge of the partner's authority is crucial in determining whether the partnership will be bound. Within a partnership there may be limits agreed to between the partners, because some are senior, or because some activities require group approval. Internal agreements between partners are not, however, applicable to outsiders, who are entitled to assume that a partner has authority if business is conducted in the usual way. Where an outsider had knowledge that a partner lacked authority, or was restricted, the partnership cannot be held responsible.[7] Similarly, where outsiders do not know of the existence of the partnership but believe that they are dealing with the partner as an individual, they cannot later hold the partnership liable once they discover its existence. It is always possible, however, for the partnership to ratify a partner's action and thus retrospectively accept responsibility for it.

The effect of this provision is that persons dealing with the partnership are protected from partners using the defence that a particular partner was acting beyond authority. Partners are also protected from liability for the personal transactions of a partner which are obviously not within the ambit of the partnership business, or where the outsider had warning. The section makes the partnership impliedly liable for transactions and activities which fall within the scope of the partnership business, such as selling goods, ordering stock related to the partnership and employing personnel. It could be said that the partnership is liable for all transactions within the scope of the business except for those specifically exempted, such as the pledging of the partnership's credit for matters not connected to the partnership business.[8]

A partner will also bind other members of the partnership for any correspondence issued in the name of the partnership. A firm will be liable for any act or letter, document or written form of any type presented in the firm's name, with the intention of binding the firm, relating to the business of the firm, whether the act is by a partner or not.[9] However, a partner signing a document in a personal capacity, even for the benefit of the firm, will not commit the firm.

---

7. NSW s 5, Vic s 9, Qld s 8, SA s 5 (and NT), WA s 26, Tas s 10, ACT s 9.
8. NSW s 7, Vic s 11, Qld s 10, SA s 7 (and NT), WA s 14, Tas s 12, ACT s 11.
9. NSW s 6, Vic s 10, Qld s 9, SA s 6 (and NT), WA s 13, Tas s 11, ACT s 10.

Joint and several liability of partners for torts and contracts

[20.22]   Joint liability means that the partners are accountable together for a contractual debt or judgment by a court. Where partners are jointly liable, as designated by the Act, they must be sued altogether and there is only one action allowed. If only one partner is sued, then no further action can be taken against the other partners.

Several liability means that partners are individually liable; a litigant can pick out one or more of the partners to sue on behalf of the other partners, leaving the partners to reimburse each other for a judgment. A litigant can sue the partners one at a time, rather than being limited to one action as in joint liability. Partners can agree that, for example, one of them will not be liable, that is they will indemnify the partner against any liability. That is an internal arrangement, however, and it does not affect the rights of an outside party.

Some sections of the Partnership Act provide that liability is joint, whereas other sections stipulate that liability is both joint and several, particularly those concerning torts. The implication of this distinction between joint and several is especially pertinent for litigation. In an action involving joint liability the litigant must name all of the partners, or the rules of court may preclude action being taken against other members after a judgment is given. This problem could be overcome if the litigant takes legal action against the partners in the firm name. Where liability is several a disgruntled third party may still bring an action against other members of the partnership individually — severally. This may be useful where a particular partner does not pay up, or where a litigant chooses to sue the wealthiest member, leaving the partners to sort out the liability amongst themselves.

Liability for torts

[20.23]   Partners are jointly and severally liable for torts. The Partnership Act[10] provides that:

> … where by any wrongful act or omission of any partner acting in the ordinary course of the business of the firm, or with the authority of his or her co-partners, loss or injury is caused to any person not being a partner in the firm or any penalty is incurred the firm is liable therefor to the same extent as the partner so acting or omitting to act.

This is particularly relevant where the partners are professionals, such as auditors or medical practitioners, who must exercise a high duty of care. The law of torts overlaps other areas of law, so that a crime could also amount to a tort: see Chapter 16.

The essence of this section is that the partners are jointly and severally liable for any tort which occurred within the course of the partnership business, as distinct from torts committed by a partner acting personally outside the business of the partnership.

Activities unrelated to the business but endorsed by the partners will also make the partnership liable. Examples of torts would be an accident through careless driving, while a partner is travelling on business or negligently completing a professional service for a client so there is a loss. A common example is that of an auditor whose negligence allows fraud to continue within a company.

Contracts

[20.24]   Every partner is liable jointly with the other partners for debts and obligations while he or she is a partner in a firm.[11] Partners are liable for the debts of the partnership,

---

10. NSW s 10, Vic s 14, Qld s 13, SA s 10 (and NT), WA s 17, Tas s 15, ACT s 14
11. NSW s 9, Vic s 13, Qld s 12, SA s 9 (and NT), WA s 16, Tas s 14, ACT s 13.

even when they leave the partnership. Should a partner die, his or her estate is liable, but only for debts incurred up to when the partner died.

The partnership will be liable for all debts incurred under the umbrella of partnership activities. It will not be liable for debts incurred personally by partners outside the partnership and not in the firm's name, even if the partnership derives some benefit from the transaction. However, this situation is distinct from contracts made by a partner in the name of the firm, or within the ambit of the partnership business, where the contract has been made only for the individual benefit of a partner. This does not absolve the other partners of all responsibility merely because the firm derived no benefit from the contract.

Case Example

A partner in a firm arranged for a longstanding client, who had previously dealt with one of the other partners, to invest money in a fraudulent scheme run by that partner and an outsider. The partner absconded without any money going into the partnership. The advice was given without the permission of the other partners and without their knowledge. The client was able to sue all of the partners for her loss because the giving of financial advice was within the ordinary course of business for a solicitors' practice, and the partners were responsible for each other's activities: *Polkinghorne v Holland & Whitington* (1934) 51 CLR 143.

Liability is determined by looking at whether the partners acted within the normal course of business. In *National Commercial Banking Corporation of Australia Ltd v Batty* (1986) 160 CLR 251 an accounting partner misappropriated cheques from a third party, deposited them into the firm's bank account, drew them out and used the proceeds personally. The other partner was never aware of his activities let alone approving of them. The court found that the fraudulent partner had not been acting in the ordinary course of the firm's business and therefore the innocent partner was not liable. The distinction seems to be that the fraudulent partner was not dealing with the third party in his capacity as a partner, it was not in the ordinary course of the business, and there was no implied acceptance of the act by the innocent partner who lacked knowledge of the activities. It seems the question of liability will be decided as a question of fact.

Partners' liability for wrongs

[20.25] Partners are agents of each other and of the firm. The Partnership Act applies agency principles, whereby partners are deemed to be liable for any wrongs committed by their fellow partners.[12] Partners are liable jointly and severally for any wrongs which are committed in the ordinary course of business, or with the authority of the other partners.[13] A wrong is an act or omission which causes a loss or injury to a person who is not a partner. Wrongs cover a wide number of activities such as torts, crime and a variety of statutory breaches such as offences under the Trade Practices Act 1974 (Cth).

---

12. NSW s 10, Vic s 14, Qld s 13, SA s 10 (and NT), WA s 17, Tas s 15, ACT s 14.
13. NSW s 12, Vic s 16, Qld s 15, SA s 12 (and NT), WA s 19, Tas s 17, ACT s 16.

[20.26]   The following are examples of partners' liabilities for wrongs:

- *Mann v Hulme* (1961) 106 CLR 136   A solicitor, who was a partner in a firm, induced a third party to invest in a mortgage arrangement in which he claimed to have connections. To show his good faith the solicitor gave the third party his own promissory notes. The solicitor in fact misappropriated the funds which had been paid to him. The third party then sought to sue the partnership for recovery of the money. The partners attempted to argue that the money was not received in the firm's name but only in the name of the defaulting partner, and as such had no connection to the business of the firm. The court found, however, that the money was the responsibility of the partnership, since it was of a type which is received in the ordinary course of business by solicitors and they were therefore liable.

- *Hamlyn v Houston* [1903] 1 KB 81   One partner attempted to bribe the clerk of an opposition partnership to obtain confidential information. The partner was sued under tort and all the partners were held to be liable, despite the lack of consensus amongst the partners in approving and allowing such actions. It was sufficient to show the action was related to the ordinary course of the firm's business.

- *Clode v Barnes* [1974] 1 WLR 544   One of two partners in a firm of car dealers, without the authority of the other partner, advertised a car in a way that breached the Trade Descriptions Act 1968 (UK). The court found both partners guilty because it was in the ordinary course of the firm's business, despite the fact that one partner had no knowledge, and had given approval to the crime.

Misapplication of money or property

[20.27]   The Partnership Act makes the partners liable as a firm for a misapplication of money or property received by a partner, or by the firm, from a third party. The firm must pay back any money which has wrongfully been taken.[14]

If a partner is a trustee and improperly uses trust property in the business, or on account of the partnership, the other partners will only be liable if they had notice of the breach of trust, though the trust money can always be recovered if it is still in the possession or control of the firm.[15] This section has a different emphasis in that partners are not automatically liable unless they knew of the misappropriation and did nothing about it. Liability depends on whether the partners actually knew about the breach of trust, and if the money or property is connected to the business of the partnership. It may be that knowledge of the breach is implied if the partners should have known about the breach, for example, through normal checking of accounts. If the property is received in a capacity other than as a partner then it is not related to partnership business.

Partnership by estoppel

[20.28]   A person who expressly or otherwise represents to another that a certain relationship exists cannot later deny the truth of that representation. That is to say, they are estopped. If a partner, or partners, deliberately creates the impression that someone is their partner, then they cannot later claim that person is really not a partner.[16] Such conduct is referred to as holding out and partners will be estopped (or stopped) from denying

---

14. NSW s 11, Vic s 15, Qld s 14, SA s 11 (and NT), WA s 18, Tas s 16, ACT s 15.
15. NSW s 13, Vic s 17, Qld s 16, SA s 13 (and NT), WA s 20, Tas s 18, ACT s 17.
16. NSW s 14, Vic s 18, Qld s 17, SA s 14 (and NT), WA s 21, Tas s 19, ACT s 18.

the relationship. Similarly, a person who holds him or herself out as a partner, or allows the impression to exist that he or she is a partner, cannot later deny that a partnership exists. Thus a third party who is led to believe that a person is a partner, and deals with the person accordingly, would be able to take action against other members of the partnership.

Admissions and representations by partners

[20.29]   The Act also covers admissions and representations of partners.[17] An admission or representation made by any partner concerning partnership affairs, and in the course of business, is evidence against the firm. This may be relevant where one partner admits liability but the other partners seek to deny it.

The Act also specifies that notice to any partner, who habitually acts in the partnership, is notice to the firm as a whole concerning the business of the partnership, except where it concerns fraud on the firm committed by, or with the consent, of that particular partner.[18] Simply put, where one working partner is informed of something it can be assumed that the whole partnership has been informed.

A partner is not deemed to have had notice of any matter concerning partnership affairs that took place before joining the partnership. For instance, an employee who later becomes a partner is not deemed to have had notice of anything concerning partnership affairs. Notice to a partner who later retires is notice to the partnership as a whole. The Act distinguishes notice given to a fraudulent partner as not being notice to the whole firm where fraud is committed on the whole firm.

Relations of partners to each other

[20.30]   A partnership is based on agreement and partners will often draw up an agreement to specify their roles, rights and obligations within the partnership. The agreement can be express or implied and need not, as a matter of law, be in writing. The Act allows for the provisions of the Partnership Act to be varied by the partners' agreement. This variation of the Partnership Act can be express or implied from the partners dealings.[19] If the partners do not make their own agreement the Act will establish the legal relations between the partners.

Property

[20.31]   Partners may wish to lend their personal property to the partnership, or perhaps allow for some partners to have a greater claim over certain property. For instance, a partner may be allowed to use a car for personal purposes. In the absence of such agreements the Act has the following rules regarding partnership property.[20]

1. Property bought by the partnership belongs to the partnership and must only be used for the partnership. All property, and rights and interests in property, which was originally bought for the partnership, or later acquired in any manner for the partnership, is to be known as partnership property. This property must be used by the partners only for the purposes of the partnership and in accordance with the partnership agreement.

---

17. NSW s 15, Vic s 19, Qld s 18, SA s 15 (and NT), WA s 22, Tas s 20, ACT s 19.
18. NSW s 16, Vic s 19, Qld s 16, SA s 23 (and NT), WA s 23, Tas s 21, ACT s 20.
19. NSW s 19, Vic s 23, Qld s 22, SA s 19 (and NT), WA s 29, Tas s 24, ACT s 23.
20. NSW s 20, Vic s 24, Qld s 23, SA s 20 (and NT), WA s 30, Tas s 25, ACT s 24.

2. Land held by the partnership belongs to the partners but subject to legitimate claims by other parties, such as creditors or even the owners of the land who have leased the land to the partnership.

3. Where persons own land as co-owners, so that the land is not partnership property but used for partnership purposes, then in the absence of a contrary agreement the land belongs to the parties as co-owners rather than as partners. Property bought with partnership money is assumed to belong to the firm, unless there is a contrary agreement.[21]

[20.32]   Whether in fact particular assets become part of the partnership property will be determined by agreements between the partners. It is possible that property used in the partnership will remain the property of the individual partner who contributed it. Some difficulty can arise, therefore, when, in the absence of a clear agreement, there is a dispute as to the use of property, or if there is a dissolution of the partnership through a breakdown in relations between the partners, or through death or bankruptcy. It is advisable therefore for a partnership to make sure it anticipates the possibility of different contributions of property, and to make provision for how that property may ultimately be distributed, since the Act assumes there will be an equal distribution of assets on a dissolution.

Case Example

A diver, who held a valuable permit to fish, entered into a partnership to fish for abalone. The partnership paid the annual licence fees of the partner who held the licence. When the partnership was dissolved a dispute arose between the two partners as to who owned the licence. The unlicensed partner claimed the licence was now partnership property since partnership money had been used to pay the annual fee. The court found that one partner always retained the ownership of the licence, even though partnership money had been used. The partnership paid only for the benefit of that licence, not for its ownership: *Kelly v Kelly* (1990) 92 ALR 74.

Rights and duties between partners

[20.33]   The Act provides a set of rules governing the rights and duties which exist between partners. What is important is that the Act specifically states that these rights and duties may be modified expressly or impliedly by a partners' agreement.[22] The rules are:

1. Partners are entitled to share equally in the capital and profits of the business, and must contribute equally towards any losses by the firm, whether of capital or otherwise. This rule has implications for the partner who has contributed more capital than another, and also for the partner who perhaps puts more time into the partnership and expects a greater share of the profits. Partners should ensure their partnership agreement reflects their different contributions.

2. Partners are entitled to indemnification for any payments or personal liabilities incurred in the ordinary and proper conduct of the business of the firm, or for anything necessarily done in the interests of the business or property of the firm. This means

---

21. NSW s 21, Vic s 25, Qld s 24, SA s 21 (and NT), WA s 31, Tas s 26, ACT s 26.
22. NSW s 24, Vic s 28, Qld s 27, SA s 24 (and NT), WA s 34, Tas s 29, ACT s 29.

that they can be reimbursed for any payments they have made for the business as agents of the firm.

3. Partners who lend to the partnership more than their required contribution of capital are entitled to interest.

4. Partners are not entitled to any payment of interest on their required capital contributions until the profits of the firm have been assessed.

5. Every partner may take part in the management of the partnership business. This right to take part in the management of the partnership may be expressly excluded by the agreement, particularly in the case of a sleeping or dormant partner.

6. No partner is entitled to payment for working in the partnership business. Partners will normally modify this by drawing up an agreement whereby some partners draw more than others from the firm because they do more work. The drawings are not salary or wages but rather, are a pre-payment of the partners' share of profit.

7. No new partner can be admitted without the agreement of all the existing partners.

8. Differences of opinion between partners as to ordinary matters connected with the partnership business may be decided by a majority of the partners, but no change may be made in the nature of the partnership business without the consent of all existing partners. There is a difference between day-to-day matters within the partnership, such as the purchase of equipment, and matters which affect the very nature or essence of the partnership. Matters which require unanimous agreement include a radical change to the type of business conducted.

9. The partnership books are to be kept at the place of business of the partnership (or the principal place if there is more than one) and every partner has the right to access, inspect and copy them. This provides full disclosure of the nature of the business and recognises that all members of the partnership have a right to participate in the management of the business.

Fiduciary duties of partners

[20.34] The relationship between partners is fiduciary. That means that the standard of honesty and proper dealing that partners should display to each other is similar to that between a trustee and beneficiary. In practical terms the partners are intimately bound and must have mutual trust and confidence in each other. Duties of a fiduciary nature in the context of a partnership include a duty not to compete; to act with diligence and care; to keep confidential information; and to act at all times in the best interests of the partnership. The Partnership Act expressly states a number of fiduciary duties:

- Partners are bound to render true accounts and full information of all things affecting the partnership to any partner or a legal representative of the partner. This means that every partner is entitled to full disclosure, whether the information is in the books or not.[23]

- Every partner must account to the firm for any benefit or profit derived from the use of the partnership property, name or business connection.[24]

- A partner cannot, without the consent of the other partners, carry on any business of the same nature that competes with the firm. If a partner does compete then any profits made must be paid to the firm.[25]

---

23. NSW s 28, Vic s 32, Qld s 31, SA s 28 (and NT), WA s 39, Tas s 33, ACT s 33.
24. NSW s 21, Vic s 25, Qld s 24, SA s 21 (and NT), WA s 31, Tas s 26, ACT s 26.
25. NSW s 30, Vic s 34, Qld s 33, SA s 30 (and NT), WA s 41, Tas s 35, ACT s 35.

An illustration of the fiduciary nature of the partnerships is found in the case of *United Dominions Corp v Brian Pty Ltd* (1985) 157 CLR 1: see **[20.51]**.

Leaving a partnership

[20.35]   Leaving a partnership can occur in several ways:

* *Expulsion*   The majority members of a partnership can expel a member of the partnership if the partnership agreement allows them to do so, but in the absence of this provision they cannot expel a member.[26] If expulsion does take place it must be strictly in accordance with the provisions of the agreement (*Bond v Hale* (1969) 72 SR (NSW) 201), in good faith and not for any wrongful or unfair reason unrelated to partnership business.

* *Retirement*   In the absence of an agreement, and where there is no fixed time for the partnership to operate, a partnership may be ended by a partner giving notice to the other partners that the partnership is finished.[27]

* *Assignment*   It is possible for a partner to assign his or her share, or part of it, to another person.[28] Assigning a share means that another person has the rights of the partner to a share of the property or income of the partnership. This does not mean, however, that the assignee (the one receiving a share) becomes a partner; this can only be done with the agreement of the other partners to admit the outsider as a partner. The Act makes it clear that the assignee is not to interfere in any aspect of the partnership. The assignee therefore only has a right to receive a share of the profits as the partners determine. The assignee can only share in the assets of the partnership on the dissolution of the partnership: *Re Garwood's Trusts; Garwood v Paynter* [1903] 1 Ch 236.

The law in this area has been explained in several taxation cases, the most notable of which was *Federal Commissioner of Taxation v Everett* (1980) 143 CLR 440. In that case a solicitor by assigning part of his interest in a partnership was able to transfer income, and tax liability to the assignee — his wife.

Incoming and outgoing partner's liability

[20.36]   A person newly admitted to an existing partnership is not liable to creditors for debts incurred by the partnership before joining.[29] A partner, even after retiring, remains liable for debts and obligations incurred while a member of a partnership up to the point of retirement. This liability can be overcome by an agreement, express or implied, between the retiring partner and the remaining members of the partnership and the creditors. A new partner may accept the liability of an outgoing partner under an agreement between the partners.

It is important to make the creditors aware of the retirement of a partner. Some partnerships take elaborate steps to inform their creditors and clientele that a former partner is no longer a member of the firm, by placing advertisements in newspapers and trade or professional journals.

Notifying the public of the change to the partnership is very important for both the retiring partner and the partnership itself. Failure to do so could create a situation of

---

26. NSW s 25, Vic s 29, Qld s 28, SA s 25 (and NT), WA s 35, Tas s 30, ACT s 30
27. NSW s 26, Vic s 30, Qld s 29, SA s 26 (and NT), WA s 37, Tas s 31, ACT s 31.
28. NSW s 31, Vic s 35, Qld s 34, SA s 31 (and NT), WA s 42, Tas s 36, ACT s 36.
29. NSW s 17, Vic s 21, Qld s 20, SA s 17 (and NT), WA s 24, Tas s 22, ACT s 21.

estoppel, whereby parties dealing with the partnership who are unaware of its dissolution will be entitled to hold all apparent partners, including any outgoing partners, liable.[30]

Dissolving a partnership

[20.37] Dissolving a partnership is the ending of a partnership, after which winding up takes place, which is the distribution of the remaining assets and obligations. When a partner leaves or joins a partnership the effect is to dissolve the earlier partnership. This is a significant legal consequence which has implications in relation to the property interests in the partnership and also in relation to capital gains tax. The Act specifies a number of ways in which a partnership may be dissolved, but the provisions of the Act can be modified by express or implied agreement between the partners.

Fixed term, venture and 'on notice' partnerships

[20.38] A partnership which is to operate for a fixed term is dissolved when that term expires. If the partnership is established for a single venture, then it finishes on the conclusion of the project or venture. A partnership may be established to run for an undefined time, but will be dissolved when a partner gives notice of an intention to dissolve the partnership.[31] The remaining members of the partnership can re-form a partnership, or perhaps reconstitute a partnership for a new time period or for a new venture.

The Act allows for the possibility of a partnership continuing after the expiration of a fixed time, where the partners have made no new agreement as to their rights and duties. In that case the rights and duties of the partners remain the same as they were during the original fixed term — at least insofar as those rights and duties are consistent with a partnership at will. Where the same partners continue within the business without any settlement or liquidation of partnership affairs, there is a presumption that the partnership continues.[32] A partnership at will is a partnership with no fixed term and operates as long as the partners agree to remain in that relationship.

Bankruptcy and death

[20.39] In the absence of any agreement, a partnership will be dissolved by the death or bankruptcy of a partner. The partners can agree that death and bankruptcy will not automatically dissolve a partnership, but the bankrupt partner or the estate of the deceased partner can still apply to a court to wind the partnership up, irrespective of the agreement.

Illegal Partnerships

[20.40] A partnership may also be dissolved where the nature of the partnership becomes illegal, or when it is unlawful for the particular members of the partnership to continue the business.[33]

Dissolution by court

[20.41] A court can dissolve a partnership by decree on the application of a partner for a number of reasons such as:[34]

---

30. NSW s 36, Vic s 40, Qld s 39, SA s 36 (and NT), WA s 47, Tas s 41, ACT s 41.
31. NSW s 32, Vic s 36, Qld s 35, SA s 32 (and NT), WA s 43, Tas s 37, ACT s 37.
32. NSW s 27, Vic s 31, Qld s 30, SA s 27 (and NT), WA s 38, Tas s 32, ACT s 32.
33. NSW s 34, Vic s 38, Qld s 37, SA s 34 (and NT), WA s 45, Tas s 39, ACT s 39.
34. NSW s 35, Vic s 39, Qld s 38, SA s 35 (and NT), WA s 46, Tas s 40, ACT s 40.

- Where a partner has been declared of unsound mind and incapable of managing his or her affairs. A similar application may be made by someone who has sufficient connection to the partner suffering the mental incapacity. This would allow for the partners or family of a partner suffering permanent mental illness to make an application to the court.

- Where a partner, other than the partner making the application to the court, is incapable of performing the obligations under the partnership contract or business. This situation may arise where a partner is disabled in some way, or perhaps no longer has the trade or professional qualifications necessary to operate in the partnership.

- Where a partner, other than the partner making the application, has been found guilty of conduct which will prejudicially affect the business. The conviction would need to be such that it affects the reputation of the business, for example, where an accountant is convicted of a crime of dishonesty.

- Where a partner, other than the partner making the application, deliberately and continually commits a breach of the partnership agreement or behaves in such a manner that the other partners are unable to carry on the partnership business with that partner. Situations could arise where a partner is continually absent from the business, acts contrary to the interests of the business or perhaps is refusing to cooperate in a normal business manner with the other partners.

- Where the partnership business cannot be carried on except at a loss.

- Where the court is satisfied that circumstances have arisen whereby in the opinion of the court it is just and equitable to dissolve the partnership. This is a catch-all provision which allows the court to dissolve a partnership for some reason which has not been specifically covered in the Act. A good example is where the relationship between the partners has deteriorated to such an extent that agreement on dissolution is impossible.

Post-dissolution issues

[20.42] Following the decision to dissolve the partnership, either by agreement or otherwise, there follows a process of winding up the old partnership. This involves concluding its business affairs and distributing the property. Notifying the public of the dissolution is one important task, the method of which is outlined in the Act.[35]

Once the winding up process has commenced the remaining partners may bind the firm for any activities related to the winding up process including the completion of transactions that were unfinished at the time of dissolution.[36] This allows the completion of work that has commenced, the payment of employees, the paying off of all outstanding debts and the selling of the partnership property.

Distributing property

[20.43] On the dissolution of the partnership, the property of the partnership is used for the payment of partnership debts and obligations. The remaining surplus, if there is any, can then be claimed by the partners according to their share in the partnership. This will also apply to persons having a claim on the partnership assets through the partners, for example, where a partner owes money to a creditor, or the family of a deceased partner.[37]

---

35. NSW s 36, Vic s 40, Qld s 39, SA s 36 (and NT), WA s 47, Tas s 41, ACT s 41.
36. NSW s 34, Vic s 38, Qld s 37, SA s 34 (and NT), WA s 45, Tas s 39, ACT s 39.
37. NSW s 39, Vic s 43, Qld s 42, SA s 39 (and NT), WA s 50, Tas s 44, ACT s 45.

It is possible to 'charge' a partner's share of the partnership, which means that a creditor of an individual partner has either obtained a voluntary undertaking from the partner, or a court order, giving the creditor rights to any profits or profit eventuating from the partnership.[38]

Partners, or their representatives, have the right to apply to a court for the appointment of a receiver if they believe they will not receive their proper entitlement from the dissolution.

Partners still have a fiduciary duty to each other in the process of dissolving the partnership so that there is a proper valuation of the assets. Items such as the goodwill of the partnership may be difficult to estimate and there can be conflict amongst the partners should a member or members wish to continue on their own, or in a new partnership, and take advantage of the goodwill built up over time. The business name itself may contain elements of goodwill within the partnership, and this may cause difficulties when each of the partners wishes to use the former partnership name.

Sharing of profits after a dissolution of the partnership

[20.44]   If, following the departure of a partner, the surviving partners carry on the business without the agreement of the outgoing partner (or his or her estate), the outgoing partner or the estate is entitled to share in the profits made since the dissolution.[39]

Subject to any agreement made by the partners, the Act provides as follows in respect of the distribution of assets on a dissolution.[40]

1. Losses and deficiencies must first be paid from profits, then from the firm's capital and lastly from the partners individually. Each partner must contribute according to the proportion in which he or she shares profits.
2. The assets of the firm must be distributed in the following order:
   a) Payment of debts and liabilities on non-partners.
   b) Payment to each partner of money lent to the partnership, other than their capital contributions. This will be paid in proportion to their contribution if the funds are insufficient.
   c) Payment to each partner of his or her capital, or in proportion to their contributions if there is insufficient funds.
   d) Payment to each partner of the surplus in proportion to the agreed share of profits while the partnership was a going concern.

The rules of distribution are important and require that third parties who are owed money by the partnership must be paid first, even if that means being paid from the personal assets of the partners. The principle that the creditors must be paid first cannot be altered by any partnership agreement. Partners take only what is left over, and then in proportion to the agreed profit they were to receive, rather than the proportion of the capital they contributed. This further highlights the need for a formal partnership agreement.

Advantages of a partnership

[20.45]   The advantages of a partnership include:
* The pooling of resources and skills is a major advantage of the partnership form. Persons in the same, or even different occupations and professions, can join their skills,

38. NSW s 23, Vic s 27, Qld s 26, SA s 23 (and NT), WA s 28, Tas s 28, ACT s 28.
39. NSW s 42, Vic s 46, Qld s 45, SA s 42 (and NT), WA s 55, Tas s 47, ACT s 48.
40. NSW s 44, Vic s 48, Qld s 47, SA s 44 (and NT), WA s 57, Tas s 49, ACT s 50.

capital and property in some mutual enterprise. This allows for greater efficiency and potential profit.

- Formality is far less in the partnership form. There is no special regulation as exists with a company. A partnership can be less expensive since there are fewer steps in constructing a partnership and the costs of compliance are lower.
- Flexibility is promoted in the partnership form as there is a great deal of freedom in how the business conducts its affairs and determines the relations between partners. There is a greater degree of privacy as accounts do not have to be disclosed or audited, unless this is required by the professional body which governs its operation, such as the Law Society of each state, which requires that a solicitor's accounts be audited.
- Income splitting has made genuine partnerships a popular form of business organisation since tax is assessed on each individual partner's income.

Disadvantages of a partnership

[20.46]   The disadvantages of a partnership include:
- *Unlimited liability*   This means that the personal assets of the partners can be called upon to pay any liability which cannot be met from the resources of the partnership. While it is possible for partners to limit or have an unequal liability for partnership debt, this is an internal arrangement only and creditors can still sue any partner for outstanding debts. For example, one partner may be liable for another's negligence if the liability was incurred in the partnership business.
- The limit of 20 members on a partnership, unless it falls under one of the exceptions in s 112 of the Corporations Law, could be a disadvantage because there is less access to capital as the limit is reached.
- Partners are not separate from the partnership. This means that, unlike the situation of a company, a partner cannot be employed by the partnership and cannot obtain the benefits of an employee.
- Partners are liable for any debts or liabilities incurred during their time as a partner so that, even after a partner has left the partnership, personal property can be called upon to satisfy the partner's share of partnership debt.
- If there is a breakdown in relations between partners an application to the court might be necessary to dissolve a partnership if partners are locked into an agreement which does not provide a dissolution procedure.
- Partners cannot transfer their share of the partnership, by sale or otherwise, unless the other partners agree. This could lock a person into a relationship which is bitter and non-productive.
- The intimacy of a partnership and the agency relationship mean that partners must rely on each other to a marked degree. The negligence of one partner can be paid for by a partner who was completely unconnected with the negligent conduct. A partnership is not a relationship to be entered lightly.

Joint ventures

[20.47] A joint venture is an arrangement where separate business entities conduct a combined project or venture, sharing the resulting product, not as a business in common, but as independent operators in their own right. The definition of a joint venture is found in common law, unlike the definition of a partnership which is determined by statutory rules. Determining whether a business relationship is a joint venture, or some other relationship, is crucial when considering the liability of members for each other's actions.

The use of joint ventures

[20.48] A joint venture arrangement may be used for projects where a single party does not have capital, expertise or a licence to undertake a particular project. It might be conducted for an entertainment event, where one party conducts the publicity, another stages the event, and a third independent member provides finance. Other projects might include mining, research and development, manufacturing and housing development.

A joint venture can be an association of entities in any number of business combinations, such as two companies combining for a project, or perhaps two sole traders. Sometimes the government enters into a joint venture agreement with a business to encourage a project.

Characteristics of the joint venture

[20.49] Normally the parties would own their assets separately, with no common sharing of resources, unless specifically agreed otherwise. For example, a joint venture of miners and a petroleum company may have the miners owning their own rigs, while the petroleum company owns its tankers. Each of the parties would be responsible for their own employees and creditors, and would conduct their share of the business independently. Mutual assets might consist only of an office for which all are responsible. Accounts, contracts and the conduct of the venture would indicate very little mutuality.

Defining a joint venture

[20.50] Defining a joint venture and distinguishing it from a partnership is very difficult. In *United Dominions Corp Ltd v Brian Pty Ltd* (1985) 157 CLR 11 per Mason, Brennan and Deane JJ the High Court stated that a joint venture may also be a partnership, in circumstances where 'the joint venture takes the form of a partnership'. In the same case the judges stated that the term '"joint venture" … is not a technical one with a settled common law meaning'. There is no fixed definition of a joint venture in statute, only the occasional reference such as in the Trade Practices Act 1974 (Cth).

Section 4 of that Act describes it in the following terms:

(a) a reference to a joint venture is a reference to an activity in trade or commerce —
(i) carried on jointly by two or more persons, whether or not in partnership; or
(ii) carried on by a body corporate formed by two or more persons for the purpose of enabling those person to carry on that activity jointly by means of their joint control, or by means of the ownership of shares in the capital, of that body corporate;

A further definitional complication arises from the fact that a joint venture may still be construed as a partnership for tax purposes, irrespective of what the parties may have called themselves: see *Tikva Investments Pty Ltd v Federal Commissioner of Taxation* (1972) 128 CLR 158.

A possible definition is that a joint venture is an arrangement or contract where two or more parties enter an agreement to contribute to a specific project, where they have respective shares without forming a partnership. Each party contributes some skill or property, not necessarily of the same type, for the purposes of joint profit without binding their joint venturers as principals or agents, unless each has expressly agreed to do so.

In the *United Dominions* case, Mason, Brennan and Deane JJ, defined a joint venture as:

> ... [connoting] an association of persons for the purposes of a particular trading, commercial, mining or other financial undertaking or endeavour with a view to mutual profit, with each participant usually (but not necessarily) contributing money, property or skill.

In the same case, Dawson J suggested that a joint venture was more like an association of people who engage in an enterprise, to produce a product which will be shared amongst the participants, whereas a partnership was more like a common adventure where the outcome is profit sharing rather product sharing.

Case Example

Two farmers with adjoining farms agreed to repair a fence running between their properties. One farmer used the other's tractor and employee to do some work on the fence but was severely injured. The injured farmer then tried to show that he was working for his neighbour, so that he could claim worker's compensation which existed at that time under state legislation. The court refused the injured farmer's argument that there was an employee relationship. The court found the relationship was one of a contract, or joint venture relationship, the two parties retaining their separate existence. Neither party had control of the other like that of an employer to employee relationship: *Pursell v Newberry* [1967] 2 NSWR 305.

Distinguishing a joint venture and a partnership

[20.51]   Distinguishing a joint venture and a partnership is not merely a matter of describing the arrangement as a joint venture. The courts, in assessing whether a joint venture exists, will examine all the arrangements between the parties — the documentation as well as how the parties view themselves.

Problems can arise both between the parties or between the joint venture and a third party. Sometimes a third party will seek to prove that the parties are more like a partnership than a joint venture, so they can sue all parties for joint liability. Alternatively, disputes can arise between the parties on what basis they share the end product, or because one party attempts to push liability onto another party.

While parties may view their relationship as a joint venture it may, on an examination of the facts, be construed to be a partnership. In *Canny Gabriel Castle Jackson Advertising Pty Ltd v Volume Sales (Finance) Pty Ltd* (1974) 131 CLR 321 the parties referred to each other as joint venturers in the contract, one providing finance and the other providing management. A dispute arose as to sharing of profits. The court construed the relationship to be a partnership, despite the evidence of what the parties called themselves. The court found that it was a commercial enterprise designed to share profits, differences of opinion were to be settled by arbitration and the degree of mutuality showed there was a partnership.

Case Example

United Dominions, Security Projects and Brian were involved in developing land for the construction of a shopping centre. The land was owned by Security Projects. Before the formal agreement setting out each party's responsibilities had been drawn up, United and Security Projects, without the knowledge of Brian, organised a mortgage to cover loans made between themselves and used the land as security for loans of the joint venture, as well as for any individual borrowing they undertook. These arrangements were set down in 'collaterisation' clauses unbeknownst to Brian. Eventually the development was sold at a substantial profit and Brian received nothing. The parties claimed they could use the 'collaterisation' clauses to take profits from the sale of the shopping centre to the exclusion of Brian.

The court found, however, that the parties had acted contrary to their fiduciary duty to Brian. The arrangement was in essence a partnership despite its being described as a joint venture. Importantly, in this case the court found that there was a fiduciary relationship between the parties in the form of a relationship of mutual obligations of trust, even though a formal agreement had not been reached. The implications were, therefore, that even if no agreement was ever signed, or even if there was not a partnership expressed, the two parties had not disclosed necessary information or been proper in their dealings with Brian which was therefore able to take a share of the profits: *United Dominions Corp Ltd v Brian Pty Ltd* (1985) 157 CLR 1.

The differences between a joint venture and a partnership

[20.52]   The differences between a joint venture and partnership are:
- Each joint venturer receives a predetermined share of the produce of the enterprise, possibly a physical product which they dispose of as they wish.
- Joint venturers are not subject to the Partnership Act which determines obligations and rights between the parties.
- Joint venturers are able to sell their share in an enterprise to another venturer, or even liquidate their share, subject to a joint venture agreement.
- Each joint venturer is responsible for its own debts, obligations and liabilities, so that an individual creditor or worker would sue a particular joint venturer rather than the group.
- Joint venturers normally have little common property between them.
- Joint venturers have limited fiduciary obligations between each other, except for those set by contract or by the courts.

Why choose a joint venture?

[20.53] A joint venture may be a favoured business organisation for the following reasons:

- Joint venturers can conduct their own businesses separately from the other parties associated in the venture. This would not be possible if they were partners because it could be in breach of the partners' obligations to each other.
- Each joint venturer is able to make separate tax arrangements in respect of depreciation, negative gearing and interest payments. Similarly, capital raising can be quite separate between venturers, one party issuing equity while another borrows.
- Each joint venturer is individually responsible for its own actions and not for those of its joint venturers. One venturer cannot pledge the credit of another.
- Each joint venturer can keep secret its own affairs and does not have to disclose its profits and accounting arrangements as would a partner. There are fewer fiduciary obligations existing between the parties than in a partnership.
- A joint venture arrangement is relatively easy to set up, it can be a very flexible arrangement according to the wishes of the parties and no agreement needs to be registered.
- The joint venturers have the benefit of a contractual relationship and duties of trust between each other: for example, not making secret profits, nor defrauding the other.
- A joint venture is not subject to any specific regulation or statute, other than those which affect each individual member.

Summary

[20.54] Careful planning will minimise potential legal difficulties which characterise ad hoc joint ventures. The joint venturers should carefully plan their relationship in a joint venture agreement. There should be an agreement which specifically states the relationship as a joint venture. There needs to be a specification of contributions of property, what, if any, is common property, and how property will be disposed of. Other contractual terms which might relate to the conduct of the joint venturers are resolution of disputes, winding up of the joint venture and the sharing of income resulting from the venture property. The agreement should demonstrate a minimum of mutuality.

Syndicates

Definition

[20.55] The business arrangement known as a syndicate is similar to that of a joint venture. Syndicate members do not have a fiduciary relationship or any mutuality, nor do they accept liability for each other, as in a partnership.

A syndicate is a combination of persons who have become associated for the purpose of promoting some business enterprise. A syndicate is a relationship where the parties have fewer mutual or common interests than those existing between joint venturers. A syndicate could further be described as a loose collection of separate entities, with an interest in the end product of the enterprise, but with less mutuality amongst the members than a joint venture. A syndicate may be formed to ensure that profits made are shared in appropriate ways. There is a fine line between partnerships, joint ventures and syndicates and the difference will be a question of fact.

Case Example

Nine people formed a syndicate and purchased a submarine. The syndicate intended to renovate the vessel and make profits from the sale of tickets to the public who could inspect the ship. There was an arrangement with the Port Jackson and Manly Steamship Co, which owned a wharf, where the submarine was to be moored. The syndicate had an agreement whereby the public would be allowed to use the wharf, in exchange for a share of profits from the sale of tickets.

A storm broke out and the company owning the wharf arranged with a tug boat company to tow the submarine away from the wharf, so that neither the wharf nor the submarine would be damaged. During the towing operation the submarine was damaged and it could no longer be used as a business proposition.

The syndicate which owned the submarine then sued the Steamship Company for the loss of its property under trespass and negligence. The Steamship Co then tried to show that there was a partnership between themselves and the syndicate, so that the syndicate was not entitled to sue them as a fellow partner. The Steamship Co relied on the agreement which referred to the parties variously as 'agent' and 'venturers' and the company was to act at its discretion on behalf of itself and as an agent for the owners of the submarine. The Steamship Co pointed to the existence of a sharing of profits between the parties as proof of a partnership.

The court examined the intentions of the parties and stated that:

> ... the parties sought to avoid creation of a partnership, and, in particular, to prevent any authority from arising in the syndicate or its members to pledge the credit of the Steamship Co or the creation of any liability in the Steamship Co to third parties.

The court said there was not a partnership. Since the agreement between the parties was construed to be an attempt to avoid the creation of a partnership, the syndicate had no power to pledge credit for the other party like a partnership, there was a fixed percentage sharing of profits and the Steamship Co acted like an agent with reference to itself as a venture so that the agreement was more like a licence to use the wharf property: *Beckingham v The Port Jackson & Manly Steamship Co* (1957) 57 SR (NSW) 403.

[20.56]   The decision in *Beckingham v The Port Jackson & Manly Steamship Co* did not resolve the problem of what exactly a syndicate is but, rather, it suggested that a syndicate is probably a relationship existing between parties where there is little mutuality or very separate business interests.

A syndicate would be construed as a partnership for tax purposes because taxation law has its own definition of partnership which would catch a joint venture.

Associations

[20.57]   At common law an association is a body of two or more persons who form an organisation, whether for the purposes of profit or not. If the association shares the profit amongst its members, it may fall within the definition of a partnership and be subject to that body of law. There are two types of association — the unincorporated association and the incorporated association — and, although they are not vehicles for conducting business, they are relevant because business entities are parties to transactions with them.

Unincorporated associations

[20.58]   An unincorporated association is a collection of individuals who form an association for some common objective, usually as a club or society. The association is not required to register under statute law, and is not subject to any specific regulation.

The unincorporated association has no legal existence and in the absence of regulation the law is not clear about who will be liable for the debts and liabilities of this organisation. The association's committee may be held liable for any debts incurred by the association, since it is not a legal entity recognised by law: *Bradley Egg Farm v Clifford* [1943] 2 All ER 378; *Peckham v Moore* [1975] 1 NSWLR 353. The law is, however, clear about the fact that an unincorporated association cannot own property in its own name — that is done through trustees. Nor can it receive gifts in its own name.

Incorporated associations

[20.59]   An incorporated association is an association which has incorporated under legislation available in each state for members of clubs, societies and other groups wishing to avoid the risk of personal liability. Incorporated associations are not as expensive to run, nor so highly regulated, as a corporation. Certain bodies cannot incorporate, such as unions and cooperatives.

An incorporated association must have a minimum of five members and must register with the appropriate government agency, usually with an undertaking as to its constitution and internal workings. The incorporation creates a separate legal entity from its members, which allows it to hold money, employ people, sue and be sued. It has limited liability which means that individual members are not liable for the association's debts, beyond their outstanding membership fees. The incorporated association can 'trade' by selling goods and raising money, provided it does not distribute profits in the form of dividends to its members. An incorporated association has particular rules under which it must operate, such as not trading while insolvent, holding public liability insurance and being audited if its revenue is over a certain amount. An incorporated association has the abbreviation 'Inc' at the end of its name to indicate its status.

Relevant legislation

Jurisdiction	Legislation
New South Wales	Associations Incorporation Act 1984
Victoria	Associations Incorporation Act 1981
Queensland	Associations Incorporation Act 1981

Jurisdiction	Legislation
South Australia	Associations Incorporation Act 1985
Western Australia	Associations Incorporation Act 1987
Tasmania	Associations Incorporation Act 1964
Australian Capital Territory	Associations Incorporation Act 1991
Northern Territory	Associations Incorporation Act 1963

Trading trusts

[20.60] Another form of business arrangement is by way of a trading trust. It is not a separate legal entity as it relies on the relationship of a trust which, like a partnership, has no legal existence. The most significant driving force behind the creation of trading trusts was originally taxation. Conducting a business by way of a trading trust offered tax advantages over the use of a company. The reform of corporate taxation has, however, made trading trusts less attractive. Using a trading trust can allow a business to avoid some of the regulation associated with a company.

Structure of a trading trust

[20.61] In essence, the trading trust involves the assets of a business being put into a trust and then being used to operate the business. A common use of the trading trust was for a sole proprietor to transfer the business into the trust. The trustee is usually a corporation and the typical beneficiaries are the members of a family. The income generated by the business is distributed to a wider group of persons and usually the trust is discretionary, which allows the trustee to distribute income in a manner most advantageous for tax. The use of a corporate trustee means that the business is able to operate under conditions of limited liability. The beneficiaries of the trust will not be liable for the debts of the business unless they indemnify the trustee. If, however, the trustee is a corporation and is not indemnified by the beneficiaries, the creditors can look only to the corporate trustee. The Corporations Law protects creditors to some extent from corporate trustees which seek to take advantage of the corporate form at their expense: s 233.

Ownership of the business assets is vested in the trustee company of which the original proprietor is usually a director and retains control. From a taxation point of view it is important for the former proprietor to recognise that circumstances have changed. To act as if the trading trust did not exist could lead to a decision by the Australian Taxation Office that the trust was a sham with the result that taxation benefits are lost.

Unit trusts

[20.62] Unit trusts are trading trusts whereby individuals pool their capital and divide the ownership of it into units: for example, capital of $100 can be divided into 10 units of $10 each, with investors holding differing numbers of units. A manager is appointed to invest the capital into shares, bullion, futures, mortgages or real estate and to pay a dividend to the unit holders. The manager is appointed by the trustee, which is usually incorporated, and the business operates under a trust deed which is a type of contract.

Unit trusts can be private or public — public unit trusts can be listed and units traded on the stock exchange. Public unit trusts are subject to regulation, they are taxed as companies and must prepare a prospectus if they offer units publicly.

The use of unit trusts has grown in Australia, despite some spectacular losses in real estate trusts. Unit trusts have the advantage of allowing small investors to pool their capital in diversified undertakings, thereby spreading the risk of the investment. Unit holders have direct ownership of the property of the trust and can readily sell the units they hold. Units rise and fall in value according to how well the investment is doing, and of course how good their manager is. Unit holders have no mutuality and are separate from each other in all respects.

Summary and key terms

[20.63]   This chapter has set out to explain:
- The legal significance of operating a business in a particular, *non-incorporated* way.
- What the legal consequences are for a *sole trader*.
- How a partnership works:
  - what a partnership is;
  - how a partnership is *formed*;
  - the significance of the *partnership agreement* and the Partnership Act;
  - why knowing that a partnership exists matters;
  - what it means to be a partner;
  - the *unlimited liabilities* of partners;
  - the *fiduciary relationship* between partners;
  - the *rights of persons* dealing with the partnership;
  - how a partnership comes to an end; and
  - *advantages and disadvantages* of partnership.
- Limited liability partnerships.
- Joint ventures — their legal implications and how they differ from partnerships.
- Syndicates — their legal significance.
- How trading trusts are structured.
- What unit trusts are.

21

Trusts

What this chapter does ...

Trusts are an ancient means of transferring property from an owner to a trustee, who then holds, maintains and manages that property for the ultimate benefit of a beneficiary. Trust relationships can arise expressly, impliedly or by force of law and are used extensively as a vehicle for business.

This chapter explains the concept of a trust, the different types of trusts which can be constructed, the relationship between the different parties to a trust and its use in business in such forms as a unit trust.

Defining a trust

[21.1] Trust law has its origins in equity law which developed in the medieval Court of Chancery, and is characteristically distinct from common law or case law. Equity is based on the principles developed by the Lord Chancellor's court of the exchequer and is more a set of rules than case references.

Trusts are composed basically of three parties: the settlor, the trustee and the beneficiary (or beneficiaries). The settlor creates the trust by providing property of some type to the trustee, who then holds that property and later pays income, or passes part or all of the property, to those designated to benefit from the trust who are known as beneficiaries.

A trust may be defined as an equitable obligation which rests upon a person (called the trustee) who is personally responsible to deal with specified property (called the trust property) for the benefit of another person or persons (known as the beneficiary or beneficiaries *cestui que trust*) or for a specific purpose, for example, the Lost Dogs Home. A beneficiary has an equitable interest which is a right or claim which is not the same as legal ownership. The beneficiaries have the right to enforce the trust.

The trustee becomes the legal owner of the property and is personally responsible for any liabilities, such as taxes, which might accrue against the property: *Federal Commissioner of Taxation v Whiting* (1943) 68 CLR 199. The trustee is always liable for property in a trust because it has no separate entity from trust property; that is why some trusts are limited liability companies who appoint a manager for running the day-to-day business of a trust.

Trusts may be created deliberately, such as through a will (testamentary trust), or the writing up of a trust deed, but can sometimes arise by force of law or by an accident whereby someone finds themselves holding property as a trustee for another.

While a trust must have three different parties (except for charitable trusts), a person may occupy a number of roles: a settlor may name himself or herself as the trustee and also as one of the beneficiaries; however, the settlor cannot be the only beneficiary. Each role in a trust has a different legal status and particular rights and obligations.

Different types of trusts

Express trusts

[21.2] An express trust is a trust which is created deliberately and demonstrates, usually in writing, an intention to create a trust. Express trusts include family trusts, trading trusts, unit trusts, retirement trusts and discretionary trusts. A trading trust, for instance, is a trust which carries on a business — it is expressly created, normally by a deed, giving the trustee a great deal of discretion; for example, to manage a family or unit trust.

Different express trusts

[21.3]   Express trusts may be used in the business world, by families or benefactors wishing to leave property to some class of person or institution. Each trust will be different since they are created for a variety of purposes, which must be assessed by terms or instructions placed in the trust deed by which moneys will be given to a beneficiary.
Discretionary trust   This is a trust which expressly allows the beneficiaries to be chosen at the discretion of trustee. Of course the trust deed may specify the categories or types of persons: for example, it could be to provide scholarships for needy students or perhaps art works for the state art gallery. The trust should specify how the discretion will be exercised, who should exercise it and amounts of money that should be allocated. Normally discretionary trusts will also have a date by which the property will move from the trustee to a specified person. This is because there is a rule against remoteness of vesting — a trust cannot continue forever.

Unit trusts

[21.4]   Unit trusts are trading trusts run through a trust arrangement. A trustee, normally an incorporated company, appoints a manager to receive funds from investors/unit holders who are the settlors under the arrangement. The trustee operates under a trust deed, usually with a lot discretion, whereby they purchase shares, property or bullion according to the terms of the trust and then pay back dividends to unit holders in the capacity of beneficiaries. Unit holders have an equitable interest in the trust assets and have certain rights not available to shareholders of a company: see Chapter 20.

Superannuation trusts

[21.5]   Some superannuation schemes operate under a trust system. The trust is expressly created and designates the various parties, the trustee/s and the trust property to be managed and ultimately distributed. Superannuation schemes are highly regulated by law, whether in a trust or not, and receive certain taxation advantages.

Family trusts

[21.6]   A family may create a trust whereby a business is transferred to a trust, usually with the trust deed expressly giving control to a parent as trustee to manage the business. This arrangement allows for splitting the trust income between different family members, thereby minimising taxation. Taxation law has intervened to make some trust minimisation schemes unattractive.

Charitable trusts

[21.7]   A trust for a charitable purpose may receive preferential tax treatment where it qualifies as having a recognised charitable purpose in promoting education, religion or some other beneficial purpose to society at large: *Commissioners for Special Purposes of Income Tax v Pemsel* [1891] AC 531.

Trusts arising by operation of the law

[21.8]   A trust arising by force of law is an implied or presumptive trust because it is created by circumstances or an arrangement whereby a trust relationship is inferred. This can also be called a resulting trust. An example of an implied trust is where a purchaser of property such as shares or land directs that it be held by another on their behalf — there is then a presumption that the property is held in trust for the settlor: *Calverley v Green* (1984) 155 CLR 242; 56 ALR 483.

Another implied trust is a constructive trust which arises under circumstances whereby it would be unfair to allow the legal owner of the property not to recognise another's interest, even though that person is not registered as an owner. Examples of constructive trusts might be where a couple in a de facto relationship purchase property and begin to pay it off; if only one of the parties is the registered owner it would be unjust enrichment for the registered owner to exclude the other: *Stephenson Nominees Pty Ltd v Official Receiver in Bankruptcy* (1987) 76 ALR 485.

Constructive trusts may arise where, for instance, a joint tenant kills the co-owner of property and then assumes total ownership as the survivor. The law construes in such a case that the survivor must hold that property on trust for the deceased's beneficiaries: *Rasmanis v Jurewitsch* [1970] 1 NSWR 650. Similarly, where an employee receives moneys which should be passed to an employer, then there is an implied trust, construed by law, that the employee holds this on behalf of the employer.

Creation of express trusts

Private (non-charitable) trusts

[21.9]   The creation of a private express trust requires what are called 'the three certainties':

*   *Certainty of intention to create a trust*   This may be an issue where there was only preparation or a desire, rather than an actual intention to create a trust which is judged by the words used.
*   *Certainty of subject matter*   The subject matter of the trust must be described with sufficient certainty.
*   *Certainty of object*   The beneficiaries must be identifiable according to the class or criteria set by the trust: *McPhail v Doulton* [1971] AC 424; [1970] 2 All ER 228.

The rules regarding private express trusts can be somewhat unclear; for instance, in *Bacon v Pianta* (1966) 114 CLR 634 the High Court struck down a trust which gave property to the Communist Party of Australia, an unincorporated body with a shifting membership, making the trust uncertain as far as the beneficiaries were concerned.

An interesting variation of trusts is found in a *Quistclose* trust which was formulated by the courts in *Barclays Bank Ltd v Quistclose Investments Ltd* [1970] AC 567 and accepted into Australian law in *Australasian Conference Association Ltd v Mainline Constructions Pty Ltd (in liq)* (1979) 141 CLR 335; 22 ALR 1. A Quistclose trust arises when money is paid to another for a specific purpose — if that purpose fails then a resulting trust is created and the money is held in trust for the settlor.

There are a number of rules regarding the construction and creation of trusts:

- if land is the subject matter of a trust, then the trust must be in writing;[1]
- wills must be in writing, which means if land is to be settled it must comply with the rule of writing, the only exemption being a fully secret trust — one where the beneficiary takes property but for the benefit of someone else. A half secret trust is one which the beneficiary takes for another, but does not say for whom;
- rule against perpetuity or remoteness of vesting. Property in a trust must vest with a beneficiary within 80 or 21 years from the death of the settlor.[2] Vesting is defined as the person entitled to take the property. If the rule against perpetuities is contravened, then the gift is void.

Charitable trusts

[21.10] Charitable trusts do not require the same certainty as to the object of the trust as do other trusts. It is sufficient that the settlor intends that a charity benefit from the trust without having to specify a particular charity. If necessary, a court will approve a charity under the *cy-pres* (approximate) doctrine. However, some jurisdictions will not allow a trust to have both charitable and non-charitable purposes, except New South Wales, Victoria, Queensland and Western Australia.[3]

The rules regarding charitable trusts are more relaxed — for instance, the rule against perpetual duration of trusts does not apply, nor does the presumption of resulting trust. While courts have general jurisdiction over trusts, it is the Attorney-General of each state who has the duty of ensuring that a charitable trust performs its objectives, where this is necessary, particularly where the object has not been defined.

Changing or ending a trust

[21.11] A trust deed may make a provision for a change to the trust, but changes are normally only carried out by courts. The power of courts differs between states: for example, in Queensland, Victoria, South Australia and Western Australia[4] the courts can change the administration or management of a trust but not the beneficial interest. In New South Wales a court can change the rights of a beneficiary where that is expedient,[5] in Tasmania the court can change the administrative arrangements for a trust, but not the interests of a beneficiary.[6]

---

1. Statute of Frauds legislation: Conveyancing Act 1919 (NSW) s 23C; Property Law Act 1974 (Qld) s 11; Property Law Act 1958 (Vic) s 53; Law of Property Act 1936 (SA) s 29; Property Law Act 1969 (WA) s 34; Conveyancing and Law of Property Act 1884 (Tas) s 60(2).
2. Perpetuities and Accumulations Act 1985 (ACT); Perpetuities Act 1984 (NSW); Perpetuities Act 1984 (NT); Property Law Act 1974 (Qld) Pt XIV; Perpetuities and Accumulation Act 1992 (Tas); Perpetuities and Accumulations Act 1968 (Vic); Property Law Act 1969 (WA) Pt XI.
3. Conveyancing Act 1919 (NSW) s 37D; Property Law Act 1958 (Vic) s 131; Trusts Act 1973 (Qld) s 104; Trustees Act 1962 (WA) s 102.
4. Trusts Act 1973 (Qld) s 94; Trustee Act 1958 (Vic) s 63A; Trustee Act 1925 (NSW) s 59C; Trustees Act 1962 (WA) s 90.
5. Conveyancing Act 1919 (NSW) s 81.
6. Conveyancing and Law of Property Act 1884 (Tas) s 47.

A settlor can end a trust only on the grounds that the trust deed allows this, or if there has been misrepresentation, undue influence or mistake. The beneficiaries to a trust may end the trust by calling on the trustee to transfer the property to them, thereby ending the trust. To demand a transfer a beneficiary must be of a majority age (legally an adult), with legal capacity and have full interest in the property (vested interest): *Saunders v Vautier* (1841) 4 Beav 115; 49 ER 282. If some of the beneficiaries are not of a sufficient age, then as long as the trust property can be divided up, there can be a distribution to those eligible provided it does not prejudice those not yet eligible: *Whakatone Paper Mills Ltd v Public Trustee* (1939) 39 SR (NSW) 426.

The ending of a trust may also occur because the trust property has been fully distributed, or has been wound up for bankruptcy. A trust may be ended where the property of the trust is part of a settlement in a divorce.[7] A trust may end where it has an illegal or immoral purpose. Note also the rule of perpetuities may cause a trust to end.

Revocation, voidness and rectification

[21.12]   A trust is only revocable (able to be cancelled) if the trust deed contains the power of revocation. However, if the trust was created by fraud or undue influence, then it may be voidable and revoked by the settlor. A voidable trust has some legal defect, and is distinct from a void trust which has no legal basis because of illegality, or because it contravenes the rule against perpetuities. A trust will not usually be void for mistake, since it is created by only one person, unless the trust was a type of contract between the settlor and the beneficiary" whereby it can be rectified by a court as if a contract.

In some circumstances a court can correct a trust on the request of a settlor (or a beneficiary if not contrary to the wishes of the settlor): *Re Butlin's Settlement Trusts* [1976] Ch 251.

Trustees

[21.13]   All state jurisdictions have legislation regarding trustees, including their appointment, duties, powers and removal. A trustee is not the same as an administrator or executor (personal representative) of an estate, though they may occupy both legal positions; that is, be originally appointed as an executor and later become a trustee as well. The distinction is important since an executor must within a year distribute property, thereby completing his or her duties, whereas a trustee holds property in trust for a beneficiary. An executor would have wide powers to settle debts in the estate, whereas the trustee would not normally pay a settlor's debts and would not have the same discretion in dealing with assets as an executor.

Appointing a trustee

[21.14]   Generally any legal person, including a natural person or corporation, can be appointed as trustee. In all states except South Australia and Tasmania, there is a limit of four persons to be appointed to a single trust. A trustee would not normally be an infant,

---

7. Family Law Act 1975 (Cth) s 85.

though, with the exception of New South Wales, the appointment of an infant is automatically void.

Appointment usually takes place by the settlor under the trust deed, though an appointment could be made by someone with the authority to exercise a power of appointment, perhaps given through a statute. An appointee can refuse to accept an appointment (disclaim), which will require a replacement trustee since the rules of equity will not allow a trust to fail for lack of a trustee — a court will then appoint a trustee.[8] Similar provisions under the Trustee Acts will apply to replace or substitute trustees who have died or are absent, unless this is unnecessary due to there being more than one trustee.

Duties of a trustee

[21.15]   The trustee has a fiduciary relationship with the beneficiary, which is a duty of trust and care while acting always in good faith on behalf of the beneficiary. A duty of general good faith is found in equity law, but other duties may be imposed by the trust instrument itself, by general law or statute. A trustee's duties include:

* gathering the assets of the trust, ascertaining the whereabouts of all assets and taking possession;
* complying with the terms of the trust deed in carrying out the provisions of the trust. Except by permission of a court, a trustee should not delegate important tasks, particularly where decision-making is required. A trustee must exercise his or her own judgment and resist pressure from beneficiaries (*Re Brockbank* [1948] Ch 206), and must not fetter or limit his or her discretion under the trust;
* completing all duties personally, in good faith. As a fiduciary, a trustee must not make profits from that office and can only receive remuneration where this is provided for in the trust deed, or by a court, or by the adult beneficiaries or any other proper means. A trustee must not self-deal, that is, engage in transactions as trustee to himself or herself beneficially, or else that dealing will be voided, despite any good intention by the trustee: *Re Thompson's Settlement* [1986] Ch 99;
* maintaining and caring for trust property — including its repair, seeking good advice, taking out insurance;
* keeping accounts and informing beneficiaries of matters relating to trust property;
* acting impartially between beneficiaries.

Powers of trustees

[21.16]   A trustee has power to act according to statutes relating to trusts, the trust deed and by the court (in its power to change the administration of the trust).[9] Powers given by the trust deed are express and implied. Express powers are the terms of the trust deed, while implied terms are those which are necessary to carry out the terms of the trust deed; for example, a direction to keep accounts will imply the need to employ an accountant.

Legislation in each of the jurisdictions will also give the trustee certain powers, including the power:

* to invest in the type of securities stipulated by statute;

8. Trusts Act 1973 (Qld) s 80; Trustee Act 1958 (Vic) s 48; Trustee Act 1925 (NSW) s 70; Trustees Act 1962 (WA) s 77; Trustee Act 1936 (SA) s 36; Trustee Act 1898 (Tas) s 32.
9. Trusts Act 1973 (Qld) s 94; Trustee Act 1958 (Vic) s 63A; Trustee Act 1936 (SA) s 59c; Trustees Act 1962 (WA) s 90.

- to apply to the court for directions if clarification of trust terms is needed;
- to sell property if the property needs to be converted for use by the beneficiaries;
- to mortgage the trust property (as long as the trust deed permits this);
- to insure property;
- to delegate certain functions where necessary;
- to provide receipts for obligations given on behalf of the trust;
- to settle debts, accepting less than the full amount where this is appropriate;
- of maintenance and advancement — this allows a trustee to pay an infant beneficiary, or his or her guardian, part or all of the trust income or property, where this is for the infant's advancement in life. This would allow for support, education and training of a child as the beneficiary of a trust.

Ending a trusteeship

[21.17]   Courts have the power under equity law to remove a trustee, if this is required in the best interests of the trust. Retirement of a trustee is possible under the terms of the trust deed, or under statutory rules of the jurisdiction. Normally, for a trustee to retire, he or she must have the permission of the beneficiaries, or the ability under the terms of the trust deed to do this. A trusteeship will be ended on the death, retirement or removal of a trustee. The trustee will end his or her appointment when that trustee has completed all that was necessary under the trust deed — where all property has been distributed. A trustee's appointment may come to an end when the beneficiaries, being of an adult age (*sui juris*), agree to remove the trustee (*Saunders v Vautier* (1841) 4 Beav 115; 49 ER 282), in which case the trustee may ask for a release and indemnity from the beneficiaries.

Rights and liabilities of trustees and beneficiaries

Breach of trust

[21.18]   A trustee who does not carry out his or her duty commits a breach of trust. Examples of breaches would include a lack of diligence or non-compliance with the terms of the trust deed. A breach of trust will require the trustee to pay compensation to put the trust back in the position it was in prior to the breach: *Hagan v Waterhouse* (1992) 34 NSWLR 308. A trustee will be liable for his or her own breaches, unless that trustee has contributed or caused another trustee to breach the trust, or was aware of another trustee's breach and did not act. Trustees who together breach the trust have joint and several liability, which means that a beneficiary can sue trustees individually or together. A breach by a trustee may be relieved by statute where the trustee acted honestly and reasonably.[10]

Trustees have unlimited personal liability to third parties dealing with the trust, unless they specifically limit their liability with that other party by contract.

---

10. Trusts Act 1973 (Qld) s 76; Trustee Act 1958 (Vic) s 36; Trustee Act 1925 (NSW) s 85; Trustees Act 1962 (WA) s 75; Trustee Act 1893 (NT) s 26; Trustee Act 1936 (SA) s 56; Trustee Act 1898 (Tas) s 50.

Rights of trustees

[21.19] A trustee, under both common law and the various state Trustee Acts, has the right to be reimbursed for expenses incurred in carrying out duties related to the trust, and an indemnity from any debts and liabilities incurred on behalf of the trust. A trustee can use trust property to pay for obligations incurred on behalf of the trust, unless the terms of the trust dictate otherwise. A trust may be able to seek reimbursement from a beneficiary who is *sui juris* (of full legal capacity) and who is entitled to the trust property: *Hardoon v Belilios* [1901] AC 118 (except a beneficiary of a discretionary trust). If a trustee carries on business as authorised by the trust deed, then, even though that trustee is personally liable, he or she can seek reimbursement from the trust. If, however, the trustee carries on business for the trust without authorisation, then he or she cannot claim an indemnity from the trust. Note that creditors may be able to make a claim on the trust assets through the doctrine of *subrogation*, which means creditors can claim through the trustees' right of reimbursement (stand in his shoes): *Vacuum Oil Co Pty Ltd v Wiltshire* (1945) 72 CLR 319.

If trustees are found jointly liable for a breach of trust, and one of the trustees has paid for the restitution to the trust, then that trustee can seek a contribution from the other trustee/s (*Babin v Hughes* (1886) 31 Ch D 390), as long as the trustee seeking reimbursement did not benefit by his or her breach or intent to breach the trust.

Rights of beneficiaries

[21.20] Beneficiaries have a number of rights:
- Beneficiaries can terminate the trust if all the beneficiaries being of *sui juris* agree: *Saunders v Vautier* (1841) 4 Beav 115; 49 ER 282.
- Beneficiaries can compel performance of the trust by court order or prevent a breach of trust with an injunction. Note that beneficiaries in a discretionary trust who cannot be conclusively identified, only have a right to be considered in regards to trust property and cannot seek court orders over the administration of the trust property.
- Beneficiaries are entitled to information and to inspect trust documents (*O'Rourke v Dabishire* [1920] AC 581; [1970] All ER Rep 1), unless the information is the trustee's personal correspondence or advice on the trust: *Re Londonderry's Settlements; Peat v Walsh* [1965] Ch 918.
- Beneficiaries will lose their right of action against the trustee if they have consented to a breach of trust or contributed to that breach. Beneficiaries have the right to release the trustee from liability as long as they are *sui juris*, understand their legal rights and are not subject to undue influence;
- Beneficiaries have rights to recover, or *trace*, any trust property in which they have an interest, unless the holder is a purchaser who gave good value for the property and had no notice of another's interest: *Re Montagu's Settlement Trusts* [1987] Ch 264; [1987] 2 WLR 1192; [1992] 4 All ER 308. The right of recovery by the beneficiary remains, even where the property has been converted by the trustee.

Trustee companies

[21.21]   Trustee companies are companies licensed by statute to charge a fee as trustees, executors and administrators, particularly of wills and deceased estates.[11] Trustee companies, who have been appointed under statute, can advertise their services, which extend beyond the mere role of trustee which any corporation can be formed to undertake.

The Public Trustee

[21.22]   The Public Trustee is a trustee company created by legislation in all Australian states.[12] The Public Trustee performs a number of public functions, including drafting of wills for people appointed as an executor and acting as trustee of property in cases of incapacity, imprisonment or where a property owner has died without appointing an executor. The Public Trustee also determines who has title to property between the moment of death of the deceased and the time of the grant of probate or administration. There are differences between states as to the operation of law regarding the ultimate granting of probate, but the Office of the Public Trustee ensures that someone will be responsible until an executor is found, particularly where someone dies *intestate* (without making a will).

Summary and key terms

[21.23]   This chapter has set out to explain:
- the legal nature and definition of a *trust*;
- the parties to a *trust* and their relationship;
- the nature and characteristics of a *beneficiary* who must be *cestui que trust*;
- different types of trusts including *express*, *implied* and *resulting trusts*;
- particular trusts such as *unit trusts*, *superannuation trusts*, *family trusts* and *charitable trusts*;
- the *three certainties rule* for creating a trust;
- the means by which a *trust* comes to an end, or is changed;
- the nature, rights and legal obligations of a *trustee*;
- the nature, rights and legal obligations of a *beneficiary*;
- a *trustee company* licensed by statute;
- *the Public Trustee* and its role.

---

11. Trustee companies: Trustee Companies Act 1964 (ACT); Trustee Companies Act 1964 (NSW); Companies (Trustees and Personal Representatives) Act 1981 (NT); Trustee Companies Act 1984 (Vic); State Trustees (State Owned Company) Act 1994; Trustee Companies Act 1968 (Qld); Trustee Companies Act 1988 (SA) and private acts for each company; WA private acts for each company.
12. Public Trustee Act 1985 (ACT); Public Trustee Act 1913 (NSW); Public Trustee Act 1979 (NT); Public Trustee Act 1978 (Qld); Administration and Probate Act 1919–75 (SA); Public Trust Office Act 1930–73 (Tas); State Trust Corporation of Victoria Act 1987 (Vic); Public Trustee Act 1941–75 (WA).

22

Companies

What this chapter does ...

The incorporated company is widely used in Australia as the vehicle for both large and small business.

A company provides advantages in that it offers an attractive form of investment while at the same time providing limited liability for the shareholders.

The incorporated company is the creature of statute. It is a legal person but totally artificial. It relies entirely on the body of law known as Company Law for its creation, operation and general regulation. The fundamental legislation dealing with companies is the Corporations Law 1991, recently amended in July 1998 by the Company Law Review Act.

This chapter examines the nature of companies and the law that governs them.

The origins of company law

[22.1] The development of Australian company law was based on the English model in which the law followed the development of commerce. In the seventeenth century, flourishing trade, commerce and exploration brought forth new venture capital, stock exchanges and stockbrokers. The first corporate-type bodies were the church, the trade guilds and later joint stock 'companies' which were really partnerships. There were many excesses in this time, particularly those of the famous South Seas Company, whose 'shares' were traded at inflated prices on the promise of overseas riches, only to collapse. The collapse of this company led to the Bubble Act 1719, which was the first registration and statutory regulation of companies. In 1862 English company law was consolidated into the Companies Act, on which Australian law is based.

The Australian colonies adopted the English Companies Act, but each began its own innovations, particularly Victoria, which distinguished between different types of companies such as no liability companies. With federation came a greater divergence between the states. There have been several stages in the development of the body of company law that now exists in Australia.

While the sources of company law are to be found in common law and the Corporations Law, it is worthwhile noting that there are many statutes which affect the operation of corporations, including environmental legislation, occupational health and safety legislation, taxation law, trade practices law and stock exchange regulations. Common law remains very important in the development of company law in Australia, while of course it can be overridden by statute.

The Uniform Companies Act 1961

[22.2] The growth of commerce and the growing trend of companies to operate on a national scale led to the creation of the Uniform Companies Acts in 1961. Each state adopted the uniform legislation but differences emerged as each state continued to amend the legislation. Early in this century the High Court tended to decide in favour of the states when questions of whether the states or the Commonwealth had power over company law.

The Co-operative Scheme 1980

[22.3] The states and the Commonwealth established the Commonwealth–State Scheme for Co-operative Companies and Securities Regulation, under the formal agreement between the states and the Commonwealth in 1980. This scheme was more commonly known as the Co-operative Scheme and was aimed at cooperation between the states and the Commonwealth, achieving uniformity of legislation and administration of company law on a national basis, and promotion of the development of the law. Much of the development of this cooperation was as a result of the excesses of the mining boom which occurred in Australia, and the unregulated practices of many companies.

Under this legislation the National Companies and Securities Commission (NCSC) was the enforcement body. The Commonwealth passed a Companies Act for the Australian Capital Territory which was adopted by states as the Companies Code. Under the Scheme there was uniform legislation regulating companies, the securities industry and takeovers.

The Corporations Law

[22.4] In 1989 the Commonwealth passed the Corporations Act. New South Wales and other states challenged the constitutional power of the Commonwealth to do so. The High Court found that the Commonwealth had the power to make laws regarding incorporated companies, but not for the registration process: *New South Wales v Commonwealth* (1990) 169 CLR 482; 90 ALR 355. The Commonwealth legislation was fatally flawed and the concept of national legislation to regulate companies was impossible. The result of the constitutional challenge was a new agreement between the Commonwealth and the states, which ultimately resulted in legislation operating from 1 January 1991, renamed as the Corporations Law to distinguish it from the first Corporations Act.

The legislation is a cooperative scheme, with the Commonwealth having sole responsibility for initiating reform and amending the legislation. The Corporations Law and any changes to it are passed by the Commonwealth in the Australian Capital Territory, and then are adopted by each of the states through their Application Acts.

The Australian Securities Commission (ASC) replaced the NCSC and the state Corporate Affairs Commissions. In 1998, under the Company Law Review Act, the ASC became the Australian Securities and Investments Commission (ASIC) to reflect its expanded role in regulating financial services for the purposes of consumer protection, along with further corporate regulation. The ASIC has the role of administering the Corporations Law, the Insurance (Agents and Brokers) Act 1984 and the Superannuation Industry (Supervision) Act 1993, along with various other financial Acts in its capacity as a consumer watchdog. The ASIC is an independent authority accountable only to the Commonwealth Treasurer and the Commonwealth Parliament. It is composed of eight members, three who are full-time and others as the Minister nominates. The ASIC is the principal administrator of the Corporations Law, with the power to delegate authority where necessary. The ASIC has the power to investigate contraventions of the law or unacceptable situations, including the power to examine a person on oath. The ASIC can exempt persons and institutions in situations where it sees fit. It can seek prosecutions through the office of the Director of Public Prosecutions (DPP); in fact, in 1996–97 some 23 people were imprisoned as a result of legal actions initiated by the former ASC. A number of bodies have been constructed to work with the ASIC, such as the Companies and Securities Advisory Committee which advises the Minister about the content, operation and administration of the Corporations Law. This body has been responsible for law reform which simplifies the legislation. The Corporations and Securities Panel, referred to as 'the Panel', adjudicates on unacceptable takeover situations referred to it by the ASIC. Other bodies include the Company and Security Advisory Committee, the Australian Accounting Standards Board (AASB) and the Companies Auditors and Liquidators Disciplinary Boards.

The state Supreme Courts and Federal Courts both have jurisdiction over company law matters and consequent appeals. The courts are encouraged for the sake of consistency to follow each other's decisions: *Australian Securities Commission v Marlborough Gold Mines Ltd* (1993) 177 CLR 485; 112 ALR 627.

The Simplification Acts

[22.5]   There are some significant changes occurring in Corporations Law. The First Corporate Law Simplification Act came into law on 9 December 1995 and was to be followed by the Second Simplification Act. The First Simplification Act has made some very significant changes such as:

- A proprietary company can form with only one shareholder and director, whereas previously two were required.
- The distinction between exempt and non-exempt proprietary companies has been replaced with large and small proprietary companies.
- No new company limited both by guarantee and shares can be registered, while existing companies are allowed to remain.
- The need for a proprietary company to restrict the transfer of its shares has been abolished.
- A proprietary company can invite the public to buy its securities where a prospectus is not required, so that some limited fund raising can take place.
- Proprietary companies can have more than 50 members where extra members are employee shareholders.

The Second Simplification Act, which was to supplement the first Act, has now been overtaken by the Company Law Review Act 1998 which has made significant changes throughout the Corporations Law. The Company Law Review Act has streamlined the Corporations Law, making it easier to establish and manage a company, while abolishing many old sections in the process. The Company Law Review Act introduces more explanation of company law into the Corporations Law, and uses plain English throughout the legislation.

The concept of an incorporated company

[22.6] While many bodies such as partnerships may legitimately refer to themselves as companies, they are not companies under the Corporations Law. They have not been registered under that legislation but, more importantly, they do not exhibit the features which distinguish such a company. It is registration under the Corporations Law — the process of incorporation — which creates a corporation, and it is therefore not uncommon to see companies referred to as corporations. There are many bodies which have a corporate nature but are not created under, nor regulated by, the Corporations Law. Bodies such as universities, incorporated associations and statutory corporations have their own legal entity which is separate from its employees, management and members, but is created in different ways. The Corporations Law, however, does apply to 'registrable bodies' (s 601CA) such as incorporated associations or trade unions which are not regulated by the Corporations Law while they operate only in their home state, but will come within its ambit if they do business across state borders into Commonwealth jurisdiction.

A partnership of more than 20 people, unless of an exempt type, is an outsized partnership and must incorporate: s 115.

The powers of a company incorporated under the Corporations Law are set out in s 124 which provides that a company has the legal capacity and powers of an individual both in and outside this jurisdiction. A company also has all the powers of a body corporate, including the power to:

a) issue and cancel shares in the company;

b) issue debentures;

c) grant options over unissued shares in the company;

d) distribute any of the company's property among the members, in kind or otherwise;

e) give security by charging uncalled capital;

f) grant a floating charge over the company's property; and

g) do anything that it is authorised to do by any other law (including a law of a foreign country).

These features mean that:

- a company is a legal person in its own right (s 124);
- a company has a legal personality distinct from that of its shareholders;
- a company is endowed with capacities similar to those of a natural person; and
- when a company is limited by shares, the liability of its shareholders is limited to the amount which remains uncalled (and unpaid) on their shares: s 516.

In a recent unreported English case, the fast food company McDonalds successfully sued two people for defamation of the company, reinforcing the principle that a company has the same rights as a person. The action has become known as the McLibel case.

The company has a separate existence from its owners, the shareholders, and from the people who work for the company. Indeed, it is common that in a small company where the shares are owned by a husband and wife, they will also be employed by the company. The managers, directors and other employees act as agents in the name of the company. Because the company has a separate existence from its members, it is said to have a perpetual existence. Perpetuity is possible even in a one-person company where the member dies — a representative can keep the company going until a new member is found: s 224A.

The company takes liability for the actions of its employees and business conducted on its behalf. Similarly, shareholders are not liable for the actions of the company in which they hold shares; their liability is limited to the payment of their shares: s 516. If a company is unable to pay its debts, the shareholders will not be liable to creditors. A company must include the words 'Co Ltd' in its name to signify that it is a company limited by shares.

Advantages and disadvantages

[22.7]   The corporate form therefore has a number of advantages which include the following:

- its members have limited liability to the paid-up amount of a share;
- the members, management and employees of a company are separate entities to the company, which allows members to have contracts with their own company;
- the transfer of shares is relatively simple according to its constitution;
- the company is a separate legal entity and owns its own property;
- it has a greater facility for raising funds than an individual;
- it is a good form for undertaking large projects;
- a company can sue and be sued in its own name;
- the members can elect the management of the company; and
- it has certain tax advantages such as franking of dividends on Australian shares and company tax is lower than the highest personal marginal rates of tax.
   There are, however, disadvantages, such as:
- there are significant establishment costs for a company;
- it has a more public financial position;
- it can be required to undertake a compulsory audit;
- members cannot always take part in the company management;
- there may be difficulties in changing the company constitution;
- it has a liability to pay income tax;
- corporations are highly regulated and there are significant penalties for breaches of law, both on the company and its officers; and
- the founders and original owners of the company can lose control of the company if an outsider purchases significant numbers of shares.

Separate legal personality

[22.8]   The significance of incorporation is that when a business incorporates a separate entity or personality is established. It is distinct from its owners.

Case Example

Salomon, a sole proprietor, sold his business to a company for $39,000. He received 20,000 shares and his wife and five children each received one share. He was paid $1000 in cash. He also received debentures to the value of $10,000 which meant that he became a secured creditor. The remainder of the purchase price was used to pay business debts.

The company encountered difficulties and Salomon borrowed $5000 on security of his debentures to put money into the company. The company eventually became insolvent and a lender appointed a liquidator. The liquidator gathered the assets of the company and could pay the $5000 secured borrowing and a further $1000 to Salomon on security of his debentures, which left nothing for the unsecured creditors who were owed about $8000. The liquidator claimed that Salomon should not be paid as a secured creditor, ahead of the unsecured creditors, because the company was a sham designed to defraud the unsecured creditors. The liquidator tried to show that Salomon was not a separate entity from the company and therefore not entitled to payment as a separate entity.

The House of Lords found that Salomon as owner was indeed a separate entity from the company, even if he was also a creditor. Salomon had established the company when it was a valuable business and there was no intention of fraud. The court established that a company is a separate entity if properly incorporated, unless it can be shown that the company was being used for improper purposes. Lord Macnaghten said in the course of his judgment that:

> … When the memorandum is duly signed and registered, though there be only seven shares taken, the subscribers are a body corporate 'capable forthwith' to use the words of the enactment, 'of exercising all the functions of an incorporated company'. Those are strong words. The company attains maturity on its birth. There is no period of minority — no interval of incapacity. I cannot understand how a body corporate thus made 'capable' by statute can lose its individuality by issuing the bulk of its capital to one person, whether he be a subscriber to the memorandum or not. The company is at law a different person altogether from the subscribers to the memorandum; and, though it may be that after incorporation the business is precisely the same as it was before, and the same persons are managers, and the same hands receive the profits, the company is not in law the agent of the subscribers or the trustee for them. Nor are the members liable, in any shape or form, except to the extent and in the manner provided by the act. That is, I think, the declared intention of the enactment …

Salomon v Salomon & Co [1897] AC 22.

Case Example

A fire destroyed timber owned by the company. It had been established to take over Macaura's sole trader business The timber had been insured in Macaura's name but he did not take out a policy in the name of the company. Macaura's argument boiled down to saying that since he was the major shareholder the timber was his anyway. The court said that shareholders have no interest in the property of the company. Their interest in the company is restricted to the rights attached to their shares: *Macaura v Northern Assurance Co Ltd* [1925] AC 619.

Case Example

A pilot established a company to conduct his business as a crop duster. He held 2999 shares and one was held by a solicitor as his nominee. The pilot died and his widow sought workers compensation. The insurance company claimed that the company was a fraudulent pretence since the owner of a company could not be an employee. The court, however, upheld the principle that a company is a separate entity from its owners who can also be company employees. The wife was entitled to the insurance as the widow of an employee: *Lee v Lee's Air Farming Ltd* [1961] AC 12; [1960] 3 All ER 420.

Lifting the corporate veil

[22.9]   Where the company form is used to mask, cover or 'veil' activities which would otherwise be illegal, fraudulent or contrary to public interest the courts may examine the activities of individuals acting within and on behalf of the company. If a court is satisfied that the facade of the company is being used for improper purposes, it may hold the individual personally liable. This is referred to as piercing the veil of incorporation. Australian courts are reluctant to take this action unless there is some statutory instruction to do so. In *Industrial Equity Ltd v Blackburn* (1977) 137 CLR 567; 17 ALR 575 a holding company tried to show that its subsidiary's profits were really its own so that it would not have to pay tax on receiving its subsidiary's dividend. The court followed the *Salomon* principle and would not allow the veil to be pierced, finding that they were separate companies which had been incorporated for proper purposes. Unlike English law, Australian courts are very unwilling to pierce the veil and hold subsidiaries as mere agents and therefore part of the parent company: *Pioneer Concrete Services Ltd v Yelnah Pty Ltd* (1986) 5 NSWLR 254; 11 ACLR 108.

One example of an Australian court lifting the veil is in *Green v Bestobell Industries Pty Ltd* [1982] WAR 1 where Green abused his fiduciary position as a former manager and incorporated a company in order to use information improperly for his own purposes. The court held that Green had breached his fiduciary duty to Bestobell, and that his company had assisted him in doing so. The court ordered that the benefits gained by the company were to be repaid to Bestobell and that Green could not shield himself from liability behind a company. There are a number of principles under which the courts may pierce the veil of incorporation, which include:

- *Determining the residence of a company*   A company may claim to have its residence in the country in which it is incorporated, possibly a low-tax regime, but in fact all its members and management live and work elsewhere.

- *Fraud or breach of an agreement being the reason for incorporation*   If a person avoids a personal agreement such as a contract of employment by, for example, setting up a company to do something he or she could not do personally, the courts may not allow that person to hide behind the corporation: *Gilford Motor Co v Horne* [1933] Ch 935.

- *Inequitable or unforeseen circumstances*   If the corporate form results in an unfair situation, such as a partner being removed from a company after the partnership was incorporated, then the courts may look behind the company form: *Ebrahimi v West-bourne Galleries Ltd* [1973] AC 360; [1972] 2 All ER 492.

The Corporations Law contains many provisions in which the corporate veil is lifted. These include, for example:

- company officers being personally liable if they authorise the payment of a dividend when there are insufficient profits (s 254T);

- trading while insolvent (s 588G) places liability on a director who incurs a debt on behalf of the company at a time when there are reasonable grounds to expect that the company will be unable to pay all its debts;

- issuing documents which do not have the company name makes the issuer personally liable (s 123, 144).

There are other statutes such as the Taxation Administration Act 1953 (Cth) which similarly provide for personal liability of directors.

Companies regulated by the Corporations Law

[22.10]   In s 9 of the Corporations Law — the definition section — a company is variously described as a company incorporated under the Corporations Law, a body corporate, a recognised company and an unincorporated company which operates in more than one state. The Corporations Law excludes from its coverage exempt public authorities such as statutory corporations and incorporated associations. It also exempts bodies designated in s 66A, such as trade unions (s 116) and building societies, which are regulated by other legislation.

While most companies are registered by the ASIC, or previous authorities, there are some corporations which gained their status through other means, by Royal Charter or through special legislation such as a university. The use of corporations is increasing — in 1998 there were more than one million registered companies in Australia, and more than 90,000 new companies were registered in that year.

Classification of companies

[22.11]   The Corporations Law classifies a company by reference to:

- the liability of company members;
- its status as a public or proprietary company;
- its status as a holding or subsidiary company;
- its status as a foreign or domestic company; and
- whether it falls within a special category such as investment companies or trustee companies.

A company can change its liability status from one company form to another by complying with the procedures set out in s 162–166, though there are some restrictions; for example, a proprietary company is not permitted to change from a limited liability company to a no liability company: s 162(1).

Liability of members

[22.12]   The Corporations Law s 112 designates four different classes of company which may be registered under the Corporations Law. These are as follows.

A company limited by shares

[22.13]   The capital of the company has been divided into units known as shares which are then issued to shareholders as owners of the company. If the company has insufficient assets to pay all its debts, the shareholders are only liable for the uncalled value of their shares. A company with capital of $100,000 may have issued shares valued at, for example, $1 each. These shares are issued to investors and the proceeds represent the paid-up capital of the company. The purchasers of the shares — the shareholders — are the owners of the company. If the shares are listed on the stock exchange they can be bought and sold by the public at a price set by the market. This price bears no relationship to the issued value of the shares. More than 90 per cent of Australia's million companies are limited by shares.

A company limited by guarantee

[22.14]   Members of this form of company are liable only for a limited amount specified in the original application for registration, should there be a default or winding up. It has no shares and members guarantee that they will contribute a certain sum, usually a nominal amount, this liability ceasing on death or the departure of a member. Because a guarantee company has no subscribed capital it is a form often used by clubs and societies who do not have a profit-making motive and do not need capital to operate. These companies would have membership subscriptions. A guarantee company must be a public company. There are comparatively few of these companies in Australia.

A company limited by shares and guarantee

[22.15]   This is a company with both shares and an undertaking from members to be liable for a limited amount specified in the company constitution. No new companies limited both by guarantee and shares can be registered with the ASIC following the First Simplification Act.

An unlimited company

[22.16]   This is a company where the members agree to have unlimited personal liability for the debts of the company. This is an unusual type of company, a form which might be used by an investment company or assurance company that wishes to show its good faith. It does have some advantages under the Corporations Law in that it can reduce its capital at any time. There are only 570 such companies in Australia, and increasingly fewer with demutualisation.

A no liability company

[22.17]   This classification is only available for mining enterprises under the Mining Companies Act and represents a high risk type of company: Corporations Law s 112(2), (3). There is no liability on members to pay calls on unpaid capital to the company, though a member may have his or her shares confiscated if that member fails to do so. A no liability company cannot be a proprietary company: s 112(1).

Proprietary companies

[22.18]   A proprietary company is usually a smaller company than a public company. It is often used for family enterprises or small businesses and may be the first type of incorporation for a business moving from a sole tradership or partnership. More than 90 per cent of companies in Australia are proprietary companies.

A company is a proprietary company if it meets the requirements of s 113:

- *It is a company having share capital*   A proprietary company must be a company limited by shares or an unlimited company that has a share capital. A guarantee company cannot be a proprietary company because it has no share capital.
- *It limits its non-employee shareholders to 50*   A proprietary company may have more than 50 members as long as those over the limit are employee shareholders: s 113(1). The possibility of more than 50 members reflects an encouragement of employees participating in company affairs as members.
- *It must not engage in any activity that would require the lodgement with the ASIC of a prospectus: s 113(3)*   This would prevent a proprietary company from being listed on the stock exchange. A proprietary company would, however, be able to raise funds where the fundraising would not require a prospectus, for example, to fewer than 20 people.

If a proprietary company does not comply with the Corporations Law then the ASIC may determine that it ceases to be a proprietary company (s 165) and order that it convert to a public company.

Characteristics of a proprietary company

[22.19]   The characteristics of a proprietary company include the following:

- It can incorporate with one shareholder (s 114) and one director: s 221(1). A one-person company need only record and sign a resolution without holding a meeting (s 249B(1)), though if there is more than one member then a meeting can be held with a minimum of two members (s 249T), unless the company has something different in its constitution.
- There is no age limit on directors — under s 228 directors of public companies must retire at 72 years of age.
- A proprietary company does not have to hold an annual general meeting, nor a statutory meeting: s 250N. In a single shareholder company a resolution may be made by a statement in writing (s 249B(1)) in lieu of a meeting.
- A proprietary company must have 'Proprietary' (s 148) or an abbreviation such as 'Pty Ltd' in its name: s 149.
- A proprietary company must have share capital, which therefore excludes guarantee companies.
- Proprietary companies are easier to maintain than public companies, which have extra conditions imposed on them throughout the Corporations Law.
- The proprietary company has the disadvantage of not being able to increase its shareholdings to over 50 non-employee members, and further it cannot advertise its shares or securities, thereby restricting its capacity to raise equity capital and its ability to expand.

Large and small proprietary companies

[22.20] Proprietary companies were changed significantly with the First Corporate Law Simplification Act 1995, which introduced small and large proprietary companies as a replacement for exempt and non-exempt proprietary companies. The First Simplification Act was the first stage of streamlining and simplifying the language, procedures and regulations of the Corporations Law followed by the Company Law Review Act 1998. As part of the simplification process the Corporations Law includes a Small Business Guide which uses plain language to summarise the rules applying to proprietary companies limited by shares. Most importantly, the Corporations Law recognises that small enterprises should be treated differently to larger businesses, which normally have many shareholders and directors.

A small proprietary company is distinguished from a large proprietary company in s 45A(2) whereby a small proprietary company is one which has two of the following characteristics:

- the consolidated gross revenue for the financial year of the company is less than $10m;
- the value of gross assets at the end of the financial year of the company is less than $5m; and
- the company has fewer than 50 employees at the end of the financial year.

If a proprietary company is not a small proprietary company, then it is deemed to be a large proprietary company: s 45A(3).

The great advantage of being defined as a small proprietary company is that they do not have to prepare, audit and lodge annual accounts in their annual return, which is an enormous saving for a small enterprise: ss 292, 293. Of course the ASIC or shareholders can demand that accounts be prepared. Before the First Simplification Act a company defined as an exempt proprietary company had the privilege of not having to prepare its annual accounts, whereas non-exempt proprietary companies had to. An exempt proprietary company was a proprietary company recognised by the ASIC as having none of its shares owned by a public company. The First Simplification Act had taken account of the fact that some ongoing exempt companies may not qualify as small proprietary companies, but has allowed them to continue with that exempt status: s 319(4).

Public companies

[22.21] A company which is not registered as a proprietary company is a public company: s 9. A public company can incorporate with one shareholder (s 114) but must have three directors: s 221(2). Public companies are not restricted in their ability to raise capital from the public through an issue of shares or borrowing.

Holding and subsidiary companies

[22.22] A holding company is a company which owns or controls another company, known as a subsidiary. The Corporations Law requires a holding company to prepare group accounts so that assets cannot be hidden. Further, there is a prohibition on a subsidiary owning shares in its holding company, since this is seen as a company purchasing its own shares: s 259B. A company is classified as a subsidiary according to ss 46 and 9 where another body controls the board of directors, or where it controls the majority of votes, or holds more than half of the issued shares of the subsidiary.

Foreign companies

[22.23]   A company which is incorporated in another country is a foreign company. Foreign companies must register in one of the states or territories before carrying on business in Australia.

Particular company enterprises

[22.24]   There are some specific types of enterprise for which the Corporations Law makes a special provision. The main examples are investment companies and trustee companies.

A company can seek a declaration from the ASIC naming it as an investment company. As an investment company the corporation can advertise an expert and professional service. To protect potential investors the company must do business predominantly in the buying and selling of securities, such as shares, debentures and bonds. There is also a borrowing limit of no more than 50 per cent of its assets. Some of the other restrictions are that it must not invest more than 10 per cent of its funds in one company; it is restricted in underwriting; and it has extensive disclosure and accounting requirements.

A trustee company is another example of a named company. Trustee companies are in a special position under state legislation which allows for a limited number of companies to act as executors of estates. Corporate trustees are another form of trustee company. The Corporations Law imposes special requirements as to disclosure, accounting and the ultimate responsibility of directors.

Criminal liability of corporations

[22.25]   Even though it is an artificial entity a company can be liable for any crime, unless it is particular to a human, for instance perjury. Crimes for which a company may be liable can be committed by the company itself, its directors and officers, or employees and agents. When an act, constituting a crime, is authorised by the company, or perhaps committed during the course of employment on behalf of the company, then the company will be liable. In the recent case of *R v Denbo Pty Ltd* (SC(Vic), Teague J, JBC9405103, 14 June 1994, unreported) a company was convicted of manslaughter for criminal negligence and fined $120,000 for criminal negligence having allowed an employee to drive a vehicle with defective brakes. In that case the directors were also fined and the company was wound up.

The will and mind of a company

[22.26]   Because a company is a non-human entity, criminal action on its part is represented by the actions of its officers and employees. The board of directors is said to be the will and mind of the company. If the directors authorise or knowingly allow a wrongful act to occur, that will supply the mental element *(mens rea)* necessary for the commission of a crime: *HL Bolton (Engineering) Co Ltd v TJ Graham & Sons Ltd* [1956] 3 All ER 624; [1957] 1 QB 159. Where, however, a company gives decision-making power normally reserved for directors to employees, it is those persons who can form the wrongful intention for the company. Where knowledge of a wrongdoing is required by

573

law, then a company can be said to have that through the collective mind of directors: *Brambles Holdings Ltd v Carey* (1976) 15 SASR 270; 2 ACLR 176. A company is defined by the various federal and state Acts Interpretation Acts as being a person for the application of most legislation, for example in the Crimes Acts, Trade Practices Act and Environmental Protection Acts.

Case Example

A shop assistant placed an advertisement for a discounted item in the window of a supermarket. In fact, the discount had ended and the advertisement amounted to false advertising under the English legislation. There was a defence to the charge if the breach was due to the actions of a person who lacked authority and was not in a position of power, or if the person had so acted despite the due diligence and care of the management. The court looked at the question of the controlling mind and will of the company and found that the shop assistant and indeed the store manager who was to supervise the assistant, did not have the will and mind of the company. Both lacked discretion and no powers had been delegated to them. Their actions were therefore not on behalf of the company. It had exercised all care and diligence and therefore could use the defence that a mere employee had exceeded authority: *Tesco Supermarkets Ltd v Nattrass* [1972] AC 153; [1971] 2 All ER 127.

Determining the criminal liability of a corporation

[22.27] In order to establish the criminal liability of a company, the following must be considered:

- The company must have committed a wrongful act or omission. Whether there has been an act amounting to a criminal offence must be determined by examining the criteria set out in the particular statute and the relevant precedent. Some Acts will determine that a company is liable, even if it is not aware of the illegal act, making the company vicariously liable: *Beach Petroleum NL v Johnson* (1993) 115 ALR 411; 43 FCR 1.

- The particular statute must be examined to determine who exactly is liable for any crime committed. The particular statute may make the person committing the offence personally liable, or rather the company as the employer, or both the perpetrator of the offence and the company.

- The statute may provide some defences against prosecution where the offence has occurred because of some mistake, or because an employee has acted entirely out of his or her authority and beyond the control of the company. The statute may, therefore, require a wrongful intention on behalf of the company, to which a company has a defence. Some statutes, however, will make a company strictly liable for a breach of a law. Where this is so, a company has no defences and is liable once the wrongful act is proved.

A company's liability for torts

[22.28] A tort is a wrongful action which allows the person suffering an injury to sue for damages. A company is liable for torts committed by its management, employees and agents on behalf of the company.

A company must take responsibility for the actions of its employees through the doctrine of vicarious liability. Alternatively, a company may be liable where the management's actions are taken to be those of the company. If the will and mind of the company intended a wrongful action, then this is taken to be the company's intention: *Lennard's Carrying Co Ltd v Asiatic Petroleum Coy* [1915] AC 705.

Bringing a company into existence

[22.29] The creation of a company is a process governed by a statutory procedure. Put simply, it is a matter of having the company registered by the ASIC.

Before registration, however, it is necessary to undertake preliminary steps such as bringing together the parties who wish to form the company, raising the capital, deciding on the internal rules for running the company and, if necessary, entering into business arrangements prior to the company being incorporated. Where time is of the essence a shelf company can be purchased — this is a company that has been incorporated in the usual way but is held 'on the shelf' until it is needed for a specific and usually urgent purpose.

Registration of a company

[22.30] The Corporations Law provides that 'to register a company, a person must lodge an application with the ASIC': s 117. The procedure for registration of a company is now much simpler under the Company Law Review Act.

There is only one form needed for registration, and it must contain the following:

- the type of company that is proposed;
- the company's proposed name (unless the ACN is to be used in its name);
- the name and address of each person who consents to become a member;
- the names and birth dates of those consenting in writing to become directors;
- the names and birth dates of those consenting to become the company secretary;
- the address of each person who consents in writing to become a director or company secretary;
- the address of the company's proposed registered office;
- the proposed opening hours of the registered office (if not the standard opening hours) for a public company;
- the address of the company's principal place of business (if not the address of the proposed registered office);
- for a company limited by shares or an unlimited company — the number and class of shares, the amount agreed to be paid for each share (in writing), and if not fully paid, the amount agreed to be unpaid (in writing) on each share;

575

- for a public company limited by shares, or an unlimited company, the details of an issue of shares for other than money;

- for a company limited by guarantee — the proposed amount of the guarantee (in writing) by each member;

Where the ASIC is satisfied that an application has been made in accordance with s 117(2) it shall register the company and issue it with a certificate: s 118. The certificate records the company's name, ACN, type of company, a statement that it is registered and the date of registration. A company comes into existence on receiving that certificate: s119.

Once the company is registered:

- the persons consenting to become a member, director or company secretary on the application are deemed to take their role (s 120(1));

- the company can choose to have a seal, and if it does the seal must contain the ACN in the company name (s 123(1));

- the company must establish registers of shareholders, charges and debentures. Minute books must also be established; and

- the company must issue shares: s 1096.

Promoters

[22.31]   Forming a company involves the association of a number of persons. The party who brings together interested parties for the registration of a company is referred to as the promoter, who could be a merchant banker, a broker, a lawyer or the person who wishes to establish a company. The promoter arranges the share subscription, and begins the formal process of registration by organising the various necessary parties.

Company law does not provide a concrete definition of what a promoter is, but the designation of a person as a promoter is crucial, since specific duties and liabilities are imposed on that person. The Corporations Law s 9 merely defines a promoter as a party to the preparation of the prospectus, but does not include a person contributing to the prospectus in a purely professional capacity. The common law provides a wider definition. In *Twycross v Grant* (1877) 2 CPD 469 the court said that a promoter is one who undertakes to form a company with reference to a given project to set it going, and who takes the necessary steps to accomplish that purpose. The High Court in *Tracy v Mandalay* (1953) 88 CLR 215 at 241 said that 'it is not only the persons who take an active part in the formation of a company and the raising of the necessary share capital to enable it to carry on business who are promoters'. The High Court said that the term 'promoter' would apply to the parties who leave it to others to set the company up on the understanding that they will profit from the company. Thus a sole trader who engaged a lawyer to set up a company to buy the business would be regarded as a promoter.

It is important to distinguish those parties who are not promoters, but who are involved in the formation of the company as a professional or a 'passenger'. In the case of *Tracy v Mandalay* (1953) 88 CLR 215 at 241 the High Court said that the term 'promoter' involves 'the idea of exertion for the purpose of getting up and starting a company (or what is called floating it) and also the idea of some duty towards the company imposed by or arising from the position which the so-called promoter assumes towards it …'. Whether a person is providing paid professional services or actively involved is a question of fact. Problems can arise where a person plays a dual role in the formation of a company; for instance, a solicitor who also becomes a shareholder in the company.

The promoter once identified has a fiduciary duty to the company and its members: he or she must not make secret profits, must act honestly, diligently and carefully. A promoter often seeks to sell a business to the company, or perhaps provide the company with a mining lease, a patent or some land. All profits made in transferring property, or providing services to the newly formed company must be disclosed and if not then the benefiting parties may have to hand back profits: *Gluckstein v Barnes* [1900] AC 240. This is an important duty and a promoter must disclose profits made in prior transactions, from whatever source. Disclosure to a fellow promoter is not sufficient, it must be a disclosure of all profits to the company concerned and especially to shareholders and other capital providers to the new company who are entitled to know what profits the promoter will make, so they can make an informed assessment of the value of the company: *Erlanger v New Sombrero Phosphate Co* (1878) 3 App Cas 1218.

A breach of a promoter's fiduciary duty makes the promoter liable to account for profits made, return property received (s 598(4)) and make good any losses incurred by the company. The promoter in these circumstances may be sued for damages, perhaps for negligence or improper conduct.

Pre-incorporation contracts

[22.32]   In the course of making arrangements for the incorporation of a company the promoter will encounter expenses or will be asked to make commitments on behalf of the emerging company. These are referred to as pre-incorporation contracts.

Because the company is not in existence it cannot make contracts or transact any business and therefore the promoter cannot be authorised to incur obligations on behalf of the company. The promoter cannot contract as an agent. There is risk that contracts and debts which are to be paid on the formation of the company will become the personal obligation of the promoter if, for example, the company does not form, is unable to pay its debts, or refuses to accept liability. Under the common law a person making a contract is always liable until the company, once formed, accepts the obligation: *Kelner v Baxter* (1862) LR 2 CP 170.

The Corporations Law stipulates that if a person enters into a contract on behalf of a company before it is registered, then the company will be bound, once it registers and ratifies the contract within a reasonable period of time: s 131(1).

If the contract is ratified the company becomes bound by it as if it had been a party to the original transaction. If the contract is not ratified, or the company is not formed within a reasonable time, the promoter is liable to the other party for damages: s 131(2). That is to say that the promoter is not required to perform the contract, but must pay the damages that would have been awarded had the contract been ratified but not performed by the company. The promoter may avoid liability by obtaining a written agreement from the other party by which an exemption from liability is given: s 132(1). If a company refuses to ratify a contract and the promoter is sued, then a court can apportion the damages as they see fit (s 131(3)), and generally against the company if it has benefited from the contract.

The company constitution

[22.33]   The constitution of a company can determine many of the rules and relationships which make up the operation of a company, in both the rights and duties of different parties — members, employees and the management — and may even restrict the way the company operates. The Company Law Review Act has made substantial changes to the concept and components of a company constitution. Before the Company Law Review Act all companies had to have a Memorandum of Association and Articles of Association, which were the fundamental documents of a company and formed its constitution. Companies that were registered before July 1988 would therefore have a constitution composed of a memorandum and articles, but now have the option of repealing their existing constitutions by special resolution: s 137.

A company on registering no longer needs to have a constitution (s 134): instead, single-person companies will be governed by particular Corporations Law sections which refer only to that type of company, for example, s 224B which governs the role of a single director in a one-member company. All other companies can elect to be governed by the replaceable rules in the Corporations Law: some of these apply to all companies, but others are specific to proprietary or public companies. Replaceable rules is the term used because a company can choose to be governed by the rules set out in the Corporations Law or it can replace some of the rules according to its own requirements, thereby creating a partial constitution: s 134. A public company is subject to some mandatory replaceable rules which cannot be changed. A company which elects not to have a constitution, or merely displaces some of the rules, will then be governed by whatever rules exist in the Corporations Law, which means if the parliament changes any rules then this will automatically change the internal management of the company. A company can therefore have no constitution, or have a partial constitution (by replacing some of the rules) or a full constitution of its own. Two companies which must have a constitution are a no liability company and a guarantee company — which removes the word limited from its name, because of its particular relationship with members.

The replaceable rules are found in a table under s 141 whereby 39 sections of the Corporations Law are designated. These relate to:

- directors, their appointment, powers, removal, contracts with the company and remuneration;
- directors' meetings and their conduct;
- meetings of members, the rights of members and the procedures which must be adopted;
- the company secretary;
- the inspection of books;
- shares, the right of pre-emption and dividends; and
- transfer of shares.

A company can pass a resolution to displace any of the replaceable rules; for example, where the company had different classes of shares, or wishes to restrict its management or is subject to external requirements such those required to hold a particular licence. The more resolutions a company has, the more likely it will need its own constitution.

The memorandum of association and the articles of association

[22.34] While the need for a memorandum of association and articles of association at the point of registration has been dispensed with, many companies would still have a constitution structured in this way until, or unless, they change their constitution. The memorandum of association has always been the most fundamental and important document — it determines the type of company it is in terms of its liability, its capital, its name and liability of its members. The articles of association were, on the other hand, designed to set out all the rules and regulations by which the company would operate; such as the election of directors, the transfer of shares and procedures at meetings. If there was any inconsistency between the two documents then the memorandum would prevail.

The contractual effect of the constitution and the replaceable rules

[22.35] The company constitution and the replaceable rules under s 140(1) have the effect of a contract between:
- the company and each member;
- the company and each director and company secretary; and
- a member and each other member of the company.

This means that all members, directors and company secretaries must observe and perform according to the company constitution or rules as they apply.

Case Example

The articles of the company stipulated that any dispute between a member and the company must first be decided by arbitration. A member tried to take a dispute with the company to court, but was refused a hearing since they were contractually bound by the articles which required arbitration: *Hickman v Kent or Romney Marsh Sheep-Breeders Association* [1915] 1 Ch 881.

The scope of the contract

[22.36] The rights and obligations specified in the constitution can be enforced only where they relate to membership of a company.

Case Example

A company proposed removing its solicitor who had been appointed for life within the articles, despite a provision which stated that his removal was only possible for misconduct. The court found the company was not contractually bound because the solicitor was enforcing rights as a contracted solicitor, rather than as a member. He was enforcing rights in a capacity other than as a member: *Eley v Positive Government Security Life Assurance* (1875) 1 Ex D 20.

A non-member cannot enforce any rights in the company constitution. In *Forbes v NSW Trotting Club Ltd* [1977] 2 NSWLR 515; (1977) 3 ACLR 145 a professional punter tried to use the articles of the company to prevent him from being excluded from the course. Because he was not a member of the club the court held that he was unable to enforce the articles.

Alteration of the company constitution

[22.37]   If a company has a constitution, rather than replaceable rules, it can be altered. The company can repeal its constitution (s 137), or adopt a constitution after registration (s 136(1)) or modify any part of its constitution after registration: s 136(2). There are many reasons why a company might wish to change its constitution, including the need to change its name, remove an objects clause, change rights attaching to shares or even change the type of company it is.

A company can change its constitution by special resolution (s 137(1)) except in certain instances where extra procedures must be complied with under the Corporations Law. A change of name requires both a special resolution and application with the ASIC (s 157), a change in the type of company requires a special resolution and an application to the ASIC (s 164(5)), and a change in class rights attaching to shares will require agreement from the members affected: s 246C–D. A company can make a part of its constitution difficult to change (s 136(3)) — this is called entrenching and means that a rule cannot be changed except by special procedures, such as lengthy notice of a change or perhaps a 100 per cent vote of agreement by members.

Certain modifications to the constitution will not be binding on existing members at the time of the modification, unless they agree in writing to be bound. These changes are set out in (s 140(2)) and relate to any change where:

a) a member must take additional shares; or

b) it increases the members' liability to contribute to share capital or pay further money; or

c) imposes or increases any restrictions on the right to transfer shares; unless

- it relates to the company changing from a public company to a proprietary company; or
- to insert takeover approval provisions.

A public company must inform the ASIC of any changes in its constitution (s 136(5)), but this does not apply to proprietary company except where the company is changing its name, type or the class rights attaching to shares.

Changes must be in good faith

[22.38]   Any change to the constitution must be in good faith (*Greenhalgh v Arderne Cinemas* [1951] Ch 286) and in the best interests of all members of the company: *Allen v Gold Reefs of West Africa Ltd* [1900] 1 Ch D 656. Where a majority interest uses its voting power to change the constitution for its own purposes, or where a shareholder suffers as a result of a change in the constitution, with no overall benefit achieved, then this may allow a member to complain to the Supreme Court for oppression: *Brown v British Abrasive Wheel Co Ltd* [1919] 1 Ch 290. A company can change its constitution and expropriate shares where it can justify it; for example, where the expropriation is aimed at a member who competes with the company. If the court is satisfied that there has been oppressive behaviour it may overturn the change: s 246AA.

In a recent decision it seems that what is in the interest of the company as a whole needs to be substantial if it affects a member's rights so that even if a company saves money by expropriating smaller shareholdings, this is not a good enough reason. This issue is considered in the rights of minorities.

Authority to act for the company

[22.39] A company, being an artificial entity, must act through its officers and employees. They act as agents who will bind the company for agreements, undertakings and arrangements made on behalf of the company with an outsider.

A company's agents have either actual authority or apparent (ostensible or implied) authority; for example, the board of directors is empowered under the company constitution with actual authority to enter into agreements on behalf of the company which will bind it. Where a person is appointed to an important position in the company such as company secretary, then he or she is an agent with apparent or ostensible authority and will bind the company. A company which allows someone to appear as an agent, or as an important officer, will be bound by that person's actions, even though the person has not been properly appointed. A outsider can assume that a company has complied with its internal procedures and its constitution when appointing an officer: *Northside Developments Pty Ltd v Registrar General* (1987) 5 ACLC 642; 11 ACLR 513. A company cannot avoid responsibility for an agent's actions by claiming that an officer or employee has acted outside his or her power, or outside the company constitution, unless the outside party actually knew or should have known that the agreement was improper.

There are various assumptions that an outsider can make regarding the actions of agents, including s 128:

- that the company constitution has been complied with in any dealings (s 129(1));
- that a person who appears from information supplied by the company, or the ASIC, has been duly appointed and has authority to exercise the powers usually performed by a director or company secretary in a similar company (s 129(2));
- that any officer or agent who is held out by the company has been properly appointed and has the authority to perform the duties customarily exercised by the officer or agent in a similar company (s 129(3));
- that officers and agents of the company properly perform their duties to the company (s 129(4));
- that any signed documents have been properly authorised (s 129(5)) and sealed documents have similarly been authorised (s 129(6)); and
- that authorised officers or agents can promise that a document is genuine: s 129(7).

The effect of these sections is that an outsider acting in good faith can presume that the person with whom his or she is dealing has authority to bind the company and all procedures and documentation are appropriate. The only exception to this rule is where the outsider knew, or should have known, perhaps by some long association, that the agent did not have authority to enter into the agreement: s 128(4). If a bank, for instance, lends money to a company which is a longstanding client, and the money does not even go to the company itself, this may put the bank on notice that the agent is not acting properly: *Northside Developments Pty Ltd v Registrar General* (1987) 5 ACLC 642. Where there is a connection between the parties, then it may amount to a relationship which puts the parties on notice of a need to make further inquiries: *Pyramid Building Society v Scorpion Hotels Pty Ltd (in liq)* (1976) 14 ACLC 679; 136 ALR 166.

Raising the money

[22.40]   One of the factors that allowed limited liability companies to develop was their potential for raising money from investors. In the case of public companies there are no restrictions on raising finance. Proprietary companies cannot invite the public to subscribe funds to them where a prospectus is required. Both forms of company, however, recognise the subscription of equity capital by issuing shares. Other forms of funding include normal trade credit, secured and unsecured borrowings and the unique company form of financing: debentures. Shares and debentures are both securities and subject to regulations governing securities. Securities are defined in s 92(1) as meaning debentures, stocks or bonds issued by a government or shares, debentures, managed investment schemes, units of shares or option contracts. Managed investment schemes are a participation interest or right to join some scheme such as a unit trust or time-share arrangement: s 9. A managed investment scheme which offers such rights to the public requires a prospectus.

The prospectus

[22.41]   One matter to be considered when a company seeks to raise funds is the need for a prospectus: s 1020. As the name implies, the prospectus sets out the situation of the company and what it believes to be its prospects. In 1997–98 there were 602 prospectuses registered with the ASC.

A prospectus is defined in the Corporations Law s 9 as any written notice which invites applications or offers to subscribe for or buy the securities of a body corporate. Securities are defined in s 92 as shares, debentures, managed investment schemes, units of such shares or an option contract. A prospectus is therefore required whenever there is a public fund raising and the issue of securities or quasi-securities, such as managed investment schemes which covers time-share and unit trust arrangements.

Any fundraising that involves the issuing of securities requires a prospectus to be prepared, lodged with the ASIC and registered, unless it falls within an exempt provision: s 1018. The exemptions defined by s 66(2), (3) are:

* large investor offers where the minimum subscription is $500,000 by each person;
* offers to underwriters;
* where no consideration is paid for the acceptance of an offer;
* where shares and debentures are offered personally to no more than a group of 20 people;
* where an offer or invitation is made to an executive officer of a corporation (or a close relative of the officer);
* where there is an offer to shareholders by a liquidator of shares in exchange for the assets of a company in liquidation;
* where the offer is for debentures of an excluded corporation;
* where the offer or invitation is exempt as declared by the regulations — the regulations give exemptions to takeover schemes, holders of dealers' licences, life insurance companies, superannuation funds, investment fund managers who control a minimum amount of $10 million; and
* a further offer of debentures to existing holders of debentures, or offer of convertible notes to existing convertible note holders.

In some circumstances a prospectus is required to be prepared and lodged, but does not have to be registered (s 1017A):

- where the securities are listed for quotation on the stock exchange;
- where there is an offer to existing members for bonus shares; or
- the offer is to an exempt recipient such as the employees of a corporation.

What are the requirements for a prospectus?

[22.42]   A company must ensure that the prospectus complies with the Corporations Law and must lodge it with the ASIC: s 1020. If the prospectus is registrable it should registered by the ASIC within 14 days. The company cannot issue invitations until the prospectus is registered, unless it is in an exempt category. The ASIC will register the prospectus unless it believes that the prospectus contains false or misleading information or does not comply with the provisions of the Law. The ASIC will not make a detailed analysis of a prospectus, and places the responsibility of compliance and truthfulness generally on the company seeking to register the prospectus.

The ASIC can, however, at any time begin an investigation, use stop orders and prosecute should there be a breach of the Corporations Law. Stop orders will be issued by the ASIC wherever there is a contravention of the Law and where there are false, deceptive or misleading statements in the prospectus: s 1033.

The content of a prospectus

[22.43]   The Corporations Law imposes only minimal requirements of what must be included in the prospectus. The basic requirement is that the prospectus is legible, printed in a readily readable form, states the date of issue, is signed by the directors and contains a statement that the securities will be allotted within 12 months of the issue of the prospectus: s 1021.

The purpose of the prospectus is to disclose information to prospective investors. In keeping with that objective the Corporations Law s 1022 imposes the requirement that:

A prospectus shall contain all such information as investors and their professional advisers would reasonably require, and reasonably expect to find in the prospectus, for the purpose of making an informed assessment of:
(a) the assets and liabilities, financial position, profits and losses and prospects of the corporation; and
(b) the rights attaching to the securities.

The onus for determining what should be in the prospectus is placed upon the company and those preparing the prospectus. Directors and their advisers must make reasonable inquiries according to the information they have available. The more public the offer is, the greater must be the care of preparation as the target group will have different levels of competency. If new information comes to light after the issue of a prospectus then a company can issue a supplementary prospectus: s 1082.

Liability for a prospectus

[22.44]   There is both civil and criminal liability for issuing a prospectus which does not meet the requirements of the Corporations Law. Subscribers to securities can claim damages if it can be shown that they have suffered loss or damage because of a reliance on the prospectus which contravened the Act's provisions regarding misleading or deceptive conduct (s 995) and for which they can recover their losses: ss 1005, 1006. There are defences, however; for instance, where a party to the prospectus withdrew his or her consent to the prospectus: s 1008.

Liability for the preparation of the prospectus rests on the corporation, directors of the company, promoters, experts referred to in the prospectus, stockbrokers, underwriters, the auditors, the banker, the solicitor, the professional adviser named or involved, or any other person who was involved in the preparation of the prospectus: s 1006. The Act allows for defences where the person preparing the prospectus had no knowledge of false information when accepting the offer: s 1008A.

Persons who issue or authorise a prospectus knowing it contains false or misleading statements, or in which there are important omissions are guilty of a criminal offence: s 996. There are defences where parties can show that they made proper inquiries, or had no reason to believe there was something untruthful in the prospectus: s 1006. Due diligence in checking and preparation is the best defence: s 1011.

In the recent case of *Fraser v NRMA Holdings Ltd* (1995) 14 ACLC 132; 127 ALR 577 a disgruntled member used s 52 of the Trade Practices Act successfully to stop a misleading prospectus. While the action did not revolve around the provisions of the Corporations Law, the case established that a prospectus must disclose all information relevant to the securities, and in the case of a merger must put the negatives as well as the positives to fulfil the spirit of the prospectus.

Publicising the prospectus

[22.45]   The Corporations Law prohibits a company from advertising its prospectus, other than stating that the prospectus is available for any interested party: s 1026. An advertisement must do no more than call attention to the prospectus in an informative way. The Act sets out certain minimum information which must be stated in the advertisement, such as the fact that it has been lodged, where a copy of the prospectus can be obtained and that an application can only be obtained if attached to a prospectus: s 1025. A company is prohibited from avoiding these provisions by making press statements, which are a disguised form of advertising. In recent times there has been a much more relaxed attitude to publicising a prospectus and some big corporations such as the Commonwealth Bank and Telstra have been able to do some careful preliminary advertising which raises awareness without actually discussing the content of a prospectus.

Company capital

[22.46]   Capital is raised by issuing shares: see **[22.47]**. This can increase the number of members of the company. It is referred to as equity capital and is not required to be repaid to the subscriber unless the company is wound up — but only if there is a surplus after liquidating the company's assets and settling its liabilities. Money which is borrowed, by the issue of debentures (see **[22.65]**) or from bank loans, is referred to as debt capital. The parties who provide debt capital are not company members and have no rights associated with membership.

Shares

[22.47]   A shareholder, by contributing capital (or buying shares on the stock exchange) becomes an owner of the company and receives certain rights by force of the Corporations Law, and the contractual effect of the constitution. Holding shares gives rights in the form of voting, participation in dividends and a share of capital in the event of the winding up of the company. The rights attached to a share can vary so that, for example, there is no right to vote or there are preferences as to dividends. The rights attached to shares are determined by the company constitution. A shareholder can be a company, an infant, or any other entity capable of owning property.

A shareholder becomes a member of the company when his or her name is entered on the shareholders register (ss 246A, 168A), except of course a member of a guarantee company where an individual signs the memorandum. The register then acts as proof of membership (s 176) which means that a shareholder has the benefits of membership, including the right to vote, attend meetings and protest at oppressive behaviour. If an individual's membership is not recorded properly then that person has no standing in the company: *Maddocks v DJE Constructions Pty Ltd* (1982) 148 CLR 104; 40 ALR 283. A person refused membership after the purchase of shares may ask for reasons for refusal (s 1093) and then ask the court to rectify the register by recording his or her name: s 1094. Membership also means that a shareholder is bound by the company constitution (s 140) and must pay calls on the unpaid proportion of shares.

A company may wish to issue new shares to raise capital. The raising of capital works on the rules of contract whereby a potential member must apply for shares, which is an offer to the company to buy shares. The company may allot shares in preparation for an issue, but this is not acceptance till the company actually communicates this to the shareholder.

The nature of a share

[22.48]   A share is a form of property which can be sold or transferred in any manner to another. A share is not physical property but rather is a bundle of rights, or a claim, evidenced by a certificate which must be issued: s 1096. Section 1085(1) defines the nature of a share as personal property which can be transferred, or willed, to another subject to the constitution of the company. Section 9 defines a share as a 'share in the share capital of a body corporate, and includes stock except where a distinction between stock and shares is expressed or implied'. A share represents a slice of ownership of the company. Because of the principle of separate legal entity it does not give the shareholder ownership of the company's property. A person who owns, say, a quarter of a company's issued capital does not own a quarter of the company's net assets.

Share capital

Authorised capital and issued capital

[22.49]   Shares are not issued with a face value or par value. Under the Company Law Review Act the concept of par value is abolished (s 254C), which means that a company can issue a share for any price it wishes, and change the price from issue to issue. The changes to the law also mean that even shares issued prior to July 1998, and bearing a face value, no longer have a par value. The abolition of par value by the Company Law Review Act is quite profound because there is now no longer any concept of discounting of shares (issuing them at less than face value), or shares issued at a premium (more than their face value).

Before the Company Law Review Act a company had to specify an upper limit to which it could issue shares in its constitution — this was known as the authorised capital. The authorised capital was divided into shares according to their par value and the company could not issue shares which exceeded its authorised capital. The requirement of an authorised capital for registration purposes has now been omitted from the registration procedures in s 117. A company can elect to restrict the number of shares that it issues by placing this provision in its constitution: s 1427.

Issued capital is the amount of capital raised from shares which have been issued. These shares can be partly or fully paid for, the balance being uncalled capital.

Uncalled capital

[22.50]   This is reserve capital, or the unpaid proportion of a share, which the company may choose to hold in reserve as security for creditors. Thus, if shares are issued at a price of $1 and only 60 cents has been paid, the amount of uncalled capital is 40 cents per share. The uncalled proportion will always be the difference between the issue price of the share and what was actually paid, and each shareholder may purchase shares for different prices (since there is no par value) and hence owe different amounts on his or her holding of shares: s 254M. Uncalled capital represents the amount which members must contribute to the company at the time of winding up if there is a deficiency. A company can resolve that only in the event of a liquidation will reserved capital be called up: s 254N. Uncalled capital can be treated like an asset and used as security for borrowing by the company, since it can always be called up.

Different types of shares

[22.51]   Different shares may have different rights attaching them so that there can be classes of shares: s 254A. These different rights may give a priority of dividends, different voting rights or priority of repayment should the company be liquidated. The rights attaching to different shares may be specified in the constitution, which may also determine how those rights may be changed. If the company has not provided in its constitution, or elsewhere, for a distinction between shares, then they are presumed to have the same rights.

Ordinary shares

[22.52]   An ordinary share carries the usual rights such as a right to receive dividends, receive a share of a profit surplus and participate in the distribution of a company's assets on a winding up. Ordinary shares may be inferior in some respects to preference shares if preference shareholders must receive dividends first out of profits.

Preference shares

[22.53]   A preference share receives specified preferential treatment against other shares. The rights attaching to a preference share must be specified, according to the criteria in s 254A(2) and in the constitution, before they can be issued. The preference can take the form of a cumulative dividend, a priority in payment of a dividend or a priority in the repayment of capital in the event of a winding up of the company. A preference shareholder may sometimes not have voting rights.

Redeemable preference shares

[22.54]   These are shares which allow for the repayment of capital at a later time: s 254J–L. Any redemption of shares must be on the terms in which they were issued and can only be redeemed if the shares are fully paid up, and paid out of profits or a new issue of shares: s 254J.

Deferred shares

[22.55]   These are shares where the dividend may be deferred until dividends have been paid out to other shareholders. These shares may be taken by the former owner of a business, who having transferred the business into a company, as an act of good faith takes dividends last of all or deferred right of a return of capital.

Share hawking

[22.56]   Share hawking takes place by visiting, phoning or some other means where the seller of securities goes about asking people to buy securities. It is prohibited by s 1078. There is an exception, however, where securities are listed on the stock exchange and offered by a person with a dealer's licence. The offer may be made by fax as long as the offer is attached to a prospectus.

The issue and allotment of shares

[22.57]   The issue of shares follows the rules of contract law in terms of offer and acceptance. The potential buyer of shares makes an offer to the company to purchase shares by filling out the application form attached to the prospectus: s 1020. The company in turn can decide whether to accept or reject the offer and, after acceptance, allot shares.

Before an allotment can take place the company must have received enough offers, with attached deposit, to cover the minimum subscription determined by the board of directors: s 1035. The minimum subscription is designed to cover the expenses of the issue. The directors must hold the application money in trust (s 1043) and return it if the share allotment does not take place: s 1036.

Where the allotment of shares has not been according to the constitution of the company, or is in contravention of the Corporations Law, the Supreme Court can validate, or approve of, an irregular allotment where it just and equitable: s 254E.

The consideration for shares

[22.58]   Shares can be paid for with money, or exchanged for property provided it is valuable consideration of equivalent value. If the exchange of property for shares is insufficient it may amount to a reduction in the capital of the company. Section 254X requires that an allotment of shares for other than cash be recorded and a copy of the contract be lodged with the ASIC within a month.

Options

[22.59]   An option is a contractual right to take up unissued shares in the future. A right to purchase shares at a fixed price might be valuable if the share price rises above the contract price. Options can be used to offer shares to employees or to debenture holders in exchange for a debenture payout. Option details must be placed in a register: s 170.

Maintaining the capital base

[22.60]   The common law and the Corporations Law place considerable importance on a company preserving its capital base. This rule is reflected in the prohibition on a company paying dividends except out of profits (s 254T) or assisting another to buy company shares: s 260A. Although the capital, or worth, of a company might deteriorate with poor trading, it should not be diminished deliberately by the actions of the company. There is a duty on the company to preserve the worth of the company in the interests of shareholders and creditors, who deal with the company on the basis that it has good security of assets: *Trevor v Whitworth* (1887) 12 App Cas 409. However, there are exceptions to the rule such as an orderly reduction of capital (s 256A–E), buy-backs of shares, payment of shares out of bonus payments and forfeiture of shares.

Purchasing own shares

[22.61]   The rule about protecting the capital base is further emphasised in the prohibition on a company purchasing its own shares (s 259A) or assisting another to purchase shares, directly or indirectly (s 260A), unless under one of the exceptions to law. For instance, a subsidiary company is not allowed to purchase shares in its parent. Any officer of a company who assists in a scheme of self-purchase is liable to prosecution. The courts take a very wide view of what amounts to giving of financial assistance: *North Sydney Brick and Tile Co Ltd v Darvall* (No 2) 15 ACLR 230. The prohibition on financial assistance is fairly wide, and does not have to result in the diminution of company financial resources. Assisting another to purchase shares, even if indirectly, will be a breach of the s 260A provisions: note *Dempster v NCSC* (1993) 10 ACSR 297, where money was lent to a party and then ended up being used to purchase shares in Rothwells.

The prohibition on the self-purchase of shares is to prevent a company giving away money and diminishing the capital base. It dilutes the value of remaining shares, since they have less capital backing, and the purchasers may not be paying the true value for shares as there could be manipulation of the market price. There are problems of voting and dividend rights attached to shares which are held by the company.

There are exceptions to the rule against self-purchase of shares set out in s 260C. They allow a company to purchase its own shares under a reduction of capital scheme, provided the court is satisfied it is in the best interests of the company: s 256A–E. The court will not approve the scheme where there is prejudice to any interest group such as creditors and creditors can object. A forfeiture of shares, for example, because of a refusal to pay a call on capital, is not regarded as a reduction of capital.

Share buy-backs

[22.62]   The Corporations Law recognises the need for a company in some instances to buy its own shares. The reasons range from allowing employees to buy shares on the promise of repurchase, or for a company to downsize its operations and allow shareholders to reinvest elsewhere. A company can reduce its share capital according to the rules of Chapter 2J of the Corporations Law, which are designed to avoid the company becoming insolvent, to protect shareholders and creditors: s 256A. A company can reduce its share capital under s 256B as long as:

- it is fair and reasonable to the company's shareholders as a whole;
- it does not materially prejudice the company's ability to pay its creditors; and
- it is approved by shareholders under s 256C.

Under s 256C the shareholders must give their approval and certain procedures must be followed:

- an ordinary resolution is required at a general meeting for an equal reduction of shares;

- a special shareholder approval is needed for selective reduction with a special resolution, or an ordinary resolution by all shareholders;
- a resolution to purchases shares must be lodged with the ASIC; and
- proper notices of the meeting must be given, both to shareholders and the ASIC.

There are a number of safeguards in the ability of a company to reduce its capital under these provisions. If the reduction in capital leads to insolvency then the directors will be personally liable: s 588G. If there is any contravention of law then a court can grant an injunction (s 1324) and the ASIC can also intervene if there is inappropriate conduct: s 733.

A company can buy back its own shares if (s 257A):

- the buy-back does not materially prejudice the company's ability to pay its creditors; and
- the company follows the procedures laid down in the law.

One of the rules which may apply is that no more than 10 per cent of shares may be purchased in 12 months — this is the 10/12 rule.

The types of buy-back schemes permitted are:

- *Buy-back schemes with identical offers*   This is where the company makes an offer to purchase the same number of shares from all shareholders, known also as an equal access scheme. The 10/12 rule also applies to this scheme.
- *Employee share purchase schemes*   This is where the company purchases shares from participating employees.
- *Selective buy-back schemes*   This is where there is an arrangement between a company and individual shareholders. There are special procedures involved in this type of scheme, such as approval by unanimous resolution, so that the interests of shareholders are not prejudiced.
- *Minimum holding buy-backs*   These are buy-backs of shares from a listed company where the number of shares is not in a marketable package which can be sold on the stock exchange.
- *On market buy-backs*   These are permitted according to special rules of the stock exchange and Corporations Law allowing for sale through the ordinary course of trading.

Dividends

[22.63]   Dividends represent the return on the shareholders' investment. They are payments divided among shareholders from the trading profits of a company, according to their rights as governed by the constitution. Some companies distinguish between shares, giving priority of dividend payment to certain shares — for instance, preference shares. Sometimes a dividend may be paid in the form of bonus shares. Under the replaceable rules (s 254U), the directors will determine that a dividend is payable and fix the amount, the time of payment and how the dividends will be paid.

Dividends must come from profits

[22.64]   Dividends must be paid from profits and not out of capital: s 254T. This rule is to ensure that the capital of a company is preserved and to protect the interests of creditors. A company must not pay a dividend if it will become insolvent. A company is under no compulsion to pay dividends, even when it has had good profits (*Burland v Earle*

[1902] AC 83), unless the refusal to declare dividends amounts to a form of oppression: see **[22.81]**ff.

Before the Company Law Review Act there was a distinction between final and interim dividends, so that final dividends once declared had to be paid to shareholders as if they were a debt (*Marra Developments Ltd v BW Rofe Pty Ltd* [1977] 2 NSWLR 616; (1977) 3 ACLR 185), whereas interim dividends did not similarly have to be paid. Under s 254V a company is only liable to pay dividends when the time for payment arises, and the company can withdraw any decision to pay dividends before the time of payment, unless the constitution states otherwise.

While a company makes profits, it is possible to pay dividends, even if the assets of the company have declined. In *Lee v Neuchatel Asphalte Co* (1889) 41 Ch D 1 a company which owned a deteriorating mine, but making profits, was able to pay dividends.

A company may pay dividends out of current profits, despite making losses in previous years — there is no compulsion to account for previous losses: *Ammonia Soda Co Ltd v Chamberlain* [1918] 1 Ch 266. A company can also revalue assets which have appreciated in value and determine profits from this revaluation: *Dimbula Valley (Ceylon) Tea Co Ltd v Laurie* [1961] Ch 353. As long as the original capital of the company is preserved and dividends are paid from profit, a company is free to make its own assessment of profit from any source and in any circumstance. Profits must be determined according to the accounting standards set in the Corporations Law.

Debentures

[22.65]   A company may, if it is permitted to do so, prefer to raise capital by borrowing from the public. This can be done through an issue of securities, known as debentures. Whereas the issue of shares allows a shareholder to become a member of the company, debenture holders are lenders and not owners of the company. A company may seek capital through an issue of debentures so as not to issue more equity. Furthermore, the interest on debentures is a tax deduction. A debenture-holder can wind up the company in the event of a default of the loan.

Debenture defined

[22.66]   A debenture has a wide meaning according to s 9 of the Corporations Law. It is any document which evidences, or acknowledges, money lent or deposited with the company, whether backed by a charge or not. A charge is dealt with later and refers to security over assets given by a company for its borrowing. Most important in the definition is that a lender has some document or certificate showing what has been lent. This is evidence that they are owed money by the company. Section 9, however, distinguishes certain transactions which are not debentures, such as a document that shows a debt which is merely in the ordinary course of business, or money lent to another in the ordinary course of business.

If a corporation is borrowing in the form of debentures then it must comply with the procedures of the Corporations Law; debenture holders also gain particular rights under this legislation.

Description of debentures

[22.67]   Where a company makes an invitation or offer to the public to subscribe in securities which are debentures, then a prospectus must be issued and the securities offered can only be referred to as:

* an unsecured note or an unsecured deposit note;
* a mortgage debenture or certificate of mortgage debenture stock; and
* a debenture or certificate of debenture stock: s 1045.

An *unsecured note* or *deposit* is a certificate evidencing a loan for which no security is given. Holders of these rank after secured creditors.

A debenture can be described as a *mortgage debenture* in a prospectus only where the company states the money lent is secured by a first mortgage on land, the mortgage is registered and the mortgage does not represent more than 60 per cent of the value of the land.

A *debenture or certificate of debenture stock*, to be described as such, must be secured by a charge on part of or all the assets of the company. Debentures are secured by a floating charge or specific charge on the property of the company. If no security is given then the certificate must be referred to as an unsecured note.

The purpose of this section is to make the lending public aware of the different security it gets with its lending. Under s 1020 no application for debentures can be supplied unless it is attached to a prospectus, which must conform to the Corporations Law.

Trustee for debenture-holders

[22.68]   Where a company issues debentures a trustee must be appointed to look after the interests of the debenture holders: s 1052. The qualifications of the trustee are set out in s 1052(1), and these bodies include a Public Trustee, a body corporate which is registered under the Life Insurance Act, an Australian bank and certain corporations approved under the Corporations Law or by the ASIC.

The duties of the trustee set out in s 1056 include:

* to exercise diligence and care in ascertaining whether the company has sufficient property to cover the principal debt when it becomes due;
* to make the sure the prospectus does not contain any material which is inconsistent with the terms of the trust deed or the debentures;
* to ensure that the company complies with the Corporations Law;
* to remedy any breach which may occur in relation to the debentures so as to ensure the interests of debenture-holders; and
* to recommend any course of actions should the debentures be unable to be paid.

Under s 1058 the directors of the company must report to the trustee on any matters affecting the interests of the debenture holders. Directors must report any exceeding of borrowing limits, any breach of conditions relating to the deed, and any event or change in the company which affects the company's security or ability to pay back the borrowing.

Role of the trustee

[22.69]   The trustee, under s 1057, has the power to assess that the company will be unable to pay its debentures when they become due. The trustee can then apply to the ASIC for an order that the company limit its activities to protect the interests of the debenture-holders. A company may, for instance, be prohibited from selling off property or raising new loans.

A trustee has a fiduciary duty to the debenture-holders and is personally liable for the discharge of duties to them. The trustee's duties may be inserted in the trust deed. A trustee can apply to the court for directions on any matter concerning the interests of debenture-holders: s 1057.

Contents of the trust deed

[22.70]   The terms and description of the debenture offer must be set out in a trust deed: s 1054. The deed is the contract between the company and the debenture-holders which prescribes the conditions under the which the borrowing takes place. Section 1054 sets out specific provisions which must be included. If the terms are not stated in the trust deed they are deemed by the Corporations Law to be stated. The undertakings in a trust deed include that:

- the company will use its best efforts to conduct its business in an efficient manner;
- the company's accounting records will be made available to the trustee or an auditor along with any information necessary;
- the company will call a meeting of debenture-holders at the request of a 10 per cent holding of debenture holders; and
- the company will lay before the debenture-holders all the accounts and balance sheets from the general meeting of shareholders.

The trust deed may contain further provisions such as a requirement that the company keep property in good repair or restrict future borrowing.

Events to make the money repayable

[22.71]   The trust deed will set out the events making the principal money repayable — such as a non-payment of interest, cessation of trading, a failure by the company to follow the terms of the trust deed, or any other event which drastically affects the business of the company.

Charges

[22.72]   Charging property is the process whereby a company designates property as security for a loan from a creditor. Practically any property of value can be charged, whether physical or intangible, such as goodwill. The law recognises that persons dealing with a company need to know whether its property is encumbered and, as with mortgages on land, there is a registration procedure. Property which is charged restricts the ability of the company to deal freely with that property. A company cannot deal with its assets which are subject to a charge so as to frustrate the interests of the person holding the floating charge: *Hamilton v Hunter* (1983) 8 ACLR 295.

Registering a charge

[22.73]   The Corporations Law requires a company to register a charge if it falls within those listed under s 262. These include floating charges, charges on uncalled capital, charges on a personal chattels, charges on goodwill, a licence or patent and book debts.

A mortgage on land does not have to be registered in the same way as other property since it will be registered on the title of the land.

Under s 263 a company must record any charge on its register of charges, and inform the ASIC within 45 days of the charge being incurred. The ASIC then enters a charge on the Australian Register of Company Charges. This is a register which is open to the public for inspection and is constructive notice to all persons dealing with a company. A creditor, before lending to a company, should check the register to see if there are any other creditors who have a charge on the assets being offered as security.

Floating charges

[22.74] A floating charge is a charge placed on property which characteristically fluctuates. The trading stock of a company, for example, has the characteristic of increasing, decreasing and constantly turning over according to the activities of the company. A floating charge is placed generally over the stock of the company and only fixes, or crystallises, when the creditor exercises the right to take possession of the stock as security. This type of security allows a company to deal with the assets under security unless the creditor has called up the security in the event of some default or some event of significance.

Fixed charges

[22.75] A fixed charge is where a specific asset has been designated as security, and the charge therefore affixes to that asset. The creditor, in the event of a default, would be able to seize that particular asset. A mortgage, either on goods or land, is a fixed charge.

Priorities of charges

[22.76] If a creditor has a charge over property and it is not registered according to the Corporations Law, then it is an unregistered or 'equitable charge'. An equitable charge is a right, but an inferior one, to a 'legal charge' which is a properly registered charge according to the Corporations Law. A registered charge will always take priority over the equitable charge. A party who has checked to see if there are any prior claims to property as security, and none are registered, is entitled to assume he or she has first claim over assets.

Sections 278–282 set out the priorities of charges and these are basically that:

* the registered charge takes priority over an unregistered charge; and
* an earlier registered charge takes priority over a later registered charge.

This priority may be crucial where creditors have security over the assets of a company in liquidation, and there are insufficient funds to pay off all the creditors.

Shareholders and the company

[22.77] Shareholders are the owners of the company and the relationship between them and the company is according to the contract made by the company constitution. The capital of the company is subscribed by shareholders and they have an interest in their investment. The position of shareholders in public companies is more flexible than those in proprietary companies — the shares in a public company can be freely transferred and if the shares are listed there is a ready market for them. A shareholder in a proprietary company could be trapped if the company chooses to restrict the transfer of shares.

Requirement to prepare financial reports

[22.78]   When it is considered that a public company raises money from the public, the need for accountability by the controllers of the company becomes apparent. In this respect the financial reports of a company are vital documents.

The financial reports are a means by which shareholders can gauge how well the company is doing. Similarly, they provide a means by which creditors can assess the profitability and stability of the company. Potential investors also find the financial reports useful in providing information.

A company is required to keep written financial records that:

a) correctly record and explain its transactions and financial position and performance; and

b) would enable true and fair financial statements to be prepared: s 286(1).

A company must keep its financial records in a proper accounting form of ledgers and not just a collection of butts and receipts: *Daniels v Anderson (formerly trading as Deloitte Haskins & Sells)* (1995) 16 ACSR 607. This is so that financial reports can be prepared if required.

A small proprietary company and an ongoing exempt proprietary company do not have to prepare or lodge financial reports with the ASIC each year (s 292(2)), unless specifically ordered to do so by the ASIC (s 294)), or if the members demand them: s 293. Large proprietary companies and public companies must lodge their financial reports each year: s 292.

To ensure that the financial reports of a company reflect its business, and that they are prepared properly, the Corporations Law imposes particular requirements on their method of preparation. The accounting requirements are found in Chapter 2M.

The Australian Accounting Standards Board has the role of developing accounting standards and the Australian Stock Exchange also stipulates rules which must be complied with by listed companies. All the regulations and rules are designed to make the financial reports as true and fair as possible.

The basic accounting requirements are that:

*   A company must keep financial records to correctly record all its transactions in the prescribed form: s 334–339. These financial records must be in English and retained for seven years: s 287.

*   The directors of a company have a number of duties in relation to financial records. They must ensure that a profit and loss statement, balance sheet and cash flow statement are prepared (ss 295) and these financial records must be in the required format and contain particular information as per the accounting regulations. The directors must present the financial reports to the annual general meeting (s 317), and have a duty to state that the financial reports are true and fair and comment on the company's business: s 295(4). Directors must report on the financial reports of the company: ss 298–300. Directors can be charged for failing to maintain the financial records: *Australian Securities Commission v Fairlie* (1993) 11 ACLC 669.

*   An auditor must be appointed, unless it is a small proprietary company. The auditor, who must be an independent person and registered as an auditor, must comment on

the financial reports and their reliability: s 307. Negligence on the part of the auditor in this regard can lead to litigation.

- The members of a company are entitled to receive a copy of the financial reports (ss 315–316), though this can now be in a concise form: s 314. Members can also seek a court order to inspect the company's financial records where the request is made in good faith (s 247A–247B), even where the member is seeking evidence for a claim of oppression: *Cescastle Pty Ltd v Renak Holdings Ltd* (1991) 9 ACLC 1333; 6 ACSR 115; see also [22.81]ff.

Company meetings

[22.79]   Meetings are the vehicle by which members are able to transact company business and hold the company controllers to account. Only a public company must hold an annual general meeting, and its first must be held within 18 months of registration: s 250N. A public company must have an annual general meeting (AGM) each calendar year and within five months of the financial year ending, and the meeting must comply with the procedures and requirements of the company's constitution (if it has one). At the AGM there is usually an election of directors, declaration of dividends, tabling of financial reports and ordinary business where the shareholders can ask questions. A proprietary company with one member does not need to hold an AGM (s 250N(4)), and can make any resolution by recording and signing it: s 249B. A proprietary company with more than one member can also dispense with the need for holding an AGM: this is done by circulating resolutions in writing and getting the members to sign: s 249A. Circulating resolutions cannot be used for special resolutions or where such a resolution would not be allowed; for example, to remove an auditor: s 329.

A general meeting other than the annual general meeting is referred to as an extraordinary general meeting. Under the Corporations Law some matters must be decided by a meeting, such as, for example, a change of status (ss 162–163) or removal of directors: s 227.

Notice and meeting procedure

[22.80]   A meeting will consider various resolutions put to it. These can be ordinary or special resolutions. An ordinary resolution requires only a simple majority of members to approve it, while a special resolution requires 75 per cent member approval: s 9. Whether a matter requires an ordinary or special resolution is determined by the Corporations Law and the company's constitution. Any notice of a meeting must set out the place, date and time of the meeting; it must also state the general nature of the meeting's business and any special resolution which is to be put: s 249L. Shareholders must receive sufficient notice of any meeting, whether a general meeting or some other type. Notice must be in writing, delivered to each member entitled to vote, though this can be done electronically: s 249J. Under s 249H all resolutions, whether special or ordinary, requires 21 days' notice be given to shareholders, though listed companies must give 28 days' notice: s 249HA. If a company has a constitution, the period of notice may be longer.

In circumstances where shareholders regard it as necessary to hold a meeting outside the usual times the Corporations Law allows them to convene one. A meeting may be called by a member holding 5 per cent of the votes which can be cast, or by 100 members entitled to vote at the meeting: s 249D. Directors will be penalised if they do not then call a requested meeting: s 249E. A court also has the power to call a meeting: s 249G.

Minutes of the meetings must be recorded with all relevant information and decisions from voting (s 251A), and must be entered within one month of a meeting being held, with members having the right to inspect them: s 251B.

Members can demand a poll (formal vote) instead of a show of hands: s 250L. Unless the constitution provides otherwise voting will take place by a show of hands. Proxies are able to be appointed in a public company as a mandatory rule, though in a proprietary company the right to appoint a proxy is a replaceable rule and a company constitution may displace this rule and require voting in person.

Protection of smaller shareholders

[22.81]   Shareholders who own the majority of shares have the ability to elect directors, and ultimately to control the company. Majority shareholders can nominate themselves as directors or control company affairs to suit their own interests. Smaller shareholders may then end up with no influence over the affairs of the company, and are subject to the wishes of majority shareholders. Courts do recognise that a majority should rule and that unpopular decisions do not always amount to oppression: *Re G Jeffery (Mens Store) Pty Ltd* (1984) 9 ACLC 193; 2 ACLC 421.

The domination of a company's affairs by majority shareholders, who use that power to further their own interests at the expense of the company, is referred to by various names such as abuse of power, oppression or fraud on the minority. There needs to be a balance between the interests of the members and the majority, who are usually the management.

Case Example

Two majority shareholders, in their capacity as directors, organised a contract for the company in which they were directors. Realising the potential profits to be made, they formed another company and transferred the valuable contract into that company. The directors then used their majority voting power to approve of the scheme. A minority shareholder successfully sued the directors on the grounds that they had misused their majority position for their own personal gain: *Cook v Deeks* [1916] 1 AC 554.

The rule in *Foss v Harbottle*

[22.82]   In the case of *Foss v Harbottle* (1843) 67 ER 189 two minority shareholders attempted to take action on behalf of the company for the negligence of the directors, which had resulted in losses for the company. The court refused to hear the shareholders, holding that since a company is a legal entity in its own right it is for the company to bring action on its own behalf against wrongdoers. This principle meant that if there was any wrongdoing by a director or member who had a majority shareholding, then the company, being controlled by a majority, was unlikely to take action against a wrongdoer.

The courts have since developed a number of exceptions to the rule in *Foss v Harbottle*:

- where a majority shareholder, or even the company itself, has acted outside the powers in the constitution;

- where the procedures of the constitution have not been complied with, such as using an ordinary resolution where a special resolution is required;
- where a member's rights have been contravened;
- where there has been a fraud on the minority. A fraud on the minority is where the majority have acted in their own interests, and not for the benefit of the company as a whole. Examples are where directors use their majority power to validate a wrongful act or organise benefits to flow to themselves personally, rather than to the company.

Protection under the Corporations Law

[22.83] In s 246AA of the Corporations Law there is a provision which allows for any aggrieved member, or the ASIC, to apply to the court for a remedy in respect of any act, or omission, which is oppressive, unfairly prejudicial, or discriminatory against a member or the members as a whole. If the court is satisfied the grounds are made out, then it may make a variety of orders, such as regulation of the affairs of the company, the institution of proceedings against a director, or even, as a last resort, the winding up of the company under s 461(e), (f) and (g). Section 246AA reinforces the exceptions to the rule of *Foss v Harbottle*.

In recent decisions there seems to be a move by the courts to support minority actions for oppression, particularly where it involves changing the company constitution to the detriment of some shareholders: *Gambotto v WCP Ltd* (1995) 182 CLR 432; 127 ALR 417; 16 ACSR 1. Some acts of oppression may be very obvious as being discriminatory or unfair, but sometimes a company when attempting to act in the best interests of all may act unfairly against one group: *Residues Treatment & Trading Co Ltd v Southern Resources Ltd* (1988) 14 ACLR 375; 6 ACLC 913.

Other protection under the Corporations Law

[22.84] There are other provisions in the Corporations Law which allow shareholders to enforce their rights. Under s 1324 a person can apply to the court for an injunction to prevent another from carrying out a contravention of the Corporations Law. The court has the power to make orders where appropriate. Under ss 246B-246E a shareholder whose rights are to be affected by a change in the constitution can apply to the court and have the change set aside if it will unfairly prejudice a class of shareholders. Members have the right to call a meeting (ss 249D), to inspect the company records (s 247A) and to claim damages for misleading conduct regarding a prospectus: ss 995, 1005.

Directors and officers

[22.85] The Corporations Law provides that a public company must have at least three directors, two of whom are resident in Australia, and a proprietary company must have at least one director, one of whom is a resident: s 221.

The role of directors

[22.86] As a general principle, directors, referred to as the board of directors, are the ultimate management and control of a company; they are more than mere employees. They constitute the 'company's will and mind' by forming the company policy and direction.

Directors must monitor all aspects of the company's functions, including management. It is the board of directors which is ultimately responsible for the company's activities and the decisions of its managers.

Directors are part of the wider group known as officers of the company. An officer is defined in ss 9 and 82A(1) to include directors, company secretary, executive officers and employees and receivers. The concept of a director is an undefined term and refers to a person involved in policy or management: *Commissioner for Corporate Affairs (Vic) v Bracht* [1989] VR 821; (1988) 14 ACLR 728. In another case it was suggested that an officer is normally a person appointed to a position with a title and specific powers: *R v Scott* (1990) 8 ACLC 752; 2 ACSR 470; 20 NSWLR 72.

Definition of director

[22.87]   The Corporations Law defines a director of a corporate body as any person who occupies or acts in the position of director: s 60. This includes a person who is not named or properly appointed as a director but assumes the powers of a director, and gives directions like a director. The section is designed to catch persons who control and direct a company but hide behind the lack of appointment. The definition of 'director' is crucial since there are special duties placed on directors, and civil and criminal penalties attaching to a breach of these duties: see **[22.25]**ff. The section does not include as a director a person who merely gives advice to the directors on a professional basis or through a business relationship, even though the directors may act upon it: s 60(1).

Appointment of a director

[22.88]   A director must be a natural person, at least 18 years and less than 72 years of age: s 228. A director over the age of 72 can be re-appointed, but only on a year-by-year basis with the approval of a meeting of shareholders. This section does not apply to proprietary companies.

Directors must be appointed according to the provisions in the constitution, which is by election of the company at the annual general meeting. The first directors are selected by the persons wishing to form a company and are named in the application, prior to registration. Under the replaceable rules a company can appoint a director (s 224C), directors can appoint other directors (s 224D), though this can be modified by the operation of the company constitution.

Qualifications of a director

[22.89]   Although the role of a company director can be demanding there are no formal educational, training or experience qualifications required. The constitution of a company may require qualifications of directors in that they hold a specific number of shares — this is known as the share qualification. The company constitution may impose particular qualifications, perhaps that a director belong to a professional organisation.

Disqualification of a director

[22.90]   The constitution of a company may contain provisions which disqualify a director. A director may be disqualified for being absent from the company, for mental illness or because a conflict of interest has arisen between the director's personal interests and those of the company.

There are a number of statutory provisions whereby a director may be prevented from taking office, or if already a director, from continuing to hold that office. The events which will result in the director's office being vacated are listed in s 224. These are:

- where the director becomes insolvent (s 229(1)), except with the leave of the court;
- where the director has been convicted of an offence under s 229(3), which prohibits certain persons from managing a company. The offences are fraud, a serious breach of corporate law, or a breach of any of the sections listed in the subsection;
- where the court has ordered a person not to manage a company under s 230 for repeated breach of the legislation, dishonesty or lack of diligence;
- where there has been a court order under s 599, where the company is insolvent under the director's management, or the person has been involved in the management of two or more companies which have failed in the past seven years;
- where the ASIC has ordered certain persons not to manage a company under s 600 because they have been directors of two or more companies which have become insolvent.

Different types of directors

[22.91] There a number of different directors, with different titles and different roles in the company. While there are accepted commercial roles, the true assessment of a director's role is obtained by examining the constitution:

- *Chairman of directors* This person controls the meetings and is usually elected by the other directors.
- *Managing director* Also referred to as the Chief Executive Officer — an executive director: s 226C.
- *Executive director* A salaried employee who has rights and duties as an employee, whereas a non-executive director is governed only by the constitution. Executive directors may each have their own portfolio, such as production or personnel.
- *Non-executive director* A non-executive director does not participate in the day-to-day running of the company, but may bring to the board of directors prestige, experience and a different perspective in the direction of the company.
- *Governing director* An executive director who commonly owns a majority of shares in a company with wide powers from the articles to control the company directly. This type of director is often the founder of a family company.
- *Nominee director* Where a company is a shareholder its interests on the board are represented by a nominee director.
- *Alternate director* A person appointed to act as a substitute and represent another on the board if permitted by the constitution: s 225A.
- *Associate directors* These are appointed by other directors to gain experience.

Loss of office

[22.92] A company is restricted in its ability to provide payments or benefits to retiring directors under s 237. Any benefits given must be approved of by a shareholders' meeting, unless they fall within the exempt benefits set out in s 237(19). These are the normal legal benefits under contract or superannuation.

Removal of directors

[22.93]   A director of a public company can be removed under s 227 by a general resolution of a shareholders' meeting, despite anything stated in the constitution or agreement between the company and the director. Special notice of 21 days is required of the meeting (s 254) and the director has the right to address the meeting: s 227(4), (5). Directors of a proprietary company can be removed by resolution under the replaceable rule of s 226E. There are certain notices which must be given to the director under this section, and there may be contractual rights applicable on removal which could result in an action for damages by the director. If a director represents a certain class of shareholder, or creditor, then another director may have to be elected to replace that particular director.

Payment of directors

[22.94]   Directors occupy a fiduciary position and therefore have no right to payment for their role as directors. Directors will only receive remuneration that the company determines by resolution: s 236A. Members can request information on directors' remuneration: s 239. Directors can be paid reasonable remuneration once approved (s 243K) and are permitted advances of up to $2000.

Loans to directors

[22.95]   Directors in proprietary companies can take loans from the company. In public companies loans are permitted but they are regulated. Basically a company cannot give a benefit to a 'related' party unless it falls within the exceptions of s 243. Related parties are directors and relatives, and associated companies of the director. The types of loans that can be made are divided into two categories. Specific benefits, which are essentially part of the payment and perks of the director's job (ss 243A–243ZI), include benefits of a reasonable remuneration (s 243K), or advances of $2000 to directors and their spouses. The second category is benefits approved by shareholders who must be given an explanatory statement which is lodged with the ASIC, to which no recipient has voted.

Powers of directors

[22.96]   Directors are empowered to manage the business of the company by law, unless restricted by the constitution: s 226A. The power is collectively exercised by the board of a company, unless the constitution of the company states that the power can be delegated to a particular director, for example, the managing director. The constitution and Corporations Law will determine the powers available and any special duties placed on directors. Under the Company Law Review Act directors are given quite wide powers to manage a corporation, unless displaced by the constitution.

A general meeting of shareholders cannot overrule the directors unless the constitution allows for it: *NRMA v Parker* (1986) 6 NSWLR 517; 11 ACLR 1. Directors once appointed have extensive powers vested in the board of directors by the constitution. In *Automatic Self Cleansing Filter Syndicate Co Ltd v Cunninghame* [1906] Ch 34 it was held that once the constitution has given power to the board of directors for management, then a general meeting cannot interfere with the exercise of that power, and thus in that case the directors could prevent the sale of company assets despite the members having voted do to so. The only remedy available to disgruntled shareholders is to remove the directors by way of an election, unless there has been a breach of law or of the company constitution, or oppression.

Duties of directors and officers

[22.97]   Directors have a range of duties relating to their position. The duties imposed on directors are derived from both common law and statute. They have both criminal and civil implications, which means that directors can be prosecuted for a breach of duty, as well as being sued by a person who has suffered a loss as a result of that breach of duty.

Statutory and common law duties overlap and complement each other. For example, a director who improperly uses that position will have contravened s 232 of the Corporations Law. The director will also have contravened a common law duty. The result could be removal from office, a criminal prosecution and civil action by the company, the shareholders and any other person who has suffered damage.

Directors are in a special position as they are given many powers in relation to the company. Under these powers a director has access to information and property, which must be administered in the best interests of the company. Directors are therefore in a position of trust and have a fiduciary duty towards the company. Directors must always act in the best interests of the company as a whole and must perform their duties properly in consideration of current and future members: *Darvall v North Sydney Brick & Tile Co Ltd* (1987) 12 ACLR 537.

Statutory duties of directors and officers

[22.98]   Throughout the Corporations Law there are various duties imposed on directors, some directly, such as calling a meeting when requested by members: s 249D. Other duties are implied by imposing a penalty; for instance, under s 588G there is personal liability on the directors for incurring a debt which cannot be repaid.

The fiduciary duties of a director are laid out in s 232 which imposes duties of trust and honesty on all officers of the company — not only directors — but also the company secretary, executive officers and others including receivers, liquidators and trustees.

The duties imposed by s 232 are:

- to act honestly (s 232(2));
- to act with care and diligence: s 232(4). A court will examine the skills of a director, the duties to be performed and make an objective test on the size of the company and time given to make decisions as to whether a director has acted diligently and carefully: *AWA Ltd v Daniels (t/as Deloitte Haskins & Sells)* (1992) 7 ACSR 759; 10 ACLC 933. A director is under a duty to familiarise himself or herself with what is happening in the company and to take an active interest;
- not to misuse information obtained from a position as a director (s 232(5)); and
- not to use a position as director improperly to gain some advantage or benefit: s 232(6).

Another major statutory duty is found in s 231 whereby a director of a proprietary company must declare any interests he or she has in the company or its subsidiaries. If the officer does not disclose an interest then the contract may become voidable, and the particular officer may be sued for any losses: *State of South Australia v Clarke* (1996) 14 ACLC 1,019; 66 SASR 199; 19 ACSR 606. Under the replaceable rule of s 231(1A) once a disclosure has been made the director can retain that interest.

Common law duties

[22.99] The common law duties relating to a director relate both to duties which are particular to a director, such as carrying out the terms of the constitution, and duties of trust, honesty and disclosure of interests. There is no absolute list of duties and since the duty of trust and to act in the best interests of the company is such a broad concept, the duties are numerous. Directors must acquire some rudimentary knowledge of the company affairs, stay informed of company affairs and business, attend board meetings and monitor corporate affairs including the financial status and statements of the company.

The duties owed by a director include:

- *A duty to act in the best interests of the company* This duty is primarily owed to the company and not to the individual shareholders: *Percival v Wright* [1902] 2 Ch 421. Decisions made on behalf of the company must be to promote the interests of the company before individual members. Where, however, company membership is small, such as in a family company, there may be a fiduciary duty to the members: *Coleman v Myers* [1977] 2 NZLR 225. This is because there is a high degree of dependence on the director for information and advice in the relationship between the parties. Similarly, where there are only two directors and one director conceals the true state of company worth by buying out his or her fellow director for less than what the company is worth, this may be a breach of duty: *Glavanics v Brunninghausen* (1996) 14 ACLC 345; 10 ACSR 204.

- *A duty of trust, so as to act in good faith and honestly* Dishonesty is a wide concept and is more than just theft; it applies to conduct which falls short of the best interests of the company. It would apply, for example, where a director has acquired assets of the company for less than their market price: *Grove v Flavel* (1986) 43 SASR 410; 111 ACLR 161.

- *A duty not to make profits from a position as a director* Where profits are made only because a person is a director — for instance, because he or she has access to information — those profits must be paid to the company. There is no breach of duty, however, where the directors have fully informed the shareholders, or company, of any potential conflict. In *Peso Silver Mines Ltd v Cropper* (1966) 58 DLR (2d) 1 a board of directors did not take up an offer of a silver mine. One of the directors, believing in its potential, formed his own company and took up the opportunity. The court found there was no breach of duty, even though the information had been gained from a position as a director, since the company had first opportunity and had rejected it. Directors should ensure that they always make full disclosure of interests to a company and get approval so there is no breach of fiduciary duty.

- *A duty to avoid a conflict of interest* Where a director is involved with a competing company, or supplies goods or property to the company, there is a potential conflict of interest. Unless the director can show full disclosure of any interest, or that the decision was made on independent advice to the company, there may be a breach of duty.

- *A duty not to misuse information gained in the position of a director* Information held by a company is a form of property and its misuse amounts to a breach of duty. In *Green & Clara Pty Ltd v Bestobell Industries Pty Ltd* [1982] WAR 1 a manager acquired information which he then used in a new company he incorporated. The court found that he had misused information gained in a position of trust, and equated the position of this officer to that of a director.

- *A duty to be diligent and careful*   Directors must act professionally; they must acquaint themselves with the company affairs and take an active role in supervising the management of the company: *AWA Ltd v Daniels (t/as Deloitte Haskins & Sells)* (1992) 7 ACSR 759; 10 ACLC 933. A non-executive director also has a duty of diligence and care — for instance, to read the company financial statements and to understand the company affairs to the extent of reaching a reasonable informed opinion of the company's financial position: *Commonwealth Bank of Australia v Friedrich* (1991) 5 ACSR 115.

Case Example

Mrs Morley was a director for 30 years in a family company, though she never participated in the business. On the death of her husband, who was a director, her son took over the running of the business. The company traded while insolvent, thus triggering personal liability. Mrs Morley sought to show she was not liable because she did not know of the breach, nor did she participate in the activities of the company. The court found her liable on the grounds that she was a director and should have known of the company's affairs; her defence of lack of knowledge was rejected, she could not hide behind ignorance: *Statewide Tobacco Services Ltd v Morley* (1990) 2 ACSR 405.

Directors' duty to creditors

[22.100]   Part of the justification for the regulation of companies is to protect creditors and in this context directors have a duty not to jeopardise the value of company assets which represent the security of investors.

A breach of the duty to creditors may occur where directors authorise a loan to a related company, while suspecting that it may not be repaid: *Walker v Wimborne* (1976) 137 CLR 1; 3 ACLR 529. The lending of money at less than market rates by directors may similarly amount to a disregard for the interests of creditors: *Ring v Sutton* (1980) 5 ACLR 546.

Directors are breaching their duty to creditors where they improperly transfer assets from the company in order to frustrate a debt. Such a breach was established in *Kinsela v Russell Kinsela Pty Ltd* (1986) 4 NSWLR 722; 10 ACLR 395, where a company in financial difficulty transferred its property and business to the directors personally, before the company went into liquidation. Similarly, in *Jeffree v NCSC* [1990] WAR 183; (1989) 15 ACLR 217 a director, expecting to lose a court case with a customer, transferred property out of the company. The customer was successful and was left with a claim against an empty company. The NCSC successfully prosecuted Jeffree for a criminal breach of s 232, because he had made improper use of his position as a director, and had acted directly against the interests of a creditor.

Liability of directors

[22.101]   Directors may be liable for civil and criminal penalties relating to negligence, breach of duty or misconduct. Sanctions against directors are set out in Pt 9.4B in ss 1317DA–1317HF which allow a court to impose civil penalties, to begin criminal proceedings, and order compensation for the company. Directors may also be ordered not to manage a corporation and disqualified from holding any future offices.

Excusing a breach of duty

[22.102] A company at its general meeting can excuse an officer for a breach of duty owed to the corporation, or even ratify an action after the event which would otherwise be a breach of duty: *Bamford v Bamford* [1968] 3 WLR 317. Ratification will not be allowed where it is not in the best interests of the company as a whole, where there is illegal actions, where there is fraud on the minority or where a third party's interest has become involved. An officer can apply to a court to excuse him or her from a possible penalty relating to a breach of duty: s 1318. A court may excuse the officer if there has been proper disclosure or if the directors can show they have acted honestly, even if negligently, and ought to be excused.

Duty of directors to outsiders

[22.103] Although the duty of directors is primarily to the company as a whole there has been discussion about widening that duty to persons outside the company. In the case of *Parke v Daily News Ltd* [1962] Ch 927; [1962] 2 All ER 929 the directors of a newspaper proposed to use company funds, from the sale of a newspaper, to make bonus payments to employees who would lose their jobs. The payments would have resulted in less money being available to shareholders. Some shareholders objected and the court stated that directors must act in the interests of the company as a whole and that there was no duty owed to the employees.

In respect of creditors there have been cases where the courts have recognised a duty. See the discussion in the context of the maintenance of capital in **[22.60]**.

The company secretary

[22.104] The directors of a company must appoint a company secretary: s 240. This section also determines the qualifications of the secretary as being over the age of 18 years, a natural person and resident in the jurisdiction of Australia. A director can be a company secretary: s 240(7).

The company secretary is not defined in the Corporations Law, but is designated as an officer in the company and has statutory duties imposed by the Corporations Law. The constitution of the company also imposes duties on the company secretary, such as maintaining all company registers, keeping minutes at directors' meetings and ensuring general company compliance with the Corporations Law. One of the most important functions of a company secretary is to lodge the company's annual return which is a public document that members and the community can inspect. The annual return contains information about changes to company affairs concerning shares, directors and other matters: s 345. In 1996 the ASC reported that it had prosecuted 3826 company secretaries for not putting in returns.

The importance and authority of a company secretary was established in the case of *Panorama Developments (Guildford) Ltd v Fidelis Furnishing Fabrics Ltd* [1971] 2 QB 711. In this case a company secretary ordered hire cars for his own use, which was an unauthorised act and outside the secretary's power. The company refused to pay for the hire of the cars and the car hire firm sued. The court held that despite the company secretary not having the power to hire the cars, the company would still be liable for the secretary's actions. A company secretary is recognised as an important officer of the company with extensive powers and duties. Outsiders are entitled to believe that the secretary has the authority to make contracts and incur liabilities on behalf of the company.

Takeovers

[22.105]   A takeover of a company occurs where someone, usually another company (the offeror), purchases sufficient shares to take control of a company (the target) from the existing controllers. The offeror buys not only the shares but also control of the target company and may have to pay above market rates to gain that control.

Control of the company

[22.106]   The diversity of shareholders and the amounts they hold means that it is possible to control a company with less than 50 plus 1 per cent of the shares. The Corporations Law takes the view that a purchaser of 20 per cent of shares in a company can have a significant influence over the affairs of the company — for instance, by electing himself or herself as a director of the company.

Purpose of regulating takeovers

[22.107]   The Corporations Law is designed to ensure that the whole market has an informed view of a takeover; that it is done in a competitive manner, that all shareholders have the opportunity to take part in any offer, and that shareholders are treated equally. The ASIC plays a considerable role in this area with wide discretionary power to modify the operation of the Law and exempt individuals from compliance: s 730. The ASIC provides guidance notes on takeovers and can intervene if it believes there has been unacceptable behaviour. The ASIC can refer certain takeovers to the Corporations and Securities Panel for adjudication, if it believes that the spirit of the Corporations Law is not being fulfilled.

Apart from the Corporations Law, the Trade Practices Act 1974 (Cth) prohibits market domination by one company: s 50. This is supervised by the Trade Practices Commission. Other relevant legislation is the Foreign Acquisitions and Takeovers Act 1975 (Cth) which regulates foreign ownership of Australian companies.

Takeover provisions under the Corporations Law

[22.108]   The Corporations Law prohibits an acquisition of shares over a benchmark of 20 per cent of the voting shares of a company, unless in compliance with the provisions of the Corporations Law: s 615. Compliance is still required by shareholders holding more than 20 per cent, but less than 90 per cent, of a company's shares.

Associated companies and individuals who have, or appear to have, some agreement between themselves in acquiring shares, will also be subject to the 20 per cent rule: s 609. Where associated persons have shares which aggregate to more than 20 per cent they fall within the rule of s 615.

The Corporations Law recognises that the 20 per cent rule can be breached by inadvertence, lack of awareness, mistake or for some reason beyond control so that takeover provisions will not apply: s 610.

Some acquisitions are not prohibited under the Corporations Law, including:

- creeping takeovers (see **[22.110]**);
- where a company has fewer than 15 members and has consented to the takeover (s 619);
- where a company allots shares on an equal basis, proportional to existing holdings (s 621);
- an acquisition made by a prospectus offer, or acquisitions by an underwriter (s 622);
- an acquisition through a compromise or arrangement approved by the Supreme Court (s 625);
- an acquisition by operation of the law (s 631); and
- an acquisition by a liquidator: s 626.

Takeover methods

[22.109]   Once the benchmark of 20 per cent has been reached, the takeover must comply with an acceptable takeover method unless it is exempt: s 615.

Once an offeror has purchased 90 per cent of the shares in a company, it can demand that the remaining 10 per cent of shareholders sell the offeror their shares at the offer price: s 701. Alternatively, the remaining 10 per cent of shareholders can give notice that they demand the offeror purchase their shares: s 703.

Creeping takeovers

[22.110]   This method of takeover allows for the purchase of 3 per cent of a company's shares each six months, provided the offeror has held a minimum 19 per cent of the shares for six months prior to a 3 per cent purchase: s 618.

Takeover scheme

[22.111]   A takeover scheme involves an offer made to all shareholders in a 'target' company, or to a particular class of shareholder: s 636. The aim of s 636 is to ensure that all shareholders, the company and the market are fully informed of an offer. Each shareholder must receive the same offer and it must be in writing. The procedure for such a scheme is as follows:

- The offeror must prepare a Pt A statement which contains prescribed information material to the offer. This statement must be served on the target company, along with the offer, before making the offer to individual shareholders: s 637. The statement and the offer must be registered with the ASIC within 21 days of service on the target company: s 644.
- If the company is listed on the stock exchange then a copy of the Pt A statement must be served on the exchange in the state in which the company operates: s 637.
- The offeror must then send the offer, attached to a Pt A statement, to all shareholders: ss 637–638. Offers can be conditional, for instance on a minimum number of offers being accepted before the takeover will proceed.
- The target company will respond with a Pt B statement: s 647. This statement must follow the format of s 750 and is the company's advice on whether shareholders should accept or reject the offer.
- The target company must send a copy of the Pt B statement to the ASIC and to its state exchange if it is a listed company. If there is an association between the offeror and the target company — for instance, there are common directors to both

companies — an expert's report must be attached to the Pt B statement. The expert must be independent and give an opinion on whether the offer should be accepted.

Takeover announcements on the stock exchange

[22.112]   If the target company is listed on the stock exchange the offeror can purchase more than 20 per cent under the procedures of a takeover announcement: s 617, ss 673–682.

A takeover announcement involves a broker announcing to the market that the offeror is willing to purchase particular shares, at a specified price for a period of not less than one month. The offeror is bound to accept all offers from shareholders once the announcement has been made. The Corporations Law specifies procedures for a takeover announcement:

- The offeror must prepare and serve a Pt C statement on the target company at the same time as the announcement is made on the stock exchange. The offeror must within 14 days of the announcement send a copy of the Pt C statement and the offer to each shareholder: s 679.
- The target company must prepare and serve a Pt D statement to the stock exchange, the offeror and the ASIC, which is a statement by the directors of the target company on whether the shareholders should accept or reject the offer made: s 683.

Defending a takeover

[22.113]   A hostile takeover bid represents a threat to the controllers of the target company and in these circumstances strenuous efforts are made to defeat the bid. The conduct of a takeover is highly regulated and in defending a takeover the target company is prohibited from using certain tactics. The target company cannot make misleading statements or omissions in its statements: s 704. Similarly, there is a prohibition on the making of false and reckless public statements: s 746. These are called bluffing bids and are designed to push the price of shares up in the market, making it more difficult to buy them.

Other prohibited defensive measures include the giving of special benefits to shareholders which have not been properly stated in the takeover documents. These are called escalator clauses whereby shareholders have an agreement with the offeror, before a takeover, to get special payments after the takeover: s 697. Also prohibited are payments or benefits not disclosed in the takeover statement: s 698.

Service agreements may be used to make the company look less attractive. These are contracts given to employees in the target company which bind a future owner, though they may be overturned by a court where they are unfair: s 740.

The directors of a target company may be able to ward off a takeover by convincing shareholders that the company is worth far more than the bid price. This can be done through the statements they must prepare. The board may be able to restructure the company, or issue small blocs of shares called share-splitting, or possibly invite another company to take it over in order to ward off a hostile takeover. The directors of any company attempting to ward off a takeover must be careful not to breach their duties as directors or contravene the Corporations Law.

The final stages in the life of a company

[22.114]   A feature of an corporation is that it has perpetual succession which means that, unlike natural persons, it cannot die. There are circumstances, however, when the company reaches the end of its useful life. A common practice is to create a company for a short term project; once the project is completed the company has no further purpose. The law provides a process of winding up and bringing the company to an end.

A company may be wound up because it has not commenced business within a year of its registration, or its members fall below the requisite number, for oppression or not complying with ASIC requirements such as the lodgement of the annual return. The company may even resolve to wind itself up.

There is a particular process of paying out debts and shareholders get what is left over after all the creditors in accordance with the company constitution: s 563A.

Companies in distress

[22.115]   A company unable to pay its debts as they fall due is insolvent. There are a number of options available to a company depending on its assets, its prospects and the wishes of its creditors. Ultimately, a company can be wound up so that its assets are sold off to pay its debts but there are procedures which stop short of that terminal process. It is sometimes in the interests of creditors to keep a company going since its business is its prime asset.

Official management

[22.116]   Prior to 23 June 1993 this process involved a manager being appointed to manage the affairs of a company in financial difficulty. It has now been replaced by a system of voluntary administration: see **[22.118]**. Official management is provided for in the Corporations Law ss 435–458 to accommodate those arrangements put in place before the law changed. The thrust of official management is to allow for a postponement or moratorium of debts until the manager comes to some arrangement with the creditors.

Receivers

[22.117]   Where a company defaults on a financial obligation — for example, in relation to debentures — the trustee for debenture-holders has traditionally been able to appoint a receiver to protect the interests of the debenture-holders: s 417. A mortgagee is similarly able to appoint a receiver if the mortgage agreement provides for it. In almost all cases the receiver is appointed privately as the exercise by creditors of a right under the security arrangement but the court has discretionary power to do so, on the application of creditors, where it considers it just or convenient to do so and that other legal remedies are inadequate. The receiver carries on the business of the company with a view to achieving the best possible result for the secured creditors — the parties who made the appointment. Unsecured creditors take a secondary position when a company goes into receivership.

Voluntary administration

[22.118]   The Corporations Law provisions dealing with insolvent companies were substantially amended in 1992. The reform package repealed the former official management procedure and introduced a new way of dealing with companies in financial difficulty. This is known as voluntary administration which may loosely be described as the corporate equivalent of Pt X of the Bankruptcy Act. The object of voluntary administration is to maximise the chances of an insolvent company continuing in existence or, if that is not possible, to achieve a better return for creditors than would have resulted if the company had been immediately wound up: s 435A.

The pivotal provisions provide the company, once the administration commences, with a moratorium on the claims of creditors against the company. Creditors' claims against the company are stayed but can be enforced with the consent of the administrator or of the court. In the case of a creditor who holds a charge over the whole or substantially the whole of a company's property it is possible to enforce the charge during the period. The administrator, who is appointed by the directors, liquidator, provisional liquidator or the holder of a charge, is required to investigate the company's affairs and report to a meeting of creditors within 21 or 28 days (depending on the time of year) from the commencement of the administration. The meeting of creditors is able to determine the future of the company and can resolve that the administration be terminated, that a deed of company arrangement be executed, or that the company be wound up.

Liquidation

[22.119]   Where a company is not solvent the creditors are able to initiate the procedure for its winding up. They may also do this as a result of the voluntary administration. Winding up is the process of bringing a company's existence to an end. A liquidator is appointed by the creditors. This person, who must be registered under the Corporations Law, becomes an officer of the company and is responsible for gathering the property of the company and distributing the proceeds of its realisation to the creditors. As with bankruptcy, the property of the company is to be distributed equally to creditors so that they are treated fairly.

Proof of debts

[22.120]   As with bankruptcy it is necessary for a creditor of a company being wound up to prove the debt. The liquidator may require them to be proved formally (Corporations Law s 553D(1)) or they can be proved informally: s 553D(2). The debts which can be proved are those which existed at the time the winding up of the company started.

Secured creditors need not prove their debts — they can rely on the asset/s which represent their security. As with bankruptcy, a secured creditor is able to surrender the security and prove as an unsecured creditor. Where the asset does not cover the amount owing, the secured creditor can prove for the shortfall: see Corporations Law s 554E.

The debts which are relevant in the proof process are those which could have been claimed at the time the winding up commenced. Debts incurred after that time should only be those related to the administration of the winding up process and would therefore be treated as priority payments. Shareholders are able to prove debts such as dividends outstanding, provided that any debts they owe the company have been paid.

Priority payments

[22.121]   Once debts have been proved they are treated in the same way as in bankruptcy. That is, the creditors are to be dealt with equally. If the property available is insufficient to satisfy the debts creditors are to be paid in proportion to their proved debts: Corporations Law s 555.

There are, however, certain payments which attract priority. These are set out in the Corporations Law s 556 and can be described as the costs of administering the winding up. The remuneration of the liquidator and administrator are no accorded priority.

Priority exists for the following classes of payment:

- employees' wages up to the time of commencing the winding up;
- workers compensation payments;
- amounts due to employees for leave; and
- retrenchment payments.

Litigation by liquidators

[22.122]   In the process of winding up a company a liquidator is required to maximise the return to creditors. It is not unusual for liquidators to launch litigation on behalf of the company. The usual targets in this regard are auditors where it is alleged that they have caused losses to the company as a result of their negligence. The directors of the company can also be pursued where it is alleged that they have caused damage to the company as a result of their breach of duty.

Insolvent trading

[22.123]   The Corporations Law offers some protection for the creditors of an insolvent company through s 588G. Under this section directors or persons involved in the management of the company are liable if the company incurs a debt whilst it is insolvent. There is criminal and civil liability. The civil liability represents a departure from the usual concept of separating the company from its members. Section 588G effectively lifts the corporate veil so that directors can become personally liable for the debts. Thus if no property is left in the company, a creditor whose debt was incurred while the company was insolvent is able to seek recovery from the directors.

Summary and key terms

[22.124]   This chapter has set out to explain:

- the nature of a *company*;
- the process of registration;
- what it means to say that a company is a *separate entity*;
- *limited liability*;
- the *constitution* of a company — the *replaceable rules*;
- *public* and *proprietary* companies;
- the steps involved in creating a company;
- *capital*;

- how *shareholders contribute* to the company;
- the role of the prospectus in raising finance for a public company;
- *equity capital*;
- *debt capital* — debentures;
- how a company is required to *maintain its capital base*;
- *directors*;
- what is involved in the *management of a company*, especially in the relationship between the *shareholders and the controllers*;
- the *accountability of directors*;
- *takeovers*;
- *receivers*;
- *voluntary administration*; and
- *liquidation* and *winding up*.

Index

references are to paragraphs

613

references are to paragraphs

references are to paragraphs

references are to paragraphs

references are to paragraphs

references are to paragraphs

Contract — *continued*
breach, 5.33–5.34
consequences of, 5.35
remedies for, 5.39
damages *see* damages
injunction, 5.43
specific performance, 5.42
capacity, 2.57
bankrupts, 2.63
corporations, 2.61
minors, 2.58–2.60, 16.13
persons of unsound mind and intoxicated
persons, 2.62, 16.13
collateral, 3.13
consent, elements affecting, 4.26
consideration
defined, 2.43–2.45
must move from the promisee, 2.46
past consideration, 2.47
promises to perform an existing obligation,
2.51–2.52
sufficient, 2.49–2.50
valuable consideration, 2.48
Contracts Review Act 1980 (NSW), 4.42
contributory negligence and, 16.13
damages for breach of, 5.46, 16.12
causation, 5.49
date of assessment of, 5.35
heads of, 5.40
measure of, 5.49
mitigation, 5.54
penalties and, 5.56
Contract — *continued*
damages for breach of — *continued*
purpose, 5.47
remoteness, 5.51
rule in *Hadley v Baxendale*, 5.52
definition, 2.5
discharge *see* termination
duress, 4.27–4.28
equitable estoppel, 2.53–2.55
relief, 2.56
exclusion clauses
consumer transactions, 3.25
ticket cases, 3.5
existence, 2.9
freedom of contract, 2.8
frustration, 5.20–5.22
consequences, 5.24
frustrating events, 5.23
statutory reform, 5.25
Hadley v Baxendale, rule in, 5.52
illegality, 5.26, 5.32
common law, 5.31

statutory, 5.27–5.30
intention, 2.40–2.42
limitation of actions, and, 16.13
misrepresentation, 4.2
existing fact, of, 4.5
falsity, 4.6
inducing the contract, 4.6
remedies, 4.9–4.10
representation, 4.3
statutory reform, 4.11
Trade Practices Act and, 4.12
types, 4.8
when significant, 4.5–4.6
mistake, 4.13
common, 4.14–4.17
identity of the other party, 4.22
money paid under, 4.25
mutual, 4.19
non est factum and, 4.24
quality, as to, 4.17
rectification for, 4.23
subject matter of the contract, existence of,
4.15
unilateral mistake, 4.20
negligence and
contributory, 16.13
professional, 16.12
offer, 2.11
communication of offer, 2.16
conditional offers, 2.21
death, effect of, 2.25, 2.26
invitation to treat, 2.14
lapse of, 2.23
mere puff, 2.12
options, 2.20
rejection, 2.24
revocation, 2.22
tenders, 2.24
termination, 2.19
to whom offers can be made, 2.17
use of the word 'offer', 2.15
part performance, 2.66
privity of contract, 2.64
third parties and, 2.65
remedies, 5.39
damages: see damages
injunction, 5.43
misrepresentation, for, 4.9–4.10
rectification, 4.23
restitution, 5.58
specific performance, 5.42
restitution, 5.58
termination, 5.1
abandonment, by, 5.18

references are to paragraphs

Corporations Law, 22.4
Countermand of payment
clear and unambiguous, must be, 12.53
effect of, 11.26, 12.53
errors by customer, and, 12.53
method of, 12.53–12.54
recovery of money, and, 12.55
verbal notice of, 12.54
Countersignature
cheques, of, 11.26
Court order
sale under, 6.20
Courts
adversary system, 1.46
appeals, 1.42
committal hearings, 1.37
cross vesting of jurisdiction, 1.45
federal courts, 1.44
government agencies, 1.84
hierarchy, 1.32
High Court, 1.43
indictable offences, 1.36
inquisitorial proceedings, 1.48
intermediate courts, 1.39
judicature, 1.21
jurisdiction, 1.35, 1.40
non-court forums, 1.88
operation of a small claims/consumer claims
    tribunal, 1.86
power to hear appeals, 1.33
self help, 1.83
small claims jurisdiction, 1.85
state courts, 1.34
summary jurisdiction, 1.34
superior courts, 1.41
taking a matter to court, 1.47
Credit
application of Consumer Credit Code, 10.8,
    10.15
avoidance of Code, 10.15
non-application, 10.13
penalties for avoidance, 10.15
statutory presumption, 10.14
codes of practice, 10.7
Credit — continued
credit contracts
relief for hardship, 10.24
re-opening by court, 10.24
unjust, 10.24, 10.25
credit defined, 10.2
disclosure regime
key disclosures, 10.19, 10.35
level of accuracy, 10.20
post contract, 10.21

requirements, 10.18
guarantees, 10.11
Credit cards
debit cards, compared with, 12.82
floor limit, and, 12.79
issuer/cardholder contract, and, 12.78
issuer/merchant contract, and, 12.79
legal character of, 12.77
merchant/cardholder contract, and, 12.80
nature of, 12.76
payment obligations under, 12.78, 12.80
security measures, and, 12.79
theft of, 12.78
three party cards, 12.76
two party cards, 12.76
Crime
torts and, compared, 16.6–16.10
Criminal law
criminal action, 1.60
examination of witnesses, 1.58
identifying the issues, 1.55
role of court, 1.59
terminology, 1.53
Criminal proceedings
arrest, 1.63
committal proceedings, 1.37, 1.64
conduct of the hearing, 1.57
investigation, 1.62
launching criminal proceedings, 1.61
offences– summary and indictable, 1.78
trial, 1.65
witnesses, 1.56, 1.58
Cross vesting, 1.45
Crossed cheque
'account payee only' crossings, 12.24
banks' liability for wrongful payment of, 12.22,
    12.65
'crossed not negotiable', 12.23
effect of, 12.22
how crossed, 12.21
multiple crossings, 12.25
not apparently crossed, 12.65
Crossing
cheques of, 12.21–12.25
Crown
interest in land of, 13.26–13.27
ownership of land, and, 13.4, 13.26
reservations by, 13.15, 13.27
resumptions by, 13.27
Customer
advice received from bank, 11.30
ambiguity, duty to avoid, 11.35
becoming a, 11.22
death of, effect on cheque, 12.57

references are to paragraphs

Debts — *continued*
  unsecured debt, 18.2
  warrant of execution, 18.40
  which court, 18.17
  whom to sue, 18.15
Debit cards
  credit cards, compared with, 12.82
  EFT Code of Conduct, and, 12.83
  law governing, 12.81
  nature of, 12.81
Deed of grant
  land, of, 13.4
  reservations in, 13.15, 13.27
Defects
  partial, effect of, 6.56
  remediable, effect of, 6.57
  sales by sample and, 6.62
Defence
  emergency, of, 16.39
  necessity, of, 16.39
  negligence, to claims of, 16.55–16.58
Defensive trade marks, 14.43
Delivery
  cheques of, defined, 12.18
  passage of risk and, 6.10–6.11
Demand
  cheque as order to pay on, 12.9
Description
  de minimis rule and, 6.41
  fitness for purpose and, 6.48
  merchantable quality and, 6.52, 6.54
  sale by, 6.14, 6.38
Designs
  account of profits from, 14.26
  damages, 14.26
  defined, 14.21
  effect of registration, 14.24
  infringements, 14.25
  novelty, 14.22
  originality, 14.22
  owner, 14.23
  priority date, 14.23
  protection, duration of, 14.23
  registrable, 14.22
  registration process, 14.23
  remedies for infringement, 14.26
  statement of monopoly, 14.23
  statement of novelty, 14.23
Detinue
  bailment and, 15.10
  conversion, compared to, 16.79
  defined, 16.79
  remedies for, 16.80
  trespass to chattels, compared to, 16.79

Directors
  appointment, 22.88
  common law duties, 22.99
  definition, 22.87
  disqualification, 22.90
  duties, 22.97, 22.98
  duty to outsiders, 22.100
  loans to, 22.95
  loss of office, 22.92
  payment, 22.94
  powers, 22.96
  qualifications, 22.89
  removal, 22.93
  role, 22.86
  statutory duties, 22.98
  types of directors, 22.91
Discharge of cheques, 12.62
Discharge of contract
  abandonment, by, 5.18
  affirmation and, 5.37
  agreement, by, 5.13
  breach, by, 5.33–5.35
  frustration, as a consequence of, 5.24
  illegality, as consequence of, 5.32
  mutual, 5.15
  novation and substitution and, 5.17
  operation of the contract, by, 5.14
  performance and, 5.2, 5.3, 5.6–5.12
  ready, willing and able rule and, 5.11, 5.38
  release and waiver and, 5.16
  strict performance and, 5.6–5.12
  time for performance and, 5.7
Discounting
  bills of exchange of, 11.18
Discrepancy
  between amounts in words and figures, 11.35, 12.12
Dishonour
  as soon as reasonably practical, defined, 12.49
  bank cheques, of, 12.70
  bankruptcy, notice of, and, 12.58
  countermand, notice of, and, 12.53–12.55
  death of drawer, notice of, and, 12.57
  defect in holder's title, notice of, and, 12.60
  discharged cheque, of, 12.62
  drawee banks' duty regarding, 12.49–12.62
  forged signature, and, 12.61
  holder in due course, and, 12.32
  mental incapacity of customer, and, 12.56
  options of holder on, 12.26
  post-dated cheques, and, 12.51
  prerequisites to, 12.42, 12.50
  rights of holder on, 12.26
  stale cheques, and, 12.52
  winding up, notice of, and, 12.58

references are to paragraphs

Exclusion clauses — *continued*
contracts, in, 3.25
insurance, 17.57
ticket cases, 3.5
Exclusive dealing
conduct prohibited, 8.30
notification, 8.34
Executive government, 1.25
Exhibiting
cheques, meaning of, 12.43, 12.46
Express terms, 3.10–3.12
collateral contracts and, 3.13
parol evidence rule and, 3.7
sale of goods contracts and, 6.26

False directory entries, 9.28
Fair Trading Acts, 7.4
Federal courts, 1.43, 1.44
Federation, 1.21
Fee simple
estate in, 13.30
Feeding title
effect of, 6.33
Fiduciary duties
company directors, 22.97, 22.98
fiduciary duties of partners, 19.24, 20.34
fiduciary obligations of agents, 19.3
accounting for all transactions, 19.9
acting in the principal's interests, 19.4
due care, skill and diligence, 19.8
payment from another party, 19.5
personal attention to the principal, 19.6
principal's instructions, 19.7
Finders
bailment and, 15.1
employees, as, 13.42–13.43
rights of, 13.39–13.44
Fitness for purpose
bailment and, 15.14
goods supplied, of, 6.42
latent defects and, 6.49, 6.51
making purpose known, 6.44
patent or trade name, sale under, 6.50
possession, passage of, and, 6.42
reliance and, 6.45
sale of goods contracts and, 6.42–6.51
seller's business and, 6.48–6.49
special needs and, 6.44
strict liability and, 6.51
Fixtures
defined, 13.5
degree of annexation, and, 13.6
injurious removal, and, 13.6
houses as, 13.8

permanance of attachment, and, 13.7
purpose of attachment, and, 13.7
tenants', 13.9
Forgeries
bank cheques, of, 12.70
customers' duty to prevent, 11.34
drawer's signature, 12.61, 12.65
indorsements, 12.65
not proper directions, 12.1
signature, of, 12.6, 12.61
Fraudulent alterations
amount payable, of, 12.65
customers' duty to prevent, 11.34
effect of on cheque, 12.62
Free trade, 1.22
Freedom of speech, 1.30
Freehold
co-ownership, 13.33–13.35
fee simple, 13.30
interests in land, 13.29–13.32
life estates, 13.31
reversionary interests, 13.31
waste, and, 13.31
Frustration, 5.20–5.22
consequences of, 5.24
frustrating events, 5.23
sale of goods contracts and, 6.29
statutory reform, 5.25
Funds
cheque not an assignment of, 12.50
Future goods
defined, 6.5
passage of property in, 6.14

Garnishee, 17.42
General crossing
effect of on cheques, 12.22
General Insurance Claims Review Panel, 1.93
Good faith
collecting bank, and, 12.66–12.67
defined, 12.67
holder in due course, and, 12.32
paying bank, and, 12.64
Goods
ascertained, 6.5
bailee's duty to retain, 15.7
bailee's duty to return, 15.10
chattels personal as, 6.4
classification of, 6.5
conversion of, 16.74–16.78
dangerous, 6.46, 15.13
defined, 6.4
destruction of, and bailment, 15.20
detention of, 16.79–16.80

Inertia selling, 9.27

Infants

contractual capacity of, 2.58–2.60

liability in contract and tort compared, 16.13

Information

banks' duties when giving, 11.30

Infringements

copyright, of, 14.14–14.15, 14.17, 14.18

designs, of, 14.25–14.26

patents, of, 14.32

trade marks, of, 14.45

Injunction

breach of contract and, 5.43

conspiracy, for, 16.96

copyright infringements, for, 14.17

design infringements, for, 14.26

intimidation, for, 16.92

passing off, for, 16.86

patent infringements, for, 14.32

procuring breach of contract, for, 16.90

trade mark infringements, for, 14.45

Injuria sine damno, 16.1, 16.5

Injurious removal

chattels, and, 13.21

fixtures, and, 13.6

Innkeepers

bailment and, 15.2, 15.23

common, defined, 15.23

liability of, 15.23

Instruments

bearer, 11.12

bills of exchange and promissory notes as, 11.10

defined, 11.1

inchoate, 12.32

negotiability of, 11.10

Insurance

agents

agent of the insurer, 17.40

agent's authority to act, 17.41

Insurance (Agents and Brokers) Act 1984, 17.38

insurer's responsibility for agent, 17.39

marketing/agency, 17.47

payments of premium to agent, 17.42

relationship with insured, 17.17

average

example, 17.101

operation, 17.99

statutory modification of average, 17.100

brokers

brokers acting under binder, 17.44

Insurance (Agents and Brokers) Act 1984, 17.38

claims

burden of proof, 17.49

general, 17.48

proof in exclusion clauses, 17.59

settlement, 17.63

classification, 17.3

general insurance, 17.4

life insurance, 17.6

marine insurance, 17.7

other classifications, 17.5

commercial purpose, 17.60

constitutional position, 17.8

contract

acceptance, 17.27

breach of conditions, 17.62

consideration — the premium, 17.23

exclusion clauses, 17.57

formation, 17.21

identity of the parties, 17.22

interim insurance — the cover note, 17.28

non-formation, 17.108, 17.109

parties, 17.36

period of the policy, 17.25

renewal of policies, 17.26

sum insured, 17.24

termination, 17.105

utmost good faith and, 17.65

disclosure

achieving disclosure questions and duty, 17.76

duty excused, 17.87

effect of misrepresentation, 17.79

fraudulent misrepresentation, 17.81

marine policy, 17.80

materiality test no longer relevant, 17.86

misrepresentation of age, 17.83

misrepresentations in life insurance, 17.82

not necessary in some forms of insurance, 17.90

notifying insured of duty to disclose, 17.91

pre-existing conditions — relief from disclosure, 17.89

s 21, components of, 17.85

significance of misrepresentation, 17.77

statutory adjustment to misrepresentations, 17.78

statutory duty of disclosure, 17.84

waiver of compliance with duty, 17.88

indemnity

agreed value, 17.95

extent, 17.93

double insurance, 17.98

market value, 17.94

maximum cover, 17.97

replacement policies, 17.96

references are to paragraphs

references are to paragraphs

references are to paragraphs

references are to paragraphs

references are to paragraphs

Tort — *continued*
conspiracy, 16.93–16.96
contract and, compared, 16.11–16.13
contributory negligence, and, 16.13
conversion, 16.74–16.78
crime and, compared, 16.6–16.10
damages in, 16.12
defamation, 16.5
defined, 16.1
detinue, 16.79–16.80
illegitimate acts and omissions, as, 16.2
infants, by, 16.13
intimidation, 16.91–16.92
limitation of actions, and, 16.13
lunatics, by, 16.13
malice, and, 16.4
negligence, 16.15–16.58
negligent misstatement, 16.59–16.66
passing off, 16.82–16.87
procuring breach of contract, 16.88–16.90
sale of goods contracts and, 6.92
third parties injured by, 16.13
trespass
    chattels, to, 16.69–16.73
    goods, to, 16.68
    land, to, 16.5, 16.68
vicarious liability, and, 16.97–16.104
Trade marks
certification trade marks, 14.42
classes of goods and services, 14.37
collective trade marks, 14.44
defensive trade marks, 14.43
defined, 14.34
distinctive, 14.37
features of, 14.34
infringements of, 14.45
invented words, 14.35
owner of, 14.40
passing off, and, 16.84
registration process, 14.38–14.40
remedies, 14.45
removal from register, 14.41
rights relating to, 14.45
sign as, defined, 14.35
use of, 14.36
Trade fixtures
tenants' fixtures as, 13.9
Trade Practices Act, 7.4
Trading trusts
operation, 20.60
structure, of, 20.61
Transfer by negotiation
cheques, of, 12.17
joint payees, by, 12.18
not negotiable crossings, and, 12.23

Transfer of property
agency and, 6.18
buyer in possession, by, 6.24
common law or statutory power, under, 6.21
court order, by, 6.20
estoppel and, 6.17
market overt, in, 6.25
mercantile agents, by, 6.19
non-owner, by, 6.16–6.25
parties' intention and, 6.12
retention of title clauses and, 6.15
risk, effect of, on, 6.10–6.12
rules governing, 6.13–6.14
seller in possession, by, 6.23
voidable title, under, 6.22
Transit
stoppage in, 6.72–6.75
Trespass
air space, to, 13.12–13.13
chattels, to *see* **Trespass to chattels**
goods, to, 16.68
land, to, 16.5, 16.68
person, to, 16.68
Trespass to chattels
damages for, 16.73
defined, 16.69
elements of, 16.69
fault, and, 16.72
harm resulting from, 16.71
possession, and, 16.69
recognised interferences, and, 16.70
remedies, 16.73
Trial, 1.54, 1.65
Trustee companies, 21.21
Trustees
appointing a trustee, 21.14
duties, 21.16
ending a trusteeship, 21.15
powers, 21.17
rights and liabilities, 21.18, 21.19
Trusts
arising by operation of law, 21.8
beneficiaries, 21.18, 21.20
changing or ending a trust, 21.11
creation of express trusts, 21.9
charitable trusts, 21.7, 21.10
definition, 21.1
express trusts, 21.2
family trusts, 21.6
private (non-express) trusts, 21.9
revocation voidness and rectification, 21.12
superannuation trusts, 21.5
types, 21.2
unit trusts, 21.3

references are to paragraphs

Related Titles

Business Law of Australia, 9th edition

R B Vermeesch, K E Lindgren

Provides a strong foundation for the study of business law and includes a comprehensive treatment of all traditional and growing areas of law impacting on business in Australia. The 9th edition has been completely revised to incorporate recent changes in legislation and discussion of new leading judgments. Much of the work has also been reorganised in order to present a more cogent and readable text. The introduction of chapter overviews and the greater use of sub-headings will considerably assist the reader's understanding of the legal principles discussed.

ISBN 0 409 31300 9 (1997)

Butterworths Course Materials: Business Law, Legislation and Cases

B Gordon, A Hargovan, A McNaughton

This work is a compilation of legislation and cases from the supplementary materials prepared for some of the subjects taught in the School of Business Law and Taxation at the University of New South Wales. It can also be adopted by other Australian universities teaching business law. It is intended to be used in conjunction with *Business Law of Australia*, 9th ed, by Vermeesch and Lindgren.

This book also supplements other textbooks and teaching materials used by the lecturers at the University of New South Wales. The materials have been selected to reinforce the fact that the primary sources of law in a common law system are cases and legislation. Certain extracts highlight the way the law has developed, or are included because they deal with a number of different areas of the law.

ISBN 0 409 31534 6 (1998)

Butterworths Business and Law Dictionary

Justice Ipp, W Weerasooria (eds), plus over 100 Contributors

This is a specialist dictionary giving detailed definitions of legal terms affecting all areas of business as well as important non-legal business terms. It comprehensively covers terms from such areas as agency, banking and finance, bankruptcy, bills of exchange, consumer credit, consumer protection, contract, corporations law, employment, trade and commerce, receivers and many more. Definitions provide encyclopaedic discourse and examples to round out the reader's understanding of the specialist areas. This publication is a must for all lawyers practising in business and commercial fields.

What the experts say...

'The *Butterworths Business and Law Dictionary* will be the first port of call for anyone in business, commercial or corporate life wanting to understand the complex and diverse terminology used in business and the law.' — *Don Munro FCIS, President, Chartered Institute of Company Secretaries in Australia Ltd*

ISBN 0 409 31400 5 (1997)

International Commercial Law

J S Mo

Suitable for undergraduate students, postgraduate students and practitioners as a concise yet comprehensive introduction to international commercial law. Includes a logical summary of Australian and common law case material and extracts from relevant legislation. In addition, a number of essential documents are included, such as the Vienna Sales Convention, Carriage of Goods by Sea Act 1991 (Cth) and OECD Guidelines for Multinational Enterprises.

ISBN 0 409 31037 9 (1996)